The History of Christian Evangelism in India

A Study in Missiology

The History of Christian Evangelism in India

A Study in Missiology

George Melvyn Ella

Go *publications*

Go Publications

3 South Parade, Seascale, Cumbria, CA20 1PZ, ENGLAND.

© Go Publications 2022

ISBN 978-1-908475-24-4

Dedication

In memory of my very good friend Sabod Sahu of Orissa who told me as a twenty-year old that I had the mind of an Indian. When I was invited to eat, or rather feast, at his house, he watched with joy and amazement as I devoured the delicious dishes. He then told me that I had also the body of an Indian because no Englishman could enjoy such spicy food without having a fit of hiccupping or gasping for water. He gave me a pod of some description full of seeds and asked me to eat it, which I did. It was very tasty. He said, 'That settles it. Only an Indian can eat that.' I took it all in my stride as hungry young students ought to do.

Sabod wanted to take me back to India with him as a fellow missionary but it was not to be. However, I am sure he would have been delighted with my present book which depicts his and my India.

Table of Contents

Part 10: *Quo Vadis* India?

Appendices

Foreword

Nowadays one finds Indians and Pakistanis in leading positions all over the world. Global progress in science, medicine, politics and education would be much less successful without them. They now play a dominant role in, for instance, the affairs of Britain and Europe, their former would-be masters.

Yet these offspring of a subcontinent long under colonial rule have almost lost their own history due to the versions penned by British, Portuguese and North American writers in past and recent times. These altered histories include the versions of Roman Catholic and Protestant churches concerning their own politico-religious actions in India. Many of these authors were quite blind to what was going on in the real India. Especially the British have been industrious in leaving posterity with the idea that Britain ruled a united India for centuries, not realising that Portugal was a colonial power in the South, East, West and North of India for several hundred years before the British claimed parts of India as their own. So, too, Portugal gave up its iron control over her Indian colonies decades after the British. Most of Britain's domination in India was not through fair-play and fair trade but through warfare and bullying. This was not only carried out against Indians but also against the Dutch, Scandinavian and French colonies and their trading companies. The British obviously thought that as much of the power in India was stolen at the time, it was fairer to consolidate all stolen power in their hands alone.

Furthermore, most of Western literature on India has highlighted one religion amongst very many and thus created much rivalry amongst the non-Christian members of Indian society leading even to warfare. The impression is left that India, besides its Christian minority, is a thoroughly Hinduized country. The tiny part the British Baptists played in India has been strangely boosted beyond all possible imagination and the fact quite ignored, at least in Britain, that the American Baptists quite outnumbered the British. However, these, in turn, were outnumbered by the Church of England missionaries and those of a large number of so-called Dissenting Churches, including the Presbyterians. For over two hundred years, these English-speaking enterprises were outnumbered by missionaries from the Continent of Europe especially those from the Netherlands, Scandinavia and Germany. The number of foreign Protestant missionaries in India from South to North before the time of William Carey had certainly reached the hundred mark and a number of foreign missionary societies were working in Serampore, besides Calcutta, long before Carey was invited there by the Danes. Happily, there are now numerous works in English by foreign scholars which look at India from refreshingly new angles, though none really please this author. Most useful here is *A History of India*, penned by Hermann Kulke and Dietmar Rothermund, published in English by Routledge in 2002 but there have been editions since 1986.

Modern free India, too, is not innocent of the many re-writings of her own history available today. Most of the recent well-researched histories of India by Indians show a great involvement of that country in creating an objective and pan-national overview of their country's past. Most of these histories, however, are written from a Buddhist, Muslim, Hindu or denominationally Christian point of view which often ignores the history of India before these religions were established and also quite ignores the work of other religions in building up modern India. Happily, we are now seeing what enormous progress was made in mathematics, astronomy, the natural sciences, agriculture, education and especially linguistics in pre-colonial days. India was no dark, primitive country before colonialism shined upon it but was ahead of the Western world in many fields. I do believe that the greatest darkness which came on India was through the Jesuits who began the re-writing of Indian history with their systematic re-classification, consolidation and amalgamation of religions which were apparently as numerous as the stars. I was amazed, however, to find one recent 'history', penned by an Indian citizen, still teaching that girls' education in India began in the late 19th century whereas such schools are recorded in the early seventeen-hundreds and even co-ed schools were long established in India before the nineteenth century. So, too, modern Indian-penned histories pay much attention to British influence in India without noting the ancient presence of numerous other colonial and trading powers which have left their mark on modern India especially in encouraging the Indians to enjoy native Indian progress.

Although both the Portuguese and the British left their former Indian colonies in a political, financial, industrial, agricultural, cultural and social turmoil, the way India has recovered from foreign tyranny has proved to be remarkable and lasting, especially when we compare India with the many other nations who have suffered from Colonialism. It is thus high time that the history of India as she was before, during and after colonial times should be adequately researched and put right. There is also a great need for the Christian public in and outside of India to be informed of the true spread of the gospel in a country which is quickly becoming the largest and may be the greatest in the world.

The author of this book has long felt that he, as a lover of historical and modern India, must play his part in the rediscovery of India for the benefit especially of South East Asians, Europeans and the English-speaking world. As his own qualifications and life-long experience are limited to the spheres of forestry, animal husbandry, history, literature, education, theology and linguistics, he has been careful not to depict ancient and modern south-east Asia outside of his own fields and his experience of India's vast peoples. He trusts that this present work will help other people, Christians especially, to appreciate God's dealings with India from the earliest times. When all is said and done, this colossal country, stretching from Sri Lanka to Afghanistan, China, Nepal, Bhutan, Pakistan, Bangladesh, the Maldives and Myanmar must be worthy of the interest of every person who dwells on this earth. We have only one world!

This book, however, really started in my youth and now old age has crept up on me and my writing scope and output has been reduced considerably. Invalidity compelled my wife and I to give up our large house and gardens in Mülheim where we had lived for fifty-two years and move into a relatively tiny flat for Old Age Pensioners in Bremerhaven. This meant my having to partly sell off and partly give away my thousands of books and study material which I had accrued throughout well over sixty years of research into church history, missiology and theology. I have thus been left over the last year or so with only the internet to rely on for procuring new source material, although I had already done the bulk of my reading and written most of my notes for the present book. A National License for free access to many archives and libraries world-wide given me by my college Martin Bucer Seminar sped this work up no end and saved me thousands of Euros. A good number of the fine lecturers at the MBS on the subject of missiology have been a constant inspiration to me as well as support gained from my fellow committee members of the Protestant Reformation Society.

Another major setback in finishing this book is my failing eye-sight and Macular Degeneration beside chronic heart trouble (8 stents) and several artificial implantations. The Lord is simply and patiently preparing me for Glory. However, I am faced with several embarrassments concerning citing sources and checking information I have gathered over the past decades. Where I have now sadly no access to the sources or my memory has failed me as to their present whereabouts, I have dropped the material for lack of current evidence. Thus, my Bibliography is much shorter than it was intended to be because I no longer have the source material available. This goes also for my hundreds of linguistic works, dictionaries and grammars to do with the Ancient Biblical Languages, Sanskrit, Pali and modern Indian languages such as Punjabi and Bengali to which I can no longer refer. However, very much is still in my memory and heart.

I cannot now keep the large scope of this book in my old head and have lost much material through my use of my computer which has become most restricted because of failing eyesight and Parkinson's disease. I have been helped greatly in keeping some overview of my work by my great friend of many decades Peter Meney and other companions such as Theodore Zacharides, Richard Schadle, Edward Malcolm and Pavel Kreko, who are all labouring in Christ's Vineyard.

Though I could write even more chapters, I have decided to send this book off to the publisher and printer before my health declines more. This will probably be my swansong and the three or so other books I have in preparation will be finished, God willing by my friends and colleagues.

My major aim throughout the book has been to fill in the quite enormous gaps in current missiological thought regarding India and explain why my task is so important in the Christian's service in the cause of God and truth. It is not that the half has not been told but that much of what has been told has been mere denominational propaganda or wishful thinking based on little research.

Some may be disappointed that I take up the radical evangelistic theories of Andrew Fuller again as I have dealt with that purveyor of a false gospel in several other books. However, Fuller is proclaimed by many, who should know better, as the missiologist and founder of Indian Missions *par excellence* and it needs to be pointed out that this unfounded view stands in stark contrast to the historical truth. I have thus been very careful to compare Francke and Ziegenbalg, whom I believe were great missiologists and missionaries, with Fuller and Carey who were very much hampered in following in their footsteps so long after. I have also dealt with a number of highly successful missionaries to India from Europe between the hundred years which separated the two teams historically and theologically from each other.

I may also annoy certain friends for dwelling somewhat on the redemptive, institutionalised duty baptism and the Lord's Supper that Fuller instituted as his very own faith. My main objection to Fuller's sacramental thinking was that he had a faulty doctrine of God's Character, Law and Revelation and had a faulty view of Christ and the Holy Spirit. He had also a faulty view of the purpose of the Word of God in salvation. He had no Biblical authority to force these views on to the citizens of India as a method of subduing them under British rule. His duty-baptism to back up his duty-faith and duty-obedience rational philosophy was not at all Christian and closely approaches the ideas behind Arian baptism rather than Christ's baptism. Fuller was not a Trinitarian in the Biblical and traditional understanding of that position. Fuller always thought it advisable to split up Christian doctrines into contradictory parts for the sake of philosophical analysis so that he lost the whole. This is not only very evident in his doctrine of God but also in his doctrine of man in his teaching concerning supposed different 'moral' and 'natural' abilities, as also man's 'inferences' and 'impressions' explaining the work of the Spirit. Supporters say Fuller took all this over from Jonathan Edwards which is, as my Scotto-Yorkshire mother always said of such fancies, 'all my eye and Peggy

Martin' as will be shown below. Fuller also applies this philosophy to examine which of the Triune Persons came first in time in past eternity. He writes, for instance, of the Son's pre-existence *after* the Father's own existence, which is a speculation foreign to the Word of God:

> And thus in the order of nature the Father must have existed before the Son; but in that of duration, he never existed without the Son.[1]

Fuller writes like this because of his rejection of the old Particular Baptist understanding of the relationship between time and eternity, Fuller trusting in a time-bound eternity.[2] However, Fuller tells us that only that which is natural according to Natural Law is eternally natural and God's Revealed Law is arbitrary and temporary. It is worthy of note that when Baptist Missionary Society missionary William Adam became an out-and-out Arian around the time of Fuller's death and explained his 'conversion' to his brother, it was his philosophical problem with the eternal nature of God that gave him the greater impulse rather than Scripture. Like most Arians, he argued that though Christ was created before time, He was neither eternal or part of the eternal Nature of the Father, thus postulating a 'time before time'.[3] This is the theory of most of Fuller's modern followers such as Curt Daniel who speak of a 'past eternity' or 'eternity past' with time stages in it which is philosophical nonsense. E. F. Clipsham, in his four Baptist Quarterly articles on 'Fuller and Fullerism',[4] relates God's actions in eternity metaphorically as referring to 'moral salvation' and 'juristic justification', nicely side-stepping the acts of God from eternity in exercising grace for undeserving man. Fuller's and the Fullerites' use of eternity as metaphor avoids most of the necessary theological

---

[1] See Fuller's 'On the Sonship of Christ' which skirts the concept of Christ's eternal Sonship and eternally being One with the Father and the Spirit. BOT edition p. 944.

[2] This is a most neglected feature of modern evangelical Reformed theology which, especially in its Fullerite form, speaks of a 'past eternity' as if eternity had a past and a future. See my *John Gill and Justification from Eternity: A Tercentenary Appreciation 1697-1997*, Go Publications, 1998.

[3] See *Letter from the Rev. William Adam, A Baptist Missionary in India to his Brother in Great Britain in defence of his own Conversion to Unitarianism*, Charleston, 1826.

[4] Now on line via BiblicalStudies.org.uk/pdf/bq/.

questions regarding how God became man. Naturally, Christ bore the just penalty for our sins so that we could be saved by grace and man's 'moral' or 'immoral' fallen will has nothing to do with God's decrees and action from eternity though much to do with God's eternal righteous Nature. This righteousness the Father shares with the Son and the Spirit and bestows as a gift to His People.

I thus cannot accept Fuller's misinterpretation of being baptised in the Name (one Name) of the Father, Son and Holy Ghost. So, too, one can only misuse Trade Union jargon to explain Fuller's view of his church which sees an open-shop Radical Christianity as the reason for his closed-shop Lord's Supper which is certainly quite foreign to Scripture and rational logic. Though Fuller's doctrinal yardstick is the 'reasonableness of things', his doctrines are without rhyme or reason. John Carlile in his 1905 work *The Story of the English Baptists*, tells us that 'Fuller became the emancipator of the Baptist denomination'. If so, it was an enforced 'emancipation' back from the Promised Land to the Fleshpots of Egypt.[5]

It is also clear that in regards to the doctrines of baptism and the Word of God which Fuller expected, even commanded, his followers to believe, Fuller left the old Particular Baptists paths. He then followed the paths of Arians such as Robinson, Gale, Whiston and Foster who refused to undersign the Salters' Hall Conference findings of 1719 establishing the doctrine of the Trinity for reasons of 'conscience'.[6] Sadly, even influential Anti-Trinitarians at this time such as Thomas Bradbury[7] taught duty-baptism as a sign of obedience. What 'obedience' could sinful man show God? It was Christ's obedience which gains salvation for sinners and this is the only obedience baptism demonstrates.

Some readers may find my spellings of Indian words rather peculiar. I can only ask them if they have ever come across consistency in spelling by any Indian scholar who dabbles in many languages? There are many officially recognized spellings for the same words which seem to be used higgledy-piggledy by scholars and writers. Most of these terms, especially family names, have been re-spelt by generations of

---

[5] Carlile, p. 182.

[6] See my *The Covenant of Grace and Christian Baptism* for more details on this topic.

[7] See Bradbury's *The Duty and Doctrine of Baptism*, London, 1759.

foreign governments in various forms and many Indians have no idea of how their names really should be spelt. Think of the fairly common Bengali name *Chatterjee*. That was the English version of *Chattopadhyay*. Some words as we shall see in this book, were merely mildly altered such as *Choromandel* which became *Coromandel*. However, when the British found words such as *Thiruvananthapuram*, they panicked and created versions that were any man's guess. To force people to use a standardized spelling is to destroy local dialects and even languages. To freeze languages is to freeze human thought.

I love the peoples of India and trust that this book will be a testimony to them of God's love for their vast country, full of great talents and opportunities to serve the Lord.

George M. Ella,
August, 2021

Introduction

A British Schoolboy's Fascination for India

My first taste of India

India has always interested me deeply. As an Elementary School child, I was influence very early by Rudyard Kipling's Mowgli stories in his *Jungle Book*, and highly entertained by his *Just So Stories*. His wonderful thought-provoking poetry brought India into the living-rooms and classrooms of my childhood contemporaries as well as my own home. Gunga Din still rings in my ears as I have often been compelled to admit of others, 'He is a better man than I am' and I will never forget Kipling's Recessional where he writes:

> If, drunk with sight of power, we loose
> Wild tongues that have not Thee in awe,
> Such boastings as the Gentiles use,
> Or lesser breeds without the Law—
> Lord God of Hosts, be with us yet,
> Lest we forget—lest we forget!

When I became a Cub Scout, I was introduced to Kipling's *Kim* and other works which widened my horizon in a Bradford slum considerably. 'Kim's Game' helped train my memory which proved a great advantage in later studies. We had several children in the Elementary and Junior School whose fathers were soldiers and moved to and fro from India. Often my school mates would accompany their parents for short periods and then send us tales from colourful India which thrust our young imaginations into scenes reminiscent of the *Arabian Nights*. I remember one girl in the class whose family lived almost as beggars and the poor girl was thin and undernourished but once in India, they even had servants! I often wondered if the poor children of India knew that there were equally poor children in Britain. When my classmate came back, she was plump and pretty. After another six months in a Bradford slum, she was again thin, grey-skinned with deeply sunken eyes.

Mahatma Gandhi the India-British hero

After the Second World War was over and eyes turned from our former hero Winston Churchill, they settled on Mahatma Gandhi who inspired us with his Sermon on the Mount ethics and his endeavours to better the state of the poor in India but also in the poverty-stricken areas in which I was brought up. When Gandhi visited Britain, he stayed amongst the lowly working class who welcomed him with open arms and hearts. This made such slum kids as myself love him. When the news that Gandhi had been brutally murdered reached our school, I, amongst several of my class mates, cried, knowing that a great apostle to the poor had gone. On reading and rereading Henty's *With Clive in India*, I sought to gain an understanding both of the national Indians and the then British raj though I, in my growing years sadly never saw another Gandhi again in India.

Living with a Sikh Punjabi family

Whilst a teenager, after my family broke up, I came under the roof and protection of a fine and upright Sikh family who told me many positive stories of their Northern Indian home from which they had fled. I had then little knowledge of languages except for School French and Swedish which I started teaching myself aged thirteen and was staggered at the richness of the Punjabi, Hindi and Urdu languages and their literature which could be traced back far beyond the origins of English literature to three thousand years ago. Starting with the history of the Punjab one moves quickly into the history of both the Near and Far East and the cradle of Christian civilisation and culture. Often, I feel that borders were fewer and easier to cross in those ancient days than they are today in our Western countries humbled by the selfish political powers and big industry. So, too, nature did not groan and bleed so much in those days. I say this as fifty-one ancient but healthy trees are now been felled near my present home in Bremerhaven to make way for gigantic buildings and parking areas.

Leaving school aged fifteen

Sadly, my hope of following an academic career ceased whilst I was very happy at a Grammar School where I had won the school prize for outstanding progress after moving from a C class to an A one. Actually, I had merely exchanged my Broad Yorkshire for Standard English but that seemed to impress the school authorities who now pronounced me 'intelligent'. To encourage me in their blindness I had to write a thousand lines almost daily containing the words 'I must not speak dialect'. Also, too, I often received six of the best for my 'brutish' ways. So, I quickly became so 'posh' that my strict but loving, honest hard-working father complained that he could not understand a word I was saying. Since then, I have discovered how all over the world social and racial inequality is enforced by one language group lording it over another. I found that this was not just a Western malady but was also rampant in that great country India. This brought Bartholomäus Ziegenbalg to my notice who translated the Scriptures into the common Tamil tongue instead of the classical language of the learned. This translation compares most favourably with Carey's alleged translations which were often in languages and script strange to the common tongues.

Due to extreme poverty, I had to leave my school and classmates in the fourth form without having the chance to go on and take my Ordinary and Advanced Levels and had now to fend for myself at barely fifteen. As I was a true lover of nature, I started an apprenticeship with the Forestry Commission and sailed off my own bat for Sweden at sixteen to continue my training.

Converted in the forests of Närke

By God's grace, I was soon led to Christ in the dark winter forests of Sweden by a friendly Methodist minister who served *in loco parentis* for me and the witness of a Christian forester. My old dream of academic studies came back to mind, this time with the work in God's harvest field as my impulse. So, I worked hard in my spare time to obtain matriculation qualifications and found that the gates leading to theology and language studies were now open to me as also the prospects of becoming a pastor-teacher and missionary.

Throughout these years of preparation both in Sweden and later Britain, I continually met up with fine Indian Christians who strengthened my deep interest in Missionary Studies and India. I also met up with quite amazing signs that the main gateway to Mission Studies would be through Uppsala University. For instance, one of the marvellous interventions of God in my life happened when I was a thirteen or fourteen-year-old, learning Swedish as fast as I could and earning a few shillings doing gardening work for Canon Desmond Kendrick of St. Clement's, Bradford. This was more than three years before my conversion. One day the evangelical clergyman took me aside, put his hands on my shoulders, looked me in the eyes and told me that I would become a Christian and study at Uppsala, a city I did not know of at the time. He felt he had an unction from the Lord to inform me.

Matriculation at Uppsala

Eventually I did matriculate to Uppsala University after extending my university entrance qualifications with Latin and Classical Greek which I was allowed to do parallel with my university course. I then had the blessed privilege of sitting at the feet of Professor Bengt Sundkler, a retired missionary bishop and now Professor of Missionary Studies. At the start of my first term, I received a majority vote to lead the Department's Students' Union and was sent abroad to represent the University thus giving me further language practice. In my committee I had a bright youngster named Anders Wejrud who was to become Archbishop of Uppsala and as Archbishop helped me in my research on John Durie who spent a number of years in Sweden. Durie's lasting work was being celebrated throughout the Swedish churches when I re-visited Sweden and stayed in Prof. Sundkler's house. This great but very humble man of royal birth whom I viewed as an ideal modern missionary taught us foreign evangelism on a Reformed, ecumenical basis. His textbook in his preparation for the home and foreign mission field was William Carey's *Enquiry*. Prof. Sundkler gave all his students a free copy of Carey's *Enquiry* which he had published with a hardback cover at his own expense. This work sums up all the desires, gifts and callings of the previous foreign missionary pioneers in India such as

Ziegenbalg and Schwartz on whose progress Carey built. Prof. Sundkler also arranged that I should be presented to the King and Royal Family who were very much concerned about evangelizing the Sami people. Later, I was to assist a cousin of the King's in the work of evangelising the Sami myself. The first missionaries both to the Sami and the Indian Tamils were sent out at the same time by the Danish Royal Family at the end of the 17th century. This was over a hundred years before Carey started witnessing to the Indians.

Carey's *Enquiry* was a belated work though necessary at the time
So, too, Carey's *Enquiry* was far from being a 'First' in missions to India as so often claimed by writers on Indian Missions who start with Carey's times. Carey depended very much on the Danish-Halle missionary Schwartz for his missionary ideas and ideals and also on Joseph White's *On the Duty of Attempting the Propagation of the Gospel Among Our Mohametan and Gentoo Subjects* of 1785. White was a Church of England clergyman. The term Gentoo, a Portuguese loanword, was formerly used to describe all non-Muslim Indians but is now used as a caste name. White was also a keen, missionary-minded Regius Professor of Hebrew at Oxford University and he also held a chair in Arabic. Carey's 'Attempt great things' is in parts an almost verbatim echo of White's admonition not to forget the Indians with the gospel. Especially White's ten Bampton lectures provided a Biblical basis for the evangelization of foreign countries, in particular India. White's tenth sermon on Mark 16:15 became fundamental to Carey's theory of missions and opened my own reception wider to any Macedonian Call of the Lord's.

Carey's pleasant dreams
Carey's book also pointed to the future of India in the service of Christ on the pattern of the Danish-Halle missionaries. Sadly, Carey had not the means of putting what Andrew Fuller called scathingly such 'pleasant dreams' into practice which the many missionaries to India who had gone before him did against far greater obstacles than Carey met up with. Most of the European missionaries to India from the early seventeenth century to Carey's times were men who realised they had to shake off their Western shackles or be unsuccessful. Had Carey not been hemmed in by the narrow-minded and uninformed Baptist

Missionary Society would-be steering committee in England, we could have probably 'expected even greater things' of Carey, to adopt his own sermon motto. So, too, few European and American missionaries after 1800 succeeded in becoming Christian Indians amongst Indians and, indeed, many carried non-Christian cultures and theologies with them to India thus polluting the harvest. Britain also brought with them to India their squabbles with France, Portugal, Holland, Denmark and the American Union. They also mixed their own theology with that of Indian religions but this was mutual. By the twentieth century, the honest Christian hey-day of missionaries without denominational, social, political or even religious prejudices was, in the opinion of this writer, over and done with. India was now striving to look after herself, though hindered by colonial slaughter, plundering and extortion.

Christian evangelism knows no national, cultural, sociological and religious boundaries

Prof. Sundkler was most stringent in warning his students of racial, political and sociological traps into which missionaries fell, particular in former colonial territories where apartheid ideas prevailed or the 'Pinkies' (Whites) felt they were superior beings. Prof. Sundkler also made it clear to his students that the term 'Mission' was a very unclear and ambiguous term used by many without exact contextualization. He told us of former evangelical, Reformed missionaries who became racists as soon as they set foot in Africa. He was even scolded by a former student of his for shaking the hands of the children in a native school choir. The young anti-missionary missionary told his bishop that he should not shake black hands on any account. Sundkler warned us also not to become so 'Missions-minded' with its organizations and home-country mentality that we forgot to preach the whole gospel and nothing but the gospel. How I praise God for Professor Sundkler!

Part 1

India Receives the Gospel

Chapter One

Progression and Regression in Early Indian Missions

India: A Key Nation in the Evangelization of the World

India is a vast country occupying the greater part of South Asia. It is the second most populated country in the world after China with 1,368,095,391 inhabitants but appears to be overtaking China in population due to its higher birth-rate.

As this one country contains over a sixth of the world's inhabitants, its importance in the evangelization of this earth is immense. This obvious fact has yet to be fully grasped by both Asian and Western Christians. Indeed, Western Protestant evangelization of India after the Reformation was sadly accompanied by commercial, political and military interests which were often antagonistic to the Christian gospel. When Bartholomäus Ziegenbalg went out to evangelize Tranquebar in 1705, colonialism had already begun to grasp out at India's wealth but Ziegenbalg was sent out personally by King Frederick IV of Denmark and was able to remain independent of the Danish East India Company as the King was keen to see the gospel spreading in India without let or hindrance. It was the Danish Court, still interested in missionary work, which sheltered what became known as the Serampore Trio (William Ward, Joshua Marshman and William Carey) and fitted them out for evangelism in the tiny Danish colony.

India had changed markedly by Carey's day

By the time Carey departed for India a hundred years after the Danish-German pioneers, Christianity in India was in a turmoil mainly because of Portuguese, French and British Colonialism. That once enlightened land had become a chaotic mixture of Western culture, politics and colonial ambitions with a mitigated Christianity which was promoted as the Light that all Indian religions had been searching for all along. So, too, the organisations sending out missionaries to the supposed 'heathens' in India tended to ignore the fact that the start of Indian evangelization occurred in Apostolic times, long before the gospel came to many European countries. So, too, Western missionaries could never explain why they called Hindus and Buddhists and even Christian Indians 'heathens' or 'blacks' but did not classify Muslims as such. This is perhaps why the gospel which was preached to the Indians became more and more involved with Hindu thinking, leaving Buddhist, Jewish and Muslim people rather out of its scope while this religious Trio also fostered fierce, unbalanced criticism of the Hindus which caused inner Indian political and religious Apartheid.

The early history of Indian evangelism

Those familiar with the Book of Esther in the Old Testament will be familiar with the opening words:

> Now it came to pass in the days of Ahasuerus (this is Ahasuerus which reigned, from India even unto Ethiopia, over a hundred and seven and twenty provinces:).

The vast empire of Xerxes I in the fifth century before Christ remained something of a religious and cultural unity into relatively modern times so that when the Gospel was established in India, the Bishop who represented her at the Council of Nicea in 325 was termed 'The Bishop of India', though this was taken to include Persia. Even today, the Persian language and ancient Persian religions are part of the Indian scene and in New Testament times part of the Christian scene.

In the early years of the world-wide spread of Christianity westwards into Europe and eastwards into Asia there were already century-old trade routes established by the Philistines, Jews, Syrians and other nations in all four directions of the compass both over land

and sea. Indeed, there is early evidence, in the case of India that Jewish merchants had a base in Malabar in Southern India to which early Christians sought refuge. The many modern traditions which trace the advent of Christianity to the arrival of the Apostle Thomas around the year 52 A.D. cannot all be classified as 'myths', though the name 'Thomas' is associated with a number of early Christian leaders who settled in Southern India. The present-day Mar Thomas Syrian Church claim they were founded in the second century. In 345 A.D., according to the same sources, a large group of Christians including a bishop, presbyters and deacons settled on the Malabar Coast, including men, women and children from Jerusalem, Baghdad and Nineveh. The merchant who brought them was also allegedly called 'Thomas'. These Christians are said to have used a Chaldean liturgy and the East Syriac language. Incidentally, the first Baptist we know of who was the means of bringing the gospel successfully to Indians was also called Thomas, John Thomas. This man was the inspiration behind the founding of the then Particular Baptist Missionary Society and won Indians, Portuguese and British converts for Christ in the seventeen eighties, a decade before he returned to India accompanied this time by William Carey in 1793. Thomas was also the first of this new team to win further souls for Christ after 1793.

The high religious standards and the social outreach of the Syriac Christians in India from almost Apostolic times caused them to be reckoned as one of the highest castes and a number even became feudal lords. At this time the young Church kept up close ties with Baghdad and Persia which would account for the vestiges of their languages still found deeply intermingled with Indian languages today.

When the Dutch East Indian Company settled in Pulicat in 1609, Madras in 1647 and Nagapattinam in 1660 on the East Coast, thinking the district was 'heathen', they came into contact with the Malabar Syrian Christians who had founded churches in India many centuries before. Amongst them Syriac was spoken until well into the 18th century and though the Roman Catholic Church had subdued them for a few centuries, they blossomed out again in the period following the Reformation and churches are still to be found with Syriac liturgies. Indeed, there has been something of a revival of the Syriac language in modern India and the old Syriac churches are consolidating once again.

Suffering caused by Roman Catholic oppression

During the sixteenth century the Portuguese Jesuit infiltration into the Indian church caused splitting and suffering. The Jesuit Synod of Diamper (Udayamperoor) in 1599 put violent pressure on the Indian Christians to take over their rites. The Portuguese Roman Catholics looked down their noses at the Indians and could in no way view them as brothers and sisters and therefore equals in the Christian faith. They fostered the caste system as they felt it reflected the natural distinctions in human social structures. It offended the Portuguese view of Christianity to see the Mar Thomas believers so wrapped up in Hindu society, not realizing how much non-Christian elements if not sheer pagan elements had infiltrated their own religion. It must be said in all honesty, however, that when so-called Protestant Powers entered India, the Portuguese were also often treated as underdogs and despised. Nevertheless, the often-used quip that the ancient Indian Church had become 'Hindu in culture, Christian in Religion and oriental in worship' seems to be a fair comment. With the advent of Protestantism, a measure of peace was restored to the Indian Syriac Church but the original Church had, to a large extent, lost its unity and became closely attached to Hinduism as a form of cultural nationalism.

Some Syriac churches survived through the Roman Catholic period

There were, however, exceptions to this trend. Associate Professor J. Mallika Punniyavathi of the Lutheran College at Porayar writes explaining that not all the Thomas Christians compromised:

> It is known, however, that about the eighth century, the Christians of Malabar were so numerous and influential that they acquired from the rulers of the land a certain political status, including the right of self-government, in token of which they received two copper plate charters dated A.D. 774 and 824.[1]

The history of next six hundred years is enveloped in obscurity

Through all the vicissitudes of history they seem to have held themselves together under the Syrian liturgy and ceremonials, though

[1] The plates have enticed many scholars into arguing for or against their historical value.

probably they entirely lacked spiritual vigour and missionary zeal. When in the fifteenth century the Portuguese obtained a footing in India, they endeavoured to bring these Christians under the rule of the Pope and to substitute the Latin rite and dogmas for the Syrian. For the time being, they succeeded in doing so by force. But when in the sixteenth century, the power of the Portuguese was broken by the Dutch; many of the Syrians threw off the Papal Yoke and placed themselves under a Bishop consecrated for them by the Patriarch of Antioch. A large number, however, still clung to the Roman church and their descendants are the 'Roman-Syrian' Christians of the present day.

The Mar Thomas Church

In 1816 the Church Missionary Society sent missionaries to Travancore who started schools and colleges and these began to leaven this ancient community. A small number of Syrians joined the Church of England, and a larger number who were in favour of reform separated themselves from the old Jacobite church and constituted what is called the 'Mar Thomas' or 'Reformed Syrian Church'. This church uses in its worship a revised form of the old Syriac liturgy translated into the vernacular. Both sections are presided over by Indian Bishops, and have always been independent of any foreign support. They are the only self-supporting and self-governing Christian bodies in all India. If these ancient churches would but unite and give themselves to the evangelization of India what a power they could exert in the land. In such activity they would surely find their own fullest spiritual life.[2]

Western missionary groups have not linked up with India's past

There is abundant evidence to show there were churches in India centuries before there were churches in many European countries so the idea of the gospel having first come to India through Western influence must be abandoned. However, on the whole, Western missionary organisations have not taken the trouble to research India's Christian past. This is no easy task and is made more difficult by the fact that in very recent years there has been a bevy of pseudo-academic articles written by young students throughout the world on the early history of

[2] Journal of Economics and Sustainable Development www.iiste.org ISSN 2222-1700 (Paper) ISSN 2222-2855 (Online) Vol. 2, No. 5, 2011

Christianity in India. Most of these appear to be an attempt to catch a Professor's eye or even that of a publisher. Indian academics from most of India's universities whether Christian, Hindu, Buddhist or Muslim have become engaged in this new interest as if it were a new internet competition with a large prize at stake. Though there is some good wheat being harvested, there is an uncommon amount of chaff. Most of these works merely repeat what former or contemporary authors have said and there is very little engagement with sources.

Modern Western ignorance of the early Indian Church

On studying a good many of these accounts posted daily on the internet, one is compelled to conclude there has been little headway in discerning the faith and practice of early Christians in India in recent years. Bartholomäus Ziegenbalg studied this period diligently in the early 18th century but the material he uncovered as he told Court Chaplain Böhme in London around 1711, were merely fantasy stories of a St. Thomas who is said to have performed all the miracles of the Bible from Moses to the Apostles continually.

This is hardly surprising as many Western denominations have ignored and even suppressed the history of Christianity in their own countries and trace the history of the churches back to the origin of their own denomination which erroneously teaches there was darkness over the face of the earth until their individual gurus came along. Nor have modern Western Christians the right to complain, however true it might be, that the Indian Christians over the centuries compromised with Hinduism. Many modern Western Christian movements have also succumbed to a pseudo-religious life foreign to Christianity. The 17th century revolution and outburst of anarchy in Britain brought with it a host of sects and denominations each with its own 'Christianity'. This goes also for the growth of 'American Religion' in the U.S.A. which produced Mormonism, Campbellism, Landmarkerism and revived Freemasonism and Denominationalism. So too, my own 'Reformed camp' which produces new theologies every five years or so cannot escape this just criticism. What goes under the false title 'Calvinism' in former Reformed circles today has nothing to do with the Calvinism of half a century ago. The one thing that seems to unite evangelicals these days appears to be a stubborn ignorance of historical theology. The old

Mission Hall favourite 'Give me the old-time religion. It's good enough for me' has not lost its significance.

Western Christian activity in the East made a very bad start

Besides, the Christian missionary spirit in Europe started off on the wrong footing in the East with the anti-Muslim Crusades and the spreading of Colonialism in India, Africa and South America where evangelization was thought to go hand in hand with conquest and Western 'civilisation'. Actually, the crusaders had the same spirit as the Muslims who were not ashamed to spread their religion by conquest in a supposed 'Holy War'. Even the early seventeenth century Dutch Protestant traders, for instance, brought both blessings and horror to India in that the Dutch East India Company's chaplains preached to the Indians but many local inhabitants were transported off to work more or less as slaves for the Dutch which caused the East Coast of India to become a centre of the slave trade and even slave export and it remained so after Carey's days. The Danish East India Company also encouraged slavery but this was combatted by the Tranquebar-Serampore Mission brought to life by the Scandinavian, German and Indian missionaries who were tolerated in the territories the Company controlled from the end of the seventeenth century on. This influence dwindled with the growth and spread of Colonialism.

The Impact of Western Colonialism on the Indian Church

The British were far from being the first colonial powers in India and her dominion of large parts of India has a relative recent history. The first to subdue large parts of Southern India were the Italians and Portuguese, the latter reigning longer over their Indian subjects than the British. Italian Franciscan and Dominican friars such as John of Montecorvino (1247-1328) and Odoric of Pordenone (1286-1331), both lived some time in India and informed their churches and countrymen of the nature of Indian religions which awoke on the Pre-Reformation European mainland an interest in spreading Roman Catholicism but also education and trade throughout India.

The Italians, however, were not the first Europeans to settle down in very large numbers in India but the Portuguese who in 1518 founded a base for both the Roman Catholic Church and trade in Goa on the West Coast. It was soon to be the Jesuits who took control of large areas in

Southern, Eastern and Western India. The first major Jesuit missionary was Francois Xavier (1505-1553) who arrived in India in 1542. The Jesuits began to rule from Goa with an iron hand, wishing to colonise India as a gift for the Pope. This may seem a ridiculous aim in the modern relatively free world but we must remember that the British Government, backed by many British missionaries of all denominations wished to conquer India as a gift for Queen Victoria so that she might wear an imperial crown. British coins were thereafter stamped 'fid. def. ind. Imp.' indicating that Victoria was the defender of the faith and Empress of India under British rule.

Xavier, however, besides being a trader and politician was a man of letters and under his guidance grammars were authored in several Indian languages and translations were made of Bible passages and catechisms were compiled in classic, poetical Tamil which was, however, hardly spoken in Tamil areas at that time such as in Ceylon and Tranquebar. This work would not have been possible but for the skills of Jesuit Henrique Henriques (1520-1600), who, in the middle of the sixteenth century began studies in Tamil and produced a Tamil Grammar, several dictionaries, catechisms and confessionals to further the priests' education and help them in their work with Indians. The aim of Xavier and Henriques was to enable the priests to be able to communicate directly with the Indians and not through the medium of interpreters and translators. Sadly, these publications were hardly ever made available to the Indian peoples, however educated they were. Indeed, their punishment cells were full of Indians who presumed to read the Scriptures for themselves.

Portugal was a colonial power in India much longer than Britain

The Jesuits were as much businessmen and traders as missionaries and soon had large areas of India under control backed by their colonial-minded King and government and also Portuguese armies. The Indians of Goa were not freed from the Portuguese colonial yoke until 1964 long after India had become theoretically 'independent' of Britain. With their 400 years of colonial history in India, Portugal beat the British by a long way as the latter could only scrape together some 190 years of part control until 1947 when they lost all control. This longer Portuguese reign gave rise to much 'pidgin-Portuguese' and even new languages with Portuguese being their meta-language and which provided a basic stock of words. These are still spoken in India and can be compared to the enormous infiltration of English words into modern Indian languages. Indeed, since earliest times there has never been a 'pure' Indian language just as there has never been a 'pure' European language and certainly not a pure English language but merely a bunch of ever-changing dialects mixed today with USA linguistic novelties.

The Portuguese influence on India was not limited to the Goa state and Bombay by far but reached out through inland parts and all around the Indian coastline including especially Calcutta and the Hooghly district. The Portuguese started building up Calcutta as the main trading post of India in 1579 and were of great influence in the city until British forces and the British East India Company 'removed' them from their possessions and took over their trade in 1765. In 1877, Calcutta, really a Portuguese town, became the capital of the British raj.

The number of Portuguese Jesuits in Goa alone by 1634 was enormous. According to Julius Richter in his *Indische Missionsgeschichte* of 1906, their College housed some 130 Portuguese Jesuit priests with many novices awaiting qualification and acceptance. By Carey's time, there were also some 400 monks in Goa alone. Their 'converts', very many of whom were Christianised by force, ran into thousands. By the end of the seventeenth century some 460 Franciscans and hundreds of Dominicans were operating in India.[3]

The Dutch Calvinistic Reformed Churches

Then, throughout the 17th century European trade routes expanded and the Dutch, traditionally able seafarers and keen mapmakers, began to trade with the Far East, and as the century wore on, gained an increasingly dominant position in world trade, a position previously occupied by the Portuguese and Spanish. With trade came settlements, churches and missionary activity.

Abraham Rogerius (1609-1649)[4]

This pioneer missionary, studied for the ministry in Leyden under Prof. Antonius Walaeus, taking courses especially designed for those going

---

[3] *Indische Missionsgeschichte* p. 74 f., the English translation *A History of Missions in India*, p. 74. f.

[4] Anglicized to 'Roger'.

to the East and West Indies. After graduation he left the Netherlands for the East Indies in October 1630 for Batavia where he spent a brief period. He then moved to Surat and then was moved on by his church to the small Dutch colony of Pulicat just north of British Madras. Here Rogerius worked as a missionary chaplain preaching to and teaching the Tamils for some ten years before being returned to Batavia for a few years. In order to recover his rapidly declining health, Rogerius was sent back to the Netherlands to Gouda where he soon died aged forty years.[5]

Rogerius began his work as an author as soon as he reached Batavia, preparing Scriptural translations and school books besides Latin works. Amongst these was Rogerius' Baals Priesters which were first distributed in handwritten copies. When printed these works were quickly translated into German and French. Once in India, Rogerius continued to study the Indian mentality and learning through the aid of three Brahmin friends. He described his work and his understanding of Tamil customs, social structures and religions in his book *De Open-Deure tot het verborgen Heydenom oftewaarachtigh vertoogh van het leven ende zede, mitsgarders de relegie, ende godsdienst der Bramines, op de cust Chormandel ende landen daaromtrent*[6] which was published by his widow at Leyden in 1651. The work was translated into German in 1663 and into French in 1670 but I can find no English version apart from portions of the work translated by a Louis H. Gray whom I take to be Louis H. Gray (1875-1955) American Orientalist and Linguist. Rogerius also compiled and published multi-lingual dictionaries. Rogerius was a strong Calvinist and was most interested in the part Calvinism played in the colonial scene especially in trade and science. Modern reports tend to overlook Rogerius' evangelistic activities. A lengthy list of Rogerius' works and published contributions on them is provided by Joose in the Biographisch Lexicon.

Philippus Baldaeus or Philips Baelde (1632-1671)

Unlike Rogerius, we know a great deal about the life of Philips Baelde who followed Rogerius to the Tamil mission-field starting at Ceylon via Batavia and then moving on to the Dutch colony at Nagapattinam

[5] Dates given for Rogerius' arrival in Pulicat differ from 1631 to 1633.

[6] *The Open Door to a Hidden Heathendom.*

near Tranquebar from 1660 to 1662. He not only wrote and published a number of works on his ministry to the Tamils and their history, religions and culture but illustrated these works with his own paintings and drawings. Though Baelde was sent out as a Reformed minister of Calvinist persuasions, he found most of the Tamils whom he pastored were Roman Catholics who called their new preacher 'Father Baldaeus'. Indeed, he found himself with three other Reformed ministers having to pastor over 32 former Roman Catholic parishes, in all parts of Ceylon except Candy. These had been left without their Roman Catholic ministers through the brutal colonial wars and most of these parishes were merged and put under the above-mentioned pastors. It is said that this small group of evangelists and ministers were able to win 12,387 Tamils for the Reformed gospel, the bulk of whom had formerly been mere 'rice Christians'. Extending his witness to the Sinhalese, Baelde is said to have been responsible for the Christian education of 18,000 children.

Almost needless to say, Baelde soon angered the Dutch East Indian Company who clamped down on funds given for the missionaries' work, arguing that Christianity would do the natives no good. Baldaeus refused to conform so the Trading Company forced the Church authorities in Batavia to stop funding Baldaeus' language work. This was the great difficulty facing all missionaries from the early 17th century to the early 19th century. However, the more foreign governments supported the missionaries financially, the less the missionaries had a say in true missionary work. Thus, almost two hundred years after the initial Protestant witness in India, William Carey found himself being paid high wages from the trading companies and the British government and was also supported by the Danish Colonial powers, yet he found he had to curb his missionary activities greatly on a part-time basis, whilst living like a wealthy Indian Nabob.

Baldaeus' complaints unheeded

Baldaeus complained to the Dutch Government concerning the way they were treating the Tamils but the government and the Dutch churches, on the whole, took the side of the trader-colonists and Baldaeus found he would have to return to the Netherlands to find freedom to end and publish his major work *A True and Exact Description of the Most Celebrated East India, Malabar and*

Coromandel Coast. In this work, besides Dutch, he quotes from Hebrew, Greek, Latin, English, French, Italian, Portuguese, Sanskrit and Tamil sources. Baldaeus is said to have been fluent in Sanskrit but not in Tamil which he had, however, studied closely for ten years. This criticism is probably to be taken with a pinch of salt as it came from the same Jesuit sources which criticized all Protestant missionaries especially Bartholomäus Ziegenbalg who was most fluent in Tamil and wrote a number of books in that language. This is because the Jesuits encouraged an academic, literary Tamil and the Protestants the Tamil of the common people which had partly no alphabet to express the sounds. Baldaeus' rendering of the Lord's Prayer in Tamil was used for very many years in the Tamil-speaking districts of both Ceylon and India and is claimed as being the first Scriptural portion to be translated into colloquial Tamil. Baldaeus' *Description* was translated and published in German in 1672. Ziegenbalg was to study Baldaeus' *Description* a few decades later and there was a copy in the Tranquebar Mission Library.

Western civilisation as a product of Asian outreach

Another criticism levelled against Baldaeus' writings is that he gives the impression that much of European civilization developed from an exported Indian culture. Such ideas, of course were not at all acceptable by the colonial powers who, on the whole, claimed that the Indians were culturally and educationally inferior to Europeans and would always remain so. Any goodness in the Indian system was said to have come from the West. Sadly, this idea increasingly infiltrated the colonial ideas of many a later missionary. Obviously, especially in the case of Christianity, writing, printing, science and world trade, the East enlightened the West.

Baldaeus, like many of the early missionaries to South East Asia, died very young before reaching the age of forty.

Chapter Two

The Gospel versus Colonialism in India

A free Gospel and free trade

It was the Dano-Norwegians who really promoted the spread of the gospel and free trade in the very early 17th century on a lasting basis. Our Reforming fathers in the faith taught that through free world trade, the more underdeveloped countries would flourish equally with all and the gospel would ensure that the Restitution of All Things would come to pass. This was the vision from John Durie, through Jonathan Edwards to William Cowper and some of us have not lost this vision today. Cowper wrote in 1782 in his poem Charity:

> Again—the band of commerce was design'd
> To associate all the branches of mankind;
> And if a boundless plenty be the robe,
> Trade is the golden girdle of the globe.
> Wise to promote whatever end he means,
> God opens fruitful Nature's various scenes:
> Each climate needs what other climes produce,
> And offers something to the general use;
> No land but listens to the common call,
> And in return receives supply from all.
> This genial intercourse, and mutual aid,
> Cheers what were else a universal shade,
> Calls nature from her ivy-mantled den,
> And softens human rock-work into men.

Ingenious Art, with her expressive face,
Steps forth to fashion and refine the race;
Not only fills necessity's demand,
But overcharges her capacious hand:
Capricious taste itself can crave no more
Than she supplies from her abounding store:

* * * * * * * * * * * * * * * * *

Heaven speed the canvas gallantly unfurl'd
To furnish and accommodate a world,
To give the pole the produce of the sun,
And knit the unsocial climates into one.
Soft airs and gentle heavings of the wave
Impel the fleet, whose errand is to save,
To succour wasted regions, and replace
The smile of opulence in sorrow's face.
Let nothing adverse, nothing unforeseen,
Impede the bark that ploughs the deep serene,
Charged with a freight transcending in its worth
The gems of India, Nature's rarest birth,
That flies, like Gabriel on his Lord's commands,
A herald of God's love to pagan lands!

Sadly, profit hunters have trampled on the equality amongst men and the spread of the gospel that commerce could have engendered.

The Union of Denmark with Norway which lasted until 1814 took advantage of the dwindling powers of the Portuguese Roman Catholic dominance in India and powerful King Christian IV of Denmark sought trade alliances with present day Sri Lanka (Candy and Ceylon) and India which eventually bore fruit in the 1616 founding of the Danish-Norwegian East India Company. The King, who as Crown Prince had already shown a keen interest in missionary work, insisted that the Company took care of the spiritual need of the Indians, a desire which was eventually set down in the 5th paragraph of the 1640 statutes which stated:

> As is to be hoped that many of the Indians, when they shall be properly instructed will be turned from their heathen errors, there shall always be priests[1] in the ships and in the territory belonging to the Company, and the King promises to promote such priests who have been in the service of the company.

The British East India Company first received a clause to this effect in 1813, long, long afterwards.

Short-term chaplaincy work was ineffective in Indian evangelism

The Danish chaplaincies had their weakness as a permanent evangelistic potential. Most Danish officials appointed by the East India Company returned back to their former homes in Denmark, Norway or Germany after a service of only five years or so and the paragraph quoted above contained the promise that pastors or chaplains would be given churches on returning home from the East. Indeed, a number of Danish pastors sent to Tranquebar perished soon after reaching India and others were only too pleased to return home after their initial tenure ceased. A further set-back to the evangelization was the fact that though King Christian of Denmark entrusted this pioneering work in India to three trusty noblemen who respected the King's evangelical wishes, most of the merchants employed by them believed that the evangelization of the Indians would be counter-productive to their business schemes. This meant that many officials, who were mostly traders, ignored their King and government and lined their own pockets by most questionable trading. One of the most scandalous ways of attaining extra perks was the armed raiding of Bengal adjacent to King Christian's enclave. Helpless captives were then forcedly 'baptised', and then sold as slaves. This 'baptism' made the slaves casteless with no social rights, creating a people who were judged as being even lower than the Pariahs.

How the Danes came to Tranquebar

Finding Tharangambadi, the modern name for Tranquebar, on the map is not at all difficult. If one moves the eye from the sharp point of

[1] The protestant Danish word for 'priest' is 'praest' which is short for 'presbyter' and used for pastors.

northern Sri Lanka across the Gulf of Bengal going due north, there on the coastline you will find Tharangambadi. Actually, getting there is quite a different matter. The small town of 23,000 inhabitants with its one eight-roomed hotel and one restaurant has no railway and the various 'local' airports are all three to four taxi-hours away. Travelling to Tranquebar by a small boat in calm weather is perhaps easier but the coastland is susceptible to many storms. Perhaps this is why the town is called Tharangambadi which means 'Singing Waves' though the waves often howl. Tranquebar, the earlier name for Tharangambadi, was given to the town by its Danish occupiers in 1620 after allegedly buying it from the Raja of Thanjavur (Tanjore).

Once in the town, however, one finds it is beautifully situated. Though recent storms have removed a long piece of the coast line, this destruction is now hardly noticeable as Tharangambadi is being polished up and even becoming a tourist attraction, with the old centre, built by the Danes, being renovated and many buildings, some over 300 years old, being restored. This includes several buildings connected with Bartholomäus Ziegenbalg who arrived in Tranquebar in 1705/6 and in a very few years transformed the place.

How Tranquebar became a Danish trading centre

As Tranquebar became the centre of Protestant missions through Danish administration in the late 17th century and early 18th century it is interesting to note how this came about. Denmark, early in the 17th century had yet to establish trade with India and at first decided to start with Ceylon as a trading partner under the leadership of Admiral Ove Gjedde in 1620. However, a severe storm drove the Danish ships onto the southern coast of India where several ships were wrecked on the coast. This part of India had already been claimed by Portugal and the Danish traders and seamen were received savagely by the Portuguese who boarded the wrecks, killed most of the sailors and cut off two Danish seamen's heads and stuck them on poles to warn the rest of the fleet against entering the land. The superior Portuguese fleet soon put an end to the rest of the Danish fleet and slaughtered the Danes. However, some fourteen men including Roland Crappe (Roelant Crape) the leading trader fell into the hands of the Indians who gave them quite a different reception to the savage Portuguese and treated them kindly.

They were taken in style to the seat of Prince Raghunatha Nayak of Tanjore (now Thanjavur) who welcomed them as guests. On hearing that they were traders, the Prince declared that they could set up a trading station in Tranquebar under his protection. Meanwhile, as Admiral Gjedde of Scania, then in Danish hands, was now in Ceylon with the remnants of his small fleet, letters were dispatched to him informing him of the Tanjore warm welcome and interest in trade. Gjedde sailed to Tranquebar and entered into months of discussions with the Indians. These negotiations were so successful that Denmark received the same trading and settlement rights as the Portuguese. Gjedde was allowed to build Fort Dansborg where Ziegenbalg was later imprisoned and collect rent from the local farmers. The only condition was that he provided Nayak with trade and gave him a yearly tribute. Thus, Tranquebar remained in Danish hands for 200 years until they were ousted by the British whose rule over vast areas of India was disastrous for the country as a whole and little alleviated by Britain's very late interest in the Christian welfare of India after 1813 prompted by friends of India such as Charles Grant and William Wilberforce.

Edmund Burke on Britain's disastrous reign over 'British' India

Protests at the East India Company's and the British Government's inhuman treatment of India were aired both in Parliament and private parlours and through the voices and pens of both nominal Christians and devoted evangelicals. Alexander Haldane, of a line closely associated with the East India Company, tells us in his biography of his father and uncle:

> The great objection to the evangelization of India, was to be found in the fears and the prejudices of the East India Company. That powerful commercial body had long ruled over India, without seeming to imagine that their mission extended beyond the material arrangements necessary for the acquisition of wealth, and the dispensation of patronage. At that period they had subjected themselves to the indignant eloquence of Burke, when, in his speech on the India Bill, he exclaimed, 'With us no pride erects stately monuments which repair the mischiefs which pride has produced, and which adorn a country out of its own spoils. England has erected no churches, no hospitals, no palaces, no

> schools. England has built no bridges, made no high roads, cut no navigations, dug out no reservoirs. Every other conqueror, of every other description, has left some monument either of state or beneficence, behind him. Were we to be driven out of India this day, nothing would remain to tell that it had been possessed during the inglorious period of our dominion by anything better than the ourang-outang, or the tiger.[2]

This is a reference to Burke's 1783 speech concerning the India Bill of that date. Really it was the work of Charles James Fox. Should we think Burke had a lily-white vest in his relationship to India, this was not the case as Burke wanted more rich people to share in the Indian pie and proposed, with strong Whig backing, that India should be governed by an oligarchy with vested interests and intrigued much in Indian political affairs, particularly against Governor Hastings.

William Cowper castigates British interference in India

One 18th century figure, who influence both the common man and high royalty in his rejection of the way Britain was running, or rather ruining, India was the poet, William Cowper. He was also a member of a Whig family, but castigated the dark side of Western political interference in India from his living-room sofa. He saw British rule in India as nothing less than an attempt to enslave this vast nation for purely material gain. In his long poem Expostulation Cowper strongly criticises the British presence in India, writing:

> Hast thou, though suckl'd at fair freedom's breast,
> Exported slavery to the conquer'd East,
> Pull'd down the tyrants India served with dread,
> And raised thyself, a greater, in their stead,
> Gone thither arm'd and hungry, return'd full,
> Fed from the richest veins of the Mogul,
> A despot big with power obtain'd by wealth,
> And that obtain'd by rapine and by stealth?
> With Asiatic vices stor'd thy mind,

[2] *Memoirs of the Lives of Robert Haldane of Airthrey and of his Brother James Alexander Haldane*, New York, 1854, p. 100.

> But left their virtues and thine own behind,
> And having truck'd thy soul, brought home the fee,
> To tempt the poor to sell himself to thee?[3]

Cowper was closely attached to the so-called Clapham Sect with William Wilberforce at its centre who pioneered British protection for missionaries to India before Parliament in 1793, shortly before Thomas and Carey departed to that continent. Cowper made sure the Clapham Sect were informed about the dangers of destroying India, believing Britain would live to regret their enforced colonialization plans. Wilberforce, supported by such as John Newton had been making plans for Indian evangelism before Carey thought of co-founding the BMS. Though observing the world from his 'loophole of retreat' in the small town of Olney, as Cowper put it, he kept up his keen interest in religion, politics and social welfare by intensive reading and correspondence with Britain's leaders. This included access to Court circles through several relations who were privy to the King's ear. Writing on 3rd January, 1784, Cowper told his close friend William Unwin, who was the instrument under God of Wilberforce's conversion, concerning the British East India Company's Charter:

> It constitutes them a trading company, and gives them an exclusive right to traffic in the East Indies. But it does no more. It invests them with no sovereignty; it does not convey to them the royal prerogative of making war and peace, which the king cannot alienate if he would. But this prerogative they have exercised, and, forgetting the terms of their institution, have possessed themselves of an immense territory, which they have ruled with a rod of iron, to which they should ever have a right, unless such a one as it is a disgrace to plead, the right of conquest. The potentates of this country they dash in pieces like a potter's vessel, as often as they please, making the happiness of thirty millions of mankind a consideration subordinate to that of their own emolument, oppressing them as often as it may serve a

---

[3] Expostulation, lines 364-375.

> lucrative purpose, and in no instance, that I have ever heard, consulting their interest or advantage.[4]

On the other hand, Cowper kept a level head in the debate and when his old classmate Warren Hastings (1732-1818), the first British Governor of a large part of India, was charged with corruption by such as Edmund Burke, Cowper, who knew his friend and fellow school-mate well, went public in defending him, writing:

> To Warren Hastings, Esq.
> Hastings! I knew thee young, and of a mind
> While young humane, conversable, and kind;
> Nor can I well believe thee, gentle then,
> Now grown a villain, and the worst of men.
> But rather some suspect, who have oppressed
> And worried thee, as not themselves the best.

In those days, most Englishmen went to India thinking they might become rich and the use of elbows and intrigues was great in the fight for more power and more wealth. This rat-race did not stop at the higher politicians.

War for war's sake

Mary A. Favret takes up the British imperialistic attitude to India in her Princetown University work *War at a Distance* writing:

> When the Indian landscape was first brought to the eyes of the British public in the 1780s and 1790s; it came as a landscape of war. In this sense it was a landscape wounded, defaced and overrun by a series of military campaigns between the armies of the British East India Company and those of the French, the Marathas, and, most recently the rulers of Mysore … William Daniell writes to his mother in 1790, 'the country not long ago was uncommonly beautiful, but such destruction has been

[4] *Letters of William Cowper*, 1912, Vol. 1, p. 274.

> brought to it by war, scarcely a tree or blade of grass is to be seen.[5]

Daniell is referring to the Bengal which greeted Carey on his arrival in Calcutta in the period of surrender to the British which the Bengali poet Nabin Chandra Sen, said was 'a night of eternal gloom for India'.

Writers on Carey ignore the fact that India was a war-torn land

It is significant to note that although much of the history of the early Protestant evangelism in India, such as that of the Swede Johann Zacharias Kiernander, records the military activities which were part of that history, the story of Carey depicted in Baptist works, on the whole, deals with him in romantic isolation from the real situation of warfare and destruction into which he plunged and which went on for years and included a number of revolutions which were obviously caused by British misrule. The history of slaughter, suppression, rebellion and mutiny going on during the Baptist period of missionary work is quite ignored as well as the troubles Britain had with the American Union's 1812 Declaration of War against Great Britain which had its repercussions in both the East and West Indies but especially against the Native Americans whom the Union claimed were British spies. On the British side, the suppression of India was partly because such as Joshua Marshman and Andrew Fuller adopted the jingoistic attitude of 'My country right or wrong' and were extremely nationalistic in a British sense.

The Armenian Church in India

Most unhelpful too is the modern insistence or strict division between Protestants, Catholics and Roman Catholics which is scarcely of use in assessing world-wide Christianity and its history. When I gained a first in Hebrew at Uppsala, I was strongly criticised for using grammars and commentaries penned by Roman Catholics to gain my good marks. These were written by authors who put their scholarship before their denomination. Even Baptist John Gill called himself a Catholic as do

[5] *War at a Distance: Romanticism and the Making of Modern Warfare*, Princetown University Press and Oxford, 2010, p. 198.

those of the Reformed Church of England. We are 'Catholic' but not of the Roman kind.

This perhaps explains why Western theological writers on India who call themselves either 'Protestant' or 'Roman Catholic' have neglected to examine the work of the Armenian Church in India as it does not fall under artificial Western categories. Indeed, it appears that the Armenian Church,[6] which was established throughout India long before Ziegenbalg's and Carey's days, has taken a back seat in modern Western works on the history of Christianity in India because of writers' concentrating on either 'Protestantism' or 'Roman Catholicism'. The Armenian Christians were generally highly respected in India for not preaching the exclusiveness of a Greek Orthodox or Roman Catholic Church. When the early Continental Protestant missionaries arrived in India, they looked on the Armenian Christians as being closer to their position as the Greek and Roman Churches, worked with them and took advice gratefully from them. Though the Armenians, on the whole, remained few in numbers, relatively large congregations were founded first in Madras in the South, then Bombay, but their largest community was founded in Calcutta. This was long before the British occupation of Calcutta but they were still in Calcutta in Carey's day. However, we know that Carey became familiar with them, worked with them, profited from their help and financial support though he scarcely mentions them apart from the fact that he said they were rich.

Armenian Christians link with Reformed missionaries

It was the Armenian Christian traders in Madras who urged Ziegenbalg and Johann Ernst Gründler (1677-1720) to send missionaries to Calcutta and these earlier Protestant missionaries in Madras had close connections with Christians in Calcutta from the 17th century on. Strangely, this Tranquebar and Armenian missionary involvement in Bengal is scarcely mentioned, if ever, in modern denominational works dealing with Carey and the BMS outreach. It is as if they had never existed. However, the Armenian congregation was founded in Calcutta in the 17th century as the central organization coping with Armenian

---

[6] The terms 'Armenian', 'Arminian' and 'Arian' are often confused. 'Armenian' refers to those of the Church of Armenia; 'Arminian' to the followers of Arminius and 'Arian' to the followers of Arius of Alexandra.

Church affairs in all India. Although Carey is very careful to list the number of Christians and denominations in very many countries, he, oddly enough, does not refer to the Armenians in India in his *Enquiry* at all but places them solely in Turkey and Abyssinia and had obviously not studied the history of their presence in India before he left for that country. This is possibly because Carey's call to India came after his writing the *Enquiry*.

The Armenian Church confused with the Greek Orthodox Church

Carey relates in his *Enquiry* that the Armenian Church and the Greek Church have some 30 million members in all, apparently mistaking both churches for one though they had little to do with each other. Furthermore, Carey claims in the *Enquiry* that the Armenian Christians are 'if possible, more ignorant and vicious than Mohametans themselves'. Carey had, of course, no first-hand acquaintance of either his Armenian brethren or the Muslims. Carey's unfounded comment does not reflect the impression one receives when researching Ziegenbalg's joint interest with the Armenians for Calcutta's spiritual welfare. Nor is it the impression one gains when following Carey's steps in India. Indeed, at least one of Carey's colleagues in the school was a renowned Armenian Christian scholar to whom Carey looked for assistance and support and translation skills. This scholar, as his many colleagues who translated for Carey were, however, not in Carey's employment but paid by the Calcutta College authorities at Carey's request though Carey had a free hand in giving them work to do. This fact also appears to be ignored in modern missionary works on Carey who had also a number of paying Armenian children in his schools.

Carey's criticism of the European churches working in India

Carey also names most of the European churches of whatever denomination operating in India, with the exception of the Moravians, critically and scathingly and exercises no discernment whatsoever concerning their work in the gospel. This is strange as Carey based the main thrust of his own *Enquiry* on Lutheran and Church of England missiologist endeavours. It was their calls for missionary-minded prayers which Sutcliff took up decades later and passed on to Carey. Yet Carey repeats time and time again that he gained his inspiration from Eliot, Brainerd and the Moravians and only mentions pioneer

Ziegenbalg's name, which he confusingly misspells, merely by the way. Indeed, Carey must be accused, though not in the same degree as Fuller, of biting the hand that fed him as he was supported immensely by the very churches he strongly criticised and was encouraged to preach in their churches and chapels.

The truth is that the Moravian Mission Carey often mentions with praise, and was to take over, was far less successful in soul winning than the other Christian missions. So, too, the 'family' idea which the Serampore Trio copied rather badly from the Moravians led to the dropping of true Christian family responsibilities. Furthermore, the Lutherans, Reformed, Presbyterian, Anglican and Independent evangelicals in India whom Carey condemns had been toiling in India since the 17th century amongst the slaves and outcasts of India with both the gospel and social aid. As Reginald Heber found in Carey's days, he was free to preach to thousands of converts, albeit mostly amongst the Tamils. The Moravians had established several mission stations in India, encouraged by the Danes and Germans but kept themselves in isolation from the Indians living outside of their towns and villages and gave up each settlement after very few years.

At that time, the Armenians were supporting Danish, German and British missionaries. Unlike Carey in Calcutta as per the traditional Baptist picture, Ziegenbalg in Madras looked for and gained support from the multi-denominational Christians there, including the Armenians. So, too, most Carey biographers write concerning the Fort William College in Calcutta where Carey worked for the main part of his sojourn in India as if it were first and foremost an establishment for Christian outreach. It is even referred to by the unknowing as a theological training centre! The College purpose was entirely secular and if religious, then inter-religious, although it contained initially a number of staunch evangelicals such as Brown, Buchanan[7] besides Carey, there were those on the staff who were of other religions or who were down-right anti-Christian. Even Brown and Buchanan pulled out of the Fort William work after a brief time, determined to work fully

[7] We are indebted to Claudius Buchanan who joined Brown in pastoring the Old Mission Church in Calcutta for his fine history of Indian evangelism, *Christian Researches in India*, The Society for the Promotion of Popular Instruction, 1840.

for the gospel elsewhere but Carey remained and worked within its secular system until his death.

The Greek Orthodox Church

Even Carey's strong criticism of the Greek Orthodox Church, especially in its relationship to Turkey needs to be qualified and corrected. A hundred years before Carey's birth strong Protestant and Reformed teaching had triumphed in Turkey through the Greek Orthodox Patriarch of Constantinople Cyril Lucaris (1572-1638) who was born in Crete then under the control of Venice who had become most sympathetic to the Reformation. Lucaris was educated in Padova, Wittenberg and Geneva and fully embraced the Reformed Doctrines and faith and campaigned most strongly against both Rome and Islam. Only Baptist leaders such as Gill, Brine and John Ryland Senior could be counted amongst those of Lucaris' Reformed theological acumen and evangelical outreach. This shows that even the Greek Orthodox Church as well as the more Reformed Armenian Church are in principle open to New Testament teaching and ought not to be likened to the heathen or claimed to be 'worse than the Muslims' and either scorned or ignored in the way the early Baptist missionaries treated them. Those who have been given eyes to see and ears to hear look for a revival of religion in all denominations. Furthermore, one cannot evangelize others by dealing out insults. Though Baptists have obviously been pioneers of the faith many times, when I studied amongst evangelicals in Uppsala, the only Liberals amongst us were Baptists. We had, thanks be to God, Professor Gunner Westin, the only Baptist on the staff, who was as evangelical as they come as was his family who ran a church in Järpen, Jämtland where I occasionally preached.

So, too, Christians of small and peculiar denominations ought to beware of presenting Islam as being nearer to the Christian ideal than that of their more numerous Christian brethren at large. Here Ziegenbalg would have strongly contested Carey's unfounded criticisms and limited knowledge. It is also true to say that where Carey relied on Lutheran Schwartz and Church of England White for his material, his work is sound; where he departed from such wisdom at the end of his *Enquiry* and here and there with his own 'asides', he flounders for want of objective information. His 'statistics' were merely copied from other sources though he had no first-hand knowledge of them so as to judge their applicability to the Indian scene.[8]

The Church of England

This Church was active in India from the seventeenth century on. This was mainly in the form of supporting chaplaincies, caring for slaves, teaching and supporting foreign missionaries such as Ziegenbalg, Schwartz, Kiernander and many more. The bulk of those missionaries whom the Church of England supported in India were not of British nationality but were mostly Dano-Germans. Over the years this support was via societies such as the Society for Promoting Christian Knowledge (SPCK) but this early work developed into several Missionary Societies which were mostly strongly evangelical and fostered the gospel throughout the whole of India. The SPCK, however, was, at times, most uncooperative with missionaries of an independent mind such as Kiernander and felt they had some rule over other evangelical denominations. They also began to insist that missionary work should only be carried out by those ordained in the Church of England manner. This meant they boycotted much Continental and Indian work and even challenged it as being 'Christian' in a similar way to Thomas' and Fuller's pleadings for a Baptist-only Church. Originally, however, the impetus for the SPCK who established themselves in India from 1710 was given by the Danes and the Germans and not the English.

The Church Missionary Society

The most well-known of later Church of England missionary societies is probably the Church Missionary Society (CMS) which was officially founded in 1799 but based on earlier organisations in the hands of such as David Brown who welcomed Carey to Calcutta and asked him to preach in his Mission church which he had taken over from Sweden's Kiernander of the Danish-Halle Mission. At first Carey refused cooperation because of Thomas who had quarrelled with Brown but

---

[8] The Verlag für Kultur und Wissenschaft, Bonn 1998 published not only a good translation of Carey's *Enquiry* into German by Klaus Fiedler and Thomas Schirrmacher but also identified the places which Carey mentioned world-wide, rendering them into their modern English equivalents.

eventually preached in the Old Mission Church founded by Kiernander whom Carey met and was instructed by him. After 1814, the CMS had also missionaries in Madras, Bengal and Travancore.

Chaplains were often missionaries and missionaries were chaplains

In modern Baptists' books on missionary activity, we often find a line drawn between chaplains and missionaries as if chaplains as Church of England men could not be missionaries yet the same writers claim that a full-time government employee such as Carey, could also be a full-time missionary. Such distinctions are highly artificial. Church of England chaplains such as George Lewis, David Brown and Henry Martyn were certainly missionaries of the first rank but originally were sent out as chaplains. In 1813, after the British officially allowed missionaries to enter British India, the CMS sent some nine missionaries between 1813 and 1816 to India amongst whom were several Germans.

A forgotten Church of England missionary

George Lewis is the forgotten pioneer missionary and chaplain of the Church of England whom I briefly comment on from time to time in this book. He deserves a book solely based on his work amongst the slaves and schools for both Portuguese and Tamil speakers and is a hot tip for future students of early missionary work in India. He, too, performed many 'firsts' that have been attributed to Carey who followed in Lewis' footsteps well over a hundred years later. Lewis was an Oxford graduate who went out to serve the Madras slaves and Portuguese Euro-Asians in 1692. When Ziegenbalg reached India some thirteen years later, the two men planned missionary strategies together. Lewis' contribution to India's Christian past has recently been re-documented but not by a church historian but by a librarian at Cambridge University, Catherine Ansorge, who kindly sent me an essay she had penned on Lewis and gave me permission to quote from it. I informed her of my own findings regarding Lewis and sent her my bibliography.

The connections between Lewis and Ziegenbalg

George Lewis corresponded regularly with Ziegenbalg and they exchanged visits between Tranquebar and Madras. To keep up their knowledge of Portuguese which both used as a lingua franca, they corresponded in Portuguese. Lewis had studied this language before going out in 1692 to serve the slaves who mostly spoke Portuguese or a mixture of Portuguese and Tamil and were of mixed origin. He also corresponded with like-minded Englishmen serving in Cuddalore and Calcutta (Kolkata), two early missionary centres. Lewis translated letters of Ziegenbalg's into English and published them in 1715 in the work *The Propagation of the Gospel in the East* [9] which was a book the Wesleys treasured and were inspired by it in their love for evangelism. Lewis was supported by the SPCK and seems something of a free-lancer and it was the SPCK who put him in touch with Ziegenbalg and provided him with a mechanized printing machine which he gave Ziegenbalg. The SPCK also founded a work in Cuddalore in 1737 jointly with the Danish-Halle missionaries such as the pioneer Swedish missionary Kiernander. Such pioneers paved the way for later missionaries. Kiernander moved from Cuddalore to Calcutta in 1758 and founded a church and several schools there many decades before Carey became active in the same city. Such as Lewis, Ziegenbalg and Kiernander were the Morning Stars of Western missionary endeavours in India. So, too, these missionaries were full time in the work of evangelizing and were not spare-time missionaries as was Carey who was otherwise employed by the British Government and East India Company in two secular colleges.

---

[9] Part III, pp. 79-109.

Chapter Three

Paving the Way for Modern Missions to India

How the mission to Tranquebar began
Originally the Dano-Norwegian East India Company aimed to work with the King of Candy in present day Sri Lanka, assisted by a Candy prince of Dutch descent named Marcelis Boshouwer who also commanded the Candy Fleet. Boshouwer had solicited King Christian's help against the Roman Catholic Portuguese who were striving to take over Ceylon by force. At the same time, a Dane named Roelant Crape, who had spent some years at the Court of Tanjore in India, told King Christian of the great trade prospects there. To cut a long story short, the Portuguese who had colonized by force lost their influence and the Danes who seemed to have plenty of money in their purses due to the lucrative Norwegian silver mines, managed in 1620 to gain control of parts of Sri Lanka and Tanjore by more or less peaceful means. The Danish Missions Director Ferdinand Fenger says that King Christian, an absolute monarch, ruled there as he did in Denmark and his other vast domains. However, the Dano-Norwegians lost their dominance in Sri Lanka but remained in Tanjore and soon established Danish-Norwegian Tranquebar (Trankebar), now called Tharangambadi.

The dawn of Continental and British missionary work in India
From the beginning of the 17th century, almost every ship from Denmark to India carried a Protestant chaplain on board, but none seemed to mix well either with the Tamil Indians, nor the Tranquebar climate. The first pastor to Tranquebar, Pedar Strensen Aale, died after

a short term of service. So, too, the merchants soon became a law unto themselves and lived as a parallel society alongside the Indians. However, the early Dutch and British missionaries to Southern India fared quite well with their colonial governments and various East Indian companies though none of them seem to have spent more than ten years there and most died early. This period has still to be closely researched and one finds but hints to this early work in preserved documents.

The first Danish missionaries to Tranquebar

The Apostle of India: Jacob Worm (1642-1691)

Actually, it was a condemned Danish 'criminal', exiled to India as an alternative punishment to being executed, who became India's first independent Protestant missionary.[1] Jacob Worm was a free-lancer, supported by no organization or church, but helped by his own wits which were many. His success awakened Denmark to the spiritual needs of India and immediately after the death of this 'criminal', the King of Denmark sent out an appeal for more missionaries to evangelize the Tamils. This 'criminal' cum missionary was the Danish scholar-poet and pastor Jacob Worm who was born in December 1642 and died in Tranquebar on December 1691.

This most eccentric man of God came into the world at Kirke-Helsignør, Denmark on 8th December, 1642 where his father Pedar Jacobsen Worm was a prominent minister. He was home-schooled before attending the Slagelse Grammar School from where he matriculated to Copenhagen University[2] and there took his M.A.. Worm reaped great praise and promotion as a young man for his preaching, writings and teaching in his mother tongue but also for his Latin disputations, especially at Court. He was soon appointed Rector of a school at Slangerup where he remained for six years until 1677 when he was appointed pastor of the Church of the Greyfriars in Viborg. There he married Abel Achton, the daughter of his predecessor. His conduct was said to be irreproachable and his preaching most earnest especially when referring to social wrongs. This earned him much criticism from the Upper Class who feared for their reputation. The

---

[1] By 'independent' I mean one not sent out by a church institution.

[2] Copenhagen was Denmark's first university followed by Kiel and Serampore.

common people heard him gladly and flocked to hear him preach the gospel as they saw the truth in Worm's humble Practical Divinity and his condemnation of deceit and hypocrisy. Worm thus scorned the behaviour of his fellow-clergy and especially the bishops in scathing satirical poetry, challenging their right to be chosen servants of the Church by worldly means. After a period of backing Worm for his learning and fine preaching, his bishop Dr Søren Glud began to warn him that he was going too far in criticizing the Church dignitaries and politicians. He condemned Worm especially for his protests at Denmark's seemingly never-ending war with Sweden and the occupation of her southern territories. That was bad enough in the eyes of the Established Church of which he was a minister but things became worse for outspoken Reformer Worm. In 1680, on King Christian's birthday, Worm refused to propose a toast for the King's illegitimate children and when he was pressed to give his reasons, he called them the name one usually used for such offspring.

Worm tricks the royal official

This caused an officer of justice to visit Worm with a warrant for a house search for rebellious literature. Worm gave the official all his keys and told him that he could explore the whole house but without Worm's help as he had to preach the following day and needed all his time for sermon preparation. The justice officer found no incriminating documents, which was no wonder as Worm was sitting on them all the time, as they were in a compartment under his writing chair which he never left during the examination.

The officer sent by the King to incriminate Worm reported that he had found nothing worthy of criticism in Worm's possessions. On the following day, Worms' congregation were wondering how the house-search had turned out and Worm, thinking he could give them a hint, preached on Genesis 31:34, 35 as his text which tells of Rachel sitting upon her father's images so that Laban could not find them. Unhappily for Worms, he had not reckoned with the officer of justice being present in the congregation who caught the hint and immediately returned to Worm's house. On examining Worm's chair on which he had been sitting throughout the search, he found a drawer under the seat full of Worm's satirical poetry.

Worm's sufferings for his outspoken testimony

All that can be said for the dignitaries whom Worm criticized was that Worm was very indiscreet about his accusations. Thus, Worm lost his living, was imprisoned, his works were burnt by the hangman and he was then sentenced to have three of his right-hand fingers cut off followed by his head. Whilst in prison, Worm wrote:

> Da lykken slog mig feil, da laerte jeg at kjende
> Min Gud, min ven, mig selv; men allermeest min fjende.
> Min fjende var mig gram, min ven mig og forlod,
> Selv var jeg skroebelig, - Gud var alene god.

My translation would be:

> My good fortune ended and I learned to know
> My God, my friend, myself, and above all my enemy.
> My enemy brought me grief, and my friend forsook me,
> I was too frail myself – God alone was good.

Widespread protests at Worm's harsh sentence

Not only were the Danish people infuriated by the Government's and Court's handling of Worm but also a number of the reforming clergy and several men of the Court and Government. So they protested loudly before King and country against the brutal capital punishment. This led even more influential people to put in a good word for Worm and, instead of being tortured and executed, he was punished by being exiled to Tranquebar, obviously with the thought behind his banishment that the climate would kill him anyway. This climate was so adverse to Western frailty that many missionaries died shortly after arriving in Tranquebar. When the Moravian Brethren founded their own mission to Tranquebar in 1760, it was abandoned in 1795 because of the high death rates of the missionaries with lives lost every year. Worm, however had no missionary society behind him and was dumped in India as mere human refuse but he survived and was greatly used of God.

A 'criminal' leads the Tamils to Christ

Worm, with only his Lord to lean on which he found was enough, lived first as a very poor man amongst the poor. After immediately identifying himself with the Indian population, he soon mastered their Tamil dialect and preached to the native inhabitants in the fields and streets. He thus, at first, made himself unpopular with the East India Company's officers as also their chaplains but was soon extremely popular with the people just as the case had been in Denmark. After picking up the language, practising it daily in his preaching and street work, Worm began to translate the Bible into the Tamil language, writing on palm leaves. Some sources say he translated the whole Bible, others only the New Testament. Others say he translated the Bible or parts of it also into Bengali but no copies of these alleged translations have been found. I am told there are piles of palm leaf manuscripts still lying in the Halle archives from this period which have still to be researched so it would be a great discovery indeed if some scholar found Worm's work amongst them. Happily, there are a number of Indian scholars now able to do this work. Even concerning many of Bartholomäus Ziegenbalg's unpublished Tamil works, Prof. Daniel Jeyaraj says:

> Ziegenbalg's palm-leaf writings are languishing in many places, including Halle. They are waiting to be researched. The Mission archives of Francke Foundations house them as crown jewels. They are looking for Indians to decipher them. There is a collection of his ethical principles titled Darmavazhi, which is also a palm-leaf manuscript. I hope scholars will come forward to study that, too.[3]

Soon Worm, because of his success in transforming Tamil lives and his great linguistic gifts was allowed by popular demand to use the small churches of the East India Company for his evangelistic work. As the Danish church had no choir leader and being a good singer, he was asked to become the music director. It was here that the common people's love for their Tamil-speaking pastor zoomed because of an extraordinary event.

---

[3] Interview with Daniel Jeyaraj, Front-line: India's National Magazine, 27, no.15, 2010.

A Hindu procession breaks down outside Worm's church

One Sunday morning, Worm was preaching to a full church when a large, loud Hindu procession began to pass by outside to impress the Christians inside. The highlight was a carriage filled with effigies of gods and Hindu priests. Everybody wanted to run out and see what the 'opposition' was up to but Worm at once exhorted the worshipers to remain in the church until the service had ended. He told the congregation that they would be able to watch what happened to the procession after the service. During Worm's preaching, the main part of the procession had just reached the church when the richly adorned carriage and its contents fell to pieces and the procession suddenly stopped and dispersed. On leaving the church, the worshippers saw the broken-down carriage and realised the procession had come to an abrupt ending on reaching the church. The story spread rapidly that God's hand had certainly been at work.

The Danish prophet and apostle to India

When Worm died in 1691, an epitaph was set up on his grave bearing the words:

> The lover of truth, the enemy of vice,
> his fatherland's prophet, the Danish Apostle of India,
> Magister Jacob Worm,
> who knew not how to deceive, but knew well how to punish sin and vice, who taught the erring and the unbelieving both by his pen and by his mouth, rests in this place for the truth's sake; for though banished from his native country, he was not burned by the heat of the sun, but naturally and happily, after his sea-voyage, short sojourn in India, and much building up among the natives,[4] he was received by Christ into
> the heavenly kingdom.

Fenger questions Worm's right to the title 'Apostle of India' but nevertheless writes that:

---

[4] I have adopted the Indian translators rendering 'natives' here. On the Epitaph the word 'sort' is used which is Danish for 'black'.

With the exception of Jacob Worm's efforts there is nothing which resembles any Missionary activity in the 17th century on the part of the Danes amongst the heathen of the East Indies.

Fenger, however, is comparing the 17th century pioneer efforts to evangelize Tranquebar with the far greater success of Bartholomäus Ziegenbalg some fifteen years later as the 18th century was dawning.

Possible connections with Ziegenbalg's later mission

We know nothing of Worm's own family life apart from the fact he was married. However, an Andreas Worm who was born in the ancient Danish Duchy of Mecklenburg and studied in Jena and Halle was ordained in the Danish Church in Copenhagen in 1729 and became a Tranquebar missionary in 1730. He was said to be absolutely fluent in Tamil before taking on his missionary duties. Was Andreas then a grandson of Jacob Worm as he had obviously begun to speak Tamil very early in life? A plaque in the New Jerusalem Church reveals that Andreas married Catharine Hall by whom he had a daughter Augusta Regina. All three died in 1735 he aged 31, Catharine 18 and Augusta aged six months. Thus, was the short life of many missionaries. All three were buried in the New Jerusalem Church at Tranquebar.[5] Fenger refers briefly to Andreas Worm in his *History of the Tranquebar Mission* saying he was well-known in India and given the office of treasurer to the Mission. This would sound strange if it referred to Andreas' very brief life as a missionary but more understandable if he had been raised in Tranquebar as the offspring of the famous 'Apostle to India'. Another possible member of Jacob Worm's family revealed by Fenger was a missionary called Worm of Tranquebar who translated Matthew's gospel (target language not specified) with two co-workers in 1739. So, too, Francke had friends named 'Worm' but that name was common in both Denmark and Germany.

King Frederick plans a Tranquebar Mission

The good work of Jacob Worm in Tranquebar had most positive repercussions in the Danish Court. The new absolute monarch over

---

[5] I found this information in an undated Indian Government paper by Julian James Cotton entitled *List of Inscriptions on Tombs and Monuments in Madras*, Vol. 2.

Denmark and Norway Frederick IV (1671-1730), son of Christian V, came to the throne in 1699 and was already devoted to supplying the world with missionaries. The most famous Danish explorer-missionary from these times was undoubtedly Hans Egede who was born in Norway in 1686. He was a pastor who studied the history of the Viking settlement in Greenland. Finding no record of the settlers after the 15th century, he raised money to lead a search party to Greenland and look for any signs of Dano-Norwegian life there. Accompanied by Gertrude his wife, Egede sailed from Norway to Greenland in 1721. They found the colony abandoned but the couple was so moved by the need for the gospel amongst the Eskimos they stayed on to evangelize them with a good amount of success. After his wife's death in 1735, Hans moved to Denmark to train further missionaries in 1736 but his son Poul remained in Greenland to continue his father's work. Hans Egede died in 1758.

As the Dano-Norwegians led by their King decided to follow Hans Egede in sending missionaries to Greenland, they also felt they must evangelize Lapland following the advice of Thomas von Western who worked as a missionary to the Lapps from 1716 to 1727. In 1723 Knud Leem, a student of the Sami languages, joined him. They pioneered the translation of Scripture into Sami, not perhaps realising that the Sami language had major dialects within it according to the geographical situation of the Sami and their occupations. Even modern translations into Sami do not take this phenomenon into account as I found out when I distributed printed Scripture portions amongst the Lapps.

Reginald Heber (1783-1826)

Here it is appropriate to mention Reginald Heber's knowledge of the Dano-Norwegian, Russian and Indian missionary outreach which provided motives for his poems and hymns from first-hand experience. Heber had toured Northern Scandinavia and Arctic Russia with other British evangelicals such as John Thornton noting the Christian work done and the needs of the peoples he encountered. This was before he was appointed as the second Church of England Bishop of Calcutta in 1823. Heber was a peripatetic bishop who made journeys to preach in areas of India, north and south, where natives had been converted. He preached to thousands of Tamils who had been led to Christ by the Tranquebar Mission. The first Anglican Bishop of Calcutta, Thomas Middleton (1769-1822) had blocked the ordination of native pastors feeling he had no authority to ordain them but Heber was quick to have them ordained and set apart for full-time ministry with the same rights, duties and wages as their British colleagues. The bishop had long been interested in the history of missions in India and supported the CMS in its development from pre-Carey times. Reginald Heber's first-hand knowledge of territories beyond the Pole Circle and India must have been in his thoughts when he penned his great missionary hymn beginning with the words 'From Greenland's icy mountains, From India's coral strand':

From Greenland's icy mountains,
From India's coral strand,
Where Afric's sunny fountains
Roll down their golden sand;
From many an ancient river,
From many a palmy plain,
They call us to deliver
Their land from error's chain.

What though the spicy breezes
Blow soft on Ceylon's isle;
Though every prospect pleases,
And only man is vile;
In vain with lavish kindness
The gifts of God are strown;
The heathen, in his blindness,
Bows down to wood and stone.

Can we, whose souls are lighted
With wisdom from on high;
Can we to men benighted
The lamp of life deny?
Salvation! O salvation!
The joyful sound proclaim,
Till each remotest nation
Has learned Messiah's name.

Waft, waft, ye winds, His story;
And you, ye waters, roll,
Till, like a sea of glory,
It spreads from pole to pole;
Till o'er our ransomed nature,
The Lamb for sinners slain,
Redeemer, King, Creator,
In bliss returns to reign.

Frederick has a troubled mind

It appears that Frederick had had his conscience troubled regarding India by a petition from a poor Danish widow whose husband and son had been murdered in an Indian rebellion in Tranquebar and her last hope of redress lay with the King. He realised that as a Christian Monarch he ought to have sent missionaries to Tranquebar as other areas of his large Kingdom which included Greenland, Iceland, Norway, parts of Sweden and parts of India. The Indian Trade Charter, then some ninety years old, had recommended the preaching of the gospel in India but little had been done in that direction. Frederick then searched Scandinavia and his Danish realms and even beyond for suitable people to be sent out as missionaries to the Danish colony of Tranquebar.[6] In 1704 Dr Franz Julius Lütkens from the Duchy of Lauenburg[7] became Frederick's court-preacher and told the King of two young men studying under August Hermann Francke in Halle, Germany who were willing to go out as missionaries. The two pioneering missionaries he chose were two friends who were students under Francke at the Halle University; Bartholomäus Ziegenbalg (1683-1719) and Heinrich Plütschau (1676-1752).

The modern mix up over Danish and German missionary names

In modern English-speaking missionary accounts, there is usually something of a mix-up concerning Danish and German missionaries

[6] Denmark was at war with Sweden (The Great Northern War) at the time.

[7] The Duchy of Lauenburg was founded in 1269 and ruled by a succession of dynastic families and various countries until 1865. The Duchy was in the extreme southeast region of what is now Schleswig-Holstein.

and often names are anglicized radically giving no indication as to whom they might really refer. Missionaries who were not German citizens have been designated as such by the writers because of their allegedly German-sounding names. This is chiefly because the writers are unaware of the history of Denmark and her changing borders. Lütkens, for instance, is usually referred to incorrectly as a German citizen in English and even in German coverage of the Dano-Norwegian Mission. However, Lauenburg where Lütkens was born and brought up was an independent Duchy which lost its independence in 1689 when it was annexed by the Principality of Luneburg and then by the King of Denmark. The Duchy then fell to Prussia in 1864 where it remained more or less autonomous until 1876. Lauenburg was part of the Deutsche Bund (German Union) which existed from 1815 to 1866.

A European Union in the 19th century

The founders of this Union were the Kings of England (through the Kingdom of Hanover), Denmark and the Netherlands, the Grand Duke of Luxemburg, and the Duke of Limburg. This resulted in the 'Holy Alliance' which Russia, Prussia, Austria and France joined. So there was a European Union, including Britain and Russia for many years with each country being equal partners. This was similar to the plans of Polish Archbishop Jan Lasky, uncle of the Reformer, in the 16th century. As Ambassador to the Austrian-Hungarian Empire which was already a union of countries, he pleaded for a further union including the rest of Western and much of Eastern Europe. This was also the wish of the Reformed churches of the day. For Jan Lasky alias John Alasko, this Europe was his Parish. Thus, he founded several Reformed churches in Europe and worked closely with the Continental Protestant churches and especially the Church of England in striving to compose a Pan-European Prayer Book under Archbishop Cranmer which became the *Book of Common Prayer*. 'Brexit' in those days was not on the political and ecclesiastical agenda.

Denmark loses much territory

Between the times of Ziegenbalg and up to the twentieth century, Denmark lost much territory to Germany. An example of this is Kiel whose university was founded whilst under Danish rule and at which I worked for a short time as co-marker of B.A. papers. Kiel, with its university is now part of the Federal Republic of Germany. Even today there are still protected minorities of Danes in Germany numbering some 50,000 citizens. These have Danish representatives in German State Parliaments. I experienced this at first hand when invited to Germany from Sweden with representatives of all the Scandinavian countries. I was given personal hospitality by the acting President of Schleswig-Holstein who took me to Parliament and I was allowed to take the seat of the Danish MP. The border conflicts between Denmark and Germany were only finally settled in 1920 and before that much of Northern Germany was either Danish or ruled by Dukes in league with Denmark.

Part 2

August Herman Francke (1663-1727)

Polyglot, Pastor, Pietist, Social Reformer, Theologian, Evangelist and Pioneer Missiologist

Chapter Four

Francke the Language Student and Social Reformer

Francke's birth and family background

August Hermann Francke was born in the North German city of Lübeck on 22nd March, 1663. Francke was the offspring of a farming family who were able to send August's father Johannes to a Grammar School, or 'Latin School' as it was then called. This paved the way for his studies in Law which ended in his becoming Dr Jur. He eventually married Anna Glorin, the daughter of Lübeck's Lord Mayor. Johannes' work took him to many different countries so that his son August Hermann was born into a world of international events. The couple had nine children of which August was the fourth. Three died in infancy and one whilst still in his youth. Both parents were sincere Bible-believing Christians and Johannes' energies, industry and honesty soon gained the attention of the Herzog Ernst von Sachsen-Gotha who made Johannes his Hofrat[1] and personal lawyer. Duke Ernst, after the Thirty Years' War, had made Gotha a centre for educational and spiritual renewal built mostly on the work of Comenius and Ratke who in turn, built on their close cooperation with John Durie.

This family bliss ended after only four years in 1670 with the death of Johannes when August was but seven years of age. Happily, August's elder brother Balthasar, who had recently gained a doctorate in Law, was able to help Johannes' widow in the education of the children and he was also supervised in his studies by his sister Anna,

---

[1] Today we would say Senior Civil Servant.

three years his senior. At this time, August, who often suffered from bad health, was being home-schooled. When he turned eleven, he asked if he could have a room to himself as he was always being disturbed in his Bible-reading and studies. Aged thirteen, he was sent to a Grammar School where, because of his mature learning, he was placed in a top class preparing for university matriculation. He passed all the necessary exams and gained his matriculation at the age of fourteen. The school proclaimed him their 'Wunderknabe' or 'Wonder Boy'.

Francke sought broader knowledge than universities required

Though he was offered a scholarship through family connections, August, partly because of his age, chose at first not to go to university but to be left free to study independent of the restrictions of a university curriculum. For the next three years, he studied theology, ancient and foreign languages and philosophy deeply. He then entered Erfurt University, not yet seventeen years of age but the older students bullied him mercilessly because he was much younger than they were and far ahead of them in learning.

August withstood this opposition for a term but then happily gained a scholarship to the Danish University of Kiel where he began to study theology under Prof. Dr Christian Kortholt taking courses leading to a Professorship under this reform-seeking Christian and friend of Philip Spener. He was able to lodge with Professor Kortholt who proved to be a wise and learned Christian tutor. August also deepened his studies of English at the university, reading the works of numerous reformers in theology and education. After completing the course speedily and with honours, August moved to Hamburg to deepen his Hebrew studies under Esdras Edzard, working through the Old Testament verse by verse six times in great detail under Edzard's supervision before his scholarship and financial independence ended. August's Old Testament translation was published some years later. Edzard was the means of winning many Hamburg Jews for Christ and set up a Trust for their evangelization which his sons Georg Elieser and Sebastian carried on with equal success after their father's death.

The collegium philobiblicum

Now the adult and independent Francke deepened his knowledge of polyhistory through the lectures of Daniel Georg Morhof (1639-1691).

He began to study French and Italian intensively and could now preach in five modern languages. To help with finances, Francke taught students Hebrew privately at Leipzig but matriculated also as a student himself. On quickly gaining the university title of 'Magister', he was then able to lecture freely and officially at the university. Now aged twenty-two, with the assistance of his friend Paul Anton, a fellow 'Magister', Francke founded a post-graduate colloquium of Hebrew and Greek scholars which he named the collegium philobiblicum. The aim was to deepen Biblical studies beyond the normal university scope. All studies and debates were to be carried out in Latin.

Francke was always something of a rebel in his university life, always demanding that the universities extended the depth and scope of their tuition on a pansophical basis. When the universities showed reluctance to cooperate, he founded his own educational establishments, social projects and trusts such as the Franckesche Stiftungen and his many orphanages. George Müller (1805-1898), a German citizen who studied at Halle, went out to England as a missionary and founded his great orphanage work in Bristol on principles laid down by Francke.

Francke's views misused

The rebellious nature of Francke against cold orthodoxy and the narrow, limited curriculum for university students of Theology worked somewhat against Francke's reputation as an objective scholar. Many of his remarks were taken down in note form and used by other scholars and those not so scholarly, for their own interests. Often, Francke's ideas were wrenched from their polyhistorical and pansophistical contents and used in isolation as if they summed up Francke's supposed 'pietistic' sentiments. Francke protested at this misuse of his ideas which were published 'without his knowledge and desire'. Amongst such works can be counted the *Pietas et Apologia* which gave the impression that Francke was even a radical Pietist. What I believe is a reliable representative of Francke's most theological and devotional works combined into one is his *Christ, the Sum and Substance of All the Holy Scriptures* which should be read by all true Bible-believers and seekers but especially by modern Fullerites and followers of New Covenant Theology. How unbelievable is their constant boast that they cannot see Christ the Messiah of the true Church and his People in the

Old Testament which the New Testament writers used as the basis of their own Covenant teaching! Not to believe Abraham, Moses and David is not to believe the New Testament. Here, centring on the writings of the Apostle John, Francke looks at all the Hebrew and Greek references in all the Scriptures to their testimony to Christ. Francke's *Guide to the Reading and Study of the Holy Scriptures* is still of immense value and well-known Philip Doddridge, author of *Lectures on Preaching*, who appears to have had a Latin edition, says, 'It contains the best rules for studying the Scriptures that I ever remember to have read.'

The collegium draws in scholars from outside the campus

The collegium grew so rapidly that the members had repeatedly to look for larger premises for their meetings. Soon the new institution became the gathering place of students, post-grads and professors alike. It also drew in many notable Bible scholars from outside the campus such as Court Chaplain Philip Jacob Spener (1635-1705). These scholars were able to dig deep both into the academic and spiritual sides of Bible Study with no fear of bursting curricula boundaries. Degree studies were more or less abandoned as a thirst for Scriptural knowledge at a higher academic level was now given scope. Apart from such extensive and intensive studies, Francke began to translate useful passages out of Italian works which he found edifying and which later brought him much criticism because other works by the same authors were thought by other theologians to be heretical, though they knew no Italian. Soon Francke was branded as a Quietist because, as William Cowper taught in his works, he found some aspects of the Quietist faith were worthy of following as, indeed, they are.

Francke finds himself blown up in his pride and a stranger to God

The great success he was having together with much public acclaim began to destroy Francke from within. He was also obviously very much overworked and exhausted. His pride in his academic progress grew and though he pleaded with God in prayer to keep him humble and of a sound spirit, he felt he had sunk into a dangerous swamp and had not the strength to rescue himself.[2] He complained at the time that his main difficulty was that he loved the world and the world loved him.

Francke still abided by the Word of God for a solution

Francke had now ceased to find his refuge in God and decided to leave his burdensome work in Leipzig and move to Lüneburg to sit under the famous New Testament scholar Superintendent Sandhagen. He knew that if any hope were there for him to receive, it would be through God's Word. His uncle Dr Glorin found a new scholarship for him but Francke was too undecided to accept. In Lüneburg he had once again a room of his own and leisure to do that which he wanted to do more than anything else, study independently and preach the Word. The former came easy but the latter was quite a struggle as Francke realised he must erase his own pride from his actions and solely concentrate on the spiritual welfare of his hearers, ignoring himself. This was no easy task as Francke had no peace with God.

This author's first Headmaster in a Paddington elementary school for immigrant children was a convinced Atheist, or so he said. Yet he always gave a sound, Biblical testimony at Morning Assembly which thrilled both teachers and children. I asked him how he could preach the gospel so fervently, accurately and clearly though he did not believe it himself. He answered that he did that which was best for the children. This was the situation Francke was now in and the people loved to hear his uplifting sermons, though he was delighted with his own performance for quite different reasons from those of his grateful hearers.

For his first sermon in Lüneburg at the Johanniskirche, Francke chose John 20:31 as his text:

> But these are written, that ye might believe that Jesus is the Christ, the Son of God; and that believing ye might have life through his name.

---

[2] I found this verbatim account of Francke's troubles and the way out of them quoted in Ernst Bunke's work *August Hermann Francke: Der Mann des Glaubens und der Liebe*, p. 18-23.

A personal confrontation with the Word of God

Immediately on choosing his text, Francke found he was confronted face to face with a Word of God which shook him to the core. He had lost all hope of such a life in Christ himself yet he was to preach on a life-offering Word from the Lord. He felt he did not possess that life of Christ in him which Christ had gained through His atoning death due to love for His People. Suddenly, as he fell on his knees before God, he was covered in shame and embarrassment at his own arrogance, pride and self-trust and began to confess his foolishness before God and his inability to see his own sinfulness. In his diary recording the event, Francke confessed that his faith hitherto had two foundations; the promises of God and his own deeds. Such a mixed faith, he realised was a barrier between him and God who alone granted faith through His love and grace. Eight years of studying God's Word intensely showed Francke that his faith had never been totally in God. This realisation filled him with sorrow, alarm and hopelessness and he realised he could not possibly preach on the text he had chosen, nor could he preach at all in his present hopeless state. In tear-filled prayers, he pleaded with God that if He were really there, He would have pity on the poor sinner August Hermann Francke.

Whilst he was yet on his knees, Francke realised things were changing. He felt the holy presence of God around him and within him and his doubts and despairs were removed in a great cleansing action of God in his soul. Suddenly, Francke's tears were swept away and he could praise God with heart and soul for this wonderful deliverance. Looking back on this experience, Francke said it was the time when he not only found God but also found a Father. He also saw that faith was not a work of man's desiring but a sovereign work of God in Christ.

Preaching with a personal faith in the God of the Scriptures

Francke was now able to stand before his congregation on the appointed Wednesday and preach on the true Life which is found in Jesus and could now add the words of 2 Corinthians 4:5:

> We preach not ourselves, but Christ Jesus our Lord, and ourselves your servants for Christ's sake.

Many writers on Francke claim that Francke had been a stranger to God until this wonderful experience and had been a lost sinner before. In other words, he was converted to a faith in the Lord Jesus Christ at this very time. Thus, such as Johannes Wallmann in his book *Der Pietismus* argues that Francke's Lüneberger Conversion (Bekehrung) has become the proto-type of all Pietistic conversions. Happily, he does not accept this and explains that both Arndt and Spener had no such experience and did not propagate it. Nor do many self-styled Pietists I have met. However, in my teens I was plagued with such teaching in my Bradford Home Mission environment. We were shown Billy Graham films of conversion scenes imitated by paid, professional actors to make us believe our hour of decision had come. God's decision for me came in the winter forests of Sweden in His own good time a year or two afterwards. I was hardly aware of it until I knew it was there. It is very hard to believe the myth that Francke's experience must be a proto-type experience of all sinners at their conversion. Most who have experienced conversion, whether Pietist or otherwise, certainly were never in the exact situation as was Francke. God has no *ordo salutis* in the conversion of His people but treats all as individual sinners needing His grace in their special situation. The idea that every born-again Christian should be able to give the situation, the day and the minute when he became a child of God is a burden on God's children that most are unable to bear. Indeed, Francke often said that he had lost his trust in God before this event and not that he never had it. He never lost his trust in God's Word as the source of salvation. Most Christians, I would have thought from my own experience, witness such mountain top experiences when in great need. I am thankful for such experiences throughout my long Christian life. The Lord never forsakes His own!

Bringing little children to God at Hamburg

Now wishing to bring the gospel to all, Francke made a detour to Hamburg on his way back to Leipzig to visit Johann Winkler, a noted exegete, and to study the educational needs of children of all ages including two-year-olds with a view to fitting them out mentally, physically and spiritually for a life honouring to God and in His care. He found it difficult but most necessary to be able to adapt his learning to a language and style that even the tiny tots could understand. Cowper called this needy exercise 'making Divine truths palatable'. The year or so in Hamburg[3] provided Francke with impetus to found orphanages for the care and education of homeless children. Francke learnt to make the deepest Divine thoughts understandable to all so that he could teach all of Christ's mercies from the cradle to the grave. If this is 'Pietism', then may we all become Pietists!

Francke's return to Leipzig

Francke now heard that his collegium philobiblicum was floundering through lack of good, well-qualified, leadership so he made his way back to Leipzig after a detour to Spener in Dresden in 1688 with whom he spent two months. As soon as Francke reached Leipzig his collegium philobiblicum began to blossom again. This time Francke concentrated on New Testament Studies rather than the Old Testament. Again, the numbers increased rapidly to three hundred and drew in a number of theology professors with their students so new premises had again to be sought out. Now Practical and Pastoral Theology was added to the curriculum and training for evangelistic work in the parishes and further afield. The demand for Francke's lectures grew and came from all parts of society including craftsmen and housewives. The authorities gave Francke permission to extend his lectures and disputations beyond term time and continue through the summer. Francke was now compelled to drop Latin as his teaching language and use German. Lectures were often dropped to make way for free discussion and enquiries. Francke was unwittingly founding a rival university for every man and woman who longed for mental and spiritual knowledge of the Lord.

Francke's fellow-ministers protest

Because of the continuous growth of the collegium philobiblicum, study groups had to be organised in local homes due to lack of space in the church and university halls and these drew in neighbouring families. Francke's university became a veritable 'Open University' in all senses of the word. There was bound to be a reaction from the pastors of stale orthodoxy and, indeed, a lobby of Halle pastors protested that such work should be in the church buildings alone and Francke was poaching on their parish work.

---

[3] Different commentators give different periods of a few months to a year but give merely secondary sources as evidence.

The situation was something like the one Tobias Crisp experienced when he was the means of leading many to Christ and the local ministers protested. William Twisse, first Chairman of the Westminster Assembly, told these jealous ministers the plain truth about Crisp's godly service to his Lord. He was only opposed because more were converted under his ministry than under that of his critics. Even today, Crisp is criticised by the cold orthodox, so-called Reformed men who distance themselves from his evangelistic outreach and even claim he was an Antinomian and Hyper-Calvinist to boot. Francke's envious enemies called him a 'Pietist' as if that should disqualify him as an ambassador for Christ.

Francke's practical theology turned out to be such a bone of contention that the local Duke, listening to the wrong side, forbade what he called Francke's 'Conventicles' and the local educational authorities then followed the Duke and demanded that the collegium philobiblicum should only be run on academic lines which excluded spiritual matters. Because of this ruling, numerous patrons of Francke's work were compelled to withdraw their support. In Protestant Germany of Francke's day the churches could do nothing without the permission and toleration of the Dukes. The situation is not too different today in this federal country in which the rulers of each state decide separately how schools and churches, whether State or Free, ought to be run. Now, however, some evangelical Dukes came to Francke's assistance and asked him to preach in their territories. Others argued that Francke should be forbidden to preach anywhere. Francke was now given the choice of becoming either a university professor or a minister of the gospel and pastor. He was not allowed to combine both these halves of true pastoral work by either the secular or Church authorities.

Francke receives a church in Erfurt

At first, Francke decided that he should work as a pastor and was invited in 1690 to preach in the Augustine Church in Erfurt. As soon as Francke finished his first sermon the congregation believed they had found the pastor of their choice. The local orthodox pastors, however, protested against his appointment and demanded that Francke should be given a four-hour examination to test his orthodoxy. Francke passed with flying colours and he was duly ordained. He chose as his ordination text 2 Corinthians 4:1, 2:

> Therefore seeing we have this ministry, as we have received mercy, we faint not; but have renounced the hidden things of dishonesty, not walking in craftiness, nor handling the word of God deceitfully; but by manifestation of the truth commending ourselves to every man's conscience in the sight of God.

A loving church and local schools were put under Francke's care
Francke had now a loving church behind him and was happy to find that several parish schools were put under his care. After his sermons had been delivered and the service ended, he began to catechise the children under his care and a good number of adults asked to join the children and soon so many were taking part in the discussions that the church proved too small and they had to meet in one of the school halls. Then both Protestants and Roman Catholics came from other parishes to take part in the after-sermon meetings. Soon, students from Leipzig and Jena joined the worshippers and a number trained by Francke found work in well-to-do Erfurt homes as private teachers.

Francke banned from the ministry
Again, the neighbouring orthodox pastors who would not fellowship with Francke and his church protested to the ecclesiastical and secular authorities who ruled that Francke's meetings to discuss his sermons should stop as Francke's extended work gave him an unfair advantage over his fellow pastors. Francke's church quickly drew up a petition in protest at the local council's and ecclesiastical ruling and the students and visitors from outside of the church also drew up petitions. These petitions were not accepted by the church and secular authorities but were nailed on the public gallows and Francke and a number of other outstanding ministers and scholars were condemned openly by name. The opposition became so great that Francke was dismissed from office and told to leave Erfurt within two days.

Professor and pastor Francke
By this time, Francke was well-known nation-wide and even quite well-known internationally, so there was an enormous protest at the irresponsible, despotic action of the Erfurt authorities which had no

theological or legal basis. Francke had proved himself to be immaculate in his theology and conduct. This was Francke's trouble. His success had caused too much jealousy and anger. However, Francke had still a tremendous backing and as one door was shut, many were opened and an embarrassment of opportunities were laid before the ex-Erfurt minister. Spener was now more or less in charge of the founding of Halle University, made to measure for people like Francke who wished to combine strong, outgoing Christian witness with intense studies of the Greek and Hebrew Scriptures at the highest level. So, Spener lost no time in inviting Francke and members of his collegium philobiblicum such as Breithaupt to help him put the university on a solid evangelical footing. Francke now accepted a Professorship of Greek and Oriental languages and the pastorship of the parish of St. George at Glaucha bordering on Halle. He was now able to do the same work as he had done in Erfurt but without opposition. Some orthodox pastors in Halle sought to win over Francke's parishioners for themselves by tolerating their drinking habits and using such toleration as a weapon against 'strict' Francke. Tiny Glaucha had only two hundred buildings in all and thirty-seven of them were ale-houses. As Francke's parish turned to the Lord, several public houses closed and Francke bought them up to serve as schools and orphanages.

The Halle pastors sought to restrict Francke's preaching and extra services that he took so the authorities gave Francke permission to preach only in certain areas but told the Halle opposition to stop their aggression against Francke who now invited a Church Commission to examine his work. After a most careful examination the Commission ruled they were quite satisfied with Francke's Glaucha and Halle work. The Halle pastors, however, continued to invite dissatisfied, heavy-drinking Glaucha parishioners to take communion with them, though this was against the laws of the day. However, opposition weakened and eventually died out after the early death of the Halle pastor who had led the opposition against Francke.

Francke is now helped by two great supporters

Meanwhile a convert of Francke's offered to become his co-pastor if Francke could take care of his board and lodgings as Francke was unable to employ an assistant on a full wage. This person was Johann Freylinghausen who became as loved in the parish as his senior pastor and carried on Francke's work after his death. Freylinghausen was enabled to work for nineteen years in the parish without official payment.

Now settled down as Professor and pastor in a more peaceful and permanent situation with a most-capable co-pastor, bachelor Francke realised he needed a helpmeet in Christ and eventually felt he should ask Anna Magdalena Wurm for her hand in marriage. The young lady immediately gave her consent and the two were married on the fourth of July, 1696. They were to have three children, the first child dying in infancy then came Johanna and Gotthelf August both of whom survived. Their son Gotthelf August chose the same path as his father and continued his work after Francke's death alongside Johann Freylinghausen. He also kept up his father's missiological work. This was also very much the case with Johanna whose story will be continued below.

In 1715, Freylinghausen asked August Hermann and Anna Magdalena if they would consent to his marrying their daughter Johanna though he was 27 years her senior. Francke was overjoyed but Anna Magdalena protested violently at the suggestion and fell into a deep depression and refused both to make marriage preparations and attend the marriage ceremony. Through the help of a doctor skilled in handling depressions, Anna Magdalena attended the marriage and quickly saw that Johannes and Johanna made a fine couple and their joint work in the Lord was further strengthened as they continued Francke's work after his death in harmony with Gotthelf August.

Francke the orphan's father and friend

Francke had already worked with poor and homeless children in Hamburg and had catered for the education of children in the schools under his supervision and written fitting literature for them. Yet, he wanted to do more for neglected and needy children. The local authorities made regular visits to the known poor with small amounts of money for each family. In the year 1694, Francke approached the authorities to see if he could accompany the social workers who distributed the monies. He wished to give the poor, and especially their children, a word of comfort and encouragement from the Scriptures with the addition of small amounts of money provided by his church.

Francke was told that his cooperation would be gladly accepted. So the poor received both spiritual and material help at the same time.

Then Francke began to collect money for the poor on a larger scale setting up boxes for donations here and there. He began to realise that actually, the poor were kept at the poverty level by the pittance they received. Then he discovered that a number of poor were overlooked by the authorities and a number of children never went to school but were put out to work for a living. Furthermore, the school money provided for the education of poor children was used by the parents for other means, not always sensible. So, Francke decided to found a school for the poor irrespective of whether the children could use the school money or not. Francke felt the children should not suffer because of the circumstances of their parents and made public appeals for money for the children. In 1695 sufficient money came in to pay students a very meagre salary sufficient, however, to enable them to teach the poor children of the neighbourhood two hours a day. The children were given schoolbooks free of charge but most of the books were sold by the families concerned and the children were then too ashamed to attend school.

School monies set to good purposes

However, a growing number of parents said they would now give Francke's school the allowance they received for their children's education so he found he could go ahead on this basis keeping costs very low and the teacher-students agreed. Indeed, now Francke could pay his teachers a higher salary and employ them for five hours a day instead of two. Francke, insisted, however, that his hard-working students should also continue their studies. Soon a number of parents who lived far afield asked Francke to send them students to teach their children and set up further schools but this would have forced the students to ex-matriculate from the University of Halle so Francke declined the offer. He now set up a fee system ranging from free education to weekly payments of two, four or eight groats (pennies) according to the financial situation of the parents.

Francke builds boarding schools

Francke became most troubled at the thought that so many children were still receiving no education and pleaded with God for a solution.

Then he realised he must set up boarding schools in which children could be taught, clothed and fed. At first the children sent from outside Glaucha were boarded in families and local houses but as suddenly larger sums of money were sent in for the poor children's education, Francke thought of erecting a special boarding school which he called the Pädagogium. Still, however, Francke discovered children who lived quite outside of any family care or were orphans. His Pädagogium now also catered for them. At first these orphans, four in number, were placed in suitable families under the care of a student named Georg Heinrich Neubauer who served the growing number of orphans from 1697 on. Francke wanted them to experience a sound family atmosphere but soon found the number of orphans, both boys and girls, were around the twenty mark and it became difficult finding suitable families for them. Francke now had not enough students for such private tuition. However, suddenly money came in not only in groats but in thousands of talers (dollars) and Francke decided to build his first orphanage with a school attached to provide elementary and secondary education for both boys and girls.

Soon Francke had to extend the work and bought a neighbouring house and one of the neighbouring public houses for his pupils. So, there were less drunkards and more well-educated children in the vicinity. As even these facilities proved insufficient, Francke sent Neubauer to the Netherlands to inspect the orphanages there with a view to perfecting their own work in Glaucha. The result was that a large brick building was planned. This project received national interest and the King quickly donated a hundred thousand building stones and 30,000 roof tiles. The building was finished in 1699 and catered for the boarding clothing and education of 1700 children. Now gifts came in of over 1000 taler at a time but Francke was unable to thank the donors as they remained anonymous. These donations provided food for the ever-growing number of children. Soon monies even came in from foreign countries such as Sweden and England and were quickly put to use. When friends ask Francke how he could manage all this, he answered that he himself had no money but it was all the Lord's provision.

Now local tradesmen sent the orphanages cartloads of fish, wheat and vegetables and local builders sent free building materials. Pharmaceutical firms sent medicine. As the University of Halle now catered for students from all over Germany and the neighbouring countries, Francke's work became internationally known and supported. Soon Francke built a further orphanage especially for the children who were sent from England. This was indirectly the beginning of the work which George Müller, a former student at Halle, started in Bristol, in the United Kingdom. Appropriately the new orphanage was called The English House. Due to generous funding, Francke could now build a further orphanage and school and a hostel for the teachers. He also built accommodation for those studying for the ministry both at home and abroad. He also started Trade Schools for training former pupils in various crafts. In 1713, King Friedrich Wilhelm I visited the orphanages and carried on his father's support of the institution and relieved their trading, newly set up joinery and building firms, and particularly their book trade, of tax. Now Francke set up a chemist's shop for the buying and distribution of medicine. Finding that many of his students were terribly poor and some confessed to not having eaten for days, Francke provided free accommodation and food for over eighty poor students. It appeared that Francke's trust in the Lord knew no bounds and he continually found his nightly prayers were answered the following day.

When Francke died in 1727, he left behind him:

1. The Royal Pedagogium[4] with three inspectors, 82 pupils, 27 teachers and a large staff of administrators, caterers, caretakers and other workers.

2. The Latin or grammar school with its three inspectors, 32 teachers and 400 pupils.

3. The German school with four inspectors 106 teachers of both sexes and 1,725 male and female pupils.

4. Orphanages with 144 children of both sexes and 10 supervisors.

5. 255 students were fed and boarded and 360 pupils from other schools received midday and evening meals.

6. 153 people were employed in the dairy, book department, printing shop, hospital work and the pharmacist department.

7. 15 hostels for women, 8 gynaecological centres and 6 widows houses.

---

[4] See next chapter.

George Müller and his Bristol orphanages

Johann Georg Müller (1805-1898), better known as George Müller in the United Kingdom, was a graduate of Halle University and went out to England as a missionary. At first, he worked primarily amongst the British Jews but was also much concerned with the state of the poor in Britain which was similar to the state of the poor in Germany. There were now strong connections between the Halle orphanages and Great Britain as witnessed by the English House set up by Francke. This led Müller to found orphanages in England's Bristol after the pattern of Francke's work. Müller was later to ally himself with the Brethren Movement of churches.

Chapter Five

Francke the University Professor and Missiologist

It is customary for modern missiologists to attribute the founding of Missiological Studies (research into the history and methodology of missions) to Alexander Duff (1806-1878) of Edinburgh University and Gustav Warneck (1834-1910) of Halle University. This is a historical blunder to say the least as such work had been carried out by Bucer, Zwingli and Bullinger in the early 16th century with their fostering of Eastern languages which were to be used in bringing the gospel to foreign parts. Prof. Thomas Schirrmacher suggests in his 2010 work on Calvin and World Missions that 'Bucer was probably the only real missiologist among the reformers'[1] but adds that Calvin sent out two missionaries to Brazil! Schirrmacher, too, is no mean missiologist and can be counted under the major globe-trotting evangelists of today.

Both Duff and especially Warneck built on the pioneering work in missiology of August Hermann Francke who put such studies on the broader basis acknowledged today. This highly gifted man was not only one of the leading Biblical scholars of his age but pioneered the training of very many missionary candidates, and provided instruction in several East Asiatic and North African languages besides Arabic, Latin, Greek and Hebrew. His pioneer work was invaluable to the development and outreach of Indian Missions. Linguistic work was one of his priorities and Evangelical, Reformed Biblical Studies would be all the poorer

---

[1] P. 10.

were it not for the textual work done on New Testament Greek by such as Francke and Johann Albrecht Bengel (1687-1752). One might truly say that without the training and backing given missionaries by Francke, India's evangelistic clock would have been put back at least half a century. So, too, it is worthy of note that the British Crown and British evangelicals first gained a strong interest in world-wide evangelism through the witness of Halle. Furthermore, Scandinavian, German, and American missionaries and those from the East profited much by the initial missiological spade-work Francke carried out and the vast archives of the Franckesche Stiftungen still provide a mine of hands-on practical advice on missionary strategy for today's missionary students. The missionary magazine Halleschen Berichten which Francke founded in 1710 was a pioneer work informing the general public of the progress of foreign missions. A member of the Halle staff Johann Albert Fabricius (1668-1736) building primarily on the works of Francke and Ziegenbalg produced in 1731 his 1,000 page Salutis Lux Evangelii collection of missionary documents from the dawn of Christianity up to his own day. This record is a history and catalogue of works to thrill any missiologist or follower of the Great Commission.

Francke was no theorist in the use of his many gifts but as noted above became a pioneering social reformer and educator of note through the founding of his orphanages, schools, colleges and universities many of which are still active today. Thus, Francke's missiology embraced the whole range of practical divinity both at home and abroad. Many of his students became missiologists and missionaries of note. After reading of Francke's enormous pastoral and social work it is, humanly speaking, amazing to find that he was equally industrious in the founding of overseas missions and home preparations for them. Sadly, a number of major missiological works inspired at Halle such as those of Friedrich Samuel Beck (1716-1786) and Mathurin Veyssière La Croze (1661-1739) seem to be forgotten or ignored today. These were pioneering missionary works indeed.

Francke's first post at the University of Halle was a professorship in Greek and Oriental languages. He was not primarily a professor of theology. This function was filled by his friends and former fellow students Breithaupt and Anton who were one with Francke in the faith. However, Francke's lectures in Greek and Hebrew exegesis and application drew such large crowds of students that Francke virtually took over the work of his friends. Breithaupt and Anton became virtually his assistants. We must also note that for the first four years of work at the University Francke received no salary. His was a labour of love. As a pastor in a pioneer district, his salary was very small but he attempted great things for the Lord and nearly always gained the financial backing needed from supportive friends. In 1698, however, he was officially given the status of Professor of Theology with a salary. To make his theological work more practical, Francke founded the lectiones paraeneticae[2] so he could deal with the inner, spiritual life opened up in the Scriptures. The latter lectures became so successful they were added to the University's official curriculum. Thereafter, at Francke's request, lectures on dogmatics and polemics were added. The latter lectures were mostly taken up with discussions concerning other theologies and confessional stands. Soon Joachim Lange who had been Rektor in Berlin and Johann Heinrich Michaelis, a Hebrew specialist and several other well-known experts joined the University staff.

Francke, however, had to struggle with candidates for professorships in mathematics and the natural sciences who wished to teach according to the philosophy of the so-called Enlightenment which was beginning to stifle academic research. Francke complained to the king concerning would-be professors who removed the entire foundation of the Christian faith in their knowledge engineering and used fallen reason as the grounds of their system. The king responded most violently against the intruders even threatening them with the death penalty. This was not at all what Francke had expected. This most exaggerated Royal reaction, however, shows what academic and religious authority Francke now held. Nevertheless, radical critics identified Francke with the King's extreme reaction and demanded strong penalties against those who opposed them. These critics such as Prof. Christian Wolff demanded freedom of speech and action for themselves but would not grant that same freedom to others. Soon there arose a strong liberal and theological lobby within Germany against evangelical, Reformed theology whose holders were labelled all together 'Pietists'. Most of these protests came from those influenced by Enlightenment who substituted 'right reason' for the work of the Holy Spirit as evidenced in the works of Gotthold Ephraim Lessing. Francke, however, gained

[2] Lessons on Edification.

much support from Reformed evangelicals in bordering countries, especially from Norway, Denmark, Sweden, Britain, Switzerland and the Netherlands.

Not being able to attack Francke on theological grounds as his orthodoxy and Lutheran principles were fully apparent, critics began to question his social work as being outside the realms of a serious Professor of Theology. Francke discovered the unfounded opposition merely strengthened the popularity of his work. Universities and training colleges were now turning out pastors with a world-wide view of the gospel so that Prof. August Tholuck in his work on the history of Protestant theological University life could argue that the 18th century in Germany produced a remarkably large number of evangelical ministers which, however, had declined by his day. Tholuck is well-known by today's reformed evangelicals as a church historian, Bible commentator, theologian of note and supporter of overseas missions. His work *Das Akademishche Leben des Siebzehnten Jahrhunderts mit besonderer Bezeihung auf die Protestantische-Theologischen Fakultäten Deutschland Nach Handschriftlichen Quellen* of 1854 is available in the Public Domain for all to read. Tholuck was himself a Professor on the staff of the Halle University.

The Adelspädagogium

Francke believed no world-wide evangelism could be possible without the backing of Christian Statesmen and he was pleased to find a number of Kings, Princes, Lords and Dukes among his hearers and supporters. This led Francke to set up his Adelspädagogium or College for the Nobility for the instruction of the rulers of mankind. I have a Baptist friend, one of the best preachers one can hear nowadays, who prays every service for the powers that be just as the Anglicans do, whether they are Kings, Queens, Presidents or tyrants. This is their scriptural and Christian duty in the spreading of the gospel which is to all sorts and conditions of men. At least two kings who supported Francke's Adelspädagogium, now ruled that all the pastors in their states should have spent at least a term at Halle during their theological studies. One of the most well-known of these students was Graf von Zinzendorf who sat under Francke far longer than one term. Indeed, he remained Francke's student from 1710 to 1716, eating at Francke's table. Zinzendorf carried on Francke's practice amongst royalty and at one time a third of Zinzendorf's fellow-labourers were from the ruling elite. Would today that our leading politicians could further world-wide evangelism according to the Great Commission!

Another nobleman and leading Evangelist who was converted under Francke's ministry and studied under him was Ernst Christoph Hochmann von Hochenau (1660-1721) who founded the Melchizedek Priestly Order for kings, princes and dukes who wished to use their authority to serve the purpose of Christ. Sadly, not all the German nobility believed the gospel and many opposed it violently in the name of orthodox religion and persecuted a number of saints to their death. Fellow dukes had Hochmann whipped, imprisoned and then exiled. For twenty-one years, Hochmann served as an itinerant preacher Europe-wide though he was often thrown into prison through political intrigue. After spending a number of years in prison and realising his early death was near, he wrote in one of his letters, 'If I had a thousand lives, I would use all of them gladly in the service of my Redeemer.'[3] Hochmann was a worthy German equivalent of Whitefield. He prayed often that the Jews should return to their Messiah whom they had abandoned. When working in Mülheim on the Ruhr, home-town of this writer for fifty-two years, he was instrumental in the conversion of Wilhelm Hoffmann who continued Theodor Untereyck's ministry which led to the conversion of Gerhard Tersteegen in 1713-14.[4] A major reason why Hochmann was persecuted by fellow-nobles was his desire for a separation of the churches from state control.[5] German states were mostly in the hands of kings, princes and dukes at the time.

The title 'Pietist' is confusing

Francke's collegium philobiblicum is often viewed as the birth place of German Pietism. This calls for some revision of modern ideas of what Pietism is. The Francke and Spener kind was anchored firmly in textual studies in the Word of God and sound exegesis and had no sense of the

---

[3] Heiland

[4] For a more detailed account of the German nobility who served the gospel in the 17th and 18th centuries please consult Paulus Scharpff's *Geschichte der Evangelisation*, especially Chapter III.

[5] This author lived for over fifty years in Mülheim which is seeped in Reformed revival history. Sadly, those days are bygone days.

'enthusiastic' or 'sectarianism' about it. So, too, Lutheranism is seen as the cradle of the evangelical movement often wrongly called 'Pietism' although, historically speaking, it started in the Reformed circles of Switzerland, Holland and Germany long before the Lutherans were influenced by it. Mülheim was a centre of Reformed 'Pietism' almost a decade before Halle became a centre of Lutheran 'Pietism'. They had the same gospel which was far more extensive than denominational borders. However, Mülheim's ministers had profited from like-minded brethren in Utrecht and Switzerland. So, too, after the Thirty Years' War such centres of Protestant learning were being set up all over Germany and neighbouring countries pioneered on the borders of the Netherlands and in modern North-Rhine Westphalia and exported throughout Germany, the New World, Africa and Asia.

The spread of missionary-mindedness

These movements gave birth to missiological interests world-wide. It was German evangelicals from these areas who influenced Whitefield so much on the North American mission field. By the end of the 17th century, Francke, however, was sending out well trained ministers of the gospel who saw themselves as missionaries, ordained for that purpose to the Scandinavian countries, including Finland, the Netherlands, North America, Poland, Bohemia, Austria, Hungary, Russia, the Balkans, Greece, Turkey, South Africa and even the Palestinian states and not least – to Great Britain. This was before Francke was encouraged to train missionaries for India. Francke was made a member and Correspondent of the foundational English missionary societies such as the SPCK. The Archbishop of Canterbury also asked for two of Francke's graduates to open up schools based on the Halle system in London. Francke sent Anton Wilhelm Böhme a former Halle student, who became Court Chaplain at St. James' Palace in London. Böhme was a major translator of Ziegenbalg's works concerning the Royal Danish-Halle Mission and furthered missionary interests in England. As more Greek Orthodox and former Jewish Christians took part in Francke's work in Halle, he set up his Colloquium Orientale to cater for the needs of Eastern Europe, Turkey and the Near East, especially Jerusalem. The Halle Jewish Mission proper was founded, however, after Francke's death. In those days, the term 'Oriental' referred to all countries east of Europe and often even East European countries.

The Collegium Orientale Theologicum

Francke had long realised that the church of the Lord Jesus Christ was not restricted to either a local denomination or a local community. It was a world-wide entity. This motivated him to found his Collegium Orientale Theologicum so that Eastern languages could be studied with a view to spreading the gospel in the East. He also furthered Greek and Coptic studies for witness to the Russian and East European churches. So too, he brought out a new edition of the Hebrew Bible through the cooperation of Prof. Michaelis and his team of experts backed by his own expertise. As now Jewish students came from Jerusalem, Francke rejoiced in sharing the gospel with them. The title of Francke's Collegium Orientale Theologicum reflects the current understanding that the 'Orient' began at the eastern side of Europe and the emphasis was on the Greek, Coptic, Hebrew and Arabic languages. This was also the case in previous attempts to set up colleges of 'Oriental' learning by Zwingli, Bibliander, Pellican and Bullinger in Switzerland and Samuel Hartlib and John Durie in England. As Francke began sending out missionaries to India, the scope of language study at Halle was widened. Francke looked on Greek, Hebrew and Latin as living languages linking him with the needs of needy living people. Thus naturally he could not neglect the needs of the Jews.

Today's EKD forbids the evangelization of the Jews

Today's German churches have not followed the Great Commission in the sense that Francke did. Nowadays Evangelical Church of Germany (EKD) members are even told to repent of their folly if they seek to lead a Jew to Christ. These enemies of the Great Commission which started amongst Jews use evangelical terminologies to stop evangelical work amongst them. In their study of the year 2000 entitled Christen und Juden III (Christians and Jews III), they claim:

> Irrespective of their mission in the world, Christians are not called to show Israel the way to God and his salvation. All efforts to induce Jews to change their religion contradict the confession

of God's faithfulness and the continuing status of Israel as God's chosen people.

This clearly contradicts the work of Christ who would have all men turn to Him and in matters of salvation taught that there is no difference between Jews and Gentiles. The EKG claim that God will lead the Jews all together to Christ in His own good time, and not merely the believing remnant as the Scriptures teach. This 'time' they project into eschatological speculations so it does not get in the way of their un-Biblical thinking. Apparently, they do not think of faith in Christ being brought to the Jews via the gospel of God's loving grace. They continue the narrow teaching of the old Gnesio-Lutheran Orthodoxy[6] of a type Luther never dreamed of and thus ignore the testimony of the Scriptures, the Ancient Church, Reformed Germany and, above all, the needs of the Jews. Indeed, the ruling is anti-Jewish to the core or 'anti-Semitic' in modern jargon. The term anti-Semitic is used incorrectly as many nations devoted to Mohammed and Islam are Semitic and the Semitic languages and peoples are older than the Jews. What is more significant for a professing body of churches is that the EKD ruling is thoroughly anti-Christian as they forbid the preaching of the good news of salvation to a needy people.

German pro-missionary work was pre-Francke

I do not pick out the EKD solely for criticism as I have even come across this attitude amongst a number of so-called Free Churches including Baptists. I mentioned the German churches here because this was the attitude in German Lutheran orthodoxy that Francke and his missionary-minded friends had to face and with which they had to contend just as we Christians today. Happily, the pro-missionary churches grew greatly in Francke's day and the numbers of church-goers rocketed and revivals were experienced throughout Germany. Actually, this movement was spreading in Reformed churches long before Francke and Spener came on the scene. This was chiefly through the work of Theodor Untereyck (1635-1693) of Mülheim an der Ruhr

[6] Lutheranism quickly developed into two factions: the Gnesio-Lutherans and the Philippian-Lutherans. The former claimed to be genuine Lutherans (gnesio=genuine or 'echt'), the latter were the followers of Philip Melanchthon and were less conservative.

who was supported by Joachim Neander (1650-1680) and Theodor J. Frelinghuysen[7] of the Netherlands who prepared the way for George Whitfield in the New World. William Tennent and his son Gilbert, the Irish Presbyterians, and founders of the Log-House College, also leaned heavily on the pioneering activities of early Dutch and German missionaries to North America. This work is now happily being brought back to mind on both sides of the Atlantic. Out of this movement Gerhard Tersteegen (1697-1763) of Mülheim was to emerge. Jung Stilling (1740-1817), a great soul-winner himself, said that since the days of the Apostles no one has led as many souls to Christ as Tersteegen.[8] These were all friends of the Jews.

Modern Christian denominations unclear about evangelising Jews

Most denominations world-wide nowadays give embarrassed and unclear answers when asked to state their attitude to the Jews. The infiltration of Dispensationalism into evangelical, Reformed circles is a main reason for this embarrassment. These churches are equally embarrassed and vague when asked to define who a Jew is. However, it was a Jew, Jesus Christ, who gave a further eleven Jews, after they had worshipped Him, the command to go into the whole world to preach the gospel. The Great Commission was thus begun by Jews but many modern Christians deny the Jews of today such a ministry. However, Jesus certainly did not exclude the Jews from the Christian gospel but established it in them.[9] Luke who was not a Jew by either birth or religion continued to promote the Gospel together with his Jewish brethren as being for the whole world, especially in his description of the work of the Jew Saul who became Paul, the Apostle to the Gentiles. Indeed, Luke traces the gospel back to pre-Jewish days and sees it

---

[7] Not to be confused with J. A. Freylinghausen (1670-1739), theologian, hymnwriter and Francke's son-in-law and successor.

[8] See Paulus Scharpff's *Geschichte der Evangelisation*, p. 41. I no longer have my copies of Jung v Stilling's works. Modern Reformed critics tend to play down Tersteegen's great work as being that of a 'Pietistic Mystic'. They are obviously ignorant of Tersteegen's many writings and sound Reformed exegetical works. His school literature was used for many years in Germany's Reformed schools. When I had to give up my large library to move into o.a.p. quarters, I kept my Tersteegen books as too precious for my personal spiritual well-being to sell or give away.

[9] Matthew 28:16-20.

triumphing in all lands and nations, way beyond Judaism. It was thus from pre-Jewish nations that the Jews received the gospel and the Gentiles in New Testament times received the gospel from the Jews and have shared it with them until today. New Testament Christians are grafted in to Old Testament teaching concerning the Covenant People of God. The Old Testament shows through its accounts of Melchizedek, Job and Abraham and many others that the Church was established for a Jewish and Gentile remnant from the dawn of time. We note that Christ, as David, was of the priestly order of Melchizedek, not Aaron. Indeed, the Priesthood of all believers was always international and not limited to either Jews or Gentiles. This is perhaps why Germans in their times of revival associated themselves with the priesthood of Melchizedek which was the Priesthood of Christ.

Throughout this period of thousands of years Moses' prayer in Psalm 90 has remained valid. 'Lord, thou hast remained our dwelling place in all generations.' Both Testaments teach that the home of God's people everywhere is in God. 'Sion' signifies a spiritual identity in God. Our 'City on the Hill' is the New Jerusalem established by God for His People. The gospel is thus not land-bound nor is it bound to certain peoples and certainly not to certain 'races'. Indeed, the saving gospel of Christ breaks down all language, ethnic and religious barriers, especially those between Jews and Gentles. Christians who behave as if these barriers still exist must remain corrected by the Holy Scriptures. Salvation is not an ethnic entity. The truth is that as many as are ordained to eternal life believe whether one formerly called them Jews or Gentiles.[10] Luke's Book of Acts moves over into the Book of Romans where Christians who were former Jews and Gentiles are taught as one in the faith. These are not Jewish proselytes to Judaism or Gentile proselytes to some new post-Jewish religion but joint members of the Church of the Lord Jesus Christ.

To return from considering the Jews back to their one-time language, nowadays, Bible students have a much easier task in learning Biblical Hebrew thanks to the pioneering work of such men as Edzard

---

[10] See especially Acts 13:48.

and Francke, and one can even download excellent daily teaching on the Hebrew text from Christian experts free of charge.[11]

The Seminarium Universale

Francke now founded his Seminarium Universale for world-wide studies concerning the spread and propagation of the Christian faith and began sending out missionaries starting with Russia. From now on, the World was Francke's parish and this conviction was followed in Halle until long after Francke's death.

With the help of a supportive nobleman, Francke began mass-distributing Bibles for a very few pennies so all could read the Word of God. These Bibles and Testaments were quickly snapped up and ran into some thirty editions and the Word of God became a 'bestseller'. These works were all printed in the orphanages' printing shops and developed into the large Bible societies still doing good work in the world today. When starting on Prelim Greek and basic Hebrew in 1959, my fellow students and I at the London Bible College all received Hebrew (Kittel) and Greek (Nestle) Bibles free of charge from German Bible Societies. They were so well-bound that I have used them at least weekly and often daily ever since without having to re-bind them.

Germany in those days had been mostly cut off from Asian Indian and African affairs. The Thirty Years' War had given Germany enough inner troubles to keep her from thinking of other countries. The orthodox Lutheran churches were also extreme anti-missionary minded. Many of their theologians argued that after the New Testament era the whole world had already been evangelized. However, the East had given up their Christian heritage so it was their own fault they were now

---

[11] This author is currently going through a daily refresher course sponsored by the Theologische Seminar Rheinland (TSR) and various evangelical bodies. All who wish to profit by these courses in other countries will not find the instructions difficult as the meta-language is the same. One only needs a computer and headphones. A more than basic knowledge of Hebrew is essential for pastors and preachers. Beware, however, of 'preachers' who claim knowledge of Hebrew who have merely learnt to translate by the help of a 'do-it-yourself dictionary' taking the first 'translation' they find as being 'an exact interpretation' of the original. I had a student once who explained the word 'dumbbell' quite out of context as meaning 'a stupid pretty girl'. It was all in his dictionary!

in spiritual darkness and the Western world was free of responsibility to evangelize countries which wished to remain heathen.

The reaction to this most un-Christian way of thinking came in the growth of both the rational liberal and the evangelical movements. In Francke's day it was common to hear preachers say that in the old days we were told to go into all the world and preach the gospel but now a Christian should stay where God has put him. Some of the finest evangelical hymns in German hymn books were written by men such as Erdmann Neumeister who felt that evangelism ended at the parish borders. Sadly, this thinking is still prevalent in much of German Lutheran and Reformed Christianity. In my travels in America, I found this strange idea even amongst the so-called Free Churches. Happily, Francke had kept his New Testament spirit.

Confucius versus Christ

In seventeenth and eighteenth century Germany it was becoming more and more popular to proclaim that the teaching of Confucius was higher than that of the Bible, Francke first thought of sending missionaries to China and corresponded with Christian philosopher Leibniz, a strong supporter of missions, concerning sending missionaries via Russia to China. As it was considered intellectual to have an inkling of Confucius' philosophy, we note that the Serampore Trio in India a hundred years later still spent much of their energies in translating Confucius. Leibniz opened the doors for Francke to become a member of the learned academies and societies in Berlin so he could put forward his ideas to the most prominent German citizens. However, doors opened through the Danish Royal family to send missionaries to India and King Friedrich of Denmark sent his royal chaplain Lütkens to ask prominent Berlin Christians such as Johann Joachim Lange, who later became a Halle Professor, if he knew of any possible missionaries prepared to go out to India and Lange passed the request on to Francke.

Part 3

Establishing a Permanent Witness in India

Chapter Six

Bartholomäus Ziegenbalg and the Royal Call to Tranquebar

Ziegenbalg and Plütschau are sent to India

The first Western pioneers of Indian missions who were sent out officially as 'missionaries' were Bartholomäus Ziegenbalg and Heinrich Plütschau who had studied under Francke at Halle. Plütschau gave up his post after labouring bravely for some five years, but Ziegenbalg, who had been the natural leader from the start and who died at his post, is seen as the most successful missionary of the day. Ziegenbalg was the son of a corn merchant of the same name, and was born in the ancient Sorbian town of Pulsnitz on the 24th of June, 1683 but was orphaned early in his life. The Sorbs or Sorbians, also called Lusatians or Wends, are a West Slavic people who live in the border regions of Germany and Poland and the majority still speak a Slavic language though all the Sorbs on the German side of the border also speak German. They were severely persecuted by the Nazis as Hitler could not tolerate minority peoples in his realm. He pretended the Sorbs just did not exist. The former President or Prime Minister of Saxony Stanislaw Tillich, a most popular man in Germany, is a Sorb.

Ziegenbalg's early life and upbringing

Ziegenbalg became an orphan whilst still only a small boy but both parents left strong death-bed impressions on his memory. Before his mother Catharina breathed her last, she called her family around her and told them that poor as she was, she was leaving them a great treasure behind. The children asked where they could find the treasure and their mother smiled and told them that God's treasures were revealed in His Word. Ziegenbalg did not have such happy memories of his father who married another woman a few months after his wife's death and estranged the children. When Ziegenbalg was only six, his father became seriously ill and, in anticipation of his death, he had his coffin made and placed in the house. A great fire broke out nearby and the neighbours told Ziegenbalg senior that he must flee for his life as his house was catching fire. The sick man confessed that he was not strong enough to leave his bed so the neighbours laid him in his coffin and carried him out to the open market place in safety. In the commotion, a neighbour took a quick glance at the coffin to see how the sick man was faring. He was dead.

Schooling in Kamenz and Görlitz

Three of Bartholomäus' and Catharina's children died very young and the eldest daughter Anna and her brother Bartholomäus were often ill and remained in poor health all their lives. This, rather than the Indian climate, and the sorrows caused by Danish enemies of the Indian Mission is responsible under God for Ziegenbalg's early death. Anna Ziegenbalg had a strong trust in the Lord but she was married early to a very stern husband. She took Bartholomäus into her family and sent him to a primary school in Kamenz and then to the Grammar School at Görlitz where he seemed, at first, to be more interested in music than anything else and joined a band of the Grammar School's musicians who called themselves the 'Collegium musicum'.

One day, however, as they were playing some old folksongs, there was a knock at the door and a young man, called Johannes, scarcely out of his teens himself, asked if he could come in. Once he had been given a seat, he explained that he was an itinerant preacher and wished to tell them that though it is a fine thing to play and sing songs praising the beautiful countryside as they did, music was much more designed for praising the Lord who on such a fine summer's day has made all things bright and beautiful. Most of the musicians mocked the well-meant words of the preacher and the 'collegium' session was quickly stopped. Ziegenbalg, however, hung on to the young man's words and was to hear him often over the next six months witnessing to the need to be born again in Christ and follow the path of the gospel. Though

Ziegenbalg had neglected his studies somewhat when playing in the pupils' band, which he now left, he neglected his school work almost altogether by meeting Johannes for prayer and fellowship every day and, after some time, accompanying him on his preaching trips. He believed Johannes, who was rather a mystic, was leading him to have peace with God. When Johannes moved out of the district Ziegenbalg felt he had been left in the dark with his only light and hope gone.

A mother's care for her son lasts longer than her life

Since he was a small child, Ziegenbalg had been convinced he would one day study for the Christian ministry but now he found himself most unworthy to take on such a task. During one night of torment, Ziegenbalg forgot the preacher who had become his idol and his thoughts returned to his mother whose last words were of the treasure she had left. He now realised his mother's great faith was schooled by the Word of God and left his bed, lit a candle and took out his mother's old Bible and turned to the text his mother had so often read for her children. It was Psalm 23. From that night on, Ziegenbalg became a man of the Bible, loathing sin and all worldliness, but for nine months he could not find mercy and forgiveness in Christ and his friends and teachers wondered at his melancholy and disinterest in life. Then, quite suddenly he realised all that his Saviour had done for him and found forgiveness, peace and joy in believing. He then took up his studies again with great eagerness and earned not only good marks but the praise of his teachers.

August Hermann Francke supplies a missing fatherly hand

Ziegenbalg, happy in his memories of his mother, felt the absence of a guiding fatherly hand badly and he longed for an earthly father with the faith of his mother. One of his teachers gave him the advice to seek out Professor Francke at Halle who had devoted his life to being a father to the fatherless. Ziegenbalg knew of Francke's work amongst orphans and decided to write to him seeking guidance. Francke replied swiftly, encouraging Bartholomäus to keep up his former ideas of entering the ministry and advised him to deepen and complete his Grammar School learning by joining Joachim Lange's famous Friedrich-Werder Grammar School in Berlin for the final instruction he needed before studying theology. In Berlin, Bartholomäus deepened his Latin and

Greek studies. Professor Francke arranged everything for Ziegenbalg who was still unsure of his suitability for the ministry.

Joachim Lange (1670-1744)

Lange had been a penniless student in Leipzig and shared a room with Francke which paved the way for a life-long friendship. Lange was eventually to become Professor of Biblical Exegesis in Halle where Francke had long wished to have him. Lange is better known in England through his hymns, a number of which appear in the hymn-books of English-speaking countries such as the Wesleyan Hymn Book of 1780 where we find Wesley's very free translation 'O God what offering shall I give'. A number of English and American hymn-writers have 'mended' Lange's hymns and incorporated them into their own works instead of publishing accurate translations into English under Lange's name. Some four of Lange's hymns, especially his 'O Jesus süßes Licht' (O Jesus sweet Light) are still sung in Germany to tunes composed by Mendelssohn-Bartholdy and Bach or the Bach School.

Lange, together with his close friend Philipp Jacob Spener (1635-1705) took Ziegenbalg under their wings and the young scholar studied Spener's *Pia Desideria* to his spiritual edification. A number of scholars believe Spener was influenced in this work by Scotland's John Durie. Ziegenbalg soon showed his maturity in the faith as well as academic abilities. After matriculation, Ziegenbalg spent several weeks at Leipzig, Wittenberg and Jena universities to see what courses they provided. Although still in poor health, he opted for Halle under the guidance of Francke.

Ziegenbalg's mistrust in his own abilities grows

This peace was somewhat disturbed by a letter from his elder sister Anna telling him that they had inherited a farm and her younger brother was needed back home to manage it. Ziegenbalg's old stomach trouble broke out again and he had to return home, not to take over the farm but to recuperate under Anna's care before returning to Halle feeling much stronger in body and spirit. His bags were all packed and he was ready to depart for Halle but two events hindered his return. The first was that a friend, faced with an eight-week absence from his church and school begged Ziegenbalg to take over both tasks for him until his return. Ziegenbalg felt duty-bound to help and reaped great blessings in the work. His friend returned with a young lady on his arm whom he swiftly married with Ziegenbalg being an honoured wedding guest, Ziegenbalg packed his bags again for Halle but suddenly Director Lange sent him a message to say that he had an earnest proposal to set before him prompted by a letter from Professor Francke and news from Denmark. The interview with his friend and former teacher was to alter Ziegenbalg's life completely. Lange greeted Ziegenbalg with the news that the King of Denmark, was looking for missionaries gifted in preaching and teaching to pioneer a church and school founding work in Tranquebar. He had found none in Denmark equal to the task and through his court chaplain had turned to Professor Francke for help. After deep consultation and prayer between Lange, Spener and Francke, it had been decided that Ziegenbalg and his friend, brother and fellow-student Heinrich Plütschau were ideally gifted to represent the Danish missionary outreach in India.

Heinrich Plütschau

There is comparatively little to be found about the life of Heinrich Plütschau (1676-1752), especially in modern works. Perhaps the best introduction to his biography is Wilhelm Germann's *Ziegenbalg und Plütschau: Die Gründungsjahre d. Trankebarschen Mission* written in 1868 and published in Erlangen. Plütschau was born six years before Ziegenbalg in Wesenberg in Mecklenburg, Western Pomerania. Mecklenburg had been formerly a Danish Dukedom but was captured by foreign Roman Catholic troops in the Thirty Years' War and rescued by Swedish intervention. Plütschau moved to Berlin for his secondary school education at Joachim Lange's Friedrich-Werder Grammar School which Ziegenbalg also visited for some time before matriculation. As Plütschau's parents pressed him to study theology and he was keenly evangelical in his approach to the gospel, he also opted for Halle University under the renowned Professor August Hermann Francke. Technically, he was more qualified than Ziegenbalg in academic studies but always looked to Ziegenbalg for leadership and played a lesser role in the affairs of the Mission, eventually leaving it after his first tenure there. Perhaps this is why we know so little of him in contrast to Ziegenbalg who became famous throughout Christendom.

Becoming proficient in Hebrew and Greek

At Halle Plütschau and Ziegenbalg concentrated on becoming more proficient in Hebrew and Greek, following their plan to read through the Greek New Testament three times a year and the Hebrew Old Testament once a year. Plütschau became convinced he should become a foreign missionary earlier than Ziegenbalg and was the first to follow the appeal for missionaries to India which both he and Ziegenbalg heard through the general search for suitable missionaries exercised by Court chaplain Dr Lütkens though he had originally, as Ziegenbalg, thought of going to Africa. Martin Tamcke calls Plütschau 'The man in Ziegenbalg's shadow' in an essay of that name. Nevertheless, it was Plütschau who took the initiative in leading Ziegenbalg to his true calling. Though Plütschau returned to Germany after five years' service, he continued to be a strong supporter of the Mission and taught Tamil for a time at the university. Plütschau moved Francke to set up a special department for the study of Indian languages. This had theoretically been the task of the Collegium Orientale, founded in 1703 but only Arabic was now being taught there so Plütschau became the first Tamil tutor at the University though other Dravidian languages were soon taught by other Professors besides studies in Jewish and Muslim literature and culture. It was through Plütschau that the mission was persuaded to upgrade the financing of the Tranquebar Mission which for five years had been very poor. However, it is said that Plütschau did not show the necessary gift of leadership needed to preside over the new college he had helped found and through Francke's intervention in 1714 he was called to a pastorate at Beidenfleth, Holstein, Germany though he kept in close touch with Halle.

It is clear, however, that Plütschau's view of missionary work which closely resembled Ziegenbalg's was rejected in 1714 by the new Missionary Society under Christian Wendt, which would explain why Plütschau was suddenly compelled to leave Halle. This is a matter which needs more careful examination as Wendt had protested greatly at Halle's intervention in Tranquebar and against all the universities at home and abroad who supported the missionary idea as propagated by Ziegenbalg. At this time, there were a number of leading universities in the Western world who were keen to promote foreign missionary enterprises. Wendt rejected their 'interference'. He maintained that missionaries should merely preach the gospel and then move on and church and school building and aids to the poor were no part of their calling. No Danish money was to be wasted in India. It was up to the Indians to look after their own welfare. Wendt's highly critical letters to Francke for interfering in 'his' mission are in the Halle archives and are available to all.

Ziegenbalg hesitates at the thought of becoming a missionary

When Ziegenbalg first heard the news that he was thought suitable to be a missionary, he could scarcely understand what this entailed so he asked for a time to organize his mind and heart. After a few days, he wrote a letter to his advisors claiming that on grounds of unsuitability he must reject the proposal. Professor Francke and his brethren took this merely as a sign of Ziegenbalg's humility and re-emphasized their conviction that he was the right man for the task. Ziegenbalg then visited his friend Plütschau to discuss the matter and found him convinced it was the Lord's will that they should go into all the world and preach the gospel. Plütschau told Ziegenbalg that he had often heard this from his friend's lips and said, 'Why not start with India?' Both friends committed the matter to prayer and all doubts and difficulties disappeared from their minds. They now both felt a strong call that they should follow Christ in His work in Tranquebar.

No time to say goodbye

After accepting the call, Ziegenbalg and Plütschau were immediately transported off to Copenhagen by the King's command with one hundred dollars each in their pockets and had no time to say goodbye to their families and friends. Not even Professor Francke knew of the final decision until he received a letter from Ziegenbalg on his arrival in India. The two friends had to leave their libraries, study materials and much of their personal possessions behind as there was no room in the post coach they took to the harbour. Ziegenbalg was happy he had at least his mother's Bible in his luggage. His last words to Plütschau before boarding the coach were, 'I am convinced that it is God's will to send us to the heathen but will I be fit for the task?' Then they travelled through Mecklenburg towards Rostock where the ship was at anchor to take them to Denmark.

Difficulties not envisaged

They were received in Copenhagen by the court chaplain Dr Lütkens but as the two men had not yet been ordained, they were sent off to the Bishop of Zealand, Dr Henrik Bornemann for the ceremony. To their surprise, the good bishop refused to ordain the two men without a strict examination in Latin and commenced his examination on an encouraging note by asking the question 'Quid est regeneratio', or 'What is the New Birth?' This posed no difficulty for the men who were well-versed in expressing themselves theologically in Latin enhanced by their great command of Biblical Hebrew and Greek. It was also a wonderful theme for Bible-believing evangelicals. Both Ziegenbalg and Plütschau had become used to reading and writing Latin texts regularly as schoolboys and students so they therefore replied quickly in Latin that 'the New Birth is an act of grace which transfers a person into life'. Further questions ensued concerning the state of the wicked outside of Christ and what is the content of the gospel to be preached to them.

A 'white supremacy' Bishop

However, the bishop who apparently believed in European supremacy grew wary on hearing that the candidates wished to take the gospel to India and pressed Ziegenbalg and Plütschau to confess that 'heathen Christians' were inferior to citizens of 'Christian' countries, though the latter might take their professed faith less seriously. Both men disagreed strongly with the Bishop and affirmed that all are lost in Adam and all are equally saved who have Christ as their Redeemer. On hearing this, Bornemann refused to ordain them. Dr Lütkens, who was present throughout the examination, told the King that all the essential questions had been adequately and correctly answered and that the Bishop was a 'hot head'. Frederick demanded a second examination, this time a fair and objective one, to take place within three days by Bornemann, who was warned that another bishop could easily be found. After examining the candidates again, Bornemann said he was surprised and pleased they had changed their opinions, which was quite untrue. Ziegenbalg and Plütschau were promptly ordained.

Perhaps we must not be too critical of Bornemann

Here Sarah Hinlicky Wilson in her Lutheran Saints comes to our aid in her article on Ziegenbalg with a further reason why Bornemann, whom she wrongly calls the 'Bishop of Denmark', refused to ordain Ziegenbalg writing, 'The bishop of Denmark initially refused to ordain Ziegenbalg because there was no pre-existing congregation to which he could be ordained.' Though I completed the requirements of ordination at a Scandinavian Theological Seminary at Uppsala University, I could not be ordained as I had no congregation to be called to. Instead, I received the venia concionandi from the Norrland bishop so that I could preach and administer communion in the national church and amongst the Samë people of which I took grateful advantage. A similar ruling is still practised throughout Europe. It seems that Bishop Bornemann altered his own opinions as he continued to ordain the Royal Danish missionary candidates throughout the following years.

Free to go abroad

Their first given task as ordained men was to preach before the King and his family on Acts 26:16-18, Paul's conversion and commission:

> I will appear unto thee; Delivering thee from the people, and from the Gentiles, unto whom now I send thee, to open their eyes, and to turn them from darkness to light, and from the power of Satan unto God, that they may receive forgiveness of sins, and inheritance among them which are sanctified by faith that is in me.

After this, the Danish brethren fitted Ziegenbalg and Plütschau out for the journey and made sure they had sufficient money to finance the start of their ministry, promising them annual funds. On 30 November, 1705, the two missionaries boarded the Princessa Sofia Hedwiga and started on their dangerous sea-voyage to Calcutta (Kolkata) which was to last until June of the following year.

Opposition from the Danish East India Company

One party, the Danish East India Company who felt they ruled over Tranquebar and not the King, was not at all pleased with the idea of missionaries starting their work in the colony which they were misruling and misusing simply as a means of making money for themselves but not for the Indian citizens. They claimed that the missionaries would convert and educate the natives and so they would soon have rebellion on their hands. They felt also that the missionaries themselves would challenge their authority and lead the Indians into rebellion. So, in secret, unknown to the King, his advisors and the two missionaries, the Company reacted quickly and sent off a faster ship to India to order the Governor of Tranquebar, the Norwegian Johan Sigismund Hassius, to do all he could do to prevent the missionaries from landing and gaining access to the inhabitants.

The Academy of Death

Once at sea, Ziegenbalg soon came to call life on board the Sofia Hedwiga, 'The Academy of Death' as there were several fatal accidents and serious injuries on board. Close to Helsingö a sailor fell from the top of the mast in the storms which had suddenly risen and was drowned. A boat's man fell overboard but was rescued by someone by grabbing his long hair as he drifted past the ship. The vessel was then driven by savage winds in the wrong direction towards Gothenburg and both Ziegenbalg and Plütschau became terribly seasick. On 16th of December a boy died on board from the pox and was buried at sea. Then the Sofia Hedwiga left Norway, Scotland and Ireland soon behind her but entered into more storms off the coast of Spain where two very suspicious ships, which appeared to be pirates, approached them closely but the canons on board the Sofia Hedwiga were loaded and fired and the threatening ships drew back. Further pirates chased the ship whilst in open sea and for eight days they experienced contrary winds as they were driven down the coast of Brazil. For a short time, the storms ceased but the heat became so intense that the sailors had to keep leaving off their work to cool down and once spent a whole day refreshing themselves in the now calm water. Then fierce winds arose again and drove the ship down towards the Antarctic Ocean. For weeks, the only food on board was 'mouldy bread, dead beer and stinking water'. This was quite different to seafaring in Carey's days when he could sit down in comfort on a ship bound for India and eat a heavy meat supper washed down by two glasses of wine.

Refreshing times in Cape Town

The Sofia Hedwiga happily reached Cape Town on 16th April where the crew and passengers stayed for some weeks. There were many damages to be repaired and food and water needed to be stocked up. The weather was pleasant and the missionaries immediately contacted the native Africans whom the found most friendly. They were not impressed by the witness of the Germans but found fellow believers under the Dutch. Ziegenbalg wrote in his first letter home to say that the Germans had given up their faith on leaving Germany and there was no German pastor in the city. They had an opposite experience on becoming familiar with the Dutch colonists. They were busy catechizing native children in the gospel and carried their Bibles with them openly in their hands to testify to their faith. Ziegenbalg writes that they love to talk to him about their joint faith. They had also many good theological books and accepted a copy of Freylinghausen's *Fundamental Principles of Divinity*, a work recommended by Louis Berkhof in his *Systematic Theology* for bringing piety into dogmatic theology.

Ziegenbalg was delighted to meet African children who were being catechised by the Dutch but was sad to see that the Dutch enslaved the Africans and did not allow them to be baptised even if they were taught and showed a true delight in the gospel. Ziegenbalg was appalled by this racist tyranny and misuse of the Great Commission. It was as if the Dutch were keen on introducing the natives to Christian doctrines to keep them docile but not keen on introducing them to Christ.

From South Africa to India

Ziegenbalg and Plütschau continued their journey on 8th May but the Sofia Hedwiga was driven helplessly by fierce winds eastwards, westwards and southwards in bitterly cold weather, thunder, lightning and hail. The ship's main mast was broken into three pieces and the foremast was shredded a few days later. Now the ship floundered to one side and water poured over the decks and everything in the ship was thrown in disorder.

After May 21 the passage became calmer and as the coasts of Madagascar and Mauritius were passed. Ziegenbalg had leisure to write letters home and start on a book concerning true wisdom, inspired by the boat's name 'Sofia'. Writing from Tranquebar on 25th September, 1706, he states that he had only time to write 26 chapters so could not post the book off during the journey as it was only half finished! On 13th June the party passed the Tropic of Capricorn for the second time on their zigzag course and the climate became warmer and on June 22nd they passed the Equator. Then the ship lost trace of its exact position and drifted on until 5th July when panic almost overcame the crew and passengers as there was still no land in sight and the ship found itself amongst treacherous rocks looming out of the sea. A strong wind now drove them mercifully out of the danger area towards the coast of Ceylon but storms prevented them from going on land. However, on 9th July, they finally reached the Malabar Coast and Tranquebar.

An Unwelcome Start in India

On arriving at Tranquebar on 9th July, 1706, Ziegenbalg and Plütschau found unexpected difficulties awaiting them. The captain had been angered by the Christian testimony of the two missionaries on board, especially at their protests when he made immodest advances to lady passengers both single and married. He refused to allow them to leave the ship even after all the other passengers had disembarked and the cargo had been stored on land. The Captain told Ziegenbalg and Plütschau that missionaries should learn to have patience. After three days prevention from going ashore, a German Captain named Mincke visited the Danish ship and persuaded its captain to place the two men in his care. The captain of Ziegenbalg's vessel seemed to think that the two arrested passengers would fare even worse under Mincke's 'care'. However, Captain Mincke turned out to be a most friendly man and quickly put Ziegenbalg and Plütschau on a boat set for the shore. The waves were most troublesome and soon the native vessel was about to capsize in the stormy waters but many brave native Indians sprang into the raging waves from the shore and steadied the boat, bringing it safe to harbour. Sadly, the enraged Danish Captain, now himself on land, seeing he had been tricked, flew at the native youngsters who had helped the missionaries, beating them wildly with a long, thick stick. He then turned on Ziegenbalg but Captain Mincke took hold of the aggressor's arm with a powerful grip, removed his stick and led the Captain away. Though the bully cursed and threatened he was no match for the big German.

Now, hoping all was well, Ziegenbalg and Plütschau looked forward to settling down with the natives who had proved so helpful and kind. Their first communications with the natives were in Danish as they had not yet learnt Tamil and Portuguese. One of native Indians, a fine young man of noble blood, offered himself as a helper and servant. He was to be the missionaries' first teacher in the Portuguese language and Tamil, their first interpreter and their first convert. The friendly Indians now gathered around the two missionaries and asked them who they were and for what purpose they had come to Tranquebar, and showed clear signs that the missionaries were welcome. Ziegenbalg and Plütschau had been called to the Indians who were now welcoming them so they realised they had found a new home from home.

Puzzling statements found in Ziegenbalg's Correspondence

It is at this point in Ziegenbalg's written testimonies since his departure from Copenhagen until his establishing himself as a missionary that Ziegenbalg's accounts become puzzling to me and apparently self-contradictory. When writing to the King and the authorities at large, Ziegenbalg describes events as if everything went according to plan with no opposition. Plütschau's reports were much blunter and explicit. However, we know that Ziegenbalg's correspondence was, at least in his initial period, heavily edited by his, at times, 'over pietistic' friends and some correspondence was even suppressed. So, too, Ziegenbalg's letters were immediately translated by his supporters into English. After studying German in several universities and teaching in that language for over fifty years, I still find Ziegenbalg's German extremely difficult so I understand the difficulties of those who have rendered his works into English. On reading English translations of Calvin's works, I found the translators had put words and thoughts into Calvin's head which he had never uttered. We also know, however, that Ziegenbalg was most cautious in writing anything which might hinder the work in India and support from abroad. Another feature of Ziegenbalg's character is hinted at with great respect by Plütschau. Ziegenbalg during the first years of his work in India was quite immune to the negative attitude of the East India Company. He could ignore it and forget it. He was so intent on reaching the Tamils and mixed races with the gospel and so stable in his faith that the Lord would conquer any opposition, that he just did not think about opposition at all. This 'stickability' was not Plütschau's who after five years worrying about such matters resigned from the Mission field. Then even Ziegenbalg became more critical of the behaviour of the Norwegian governor and his henchmen.

Chapter Seven

Uneasy Times for the Missionaries

Protests from the Danish and Norwegian authorities

Scarcely, however, were the troubles with their sea captain on land over when further opposition arose on the part of the Tranquebar Danish and Norwegian authorities. Whilst still on the dockside, the Vice-Commandant of Tranquebar, Krahe,[1] approached Ziegenbalg and Plütschau with anger on his face and had the missionaries thrown into a tiny, dark cell which was so hot and stuffy that one could hardly breathe. There they were left from morning until late evening without food or drink though their thirst was great. At last Commandant Hassius, a Norwegian of German stock and a graduate of Wittenberg University,[2] appeared with four officials and two chaplains and, though he knew all about Ziegenbalg's mission, asked for documentary proof that the missionaries had a right to land at Tranquebar, telling them that as they were not merchants, there was no place for them in the town. Ziegenbalg showed Hassius his credentials from King Frederick and the Danish-Halle Mission but Hassius ignored them protesting that he saw no use in their missionary efforts and they were not welcome in Tranquebar. He then had the two missionaries led to the market place where he left them to take care of themselves though the King had

[1] Krahe did not live long and his widow married a missionary to India.

[2] Wittenburg University lost students to Halle and was eventually merged with Halle in 1817.

commanded Hassius to welcome and look after the missionaries. Ziegenbalg and Plütschau comforted each other with the knowledge that the Lord who had brought them thus far would help them in their plight.

Ziegenbalg and Plütschau find friends amongst the Europeans

Soon a friendly Dane approached them and asked if they were looking for lodgings. On hearing this was the case, he said that his father-in-law would be glad to receive them. The Dane gave his name as Attrug and his profession as secretary to the East India Company, so he was a very useful first connection. However, Attrug told them they would never receive help from the Tranquebar authorities who were convinced that they had been sent as spies by King Frederick to report on the officials' behaviour. Attrug's father-in-law told the missionaries that he had a tiny house in the poorer part of the town which they could use. 'It is to the poor people that we are called', confessed Ziegenbalg. The neighbours in the dockside area were the down and outs of the town and mostly the offspring of Portuguese and low caste Indians who were looked down upon by most sections of the public. Here we can contrast the start of Ziegenbalg's and Plütschau's ministry in a shack amongst the Pariahs with that of Thomas and Carey who moved into a large expensive villa in a better-off region which they were unable to keep up.

Life as missionaries begins in earnest

Now happy to be with the poor, casteless people of Tranquebar, Ziegenbalg and Plütschau within a few days, and with the help of their new Tamil friend, composed a statement as to the intentions of the missionaries. This included thirty-six Christian objectives and prayers for the conversion of the Tamils and also the Lord's Prayer. This was first composed in Portuguese and then translated into Tamil to be distributed amongst the Indians and Euro-Indians in the locality so all would know that the missionary enterprise had begun. At the same time Ziegenbalg started on a Tamil dictionary with transcriptions in Latin characters and explanations in German adding words and phrases daily for their own use.

Through the help of a school-master interpreter who understood some German, Dutch, Danish and Portuguese, the latter language being the lingua franca of the area, the two friends realized that most of the natives could speak both Portuguese and Tamil so they struggled to become fluent in both languages. There is some confusion amongst writers in assessing the help given by Ziegenbalg's teachers. Two were gifted men but the elderly schoolmaster who was first employed spoke no Portuguese. Fenger, a later Director of the Danish Missionary Society writes of the missionaries' early language studies in Tranquebar:

> It was much more difficult to them to make themselves masters of the Tamil language, as all printed and written means of assistance were wanting, and at first they could not find any one who by knowing Tamil as well as some language known to them, could become their teacher. They tried it in all ways, but could not succeed. At last, after some months had passed away, they fell in with an old Malabar school-master, whom they took into their service and agreed that they should pay him a certain sum for bringing his school into their houses. Both schoolmaster and school-children were heathens, but the Missionaries wished to observe closely how the Malabarians taught children, to make acquaintance with the young people, to learn what they could, and were not ashamed of becoming pupils of the heathen schoolmaster. The two Missionaries might be seen amongst the children, seated on the ground and like them, tracing out first letters, then syllables and finally words, in the sand. Thus they learned to read, to write and to pronounce a number of words, but the meaning of words was unknown to them, for the schoolmaster did not understand Portuguese.[3]

Ziegenbalg and Plütschau's teachers

Fenger's words need correcting somewhat. The two missionaries had help from the start by an educated Indian named Modaliapen as we read in a letter from Ziegenbalg to Prof. Francke dated 1st October 1706, shortly after the missionaries arrived in Tranquebar. Modaliapen had boarded their ship before the missionaries were able to go ashore and asked them if he could enter their services. His reason was that he

[3] *History of the Tranquebar Mission* English translation p. 31.

wished to be instructed in Christianity. After being with the missionaries a week, his request to remain permanently with the Mission was accepted. This was seen as an act of God introducing the new missionaries to India and well-educated Modaliapen proved of immense value as the Europeans in Tranquebar ignored him so he was free to work for the Mission unhindered and served as a mediator and translator between the Mission and the King of Tanjore. This royal person had been 'paid off' by the Danish East India Company but still had a good deal of influence. Ziegenbalg had by this time persuaded the traders to give their slaves two hours of freedom each day to be instructed in the gospel and receive a basic education. A number of German traders (Ziegenbalg says 'viele', that is 'many'), asked Ziegenbalg to preach to them weekly. The Danish chaplains protested strongly against this move as it meant the Germans would not attend their services but receive the gospel from one more able to preach it.

Some Portuguese works used from the start by the missionaries
Furthermore, the missionaries had access to Portuguese literature from the very start of their work in Tranquebar as we see from a letter to a correspondent in Ziegenbalg's hand dated as early as 25th September 1706 informing him that he had a Portuguese New Testament and a Portuguese Grammar which aided the missionaries' studies of Portuguese. One teacher to whom the missionaries loaned their home for teaching purposes was ignorant of Portuguese though most of the Tamils were bi-lingual. Besides Tamil, some spoke either Portuguese, Danish or German. With his teachers' help Ziegenbalg began to catechise the Tamils, at first through the medium of Portuguese and then gradually Tamil.

The missionaries had access to Tamil works
So, too, Fenger is less than correct in assuming the two missionaries had no written Tamil works to help them. They had such works though they were in classical Tamil and not in the colloquial language of Ziegenbalg's quickly growing flock. Indeed, Ziegenbalg confessed that his early studies in Tamil literature showed him that they contained more good sense than 'Aristotle and other pagan writings'. He spoke of early studying the Tamils' *Arcana*. Critics unfamiliar with Indian languages quickly tell us that this word is derived from the Latin

arcanum meaning a chest in which secrets and mysteries are locked. They deduce then that Ziegenbalg learnt a nigh occult brand of Tamil. However, the term arcana is an ancient Sanskrit word, most likely much older than Latin, and means 'worship', 'respect' or 'praise'. Ziegenbalg was using literature of a high moral level and confessed that he was finding such wisdom in Tamil texts that their ancient writers would have laughed out loud at the crude material Western culture and philosophy supplied. Obviously to counteract European ideas that Indians were a bunch of savages, Ziegenbalg told Francke in October of his first year in India that the Tamils had 'many books' and claimed that they showed more respect for spiritual things than 'Christian Atheists'.

How the missionaries learnt Tamil

Now happy to be with the poor, casteless people of Tranquebar, Ziegenbalg and Plütschau made speedy headway with the languages used around them. Ziegenbalg soon started catechizing in Tamil, using Luther's catechism which he had quickly translated. Ziegenbalg himself gave a more comprehensive description than Fenger's somewhat misleading account of how he and Plütschau learnt the language:

> We did indeed have a Malabar[4] teacher of our own. However we did not know where we should get the vocabulary and an understanding of the construction of this language, since the school master could show us reading and writing but knew no Portuguese and could not explain anything to us. After this we got acquainted with a Malabaree who … besides his own language spoke Portuguese, Danish, Dutch, and German well. Him we employed at fixed pay as our translator, and through him daily acquired many Malabar words, up to several thousands, and memorized them well. After that, we busied ourselves to get the declensions and conjugations, and began to read books in this language. God let everything progress well. Then the Commandant recommended to us a grammar in the Portuguese language, written by a missionary of the King of France. We

[4] Ziegenbalg used the terms 'Malabar' and 'Tamil' interchangeably.

> obtained a number of books in the Malabar language, prepared by Catholics, which almost led us into dangerous heresies but not into an understanding of the language or a Christian style of writing. We had no means of knowing with what words and expressions we should explain spiritual matters in order not to give them a heathen flavour. The best book, so necessary and so useful, was their Gospel-book. This we examined first of all and took all the vocabulary and expressions to make ourselves well acquainted and use them in our daily conversations. After that we worked through other books so that in eight months had come so far that with God's grace I was able to read, write, and speak in this very difficult language and even understand the conversation of others.[5]

The Tamil scholar who was now employed by the missionaries was Atakapa, a former translator for the East India Company.

Three years of reading Tamil literature

In the documents preserved by Arno Lehmann, Ziegenbalg tells us that for the first three years he had hardly read a book in any other language than Tamil so that he could master the language. Each morning from seven to eight he practised the words and phrases he had just learnt in speech and writing. Then from eight until noon, he studied books in the Tamil language, writing down expressions he could use in preaching and catechising, guided by a Tamil teacher who helped Ziegenbalg put the poetic words which few ordinary Tamils understood into colloquial speech. There was no literature available in the common tongue so Bartholomäus had to be creative. Favourable books were read over a hundred times in Ziegenbalg's 'spare time' so that he could secure every word and its pronunciation in his memory. Even at meals, the missionary had Tamil texts read to him whilst eating. After preaching

[5] See E. Arno Lehmann *It Began at Tranquebar* via M. J. Lutz' translation into English, p. 24, The Christian Literature Society, Chennai, 1956. For copies of the original letters see Arno Lehmann (Mitwirkende) *Alte Briefe aus Indien: Unveröffentliche Briefe von Bartholomäus Ziegenbalg 1706-1719*. Many of these letters are in the Public Domain. Prof. Daniel Jeyaraj has translated and published much of Ziegenbalg in his works. See especially *Bartholomäus Ziegenbalg, the Father of Modern Mission: An Indian Assessment*, ISPCK, 2006.

and witnessing and organising the Mission for several hours, in the evenings, Ziegenbalg had books read to him in Tamil from seven to eight o'clock, partly to save his eyes and partly to be sure of the pronunciation. He then went out into the streets and practised what he had learnt through witnessing for Christ. He was then active until well into the night in spite of his poor health. The fact that Ziegenbalg and Plütschau learnt Tamil and Portuguese from morning to night gave them a great advantage over Thomas and Carey who were kept by secular employment using mainly English in their daily activities. Carey even corresponded with Fuller concerning using English as his main preaching language. By quickly learning Portuguese and Tamil and not being employed primarily to use their mother tongue, the two Dano-German missionaries had a start of a number of years over Thomas and Carey.

In Europe, the two missionaries had arranged that Plütschau should take care of preaching in Tamil and Ziegenbalg should use Portuguese with the half-castes and Pariahs but now the roles were reversed. Plütschau could not work at Ziegenbalg's speed and soon lagged behind in speaking Tamil fluently. Instead, he picked up Portuguese, the lingua franca of the area quickly and could soon preach in that language. Plütschau kept up his Tamil studies on leaving the Mission and even taught Tamil for a while in Halle but was turned down as Head of the Departments and Francke found a church for him to pastor.

In 1709, Ziegenbalg wrote to his friends in Halle concerning his reading at the time, saying:

> I choose such books as I should wish to imitate both in speaking and writing. I have had such authors read to me a hundred times, that there might not be a word or an expression which I did not know and could not imitate. Indeed in the three years that I have been in India, I have scarcely read a German or Latin book, but have given up all my time to reading Malabar books, have talked diligently with the heathen, and executed all my business in their tongue, so that now it is as easy to me as my mother-tongue, and in the last two years I have been enabled to write several books in Tamil.[6]

[6] Fenger, p. 31.

Ziegenbalg's single-mindedness under fierce opposition

Sarah Hinlicky Wilson places Ziegenbalg as the first of her 'Saints' in her online series 'Lutheran Saints',[7] and comments on Hassius' aggression and the East India Company's apathy towards missionary work claiming that these officials were racists and viewed the Indians as dark-skinned savages and protested at Ziegenbalg's treating their 'savages' as normal people. The Company feared their abuse of the natives, their whoring and slave-holding would end as the Indians had always shown their disgust at the European's immoral behaviour and might take action against them. They complained that it was wrong of the King to burden the colony with missionaries without consulting them. Wilson maintains that the reason Plütschau did not return to his Tranquebar post was that even he could not accept the natives as equals nor even accept their humanity. I believe Plütschau showed weariness in not returning to his post but this was mainly because of the burden of work and fear of the Norwegian, Danish and German opposition. There is nothing to show that Plütschau despised the Indians but much to show the contrary. Nevertheless, of Ziegenbalg, Wilson writes:

> But Ziegenbalg was made of sterner stuff. The persecutions didn't discourage him but sent him on the track that would overturn his own prejudices and make him not only the first Protestant missionary to India but also the first European Indologist, an educational pioneer, the founder of the Indian printing tradition, and—three hundred years later—the honoured ancestor commemorated at a weeklong celebration attended by over ten thousand Christian, Muslim, and Hindu Indians.

Wilson also says,

> Within eight months Ziegenbalg was speaking Tamil—and translating into Tamil, too, works such as the Small Catechism and the Bible. Within two years of his arrival he'd assembled a Tamil lexicon of twenty thousand words; by 1712 he had doubled the number. And Tamil was no easy language to master: it had both a poetical and a colloquial form, and the latter had not yet been codified in written form. Ziegenbalg gave the written

[7] Feb. 2019.

colloquial language to the Tamils, which is still in use to this day, and in 1716 published the first Tamil grammar to use Tamil characters.

Ziegenbalg's first mistake

As most of the Danish officials held slaves, and the caste system was prevalent, both missionaries first sought to bring the slaves and the low castes under the gospel. They provided extra care for the Pariahs or 'untouchables' who had no caste at all. It is here, however, that Ziegenbalg acted unwisely and gained opposition from a number of Indians. The event made Ziegenbalg thoroughly ashamed of his action and he confessed openly that he had done wrong, winning back those whom he had angered. Ziegenbalg visited a pagoda or small temple which displayed porcelain statues of Isparae, the local name for Siva, and being 'full of godly zeal', as he thought, on the spur of the moment knocked the heads off a number of figures and entirely smashed others. However, instead of lynching the missionaries, the priests of Siva explained courteously that the ornaments the missionaries destroyed were not gods but merely representative of the forces God employed in the world. They also explained to Ziegenbalg with many true examples how pagan they felt Europeans were. Ziegenbalg agreed with them. Indeed, Ziegenbalg could not help agreeing with the Tamils concerning many of his fellow Europeans who assumed the name of Christian.

Translation difficulties

Tamil is off-putting to Western speakers and no easy language to learn as it has eight cases in both their singular and plural forms. A Latin metalanguage describing grammar as used in most European language except for the Finno-Hungarian group is of no use here. In our English metalanguage the Tamil cases would be called the nominative, accusative, instrumental, social, dative, ablative, genitive and vocative. These cases seem to be in no wise constant as an organized framework as prepositional phrases are also used to depict a case. English grammarians often quarrel over prepositions such as Winston Churchill's quip of matters 'up with which I will not put'. As a school boy, I was not allowed to end a sentence with a preposition. Today, my English language is that of yesteryear.

Linguists speak of Old Tamil, Middle Tamil and Modern Tamil just like Old English, Middle English and Modern English. Most languages have altered their grammar for the worse by using complicated prepositional phrases instead of case endings. Even the French have stopped trying to 'freeze' their language. This has proved a major difficulty in long-term Bible translating as target languages often develop and change quicker than the translators can work. Most translations are thus 'old-fashioned' as soon as they are completed. The New English Bible is a case in point. When I return occasionally to Britain or the States after living abroad for some fifty-five years or more, I find there is much that I do not immediately understand. I met an elderly gentleman recently in Greece who had lived abroad for twenty-five years and was visiting his grandchildren. He told me that they spoke quite a different language to his now old-fashioned Greek. Even the 1979 new version of the Greek Bible presented to me by a Greek student of mine, which I often use, is now outdated. How privileged English readers are to have the Authorised Version which is still more understandable than the new dumbed-down versions! Modern Tamil Bible versions have received the same criticism in comparison to Ziegenbalg's translation.

Early successes and difficulties

Though still in their first year the missionaries made a good number of converts but these were rejected by their families and treated as Pariahs. As conversions increased, they were accepted more and more by their Hindu and Muslim neighbours as everyone saw the great change in the behaviour of the newly converted. Thankfully, Ziegenbalg found that the ancient Tamil writers criticised the caste system so he used their works to persuade the inhabitants of Tranquebar forward against the practice. It was easier to denounce the practice when it came from an Indian rather than European source. It was also his desire that when Indian's became Christians there should be no caste system to prevent them worshipping together.

Ziegenbalg and the caste system

When one reads Ziegenbalg's description of the caste system in his book *Malabarisches Heidentum* one quickly notices his descriptions neither tally closely to those of previous writers nor those of later ones.

This is perhaps because Ziegenbalg had mostly to do with the down to earth lower castes which were classified either according to occupations or to the lack of them whereas the higher castes were supposedly related to the gods and were not considered truly as people of this world. The Jesuits had kept up the caste system because they thought it reflected Western social classes which they accepted as God's will. Indeed, it is obvious that they assisted in caste classification and thus influenced the Indians. On the whole, Western Colonials kept up the caste system placing themselves at the head of it. Ziegenbalg, however, saw the caste system as more according to temporary social status rather than godly connections and sees his Sudras and other lower castes leaving room for development either up the social scale or down it. On page 198 he thus writes:

> Ein jedweder musz bey der Profession bleiben, darinnen er gebohren worden. Kan er aber durch Kunst und Klugheit zu einer Standspersohn gelangen, so stehet es ihm frey. Item wenn er durch seine Profession sich nicht ernehren kan, so stehets ihm frey einen Handel anzufangen oder bey anderen zu dienen.

> Each individual must abide by the profession into which he is born. If, however, he is able through skill or prudence to become a person of rank, he is free to do so. In the same way, if he cannot sustain himself by his profession, he can start up a business or enter the service of others.

This would mean that a person could possibly gain a higher caste or lose his caste for a lower one, or become casteless. Ziegenbalg even gives examples of castes which later dealt with different occupations and social ranks. Anyone, however, dealing with the Hindu caste system from the earliest times to the present age will see that caste theories have altered considerably over the centuries. Though Ziegenbalg taught that all were equal in Christ, some later missionaries built churches with three or four wings to isolate caste from caste.

Ziegenbalg's use of ancient Tamil poets

Ziegenbalg used the ancient poets and philosophers where they were usable, especially as a source for arguments shared by them with the

Bible. As we notice in *Malabarisches Heidentum* Ziegenbalg was fond of quoting the ancient Tamil poet Kapilar[8] who emphasised the oneness of God and the oneness of man arguing that the same rain falls on all mankind just as the same wind blows on them and the same sun shines on them. All men are of the same kind bodily and they all stand on the same earth. Surely there is an echo of Matthew 5:45 here.

Hassius allies with the Jesuits

Indeed, it was not the native Hindus with their caste-system which gave the missionaries most opposition but the Jesuits who had allied with the supposedly Protestant Danes and become extremely malignant.[9] Hassius' Jesuit-backed treatment of the missionaries became most erratic, sometimes allowing them freedom to preach and sometimes treating them as unwanted intruders. He allowed, for instance, Ziegenbalg to baptize his first converts in the Danish Zion Church in 1707 when he preached in Tamil, but when a further fifty or more were ready for baptism, Hassius became aggressive towards the Mission again. The young Church defied him by building their own place of worship in stone at the other side of the road facing the Danish Church in June 1707, just a year after Ziegenbalg's and Plütschau's arrival in Tranquebar. Because of difficulties with the Company Hassius led, this was formerly opened for worship in August of the following year. Ziegenbalg found a newly baptised convert eager to preach the gospel to his own people so started to train him as a catechist. Soon several more volunteered to go out into the highways and byways with the gospel. Here we find Ziegenbalg praising the international fellowship of evangelical Protestants who were supplementing the very sporadic monies that came from Denmark and Germany. The Tamils of Tranquebar are still praised for their excellent cooking and often Ziegenbalg and Plütschau were treated to delicacies provided by the local inhabitants, poor as they were.[10] On their part, the missionaries

---

[8] Though Kapilar's poetry has been preserved, nobody knows when he was born or died. Theories run from the first century B.C. to the second century A.D.

[9] There was a Jesuit church in Tranquebar.

[10] Modern tourist guides complain of the absence of restaurants in Tranquebar but advise their readers to visit the citizens' homes as paying guests where they will be very well fed.

taught the children without demanding payment and instructed their parents' skills in various crafts and husbandry. By the late summer of Ziegenbalg's first year in India, he was writing of daily blessings through witnessing to a responsive and friendly public and that he and Plütschau were opening a school for an awaited 20 pupils. It appears that these first pupils were children of slaves bought and freed by Ziegenbalg and Plütschau.

Hopes of financial aid followed by great disappointments

On the first of August, 1708, after living on next to nothing for two years, the news reached Ziegenbalg's and Plütschau's ears that a Danish ship had docked bringing with it the command that Commandant Hassius should pay out 2,000 dollars of the money on board to the Mission. This was accompanied by reports from both the Danish Court and Halle which were glowing in their praise of the success of the mission. Without delay, Ziegenbalg and Plütschau held a thanksgiving service in the Zion Church and the missionaries were surrounded by congratulators who rejoiced with the missionaries especially as 2,000 dollars was beyond what they had ever expected.

Scarcely had the missionaries returned home when a Portuguese friend burst in to announce that the news had reached him that the overladen boat carrying part of the cargo and monies to be administrated by the Commandant had sunk through the recklessness of the drunken Captain, the same man who had brought Ziegenbalg and Plütschau to India. The Portuguese comforted the missionaries by saying that the water was very shallow where the cargo and monies were allegedly lost and all would soon be brought on land. A friendly soldier told Ziegenbalg that even if the money was not found the missionaries were entitled to have the 2,000 dollars paid out to them as the King had commanded. However, the unbelieving Europeans laughed over the situation and told the missionaries that they had been punished by God. Then the news came that the lost cargo had been found but the money was 'missing'.

No help from Hassius

Ziegenbalg and Plütschau asked Hassius for help in finding the lost money but he paid them a haughty visit telling them that he had no interest in looking for a 'beggar's purse' at sea to aid the missionaries.

Ziegenbalg protested that one cannot call a 2,000-dollar gift from the King a 'beggar's purse'. At this, Hassius lost his temper and rushed at Ziegenbalg punching him in the chest repeatedly. After this disrespectful behaviour, the Commandant, who had been asked to be a godfather at a further baptism of one of Ziegenbalg's converts, declined the offer. When military leaders promised to pay Ziegenbalg some of the loss, Hassius refused to allow them to draw their own money out of 'his' bank. One of Ziegenbalg's party, Ole Thoren, a former sailor managed to get on board the Sofia Hedwiga heading for Denmark with letters telling of the success of the missionary outreach but also of Hassius' constant harassment and his accusation that Ziegenbalg was a 'Thomas Müntzer who opposed Luther'.[11] If Hassius felt he was a Luther, he was wide off the mark. So, too, Ziegenbalg was now refusing to be bullied by Hassius.

[11] *The First Lutheran Missionary*, p. 379 ff.

Chapter Eight

The Tranquebar Mission Grows and Prospers

Hassius as uncooperative as ever

There were now a further fifty candidates for baptism but Hassius and his henchmen threatened the newly converted with strong reprisals should they go ahead with their testimonies and prevented the new converts from publicly professing their new faith. The Commandant had allied with a Jesuit priest named Pater Guevara, against the Protestant Mission. This priest was also a merchant and feared that the missionaries would lead to his methods of employment being challenged. Julius Richter says of Hassius that 'everything he could do to hinder the Mission was done'. Hassius even stooped so low as to open the letters Ziegenbalg had sent to Germany, Denmark and England and remove from them passages which were not to his liking.[1] This could account for Ziegenbalg's early letters mentioning nothing negative about Hassius.

False charges against Ziegenbalg

Then, urged on by the priest, Hassius brought a charge against Ziegenbalg for kidnapping a child in order to have him baptized. The child had been secretly baptized by a Roman Catholic priest without the soldier father's permission who had now joined the Mission church. Ziegenbalg could easily show that the whole thing had been rigged merely to discredit the Mission and the case was quickly dropped, but

[1] *History of Indian Missions*, p.105.

in his anger Hassius had the father, who was quite innocent in the affair, run the gauntlet. He was beaten through the streets through two lines of armed soldiers until he could walk no more and collapsed from his severe injuries.

Hassius bans 'whites' from hearing Ziegenbalg

Then Hassius forbade all 'whites' to attend the Mission's services in the New Jerusalem church which the growing number of converts had built for themselves, on Pariah soil. He did not want Indians evangelising Europeans. The native church was growing in leaps and bounds and Hassius and his Danish East India Company were complaining that the natives would soon be rising against them. Now Hassius forbade all donations to the missionary enterprise and pronounced Ziegenbalg and Plütschau lawless rebels even though they could produce letters and seals from the King! His retort was that there was no place for the King's spies in his territory. Hassius then warned the European citizens that Ziegenbalg was planning to found a university for the 'stupid heathens' so that they could learn Mathematics and other subjects in order to win back their country again. The riff-raff of the community under his rule were better off without the missionaries, he argued, striving to obtain backing from those who had still not come under the gospel of peace.

Ziegenbalg arrested on trumped up charges

To back up this slander, Hassius sent twelve soldiers to arrest Ziegenbalg in November, 1708, and imprison him in Fort Dansborg. He argued that as Plütschau was a mere 'yes-man' who followed Ziegenbalg's orders, he should be left free. Having separated the two friends, Hassius felt he could 'soften' Plütschau to his side, then alienate the missionaries from each other and so destroy their work. Plütschau remained faithful to his friend and the cause of the gospel. From November, 1708, to the end of March, Ziegenbalg was left in a horridly dark and unhealthy dungeon cell without pen, paper and books. Plütschau constantly pleaded for his friend's release but was told that Ziegenbalg would be kept in prison as long as Hassius remained Commandant. As Plütschau did not stop urging Hassius to show restraint, the Commandant promised him that Ziegenbalg would be given a fair trial. Both missionaries agreed to this move.

Ziegenbalg prays for Hassius
Ziegenbalg was finally allowed pen and ink and wrote to Hassius:

> I do not feel any hate for you, nor feel any fear for you … You have forbidden me all that I have often asked of you but you have not forbidden me to pray for you which I shall continue to do.

Hassius, however, must have seen that a trial could only be in Ziegenbalg's favour so, on 17 March, 1709, after a promise from Ziegenbalg that he would keep a low profile and would accept a further prison sentence whenever he proved troublesome, Ziegenbalg was released after being imprisoned without charges for four months.

A growing congregation
Meanwhile, Ziegenbalg's congregation in his little Jerusalem Church had grown to 150 members and the Mission was strengthened by the arrival of Gründler, Bövingh and Jordan who arrived on 20th July, 1709. Ole Thoren, under extreme hardships, including a shipwreck, was still at sea. So, neither the Danish or German friends of the Mission had news from India. Thoren eventually reached Denmark a little over two years after his departure from India during which time there appears to have been no contact with him from either the European or Indian side.

Johann Ernst Gründler (1677-1720)
Gründler was of enormous help to the Mission. This faithful missionary learnt his rudiments of foreign languages at Latin Grammar Schools in Quedlinburg and Weißenfels before his studies in Wittenberg, Leipzig and Halle. He stayed on at Halle as a lecturer. When the first missionary reports came from Ziegenbalg in Tranquebar, Gründler felt himself called to go over and join the Indian Mission. Thus in 1708, after a thorough training for the mission field and with Francke's strong recommendation, Gründler applied to King Frederick IV of Denmark to be sent out to Tranquebar. Gründler was immediately sent to Denmark to be examined and was speedily ordained and shipped to India in 1709 where he died only two years later, heartbroken because of the fierce opposition of Johann Bövingh and Christian Wendt who had become President of the new Danish Missionary Society which was really an Anti-Missionary Society. Gründler served as Ziegenbalg's

right-hand man and became his successor after Ziegenbalg's death. Gründler proved invaluable both as a preacher of righteousness and organizer especially in church planting, team work, education and printing. He soon picked up both Portuguese and Tamil and proved a fine preacher and teacher to the poorer Tamils, eventually campaigning for the Tamil language to be taught in German and British universities. Immediately on Gründler's arrival, He encouraged Ziegenbalg to keep up supplying Denmark, Germany and Britain with news of activities and progress and he and Ziegenbalg informed a growing number of overseas supporters of the state of the Mission which was described as:

> Two small congregations, one Tamil speaking and the other Portuguese (Portuguese Tamils).
> Five schools including three for Tamil speakers, one for Portuguese speakers and one for Danish speakers.
> A seminary for training Indian missionaries.
> A catechism school for converts.
> A printing station provided with Tamil, Portuguese and German type.
> A foundry for moulding forms for type.
> A foundry for moulding letter type.
> A paper mill.
> A hospital.

Gründler supported Ziegenbalg strongly in his efforts to train Tamils for the ministry and was godfather to the Mission's first Tamil pastor Aron at his baptism. He is described in the National Deutsche Biographie (NDB) as managing the first printing press in Southern India which was incorrect, though Gründler did take charge of the Tranquebar press. Gründler, who was well qualified academically, began at once to research the history and scope of medicine in the South of India and wrote his *Malabarischen Medicus* for distribution in Europe. However, he sent the book to be printed to the newly formed Danish Missionary Society led by Wendt who believed such undertakings were outside the realm of the Mission and it still languishes unpublished in the Halle archives. Happily, W. Germann discovered this important work in his 1868 researches but only managed to summarise it in a few pages.

More about the legal, social and religious state of Tranquebar

Hassius strove to rule Tranquebar as if it were a colony of 200 Europeans only and the very dense population of Tamils, ex-slaves, slaves and Euro-Asians were merely goods and chattel. However, due to a letter written on 7th October, 1710, to a Rector Weitzmann of Pulsnitz by Ziegenbalg, we learn that Hassius was restricted by the Danish law of the land in his powers. This law was extremely complicated owing to the mixed population in Tranquebar. There were three courts in Tranquebar, one claimed to be 'Christian', one for the Hindus and one for the Muslims, the latter two being very particular about being overruled by the relative few Europeans in their country. However, though these were under the protection of the Danish Court, Hassius believed that the only rightful rulers of Tranquebar were the Danish East India Company directors who did not take orders from the King once they were on Tranquebar soil. Happily, Hassius lived to regret this merely theoretical stand. When the King heard of his inhuman and un-Christian behaviour, Hassius was removed from his post. This, however, was almost ten years after Ziegenbalg's first contact with Hassius. This arrangement was not always in the interests of the missionaries as by Royal law, if the Hindu and Muslim courts could not agree about certain cases, these were forwarded to the so-called 'Christian' court which often ruled in the interest of the DEIC.

Roman Catholic churches no different from Hindu pagodas

We learn in the 1710 letter that Tranquebar had also a large Roman Catholic Church run by the Jesuits but Ziegenbalg said that the liturgies and icons in the church were indistinguishable from the non-Christian pagodas. The Roman Catholics, especially when they allied with Hassius, were Ziegenbalg's greatest critics and they were particularly insistent that their baptism was the only true baptism just like the later Baptists in India who were ruled by Andrew Fuller who had broken from the old Particular Baptists. The Jesuits, however, strove to have babies speedily baptized so they could tell the Protestants, who usually catechized adults before baptizing them and their children, that the children were already 'christened' as Roman Catholics so could not become Protestant 'property'. In Tranquebar there were five large pagodas or temples and a number of smaller places for Siva worship besides a large Muslim Mosque. The Hindu temples were never used as places of instruction by their priests but purely for worship.

Bricks preferred to wood as building material

The Danish Zion Church was a fine brick building in which Ziegenbalg was allowed to preach to the German inhabitants for two years. Most of the buildings in the city, even those of the poorer inhabitants were built with bricks baked in large ovens. Indeed, brick burning was a major occupation in Tranquebar. Wooden buildings were rare because wood was so much more expensive than bricks. In a moment of kindness, Hassius himself provided the Mission with 20,000 bricks towards building their Jerusalem Church though this was also governed by Hassius' intention to keep the native church separate from the European Church.

Most Tranquebar Tamils did not own their houses

Most of the natives were not owner-occupiers of their houses and land but worked for the King of Tanjore whom Ziegenbalg describes as a king without a crown and a vassal of the Great Mogul. Many Tamils were little less than beggars as the vassal king used unpaid slaves to do the farming work. Most inhabitants lived on fish so Ziegenbalg preached on the beaches where the Tamils kept their boats and fishing gear. Craftsmen in Tranquebar were as various as in Europe.

The Mission builds a library

By this time Ziegenbalg had 145 converts, including those undergoing teaching in preparation for baptism attending his church, but not counting converts amongst the many Europeans to whom Ziegenbalg preached. The natives church-goers and school children studied sixteen books in all written by Ziegenbalg in Tamil and copied by hand on palm-leaves for their instruction. Although it was considered a crime to allow Christians to be given Hindu books or to sell them, Ziegenbalg soon built up a library of 300 of their works in Tamil. Ziegenbalg praised the widespread literacy amongst the Hindus and their progressive schools and especially their teaching on Medicine.

Meanwhile, Ziegenbalg was gathering over 600 questions together asked by Tamils concerning the Christian faith which he used as a basis for a number of sermons and for instruction in his schools. Encouraged by the growing work he visited Madras in 1710 hoping to found a Mission Centre there for the whole of Southern India.

It was not until 1710 that the next ship from Denmark reached Tranquebar and the missionaries had had no income during this time. As all the Mission's schools were free of charge and the missionaries had to feed and clothe a growing number of poor children, times were hard for the Tranquebar Mission. A few wealthy Europeans in Tranquebar assisted the Mission in secret because such help was forbidden by Hassius.

A large staff of native workers

Ziegenbalg and Gründler needed a large staff of native workers to assist the missionaries in running these churches, schools, colleges, factories and clinics so in their report they list fifty staff members in all including, church-workers, teachers, foundry and factory workers, a doctor, an agriculturist and a finance manager. These workers were divided into two groups according to their tasks which met together weekly to report on their progress. These meetings were also accompanied by much prayer especially for harvest blessings as the Mission was becoming more and more self-supplying.

The King informed of Tranquebar education

In a long letter to the King, the two missionaries stressed at length their goals in education summarized below:

> Implant true religion and piety in the souls of the pupils.
> Teach fundamental Bible principles.
> Provide a thorough grounding in the way of salvation through the use of the Bible and edifying books, showing how God works on the soul.
> Provide the children with a lamp of Christian understanding to help them through the darkness hitherto present in their country.
> Teach right Christian conduct as a means of combatting heathenism.
> Teach reading and developing a good style in writing and provide instruction in arithmetic.

Actually, the scope of education organized in Tranquebar extended far beyond this brief survey as pupils and students besides Tamil adults were being trained to take on duties as clerks, teachers, printers, paper-makers and gardeners. The younger children were not only trained in Scriptural topics, reading and writing but also in mathematics, botany, navigation and medicine. The methods of instruction were based on traditional Tamil practice and also included a knowledge of the Tamil Classics and music. As voices were now being raised amongst Lutherans in Denmark and Germany claiming that missionary help must remain 'spiritual', Ziegenbalg and Gründler were now wary about too much information being spread abroad.

Now Ziegenbalg decided to be more resolute and demanded of Hassius that he should allow him to go on furlough to Denmark, Germany and England to inform Europe about what was actually happening in India but Hassius forbade him to leave the country. He gave, however, Plütschau leave to travel back with a Tamil convert on the Sofia Hedwig which had brought the new missionaries to India.

It appears that Ziegenbalg's letters to Halle at this time did not always meet with Francke's approval as they criticized the powers that be in India openly. Francke did not want his University to be part of any political controversy. The missiologist did not have Hassius looking over his shoulder and his German work was basking in general acceptance. Missionary Director Fenger of the Danish Mission quotes from an unpublished letter from Ziegenbalg which the Halle authorities had seen fit to hold back for fear of man:

> 'God gave his rich blessing to all that we began in his name,' writes he, 'and yet we had a determined opposition, not only from the heathen, but also from the European Christians; even the Commandant and the whole Privy Council were quite opposed to us, so that not only did they not assist us in any point, but tried in every way to impede the holy work. Our congregations were increased weekly, and Heathens, Mohammedans and Christians were constrained to acknowledge that such a work was from God, but the authorities here would not acknowledge it to be so, but acted in such a manner from their hatred and envy, that even the heathen were vexed. The more we spoke the truth the more

were we persecuted, so that at last it seemed as if they wished to exterminate both us and our congregations.[2]

The rapid growth of the Tranquebar native Church

Living in the midst of the Pariah section of Tranquebar, Ziegenbalg had a large number of poor Tamils around him so he set up a large bamboo shade adjoining the outside wall of his house and announced that he would preach there three times a week at set times. This became a popular gathering point for the Tamils, both half-caste and casteless. At this time, according to the Svenska Missions Tidskrift there were 30,000 inhabitants in the colony which consisted of one town surrounded by a number of villages. Half of the inhabitants were Roman Catholics. Of the 6,000 who lived within the walled city of Tranquebar only 21 were Danes, 100 were Portuguese, 2,000 were or had been Muslims and the rest were Tamils of various Hinduistic religions, many of whom were now being won for Christ. Those then counted as 'Portuguese' were usually those of mixed racial backgrounds who were brought up speaking either Portuguese or the mixed Indian-Portuguese dialects which had evolved from it. They had received their Roman Catholic religion from their slave owners or employers.

Whilst still in their first year the missionaries had made some 35 converts but these were then rejected by their families and treated as Pariahs. In 1708 this small church had grown to 101 converted worshippers who had built a small building for worship themselves and by 1712 it had, according to various sources, at least 221 converts. Jeyaraj goes into more detail through his excellent researches and tells us that the Tranquebar Church in 1712 had 117 Tamil members and 85 'Portuguese' members besides 35 catechumens who were being prepared for baptism. Only a few years later, however, we are told that Ziegenbalg could gather seventeen hundred converts for worship and send out trained native pastors and preachers around Southern India.

An interesting anecdote concerning the Mission's press

In March 1711, Ziegenbalg at last found peace to finish his New Testament in Tamil and in 1714 the Gospels and Acts were being

[2] Fenger, p. 38.

printed off the Tranquebar press. This press had a most interesting history. The vessel on which it was sent from England, but paid for by Halle, to India was pirated by the French, captured and taken to South America. The printer who accompanied the press and was to run it in India died and the press lay undiscovered in the hold on reaching what Ziegenbalg called 'the Brazils'. The SPCK had followed the fate of the printing press and now bought it back from its new 'owners' and had it sent on to India after a year's delay. The press had only Roman and Italic types but the Germans moulded a special Tamil type and sent it on to Tranquebar. By this time, the missionaries were able to cast even better type themselves and provide paper from their own mill. When Schultz brought out a new edition of the Tranquebar New Testament, originally printed at the Tranquebar press, it had reached such recognition that a number of Bible and Missionary Societies helped fund the distribution.

Converts doubled each year

One can say that the number of converts doubled each year throughout the rest of Ziegenbalg's short life. Though Ziegenbalg had converts from the various castes, he encouraged them to ignore the caste system in fellowship with other Christians. His converts were casteless, half-castes and those of castes in equal proportions. Strangely enough he found more caste mentality in the lower castes than in the higher and it was more difficult to persuade the lower castes to sit together in church than the higher who had less inhibitions. Though mixed marriages became common between different castes, Sudras who were of the fourth or lowest caste, never married Pariahs and insisted on taking the Lord's Supper before them. Especially the Sudra Christian women caused some commotion when they objected that some Pariah men had been given the sacraments before them. The problem of the lower castes and half-castes was often one of language rather than a relic of their old religion. The half-castes of mixed extraction spoke Portuguese which they considered superior to Tamil so Ziegenbalg taught his casteless Tamils, and especially their children, Portuguese.

The Indian converts elect their own church officers

So, too, Ziegenbalg could report that he had preached the gospel to Tamils who had formed a church so the converted natives should be free to elect their own church officers and also their own disciplinary committee. He also encouraged his converts to dress traditionally and eat what they liked. Later missionaries were very critical of what they imagined was 'heathen dress' and 'heathen food', though they eventually adopted caampaar caatam (curried rice) though without the healthy husks. I would far prefer to eat Chicken Chettinad helped down by Archuvita Sambar (mixed not separate) to Fish and Chips. Thus, the natives of Tranquebar formed their own indigenous Church with Indian standards of food and clothing compatible with their Christian witness. Ziegenbalg diplomatically provided traditional clothing for the poorer Tamil children who could not afford them. Those Portuguese-speaking pupils whose parents had adopted European dress were provided with Portuguese clothing for their children. By this time, in 1715, the Mission Schools were charging no fees even for boarders irrespective of whether the parents were Christian or not.

There are two points of lasting interest raised by the above description of life in Tranquebar. First, the young Christian congregation's attitude to inter-caste marriages. Traditionally such marriages were less in Tamil Nadu than other areas of India such as Haryana and Uttar Pradesh but did occur in the Dano-Halle Mission. Ziegenbalg and his associates neither encouraged this trend nor contested it but noted that though certain of their Christian flock married up-caste, few married down the caste system. Marriages between Sudras and Dalits or Pariahs were nigh non-existent. Even today national Indian statistics claim that only 5.8% of Indian marriages are between people of different castes. Another point is the eating together of Indians and Christians and of mixed caste peoples and the problem of Indians inviting Christians to their homes. The early Baptist missionaries claimed that inter-caste marriages and also missionaries visiting Indians in their homes first started on Carey's initiative. This is quite an erroneous thought as inter-caste marriages had occurred for hundreds of years before Carey, though often under most difficult circumstances leading even to 'honour killing'. We know also from the records that Ziegenbalg and his associates regularly visited the Indians in their homes in order to catechise them and were very often the guests of Indians both Christian and Non-Christian in their gardens and houses. Buchanan and Carne both testify that Schwartz visited the Indians in their 'cottages'. Thus, all the more to be wondered at is

Carey's account of a meal in Krishna's garden after the marriage of his Christian daughter to a Brahmin, of which Carey wrote:

> This evening we all went to supper at Krishna's, and sat under the shade where the marriage ceremony had been performed. Tables, knives and forks, glasses, etc., having been taken from our house, we had a number of Bengali plain dishes, consisting of curry, fried fish, vegetables, etc., and I fancy most of us ate heartily. This is the first instance of our eating at the house of our native brethren. At this table we all sat with the greatest cheerfulness, and some of the neighbours looked on with a kind of amazement. It was a new and very singular sight in this land where clean and unclean is so much regarded. We should have gone in the daytime, but were prevented by the heat and want of leisure. We began this wedding supper with singing, and concluded with prayer: even we returned home with joy. This was a glorious triumph over the caste! A Brahman married to a soodra, in the Christian way: Englishmen eating with the married couple and their friends, at the same table, and at a native house. Allowing the Hindoo chronology to be true, there has not been such a sight in Bengal these millions of years! [3]

Since writing this account, the incident has become one of the many 'first' myths attached to Carey who wrote being blissfully ignorant of India's Christian past. We note Carey ate in Krishna's garden and does not mention entering Krishna's house though it had been common missionary practice to teach the Scriptures in private Indian homes for a very long time. This has perhaps led to the rumour that Carey never entered an Indian home. We know from Cox's portrayals of native Christians entering homes with the gospel, 'employed' as Cox words it, by Baptist missionaries. Cox, seemingly does not disapprove of this method but describes the Baptist missionaries as if they were mainly a labour management group employing native Indians to do essential missionary work on low wages which they could not do themselves.

---

[3] George Smith's *William Carey*, pp. 145, 146. Carey is referring to the most complicated Panchang, which, given its somewhat varied idea of 'millions of years' would still have pointed to an enormous exaggeration on Carey's part.

Part 4

The Ups and Downs of Missionary Life

Chapter Nine

A Mole Undermines the Work of the Mission

Johann George Bövingh (1676-1728)[1]

In 2003 Gerald Groenewald published his review article 'Two Editions of Johann George Bövingh's work Nachricht von den Hottentotten (1712 and 1714)[2] which he wrote from Cape Town for publication on his way to Tranquebar in 1709. The first edition of this published work is dated 1712 and contains also a *Kurtze Nachricht von Tranquebar und vorneemlich von den daselbsten seyenden Malababaren* and copies of letters he sent to various Europeans addressing his version of Tamil religions and his quarrels with the Tranquebar missionaries during his brief stay in India. This led Groenewald to research Bövingh's biography about which he says:

> Bövingh's career in the East is shrouded in mystery and controversy. It appears that soon after he joined the other missionaries in July 1709, he took charge of the school.[3] However, he almost immediately started meddling in the other affairs of the missionary station. Apparently, he accused his fellow-missionaries of mismanaging the financial affairs of the mission. Complaining continuously about this and other matters

[1] See Slaegten Böving www.tuyen.info/kinafarer/slaegten_boeving.pdh drawn up by Søren Bøving in 2003 for a genealogy of Bövingh's family who moved to Denmark and dropped the 'h' from the name.

[2] 'A Note on the Two Editions of Johann George Bövingh's Nachricht von den Hottentotten (1712 and 1714)', Quart Bull NLSA 57 (3) 2003.

[3] Bövingh had worked previously as a teacher in Westphalia.

to the authorities in Europe, he left the mission in Tranquebar in January 1711. According to Ziegenbalg he then spent several months in India making the missionaries and their work 'hateful' to the local authorities. Bövingh finally left India on an English ship in February or March of 1712. This caused Ziegenbalg to write to Gründler that in the two years that Bövingh spent in India, he had done no missionary work and had only caused discord among them. Bövingh's 'wilfulness and quarrelsomeness' had greatly damaged their work. What Bövingh did on his return to Europe is not known, but in 1714 Ziegenbalg wrote to Francke thanking him for having prevented Bövingh from returning to Tranquebar, thereby ensuring the 'peace, love, unity and harmony' of the missionaries.

The Apologia Epistolis Boevinghianis opposita

Groenewald, like most of modern writers on the Tranquebar Mission such as myself leans on Arno Lehmann for his quotes in English but is apparently also using a translation or part-translation of a reviewer named Raven-Hart.[4] It is interesting to note, however, that Groenewald in 2003 refers to an Apologia Epistolis Boevinghianis opposita[5] from Ziegenbalg's pen written in 1713 the whereabouts of which, he claims, is not known and does not occur in Lehmann's collection. Happily, I have had a copy of this 'Apologia' in my hand since 2002, brought to light by the research of Professor Niels-Peter Moritzen and published by the Martin Bucer Seminar.

Orthodoxy versus Biblical evangelism

Johann George Bövingh was a Westphalian born in the town of Hattingen and a believer in what then was quite falsely called 'Orthodoxy'. This was a very strict version of Lutheranism quite barren of evangelical or pietistic fervour. It was church-centred in a physical way believing that those who came to the church services could be

---

[4] I have a copy of R. Raven-Hart's book *Cape Good Hope 1652-1702* which refers to Bövingh in his Bibliography using Johann Schleyer's works on the Hottentotts for his brief publication but have not found the work Groenewald mentions.

[5] Against Bövingh's *Letters*.

preached to but not those outside of the buildings. This extremely narrow-minded and institutionalised form of religion in a way gave birth to modern Liberalism in its fight against such 'Orthodoxy'. It was Ephraim Lessing's protests at the hardness, bigotry and lovelessness of Orthodoxy in his quarrels with Pastor J. M. Goetze of Hamburg which led to his Anti-Goetze writings of 1778 and his publication of *Fragmente eines Ungennanten (1724-77)* which laid the foundation of modern Liberalism in theology.[6] William Fleming Stevenson in his work *The Dawn of the Modern Mission* says of the movement within the Lutheran Church:

> A purely logical theology controlled the pulpit, and dried up the springs of spiritual life: the sermons were strings of formal propositions formally stated, while the Bible was scarcely mentioned; and candidates for the ministry did not profess to understand the language of the Old Testament, broke down in the most superficial acquaintance with Biblical Greek, and frequently did not know a word of Greek at all.

This was the religion of Bövingh and one wonders why he was sent to plague Ziegenbalg in Tranquebar. Later, as we shall see in this book, it was a planned move by the usurpers of the Home Board which developed into a downgrading of Christian religion and threatened to extinguish the Indian Mission.

Bövingh was not recognised as a missionary but as a schoolteacher
However, Bövingh was not sent out, like Gründler, as a missionary but solely as a teacher in the Mission's schools. Furthermore, he was supported and encouraged by a group of Orthodox men who were entirely against Ziegenbalg's evangelistic work. These men eventually founded a Danish Missionary Society clandestinely based on their own principles of which the Danish King was unaware. They then insisted that they were the true employers of the Tranquebar Mission. When the King was informed of the Mission Board's anti-missionary tactics, he stopped them but not before they had almost ruined the Danish-Halle

[6] 'Fragments from Anonymous'. The writings in question were from the pen of H. S. Reimarus.

Mission and driven Ziegenbalg and Gründler to the grave. Sadly, it appears that Bövingh who declared himself superior to the other missionaries in knowledge and Christian integrity was sent as a mole inside the Mission to spread evil rumours of the missionaries abroad which he used to establish his own importance in Tranquebar and create a friendship with Hassius.

Gründler was one heart and one soul with Ziegenbalg

Gründler, however, was one heart and one soul with Ziegenbalg and shared his great sorrow at the down-grading going on in the new, self-appointed Mission Board. This oncoming trouble was known to the Tranquebar Mission's old supporters who placed funds in the hands of Gründler only before he embarked with Bövingh for India. This was taken as a great insult to his own person by Bövingh who felt his position as a representative of Orthodoxy was senior to that of Gründler though the latter was better qualified theologically and academically.

New discoveries in 2002

Ziegenbalg researchers are most indebted to the archive discoveries of Professor Niels-Peter Moritzen who found Ziegenbalg's own handwritten account of Bövingh's opposition to the Mission at Halle. This 'Apologia' was written as a defence against a work published by Bövingh in Denmark after he left the Mission. I obtained a copy of Prof. Moritzen's transcription from my colleagues in the Martin Bucer Seminar, Bonn in 2002 which was published as written but without further documentation, commentaries and footnotes.[7] Ziegenbalg's early 17th century German is not at all easy to understand by the modern educated Germans to whom I have shown Prof. Moritzen's transcribed copy which is heavy with Latinisms and many now redundant expressions. Previous publications of Ziegenbalg's letters show signs of being edited and updated in the language. I shall therefore not quote the original verbatim but give the gist of what Ziegenbalg has to say.

---

[7] Published by the Verlag für Kultur und Wissenshaft (Culture and Science Publications) who also kindly published my *The Covenant of Grace and Christian Baptism* (2007) and *The Practical Divinity of Universal Learning: John Durie's Educational Pansophism* (2011) and our co-production in *William Carey: Theologian- – Linguist – Social Reformer* (2013)

The original document covers some 100 printed pages and is invaluable in understanding the different attitudes to church planting introduced into India by Westerners of various understandings concerning missionary work which certainly hindered the spreading of the gospel in India. Prof. Moritzen's major reason for publishing this hitherto unpublished document is because he finds the discussions Bövingh raised typical of much missionary work which is passed for such today. The Bövinghs of this world are sadly still with us. Missionary Societies often seek to determine the policies of Missions as governing owners without understanding the needs and conditions of the peoples to whom they send missionaries.

Ziegenbalg's 'Apologia'

Trouble often begins in organisations over what is to be done with the kitty. Such squabbles started in the Tranquebar Mission in Copenhagen before Gründler, Jordan and Bövingh boarded the ship bound for India. Bövingh complained he should have been given charge of the monies which Gründler had received for the Mission. Gründler had been presented with a locked cashbox at the dock by Danish and German supporters with their donations in it and the key was entrusted to Gründler alone. Bövingh immediately objected that this was an insult to his own person. During the journey and as soon as he reached India Bövingh attacked the theological position of Gründler, the entire teaching of the Halle University and especially Ziegenbalg's leadership of the Mission. Bövingh had been educated at the Danish University in Kiel which saw itself as a rival to Halle and looked down their noses at the respect for the Bible taught and practised there. However, nearly all of the missionaries to India sent by Denmark were graduates of Halle and this was to continue for many years. The situation was something like the rivalry between Uppsala and Lund in Sweden; Marburg and Wuppertal in Germany and Oxford and Cambridge in England but Bövingh forced the rivalry to extremes.

Bövingh and the New Birth

Bövingh accused Gründler of thinking that he was an 'irregenitus' or one who was not a born-again Christian and aired his complaints in his many letters back to Europe. This lack of understanding concerning the aim of Christian evangelism caused perpetual animosity against the missionaries' main calling to take the gospel to the poor in the areas where they lived. Bövingh, who protested strongly and permanently over what he called the Mission's Bekehrungswerk or preaching that one must be born again, thought that the church building was the place for correct preaching and not the highways and byways. He felt that church life should be building-based and form the Christian within that cocoon from the cradle to the grave. The idea of winning souls for Christ which was the foundation of a true, spiritual Church seemed foreign to Bövingh as it was foreign to the Danish Missionary Society which was soon to be set up to follow his ideas. Yet Bövingh boasted that he alone was the true Orthodox representative of the Lutheran faith from which his colleagues had departed. This, he felt, gave him the right to leadership in the Mission community.

Bövingh given a hearty welcome in Tranquebar

On Bövingh's arrival in Tranquebar, he was welcomed heartily by Ziegenbalg who told him how things were being managed and gave Bövingh his own diary and journals to read and showed him all the account books of the Mission to help him obtain a grasp of what the Mission was all about. Bövingh met Ziegenbalg's friendly approach most coldly and accused him and his fellow missionaries at once of misusing funds in their care. This was chiefly because the missionaries were caring for the physical welfare of the very poor Indians in their district which Bövingh called a misuse of funds. Then Bövingh protested that he was not given the correct respect and acknowledgement by the missionaries and kept complaining of quite imaginary wrongs done to him by Gründler besides demanding that all matters of finance should be discussed in his presence. He felt strongly that the missionaries were being favoured more than he in their salaries ignoring the fact that all the missionaries worked far harder than he did, gave half of their meagre salaries back to the Mission and he was paid a good wage by the Mission as a teacher with far less responsibility than the missionaries. He had also far more time at his own disposal which he chiefly used to misinform the Mission's supporters.

Bövingh refuses to learn Tamil

The first major sign of non-cooperation on Bövingh's part was that he refused to learn Tamil. Ziegenbalg who now was very fluent in the language offered to coach Bövingh who refused the offer hinting that it was below his pride to be instructed by those he did not trust. Though Bövingh was very aware of his linguistic deficiency and felt he was being laughed at by the missionaries and Christian natives behind his back, he insisted, nevertheless, on teaching in either a language the Indians did not understand or a broken Tamil of his own invention which he felt all should comprehend. He obviously preferred to learn Portuguese but did not become proficient enough to preach in that language, either. On the few occasions he did, he had his text written out for him and then learnt it off by heart, which showed he could work intelligently when needed. However, he forbade the other missionaries to listen in to his sermons.

From bad to worse

Just when Bövingh appeared to have cooled down and even confessed that the Mission's account books had been well-kept, he still refused to add his signature to future investments in property which the missionaries had planned at his bidding and even told those who engaged in business with the missionaries that his colleagues could not be trusted. Things then became worse when Plütschau cooked a meal for Bövingh when he was ill but instead of thanking Plütschau, Bövingh complained that Plütschau was trying to poison him. Then he persuaded a Danish priest, who was antagonistic to the Mission to become his Beichtvater or confessor in whom he confided rather than the missionaries. Again, Bövingh appeared to repent of his aggression against his brethren and demanded they should attend him in his room when he was feeling unwell. He asked all to forgive him which they did with great joy and relief and shared the Lord's Supper with him.

This too, was a matter of moments only as Bövingh, after his recovery, sought to turn his fellow Danish teacher against the Mission by pretending to have inside information against the missionaries. The Danish teacher believed Bövingh and promptly handed in his notice. Again, Bövingh refused to sign the monthly accounts and torpedoed transactions which were not to his liking, always acting as one against three. Then Bövingh said he wished to set up a work of his own in another area. The missionaries agreed to this so that peace in Tranquebar might return but then Bövingh started to quarrel over the property put to his disposal and his pupils rebelled complaining that they could not understand him and needed a teacher who both understood them and they him. The whole school system was jeopardised by his incompetence.

Bövingh demands control over the Mission

Bövingh then became so blown up with his own ego that he demanded he should govern the affairs of the Mission complaining that the other missionaries were not competent enough to do such work. Then he printed a petition for circulation at home and abroad condemning the Mission on seven points. He maintained that Mission funding was not being used efficiently and he was not party to all that went on allegedly behind his back. One point was that he maintained that Ziegenbalg, Gründler and Jordan behaved Pharisaically against him and did not conform rigidly to the traditional Lutheran structures in worship. Again, this was really Bövingh's fault as he insisted in using the chapel for meetings for Portuguese-speaking people immediately before the usual Tamil services began which then had to be shortened because of his demands. He refused to have the missionaries in the church when he was allegedly taking services which was not part of his duties anyway. Indeed, Ziegenbalg and Gründler argued that Bövingh's seven complaints had only arisen because of troubles that Bövingh himself had caused. An example of this was that Bövingh censored Ziegenbalg and Gründler for cancelling the communi consilo or regular joint discussions concerning the work yet the missionaries protested that Bövingh would not attend the meetings or insisted on using them merely as a platform to air his protests and demanded a written agreement to his favour on the spot. Even when Bövingh agreed with his colleagues in the conferences, however, he refused to sign such agreements which were to be sent to the supporters in Denmark fearing it would be thought he had accepted the status quo of the Mission.

Bövingh also complained that monies from Europe were sent directly to the missionaries and not to him personally and that the Mission had made communication with Hassius most difficult whereas he claimed to be of one opinion with the Commandant himself. Sadly, Bövingh's many letters and publications to Europe now fostered a group of do-gooders in Copenhagen who became bent on having the Mission stopped in the evangelistic, outreaching form it had begun with so much success. This group set themselves up as being independent of the King and the Europe-wide universities who sympathized with Ziegenbalg's combination of a scholarly yet evangelistic spirit. Ziegenbalg's and Gründler's main argument against Bövingh was that he refused to witness to unbelievers even after spending two years in India, thus ignoring the main work of the Mission.

Bövingh wanted above all to manage the funds

Bövingh pestered the missionaries so long concerning his demands for access to the funds and the key to the safe that they gave Bövingh the key to end the squabbling. However, when quarterly payments were due Bövingh moved off to his new sphere of service taking the key of the Cassa with him. This seems to have been a move purely motivated by spite. The missionaries had to break open the cashbox to take out the money. It was then found out, however, that Bövingh had plundered the funds to finance projects behind the backs of his colleagues all of which came to naught.

Bövingh objected to a mission to the poor

Now Bövingh complained that the new converts were all of the poorer classes who only professed faith in Christ so that they could obtain free food and clothing. This, he argued, was a misuse of funds. Bövingh also maintained that the wealthier populace should be attracted to the Church so that it could pay its way. Besides, he argued, the poor were mostly former Roman Catholics of the kind we now call 'Rice Christians' who pretend to be converted in order to be fed. Neither argument was true as the new converts were catechized diligently in the faith over a lengthy period and were only baptized when they gave obvious evidence of their trust in Christ. Nor were these converts mostly former Roman Catholics but mostly former followers of Hinduism, Jainism, Islam or other religions. These converts proved their faith through much opposition by their former religious leaders but also from many Europeans in Tranquebar, including the Commandant with whom Bövingh sided.

Bövingh denied all the Mission stood for

Bövingh in arguing that the pupils were from the wrong section of the public and were a financial burden to the Mission was denying what the Mission was all about. The missionaries did not believe in preaching to empty stomachs but believed that care of the poor is a loving Christian duty. Furthermore, Bövingh's negative view of the Mission's converts was not based on actual contact with the Indians because Bövingh refused to learn their language and could not communicate with them. As Ziegenbalg concluded, and this must have stared him in the face from the start, Bövingh was quite incapable of doing the work he was supposed to do, and was allegedly called to do, yet he was most particular at being paid for doing little or nothing.

Peace could only be maintained in Bövingh's absence

The final break with Bövingh came when he confessed that a Mission to the Indians on the Malabar Coast was impossible as the people were so evil that even when they embraced Christianity, they could not part from their evil ways. Sadly, this became the argument of a number of Western missionaries particular amongst the British such as Marshman and Fuller who believed that to keep up their Christianity native converts must put themselves under the control of the British Raj as they were incapable of looking after themselves. This was not Ziegenbalg's view as he was amazed at the industry of most Indians, especially the many craftsmen, fishermen, farmers and scholars amongst them.

Bövingh's protests and his long campaign to 'reform' the Tranquebar Mission according to his idea of Orthodoxy when he returned to Denmark and Germany caused the Mission great problems which were to last many years after Ziegenbalg's death. The more positive side of the advent of Gründler, Jordan and Bövingh was that the new missionaries brought with them a number of books to add to the still rather scanty Tranquebar library and badly needed medicine for the missionaries' health work. Ziegenbalg was also able to finish his Tamil New Testament which he had translated directly from the Greek into Tamil.[8] He also published his *The Propagation of the Gospel in the East* in the same year via the English missionary-chaplain Lewis. This moved the Church of England SPCK to donate funds to help support the Tranquebar schools.

---

[8] There is some confusion as to the publication of this work. It was printed in July, 1715 as a 'finished work' but had obviously been circulated before this date.

Chapter Ten

The Tranquebar Mission Schools 1712-1715

Ziegenbalg's cooperation with Lewis

Ziegenbalg's correspondence and conversations in 1713 with George Lewis, the Church of England chaplain and missionary to the slaves in Madras, reveal that by that year the Mission's schoolchildren in Tranquebar were all provided with textbooks in their appropriate languages and the Tamils were well supplied with teaching material in their mother tongue and text books translated into Tamil by Ziegenbalg and his team which also included some 20 works authored by Roman Catholics, altogether amounting to 237 volumes. They had already a large staff of paid co-workers, mostly native Tamil teachers, catechists, gardeners, accountants, one Tamil doctor, two Tamil lady water-carriers and a laundryman, besides the Dutch and Danish co-workers. The five schools set up between 1712 and 1715 by Ziegenbalg and Gründler used the most modern methods of education known to that age and had caused a sensation as the Mission set up two co-ed schools, one for Portuguese speaking Indians of both sexes which then numbered 21 boys and girls under one master and one for Danish-speaking pupils of both sexes with fourteen pupils under one master besides the two schools purely for Tamils who could neither speak Portuguese nor Danish. Ziegenbalg and Gründler, however, gave all the pupils instruction in Tamil, Portuguese and Danish and catechised the children of the Germans through adding the fourth language, German.

The Tranquebar schools compared with Carey's schools a hundred years later

This must be noted by modern writers on William Carey who claim he was the first to found schools in India for girls. Yet, we find that a hundred years before him, there were not only girls' schools in India but co-eds for boys and girls together. Indeed, it is very necessary to compare the growth and extension of the Tranquebar schools with those of the BMS missionaries a hundred years later because of the many myths and legends surrounding the Baptist Missionary Society (BMS) thrust in India. The Royal Danish Mission started in 1706 and six years later there were a growing number of schools founded for boys and girls teaching many subjects including science, medicine and navigation, backing up the work of a thriving native church. Carey reached Bengal with a far more favourable reception but for the six or seven years following there was hardly any sign of missionary work done besides Carey's preaching to the European traders. We must also add that the Tranquebar Mission was printing school literature from their press also a century before Carey.

Twinning up Tranquebar with Halle

One of the most delightful stories of Ziegenbalg's educational strategies and a major 'First' in Ziegenbalg's missionary outreach was to twin-up his school-children with those of a Halle school so they could exchange ideas and describe their country and faith to each other. Prof. Jeyaraj writes in page 88 of his major work on Ziegenbalg:

> Another important intercultural relationship was the letter correspondence between the school children in Halle and Tranquebar. It was amazing that the Pietists encouraged their school children in Germany and in Tranquebar to pray for one another and exchange letters. Thus, they contributed to intercultural learning: in 1711 the school children in Tranquebar wrote a letter to the children of the Francke Foundations in Halle (Saale). When the children in Halle received the letter a year later, they rejoiced. On December 21, 1712 they sent their reply to the school children in Tranquebar. The content of their long letter can be summarized as follows:

> The children of the Francke Foundations in Halle wish the children of the Jerusalem School in Tranquebar grace and blessings from God the Father, and our Lord Jesus Christ. We write this letter to show you our brotherly love to you.
>
> Just now we have received your letter of last year. You can be sure of our love to you. We are about the grace of our heavenly Father through His Son Jesus Christ; this grace of God looks for justice and redemption. The news of your conversion in East India has spread here all over Europe. Dear Brothers and Sisters, do you know that those who accept Jesus Christ indeed become God's children? Persist in the Word of God; may it richly live among you, and help you to bear a thousand-fold the fruits of faith, love, obedience, discipline, chastity, civilized life, meekness, and humility. It may be possible that one day we will learn your language, similarly, if you would learn our language, we can correspond more easily and more frequently. In the meantime, we greet you, and commit you to the care of Jesus Christ.

In 1713, Ziegenbalg and Gründler wrote to their supporters and friends in Europe outlining their work in ten points:

1. We missionaries request God to use us as His instruments.
2. Conversion is entirely God's work; it happens through God's power, support, work and the blessings. We commit everything to God in prayer.
3. We teach the Tamil people in their own mother tongue and write books about the pure Word of God.
4. We have established charity schools to train able co-workers for our congregations and schools.
5. We seek to teach God's Word in our schools, and print books about the Word of God so that many people can read and understand God's Word.
6. We teach catechism to inquirers. Our catechists visit the inquirers in their homes and teach them.

> 7. We are not satisfied with an outward change of religion. We insist on complete transformation of the heart in obedience to faith. Therefore we are not interested in increasing the number of converts. Rather, we make sure that those who become Lutherans grow in active knowledge of the truth, holy life, and real Christianity.
> 8. We establish good institutions to achieve our final goal, and keep them in good order.
> 9. We depend on Indian co-workers and other staff members who follow our instructions. Every week they give us a report on their work, and receive our guidance.
> 10. We suffer for the sake of the Gospel.

Ziegenbalg's Tranquebar education report published by Lewis

By 1715 numerous Mission reports were being printed in India, Germany and England and distributed throughout the Western world besides Asia. We still have original copies of George Lewis' thirty-one paged publication in 1715 of a report he received concerning the Tranquebar Mission's school programmes and curricula between 1714 and 1715 with his Letter to the Reader prefaced to it. It is an exact overview of the timetables and subjects taught in each school system. As there were a number of criticisms coming from Europe and several misrepresentations of Ziegenbalg's work amongst the 'Heathen', Lewis opened his introductory letter by saying:

> The Intent of the following letter was to set forth the Method used, and the Progress made by the Protestant Missionaries in Tranquebar, in converting the Gentiles in those parts to the Faith of Christ. And the directing of it to me, being then at Fort St. George, was intended to satisfy the World of the Truth of what they wrote. These Two Places being not so far asunder, but that I might easily inform myself in the Truth of these things: And therefore it must be supposed, they would not represent Matters other wise to me than indeed they were.

We note here how this forgotten missionary to the slaves does not speak of 'Heathens' as the Tamils were no more 'Heathen' than non-

Christians in Europe but that Ziegenbalg, in accordance with the Great Commission outlined in Matthew 28, was bringing the gospel to the Gentiles from other Gentile nations. Ziegenbalg had been warned before his journey to India that the natives were 'black uncivilized savages and Heathens' and he had expected to meet up with such. On learning the Tamil language and reading Tamil books and talking to people whom he found often more polite, agreeable and even basically better educated than their European counterparts he quickly called the unconverted Indians 'Gentiles'[1] as can be seen from his letters, especially this letter addressed to Lewis. So, too, Lewis did not speak of a person's duty to exercise his natural faith as became the practice in later Indian evangelism by Westerners, but declared that Ziegenbalg (as he himself taught) introduced un-believers to the faith of Christ so that they might be converted.

Lewis also tells his readers that they must accept the fact that Ziegenbalg and his fellow missionaries knew best[2] about what was necessary and acceptable in Indian education as they were there on the spot and in close cooperation with the wishes of the children's parents, who, Lewis ventured to say, were more concerned with children's education than were Westerners. So, too, Lewis argued that Indian pupils generally learnt faster than their Western counterparts. He continues:

> But what requires to be considered most of all in the following Letter is, the great Charge those Gentlemen are at in keeping of so many Schools, and in maintaining so great a Number of Children wholly upon their own Cost; for which they have very little Helps but what come from Europe; and those, we have Reason to fear, are too short to answer their constant and great Expenses.

Ziegenbalg realised if children were neglected in spreading the gospel, they would not have the calling, nor the desire, nor the ability

---

[1] Gradually the term 'Gentile' was applied solely to the Indians by Westerners as if they were not Gentiles themselves.

[2] In comparison to the unworthy suggestions they had received from absentee critics.

to bring up a future generation in the way of the Lord. So Ziegenbalg writes in his introduction translated from the Portuguese by Lewis:

> Only this we say, that we likewise[3] are fully persuaded, that true Christianity, and all that make for the common Good of the Gentiles, at least here in the East Indies, must be founded and built upon Christian Schools for Children, who, growing up from their Infancy in the Knowledge and Fear of God, may, by the Divine Blessing, become a means of planting a Church of Christ, deeply rooted in the Word of Truth. Wherefore, we being sensible of this Truth from our own Experience, and it being the End of our holy Calling, that Men may be turned away from their abominable Idolatry unto the Living God, we make it our principle Business to procure, by the divine Assistance, the Establishment of Christian Schools for Children of the Gentiles; to which we have been likewise stirr'd up by Letters from Europe.

The organisation of the Tranquebar schools

Then Ziegenbalg proceeds to outline how the Mission's three Malabar-Tamil schools and the Portuguese and Danish[4] schools were organized. All school forms attended Morning Assembly in their respective classrooms or buildings at the break of day. This was really a prayer meeting and two pupils each day were encouraged to say their own prayers in their own words besides communal prayers. The meeting was then closed with a hymn. The evenings ended with the same kind of prayer meeting. At meal times (at eight a.m., noon and eight p.m., the 78 pupils sat at three large tables and whilst eating, the Word of God was read. The eldest Tamils composed meditations on palm leaves and the Portuguese on paper which were delivered and discussed every Wednesday and commented on by the missionaries. This was all in preparation to provide India with a future indigenous Church governed by the Indians themselves under their own authority. On Sundays, the

[3] Ziegenbalg has just mentioned the Christian Charity Schools in England.

[4] The slaves and servants of the Danes had to learn to speak Danish because their masters would not 'talk native'.

children were encouraged to repeat the details of the sermon and read edifying literature and were exercised in their understanding of Christian doctrine outside of the school grounds where adult Tamils gathered. Regular times were organized for the Portuguese boys to wash but the girls washed at home. On Mondays, the catechizing was done in nearby villages with the adults listening in to the pupils' work. Time was then given for personal hygiene and recreation in a large garden. During the evening lessons singing was practised accompanied by Tamil music. We remember here that Carey condemned Indian music strongly.

Whenever outdoor meetings were organized, the children were present with their Bibles in their hands and followed the exegesis from the text. Prayers were said for the rulers and people in authority. On Friday evenings, the missionaries, their assistants, the school-teachers the Catechist and Steward met to discuss critically the results of the week's tuition, noting failures where these had occurred. At the start of each month there was a general examination of all the pupils, both girls and boys who gathered together for this occasion. Though visits were organized for parents and adults during special lessons, the general public were always invited to witness all the tuition and examinations when they so wished.[5]

There was no special fund or bursary for the five schools which often did not know where the next day's food supplies, clothing and other supplies would come from. The Tranquebar printing press sent out regular flyers for world-distribution concerning the 'End or Design of the Charity Schools' which were worded under three headings:

> The laying a Foundation of true Christianity in tender souls.
> The preparation of disciples for the future service of Christ's Church.

[5] When teaching in the USA and when teaching scouts, I have witnessed a similar practice and in Germany we had regular 'open days' at schools when parents could sit in on their children's lessons. There were also 'open days' for the Gideons to visit state schools and distribute New Testaments and give testimonies. Sadly, this was not possible in North America and Britain but possible in Sweden, at least in the Sami Boarding School where I taught for a number of years.

> The bringing in the use of books among Christians in the East Indies.

Here we notice that the word 'Church' was used here by the Mission, meaning the general community of believers without such epithets as 'Lutheran', 'Church of England', 'Presbyterian' or 'Baptist' to limit its work. This was an intentional usage.

Ziegenbalg and Gründler now expand what they mean by The Three Designs

> The laying of a foundation of true Christianity in tender souls:
>
> Concerning the first Design, which is to lay the Foundation of true Christianity in tender Souls: We find, by daily Experience, that such as are in Years are not so well disposed, or able to apprehend Christian Doctrines, and attain to the Knowledge of spiritual things, as younger Minds are; besides, those that are grown up, being forced to work hard to get a poor Livelihood, cannot spare time for frequent Instruction: Wherefore it is our earnest Care, that our Scholars, of either Sex, should, in the time of their Childhood and Youth, be fed, as it were, and nourish'd with Christian Doctrines; so as that they may not attain to a bare historical Knowledge, or even an outward Practice of many Christian Truths, thereby to become like tinkling Cymbals; but that their Minds, by means of what they learn, may be sanctified, regenerated, and renew'd, feeling within, themselves the good and lively Word of God, and knowing, by their own Experience, that true Christianity, and the Kingdom of God in the Soul, doth not consist in Words, but in a divine Power, and a real taste of God's Goodness in the Heart; consequently that the holy Doctrine of Jesus Christ, when, learnt with such divine Efficacy, must necessarily be accompanied with a pious Life, and a holy Conversation.
>
> This is the first and principal Point, which, by the divine Assistance, we are perpetually labouring to inculcate to our Children in the Schools, by continual Precepts, Admonitions, and Prayers.

The preparation of disciples for the future service of Christ's Church

Touching the second End, which is a worthy Preparation of Disciples for the future Service of the Church, and the Schools in India; Every Day's Experience gives us to understand, that in order to have good and sufficient Matters, Catechists, Writers, and such others as may be useful on several Occasions, it is necessary they should be bred up in good Schools; and that not only on account of their being well rooted and grounded in all good Learning and Piety, but of their being skilful in such Methods of teaching as may be most for the Advantage of others. For the Missionaries cannot do all themselves that is needful to be done in the Church and Schools, and therefore such, Catechists and Masters as have been trained up in Schools, from their Youth, to a mature Age, and fitted for such Employments, will be a mighty Help to them in their Ministry. And this Hope, which we conceive of our Scholars, will not, we are sure, be in vain; since God gives the Increase to such an Education, for his own Glory, and the future happy Enlargement of Christ's Church in the East.

The bringing in the use of books among Christians in the East-Indies

As to the Third and last Design, which is, the bringing in a right Use of Books among Christians in the Indies; We know it, for a Truth, that the Want and Disuse of Books is that which chiefly hinders true Christianity, and such a holy Conversation as becomes the Gospel, from being introduced and propagated among Christians and Gentiles. How greatly the Distribution of religious Books tends to the Advancement of true Piety in Europe, is well known to those Persons who have made it their Business to promote Religion and Virtue. Now this Want of Books in the Indies proceeds, in Truth, from the Want of well-order'd Schools, for the good Education of Children. Who can doubt but that the Corruption of the Portuguese-Language, in the East-Indies, proceeds, in a great Measure, from this Want of good Schools, and the Scarcity of Books? We say nothing of the Gentiles, and their Neglect of so necessary a thing; but only speak of those who call themselves Christians, and profess to be Converts from Heathenism, who, by reason of their great Neglect of this Matter, know very little of the Christian Religion, either they, or their Children; and for the most part, cannot so much as write or read.

The Care of procuring good Schools belongs, in a special manner, to the Missionaries, and the Padres, who are set over the Flock in India. But it is no small Grief to us, when we consider, that there are such in the Indies, as seek their own things, and not the things of Jesus Christ. Wherefore we earnestly beseech them, in the Name of the Lord, that they will, for the future, lay this Matter more to heart, and show a more tender Concern for the Institution of good Schools, and religious Education of Youth: this being the only way to raise a holy Church in India, that shall be well-pleasing unto God, in his Son. For ourselves, though unworthy, we are very careful, that such as are under our Discipline, be they of either Sex, whilst they are instructed in Matters, the most necessary to be learnt, shall, at the same time, be taught to read and write well; this being a Means to promote the Desire and Use of Books in the Indies. For in case those who shall hereafter become Christians, shall be able to search for the divine Truths in Books, there is no doubt, but such a Search, accompanied with the Operation of the holy Spirit, will mightily conduce to attaining the true Knowledge of Jesus Christ, and his heavenly Doctrine, to a pious Life, and holy Conversation of Christians among the Gentiles.

The first Tamil Elementary School

This School had eleven pupils and one master. However, parents and the adult inhabitants of Tranquebar were free to join the pupils for the early morning tuition from six until seven as then the trained Catechist taught Ziegenbalg's adaption of Luther's Catechism.

From seven to eight the children were guided through the major doctrines discovered on reading the New Testament. From eight to nine the children had a short break for breakfast and read out loud in turns either from the New Testament or books on Old Testament history, with due attention to correct pronunciation and delivery. From nine to ten the pupils studied how all the doctrines of Christianity merged with each other into one great plan of salvation. The following two hours were devoted to Tamil poetry and letter writing after which there was a well-earned break of an hour when food was served.

German children now go home after six lessons of three-quarters of an hour each day starting at 8:30 a.m. Morning assemblies have been almost abolished. In contrast, the Tamil children assembled at daybreak for prayer and studied from six in the morning until half-past seven in the evening with breaks for meals. After one in the afternoon, the pupils were taken to the Portuguese school and instructed for an hour in that language. From two to four, the pupils then transcribed works from the school library with a steel pen on palm leaves just as Ziegenbalg had composed his first works. The next two hours were taken up with learning arithmetic in the Tamil way. From six to half-past seven the class was divided; the younger children being again catechized in Christian doctrine by older prefects. The time between six and half past seven was set apart on Sundays and Fridays to discuss the sermons held at church. This discussion was also carried out by a system of questions and answers.

The Second Tamil Elementary School

The second Tamil school had twenty-one younger boys under one master. These pupils contained pupils of various reading and writing standards. School started at six for them, too, and the first lesson was taken up with catechising. From seven to eight they repeated the lessons taught the day before. From eight to ten the young boys learnt the Tamil Alphabet with its variations and how to spell, and simple reading exercises were given based on hymn books, catechisms or a book named *The Method of Salvation* which was used as a text book. This was continued throughout the next two hours with part of the class working in private study but those who were slow at reading were given extra tuition.

In the afternoon the pupils sat on the sand floor, writing their letters with their fingers, chanting the names of the letters as they wrote them. In his first year, Ziegenbalg learnt his Tamil letters with the children in this way. The rest of the school day until 7:30 p.m. was similar to the timetable of the first school.

Tranquebar teaching methods were not inferior to relatively modern European methods

This all reminds me of the time I worked in Switzerland during my teacher-training as a fill-in teacher in a junior school during the early sixties. All the classes met in one large hall as they had no separate classrooms as in Tranquebar. Here, they sat in groups according to proficiency. I had to give different lessons to different groups who chanted out what they were doing so I could hear how they were progressing and then, when they thought everyone in the group had mastered the exercise, the whole group would clap their hands so that I could go and check their work. As most of the pupils were quite bright and quick to learn, I had to be off like a rocket every few minutes to check one group after the other. The poor children from around six to ten years of age were very small of stature and fitted out with clothing which seemed to consist of a long black cloak with a large hood which encompassed the children fully so that one could hardly tell who was a boy and who a girl and how old they were. Instead of sand, they had slates. Even as late as the nineties, in Germany, I had to carry a class-set of text books from classroom to classroom as the schools could not provide every pupil with books. I relate this to show that Ziegenbalg's five schools could well compete with the many relatively modern schools I have taught in throughout the Western world for over forty years.

The Girls' School

The third school catered for eleven girls with one mistress. The older and younger girls met with the missionaries for catechizing in the first hour from six to seven and these were also joined by the adult catechumens. The second lesson was for learning Scriptural proofs off-by-heart and the third lesson took the form of a conference where the older girls discussed items of the Christian faith and practice with one another. The younger girls during this period learnt their catechism, some doctrine and sang spiritual songs to Tamil tunes. The rest of the school hours were taken up by repeating texts or questions and answers off-by-heart, the elder girls learning to sew and the younger ones to write in the sand. In the last few lessons, the older girls practised hand-writing with a pen on palm leaves with attention given to composition and style. The younger pupils read aloud from their school books.

The Portuguese Co-Ed School

The Portuguese school catered for twenty-one boys and girls, most of 'mixed' parentage, under one master. These shared the first catechism lesson with the pupils of the Danish school and adults from the town. From seven to eight the girls and boys studied two chapters of the New Testament, reading them out loud. Then the teacher expounded the chapters and examined the pupils to see if everything had been understood. Those who had made a profession of Christ were prepared by the catechist for baptism. From eight to ten the twenty-one pupils were trained in the Catechism by questions and answers. One part was worked through in a month and the whole Catechism was gone through in a year. The younger members of the class either read the *Method of Salvation* or practised spelling aided by a Primer. Some were taught the significance of baptism and the already baptised are prepared for the Lord's Supper. The older pupils practised maths and accounting from ten to eleven whilst the young ones learnt Scriptural proofs for the Biblical teaching found in the *Method of Salvation.* From eleven to twelve the older pupils join with the Tamils and the Danes twice a week to study geography and the globe and on the other days they studied works in Portuguese which had an elegant style or bettered their writing skills. The little children were catechized through the *Method of Salvation.*

In the afternoons, the older children went over to the Tamil school for an hour to learn to read and write their mother tongue and the younger ones learnt Old Testament and New Testament history. Then for two hours the older children improved their hand-writing and the younger their reading. From four to five maths was again on the curriculum and the youngsters carried on with their reading. Then from five to six the class was again split up with the older children spending an hour learning Tamil and the younger ones summarizing a book on Christian doctrine of which the school library had now quite a stock. In the evening lessons the older children discussed and questioned one another on the catechism and the small children were catechised by the master.

The Danish Co-Ed School

This school consisted of fourteen scholars of both sexes under one master. The pupils were mostly the offspring of Danish Europeans and their Indian Concubines or Danish slaves who were compelled to speak the language of their masters. A number of these slaves were not Tamils but Bengalis. Tuition in this school started at seven o'clock after breakfast.

The lesson began with one pupil reading a chapter from the New Testament and the master asking the pupils what they have gained from the chapter for their own edification. When time allowed, the master picked out a text for extra scrutiny. From eight to nine the elder pupils learnt maths, others perfected their reading, some in the Gospels, others in the Psalms and still others in The Song of Songs (Canticles). From nine to ten work was done on the Catechism, Psalms and other books of the Bible. On Saturdays, they learnt the gospel appointed for the Sunday services. From ten to eleven the pupils worked on the Catechism and on Wednesdays they were examined in the doctrines outlined in the *Method of Salvation*. This school officially closed the morning lessons for all at eleven a.m. but on Tuesdays and Thursdays the 'head scholars' learned Geography and the usage of the globe with their counterparts in the other schools. School continued in the afternoons from two to four by studies in the Old Testament or writing practise or taking down dictations to perfect their orthography. The younger pupils continued their work started in the eight o'clock lesson. From four to six, the older pupils learnt and practised Arithmetic or studied Danish letters so as to better their own letter-writing skills. Others worked on their text books or read the New Testament in Portuguese.

The Danish-speaking pupils had less schoolwork to do than the others. This was not because they were privileged but because, though children, they were in employment by their masters and mistresses at certain times of the day.

The educational progress shown in the Tranquebar schools

Still today, there are educationalists who turn their noses up at Christian education and believe that religion has no place in either literature or education so we must accept that Ziegenbalg's schools reflected an educational progress not yet anchored in most modern educational theories which are highly restrictive in their knowledge engineering. During my own international training in four countries, I had to teach Scripture in several classes, including a British Grammar School where the standard was far lower than at Tranquebar. There were also fewer Bibles and textbooks to be had. In Britain and Germany, I had some fifty pupils in my classes and those pupils who came late had to either sit on the floor or on the window-sills as there were no chairs left. As school librarian I had pitifully few books to manage and my meagre annual budget after two years was reduced to nothing at all.

One may criticize the idea of co-ed schools as did C. S. Lewis and I, as an educationalist, would agree with his reasons. However, this 'politically correct' method of gender mismanagement is now considered 'modern' all over Europe and in the United States of America. Ziegenbalg was therefore 'modern' long before the rest of the world caught up and introduced the method and practised it over three hundred years ago. It is now also 'modern' to use a multi-lingual approach to education, though this is proving difficult to manage in the Western world. Here in Germany in the Grammar Schools some six lessons per week in several subjects are taught in a second language but English and French in the elementary schools are sadly gradually disappearing. Which school we may ask nowadays teaches general education at elementary school level in three and more languages? Western education mis-trains reading learners so that they can scarcely compose meaningful sentences after a year's schooling. I was not taught a foreign language in the Elementary or Junior School in Bradford, England at all and had only one grammar-based foreign language at a British Grammar school, French. Most of the G.C.E.'s at Ordinary and Advanced Level which I took at eighteen and twenty respectively because of leaving school prematurely, including German, Swedish, Latin, Greek and Ancient History were not on the curriculum of my class at day school, though Geography was. Even the latter subject was not taught in several of my subsequent schools. When I taught in a Primary School in Paddington, London, during my teacher-training, the only foreign language element taught there was the singing of *Meunier tu dors* and *Sur le pont D'Avignon*.

The Western World is still basically mono-linguistic

The trouble with research into Indian religions and history in the Anglo-Saxon world, as foreigners are quick to point out, is that English-speaking academics are still mostly monolingual. The joy and thrill of research demands that the researcher be multi-lingual to be able to at least understand the written words of source materials. The reward, however, for this uplifting learning is great. Ziegenbalg always emphasized that the learning of languages was essential to the Great Commission. As India is a polyglot and multi-cultural nation, there is no sense in sending out missionaries such as Bövingh who refuse to learn and speak the indigenous languages and look down on the people to whom they yet believe themselves called. Do-gooders often do badly. Yet some sociolects in Indian society itself also show signs of a dumbing-down in learning and religious freedom in their usages. There is a strong movement in India today to cut all religions down to a syncretistic Hinduism and all languages down to Hindi and English. Religious freedom used to be one of the crowns which fitted India's head perfectly. This causes strife between the remaining religions. Now the great dumbing-down of learning, in a social, religious and political sense hinders gospel preaching in India no end and this is not basically the fault of the Indians themselves. The Western world has just messed things up, to be blunt. It was this kind of attitude which caused India as a single, united country to split up into religious and linguistic elements in the 1940s which is continuing in the present day. Hence, Pakistan's, Bangladesh' and today's Kashmir's attitude to a shrunken India. Religion goes hand in hand with linguistic and political warfare in these four divided countries. There are, however, a growing number of smaller enclaves of the dissatisfied which point to future problems for India. Even Christianity in India is divided geographically between the South and the North which occasionally causes unrest and rivalry amongst the churches because of different approaches and theologies.

Chapter Eleven

The Tranquebar Church Outreach Receives International Praise

Planting missionary stations in British and Dutch controlled India

As Hassius would not allow Ziegenbalg to extend his work in and around Tranquebar, Ziegenbalg travelled to British Madras to the North and to Dutch Negapatam[1] in the South in order to have Mission Stations placed there. He was pleased to find that missionary-minded universities in Denmark, The Netherlands and Germany were backing him with interest now growing in other countries such as the U.S.A. Ziegenbalg's interest in planting a Mission in Madras where he worked for six months found mutual support and backing from like-minded George Lewis which opened up doors in Britain for the future of the Tranquebar work and outreach. The Armenian merchants in Madras also gave Ziegenbalg their support and backing which Prof. Jeyaraj says was none too soon as by 1712 four years had gone by without funding from Denmark and when this came its distribution was heavily curbed by Bövingh's protests.

Hassius claims he has orders to close down the Mission

Any news from Plütschau which might have eased Ziegenbalg's mind took several years before it came through and the situation in Tranquebar became more difficult because of Hassius' aggression and

[1] Now Nagapattinam

the lack of support from the Danish East India Company. Hassius, now called the missionaries to his headquarters and read to them secret orders he claimed he had received from the East Indian Company's directors which commanded him to use all his authority to stop the work of the Tranquebar Mission. This was obviously bluff and Hassius was powerless to implement the order but he still tried his level best to suppress Ziegenbalg's work by means more foul than fair. This opposition forced Ziegenbalg to look for sympathy, understanding and support further afield.

It is thus absolutely amazing that in times of great trouble when Bövingh and others were broadcasting that foreign missionary work was doomed to failure, the Tranquebar Church began to grow and extend its outreach.

Friends in England

Ziegenbalg had now many friends and followers in Britain, particularly in Court and government circles due to the Danish and Hanoverian presence there. Now a good number of evangelical and missionary-minded people in high places kept in touch with Ziegenbalg, especially through the encouragement of Court Chaplain Böhme. It is constantly argued in works on Ziegenbalg that he was supported by the Church of England. Actually, the initial support was from Lutheran evangelicals and Pietists in Britain and through the international connections between the royal houses of Europe who supported the work of several early missionary societies. These displayed a healthy combination of Lutheran and Reformed principles and provided Britain with the impetus to send out missionaries throughout the world, especially to the Americas and India.

The closest ties between Britain and Denmark

At this point in history, Britain and Denmark enjoyed the closest ties. George, Prince of Denmark and Norway and son of King Frederick III of Denmark and uncle of King Frederick IV of Denmark married Queen Anne of England in 1683 and both he and the Queen expressed the need to send out missionaries to all the world. Anton Wilhelm Böhme (1679-1722) was a graduate of Halle under Prof. Francke and would have known Ziegenbalg and Plütschau in their student years. He was also good friends with the Danish Court and especially with Prince George's

Personal Secretary Heinrich Wilhelm Ludolf. In 1705, the year Ziegenbalg sailed for India, Böhme became Chaplain to Prince George who was now also the Duke of Cumberland. George, being a Nonconformist and Whig and backed by his wife who had the larger purse being the Queen, supported the rights of British Nonconformists. At the instigation of Queen Anne, Böhme introduced the *Book of Common Prayer* into George's St. James Chapel which eventually merged Lutheran and Reformed Church of England worship. George died in 1708 smitten with the dropsy and other lethal ailments. When George I, Anne's second cousin, took over the British throne, Böhme remained Court Chaplain until his own death on 27th May, 1722 aged only 48 years.

Böhme left some impact on the evangelical Reformed scene and several of his works gained a wide circulation in their Latin, German and English editions. Isaac Watts wrote in praise of Böhme's *Encridion*, published in 1707 and his *Duty of the Reformation* (1718) was much appreciated as also his *Doctrine of Godly Sorrow* (1720). Böhme was a keen supporter of the Society for Promoting Christian Knowledge and its world-wide missionary outreach. This missionary organization, founded in 1698, is one of the oldest in the world, beating the Royal Danish Mission by seven years. Böhme's writings emphasized Practical Christianity and were collected at Halle for publication as Böhme's legacy to the Church and what was not already in English was translated for the British public by Johann Christian Jacobi in 1735.

Close connections between the Danish-Halle Mission and Britain

Throughout the 100 years of missionary endeavours in India prior to Carey, the British SPCK supported the Indian Mission though at times more weakly than strongly. Daniel Jeyaraj in his *Lutheran Churches in Eighteenth Century India* writes:

> Heinrich Wilhelm Ludolf (1655-1712), secretary to George, the Lutheran Danish Prince Consort of Queen Anne of England, knew August Hermann Francke and his orphanage in Halle. Ludolf recommended Anton Wilhelm Böhme (1673-1722), a student of Francke, to be the Lutheran chaplain to Prince George in London. Böhme translated some writings of Francke into English and drew the attention of his readers to the distinctive

elements of the Halle Pietism. After he had become a member of the Society for Promoting Christian Knowledge (SPCK), established in London in 1698, he translated some selected letters and reports of Ziegenbalg on the mission work in India. The leaders of SPCK took much interest in the function of the Tranquebar Mission. They sent a printing press to Tranquebar. They secured free travel and transportation of letters and goods on the ships of the British East India Company for the missionaries in Tranquebar. When Ziegenbalg visited London in 1716, the leaders of SPCK introduced him to King George I (who was from Hanover, Germany). King George I expressed his great pleasure in the work of the Tranquebar missionaries. The SPCK was aware of the co-operation between the Anglicans in England and the Lutherans in Germany. The Charter of the British East India Company demanded that in all their colonies in India, a charity school should be established for the education of children. For a very long time, this need remained unfulfilled. In 1717, at the invitation of the officers of the East India Company, the Tranquebar missionaries established a charity school in Cuddalore. Another Tranquebar missionary, Benjamin Schultze (1689-1760), from 1719 until 1725 in Tranquebar, from 1741 in Halle, Germany, became the first Lutheran missionary in India to be sponsored by the Anglican SPCK. Schultze established a school and a church in the Black Town in Madras. At the request of the SPCK, the Lutheran Court Chaplain Ruperti in London ordained the German Lutheran, J. A. Sartorius, as a missionary to the English colony Cuddalore (known as Fort St. David). The results of the labour of Sartorius and his successors are evident even to this day.[2]

Ziegenbalg demands he be allowed to visit Denmark, Germany and Britain

Now Ziegenbalg became more determined than ever to visit Denmark, Germany and England and argued long with Hassius who at last gave in and Ziegenbalg received permission to leave the colony. One of

[2] *Lutheran Churches in Eighteenth Century India*, p. 86.

Ziegenbalg's aims was to inform the three supporting countries of the state of affairs in Tranquebar of which their governments knew nothing. Ziegenbalg also wanted Halle to publish and print his new Tamil grammar for use in the University and other colleges abroad which taught Tamil. For this cause, he had written all the explanatory notes in Latin so it could be used throughout Europe including Britain. He also wanted to consult with the King of Denmark concerning the future of the Mission. Also high on his 'to do' agenda in Europe was to find a wife to share his life and work in Tranquebar and perhaps raise a family.

Hassius realising all too well that Ziegenbalg would complain of him before the Danish King suddenly stopped his harassment of the Tranquebar Mission and said he was willing to live peacefully with the missionaries. This led to him to cooperate with the missionaries in drawing up a pact of mutual trust which reads:

> I Johann Sigismund Hassius, Commandant of Dansborg in Tranquebar, and Chief of the states of the chartered India Company, and we Missionaries Ziegenbalg and Gründler, have several times consulted together, whether the differences which took place between us several years ago, might not be arranged to the satisfaction of both parties and to the requirements of our employments, so that the past might be forgotten and forgiven; but this has never come to pass, because each wished to show his zeal in the exercise of his profession and was determined to stand by his rights to the uttermost. But as we learn from the letters we have lately received from Copenhagen that an amnesty is much desired there, and do not doubt that his Royal Majesty of Denmark and Norway would confirm it, we the undersigned, in the name of God and in consideration of our christian obligations, as also for the furtherance of the work of conversion amongst the heathen and for the general good, have taken the christian and firm determination to forget and forgive forever all those quarrels which have taken place between us, by whatsoever name they may be called; and on account of this christian compact they are to be abrogated for all time and we give each other the assurance that we at all times and on all occasions will seek the advantage of each other. On both sides we feel assured that when his Royal Majesty of Denmark and Norway shall receive this amnesty by

> the hands of Bartholomaus Ziegenbalg, the Missionary, who is now about to start for Denmark, he will give his most gracious consent thereto, and will allow both sides to continue to enjoy his royal favour. For the greater security of both parties, two similar copies of this have been prepared, to which correct signatures have been signed, and of which each party retains one.
>
> J. S. Hassius. Bartholomaus Ziegenbalg, Andreas Krahe, Johannes Ernestus Gründler, C. Brun, Jacob Panck.
> Tranquebar, 15th October 1714.

Ziegenbalg now sailed for Denmark but whilst he was still on the voyage, a royal warrant was proclaimed for the setting up of a missionary society to be called the collegium de cursu evangelii promovendo for the propagation of the gospel in foreign parts. However, once the King had founded the collegium, he left it to run itself and it was sadly manned by 'Orthodox' men of the Bövingh kind who were bent on ignoring the King's wishes. The King now appointed Ziegenbalg as the Tranquebar Mission's Provost so that he could now ordain suitable Indian Christians as preachers and pastors, little realizing that the collegium could not stomach Ziegenbalg's missionary activities. Nevertheless, news of Hassius' wrong-doings had reached the Court from various trustworthy sources and the King recalled Hassius back to Denmark and a new Commandant who was most missionary-minded was sent out to replace him. Rather than being the good news it appeared to be at first concerning the Missionary Society, the move became a great hindrance to the work in Tranquebar as the new quite inexperienced, incapable Society treated the now well-experienced and well-qualified missionaries as servants at their beck and call. Like the BMS in the case of Carey, they believed that Missionaries should be ruled by non-missionaries.

Ziegenbalg in Europe

When Ziegenbalg arrived in Europe, he was given a very warm welcome throughout the countries he visited and very especially in England. Whilst in Halle, he visited his old friends the Saltzmanns and within a few days had fallen in love with their daughter Maria whom he had known from earlier days, indeed, she had been a pupil in a class he had taught. Again, there is a connection with Carey whose second wife was his private pupil at the time of his first wife's death. Maria was quick to agree with Ziegenbalg's proposal of marriage. There was some trouble with Prof Francke who was under great pressure by Christian Wendt, the new leader of the Danish Missionary Society, not to allow missionaries to marry. In a letter to Francke dated 8th November, 1718, Wendt called the marriages of Ziegenbalg and Gründler 'a plague'.[3] Some accounts say that Francke turned up at the wedding, others say he did not attend the service. However, Francke soon made up to his friend. Happily, Francke came down on Bartholomäus' and Maria's side before the young couple left for India. Here is a parallel with Luther and Melanchthon who were estranged for a time due to Luther's opposition to his marriage on the grounds that the clergy should not marry. Of course, when Luther came under his Käthe's influence, Luther changed his views and married. Francke, however, had already married his Anna Magdalena von Wurmb (1670-1734) and the couple had three children, one girl and two boys. It appears that Francke did for a while distinguish between the needs of those at home and those on the foreign mission field.

Honey-moon in England

Bartholomäus and Maria after the wedding celebrations were over decided to visit England before departing from there on a British ship to India in 1716. Ziegenbalg and his wife were given a reception otherwise only due to high diplomats. They were hosted by King George and Ziegenbalg was invited to preach several times in the Royal Chapels. He was given a very warm welcome by the SPCK who honoured him with a special address in Latin, which led to his making a speech of thanks in Tamil, hopefully with an interpreter being present. Archbishop Wake was thrilled by Ziegenbalg's testimony and from then on corresponded diligently with the missionary. Jeyaraj says of Maria Dorothea Saltzmann, 'She proved to be an outstanding companion and loved the Tamils as well as her husband did, earning her the distinction of being the first female Protestant missionary'. However, in Ziegenbalg's absence, Gründler had married Danish Utilia Elizabeth Krahe of Copenhagen who was the widow of Andreas Krahe,

[3] See *Mission in Quellen Texten* (Mission in the Source Texts), p. 150.

a former member of the East India Company and co-worker with Hassius who had opposed Ziegenbalg and Plütschau. Utilia, too, played a positive part in the work of the Mission and as Jeyaraj says she 'proved enormously helpful in resolving the lingering tensions between mission and colony'. This role was also played by Charlotte Carey.

Gründler' missionary successes in Ziegenbalg's absence

Meanwhile Gründler had been very successful in increasing the Tamil church members in the city so when Ziegenbalg and his bride returned to Tranquebar, they found that the original Tamil church was now far too small for the great number of converts so they built their much larger New Jerusalem Church which was dedicated on October 11, 1718. This church still stands today and has a Tamil minister who looks back on a continual ministry since the foundation of the church. With the backing of the new Governor, Ziegenbalg founded the first Protestant Seminary in India for the training of native teachers, preacher, pastors but it was not until 1733 that the first graduate was ordained, this being Rumukam Pillai whom all called Aaron. The founding purpose of the college was to train native missionaries to establish churches in Poriar, and beyond.[4]

The brevis deliniatio of 1717

Soon after Ziegenbalg's return to Tranquebar, he and Gründler printed out their brevis deliniato or Brief Report from the Mission's press which they dedicated to Joseph Collet the new President of the British East India Company whom they hoped would be sympathetic to the Mission's cause. Collet was stationed in Madras (Madraspatna) where Lewis had had his chaplaincy and where Ziegenbalg had also started a work. The missionaries dedicate the work to their 'Honourable Patron' or Guardian (Beschützer) so it seems that Collet had proved most helpful hitherto to the Mission. The report was primarily intended for British readers so was written in Latin which was still the lingua franca of pastors and scholars in England and neither Ziegenbalg nor Gründler had much proficiency in English. They had relied more on the Scandinavian, German and Portuguese languages besides their now

---

[4] See Ziegenbalg's letter to Lange dated 27th September, 1709, concerning Ziegenbalg's concept for a missionary training centre in India.

profound knowledge of Tamil and a smattering of other Indian tongues. When they met British Christian workers or merchants in India, they spoke either Latin or Portuguese with them. The report was certainly not so 'brief' as the title suggests as it covers forty points dealing with the various aspects of the Mission from its beginnings to the time of writing. It was really a presentation for the use of the SPCK.

The way Collet is addressed in the work is probably more diplomatic than a sign of Christian fellowship with the new President as he was a most stern and cruel self-appointed ruler of the Indians, especially the Chetties and in two years had made a huge fortune through his colonial policies and lack of respect for the Indians. As a Semi-Arian, he would have had little in common with Ziegenbalg but nevertheless followed Lewis' and Ziegenbalg's example by founding two charity schools for slaves, one in Madras and one in Kudulur (formerly Gudulore or Cuddalore and now Gudulur). He also commissioned Ziegenbalg to print a new version of the Psalms set to Indian music. It was at his request that Ziegenbalg and Gründler authored the report which possibly explains the highly flattering way the missionaries addressed Collet. By 1720 Collet was so surrounded with troubles, mostly of his own making, that he gave up his post and retired to England where he entered into politics. He died in 1725 and was buried in Bunhill Fields.

One congregation for Tamil-speakers and one for Portuguese-speakers

In the report we find that the missionaries had divided their work into two congregations: one for those who spoke mostly Portuguese and one for those who spoke mostly Tamil. The large number of adults who spoke either the one language or the other had not had the privilege of a multi-lingual education like their children so needed to be evangelized in the one language they knew best. The schools were flourishing and growing and providing India with bilingual, trilingual, and even quadlingual well-spoken teachers, clerks, trades men and women and ministers of the gospel who were to take up leading posts in Indian society.

The Indian Seminary for training in Practical Divinity was up and functioning as well as the work of catechising those who wished to know more of the gospel. The printing press was now printing works in Tamil, Portuguese, Danish and German. Because this work had grown rapidly the Mission had two foundries, one for smelting and one for pattern-making, mainly for moveable type. One of the paragraphs in the Brief Report deals with the different fonts the missionaries used, especially the Cicero Antiqua.

We note here that when Carey started his printing work many decades later, he used wooden type, each letter having to be carved separately. Carey only started using metal type after a fire destroyed his wooden letters in 1812. Metal type, however, had been mass-produced in Tranquebar from almost the start of the Mission. So, too, paper was produced on the premises. The Mission also ran a hospital with an international team of doctors and nurses.

Ziegenbalg and Gründler did not include a description of the horticultural and agricultural work of the Mission in their report as it would have probably challenged British methods of reaping profits from Indian agriculture and angered certain members of the Mission Board in Denmark. We remember how Staughton of the Kettering Board would not support Carey's work in Serampore because he taught Chemistry and Horticulture. Though the Serampore Trio had very many servants, they did not have a highly trained Mission team like the one in Tranquebar but had much of their work done by outside people and government employers. Now fifty persons were managing the affairs of the spiritual and physical needs of the Tranquebar Mission which included a professionally trained economist who made sure that the monies coming in were rightly used. These were all paid by the Mission and not financed by secular bodies.

The missionary went on to describe how the preaching, teaching, catechizing, private counselling, prayer meetings, Bible studies and house visiting were organized. As everything had to be done in four or five different languages, this entailed much coordination especially on Sundays when four or five different services were held in the various languages in churches, homes and in the open-air. The work in the various schools from Kindergarten to High School level was explained class for class and school year for school year bearing in mind that the tuition in the five schools was for several hours in the week trilingual. The subjects were now more akin to modern European schools or the pansophist schools influenced world-wide by John Durie or Comenius[5] but the emphasis was on learning to know the God-Only-wise who was the source of all knowledge.

The children were fed three times a day and many of the poor clothed but now school fees had to be paid by those who could afford it such as the Danes, Germans and some Portuguese. Now all the children were taught the rudiments of hygiene and were able to wash themselves on the school premises and use the toilets as the children's homes lacked sanitation. In all, the Mission catered now for 121 full-time pupils and in the two Tranquebar congregations there were 354 catechised and baptized members of which the majority were Tamils. Muslims were now showing a keen interest in the work of the schools. As the British were causing them great difficulties, they looked on the peace of the Tranquebar Mission with envy.

The Collegium Biblicum et Exegeticum

In the Missionary Seminary connected to the already instituted Collegium Biblicum et Exegeticum eight students were being trained in 1717 to evangelize their own people. The emphasis was on a sound grasp of evangelical theology, Bible exposition in both Testaments, and language proficiency in speaking and writing. The Tamil and Portuguese speakers were trained in each other's languages but also in their various histories and geographies. They were especially instructed in Medicine according to the Tamil system which relied very much on the horticulture and Flora of Tamil Nadu and the Coromandel Coast. The Mission's European and Tamil doctors worked well with one another. So as to be quite frank and open with Collet over the affairs of the Mission, the missionaries gave a most detailed account of their finances during the last year almost down to a penny.

Work on suitable literature

The literature produced by the Mission was both numerous and varied but much of it was printed on the European Continent or Britain through

---

[5] See my book and Dr theol. thesis *The Practical Divinity of Universal Learning: John Durie's Educational Pansophism* for 'modern' educational practices which have remained dormant for centuries but are now being practised again throughout the world based on the principle of synergisation.

the donations of friends outside of India. There were some 22 major and minor productions up to and including 1717. Most of the educational material for the schools was printed on the Tranquebar press in Tamil and Portuguese. The Tamil material included a New Testament translated by the missionaries, a hymn book mostly with indigenous tunes, Luther's *Shorter Catechism*, a book comparing Christianity with the Indian religions, a book of Christian doctrines, and a book on the way of salvation. The books in Portuguese were more numerous because those skilled in Portuguese at the Mission Station outnumbered those who only spoke Tamil and it was easier to tap Portuguese sources. However, a number of the publications were bi-lingual. These included correspondence with George Lewis, creeds, several Old Testament books and works on theology. Several books in English were printed in Madras, probably by Lewis, a translation of the Psalms to be sung, a volume in evangelical strategy and a yearly bi-lingual calendar. The press had not hitherto been used to its fullest capacity owing to lack of paper but now there was a good stack of paper for further works manufactured on the Mission's premises.

The Mission Station had now a relatively large library, most of the books being gifts from Denmark, Germany and Britain and a catalogue had been maintained since 1714 printed on the Mission's press. Ziegenbalg called his printed book catalogue and collection the Bibliotheca Malabrica which went through several editions as the library grew starting at some 175 volumes in 1719 and some 300 books from Tamil sources added in later years. These works were mainly for a readership throughout the colony and not only for the Mission staff, pupils and students.

One 'first' in missionary work in India was a regularly printed journal of missionary reports starting 1710 and continuing until 1772. This series was continued with one or two short breaks and under various titles until 1880. These were mostly printed in Halle for European distribution. The subject matter of these regular reports which eventually became quarterly magazines between 1849 and 1880 included not only religious matters but also discussions concerning arithmetic, social structures, literature, languages, agriculture and handicrafts under the guidance of the Mission.

In order to answer all the questions sent to the Mission concerning the Mission and Indian cultures, the missionaries put together collections of non-Christian Tamil beliefs, religious practices, philosophy and poetry. They also referred to a number of horticultural an agricultural works though these are not mentioned in the Brief Report. These works amounted to some eleven volumes in all. Older Dutch works such van Rheede's mammoth 12 volumed *Hortus Malabaricus* published between 1678 and 1693 helped Ziegenbalg gain knowledge of the Indian flora and taxonomy. This was one of two works, the other on English horticulture the *Hortus Elthamensis* by John Jacob Dillenius, which won Carl Linné's praise and attention. A number of Indian botanists and taxonomists prepared much of the material for van Rheede's work but these scholars have gained attention only in modern times. K. S. Manilal, a leading horticulturalist, botanist and taxonomist sums this work up in his *Hortus Malabaricus* and *The Socio-Cultural Heritage of India* published in 2012.[6]

A mixed reception of Ziegenbalg's many works

Some twenty-two volumes of 'background information' concerning the Mission, several running into many hundreds of pages, were printed and distributed in Europe in five languages (Latin, Danish, Portuguese, English and German) and these on reaching their destination were immediately translated into further languages such as French. Some of these, especially those on Indology, were early suppressed by Halle and other perhaps too pious sources. One of Ziegenbalg's major works, for instance, which became of historical importance for India and for future students of Indian religions was his *Genealogy of the Malabarian Gods* which only saw the light of a publisher's day in relatively modern times. So, too, records of Ziegenbalg's positive records of Indian medicine were suppressed by the Halle 'Holier-than-thous' who seemed to think Indian medicine was some sort of sorcery. Indeed, some of Ziegenbalg's works, particularly the early ones, have probably still to be published and are still in the Halle Archives as Prof. Moritzen has discovered. Happily, such works, as I have discovered in my research, are as good as published as the Franckesche Stiftungen is open to all. Ziegenbalg's work on the genealogy of Indian deities was written in 1713 but not published until 2003 in an English translation by Prof. Daniel Jeyaraj. However, the publisher's note that this was a 'first'

[6] Association for Angiosperm Taxonomy, India.

publication is incorrect according to records I have archived. W. Germann of the London Missionary Society published an early German version which was translated and published in Madras by G. J. Metzger of the Madras Free Church of Scotland. This version is available as a free download on the internet.

House visiting

The information concerning the missionaries' house-visits is worthy of note. Because of their religious beliefs and perhaps because of their poverty, the Tamils were at first reluctant to invite Ziegenbalg and his colleagues into their homes. However, the moon played a great part in their beliefs and families sat outside of their houses on moonlight nights and were then most sociable and welcomed visitors. So Ziegenbalg and Gründler informed Collet of the topics they spoke about on moonlit evenings such as responsibility to God, the Fall and how sin came into the world. They spoke of God's good grace, the salvation wrought out by Christ and about eternal fellowship with God. When firmer contacts were cemented, the missionaries were invited into the Indians' homes where fellowship and catechising continued.

Most of the Tamils, according to Ziegenbalg's testimony, believed in a God over all gods so Ziegenbalg started off with this mutual thought. As they believed also that their gods were but representative of the one God, the missionaries could then talk about the relationship of the Father to the Son. Otherwise, the missionaries now preached daily from a shaded platform they had set up in the town and very bravely spoke at the Tamils' religious festivals and distributed tracts and books. This shows the kind nature of the Tamils who very rarely showed opposition. This is a miracle in itself as Governor Collet was busy suppressing the people of Tamil Nadu by conquest and slaughter. This evangelical witness would have been good for his soul and an appeal to his conscience as he professed to be an evangelical Christian. Sadly, the conflicts the British had with the Muslims which had nothing to do with religion began to weaken Muslim interest in the Mission.

The missionaries also outlined their efforts to bring the gospel to areas beyond the colony and their travels for the sake of the gospel and emphasized their work amongst the children. Finally, in this section Ziegenbalg and Gründler informed Collet that they were in personal correspondence with many Tamils. This was a most important, even daring, confession to make as many British Governors and EIC Presidents believed the Indians to be an un-cultured and analphabetic people. This was very far from being the case. I remember with sorrow how I fellowshipped with Sami people who were as well educated as I was in Jämtland, Sweden and how Swedish visitors would surround my friends and young, ignorant, even vulgar ladies of fashion would force elderly heads forwards and look down their necks saying that they knew the Sami never washed themselves. The church verger took me aside and told me that the Swedes treated the Sami even worse than some white Americans treated the Afro-Americans. I gave these dirty-minded people a piece of my mind and thereafter I was given the title of 'Samernas vän' or 'friend of the Sami'. Ziegenbalg had a number of similar experiences with such ignorant 'Whites' in India. In the U.S.A. I felt compelled to reprimand Reformed Evangelical pastors who cracked racist jokes over the local Native Americans whose history I was writing. I quoted an old Sunday-School chorus I had learnt as a three-year-old at the Bradford Home Mission, 'Red or yellow, black or white (and we could also add "pink") all are precious in His sight'.

Correspondence with Danes, Germans and the British

The last three points in the missionaries' report concerned the correspondence they had enjoyed with Danes, Germans and the British over the past years. Several letters with their replies are recorded, the last one being a very long letter from the Secretary of the SPCK dated London, 24th December, 1714, and signed Heinrich Neumann. The British had learnt to engage in missionary work from the Stuarts in Germany and Denmark who were all the descendants of Elizabeth Stuart and King Frederick V of the Palatine and Bohemia who were both very evangelical, Reformed monarchs leading the Protestants in the early years of the Thirty Years' War, allied with Sweden. Elizabeth was the sister of Charles I and her son, Prince Rupert, became heir to the British throne. After Rupert's death the heirship passed on to Frederick and Elizabeth's grandchild, George. Elizabeth and Frederick were commonly called 'The Winter King and Queen' because of their short rule in Bohemia from where they were driven out during the Thirty Years' War. After Frederick's death in the King of Sweden's service, Elizabeth set up her court in the Hague and was known as 'The Queen of Hearts'.

Disaster occurs

Whilst all was going well in Tranquebar and Ziegenbalg with his wife and Gründler were rejoicing at the healthy growth of the church, Bövingh had been making a thorough nuisance of himself and rebelled against the work he was supposed to do. He left off being a missionary, though he never really started, and wrote numerous letters to the home-front complaining against his fellow missionaries, accusing them of mismanaging the Mission. As he was in charge of the Mission's funds and was guilty of many irregularities, his protests were obviously meant to cover his own mismanagements by accusing others of the same. This led to a severe move in the Danish Mission Headquarters which meant the end of the mission as Ziegenbalg had planned and the speedy end of Ziegenbalg's and Gründler's lives who became seriously ill with the horrible accusations and impossible working conditions which ensued leaving them without money and food. A recent Indian film I saw celebrating Ziegenbalg's great importance for India declared that Ziegenbalg was one of the greatest Indian heroes but was persecuted to death by narrow-minded, ignorant people on the home-front who were supposed to be holding the ropes for him but they let them all go. This picture is sadly truthful.

Things go wrong in Denmark

As soon as the missionary society had been founded in Copenhagen, things began to go wrong. Through elbowing out representatives of the churches and universities both at home and abroad, it became a layman's organisation claiming the sole right to act for all Denmark's missionaries including Ziegenbalg. The new Secretary-Chairman Christian Wendt had no missionary experience of his own and was a vowed opponent of Ziegenbalg's evangelical theology. He had also a most narrow and naïve idea of what missionary work entailed. He thus announced that, from then on, the Board's policy was that:

> Missionaries should not marry.
> No church buildings were to be erected.
> No schools or colleges were to be maintained.
> No orphanages were to be set up or any kind of boarding house for pupils.

Missionaries should not rely on foreign financing but live off donations from their converts.
Missionaries should have no private property.
Missionaries should establish no Mission Station but engage solely in an itinerant ministry.
Ziegenbalg's mission did not live according to these proposals so the Board must stop all funding of the Mission.
Tranquebar was not a missionary prospect at all as missionaries should not build churches, schools and missionary housing nor should they have libraries or possess personal goods but be solely itinerant preachers relying on the Lord for their upkeep. They should thus wander from place to place without any luggage whatsoever and preach the gospel.

This shocking and scarcely believable news came when the Tranquebar Mission, with help from England, had just set up a charity school for borders and the training Seminar for training native missionary workers and ordained pastors was well under way. The printing presses were turning out a large series of Tamil and Portuguese Christian Literature including the Tamil New Testament which Ziegenbalg had finished in 1715 and their new large church was full of native worshippers. Jeyaraj comments:

> Wendt held Pietists like Ziegenbalg in contempt. He had no first-hand experience of mission work or cross-cultural encounter, but that in no way deterred him from shaming, slandering, and attacking every last undertaking of Ziegenbalg and Gründler's. Wendt thought they should simply preach the gospel and move on, not wasting their time building churches, schools, orphanages, hospitals, or printing presses. Accordingly, he cut off their funding. He had no understanding of the social cost to Tamils of turning their backs on caste and family, or the need of the church to provide them with a new family and a new vocation along with the new faith. Ziegenbalg, by contrast, had cultivated Tamil doctors, poets, and teachers and hired a vast staff to do everything from operating the printing press to fetching the water. His church was truly an ekklesia, a body

'called out' of its society and yet commissioned to serve that same society.

Now, after cutting off all financial aid from Denmark, Wendt insisted that the entire Mission Station should be dispersed. He actually believed naïvely that if the poorer Tamils wanted to be evangelized, they should pay for this themselves as if Ziegenbalg's converts, mostly the poorest of the poor, had money to burn. Wendt's move meant the large staff of Tamil workers and the teachers and medical team of Europeans and Tamils should be disbanded. Then there were the printers, the farmers, the gardeners, the caretakers, the laundry men and the water carriers who were now faced with being without an occupation and without an income. What Wendt strove to do was to impoverish a large society of industrious Indians. Wendt had simply no idea of the great and godly work he was destroying. He was also destroying his own reputation which led to his dismissal by the Danish King.

Bövingh was in his element as he felt he had broken the back of the Mission which he had grown to hate and now Wendt sent out three new Missionaries Schultze, Dal and Kistenmacher carrying a letter of scathing condemnation of Ziegenbalg, hoping that the three new recruits would obey his orders. The three arrived in Tranquebar in July, 1719 ready to carry out Wendt's demands but soon realised that Wendt had totally misjudged the situation. By then, however both Ziegenbalg and Gründler were broken men. Ziegenbalg's old stomach trouble had come back in an even severer form and the missionary, still a relatively young man was at death's door and Gründler was constantly in tears because of the sad turn of events and became most ill, more from sorrow than anything else.

Ziegenbalg's earthly pilgrimage ends

Though Ziegenbalg had a setback in health with terrible pains and a most troublesome cough, he kept at his work for a further six months until he could scarcely stand. A few days before his death he felt rather better, prayed with his wife and, realising the Lord was giving him peace before taking him Home, he asked his congregation to come together to share the Lord's Supper with him and preached the gospel to them for the last time. Gründler, realising that his friend was about to leave this world, told him that to be with Christ was a far better state and Ziegenbalg replied that summed up his thoughts exactly, adding that he would enter Glory washed from his sins and clothed in Christ's righteousness. After hearing his congregation sing of the love of the Saviour he departed forever to be with his beloved Lord.

Jeyaraj sums up the entire situation well by writing:

> Wendt's letters were so nasty that Ziegenbalg fell ill again, a relapse of his youthful malady, complete with fatigue, headaches, chest pains, and vomiting. He declined steadily and in February of 1719 commended care of the mission to Gründler. He died while his friends and family around him sang Jesu, Meine Zuversicht, at the age of thirty-five. Dorothea[7] was left bereft with two small sons and a third on the way, but the second died three months after his father and the new-born just days after his birth. In time she remarried and moved back to Denmark. Gründler also fell to the attacks of Wendt and followed Ziegenbalg to the grave just a year later. By then other missionaries who shared their point of view were ready to take up the torch, and the Tamil faithful were already taking the mission into their own hands.

Ziegenbalg's Epitaph

One of the finest sources of information on the lives of foreign missionaries in India is the many lists of deaths and burials preserved by the Indian Government. In search of such information, I happily stumbled on Julian James Cotton's, *List of Inscriptions on Tombs or Monuments, Madras*. Cotton gives the Latin Inscription on Ziegenbalg's extant grave in the New Jerusalem Church as:

> In spe gloriosae resurrectionis quiescunt hic ossa beati BARTHOLOMEI ZIEGENBALG Sacr. Reg. Maj. Dan. et Norw. missionariiad Tamulos, viri doctissimi gravissimi fidelissimi et per XIII annos ecclesiae evangelicae ex iisdem

[7] Maria was the first name of Ziegenbalg's wife but Jeyaraj called her by her second name 'Dorothea' which was also the name of Carey's first wife.

collectae Praepositi praeclarissimi nati 24 Jun. 1683, denati 23 Feb. 1719 [8]

and comments:

Native of Pulsnitz in Saxony, graduate of Halle; arrived 1706. Praepositus is the translation of the German 'Propst' or Provost. As Ziegenbalg was the first to preach in New Jerusalem Church, so he was the first to be buried there. He lies on the right hand of the altar, opposite his colleague Grundler. Their places are marked by thin copper-plates let into the wall, with Latin inscriptions from the pen of Schultze, who was like Schwartz a native of Sonnenburg in Brandenburg. The Latinity is not remarkable, except for the use of the ante-classical word 'dinatus,' which is found all over Tranquebar. Ziegenbalg is the father of Protestant Missions in India. His name, though little known among Englishmen to-day, was once received with enthusiasm in London. He had audiences of King George in 1716, and preached many times in the Chapels Royal and Savoy. The S.P.C.K. gave him a congratulatory address in Latin, to which he returned a reply in Tamil. Encouraging letters were written to him by Dr Wake, Archbishop of Canterbury, and one communication, received in India from the Archbishop too late for Ziegenbalg's earthly eyes, bears the following testimony to his apostolic usefulness:

> I consider that your lot is far higher than all church dignities. Let others be prelates, patriarchs and popes: let them be adorned with purple and scarlet, let them desire bowings and genuflections. You have won a greater honour than all these and a far more magnificent recompense shall be given you.

---

[8] Here rests the blessed bones of Bartholomäus Ziegenbalg chaplain to the most noble King of Denmark and Norway, learned, venerable and most faithful missionary to the Tamils for thirteen years in the evangelical (Protestant) church and renowned provost of the same assembly, born 24 June 1683, died 23 February 1719.

There is also a plaque in memory of Ziegenbalg and Plütschau on the Tranquebar beach. A more modern grave inscription says in English that Ziegenbalg, 'died in harness'. May we also so die.

On dealing with Ziegenbalg's life and death for a work which was without precedent from the point of view of a Tamil Christian, Jeyaraj relates how Ziegenbalg's missionary work was considered incomprehensible by his Lutheran contemporaries, yet Ziegenbalg triumphed against all odds because of his faith in the world-wide provisions of the Lord, his ministry becoming from its very humble origins the mother of Protestant Christianity in India. He finishes his praise of Ziegenbalg's work by quoting Luke 13:18, 19.

> What is the kingdom of God like? And to what shall I compare it? It is like a grain of mustard seed that a man took and sowed in his garden, and it grew and became a tree, and the birds of the air nest in its branches.

Part 5

A Hundred Years of Missionary Endeavours from Tamil Nadu to Bengal

Chapter Twelve

From Tranquebar to Cuddalore

Ziegenbalg set the pattern for many to follow him

After Ziegenbalg, scores of missionaries, from Scandinavia and Germany accompanied by their British, Asian and American brethren evangelized the areas between Tranquebar and Calcutta before the arrival of William Carey. After Wendt had been removed from office and Schultze, Dal and Kistenmacher had seen what great work Ziegenbalg had done, the work in Tranquebar continued with renewed vigour. Most of Ziegenbalg's successors in the Mission were trained academically in Latin, Greek and Hebrew and most, like Schwartz, had been able to study various Indian languages besides Farsi and Arabic so they could start at once on translating the Scriptures on their arrival in Southern India. Schwartz also became fluent in Syriac and translated a number of Syriac works into German. Buchanan in his 'Researches' and missionary journeys found some 100 churches whose congregation read the Syriac Bible, known to them since at least the fourth century. He also discovered a number of ancient Christian Colleges where the Indians were trained to read the Syriac Bible. Schwartz and his team also founded schools, printing works and paper mills in a number of new areas and trained Indian citizens in their colleges to take over their tasks. Carey thus stepped into the footprints of many illustrious men and women of God when he landed in Calcutta in 1793 but waited until 1800 before he became active as a part-time missionary. Up to then he had been a part-time pastor amongst his employees and business colleagues. Yet Baptist authors such as George Winfred Hervey writing in 1884 tell us that there was no real Indian evangelism until 1793 and the really successful work was done by the American Baptists.[1]

The lasting Tranquebar Mission in Calcutta

The missions Ziegenbalg had founded were still intact in the early nineteenth century under the care of the Danish King Frederick VI whose ancestor Frederick IV had sent out Bartholomäus Ziegenbalg in 1705 to evangelize Tranquebar and train native pastors. The strong Christian witness at Calcutta (Kolkata) and Serampore (Srirampur), to which Carey attached himself, was an extension of the Tranquebar Mission and had thus been established long, long before Carey set foot on Indian soil. It had an immediate and direct contact with Ziegenbalg's family as his son Gottlieb Ernst Ziegenbalg became Director of the Danish East India Company in the 1750s and took with him missionaries who were formerly at Tranquebar to Serampore. Gottlieb Ziegenbalg differed greatly from the usual East India Company directors as he did not obtain his high position via politics or a military background but was an intellectual and former University Professor in Germany and deeply evangelical.

Sadly, the work of the many indigenous evangelists and pastors of this time have either not been recorded or have gained little interest world-wide. Indeed, Indians who professed and witnessed to Christ and were carrying out pastoral and itinerant work were still called 'Heathens' or 'Blacks' by many so-called Christian commentators for two hundred years after Ziegenbalg. The Dano-German missionaries had shown that methods of education and scholarly approach amongst the Tamils were quite equal to European standards and that many so-called 'pagan' Tamils led more upright lives than many 'Christians' who looked down on them.

Rectifying former errors

One of the few Westerners to pioneer studies in this area was the Swedish Professor, Bishop and missionary Bengt Sundkler (1908-1995), as testified in his book *Missionens Värld* from which I have gained some of my Indian statistics. Sundkler (Sinclair) was a

---

[1] Introduction to *The Story of Baptist Missions in Foreign Lands: From the Time of Carey until the Present Date.*

missionary in Africa for many years and Mission Supervisor and I had the enormous privilege of being tutored by him in missionary strategy for three terms at Uppsala University in the sixties. Sundkler estimated that the Tranquebar-Serampore Mission alone had enriched their churches by some 35,000 baptised worshippers before Carey's arrival in India. My dear Professor objected strongly to the title of 'missionary' being used solely for Westerners and told us that the term applied to every ambassador for Christ irrespective of nationality, race, social status or language.

Sundkler complained strongly of racism amongst missionaries, especially in Africa and gave us numerous examples of missionaries who had put Western 'culture', politics and racism before their work in the gospel and warned us severely concerning the follies of doing likewise. He thus pays tribute in his books to Indian missionaries in their own country as also native African, Korean, Philippine, Japanese and Chinese missionaries who have helped to evangelize the world but are little remembered.

Happily, a number of Indian Christian scholars are now rectifying this inexcusable attitude and neglect. The first Tamil to be ordained and sent out as a missionary to his own people, Aaron, was set apart for his new duties in 1733 and a further thirteen ordained Indian missionaries, pastors and preachers, including most successful Diego, followed Aaron before 1813. We read in the missionary reports prefixed to Buchanan's Researches of Aaron and Diego:

> The two native preachers, Aaron and Diego, in their travels through the villages, were eminently useful; and so numerous were their converts in some of them, that it became necessary to appoint a special superintendent over them.[2]

The 'Superintendents' were Europeans who we can be sure reaped the laurels for the indigenous missionaries' work. Here Buchanan is speaking of native Indians who were prior to and more successful than many Europeans and we must ask where are the fitting biographies of these Christian heroes? The lives of college-trained Indian pastors and evangelists must be relatively easy to investigate. We have still,

---

[2] Buchanan, p. 41.

however, to find material on and research into the large number of pioneer Indian missionaries from humbler circumstances. It is also a puzzle why well-trained Aaron had to wait until 1733 for his ordination though he had been with the Mission over a decade. Was this because of post-Ziegenbalg Western superstition concerning 'natives'? Reginald Heber had no such thoughts and had commenced to ordain native pastors and preachers in India ten years previously.

At least two Indian missionaries converted through Thomas and Carey took up the great itinerant church-building work which the Serampore trio; Carey, Ward and Marshman, failed to do themselves. So, too, there were well over eighty Scandinavian-German pioneers of Protestant evangelism before Carey besides missionaries from other countries. The records of European missionaries from Ziegenbalg in Tranquebar and Kiernander who founded the Calcutta work, are often most copiously documented which causes one to wonder why this history is so neglected amongst many modern writers of missionary activity particularly in the Baptist fold. The Gaebler Info und Geneologie Website list the names, dates and years of service of no less than fifty Dano-Halle missionaries, besides providing information as to their services and writings. As there were so many missionaries active in India before Carey's time, I am thus devoting two chapters on their lives and work. Amongst the most still well-known representatives of the Danish Mission before Carey's day were:

Benjamin Schultze (1689-1760)

Halle graduate Schulze took over from Ziegenbalg and managed the Tranquebar Mission from 1719-1743. He appears to have been the only one of the three new missionaries who was able to shoulder the real work of a missionary. The Danish Missionary Society's Chairman Fenger, who put the Society back on the missionary agenda, tells us that Kistenmacher was too sickly and Dal too dilatory.

Schulze extended the Madras Mission which Ziegenbalg had started with Lewis' help and had a church building erected there in 1726. He also planted mission stations in Cuddalore which later Kiernander took over before the French threw him out, and also Calcutta to where Kiernander moved after Cuddalore. The old church building in Calcutta had been destroyed in the conflicts with the British so Kiernander built a new one. Never resting, Schulze also founded mission stations at

Tiruchirappalli and Tanjore. By the end of his service, the Danish-Halle Mission had become a pan-Indian mission, stretching far northwards from its starting point in the South. Obviously owing to the anti-missionary strategy of the Danish Board, Schultze was worried about the assets of the Mission so he put all accounts into the hands of the SPCK which was originally in Dano-German hands. Once the Danish Missionary Society was reformed and again took its former pre-Wendt line, this caused difficulties between the Danish and British supporter. The SPCK was now considered part of the Church of England and considered the Tranquebar Mission as under their authority. Few Danes and Germans, however, were unwilling to receive British funding though they wished to keep their independence. The matter of ownership only escalated in the time of Kiernander who refused to hand over the Missions' assets to the British, possibly because nearly all the funding had been from his own and his family's pockets.

Further work on Tamil, Telugu, Arabic and Hindi

Schultze, with his colleagues, revised Ziegenbalg's Tamil Dictionary and completed Ziegenbalg's Tamil Bible. He then translated the New Testament into Telugu and also parts of Genesis. He worked on several Hindustani dialects and printed the Psalms, Gospels and Epistles in Arabic characters for his Muslim readers. The use of Hindustani at that time was not identified with a specific religion but was widely spoken in its various dialects, especially by the Muslims. Schultze wrote a refutation of Islam in both Latin and German but found his work amongst the Muslims quite different to what he had expected as the Muslims in Southern India could not understand Arabic either in speech or writing. These times have changed in modern India.

During Schultze's ministry, some four or five new missionaries were sent out from Denmark but were also 'dilatory' as Fenger described Dal. Sadly, keeping charge of the Mission's funds proved too much of a temptation for at least five of the missionaries over the years and one missionary was dismissed for misusing his cash-keeping powers and excessive drunkenness.

Schultze campaigned strongly against slavery in the Danish colonies but the Danish government in Tranquebar could only be moved to abolish the horrible trade in 1783, long after his death. One noble gesture was that very many Danish officials who had to leave India for

Denmark, often due to French and British pressure, transferred their property to their former slaves. Schultze's Telugu Grammar was completed for publication in 1728 and his Hindi Grammar in 1745. Besides Royal Danish and German support, Schultze was supported by the London SPCK in their endeavours to set up what came to be called 'the English Mission to India' though most of the missionaries were Scandinavian or German. Later missionaries, such as those from the BMS, CMS and LMS[3] besides the American Societies were able to take advantage of this linguistic and lingual work in Bengal.

Johann Anton Sartorius (1704-1738)

Whilst Schultze was labouring in India, Sartorius was sent out to assist him. The SPCK had been striving for some time to send a British missionary to India but found no one in Britain who wished to take up the task. Hearing there were still Danes and Germans willing to take up the call to the foreign mission field, especially at Halle, they approached Johann Anton Sartorius and asked him if he would consider going to India as a missionary. Sartorius asked for one night's delay so that he could pray over the matter and accepted the call on the following morning. Sartorius travelled to England and was well-received by Queen Caroline, Archbishop Wake and the East India Company Directors. Wake sent a letter in Latin to the missionary team via Sartorius which Westcott gives in parts which he has translated:

> The most welcome news which I have now received from you concerning the newly commenced conversion of the Indians at Madras, and the flourishing condition of that mission, and that nothing is lacking to the furtherance of the work save that a helper be sent to you by us from these shores, no longer permits me to neglect the duty of writing. What you have asked is done. We send to you Mr. Sartorius who has been trained at the College at Halle, which has been most fruitful in good and learned men, a man too as it were formed and fashioned by nature for mission work and long proved, tried and approved in action. Receive him as a most loving brother sent from heaven and treat him with all kindness.

[3] Baptist, Church and London Missionary Societies

> May God Almighty grant you both a long life and sound minds in sound bodies. May He support you in His work and protect you against all snares of the enemy, and may He grant you success in converting the heathen, if not beyond what you hope, yet such as we desire for you, and such as He in His infinite wisdom shall see to be for your good, that so in those uttermost parts of the Earth, the true knowledge of Him may be preached, and the light of the Gospel shed abroad, and many souls be converted, and by your work that prophecy concerning Christ be fulfilled, wherein God Himself has promised that He will give to His son the heathen for His heritage and the uttermost bounds for His possession. Grant this in our days Most Gracious Father, to whom with the Son our Redeemer, and the Holy Spirit be praise and glory for ever. Amen.

Far-seeing Wake also wrote to the missionaries urging them to double their energies in making sure suitable Indians were trained to carry on the Christian work in India.

Sartorius arrived in India in 1730 and his early reports, like those of Ziegenbalg, were most detrimental to the Indians but became more positive when he was able to cross the language barriers and speak to the native Indians in their own tongues. He was to serve eight years on the mission field. Westcott gives him a rather negative write-up but Fenger, who was nearer to the sources, gives a most balanced and comprehensive review of the missionary's life. Sartorius had probably been warned in Germany and England of alleged primitive savages in India, as in Ziegenbalg's case but was soon comparing them to the primitive savages in Europe. Sartorius became more and more critical of his fellow-Europeans and especially the Jesuit rulers of Goa who had the Dano-German-British Mission's native co-workers beaten up. They tried to drag them before their Goa Inquisition but Westcott tells us this was stopped 'by the government' without saying which government was meant. Sartorius picked up English, Portuguese and Tamil quickly and could preach in Portuguese and Tamil within a year.

Missing the notes

Fenger relates how Schulze had not followed Ziegenbalg in encouraging the Tamils to praise God with their own music and hymn-singing. He gave up trying to teach the children Western music as they could not manage the Western scales and often missed the notes. Schulze left the matter to Sartorius who tried to teach Western scales and chords without explaining the difference in Western and Eastern music between notes, intervals, octaves and pitches. The Indian children were brought up on Raga music which is far more harmonic than Western scaled music. One note in a normal octave is considered absolute by Westerners though this can be represented by numerous pitches in the hundreds of thousands of Indian Ragas. Thus, a piano is no use for Indian singing as it has not enough keys to the octave. The chromatic scale has 12 notes (13 counting the octave) but again this cannot be used to produce the Ragas. Ziegenbalg knew this but most of the other Western missionaries after him did not and seemingly did not bother to learn. Schulze and Sartorius concluded that Tamils were unmusical as Carey also did on hearing the Bengalis sing to his Western tunes such as Redhead for Rock of Ages. I was used to singing Rock of Ages to both the 'Redhead' and 'Toplady' tunes at a very slow pace but in Lapland I did not recognise the tunes as they were sung to a galloping rhythm to which I could not keep up without tripping up over my words. 'Music' for the one is not always 'music' for the other.

Archbishop Wake finances a new Madras school

Schulze was able to open a second school in Madras in 1731 through the generosity of Archbishop Wake. Up to 1731 Schultze had baptised 400 converts in Madras and 45 pupils were being educated, clothed and fed at the expense of the Mission but soon funds coming in were not sufficient to meet expenses. This deficit was filled by a certain Mr Hollis who had continually supplied the Mission with money gifts and now left the work a substantial legacy. Plans were now made to erect a further church building in British Fort St. David and Johan Ernest Geister, a German missionary who had joined the Madras team in 1732 started a further work at Cuddalore.

Again, a Ziegenbalg tradition was broken and Sartorius and the SPCK insisted on a church which not only kept the men from their woman folk but also the castes from one another. However, this backwards-looking enterprise came to naught when the French threw out the British. Meanwhile, the fact that Schulze could not work with the other missionaries profited the Mission as those whom he could not tolerate left Madras for other areas. Schulze was a 'go-it-alone' man and no team-player.

Sartorius also left for Cuddalore but died there only a year later in 1738. He left behind him a number of works in Tamil, an extension of Ziegenbalg's dictionary, a work on geography, a Gospel Harmony and a detailed Introduction to the Scriptures. These, however, do not seem to have survived until the present day. The journals of Sartorius, Schulze and Johan Ernest Geister in a most clear and readable handwritten form are available online at the Franckesche Stiftungen.

In 1733 Aaron (re-named after Sartorius) was ordained for the ministry and all the missionaries gathered in Tranquebar for the ceremony. This produced something of a rivalry between Madras and Tranquebar as to who could open the door for further native evangelists. Schulze's brave catechist Enoch, brutally attacked for his faith by Jesuit henchmen, was sent from Tranquebar to help him but Schulze soon had two of his own converts working as schoolmasters and copyists. Fender, perhaps reflecting the scepticism of the times, in his chapter on native pastors and catechists rather stresses the biographies of those natives who did not make it rather than those who did. However, his descriptions of the Jesuit persecution of new converts serves to illustrate the bravery of Indian Christians such as Aaron and Enoch who remained faithful to the Lord's work and never gave up.

On looking back on the state of the Tranquebar Mission at this time, we read in the *Introductory Sketch of Protestant Missions in India* published with Buchanan's *Christian Researches in India*:

> On a review of the past, we are constrained to explain, 'What hath God wrought'. It appears, by official returns, that from the arrival of Ziegenbalg, in 1705, to the year 1750, the number of converts, at Tranquebar and the neighbouring districts, amounted to nearly 8000; and that from 1728 to the same period, the converts at Madras and Cuddalore, and along the coast of Coromandel, might be estimated at more than 1000. A few only of these were Roman Catholics, and a few Mahomedans; but the great majority were native Hindus, chiefly, though not exclusively, of the inferior Castes.[4]

[4] *Christian Researches in India*, p.41.

Schultze returned to Halle to take over Francke's orphanages in 1745. His health, however, was ruined but he spent his last few years making sure that the Tamil Bible and other Indian language works were printed and distributed. During his time at Halle, he met a young student by the name of Christian Friedrich Schwartz who showed a strong interest in India. Schultze encouraged Schwartz to learn Tamil with a view to becoming a missionary in India, perhaps the most successful.

Johann Philipp Fabricius (1740-91)

Benjamin Schultze was succeeded in 1745 by the scholar-evangelist Fabricius who had already spent five years in India and was to complete 51 years in all. Working on Ziegenbalg's Scripture translations, he completed what became known as 'The Golden Translation' of the Tamil Bible. Fabricius composed many hymns in Tamil and compiled a Tamil-English dictionary besides translating Bunyan's *Pilgrim's Progress* into Tamil. Fabricius also evangelized the East India Company soldiers and was also supported by the SPCK.

It is strange that modern books on pioneer missionaries often criticise the fact that these early missionaries preached to all they met up with as India was already very multi-national at that time. Kiernander has especially been criticized by modern pro-Carey commentators for preaching to 'mix-bloods' rather than 'full-bloods' which is quite untrue and strangely racist. Furthermore, Carey, too, catered for an international community, especially in his schools. The gospel these pioneer missionaries preached was not merely for Tamils, Bengalis, Portuguese, Danes, Germans, French and British it was for all people everywhere. The Church that Buchanan pastored parallel with Carey's work in Calcutta was quite international and inter-denominational. Carne quotes Buchanan as writing that the Christian public in Calcutta consisted of:

> Presbyterians, Independents, Baptists, Armenians, Greeks, and Nestorians; and some of these are part of my audience at the English church. But a name, or a sect, is never mentioned from the pulpit; and thus, the word preached comes profitable to all.[5]

---

[5] Carne, *List of Eminent Missionaries*, Vol. II, p. 169.

Fabricius' work suffered very much from the continuous warfare going on between Britain, France, the Netherlands and Denmark which was bitter and lasting. At times, it actually brought advantages. Sometimes, Fabricius suffered under a governor who was not in favour of missions but many times he encountered military people who sought to aid him. So, when the British drove out the French at Pondicherry (Puducherry) in 1769 and confiscated the French printing press, having no use for it themselves, they presented it to Fabricius. The missionary was thus able to use Pondicherry as a publishing centre and distributed works throughout the Mission's outstations in and around Madras such as Pulicat, Sadras, Chingleput and Vellore. Again, this fact is seldom mentioned by modern writers on the BMS such as Michael Haykin who in their numerous works on Andrew Fuller's pioneer literary outreach do not realise how much printed works served in evangelising India and other countries long before Fuller. It appears that Haykin feels this productive work was another 'first' of Fuller's as an opener of mission-fields through literature. In his long essay, A Great Thirst for Reading: Andrew Fuller the Theological Reader, after commenting on Fuller's correspondence with New Divinity Samuel Hopkins, Haykin says:

> Thus, despite the fact that England had an abundance of copies of the Scriptures, a result of the invention of printing and which gave Fuller and his contemporaries a distinct advantage over many previous generations of the Church who had not had the benefit of printed texts.

Such a statement must be challenged from history. Haykin often pushes forward Fuller as a pioneer author and distributor of Christian books both in Britain and Europe but the Baptist output was minimal to that of true pioneers in printing and distributing Christian literature from over 200 years before his Secretaryship for the BMS. We remember that John Durie was producing some three to four booklets and books in five languages monthly which appeared simultaneously in print in several Continents and several generations of the Mather family were also writing and distributing multi-lingual works in several Continents and were in close touch with Halle's Francke who produced a massive amount of printed works. The volume of SPCK publications in the 18th century throughout the world was enormous in the days before Fuller. Thomas Bray in those days was setting up Christian libraries all over Britain and did not neglect such work in India. The printing presses at Halle were churning out book after book and magazine after magazine long before Fuller came on the scene and Indian production was not to be trifled with either. Furthermore, the output of the Serampore Press and the rival printing press or presses the BMS set up were hardly anything in comparison to the Indian owned Fort William presses Carey's own college were running translating Bibles and edifying works. So, too, the results of people being led to Christ through Bibles and other Christian literature in Fuller's day outnumbered Baptist successes greatly.

Fabricius was enabled to add 4,000 souls to Christ's Church
Fabricius increased the mission's converts by a further 4,000 souls. However, because of the uncertain political situation which left its marks on the banking system, Fabricius suddenly amassed great debts. Most of the missionaries had no idea of accounting and bookkeeping and invariably left the task to others who knew almost as little as they did about investing money. Fabricius who was now in charge of the Tranquebar Mission was happy to give the job of treasurer to one of his converts named Gurupadam. This person who was suddenly in possession of relatively large amounts of money though faithful to the mission, invested the missionaries' savings in extremely risky business schemes which came to naught and both the banks and the investors lost huge sums of money. As Fabricius was officially in charge of the Mission's monies, he was held responsible and thrown into a debtor's prison as the Mission was allegedly 100,000 dollars in debt. Schwartz who put Fabricius in charge of his entire savings, lost almost all he had.

Christian Friedrich Schwartz (1726-1798)
Schwartz arrived in India in 1750 and was to serve 48 years there. He became internationally famous because of his success as an evangelist, Christian scholar and diplomat and was one of the most successful missionaries to India of all time. So high was the Indians' respect for him and thankfulness for his work that they treated him wherever he went as an Indian noble. The Indian nobles themselves treated Schwartz as their equal and even mentor. The French, Danish, Dutch and English Colonialists appreciated Schwartz' Christian input as much as the

Indians so he was thus widely proclaimed in India, on the Continent and in Britain as the Jewel of the Tranquebar Mission and Brightest Star in the Constellation of Danish-Halle Missionaries.[6] Schwartz was well-known to Carey who, he confessed, had led him to write his famous *Enquiry* and follow Schwartz' evangelistic course. Carey, however, appears not to have written to or visited Schwartz whilst both were in India and within easy travelling distance. Indeed, Carey's refusal to enter into the fellowship and work of the scores of missionaries who had gone before him and prepared his way is extremely difficult to understand. As in Fabricius' case, the British SPCK helped support Schwartz. A major 'First' in missionary outreach was Schwartz' highly skilled translation of the whole Bible into Telugu.

Daniel Jeyaraj claims in his work *Lutheran Churches in India* that the vast contribution Schwartz made to Christian India and far beyond is still to be chronicled and analysed and writes concerning Schwartz:

> One of the most influential Lutheran missionaries in India was Christian Friedrich Schwartz (1726-1798, from 1750 in South India). In 1762, he visited the Christians in the city of Tiruchirappalli, the Residence City of the Nawab, who was the official representative of the Mogul Empire of India. The Nawab had invited an army of the British East India Company to assist him in collecting revenues from local Tamil kings. Schwartz met Major Preston in Tiruchirappalli. Preston requested him to minister to the spiritual needs of the English soldiers. In 1763, the British soldiers started a LUTHERAN QUARTERLY school for those English children who had lost their fathers in the wars. Major Preston assigned a small place to build the first Lutheran church in Tiruchirappalli. The church was dedicated as 'Christ Church'. Now it belongs to the Church of South India. In 1769 Tulasiraja, the King of Tanjore, invited Schwartz to settle down in Tanjore permanently. Tulasiraja knew that Schwartz enjoyed the trust of the Tamils, Muslims, Christians, and the British people in the Tamil Country. He was also aware that Schwartz

[6] For a quick overview of Schwartz' life in English see 'The Legacy of Christian Friedrich Schwartz' by Robert Eric Frykenberg, International Bulletin of Missionary Research, July, 1999, University of Wisconsin.

was not in need of interpreters because he was fluent in Tamil (the language of the people), Persian (the language of the Muslim administration), Marathi (the administrative language of the Tanjore Kings), English (the language of the British), Latin, Greek and Hebrew. On his deathbed, Tulasiraja entrusted his adopted son, Serfojee II, to the care of Schwartz. Schwartz taught him English, the values of good administration, and the determination to collect manuscripts in different languages. He never tried to compel him to change his faith. Thus, Schwartz has left behind him an indelible influence in South India. The Saraswathi Mahal Library in Tanjore, which now houses several thousands of manuscripts in many different Indian and European languages, testifies to the abiding influence of Schwartz on the South Indians. Some of the converts and co-workers of Schwartz became outstanding missionaries and church planters. He baptized Clarinda, a Maratha Brahmin woman convert. She established the first Lutheran church at Palayamkottai in the District of Tirunelveli which is still witnessing for Christ today. Schwartz ordained Sattiyanathan, a catechist, in 1790 to be the pastor of the church at Palayamkottai. Although Schwartz did not possess the ecclesiastical authority of a bishop to ordain others for Christian ministry, no one in India or in Europe questioned him. His life and service earned him fame and acceptance. His contributions to the welfare of Indians are yet to be written.

Schwartz probably stands alone as the most successful of foreign missionaries to India

This author has found enough evidence of Schwartz' life and work in India to indicate that it was much greater and lasting than most, if not all, foreign missionaries who came after him. With hindsight, Schwartz' influence was perhaps also even greater than Ziegenbalg's. The bulk of my knowledge came from Scandinavian and German articles but also from an early work of 1835 by Hugh Pearson, Oxford graduate, Dean of Salisbury and Committee Member of the Church Missionary Society. Pearson, friend of Thomas Haweis, John Venn, Richard Cecil and Brownlow North, who ordained him, and Member of the Clapham Sect began to collect everything he could lay his hands on in the form of documents appertaining to the history of Christianity in India three years after Schwartz' Home call in 1798. In other words, the history of many successful missionaries in India must have been well known in Britain at the time of Carey's start-up of part-time missionary ventures.

Pearson wins a prize for his reports on Asia

Claudius Buchanan who started to assist the Calcutta Mission Church towards the end of the 18th century offered a prize of £500 to anyone who prepared the best written work concerning the advancement of the gospel in Asia and the problems involved in translating the Scriptures. Pearson accepted the challenge and wrote on the propagation of the gospel in Asia, and handed in his findings to Grant in 1808 and won the competition. Besides his general work on the evangelization of Asia, Pearson wrote his *Memoirs of the Life and Correspondence of Christian Frederick Swartz*[7] *to Which is Prefixed a Sketch of the History of Christianity in India*, published in 1835. This enormous work is a 'must' for friends of India and is freely available in the Public Domain.

Schwartz served the gospel faithfully until his death

In the above cited work, we find that Schwartz, up to shortly before his death, preached weekly and regularly in the native and colonial districts using Tamil and Telugu to communicate with the Indians and Portuguese, English and German for the other communities. On realizing that he was approaching the end of his services on earth, he had the children in his neighbourhood enter his house and sing Isaac Watts' hymn of worship:

> Far from my thoughts, vain world begone,
> Let my religious hours alone;
> Fain would my eyes my Saviour see,
> I wait a visit, Lord from thee!
>
> My heart grows warm with holy fire,
> And kindles with a pure desire:
> Come, my dear Jesus from above,
> And feed my soul with heavenly love.

---

[7] A widely used attempted Anglicism of Schwartz' name.

The trees of life immortal stand
In fragrant rows at thy right hand
And in sweet murmurs, by their side,
Rivers of bliss perpetual glide.

Haste, then, but with a smiling face,
And spread the table of thy grace;
Bring down a taste of fruit divine,
And cheer my heart with sacred wine.

Blest Jesus what delicious fare!
How sweet thy entertainments are!
Never did angels taste above
Redeeming grace, and dying love.

Hail, great Immanuel, all divine!
In thee thy Father's glories shine;
Thou brightest, sweetest, fairest one,
That eyes have seen or angels known.

Johann Zacharias Kiernander (1711-1799)

Kiernander was a Swedish missionary who was born in 1711 at Akstad near Lidköping. After matriculating from the Lidköping Grammar School he continued his education at Uppsala[8] and after graduation there in Theology, Latin, Greek, Hebrew and Missionary Outreach decided to continue his theological education and the Biblical languages at Halle University under Emil Francke.

After spending four years in Halle both teaching and studying, Kiernander decided to return to Sweden but the British Society for the Promotion of Christian Knowledge approached Francke saying they wished to support a missionary at Cuddalore, in Tamil Nadu, just north of Tharangambadi (Tranquebar), India. Tamil was being taught at Halle

[8] The same courses as Kiernander took at Uppsala and the same intense study of the original Scriptural languages and also missionary strategies were also my lot when I studied theology at Uppsala. Of the six European Universities from which I have graduated, Uppsala beat all in its academic standards and good teaching.

at this time so I presume Kiernander received such instruction making him more eligible for the post. Kiernander's curriculum at Uppsala is well-known but I have no documentation for Halle's exact curriculum at this time. Francke discussed the proposal with Kiernander who then felt sure he should take up the post.

Denmark at war with Sweden

As Denmark was at war with Sweden at the time, it was a daring thing to acknowledge Kiernander as a Dano-Halle-SPCK missionary but his character, qualifications and a good word from Francke settled the issue. Kiernander thus found he had Scandinavian, German and British supporters and the records say he was most liberally assisted by these sources. This seems to have caused other missionaries in India to be rather jealous of Kiernander as they claimed he had too much money at his disposal. However, Kiernander was not at all poor himself, especially after inheriting the family property and income and both his first and second wife were wealthy people. All three pooled almost all their fortunes into the Mission.

Kiernander was duly ordained on 20th November, 1739 and immediately set out for London to be shipped out to India. King George gave Kiernander a personal welcome and he was quartered in the house of his chaplain Ziegenhagen from December to 20th April when he boarded the Indiaman Colchester which set sail for India. Kiernander was never to see Sweden, Germany and Britain again.

Kiernander was introduced to the mission work at Cuddalore by missionary John Ernest Geister who later moved to Madras. The Mission church had 154 members, 99 of whom were Malabars or Tamil speakers, and 55 Portuguese speaking Christians. Two schools had been founded, the Malabarian School had 20 pupils and the Portuguese school 28. Immediately on the starting up of Kiernander's work, his congregation grew. Writing in 1833 of Kiernander's years at Cuddalore, John Carne[9] says:

> At Cuddalore he found a congregation, left by Sartorius, now removed to Madras, and he was appointed to be the successor. He was treated with the politest attention by Admiral Boscawen,

[9] *The Lives of Eminent Missionaries*, Vol. I, p. 300.

> and the English settlement of Fort St. David, who having judged it necessary, as a measure of policy, to expel all popish priests from this part of the Company's territories, put Kiernander into possession of the Portuguese church. It was solemnly dedicated anew, and from this time the mission at Cuddalore prospered under his care. He seems to have been delighted with the situation and climate, so different from those of his native Akstad; whose barren hills and rocks, and eternal snows,[10] were exchanged for a noble plain, amidst whose wild and glowing vegetation rose the city of Cuddalore. In the first letter to the Society, he writes, 'that his prospects were good; that he went out into the villages several times a week, to make known to the people the truths of Christianity; that his congregation in the town was increased. In the year 1745, its number amounted to near 200 persons, including those who were left by Sartorius, and, in the following year, it received an increase of a hundred and sixty converts.' In more than one place, he speaks of the happiness he felt: he had reason to be satisfied; *for no mission in India prospered so rapidly at this time, as that of Cuddalore.*[11]

Kiernander renamed the old Portuguese Roman Catholic church in Cuddalore for his reformed evangelical preaching 'Christ Church'. His happy position became even more attractive to him as he met Wendela Fischer, a young lady described in the Calcutta Christian Observer as 'a lady of some property'[12]. She was an amiable woman, an attached wife, and, being faithful to God, was a helpmeet for him in the preaching of the gospel. With this woman, he lived in happiness many years, and the Lord prospered his labours.[13]

---

[10] The author was obviously ignorant of the beautiful area around Akstad where I camped several times in winter and in summer with my scout troop and individual scouting friends. In winter, I learnt to ski there and do backwoodsman activities. The countryside is woody and fertile and the summers can be very hot and midge-infested.

[11] My italics.

[12] Miss Fischer was the sister of Colonel Fischer of the Madras Army.

[13] Calcutta Christian Observer of May, 1837, p. 232.

Chapter Thirteen

From Cuddalore to Calcutta

Kiernander is forced to leave Cuddalore and moves via Tranquebar to Serampore and Calcutta

On the 4th of May, 1758 the French under Thomas Arthur Comte de Lally threw out the British under Robert Clive from Cuddalore. When British Fort David fell to the French on 2nd June of the same year there appeared no hope of returning to the district where Kiernander had been very successful as a missionary. The Kiernanders were told there was no room for Protestant missionaries in French possessions but given a pass to leave Cuddalore. They fled to Tranquebar, possessing only the clothes they had on their backs. However, General de Lally, on hearing of the missionary's plight, kindly made good Kiernander's loss.

Whilst in Tranquebar, the Kiernanders received an invitation from Ziegenbalg's son Bartholomäus Lebrecht Ziegenbalg to join him in Serampore and Clive also welcomed his services in Calcutta which had also come under Tranquebar's gospel influence through earlier Dano-Halle missionaries. Ziegenbalg junior was now the Director of the Danish East India Company with his headquarters in Bengal but was as missionary-minded as ever. So the Kiernanders left Tranquebar on 11th September, well-provisioned for the start of a new missionary ministry by the Danes and arrived at Calcutta on the 29th September after a safe sea journey along an otherwise stormy coast.

Kiernander, supported by Clive founded a Mission Station and schools. Clive, who had fled from Fort David had now been made Governor of Calcutta and he and his Council welcomed Kiernander.

Soon afterwards, Mrs Kiernander gave birth to a son named Robert William after the Governor who stood with his wife and Mr and Mrs Francis Watts[1] as sponsors for him. So now the Kiernanders became the first permanent Protestant European missionaries to Calcutta helped by the Danes and Governor Clive who gave Kiernander a house to be used as a mission station.

Kiernander founded the Mission School at Calcutta in December 1758, and within a year, it was catering for some 175 children. Wealthy pupils paid their own way and others received bursaries from the Mission funds but the Kiernanders paid for the tuition and board of 37 poor scholars out of their own pockets. Whether wise, or not, they had declined support from Denmark and Germany and funds from England and the SPCK had become most erratic. The Kiernanders had now sufficient funds themselves and had received several large subscriptions through the agency of the two British chaplains in India, Henry Butler and John Cape, who were of great service to the mission. The Danes in Serampore asked Kiernander to fill in as a chaplain there and preach regularly with a good salary. Most of the Kiernanders' joint income was ploughed back into the mission. Thus, Serampore had a permanent evangelical witness some 22 years before Carey moved to Serampore.

Kiernander used his legacies for the Mission

A hard blow for Kiernander came on the 9th of May, 1759. His wife and co-missionary Wendela suddenly took ill of the cholera and died. Kiernander had six fierce attacks of the disease and was near death's door but survived. The two British Chaplains in Calcutta, Henry Butler and John Cape, also died of the cholera at this time. As Kiernander inherited a small fortune from Wendela, he is often criticized for living on her money though it is natural that one spouse inherits from the other and most spouses have a common kitty. However, at the time of Wendela's death, the news reached Kiernander that his wealthy brother had also died in Sweden and our Kiernander was the sole inheritor. A year later, Kiernander married a widow by the name of Anne Wooley who also enjoyed a degree of wealth.

It is strange that so many pro-Baptist accounts of the mission in Calcutta have criticised Kiernander for living off joint family income

---

[1] Watts was a Member of the Council.

whereas the Serampore Trio were financed through appeals for money outside of the Mission and gained the bulk of their income from secular financing. When Carey married Charlotte Emilia de Rumohr of noble birth in 1808, Carey's new wife immediately transferred her property and fortune to the ownership of the Mission and no one has had the silliness to challenge that. I have read very many accounts of the Serampore Trio's 'missionary' work but no pro-Carey writer has criticised the fact that their idol was financed mainly through secular organisations and not through Christian support, and had a wealthy wife. Besides, Carey was quite well-off himself before marrying Charlotte though he ploughed everything into the Baptist work in India as did his new wife and Mr and Mrs Kiernander. So too, the Serampore Press ran a flourishing business for several years and gained much profit from producing secular works.

Kiernander's work in 1760

Michael Wilkinson, who had access to Kiernander's papers recorded in 1844 concerning Kiernander's work in Calcutta and Serampore, writes:

> At the end of 1760, being the second year of his abode in that city, Mr Kiernander gave the following account of his school and ministry: 'that there remained 231 scholars, all of whom are taught reading, writing, cyphering, and the principles of Christianity'; and, he says, their inclination to learn, and the emulation that he perceives among them, make him go on with pleasure in his labour'. The number increasing obliged him to employ more assistants, and he was supplied with them from those brought up in the school. This is a pleasing fact in this early part of the history of the mission. It is further stated, that he had been enabled to supply 154 rupees monthly, for the salaries of those assistants, besides books, ink, and some small wages for servants, all which large expense had been defrayed, without putting the Society to any costs. Kiernander was at that time bargaining for a further house to accommodate a further school.
>
> He had baptized, beside children of Portuguese, German, and Dutch parents, one adult Tamulcan, seventeen years old, and was preparing three other adults for baptism. Of his Portuguese congregation, two adult persons and four children had died. He

> had that year sixty-one communicants; he continued preaching in the Portuguese language, had no time to apply himself fully to learn the language of the country, and was desirous of an associate to assist him in his growing labours.[2]

However, Wilkinson not only records a growth in the number of pupils in the following years but also in the number of native Indians who were converted and baptised yearly which were well over a dozen and Portuguese-speaking natives at times reached well over a score converted annually.

New language problems for Kiernander

Kiernander's transfer to Calcutta was a rushed affair due to the war conditions in Cuddalore and he had concentrated on Swedish, Danish, German, Portuguese and Tamil and he now had to learn Hindi and Bengali, so this obviously took some time and his situation was no different from most of the foreign missionaries. He was not, however, like Bövingh who refused to learn a native language. We must also take into account that times were very hard for missionaries due to the constant battles and uprisings going on in the area. Calcutta was a city of many nationalities, peoples and religions and the Bengali that Kiernander is often accused of not knowing was only one of the ten languages or so spoken in the city. Hindi, which Kiernander, Brown, Grant and Buchanan used, was the more widespread of languages in the North and was also used throughout India. Western missionaries and Indian evangelists had often to preach in Portuguese so that the highly mixed congregation both in the church and in the streets and surrounding villages could receive the gospel.

Kiernander stays independent of the SPCK

Wilkinson probably had favourable connections with the SPCK as he mentions several times that Kiernander would not dance to their pipe and preferred to keep the Mission under his own leadership and within the Danish-Halle fold. Wilkinson's reports on Kiernander's work, when quoting archived documents is most positive and he records how regular conversions were made through Kiernander's work. However,

[2] *Sketches of Christianity in North India*, p. 11.

he is most personal and critical in assuming that, in spite of Kiernander's great success, he was a man of little spiritual status. The records he uses and the examples he gives do not verify this in any way.

Kiernander builds a church using mostly his own money

The settlement's churches had been razed in uprisings during 1756 by oppositional native factions and the Kiernanders' funds were not sufficient to start building a mission church building for his native Indian, Euro-Indian, Portuguese, Scandinavian and British converts until 1767. The building was delayed through the death of the Danish architect but it was eventually finished in 1770 and paid for almost entirely at Kiernander's expense. Eyre Chatterton reports concerning this financing:

> It is no small thing that he, mainly at his own expense, erected a Church where no Church was, and thus restored to the inhabitants of the chief city of British India the long-forfeited privileges of worshipping God in a public place consecrated to His Service. Calcutta was without a Protestant Church, and without a Protestant Church it would have remained many years longer, if Kiernander had not thought of erecting one for missionary purposes at his own expense.

It was this church that the grasping SPCK demanded should be made over to them reminding one of the later BMS who burdened the Serampore Trio with similar demands. Chatterton continues:

> Certainly no Church in India has passed through such strange vicissitudes of fortune, or has ministered more effectively to the spiritual needs of men, than has the Old Mission Church in Calcutta.[3]

Mrs David Brown, widow of Kiernander's successor, wrote in the biography of her husband that Kiernander's church-building was thought unfit at the time for European worship but it was well used by

[3] *A History of the Church of England in India*, beginning of Chapter V 'Calcutta Continued'. No pagination.

Indians and Euro-Asians, the people to whom Kiernander had been called. It served an initial purpose for Kiernander's immediate missionary work as it could seat 200 souls. Kiernander named the mission church Beth-Tiphillah, the House of Prayer. It is still standing, though extended by Kiernander's successor David Brown, and in use but the locals call it either Lal Girja or The Old Church.

The Emperor asks Kiernander for Bible works in Arabic

The Emperor Shah Allum now asked Kiernander to translate the Psalter and New Testament into Arabic so that his Mullahs could read the gospel which, apparently, they did avidly. Jeyaraj believes that Carey would have been assisted by Kiernander's former students in establishing himself in Calcutta. Be that as it may, Kiernander certainly pioneered the gospel in Calcutta via the Danish-Halle Mission long before Carey entered into the field. Massive criticism from later British evangelicals during the following 30 years or so centred around Kiernander's care of children of 'mixed' blood as these were often not accepted as equal humans by both 'Christians' and Indians within their respective caste systems. In such cases Kiernander was happily 'colour blind'. I usually tease those missionary-minded who wish to take the gospel to 'full-blooded' Indians by informing them that one can scarcely find a human being on this earth today who is not an immigrant from somewhere. My Yorkshire father, who could look back on ancient Saxon and Irish-Scottish roots, always told me he was really a Dane! My mother, being closely related to my father, had the same 'mixed' roots. My wife has Franco-German roots and my children were born each in a different country. Everybody today has mixed origins.

Conversions amongst the Portuguese priests

The Portuguese priests in Calcutta were thrilled by Kiernander's clear grasp of a Christianity far more favourable to sinners than theirs and no less than five priests were converted through Kiernander's ministry and joined the Calcutta church. The Goa Portuguese Headquarters took this matter so seriously they sent a Jesuit ambassador over to Calcutta to officially excommunicate the converted priests. Two of these former Jesuits, Bento de Silvestre and Manuel Joze de Costa, became Kiernander's assistants. Chatterton writes in his *History*, Chapter V:

Kiernander was a whole-hearted missionary. His missionary zeal, however, led him just as strongly towards the conversion of the Roman Catholic community as it did towards that of the non-Christian world. After eight years' work in Calcutta, he reported to the S.P.C.K. that from December 1, 1758, to the end of the year 1766, he had made 189 converts, of whom one-half were Romanists, one-third the children of Roman Catholic parents, and thirty were heathen. Of his Roman Catholic converts no less than five were priests of that Church. Several of the priests afterwards assisted in his work.

It must be a sobering thought for many here to note that Carey, in the same time had made no known converts, yet he is praised as the missionary pioneer *par excellence*.

The loss of his wife and his son's mismanagement

In June, 1773 Kiernander lost his second wife after a serious illness lasting six months. Anne was devoted to the Mission and used up all her money in its service except her jewellery which she now left to the Mission School which was rebuilt to hold 250 pupils. In 1773 the Mission was given a 500 rupees gift via Chaplain Westrow Hulse on behalf of Sir and Lady Eyre Coote. It is also recorded that Kiernander donated 1,000 rupees to the Mission and his son Robert William 3,000 rupees. Now aged 76, Kiernander realised he could not carry the sole burden of the Mission alone and planned to visit England to arrange for some form of cooperation 'lest his congregation should be forsaken and his Church shut up'. However, Kiernander now found little interest in England for his Mission.

The situation of the SPCK at the time

The SPCK's lack of interest in Kiernander's wish to be independent of the Church of England became of little importance as parallel with Kiernander's refusal to comply with the SPCK's wishes, the society decided to stop sending missionaries to India and concentrate on other matters such as book distribution. Missionary work in India was to be handed over to the sister society The United Society for the Propagation of the Gospel (USPG) and the Irish based The Association for Promoting Christian Knowledge (APCK). The APCK's interest in India started in 1792 and was strongest in the South where the bulk of their former work had been done. Thus, the weight of British Episcopalian missionary support furthered the Church of South India.[4] However, in 1825, the British authorities allowed the High-Church American missionary organisation SPG to take over the Tranquebar missions in Madras, Cuddalore, Tanjore, Tritschinopoli and Tinnevelly. Thus, without asking the native Indian Christians if they were in agreement or not, the young Southern Indian, relatively independent and nominally Lutheran churches were turned into episcopalian 'Anglican' churches by decision of the colonial occupiers.[5] Though the Baptist missionaries had been in India for thirty-two years, they yet backed, or were compelled to back, the enforced transfer of thousands of Christian Indians to an American denomination. No foreign power campaigned to allow the Indian churches to rule themselves.

Kiernander's church was eventually taken over by the CMS and not the SPCK.

Bankruptcy threatens to close the Mission

Meanwhile, by 1786 Kiernander was almost blind so he looked to his son Robert, also educated at Halle, to take care of the mission's finances. Robert helped his father in the ministry and was known for his generous giving to the Mission. Not having his father's head for thrift and business, however, Robert soon invested in schemes which left the Kiernanders almost bankrupt. Once again, the Mission was almost destroyed because of the treasurer's failure in balancing the books. This was not entirely Robert's fault as, in order to finance the Mission, he had invested in land which became worthless when the British wars caused land prices to sink. The SPCK now answered Kiernander's plea for more missionaries by urging him to write over the ownership of the Mission to them and then they would supply missionaries. It is an ever-repeated story in world evangelism that home societies wish to have missionaries as their employees and dictate what they should do though having little knowledge of what is at stake. To

[4] It is a popular misconception that Tranquebar and Calcutta must be near each other as they are both in the Bay of Bengal. That bay, however, stretches from Sri Lanka to Indonesia!

[5] See Raupp's *Mission in Quellentexten*, p. 155.

put pressure on Kiernander, the SPCK told him that if he did not hand over the ownership of the Mission and its considerable property, they would not help fund him. Kiernander refused to write over the Mission with the result that Kiernander was soon faced with a debt of 10,000 rupees.

Abortive attempts to oust Kiernander from his mission
The SPCK did send out Johann Christian Diemar (1745-1799) who had spent some time in Calcutta before journeying to England to be ordained and return as a SPCK missionary assigned to assist Kiernander but obviously with the intention of forcing Kiernander out. One is reminded of similar attempts by the BMS to oust the Serampore Trio. Diemar opposed Kiernander violently and strove to force him to sign over the entire Mission with its property to the SPCK. As Kiernander refused, Diemar robbed the Mission of the money used for schools for his own private use. This must have been about the sixth case of the Mission's treasurers' fiddling of the Mission's books. Diemar then married Mary Weston, the daughter of a wealthy English business man who supported both the Mission Church and the SPCK. Probably Diemar thought Weston and the SPCK could be influential in his taking over the Mission on their behalf and pestered Kiernander mercilessly and continually to sign over the Mission to the SPCK. The SPCK asked the other Tranquebar missionaries to intercede on their behalf but to no avail. Obviously, this was not in the Mission's interest. The SPCK then appealed to the Mission's supporters at Halle but they, too, gave them a rebuff which led to a violent quarrel. Nothing daunting the SPCK sent another missionary named Gerlach to Calcutta as their spokesman but the German showed almost no interest in the affairs of the Mission. At last, the SPCK found an Englishman to go over to Calcutta to help them. This was A. T. Clark, a Cambridge man. Kiernander now trusting that Clark would take on all the burdens of the Mission resigned his post but his joy at having been sent a successor was very brief. The new post was apparently too tough for the Cambridge graduate and the Christian Observer continues:

> But after having resided a few months at Calcutta, he (Clark) abandoned his mission, but David Brown took over assisted by

John Owen. Soon Buchanan and several other missionaries and chaplains joined the Old Church ministry.[6]

The Christian Observer of October, 1814, also records the arrival of Clark:

> In the report of 1788, it appears that Mr. Kiernander, the society's missionary at Calcutta, had been obliged, from age and infirmities to relinquish the service of the mission, and to transfer the mission church, school, etc., to the Rev David Brown, W. Chambers, Esq, and C. Grant Esq, … In consequence of the communications made by these gentlemen to the board, in which they set forth the importance of Calcutta as a station from whence the knowledge of Christianity might be defused, considerable efforts were made to procure a suitable missionary to succeed Mr Kiernander. The Rev A. T. Clark, of Cambridge was nominated to this office.

Kathleen Blechynden remarks in her book *Calcutta: Past and Present*:

> While Kiernander was the first Protestant missionary to Bengal, his successor, the Rev. A. T. Clarke, was the first Protestant missionary of English nationality in Bengal, his arrival, in 1789, preceding by four years that of the Baptist missionary, Dr Carey, for whom the honour is sometimes claimed.[7]

These statements are quite misleading. Although Grant, Brown and Chambers did save Kiernander from financial embarrassment, Clark was of little help to Kiernander and did not take up his mantel. Indeed, he broke with the Mission after a few months. Nor was Carey Clark's successor as he never joined the band of the mixed denominations who ran the Mission though he preached there occasionally.

---

[6] Christian Observer, Oct. 1814, No 154, Vol. XIII, p. 637.
[7] *Calcutta: Past and Present*, London, 1905, p. 84.

Grant, Brown and Chambers did not favour the SPCK's demands, so they formed their own missionary society with the help of the so-called Clapham Sect. Clark was replaced by a German called William Tobias Ringeltaube (1770- ?), another graduate of Halle and son of a Silesian Court Chaplain and area Superintendent. Ringeltaube was ordained for the mission field in 1796 in Wernigerode. Ringeltaube was a fine man of God but also turned quickly from the Danish-Halle Mission and affiliated himself with the Moravians in Calcutta. The latter, however, were rapidly forsaking Bengal and their property was eventually taken over by Carey. Ringeltaube left Calcutta around 1803 and became a London Missionary Society missionary in Travancore. Thus, all attempts to oust Kiernander by the SPCK failed but put unhealthy pressure on the aged Swedish missionary and were of no help to him in his ministry.

At this time the British Government were clamping down on evangelical Church of England missionaries, giving others who accepted Britain's foreign policies, the preference. The Serampore Trio who professed to be true servants of the British Raj nevertheless survived because they put themselves under Danish protection in Serampore and Carey, after 1800, was in the East Indian Company's and Governmental employment in Calcutta.

Kiernander gives up his Mission work

Kiernander now handed over his pastorate completely to David Brown. This did not mean retirement for him by a long way. He set up a new work in Dutch Chinsurah (now Chuchura), some 30 miles up the Hooghly River. Governor Isaac Titsingh (1745-1812) found himself without a chaplain and after gaining some insight into Kiernander's ministry invited him to take on the post with a monthly salary of 50 rupees which put Kiernander back on his financial feet. Sadly, Kiernander's work for the gospel was soon hindered by the British war with the Dutch and Chinsurah came under British control and Swedish Kiernander was made a Dutch prisoner of war on the grounds that he had preached to Dutch soldiers. So now Kiernander who had once been driven out of his southern Indian home by the French was now driven out of his northern home by the British.

However, as in the case of the French, Kiernander was dealt with kindly by the British after the initial smoke of conflict had disappeared and he was not only set free but the British Commissioner Birch who took over from Titsingh even continued to pay Kiernander his salary in lieu of the Dutch and he was allowed to preach freely. The SPCK and the Church of England now stopped supplying Kiernander with funds and his son Robert died intestate and left Kiernander to look after his widow and six children. Brown asked the SPCK to award Kiernander a generous money gift for his past services. Their response was to send Kiernander a mere £40. Then Brown repaired, improved and extended the Old Church, adding a chancel and asked Kiernander to take the opening service and officiate over the Lord's Supper. Kiernander remained on most amiable terms with the new pastor and Superintendent. The number of Christians in Calcutta both native and European, was growing so rapidly that Brown had to build a second, much larger church as well as keeping the old congregation going. The new church building was frequented mostly by Europeans and the Old Church by a mixed community. These were the churches that modern Baptists wrongly claim maintained no continued Christian witness after Kiernander, yet the Baptists had to wait decades before they could speak of such Christian outreach themselves though they had, at times, far larger teams of workers.

Kiernander takes Carey under his wing

Soon the pioneer missionary due to blindness and old age became overburdened by his gospel work, but was providentially able to take over his old house in Calcutta and lived there with his widowed daughter-in-law and his many grandchildren. Even then when well over eighty years of age Kiernander did not fully retire from preaching and assisted his successor David Brown regularly until his death. One of Kiernander's last tasks was to take Carey under his wing and introduce him to field preaching along the Hooghly River on whose banks lay Calcutta, Serampore and Chinsurah, Carey's future sphere of work. Carey rejected Kiernander's advice and practical experience and took up secular work instead. He told Kiernander, however, that he wanted to build a hut in the wilderness and live off the land.

Mixed up thinking concerning Kiernander

Baptist writers have criticized Kiernander for spending much (about a third) of his time preaching to Eurasians instead of 'pure' Indians which is a very odd criticism indeed. However, Carey is rarely criticised for spending most of his time not preaching at all but working mainly with British Government and East India Company employees. In Serampore, he worked as a Dane amongst Danes in a Danish college under the Danish King's charter. By the end of the 18th century a very large population of Indians were of 'mixed' origin and even before the time of Western invasions and their debauchery with Indian women, the Indians had absorbed the peoples of many countries into their families. Several of their religions such as Islam were not native to India. Nor was much of its folklore which came from Persia. On the other hand, Carey is supposed to have spent all his missionary energies in evangelizing native Indians only. This is quite incorrect as Carey's students were mostly British citizens or Anglo-Indians. Carey's teaching language, as much of his preaching language, was English and he campaigned to use English as the language of evangelism. The so-called 'vernacular schools', which Carey is famed for having set up, were taught by Indians who were often not Christians. Where the Serampore Trio were involved in Indian evangelism it was via employing and superintending Christian native evangelists.

Evangelising the Adivasi

Today, many Western Christian missiologists spoil their testimony by wasting time looking for the Adivasi in India or the original Indians. Such people, if they can be found, which I very much doubt, are then made the subject of special missions with special money raising campaigns. A missionary who is called to India is not called to search out a lost piece of alleged history but called to her actual peoples whatever their genetics have made them and is no respecter of persons in this sense. To try and divide the Indians, or any other peoples, into 'races' is racism itself. Months after writing this, I came across two articles on the Adivasi, one entitled 'The Indigenous Peoples of India', dated 1995, published by the Association of Asian Studies and another sent me via academia.edu on 31st of May 2021 entitled 'Lost innocents and the loss of innocence': interpreting Adivasi movements in South Asia by Crispin Bates, Department of History, Edinburgh University. Both articles looked at the idea of seeking out 'the lost innocents' most critically. Dr Bates amusingly, but quite truly, ended his enlightening long essay by claiming, 'All Indians are, in one sense 'Adivasis'!

Ziegenbalg and Kiernander did not look to the colour of skins or examine genes and DNAs but the state of the human heart. Kiernander's converts were all sorts of mixtures and came from eight different religious backgrounds if not more because that was the mixed ethnical religious state of Calcutta at the time. What would the British think if Indians were to evangelize the multi-racial UK but insist on only preaching to the 'original British'? Does anyone know who they were and where they are now? Most present Evolutionists are bent on a search for a pre-historic 'Adivasi' and even tell us that Westerners are descended from the Neanderthal Man, but how that helps or interests us, I do not know, even if they do trace the Neanderthal Man back to an ever-changing amoeba. Calcutta was international, multi-national and 'transformational' even before early Portuguese ownership. Many of the converts of other missionaries who came after Kiernander were also of mixed blood because, after centuries of European Colonists and traders in India, this was the mixed state of things. Nowadays, missionaries to India of whatever nationality are also missionaries to the Portuguese-Indians and the Anglo-Indians who nevertheless are 'full-blooded' Indians as far as citizenship and loyalty are concerned.

Kiernander's Indian converts were proportionally high

The truth is, however, that though the population was very mixed, Kiernander always had more native Indian converts than those of mixed races. Looking back over Kiernander's last years of soul-winning, at an age when most other missionaries were retired or probably dead, I can find no exact annual statistics, however trustworthy 'now and then' official records for most of Kiernander's last years as pastor of the Calcutta Church have been preserved. So, we find that Kiernander in 1776 had been the means of converting and baptizing 27 natives and together with those designated 'Portuguese' and English had 88 converts that year. In 1780, Kiernander had ten native converts both Hindus and Muslims and four previous Roman Catholics, probably Portuguese. In 1781 he made six native converts and two converts from the Roman Catholics. In 1783 he made 27 native converts of various religious backgrounds, and also one Chinese and one Roman Catholic convert. In 1785 there were 19 Indian converts, ten from the Roman Catholics whose race was not specified. In 1786 he baptised 20 Indians and 15 Roman Catholics (again nationality not specified) and had to split the church into two congregations as they could not all gather at once. Few Christians I know of were so successful in soul-winning.

But yet, a picture is often given us in ill-researched missionary studies of a helpless old man working alone at a failing cause who was quite unable to lead a soul to Christ. There is no evidence whatsoever for this distorted picture which is even attributed partly to Carey. Actually, the very opposite was the case. Kiernander's congregation numbered at least 290 worshippers before his retirement to take on new duties. What missionary pastor at the time and at such a high age could compete with that? Furthermore, Kiernander had a fine team of faithful helpers such as de Sausa who had been a leading Jesuit and had been converted through Kiernander's ministry and Charles Weston, another convert, besides W. Chambers the Bible translator. These many assistants included at least four ordained missionaries such as Frenzel, Gerlach, Obeck and Diemar, though Gerlach and Diemar proved of little help. Johann Christian Obeck had started his Christian outreach in Tranquebar in 1755, then aged 26, and moved to Calcutta in 1777. Up to this time, the British missionary societies could not find many missionaries in Britain so they mostly sent out foreigners such as Obeck with a call to India.

Though one often reads that Kiernander was inefficient as a missionary between the ages of 75 and 88, this criticism is quite unjust though it is repeated as a mantra by many writers who obviously wish to place him in Carey's shade. Anyway, most missionaries nowadays retire at 65 if not earlier. The many negative tales concerning Kiernander's use of funds, which were always given most generously, and that he neglected the natives in preference to mixed bloods are all parts of the mythology surrounding Indian Missions and party-mindedness in general.

After eye operations, old Kiernander begins anew

Besides, after successful eye operations (couching) in extreme old age, Kiernander could once again take on many responsibilities and he continued to be a soul winner in the Dutch colony near at hand and in the Hooghly district until his death aged 88. The statistics of conversions mentioned above were obtained from the writings of Michael Wilkinson, a Church of England missionary, who was familiar with the churches in Calcutta during Carey's day but evangelized an area as large as Wales in Uttar Pradesh from 1824 to 1848 from his base in Goruckpore. Wilkinson's works which display a first-hand knowledge of Indian Missions are happily still in print and veritable eye-openers concerning the stalwarts he followed and his contemporary missionaries. Wilkinson mentions men and women of God whose lives still require much attention for the benefit of the cause of God and truth. I would like to research further the life of Obeck mentioned in several books, magazines and newspapers of the day for his great practical piety.

Kiernander did not die penniless

Most biographies of Kiernander, especially those who will not accept Kiernander's contribution to Indian evangelism because of Hyper-Denominationalism, politics and racism,[8] say that he died in absolute poverty which is quite incorrect. Though he again became blind after the couching operation, and aged as he was, he was still able to recover some of his deceased wife's fortune and, with occasional funding from international missionary organisations, he is said to have had an income of some 800 rupees a month throughout the last few years of his life which was not too little to cover the costs of his admittedly now large family. In 1799, he fell badly and broke a thighbone which would not heal and he died a month later aged eighty-eight. So, it was not old age which ended Kiernander's service but a bad fall. After Kiernander a further twenty-five or so Swedish missionaries were sent out from Uppsala and the Leipzig Missionary Society in the 19th century. Most famous of these, at least, as far as length of service goes, was the Sandegren family who provided missionaries over several generations of sons and daughters. The Swedes added to their women born in India a relatively large percentage of well-educated Swedish women missionaries sent out from Sweden. Their histories are still to be adequately researched and published. When the British drove out German missionaries from India in the last century, the Swedes took

---

[8] It is surprising how many 'Christian' writers have criticized Kiernander for his evangelizing the down-and-out half-castes and people of mixed blood often called 'Portuguese' for want of a more exact, objective term. It is also a puzzle to me why Westerners speak of 'Hindu Christians', 'Muslim Christians', 'Jewish Christians' and even 'Heathen Christians'!

over much of their work.[9] It was through the Sandegrens that the Baptist churches were informed about the connection between Tranquebar and Serampore, a fact which does not appear to have been given much attention on the Baptist side.

George Smith's historical blunder

George Smith in his 1885 *Life of William Carey* tells us that 'Carey could find no trace of Kiernander's work amongst the natives six years after his death'.[10] This is a most surprising statement as Grant, Brown, Buchanan and Chambers were all carrying on the good work but Carey had not joined it and was still without converts himself. Brown preferred working amongst Kiernander's converts and his own in the Old Mission Church. The new Church was mostly for the Colonists. So, too, one can only ask what Carey was doing during these six or seven years in and around Calcutta and why had he not continued where Kiernander left off. It is pointless to criticise the work of others when one does such little work oneself. Carey had also been given ample opportunities to be active in missionary work during Kiernander's life-time. Thomas had already backed out of supporting the Calcutta work before returning to England to canvas for funds and assistants. Smith had not bothered to look over Carey's shoulder and read the accounts of John Thomas and the church which had welcomed him and in which he preached before his Baptist days. During Carey's day a number of missionaries in Calcutta from several countries besides Indian ministers were carrying on Kiernander's work in the city so there is sufficient documentation to refute fully Smith's claim. One can hardly imagine Carey saying such things. When Thomas first visited Calcutta in the 1780s, he also thought that there would be no witness there but soon found things to be quite different. Carey obviously knew of the Calcutta church not only through Thomas but also through his own experience as he eventually occasionally preached there. Carey thus became part of the work Kiernander founded himself. Kiernander had taken Carey with him shortly before his death and shown him how to preach in the highways and byways. Kiernander had also given Carey sound advice as to where and how to set up a mission station, suggesting nearby

[9] See Johannes Sandegren's *From Tranquebar to Serampore*, Serampore College, 1956.
[10] *Life of William Carey*, p. 78.

Bandel, but Carey refused the idea and said hiring or buying a house would be too expensive and he wished to 'go into the Country, build a hut and live like the natives'.[11] This reminded me of a poem I learnt as a young boy with similar dreams as Carey from the pen of William Butler Yeats. It was called The Lake Isle of Innisfree:

> I will arise and go now, and go to Innisfree,
> And a small cabin build there, of clay and wattles made;
> Nine bean rows will I have there, a hive for the honey bee,
> And live alone in the bee-loud glade.

This moved me to build such a hide-away in Cottingley Woods near Bingley, Yorkshire as an early teenager, where I spent many weekends scouting and eating self-snared rabbits, twists and dampers. This was good preparation for my work amongst charcoal-burners in the forests of Sweden and later living in the Kåtas (birch bark and sod huts) of the Samë. I found my little Eden on earth and was able to serve the Lord in it but Carey gave up the idea of his wee self-built hut and desire to live like the natives. Though the kind natives offered him a hut and garden free of charge, he opted for a mansion-like house with many servants bought initially on borrowed money.

Perhaps Carey's reluctance to settle in Bandel was because the local inhabitants mostly spoke Portuguese and, at first, Carey could only preach in English. Carey's dream was never to be, though we soon read that he was assisting Kiernander's successors in the Old Mission Church now greatly extended and drawing in increasing numbers. The reality is that years after Kiernander's home-call, Carey had still seen no converts himself. Kiernander had hundreds in the same period at the start of his mission and continued to have them.[12] This reminds me that when Carey failed in his later writings, he blamed this on his numerous native scholarly assistants who had merely done what he had told them to do.

---

[11] Carey's Journal, Jan. 1794.

[12] By that time a New Church had been set up by Brown who now pastored both churches, opening up a third 'preaching house' in an old temple in which Henry Martyn and Carey also preached.

The perpetuation of many legends

Julius Richter perpetuated the missionary legends of Smith writing in 1906, that 'when Carey arrived at Calcutta, seven years after Kiernander's death, he was hardly able to discover a single vestige of Kiernander's missionary activity'.[13] He writes this though he had just written that Kiernander's ministry was 'much blessed'. However, Richter counts his years wrongly, apparently believing that Kiernander's ministry ended in 1786 with his death and seven years later Carey arrived in Calcutta and allegedly found no trace of Kiernander's pioneering missionary work. The Swede was, however, still very much alive and still winning converts for Christ when Carey accompanied him in his field preaching, the older missionary obviously thinking he had a successor who needed to be encouraged.

It was apparently John Thomas who persuaded Carey, against his friend's ideals, to ignore Kiernander's advice and example and settle in Calcutta in a large expensive villa to keep up European appearances. The wide-spread myth that Carey found no trace of Kiernander's work in Calcutta is without any foundation whatsoever. Kiernander's work was being continued by most capable men who even financed Carey's first attempts at translations and helped Thomas and Carey to settle down in India, even providing occupation for them.

Opportunities and open-doors ignored

Charles Grant, a Senior East India Company Director and evangelical Christian, encouraged by Schwartz' writings on missionary work like Carey after him, backed by Kiernander, Chambers and David Brown in Calcutta, had been campaigning for Britain to send out missionaries to India with a small measure of success long before the BMS was set up and had also advised Carey to take over Kiernander's Old Church as a missionary base. It is here that a good number of biographers lose track of Kiernander's history – and Carey's. Carey did little to carry on Kiernander's work at all between 1793 and 1800 and even afterwards, when he had the opportunity and all doors were opened for him. He left Kiernander's work in Brown's and Buchanan's full-time capable hands assisted by several other British, German and Swedish missionaries. At this time Carey was making a living as an indigo trader.

---

[13] *A History of Missions in India*, p. 130.

On taking over Kiernander's church, Brown realised it was too small for the large number of worshippers, so extended it. He immediately founded a further school for native children. There were already schools for older native children but Brown's school catered for Elementary School children from four years of age up to Secondary School entrance. Ignorance of these facts in modern missionary mythology is not to be excused.

What is also surprising to this author is that Schwartz corresponded with several members of the Calcutta Mission Church, especially with Mr and Mrs Chambers, Buchannan and Grant up to 1798 but no mention is made of Carey who was engaged in secular business outside of Calcutta at the time and appeared not to be in the 'inner circle' of the missionaries. Furthermore, in the condolences which came from Calcutta after Schwartz' death in that year, I have found no trace of Carey's name after searching the records diligently. This would indicate that Carey was inactive in Calcutta and had possibly cut himself off from Schwartz. Yet Carey had been very much influenced by Schwartz in his first missionary thoughts back in England. Somehow, Carey was keeping a low profile away from the currently large family of evangelical Christians both locally and in India at large at that time. He was perhaps too much involved in business matters. It was members of the Old Mission Church such as George Udny, however, who had found Carey the secular work which he and Thomas had sought. Brown gave Carey a post in the college where he was on the governing Board. Gradually, rather belatedly, Carey did join in with the members of the Old Church, even preaching there, but Andrew Fuller pulled him back.

Kiernander was buried in the tomb of his second wife in the Calcutta cemetery he had purchased for the Mission. Wilkinson quotes one of Kiernander's last letters to his Swedish home in Akstad which he had given up so many decades before:

> My heart is full, but my hand is weak. The world is yet the same; there are many cold friends, others like broken reeds, but God makes the heaviest burden light and easy. I rejoice to see the poor mission prosper; this comforts me amidst all.[14]

---

[14] Wilkinson, p. 33.

Perhaps it is best not to enquire too deeply as to whom those 'many cold friends and broken reeds' were. However, Kiernander's words indicate that when he died, his successor David Brown took over a prospering work. This is also clearly how Brown judged the situation, the number of communicants (those catechized and baptised) being at the takeover 266, 119 of which were Indian natives. Indeed, Wilkinson says:

> Mr Brown found in Calcutta, in 1786, a small body of pious Christians, and in a course of years had the happiness of discovering that in hidden and unexplored retreats, there were unthought-of individuals who lived the life of faith on the Son of God, and walked in the paths of his commandments; and some who in the utmost privacy, had exerted themselves to stem the torrent of surrounding evil by their religious example in their families, and in maintaining and superintending schools for the instruction of heathen children.[15]

Though modern Baptist writers tend to ignore Kiernander's missionary zeal, older writers were not so inclined. James Foot Holcomb in his Introduction to Helen Holcomb's *Men of Might in India Missions*, tells us that when Kiernander was 83 years of age 'he received a visit from Carey, who records the fresh ardour he derived from the *still burning fire* of the aged saint.'[16]

This 'fresh ardour from the aged saint' ought to be given more attention.

Arthur C. Chute's historical blunder

Given such praise for the spirituality and success of Kiernander's preaching and teaching, it is quite astonishing that Arthur C. Chute says in his 1893 work *John Thomas: First Baptist Missionary to Bengal 1757-1801*[17] of Kiernander, 'Though Kiernander was a benevolent man, it does not appear that he greatly gloried in the Cross of Christ'.[18]

---

[15] Wilkinson, p. 37.
[16] My italics, p. 12 in Holcomb's work.
[17] Baptist Book & Tract Society.
[18] Chute, p. 8.

He also claims that Brown, who actually ministered to a multi-national congregation of growing numbers so that he had to extend Kiernander's Old Church and build a second one which continued together under Brown's supervision, 'preached to a small audience of his own countrymen'.[19] Sadly, this most incorrect and highly prejudiced view, void of all documentation, is repeated as a mantra through numerous later works written by writers not prepared to research their subjects themselves. There is blindness in part in the Christian churches.

A controversial inscription on Kiernander's tomb

The inscription on Kiernander's tomb, however, caused some considerable discussion. It reads:

JOHANN ZACHRIAS KIERNANDER,
born in Sweden on 1st December 1710,
Went in 1739 as English Missionary to Cuddalore,
Founded in 1758 the Mission in Bengal, and built for the same
out of his own money a Church which he called
Beth Tephillah.

It was set up by Kiernander's grandson who wrongly believed that Kiernander was sent out to Cuddalore by the Church of England and not the Dano-Halle Mission.[20] Kiernander, however, was and remained a missionary of the Danish-Halle Mission.

Bishop Chatterton of Nagpur in his *History of the Church of England* gives a long vindication of Kiernander and praise for his work but tells us that the SPCK did not pay a penny to help Kiernander build a church. The SPCK did, however, help Kiernander to travel from Tranquebar to Calcutta with no ulterior motives then but later claimed that Kiernander's work was bound to fail unless it was placed in their hands. Carey at last gave in to BMS demands and signed his Mission over to his Society but Kiernander remained in the Danish-Halle Mission and withstood the demands of the SPCK. For this stance, he was greatly criticised by British missionaries who were either fully under the SPCK's support or received generous grants from them.

---

[19] Chute, p. 9.

[20] Here Richter is accurate in stressing this fact on page 113 of his *History*.

Anglicans in India such as Chatterton knew Kiernander's value and praised his pioneering work. Chatterton explains that most of the SPCK's missionaries were Danes and Germans who were not Anglicans. When it appeared that Kiernander was heading for bankruptcy, the SPCK did not see fit to help him out but Brown intervened and appealed to the SPCK conscience as Kiernander had served them well. The SPCK then gave Kiernander a grant of £40. As Kiernander needed thousands of pounds at the time to pay off his debts, he had to be thankful for small mercies.

Praise for Kiernander was slow in coming

After Kiernander's home-call, praise for the Swede Kiernander was slow in coming, chiefly for political reasons. Sweden was still warring with Denmark but Denmark was being thrown out of India by British expansionism and Britain was using all means at their disposal to force the Danish King to give up Serampore. Now the Scandinavians were considered enemies of Britain. Serampore was forced to give in to the British in 1845 which more or less ended the Danish-Norwegian influence in missionary matters. This may partly explain why British Baptist write-ups became, on the whole, unfavourable to previous Serampore and Calcutta Missions which had been pioneered by the Danes, Norwegians and Swedes beside the Germans whose work was also ended by the British. By 1847, such anti-Kiernander pressures were lessening and the Calcutta Review (Vol. 4), took a new look at the history of missions in Bengal and dedicated a detailed and lengthy tribute to 'The First Protestant Missionary to Bengal, Johann Zacharias Kiernander'. This account is freely available on the Public Domain and ought to be studied by all those interested in the spread of the Gospel in India.

Chapter Fourteen

British Multi-Denominational Presence in Calcutta before 1800

David Brown (1763-1812)

The work of Brown in Calcutta and Serampore especially prior to and after Carey's arrival in India must be emphasized here as Brown did all in his power to make Carey welcome in both cities and was the man who secured for him a living wage when Carey's business dreams ended in bankruptcy. Brown's support of Carey was far more effective than that of the Baptist Missionary Society both spiritually and financially. Brown was a native of Hull in East Yorkshire and was home-schooled in Scarborough before matriculation to Magdalene College, Cambridge, through the Hull Grammar School. Brown broke off his studies before graduation and was ordained as a deacon of the Church of England in 1785 and a year later made a chaplain of the British East India Company and sent to India. He was placed in charge of a company orphanage for the unwanted 'mixed' offspring of the British in Calcutta. After meeting ageing Kiernander he took over the Mission church as pastor soon after settling in Calcutta in 1786. Chatterton tells us in Chapter V of his *History* that;

> From this time onwards this Church became famous as a great centre of evangelicalism in India. Here preachers such as David Brown, Claudius Buchanan, Henry Martyn, Daniel Corrie (first Bishop of Madras), and Dealtry (third Bishop of Madras) and

many others drew large crowds, which often included the leaders of Calcutta society.

As the church built by Kiernander only seated some 200 souls, Brown had it extended to make room for 800 worshippers, including Europeans. This Mission church was still going strong when Carey sailed to India in 1793 and joined the Christians there. Carey was also invited to preach in the church, an invitation he eventually accepted. This must be noted in contrast to contrary reports such as those of Chute noted above.

Brown had effective plans for a Missionary Society before the BMS
Shortly after settling in Calcutta, Brown founded a missionary society in conjunction with Charles Grant, George Simeon, William Wilberforce and John Newton which went through several names but which was eventually called the Church Missionary Society.[1] Besides pastoring Kiernander's old church, Brown's ministry spread throughout all Calcutta so he had a much larger church built in a quarter occupied by British officials and civil servants which he named St. John's. Most of the British officials and their staffs attended this church. We might thus rightly call Brown a missionary-chaplain as he served both the native Indians and the English East Indian company workers who were becoming more and more of mixed races. It must also be said that he pastored the Old Mission Church in Calcutta for twenty-three years non-stop without being paid any salary whatsoever but he claimed his other incomes kept the wolf from the door. He preferred working at the Mission Church than working in the British Church.

Rather than this evangelical Mission Church being run down in 1793, as so often reported, fellow-Indian missionary Michael Wilkinson relates:

> During this year (1793) the increased attendance at the Mission Church, rendered the enlargement of the building necessary. When it first devolved to Mr. Brown's care, as the 'Bethtiphla' of the aged Zacharias Kiernander, it was in a very

[1] The Church was still run by the CMS into the 20th century.

> different style to the elegant structure now presented to the eye, as one of the ornaments of the 'city of palaces'.
>
> From its original appearance it was designated by the natives Lai Girja, (Lai, red; and Girja, church;) with which appellation it is still best known, though now presenting the appearance of a massy stone edifice. Those who remember the old building describe its internal fittings-up and furniture, as consisting of a brick pulpit built against the wall, its aisle rough uncovered tiling, a few rude benches and pews of unpainted plank, formed the general seats, with a small number of chairs without pews for the gentry, and it did not accommodate at that time more than two hundred persons; yet was it strongly built of good masonry, and very lofty, so as to be an object of attraction. Encouraged and assisted by the fine taste and scientific abilities of his friend Mr. W. Chambers, Mr. Brown was not long in making a beginning, to enlarge and improve the building. The inner east wall which then divided the chancel was removed, and some beautiful highly finished Corinthian pillars were substituted, to support the roof, or break the ill-proportioned length. The increasing congregation soon required the space these pillars occupied. They were first decreased in number, and then reluctantly removed altogether, and other means of preserving the proportion as well as enlarging the space were resorted to, by extensive bows thrown out in the centre, and galleries erected at the extremities. It also was gradually fitted up in a manner suitable to the climate, abundantly lighted, supplied with an excellent organ and handsome pulpit and desks, to correspond with the general neatness of the whole.[2]

Again, this does not sound as if there were no Christian activity in Calcutta during this time and the work started by Kiernander was dead. Prominent members of Brown's congregations were Governor General Wellesley and his brother Arthur who became the famous Duke of Wellington. When Wellesley founded the Fort William College for Indian civil servants in 1800, he made Brown Provost and Buchanan Vice-Provost. Brown, realising that Wellesley disdained evangelical Church of England men in India called Baptist Carey who was said to

[2] Wilkinson, pp. 79, 80.

be 'well affected' to the British Government and several of his Christian and non-Christian friends to the staff. So, Carey's appointment was really political. In this way, however, Brown secured a stable income for Carey. Brown retired from the project in 1806-7 after the East Indian Company withdrew their support. The EIC were dissatisfied with Lord Wellesley's management, aims and educational methods and demanded that the college should be closed but Wellesley decided to continue the work under his own supervision. The EIC founded a new college in Haileybury, England in 1806 solely for their own representatives abroad. The Wellesley Fort William College found enough support, however, to continue and Carey remained as a teacher of vernacular languages for 31 years at the school on a relatively high salary, with extra perks from the Asiatic Society. The college itself was continued under various supporters until 1854. By 1831, however, most of Carey's work was rejected, not that the new language reforms and translations were very much better. Indeed, the dumbing down of scripts, vocabulary and grammar in their published works continued.

Life at the Fort William College

Carey is often described as a Professor of Bengali and Sanskrit at Fort William but in her Florida State University MA thesis Kelly Rebecca Cross Elliot argues that this title was never officially given Carey. In this she was correct concerning the first seven years of Carey's work at the College but on Jan. 1, 1807, Carey, in view of the honorary academic titles given him, was officially appointed as 'Professor' or 'Head of Department' within a leading team of scholars. His achievements were in simplifying the Indian languages on the basis of the Sanskrit he was still studying and popularizing his Devanagari script. However, the Fort William College was never given university status and never trained students in theology.[3] Indeed, Michael Wilkinson quotes from a letter penned by Buchanan to Grant saying:

[3] *Baptist Missions in the British Empire: Jamaica and Serampore in the First Half of the Nineteenth Century*, Florida State University, 2007, p. 16. See also Buchannan's *The College of Fort William in Bengal*, 1805.

> Lord Wellesley is at present engaged in founding a college for the instruction of young civil servants in eastern literature and general learning.[4]

Buchanan was to write on the founding and progress of the College in his, *The College of Fort William in Bengal* of 1805. Whilst on the governing board of the college, Buchanan, Grant and Brown took the initiative of making sure that the college day started with a Christian Assembly for worship and the Indian students were encouraged to attend the Mission Church. This was in Lord Wellesley's interest but did not quite please the EIC who eventually broke with Wellesley.

We read concerning the founding of Fort William College:

> The educational standards required for judges, magistrates, collectors and ambassadors had not changed since the early days of the Company, when legible hand-writing and book-keeping skills were all that was required of candidates. Some of the clerks, known as 'writers', had left public school in England at fourteen or fifteen. There were no facilities in India to prepare them for their duties. Lord Wellesley fixed January 1801 as the date after which no appointments could be made without candidates having passed examinations in the native languages. He founded Fort William College to teach Modern European Languages, Latin, Greek, English Classics, Geography, Mathematics, History, Natural History, Botany, Chemistry, Astronomy, Ethics and Jurisprudence. As regards Indian studies, it was to teach Arabic, Persian, Sanskrit, Hindi, Bengali, Telugu, Marathi and Tamil. No promotion was to be given in the whole Presidency except through the College. It was to be considered one of the most important departments of state and senior members of the government were expected to take a share in its management. Men of learning from all over India were advised to proceed to Calcutta and become teachers. More than 50 did so.[5]

---

[4] Wilkinson, p. 107.

[5] *William Ward*, Chapter 8 – William Carey University, Online Account.

Indeed, the number of staff members, including military personnel, was at times over double that of the students as the experts only attended the college to give occasional lectures. Because of the large number of part-time lecturers, the College could keep up a full curriculum of instruction for the youths being taught. Happily, there are a number of works still extent concerning the founding and organisation of the college.

One of the most detailed and lengthy accounts of the Fort William College was penned by the Assistant Secretary to the Council of the College of Fort William, Thomas Roebuck in 1819 entitled *The Annals of the College of Fort William With Appendix in 1819*. That wonderful institution the Internet Archive provides a download of this valuable work free of charge. It is full of surprises for those brought up with the dozen or so standard biographies of Carey. We read of much more Indian co-working in the College than is usually portrayed in Western books. For instance, though Carey is mentioned as Head of the Vernacular Language Department, we read that Moonshee Meer Sher Ulee was Head of the Hindustani Department and that a Sanskrit dictionary was being compiled by learned natives employed by the College and not Carey. It is also reported that the College was supporting Carey and Marshman in their translations of Ramayana and further works on Hindu philosophy. A number of native scholars were working on modernizing, and codifying Sanskrit, Tamil and Farsi for the use of the British.

We read on page 155,

> A printing press has been established by learned Hindoos, furnished with complete founts of improved Nagree types of different sizes, for the printing of books in the Sunskrit language. This press has been encouraged by the College to undertake an edition of the best Sunskrit Dictionaries, and a compilation of the Sunskrit rules of Grammar. The first of these works is completed, and with the second, which is in considerable forwardness, will form a valuable collection of Sunskrit Philology. It may be hoped, that the introduction of the art of printing among the Hindoos, which has been thus begun by the institution of a Sunskrit press, will promote the general diffusion of knowledge among this numerous and very ancient people; at the same time

> that it becomes the means of preserving the classic remains of their literature and sciences.

It would thus appear that the College before 1819 had its own Indian run printing works and did not have to rely on the printing works run by the Serampore Trio. However, Roebuck refers to the type-casting of the Serampore press so there was obviously close cooperation between Serampore and the Fort William College. Scripture translations of parts of Genesis, John and Matthew were commissioned by the College to be printed at Serampore in 1815. These were passages pioneered by Thomas in the seventeen nineties which Carey had now published at the College's expense. Carey is reported to have compiled a dictionary of the Marathi language and printed by him though such dictionaries had been in existence for some time. Also, a number of Bible portions and whole Bibles had been produced in Indian languages such as Teluga and Hindi so that the College's printings were often mere reprints and not original works as often claimed. Henry Pitts Forster had produced dictionaries in Sanskrit and Bengali, which were in use at the College by 1807 if not before.[6] This would suggest that Carey's dictionary had a very short life at the College. The trouble was that Carey's dictionary was continually being held up in its printing because of obvious improvements which needed to be made, so whilst moving over to Forster's dictionary, Roebuck writes of Carey's production:

> A Dictionary of the Vernacular Dialect of Bengal which was mentioned in the Visitor's last Discourse as undertaken by the Professor of Sanskrit and Bengalee Languages, is now in the Serampore Press: but from the extent of the work and labour employed in tracing the Etymologies, with a view to its more perfect execution, a considerable time will yet be required for the completion of it.[7]

---

[6] *Annals,* p. 158. Dating the events described by Roebuck accurately is not always easy but, apparently, he is writing concerning the state of the college in 1807, see page 143.
[7] *Annals,* pp. 291-293.

The Secretary speaks of Carey's Marathi Dictionary which 'has been some time in the press'. Concerning the native printing works produced by the College Press, Roebuck says:

> The dissemination, by means of the press, of works composed by Natives eminent for their knowledge and practical skill in this dialect, must gradually polish, and fix a standard of excellence in a language, which, though long employed as an elegant medium of colloquial intercourse, and as the vehicle of poetical imagery, has hitherto been little used for prose composition.[8]

Carey's duties at the Fort William College

It is not easy to work out exactly what Carey's duties were at the College as Head of the Sanskrit and Bengali departments. Carey confessed to having no knowledge of Sanskrit before his appointment and we read that he was being taught Sanskrit by an Indian lady member of the staff. He, however, assisted by very many pundits, taught Marathi in his own right which he based on his growing Sanskrit knowledge and regularly 'up-dated'. In this way Carey altered Marathi as it had been written and spoken hitherto. Carey did not feel comfortable in preaching in Bengali before 1807. In the very thick volume of the *Annals* Carey is referred to variously as professor, teacher, moderator and superintendent or the Rev. Carey or plain Mr Carey. However, he did not lead the department alone but his duties were apparently performed within a team consisting of H. Colebrooke, Carey and H. H. Wilson in the order of their signatures under their joint works.[9]

Marathi is one of the most widespread languages of India after Hindi and Bengali but was simplified and altered into 'Missionary Marathi' by Carey who used his recently acquired knowledge of Sanskrit to modify the language and altered the scripts to his own Devanagari, the possible reason being that those were the only fonts available to him at the time. In 1831 a new dictionary was brought out by J. T. Molesworth and his Indian assistants which further 'Sanskritised' the language in the way the pidginised Sanskrit was currently being used. Concerning

---

[8] *Annals*, p. 158.

[9] *Annals*, p. 365.

Marathi which Carey taught in a simplified form, there are now 42 officially recognised dialects of that language so any attempt at compiling a dictionary could lead to a further dumbing down of the language. I have Punjabi, Bengali and Marathi speaking friends who quarrel amiably about who is speaking the correct language. This applies also to Sanskrit, Pali, and a host of other Indian language groups. Of course, we have this problem in English and German, too. The old way of learning a language via a grammar and a dictionary just does not work today, if it ever did. Although the Goa Marathi is widely spoken in Western India, its 'modern' origin is in the work of the Fort William College in Calcutta on the Eastern Coast. Once, when travelling by bus to Trondheim from Jämtland, an elderly lady addressed me and I answered in Swedish, not realising from her language at first that she was Norwegian. The lady immediately congratulated me on my 'good Norwegian' and we chatted away in 'Scandinavian' for the rest of the journey. The Norwegian and Swedish dictionaries and grammars, however, tell us that these are two different languages. Such 'linguistic kidding' is very much rampant also in India. It is rather a foolish enterprise to 'standardise any language as this creates a new dialect and separates the people from their written history as it has destroyed much of the culture of the Sami who have had a standardised, artificial Sami enforced on them under various names. The beautiful sing-song joiking of the Lapps which is at least two thousand years old has become a mixture of Heavy Metal and Dolly Parton's 'Western Country' songs performed by youngsters in competitions and tourist attractions. The unmusical missionaries banned it as 'pagan' because they could not understand it. Now it brings with it a generation gap.

What is rather puzzling to a language instructor such as myself is that Carey did not moderate or superintend the Sanskrit and Bengali disputation in these tongues but in English. A knowledge of Sanskrit and Bengali was, however, demanded of the pupils who were mostly native English-speakers. Today, such disputations in grammar school and university courses are mono-lingual. The Sanskrit disputations bore such titles as 'The Greek systems of Philosophy are derived from the Hindoos'. The Bengali disputations had such titles as 'The Advantage of the Oriental method of conveying instructions by means of Parables or Tales, is particularly conspicuous in the Bengali Language'. This was all good practice in debate and apologetics though not at a particularly high academic level. We expect that the students could show proficiencies in the target language by giving examples to back up their arguments. The candidates were seventeen to nineteen years old who usually had stayed only a year at the College. 'Honours' and 'passes' were given but not at degree level as the college had no university status. This was all far from being of university academic standard.

Brown was more at home in the Old Church

Although Brown was now officially pastor of two quite different congregations, he spent the bulk of his time looking after his fold at the Mission church, now called the Old Church to distinguish it from St. John's, the New Church. To ease the burden, he resigned from his Orphanage tasks in 1788. Brown's first wife a Miss Robertson of Hull died in 1794 and he then married Francis Cowley in 1796, fathering nine children in all. His call for missionaries world-wide was started a good number of years before the Baptist Missionary Society and backed by most prominent and godly evangelicals. So, too, the Calcutta Bible Society which he helped found was one of the first of its kind.

Brown invites Carey to preach in his Serampore chapel

In 1803, Brown bought Alden House in Serampore with a view to using it as a guest house for his many evangelical friends of several denominations, including Baptist preachers. So again, we see Brown ignoring denominational barriers. Apparently, the Browns' house was always full to bursting point as Brown's hospitality was well-known. In the garden was an old Hindu temple which Brown turned into a preaching chapel where both Carey and Henry Martyn preached. Brown opposed the strange action of the Baptist Missionary Society to go it alone in Serampore whilst still demanding funding from the international supporters whom Fuller would not recognize as 'pure' Christians. Thus, the British Baptists broke the quite idyllic Christian fellowship under Brown's leadership but Brown did not break with his Baptist friends and supported Carey and others solidly, especially when the BMS elbowed the Serampore Trio out of their mission strategy altogether. Without the support of the CMS, the LMS and the Church of England and men such as Grant, Buchanan, Brown and Udney, and Lutherans such as Bie and King Frederick of Denmark and Norway, there would have been no Baptist work done at all in Calcutta and Serampore.

Brown died in 1812 from a grave illness under most tragic circumstances including the shipwreck of the vessel taking him to a healthier climate for healing. His last days were spent at the home of John Herbert Harington, president of the Bible Society which he and Brown had founded the previous year. Brown was 'modern' in the sense that he combined missionary work with that of an East India Company employee and government civil servant. Carey followed him in this dual capacity.

John Thomas (1757-1801)

A. J. Gordon in his Introduction to Arthur C. Chute's *John Thomas: First Baptist Missionary to Bengal* claims that, 'If William Carey was the pioneer of Modern Missions, John Thomas was the pioneer of Carey'. The 'if clause' is fitting as Carey can hardly be called 'the pioneer of modern missions' but Thomas was certainly the pioneer of Carey and of Fuller. Gordon goes on to say of Carey, 'As far as we can see, the great missionary translator and preacher might not have had his face turned towards India, had not the missionary doctor gone before him to pave the way'.

Chute in his first chapter argues that Thomas is given such a negative write-up by Baptist authors because they wish to compare him with Carey whom they see in a better light. There is much truth in this theory and it is obvious that Thomas, as Kiernander, Brown and many others is played down to play up on Carey. This is not a satisfying approach to the truth. However, Chute is leaning on C. B. Lewis here whose larger biography was acknowledged by Chute as his inspiration in writing his shorter work. At the beginning of his book, Lewis records that:

> Many facts in Mr Thomas' history were withheld from publication by the early friends of the Baptist Mission, there can be no doubt, because they were felt to be discreditable. His debts and his misunderstandings with his friends involved so much that was unpleasant, that it was thought well to keep them out of sight, and himself with them.

Lewis also claims that Thomas was (mis)used:

> as a fail setting off the excellences of others, rather than to wish to relate his services to the cause of Christ.[10]

Though Lewis feels Thomas has suffered under the hands of later Baptist writers, he nevertheless confesses to heavily editing Thomas' words in his many quotes from Thomas' writings himself and has altered his grammar. It is often frustrating to read how Carey, who was in many ways similar to Thomas, has been praised for his 'excellences' in comparison to Thomas' 'discreditable' nature. In recent years, however, the 'other side' of Carey is coming to light, particular in his attitude to Thomas, his wife and his children but also in his eagerness to have governmental honours and salaries. This separated him from the full-time work of a missionary. Thomas was certainly a more out-and-out evangelist than Carey though much less of a politician.

Thomas' early life

We gather from Lewis, whom Chute follows, that Thomas was born in Fairford, Gloucestershire in May 1757, so he was some four years older than Carey. His father was a Deacon in the town's Baptist Church where Benjamin Beddome occasionally preached and took part in Association Conferences. Beddome had told Carey to make sure that his own district was evangelized before striving to evangelize those of strangers. In his youth Thomas thought of becoming a preacher and indeed, preached to his friends and the countryside from the age of five on. He had also many other interests and started several apprenticeships which he quickly gave up.

Early considered a ne'er-do-well

Because of his wild behaviour Thomas began to be considered a ne'er-do-well in his locality. On being given a place in Westminster Hospital, he found Surgery and Medicine to his liking and after successful studies was appointed assistant surgeon on one of His Majesty's ships. After a most dangerous voyage, he decided to remain on dry land and opened a Surgery and Chemist's shop in London. Then, aged 24, he married a Church of England lady but writes that he married for the wrong reasons and claims unromantically, 'I naturally exposed myself to the common

---

[10] Both quotes from Lewis, p. iv.

misery and unhappiness of a married state'. He confessed, however, that his wife loved him dearly.[11] He became influenced by Robert Robinson the former Methodist who by Thomas' day had become an Arian Baptist and introduced Arian Baptism as the Scriptural norm. Happily, he then came under the more wholesome teaching of Dr Samuel Stennett whose gospel touched Thomas' heart and led him to Christ. Then Thomas turned to Abraham Booth and asked to be baptised by him but the Particular Baptist rejected Thomas thinking him far too 'wild and enthusiastic' to be taken seriously.

Thomas flees from his debts and family responsibilities

By this time Thomas was in great debt through living beyond his income and had to sell his business and property. His 'tender and delicate wife', so Thomas, was awaiting the birth of their daughter and Thomas could not provide for a family. This did not appear to trouble Thomas too much, though now a Christian, so he joined the Earl of Oxford Indiaman in 1783 as a ship's surgeon, stating that 'My poor wife was sadly distressed at this prospect'.[12] Thomas had no qualms about leaving his expectant wife penniless hoping she would rely on the 'generosity of friends'. The only hitch was that Thomas had few friends to rely on.

Lewis strange commentary on Thomas' inexcusable behaviour would make a sensitive soul shake his head in sorrow. Yet Lewis labours at great length to express his sympathy for Thomas as if he were being a martyr and wastes not a word of sympathy for his poor abandoned wife. So, too, one cannot but challenge Lewis' defence of Colonialism by conquest which was then rampant in India and presented as a positive thing. Lewis goes back to the early seventeen fifties in his description of Calcutta which led to the 1756 Black Hole of Calcutta horror. Terrible as this was, it was nothing compared to the massive slaughter of almost defenceless Indians in the name of money-making business which reduced many surviving Indians to poverty and paved the way for the avenging 'Black Hole'. Thomas complained that the 'Heathens' were so poor that they had to sell their children to buy food, listing this to prove how uncivilized the Indians were. He did not

---

[11] Lewis, p. 7.
[12] Lewis, p. 10.

stop to ask himself who had caused this poverty or criticise himself for abandoning both wife and child to such poverty in order to make sure he had enough food in his own stomach.

However, when Thomas reached Calcutta, there was little of the past evident. The city was now rebuilt and though the original church built in 1715 had been destroyed by the local natives, it had been rebuilt decades before by Kiernander. Calcutta in 1783 was a modern, thriving city with a sound evangelical witness.

Thomas makes his project known to the British Baptists

In the 1792 edition of John Rippon's *Annual Register*, we find printed a lengthy letter from John Thomas who relates his experiences gained in two trips to Calcutta from 1783 to 1792. He reports his difficulty on his first visit to Calcutta in finding Christian fellowship so he placed an advertisement in the India Gazette under the heading Religious Society in an effort to find like-minded people. Here Thomas wrote:

> A plan is now forming for the more effectually spreading the knowledge of Jesus Christ, and his glorious gospel, in and about Bengal: any serious persons of any denomination, rich or poor, high or low, who would heartily approve of, join in, or gladly forward such an undertaking, are hereby invited to give a small testimony of their inclination, that they may enjoy the satisfaction of forming a communion, the most useful, the most comfortable, and the most exalted, in the world. Direct for A. B. C. to be left with the Editor.

The very next day Thomas received a positive answer from one who promised to open a subscription for the translation of the Scriptures into 'Persian and the Moorish languages'. The writer was sure he could collect together a group of subscribers who could manage all the financing. Another positive letter was sent by a minister whom Thomas thought was a Chaplain whom he had heard preach on 'The Unknown God' and decided not to follow up that letter. However, Thomas soon found 'truly pious people' in Calcutta, a businessman named W--- which I take to be Weston and a Mr G--- which must have been Grant and a Mr. C--- who was probably Chambers. As Thomas' ship was now due to leave for England, he had to give up his idea of forming a

Christian Mission himself, but was determined to pursue the cause in Britain. There he heard that a good gospel minister had been sent to Bengal (most likely Brown) and another Minister named N----- (Newton?) felt there were 'religious stirrings' in Bengal. Apparently, Thomas believed that N----- had merely read his India Gazette advertisement. If 'N' were Newton, then that saint had been thinking of evangelizing India for some time and Thomas was not the first to take positive action by a long way.

Thomas describes Indian 'Heathenism' vividly in the pages of the *Annual Register* forgetting that it was a running joke at the time that British officials left their religion at the Cape of Good Hope when journeying to India. While still in the Atlantic, they were 'Christian' but when they turned towards the Indian Ocean, they became thorough-going Heathens of a kind scarcely known in India.

Thomas becomes a Baptist

Once back in England, Thomas was moved to join the Baptists and hoped that they would support him but had still not undergone Baptist baptism himself. He had not been able to move Booth to baptise him. Thomas eventually found a Baptist minister who baptised him in 1785 after which he preached around the country, now suddenly calling himself The Rev. John Thomas, though he had neither ordination nor a church. Debts, however followed Thomas everywhere in his wake so he returned to India again in 1786, leaving his ailing wife once more to fend for herself and their little daughter. On arriving in Calcutta, though now an enthusiastic Baptist, he immediately sought out Church of England chaplain and missionary David Brown who was caring for cast off infants and children of Europeans, mainly British and Portuguese, who had Indian mistresses or concubines. He also now met Grant and Chambers again and a Mr U---- who must have been Udny. Thomas tells us that he preached regularly to this multi-denominational fellowship, though in a private house and not in the church. He was encouraged by Grant to stay in India, learn Hindi, which was the widest established language in the region and preach the gospel. At first, he had qualms about abandoning his family again without a husband and father and without financial support but nevertheless decided to stay somehow thinking that serving the Lord of necessity meant neglecting one's family responsibilities. He was strengthened in his decision by the conversion of two Europeans under his ministry. However, Thomas could not keep himself from going into debt and quarrelling with his fellow Christians which caused Thomas to change his plans radically. Of course, this is not mentioned in Thomas' *Annual Register* article.

Thomas and Indian religion

In that article dated 1792, Thomas in his description of Indian religions, speaks of the Vedas which are claimed to be many thousands of years old. Thomas had obviously done a little research here as he argues that other religious books in India contradict the idea of the antiquity of the Vedas. As most of the old 17th century proofs concerning Hinduism come from Jesuit pens and the ideas described are often similar to what the Jesuits taught themselves, one wonders if, after all, the Vedas are not a Western invention. At least one 'Veda' presumed to be ancient had already been proved by Ziegenbalg and other experts to be a forgery. It is certain, however, that the foreign missionaries' occupation with variants of religions which they summed up under the heading 'Hinduism' has helped to kindle the modern idea that Hinduism is the basic religion of all Indians. My own research into Hinduism shows that it contains religious views from many faiths of perhaps more ancient origin. Jainism and Sivism certainly seem to be older than Hinduism and perhaps also Buddhism but religions have been coming and going in India for many centuries and are always changing as is, sadly, the world-wide understanding of Christianity. Actually, Hinduism now embraces around a billion people who mostly live in India, Pakistan and Bangladesh. Thus some 15 per cent of the world's population follow Hinduism. Most holders of the religion appear to be born into Hindu families. Hinduism is, however, so complex that it cannot be called a single religion as it has no basic standard of orthodoxy and no standard confession or statement of faith.

Thomas' first converts

Now Thomas relates that two Hindus have been converted under his ministry, one being Bosu (Boshoo) whom he says is 'well educated in the Persian language' and 'a person of no ordinary capacity'. Bosu had composed a hymn in Bengali a copy of which Thomas sent Rippon. Thomas also speaks of a Brahmin Parbotee who wishes to be baptised with Bosu. The latter's trial was great as he was of the writer caste whom the Brahmin's would not accept as equals. Furthermore, because of Bosu's conversion, his and his wife's families had taken his wife and children into custody and declared Bosu dead with regards to them. Before we complain that this was terrible and pagan, we must realise that terrible pagan times were the lot of both Christians and Indians. Andrew Fuller campaigned soon after for the same policies which he forced on non-Baptist or non-Christian Indians, declaring that men and women who would not follow their spouses in a profession of Baptist baptism should be divorced from them.

Michael Wilkinson, a CMS missionary to India, in his 1844 work *Sketches of Christianity in North India* writes concerning the Baptist Missionary Society founded in 1792 and Thomas' call for missionaries to Bengal some ten years earlier:

> and to Mr Thomas perhaps Bengal is indebted for having led the Baptist Missionary Society to fix on India as the future scene of their labours. That gentleman, on his return to England, advertised for subscriptions for carrying on the work, which he represented as greatly favoured by several persons of influence in Calcutta, of translating the Scriptures into Bengalee. The Baptist Society forthwith invited him to return under their patronage. This invitation he accepted, and the progress by which his mind was led to this determination is thus related in the statement he made to the Society: — 'I sailed the second time to Bengal in 1786, with the same captain and officers, and in the same ship as before. That very season the Rev. D. Brown, who now preaches in Calcutta, went over and took charge of the Orphan School, where all the children of European soldiers are educated and provided for. On my arrival there I found a Mr Udny, and a Mr Chambers, and two or three more who were connected with Mr Grant's family, all serious people, and we used to go together to hear Mr Brown on the Lord's-day, who preached to the children under his charge; and after a little while, we had a prayer-meeting, and sometimes a word of exhortation given. Mr Grant removed from Maldah to Calcutta; on his coming to us we were increased and strengthened, and I preached at his house every Lord's-day evening. One day as Mr Udny and I were walking out, he gave me to understand that Mr Grant

> wished me to stay in the country, to learn the language, and preach the Gospel to the Hindoos; but I was averse to the climate, dreaded a longer separation from my family, and had no particular bent of mind to the work. Having also the charge of a ship's company as their surgeon, without any probability of the Captain giving me leave to stay, or of another surgeon being found to supply my place, I could not accede to the proposal, yet it would often return to my mind, and after a few weeks I became greatly concerned at heart for the condition of the perishing multitudes of Pagans in utter darkness, and was inflamed with fervent desires to go and declare the glory of Christ among them. Waters enough have risen since to damp, but will never extinguish what was lighted up at that time. After much prayer and many tears, I gave myself up to this work, and the Lord removed difficulties out of the way, confirmed the mission, and comforted me by adding two souls (both European) to my first labours, who continue my hope and joy, and, I trust, will be my crown at the day of Christ's appearing.[13]

Here, it appears that the impetus of enrolling Baptist missionaries for Calcutta came from Thomas who saw himself as pioneering the movement which caused him to move back to England to find support. The four or five now converted under Thomas' ministry became the nucleus of the Mission set up by the BMS in Calcutta and the first converts after 1793 such as Krishna Pal were through his ministry also. Thomas' own affiliation at the time in spite of his being a Baptist was with the Old Calcutta Church until Brown took over the pastorate from Kiernander. Thomas' description of the fellowship he enjoyed in the Old Church and Brown's work amongst Indian and European children of different national backgrounds shows that the gospel was definitely still being preached in Kiernander's day. Indeed, it was primarily Brown and Udny who supported Thomas and also Carey when they reached Calcutta in 1793. Brown, following Kiernander, encouraged both men to preach repeatedly in their church and both Brown and Udny found secular employment for Carey when he decided not to join the work of evangelism carried out by the Mission Church, not to follow

[13] Wilkinson pp. 77-79.

the demands of the BMS, and not to take up his former call to 'go native'. He saw secular employment as the only alternative which could bring him a desired income. Again, the 'Thomas' in him was gaining the upper hand but he had not Thomas' evangelistic abilities.

Thomas alienates himself from the Calcutta Mission Church

This was perhaps more Thomas' fault than Carey's as Thomas had alienated himself severely from the Calcutta church fellowship because of his debts and ecclesiastical dogmatism and he was still Carey's spokesman and even financer. Thomas had insisted on being the keeper of the initial BMS funding, small as it was, and sadly squandered their joint monies. Carey for a short while was just as unwelcome in the Mission Church as Thomas was, but, as he was not so argumentative and stubborn as Thomas, he gradually gained favour. We can understand that Thomas became a great embarrassment to Carey yet the latter could never have settled down in India without Thomas' help in obtaining the secular employment both men sought. Carey failed in the same way as Thomas in this enterprise which altered both Thomas' and Carey's calling radically and it was again Brown, Grant and Udny, three Church of England men, who came to Carey's help, not the BMS.

Thomas' debts and difficulties during his second sojourn in India

Thomas' second voyage to India did not turn out as he wished due to his heavy demands on his friends and supporters. Again, these unedifying facts are not disclosed in Thomas' *Annual Register* report. Thomas' total lack of humility and displays of thankfulness to those financing him and his strong insistence that others should maintain him adequately to his demands began to try the nerves and patience of his generous friends. So Thomas aimed high. As Kiernander was now an old man and the SPCK had dropped their support because Kiernander had refused to sign over the Mission and large property to them, Thomas now presented himself as Kiernander's successor and wished to take over all the Missions' property, income and organization. He maintained that as he was a Baptist, he wished to run the church on Baptist lines, fully knowing that those financing the Mission Church, including its governors, were opposed to the kind of Baptist ecclesiology and rites that Thomas represented. He was thus gravely disappointed when David Brown was given charge of the Mission and would not accept that he had been too ambitious though a novice in India. Then Thomas quarrelled with both Grant, who had encouraged him to become a missionary, and Brown who had nothing to do with Thomas at all but had merely been given the charge of the Mission Church without a salary, which went completely against Thomas' thwarted plans anyway. Thomas badly needed financial support again as his debts were running high. Thomas' main protest, however, was that neither Grant nor Brown were Baptists. Somehow Thomas felt that non-Baptists could not be strict enough Calvinists though Calvin was certainly not a Baptist and Thomas does not appear to have been much of a Calvinist. Indeed, Thomas was most similar to Bövingh who felt that his version of Orthodoxy made him automatically superior to those of other persuasions.

With another prospective source of income gone, Thomas was soon in great debt again. Grant, Brown and Udny felt it their Christian duty to help Thomas out of his financial misery and even bought a newly built house for him though Thomas continued to denounce them. Yet, Thomas still felt they were inferior Christians and continued to pressurise his generous friends to become institutionalised Baptists as if this were the whole point of Christian evangelism. So, he now preached his narrow, totalitarian view of Baptist baptism in India as a major part of his gospel even in the Old Mission Church. Grant, Brown and even Udny, who had befriended Thomas the most, finally ceased to support him as they felt he was doing more damage than good in striving to divide the Church. 'The waters that divide' were sadly to flow freely in the Indian churches after 1800 so that few were able to minister without this dilemma splitting the churches. With the advent of Andrew Fuller's interference in the Indian mission fields the 'great divide' was to become a chasm as Fuller, like Thomas, accepted non-Baptist financial support but claimed that the greatest initial givers and supporters such as Grant and Buchanan were deceived by 'Jezebel'. This was Jesuit thinking indeed.

The alleged 'baptism of Christ and His Apostles'

Thomas now felt himself being martyred in India for preaching what he called 'the baptism of Christ and His Apostles' and he refused to give the Lord's Supper to catechized and baptised or baptised and confirmed Christians because they were not baptised in the form recently adopted by certain Baptists of the Fullerite school who had broken with the Olney practice inherited from John Bunyan and Henry Jessey where, to use William Cowper's words, 'the dipped and sprinkled lived in peace'. Bunyan had founded the Olney Baptist Church as an Open Communion Church in 1672 and when Sutcliff took over the church in 1775, this practice continued. Fuller's break with the pioneer Baptist churches and especially the Particular Baptists introduced a new, sacramental form of Baptism unknown to previous churches, including the Baptists. The waters which were to divide the 'dipped and sprinkled' also divided the 'immersed'. Clearly Thomas saw his view of 'Christ's baptism' as indicating that Christ instituted baptism primarily for a public profession of faith leading to church membership in a local church, forgetting the teaching of Pentecost. He also believed that such a profession is part of the meaning and function of salvatory baptism for those 'of age' and 'of discretion' only, in other words, for already-believers only. He could not imagine baptism as being part of the evangelistic gospel pointing to the life, work and expiatory baptism of Christ in His atoning death with its covenant promises to both young and old. It was Christ who was baptised to fulfil all righteousness for man, not individual men for themselves only.

Thomas thus found in baptism the reasons for partaking in the Lord's Supper. Baptism certainly does not save, nor does it point to anything the baptismal candidate has done but points the way to Christ's baptism and the salvation gained by it. Thomas' baptism was a looking back to the baptismal candidate's own step in faith and not a pointer to the faith of Jesus Christ portrayed through His own baptism in death for the dead that they might be resurrected in and with Him. Grant, Brown and Udny thus saw baptism rather as an evangelistic gospel action within the gospel and not an indicator of one's own step of hopeful obedience. Many Baptists therefore can see no parallel between circumcision and baptism arguing that the latter is for the People of God but the former a mere sign of adherence to the Jewish national faith. Of course, this quite destroys the fact that the Scriptures emphasise Old Testament circumcision as a sign of God's promise to choose out His Covenant People of God as is clearly emphasised in the Old Testament just as is the case with New Testament baptism. Titus 3:4, 5 teaches:

> But after that the kindness and love of God our Saviour towards man appeared. Not by works of righteousness which we have done, but according to his mercy he saved us, by the washing of regeneration, and renewing of the Holy Ghost.

Surely this is a reference to the gospel which baptism depicts. We see this also in Ephesians 5:25, 26 where we read:

> Husbands, love your wives, even as Christ also loved the church and gave himself for it; that he might sanctify it and cleanse it with the washing of water by the word.

Here is a clear reference to the promise-carrying purpose of baptism and the fact that baptism depicts the cleansing effect of the Word through the death of Christ who thus fulfilled all righteousness. This is the gospel pointed to by baptism which is able to make a person wise unto salvation.

Thomas complains of being despised because he was poor

Thomas also complained that he was now despised because he was poor which was rather far-fetched as he was hardly undeservingly poor. Again, he fell into debt and again those whom he could not accept as true brethren, such as Udny, helped him out. Then friends in Malda, near Calcutta where Udny lived and where Thomas and Carey later gained employment through kind Udny as traders, promised to support Thomas financially. Thomas surprisingly refused the offer, though he was badly in need of funding to pay off his debts. He had now decided to return to England with his debts unsettled and raise money for greater projects. He actually felt that new supporters would finance him and cause him to be debt free. In July, 1792, he was reunited with his faithful wife and daughter who had been left without any income for six years. How they had managed throughout this time of gross neglect, Heaven only knows. A number of writers have written in deep sympathy with Thomas' plight but who will research the neglected lives of his family?

Part 6

Andrew Fuller's Role in Indian Missions

Chapter Fifteen

Andrew Fuller's Doctrine of Man and God

Fuller's theological legacy

Andrew Fuller is noted today by many writers on church history and world-wide evangelism as making a significant contribution to the revitalization of Particular (Calvinist) Baptist life in late 18th century England. He is depicted furthermore as the greatest theologian of his time, a claim sometimes restricted to his doctrinal influence on the Baptist Movement alone. In recent years he is primarily seen as a key figure in the historic turn towards the establishing of free Protestant Missionary Societies world-wide, but especially in India, at the turn of the nineteenth century. When one, however, compares Fuller's highly provincial endeavours in home and Asian evangelism with the absolutely massive European-wide and international endeavours of Francke, one can hardly believe that some Christians view Fuller as the more important man in the history of missiology. So, too, to make a Halle of Kettering demands a stubborn if not blind imagination that quite shuts the eyes to reality.

Fuller is also claimed to have put the doctrines of Jonathan Edwards into practice in a marked degree, indeed much of Fuller's claim to greatness rests on the assumption that it was Jonathan Edwards' early works which gave to Fuller his knowledge of both man and God but particularly of man. Fuller, however, is seen to have outdone even Edwards in his theology of man and God. Fuller's view of man became the basis for most of his theological works which he formed according to his own precepts which were certainly not Edwardsean. However, praise for Fuller goes far beyond merely his supposed Edwardsean studies and is based on theories of his vast theological reading and deep insight into doctrinal and pastoral matters. All this praise is used as a basis for boosting Fuller as the one and great Missiologist of all time. This writer cannot escape criticizing the mythical view of Fuller propagated today for the best of theological, doctrinal, historical, pastoral and missiological reasons.

Edwards' influence on Fuller examined

A recent firm attempt to establish Fuller as the promoter and developer of Edwards' theology is Chris Chun's doctoral thesis entitled *The Legacy of Jonathan Edwards in the Theology of Andrew Fuller* published by the Dutch publishing house Brill in the Netherlands. His supervisor was Prof. Stephen R. Holmes who kindly provided a Foreword for the published thesis.

In this work Chun has sought to gather together the sum teaching of Fullerite theology arguing that it was based on Fuller's earlier reading of Edwards resulting in Fuller's major and earliest work *The Gospel Worthy of All Acceptation.* Chun bases his entire argument on the assumption that Fuller read, learnt and inwardly digested Edwards' early work on the 'moral' and 'natural' nature of man which was published in 1771 during Fuller's Johnsonian days.

Fuller did not know Edwards before 1777

Fuller was born in 1754 in Wicken, Cambridgeshire to a farming couple of Particular Baptist persuasion and the family moved to nearby Soham seven years later where they joined a Johnsonite church pastored by a sieve-maker John Eve. Later Fuller was highly critical of the Soham church of his childhood and youth. Of Pastor Eve, he reported that his theology was 'tinged with false Calvinism' and that he had 'little to say to the unconverted', yet unconverted Fuller found Christ under Eve's ministry after experiencing a strong conviction of sin. He was baptised in 1770 when he became a Soham member. From this time on, Fuller preached regularly in the Soham church which Eve left a year later to take on a new church in 1771.

Fuller was said by the author of the Memoir prefaced to the 1841 edition of his works to have obtained 'the barest rudiments of English instruction'. Most biographers have not bothered to enquire closely into

Fuller's education and Michael Haykin merely tells us in his 'Andrew Fuller: Life and Legacy: A Brief Overview'[1] that Fuller was 'self-taught in theology'. However, we find that when Fuller accepted the call to pastor Soham in 1775, he was advised by Robert Hall Sen. to read 'Edwards on the will'.

Fuller's reaction showed that he had no idea of who Jonathan Edwards was at the time. After looking into the matter Fuller thought Hall must have meant Dr John Edwards of Cambridge (1637-1716), the author of Veritas Redux. It is strange that Fuller did not turn to Jonathan Edwards of Oxford (1629-1712), the opposer of Socinianism and Arminianism. Fuller tells us he did not discover his mistake until 1777 but even then, he gives no certain information that he had now read Edwards but takes his readers back to 1775 again before he knew Edwards. It is clear from these records, that Fuller wrote his *Gospel Worthy* at this time when he was still struggling with unresolved theological problems. It was an attempt on Fuller's part to let his faith come to an understanding of itself, especially concerning the supposed 'natural' and 'moral' capabilities of man. The resulting faith which he gained from this strictly anthropological study was duty-faith, not Christ's faith.

Indeed, as far as the evidence goes, there is very little to prove that Fuller obtained his ideas of what is 'moral' and what is 'natural' from Edwards at all, though such as Chun are firm in their belief that Fuller did not receive his ideas independently but took them from Edwards. Modern Fullerite believers have thus not progressed beyond Fuller's basic faulty thinking concerning man's 'moral' abilities which they mistake for 'spiritual' abilities. So, in spite of this uncertainty concerning Fuller's following of Edwards' philosophical work, what Fuller actually wrote is unanimously interpreted by such writers as Haykin, Chute, Daniel and Chun as the be all and end all of Edwards' and Fuller's theology. They do not stop to think that though Edwards matured greatly from a position quite foreign to Fuller's alleged interpretation, Fuller kept to the basic theology he had picked up when writing his major works in the 1770s, obviously quite independent of Edwards.

[1] Introduction to the Banner Of Truth 2007 reprint of Fuller's *Works*.

Words are nothing apart from the meaning given them

John Newton loved Edwards but was dismayed by his philosophical diversions. They have puzzled many. However, to be fair to Edwards, his explanations of these philosophical terms are diametrically opposed to how Fuller and his followers use the terms. Names say nothing apart from the meanings given them. It appears that these dualistic ideas of 'moral' and 'natural' in Edwards' earlier works, though the Bible knows no such distinctions, are Chun's whole understanding of Edwards seen through Hopkinsonian[2] via New Divinity and Fullerite eyes which Edwards did not have. The true sources of Fuller's divinity, if it can be called such, is Enlightenment Philosophy, Grotianism and New Divinity thinking. More research is needed on the supposed philosophical but threadbare influence of Edwards on Fuller for those interested in such matters.

Chun's defence of Fuller is mere 'mental gymnastics'

Chun's strenuous 'mental gymnastics' in reducing Edwards' and New Divinity influence on Fuller to the two misused terms 'natural' and 'moral' may be legitimate as an academic exercise. However, arguments limited to discussing what is natural and what is moral, which took up so much of Fuller's and Chun's time, do not produce faith nor do they do justice to Edwards' early philosophical works. Moreover, the evidence to link Edwards with Fuller before the first drafts of *The Gospel Worthy* is very threadbare indeed.

Furthermore, Chun takes what he feels are Edwards' philosophical views seen through New Divinity eyes without apparently examining the many alterations involved in this complicated transaction from one mind to the other, especially from father to son in Edwards' case. One has only to think of the English words, 'democracy', 'gaiety' and 'pride' to realise how different sections of the public attach different connotations to such words. Chun is, indeed, more interested in interpreting what is 'natural' and what is 'moral' in Fuller's sense rather than Edwards' and his understanding of 'will' is quite different to Edwards'. Fuller's position is clearly that though man is 'morally'

---

[2] Fuller's theology reflects that of Samuel Hopkins the later leader and transformer of the New Divinity School who had altered Edwards' teaching to paint his own picture of the Puritan.

fallen he is 'naturally' as he was before the Fall. What separates him from God is merely his will but he could find God if he only willed it. This is diametrically opposed to Edwards' teaching.

Furthermore, Edwards' teaching on the 'natural', and the 'moral' regarding the 'will' of man is not representative of Edwards' entire theology however Fuller and Chun might understand the terms differently as embracing their whole view of man. Furthermore, it is academic and theological folly indeed to interpret Edwards Senior's terms merely in the sense that his New Divinity son later used them. His own theology developed radically away from that of his father's. However, Chun obviously interprets the father's views by his son's misinterpretation.

A daring academic undertaking

This dissertation is thus a daring undertaking indeed and theories raised but not proven can scarcely be viewed as a basis for a doctoral work. If Chun's aim is really to reduce Edwards', Fuller's and his own theology down to seeing fallen man as 'natural' and open to God, as opposed to a 'moral' position subordinate to man's will, he must introduce sufficient evidence on which to build his thesis. This entails also studying Edwards' entire works and comparing them with Fuller's. For a Christian scholar undertaking such a comparison the whole teaching of the Bible must be presented and both Edwards' and Fuller' views compared in the presentation of it. So, anyone would expect here a full study of Edwards' gospel testimony compared to Fuller's as Chun is arguing that they overlap more or less fully. Yet Chun labours on his misunderstanding of Edwards' earlier, more philosophical works and does not provide evidence for his theory of Fuller's dependence on him even here. He merely views Edwards' sounder theology through Fuller's early and quite untrained eyes. 'Naturals' and 'morals' just do not fill the scope in Edwards' later theology though they do appear to be the basis of Fullerism and also Chunism. Thus, Chun's painting of both Edwards and Fuller remains unnatural to say the least.

Man is fallen in his nature and thus in his morals

Of course, Chun must be aware that 'natural man' is fallen just as nature is fallen with him and 'morals' become immoral when they are used as a substitute for true religion. Nature red in tooth and claw, as Matthew

Arnold puts it, is no substitute for the blood of the Lord Jesus Christ which cleanses from all sin. Man is just as fallen morally as he is fallen naturally. He is fallen in his entire being. Our Christian faith sees both man's 'natural' and 'moral' states as being at enmity with God. This is a point Edwards made quite clear when he stressed the inability of man to either approach God by any natural means as man in all aspects is fallen. Edwards' son and those his son led astray such as Fuller and Chun do not accept Edwards' theology here. Chun's argument seems to be that as Edwards was a pukka Calvinist, Fuller must also be considered such but where is the proof? Chun's own 'Calvinism' may be identical to Fuller's but this is a long way from saying it is Calvin's Calvinism. To reduce Calvin's faith to that of Fuller's would be a grave injustice to Calvin as it is quite opposed to much that he taught.

Reading Edwards not a guarantee of becoming an Edwardsean

On page 55 of his thesis Chun claims I maintain that the mere fact of reading Edwards does not make Fuller an Edwardsean. This may be a valid presumption but it is a point I have never argued though I did query whether this was Haykin's position or not.[3] Otherwise the idea cannot be challenged. Chun gives no source here but he has obviously taken the words from my argument on page 68 of my *Law and Gospel* where I maintain, alongside one of my mentors Baptist pastor Arthur Kirkby, whom I quote, that there is little evidence indeed to demonstrate that Fuller was influenced either greatly or directly by Jonathan Edwards. Indeed, the meagre and misleading evidence produced by Chun does not prove the connection which he claims. Furthermore, Chun's own theology is at such variance to Edwards', it would be highly unlikely that he has judged him objectively. He seems to read Edwards through Fullerite eyes and thus has little original evidence to go on as Fuller has very little indeed to say about Edwards with whom he became acquainted too late to use him positively in compiling his *Gospel Worthy of All Acceptation*. Sadly, the modern interest in Edwards in an attempt to display one's own Reformed acumen is backfiring radically. Most studies deal with mere aspects of Edwards' theology which he saw as a whole. One cannot isolate man as 'natural' or 'moral' from Edwards' essential gospel. Today, (on Good Friday,

---

[3] *Law and Gospel*, p. 167.

2021), I was sent a 2014 copy of the evangelical magazine Themelios via Academia.educ. The editorial by D. A. Carson presented a most confusing and highly partitioned view of what the gospel entails and Ralf Cunnington's contribution 'A critical example of Jonathan Edwards' doctrine of the Trinity with a particular focus on the Holy Spirit' shows how one can systemise anyone's views so that they appear incoherent. One would have thought anyone trying to split up and analyse the Trinity has lost all sense of who God is and has quite misunderstood Edwards' teaching.

Dating Fuller's alleged reception of Edwards

As I point out on page 68 of my *Law and Gospel*, Fuller tells us in his 1789/90 diary that he only started reading Edwards' sermons revealing his gospel theology at that date though he had written his *The Gospel Worthy of All Acceptation* in the late 1770s but left it unpublished until 1801. However, it was in these sermons that Edwards taught his theology of the Atonement which is quite different to the rationalising and theorising Fuller had written in his *Gospel Worthy* before reading Edwards. Thus, to proclaim Fuller obtained his views here from Edwards but give no documentation for it, is most unfitting for a doctoral thesis. Chun claims that Fuller had read Edwards' early work on the 'moral' and 'natural' nature of man during his Johnsonian days but this is the very dichotomy in which Fuller shows strong disagreement with Edwards but close agreement with Edwards Junior. In footnotes on page 180, Chun is obviously agreeing with those he quotes in maintaining that Fuller changed his theology between 1787 and 1799. I would lengthen this period considerably. Even if we accept these dates, they would still indicate that Fuller knew little of Edwards' distinction between 'natural' and 'moral'. As Chun has apparently studied Fuller's changing theology from 1771 up to 1799, he ought to have given documentary evidence for this in relation to Edwards' definitions and Fuller's obvious departure from Edwards in his understanding of them. After all, Chun's dissertation was allegedly designed specifically for the use of such evidence. Chun ought, too, to have outlined the alterations in Fuller's theology not only before but also after penning his *Gospel Worthy*. A number of these shifts in Fuller's position are evident in his major work and even pointed out by Fuller who, nevertheless, does not erase his altered views from the book. Indeed, Fuller even published several essays outlining his re-definitions of terms and his shifts in theology without changing his *Gospel Worthy*.

Fuller's sparse references to Edwards in his works

The one volume Banner Of Truth (BOT) edition of Fuller's former work of three volumes produced by the BOT in 2007 lists Fuller's first mention of Edwards in its Index referring to page 150 of the Second Edition of his *Gospel Worthy*. It is not clear here, however if the Preface is Fuller's own or the Editor's as the reference is to 'the author' whereas Fuller usually stands behind his own name and person. However, whoever wrote the Preface merely mentions on page 150 that Fuller had read 'Elliot(?), Brainerd, and several others', who preached Christ with so much success, with reference to the Native Americans. Is the Index compiler and Chun assuming that Edwards must have been amongst the 'several others'?

Furthermore, Fuller or his Editor is apparently writing in 1781 but claims that 'the author' had no plans to publish at that date. However, some four years later, in 1785 Fuller altered his view. During these years there is no reference to Edwards by either the Editor or Fuller by name as one who had influenced him in establishing his altered views. The first actual reference to Edwards is on page 51 of the Preface where we are told the author was fascinated by Edwards' distinctions between natural and moral inability whereas Fuller spoke of abilities. This would mean that Fuller was introduced to Edwards at least four years after he wrote his *Gospel Worthy* which he, however, according to the Preface, altered significantly before 1781.

E. F. Clipsham, in his series of essays on 'Fuller and Fullerism' in the Baptist Quarterly, starting 1963, tells us that Fuller radically changed his theology between 1787 and 1802 in three marked stages. He implies this brought Fuller up to the theology of Jonathan Edwards as outlined in his Treatise on Original Sin, and adds 'though he made surprising little use of its reasoning'. However, Clipsham gives no documentation for this and, when listing the many works he believes Fuller had read, he refers to secondary sources for verification or merely states that Fuller was influenced by A. B. and C. without giving sources. On checking through some five modern writers on Fuller, I find this is the usual course taken.

Furthermore, Edwards' views on the inabilities of man both natural and moral are far from Fuller's own position which is that man is naturally able to follow God's call, a theory which became the basic argument for his *Gospel Worthy*. Fuller also refers briefly to Edwards' 'On the Will' and to the fourth edition of his 'Treatise on the Affections' in a footnote on page 188. Edwards on 'Religious Affections' is now available as a freebie on the net and is a very good read until it falls into the hands of psychologically bent reviewers. Edwards' re-definition of commonly applied words makes following his arguments at times difficult but I would suggest that if Fuller had read Edwards and yet misinterpreted Edwards so badly, it was not all Edwards' fault. Not being as careful as Edwards who stuck to his definitions, Fuller uses the same terms higgledy-piggledy to mean, like Alice's Humpty-Dumpty, whatever he intends them to mean for the moment. This fact is not noted by Tom Nettles in his Reformation Today articles for 1984 and his Founders Journal articles on Edwards and Fuller, #53, Summer 2003 where he mentions Fuller's reading of Edwards on the *Affections* concluding that this refutes my statement that 'convincing evidence for a direct influence by Edwards on Fuller has still to be produced as Fuller's theology is radically different from Edwards'. Furthermore, Nettles is dealing in his strictures against me with Fuller's very brief essay on the Inward Witness of the Spirit or God Speaking Peace to His People, which Nettles claims is a summary of Edwards on the *Affections*. This is a comment on Psalms 85:8 and 35:3 which read:

> I will hear what God the Lord will speak: for he will speak peace unto his people, and to his saints: but let them not turn again to folly.
>
> Draw out also the spear, and stop the way against them that persecute me: say unto my soul, I am thy salvation.

In his very brief essay on 'inferences' versus 'impressions', true to his constant emphasis that Old Testament blessings to the Jews were merely physical and national in true New Covenant Theology (NCT) style, Fuller tells us that we are to understand 'peace' here as 'prosperity'. In context, however, we read in these passages of forgiveness of sin, the taking away of wrath, of mercy, salvation and righteousness which Fuller ignores in the spiritual sense or what Moses called the 'tenor' of the texts. Indeed, the spiritual side of the gospel in the Old Testament which is its main emphasis is almost totally avoided by Fuller as if the Old Testament was a mere legal document now passed away. This refusal of Fuller's to understand the 'tenor' or gospel teaching of the Old Testament is illustrated by Fuller's use of Isaiah's gospel proclamation in Chapter 55:1 stating 'Ho, every one that thirsteth'. This is no gospel appeal according to Fuller but is for those who wish for physical happiness, peace and rest only.[4]

The 'peace' thus described in the Psalms Fuller cites is not merely a state of prosperity in the material sense but a state where 'mercy and truth are met together' and 'righteousness and peace have kissed each other'. It has nothing to do with 'inferences' as Fuller supposes but with God graciously revealing His peace and salvation. The receivers of this peace and salvation are described as God's 'saints', yet Fuller claims that we must infer how God works through and reveals himself to these saints, or 'characters' as he calls them, as if he were not one of them himself. There is no hint of an indirect witness of the Spirit in the passages Fuller takes up and analyses but the Spirit's direct work. Besides, I have gone through Edwards on the *Affections* from cover to cover but I have not come across anything like Fuller's analysis of Psalm 85 and 35, let alone a summary of these passages as presented by Fuller.

Thus, Fuller's work here bears no relation to Edwards' teaching in his *Affections* and Fuller in no way refers to the supposed idea that he is summarising Edwards. When one summarises either Nettles, Fuller or Edwards one naturally mentions their names and fits the summary to the text chosen. Fuller does not claim to summarise Edwards here so why surmise that he does?

However, after telling us that peace means prosperity, Fuller starts off his book by saying his enquiry is into 'what form or manner does God communicate peace to our minds'.[5] Edwards' concern in his *Affections*, on the other hand, was to show 'what are the distinguishing signs of truly gracious and holy affections' keeping to his permanent theme of examining the 'qualifications of those that are in favour with

---

[4] *Works*, Vol. 2, p. 563.

[5] BOT edition p. 511.

God through God's grace'. Edwards' preaches the gospel of God's direct grace to man but Fuller strives to philosophise over indirect terms concerning the human mind.

Edwards centred his long study of holy affections on the 'religion of the heart' and thus moved John Wesley to summarise this aspect of Edwards' faith in his 'An Extract from a Treatise Concerning Religious Affections', 1773. Christopher Allison says of this work:

> Wesley's treatment of *Religious Affections* is the most radical of all his abridgements, inasmuch as he takes the most liberties with this text; it is the only one in which he comments directly on Edwards' content. His comments in the section 'To the Reader' is worth quoting in its entirety:
>
> > 1. The design of Mr. Edwards in the treatise, from which the following extract is made, seems to have been (chiefly, if not altogether) to serve his hypothesis. In three preceding tracts, he had given an account of a glorious work in New England; of abundance of sinners of every sort and degree, who were in a short time converted to God. But in a few years, a considerable part of these turned back as a dog to vomit. What was the plain inference to be drawn from this? Why, that a true believer may make shipwreck of the Faith. How then could he evade the force of this? Truly by eating his own words, and proving, (as well as the nature of the thing would bear) that they were no believers at all!
> >
> > 2. In order to this, he heaps together so many curious, subtle, metaphysical distinctions, as are sufficient to puzzle the brain, and confound the intellects, of all the plain men and women in the universe; and to make them doubt of, if not wholly deny, all the work which God had wrought in their souls.
> >
> > 3. Out of this dangerous heap, wherein much wholesome food is mixt with much deadly poison, I have selected many remarks and admonitions, which may be of great use to the children of God. May God write them in

> the hearts of all that desire to walk as Christ also walked!
> Bristol, Sept. 1, 1773.[6]

Wesley thus cut out most of Edwards' Reformed views on the doctrines of grace which, however, in no way denied a religion of the heart. Edwards placed his list of faithful qualifications firmly in the doctrines of grace and the full scope of the gospel. If Fuller summarised Edwards at all, he turned Edwards' religion of the heart into a religion of the head, pitting rational 'inferences' against immediate 'impressions' from the Word. He felt it was too dangerous to live on 'impressions' but, oddly enough, not 'inferences'. He will not have immediate revelation from God in the Word which is the inner working of the Spirit on the soul. He tells us that means are 'indifferent' in themselves, what matters is what one infers from them. Edwards' religion goes out from God to man whereas Fuller's religion goes out from man to God through 'character studies' and inferences one gains from them. Really, when Fuller speaks of 'inferences' he means 'impressions' but he accepts the former as they come from inward reasoning alone and rejects the latter because they are placed on us from outside of us by revelational 'means'. On these issues Edwards and Fuller could not be more different.

Following Fuller's theology from the age of sixteen

When Edwards published his *Freedom of the Will*, Fuller was sixteen or seventeen years of age and had just been baptised and had become a member of the Soham Johnsonian Church which showed alarming diversions from Christian Orthodoxy. This was the setting for Fuller's conversion. Fuller eventually became the church's pastor in 1775. By 1771/72 Fuller was leaving his Hyper-Calvinism behind helped chiefly by John Gill's *The Cause of God and Truth* with which he was delighted. Fuller also learnt to stress the human responsibility of sinners for sinning from Gill as the Soham teaching denied having such responsibility. It is surprising that modern Fullerites teach that Gill, as

---

[6] 'The Methodist Edwards: John Wesley's Abridgment of the Selected Works of Jonathan Edwards', Methodist History, 50:3 (April 2012).

opposed to Fuller, did not teach human responsibility for the Fall yet Fuller learnt this vital doctrine from Gill! However, contemporary writers claimed that Fuller gave man too much damaging responsibility in demanding that he exercised saving faith though lost in sin. Owing to quarrels at Soham, however, Fuller did not take sides as so often argued but left the church and began to attend an Independent Chapel regularly. This fact is overlooked in most descriptions of Fuller's early years as a Christian as in Haykin's BOT Introduction above named. Later, Fuller was to call such non-Baptist chapels in which he had sought for better teaching than that of Soham 'seduced by Jezebel' as he told missionary William Ward subsequently in a letter advising him not to fellowship with non-Baptists. So Fuller then returned to Soham Baptist Church though Soham had not bettered its theology. If Soham's theology was as bad as Fuller later made it out to be, why did he return? In his Memoir of his father, Andrew Gunton deals with a number of authors who may have influenced Fuller over the next years including those of John Johnson, popular at Soham whose views Fuller held for a time, but Edwards is not mentioned once.

Fuller's pastorate at Soham

In 1775 Fuller became pastor of the run down and split up Soham Baptist Church which had been reduced to 47 members. They now looked to young Fuller to unite, build up and extend the membership. The old quarrels, however, continued but Fuller was too unversed theologically to know what truths were at stake which became obvious as the quarrels escalated. Fuller's son mentions that his father met John Sutcliff of Olney in 1776 and shortly later John Ryland Junior. Both spoke of help they had found in Jonathan Edwards', Joseph Bellamy's and David Brainerd's works. We know, however, that Sutcliff's own ideas of 'natural' and 'moral' differed radically from Fuller's and were Biblical and akin to Edwards'. This is not explained in Haykin's *One Heart and One Soul* concerning the differences in Sutcliff's and Fuller's theologies, though this is a doctrine fundamental to the gospel.

Fuller's six or so references to Edwards

The fact is that in all his own hitherto published *Complete Works*, if we include the Prefaces as coming from his pen, Fuller has a mere six or so references to Edwards. Even if we could find double that amount, it would still be scanty. Haykin quotes Fuller and Edwards hundreds of times, as I do myself. This is because we have studied their works thoroughly though from two different theological approaches. I have probably written less than Fuller but mentioned those on whom I depend such as Gill, Bullinger, Hervey, Durie, Cowper and many more scores if not hundreds of times in my works. Yet, Fuller nowhere analyses Edwards' works and nowhere claims that his views are identical with Edwards and nowhere quotes Edwards as if he felt he was a mentor *par excellence*. There is thus not sufficient evidence here to justify Chun's dissertation title or the contents of his thesis which are extremely forced. Chun, to back up his theories, ought rather to have shown parallels with Edwards' works and Fuller's rationalistic approach to theology. He could then have outlined the changes which took place in Fuller's theology in relation to his reception of Edwards. Then his dissertation would have deserved the title he gave it. This necessary scholarly work is absent from Chun's academic thesis. So, too, Chun takes up Fuller's later reading of Edwards and back-projects it onto Fuller's muddled theology at Soham.

Chun does not deal with research work which contradicts him

However, in the reference Chun gives of my views, I write after studying both Edwards and Fuller carefully, comprehensively and methodically and siding with Baptist pastor Arthur Kirkby, whom Chun does not mention, in believing that Fuller's reading of Edwards was limited and, was, as Kirkby says, 'less than generally claimed'. I will deal with the neglect of Kirkby's important works in a special Appendix.

Were Edwards Senior and Edwards Junior one in the faith?

In reply to such a question the records say, sadly but clearly, 'No'. On page 161 of his thesis Chun, after browsing through my website for my remarks concerning Edwards which are mostly positive,[7] challenges my wish for clarity on whether or not there is some confusion amongst

---

[7] I refuse to bow under Fullerite pressure to merely understand Edwards philosophically or as an ambassador for Governmental Theology and I believe even Edwards' philosophical writings contained much more sound theology than Fuller's alleged theological works.

certain scholars concerning the theology of Edwards Sr and Edwards Jr. Here, as in his assurance that Fuller was 'Calvinistic', he is leaning on Tom Nettles. The main source of Chun's criticism is an essay of mine entitled 'The Atonement in Evangelical Thought Part IV' which I had posted on my website and which I have used since as part of my book on the Atonement published in 2021. Here I query Tom Nettles' views on both of the Edwards, father and son, regarding their distinctions. Nettles has been occasionally criticised for sitting on the fence and here important distinctions, I believe, were also blurred. Chun replies merely by saying, 'Nettles has not mistaken Edwards Jr for Edwards Sr.' A fair enough statement, but I wanted evidence to back this up which is not forthcoming in Chun's dissertation and I could not find it in Nettles. Clearly, Edwards Junior disagreed with his father on the nature of man, the nature of the Atonement and the nature of Christ's imputation. This envelops most of the gospel topics we ought to be preaching. When one makes such statements, evidence is required. Furthermore, it is obvious that Chun does indeed confuse the teaching of both father and son irrespective of Nettles' views which, to me, are more orthodox, on the whole, than Chun's.

Chun's unhelpful approach

Chun's interpretation seems to be more his own missionary gospel appeal to the world rather than a true analysis of Fuller's theological dependence. One of Chun's obvious mistakes is his effort to describe Fuller's Rationalism in Calvinistic and even Biblical terms which makes his dissertation seem like an attempt to square the circle. As Chun notices in my writings, I do not think this approach is at all helpful in understanding Christian doctrine. Chun, however, thinks it is so crucial that he feels he must refute the orthodox position as I understand it on pages 55, 144-45, 161, 172-73 and 180-81 of his thesis. Here it is easy to demonstrate that Chun throws out much Biblical gospel teaching and brings in very much that is adverse to it. He is so far away, however, from appreciating any views of Fuller's philosophical presumptions which are contrary to his own that he is quite unable to describe such contrary views accurately and in a trustworthy way in order to refute them. He has just not researched Fuller enough, nor his critics. Indeed, he feels that such a defence on his part is unnecessary. A good supervisor ought to have checked Chun's sources or rather lack of them and examined Chun's aims and his method of approaching them. Indeed, as a former chairman of a university faculty examination board and university marker of examination papers and theses over very many years, I would say a good supervisor ought rather to have given Chun a task he could handle.

Chapter Sixteen

Fuller the Theologian

Modern promoters of Fuller as a great theologian

Much of the Fullerite conviction that Fuller was a great theologian is based on the alleged vastness of his theological reading. Michael Haykin in his article 'A Great Thirst for Reading: Andrew Fuller the Theological Reader'[1] emphasises what he claims was the great depth and scope of Fuller's reading which prepared Fuller for his task as a great theologian. However, Haykin does not deal with a number of Fuller's contemporaries and biographers who quote works Fuller had read though Fuller himself does not mention them. Nor does he present all that Fuller has obviously read. Indeed, Haykin merely presents a Fuller who apparently read less than many of his Baptist contemporaries such as Sutcliff and Gill. This may be due to Haykin's far from full study of Fuller's reading. So, what was Haykin's aim in his article? I do believe that Fuller read more than Haykin suggests but this would still not mark him out as a prolific reader in comparison with a number of his contemporary pastors. Indeed, much of Fuller's reading Haykin sees uncritically as concentrating on New Divinity authors who introduced a form of radical rationalism. Yet Haykin offers no theological or historical explanations for his brief 'study' of New Divinity's great influence on Fuller and how its teaching pervaded Fuller's works. Indeed, Haykin writes as if it were New Divinity

[1] See my website Bibliographia Evangelica for a detailed criticism of Haykin's unconvincing study under the heading 'Fuller and his Thirst for Theological Reading'.

teaching including Fuller's sheer Grotianism which underlined Fuller's orthodoxy in Haykin's eyes. This leads me to question Haykin's own theological standing which appears very Liberal to me. Indeed, a detailed study of how New Divinity teaching influenced Fuller is absent from such as Haykin's, Chun's and Daniel's evaluations of what has come to be known as 'Fullerism'. E. F. Clipsham in his BQ essay mentioned above under the name of 'Fuller the Theologian', tells us that Fuller was 'a prophet of evangelical Calvinism', yet apparently bases his notion on Fuller's reading of Bellamy and the New Divinity School which departed radically from Calvin.

However, according to Haykin's theory aired in his article on Fuller's reading, we would expect great readers of theology to be great theologians. Haykin has neither proved the one point nor the other. So, too, Fuller was often most critical of other authors. What he learnt from them positively can scarcely be seen. Merely talking about books does not make anybody a great theologian as the following example shows.

Fuller reads Mosheim on Church History

We read in the various memoirs and biographies appertaining to Fuller that Sutcliff and Ryland gave him sound advice on what to read. In Fuller's 1841 BOT collection with an Introduction by Prof. Haykin we also read that they lived too far away for regular discussions with Fuller concerning the books they recommended. We are given no information as to whether Fuller actually read the recommended authors.

One of the major Christian writers Fuller did tackle was Johann Lorenz Mosheim (1693-1755), Chancellor of Göttingen University, the famous German Church Historian whom, according to Fuller's diary, he read on 26th and 28th June and 3rd July, 1781. However, Fuller approached Mosheim most narrowly through the eyes of one of limited theological and historical understanding and apparently read but one of Mosheim's works which was a historical overview void of much detail which was supplemented by a good number of detailed works which Fuller apparently did not read. If the work quoted by Fuller was the one mentioned below as it appears it was, then it would be a sheer impossibility to read and weigh up its contents in three short sessions. At first, Fuller was delighted at finding someone who wrote as a convinced Protestant but soon rejected Mosheim's history with harsh unschooled criticism.

The only work of Mosheim printed in English by 1781 was Archibald Maclean's 1764 translation of Mosheim's Institutes or to give it its full English title, *An Ecclesiastical History, From the birth of Christ to the Beginning of the Eighteenth Century in which the Rise, Progress and Variation of Church Power are Considered in their Connection with the State of Learning and Philosophy and the Political History of Europe During that Period.*

Michael Haykin in his essay on Fuller's reading surprisingly does not mention this pioneering work and Fuller's recorded comments on it at all. Yet he is arguing that Fuller was a prolific reader. Why does he not cite Mosheim as 'proof'? Usually, Haykin packs all he can into his evidence for his positive understanding of Fuller but here he leaves out such an important theological and church historical writer as Mosheim. It might be that he felt Fuller was merely relying on review material as we know he did with other classical Protestant authors.

Perhaps, also, Haykin's decision not to use important writers such as Mosheim as an example of Fuller's reading is because Fuller developed a strong dislike of the church historian after dipping into the one work briefly three times. He wrote in his journal that he was 'sick of it' and that Mosheim's overview of church history was 'a history of locusts', though he had no other work on church history with which to compare it. One wonders how he could come to such a conclusion so quickly without consulting Mosheim's many Latin and German works where the author goes into far more detail. Besides, it appears that this was the only work Fuller read, at least at this time, which deals with our Reformers. I remember tackling Mosheim's Latin works on only one particular theological issue with the help of five dictionaries on my writing desk. I wanted to know what he really taught. I was not disappointed. One needs to work hard for long hours to grasp Mosheim or any other church historian and theologian of note!

It soon became apparent why Fuller rejected Mosheim. He realised soon that Mosheim was not a Baptist and that made him drop the author.[2] In his Discourse XII on Papal Apostasy, he again criticises Mosheim harshly and asks concerning his work 'Where is wisdom, and where is the place of understanding?'[3] Unlike his wiser contemporary

[2] See *Memoirs of The Rev. Andrew Fuller* p. xxxiv.
[3] Banner Of Truth one volume reprint, p. 455.

John Gill, Fuller lumps Waldensians, Novatians, Cathari and Paulicans altogether as 'Baptists' and does not notice how finely Mosheim, like Gill, draws distinctions between them, comparing them with the lives and works of our Reformers. Indeed, since the First London Baptist Confession (1644), which divided the Particular Baptists from the General Baptists in Britain, the English-speaking Particular Baptists have rejected the claim that they were Anabaptists, chiefly because of the motley nature of that unspecific movement. Actually, Mosheim was most fair to the Wiedertäufer in contrast to his predecessors and prepared the way for a better understanding of their views. Today's official websites of the Mennonites argue that Mosheim was 'moderate and correct' in any criticism he made. Fuller did not have this theological insight. So, too, Mosheim authored detailed studies of the Waldensians which Fuller apparently never read. Henry Bullinger's works also dealing with the Catabaptists were featured in very many evangelical libraries in Fuller's day as were Francis Lambert's works but Fuller does not refer to them.[4]

To counteract what Mosheim taught about the Baptists, Fuller could have quoted from Thomas Crosby's four volumes of Baptist History or Joseph Ivimey's work on Baptist history in four volumes. Then Daniel Neal could have been turned to and also Robert Robinson besides Joseph and Isaac Miller. Indeed, there were many books on Church History, the Baptists, the Reformation and evangelical theology well-known to the Baptists of Fuller's Association but Fuller appears not to have known them or at least never referred to them. Indeed, Fuller obviously read very little of standard Baptist works other than John Gill and John Brine and possibly the Halls. Fuller does mention that he consulted a review of Bogue's and Bennet's *History of Dissenters* in the Quarterly Review of 1813 and then 'perused the volumes reviewed' but keeps to the review for his comments. The references to Bunyan in Fuller's BOT collection are from Fuller's 'Memoirs' written by his son and not from Fuller's works. Much of Fuller's knowledge of Christian writers came from reading reviews and magazine articles. Fuller mentions that he read about John Eliot, the British missionary to the Native Americans through 'Millar's account' but I have not been able

[4] See Heinhold Fast's *Heinrich Bullinger and the Täufer*, Mennonite Geschichtsverein, 1959.

to locate this name.[5] If the Miller brothers are meant, their multi-volume Church History does not include the New World so this mention of 'Millar' poses problems. So, too, Fuller refers to 'Elliot', not 'Eliot'. Neither 'Millar' nor 'Miller' appear in the BOT edition's index but this index omits many references to the contents of the volume. The Eliot Tracts and Eliot's correspondence with Thomas Thorowgood and Richard Baxter were published in England several times in the 17th century. Neither the three 19th century biographies I have of Eliot (Moore 1822, Wilson 1828, Adams 1847) nor Richard W. Cogley's 1999 biography refer to a work on Eliot by a Millar though especially Adams refers to earlier biographers of Eliot. Carey mentions Eliot five times in his *Enquiry* without giving the sources. Carey also misspells Eliot's name though contemporary works used the original spelling. Haykin in his work on Fuller's reading merely states that he had read about Eliot but does not comment as to the source.

Though Gill, like our Reformers and, indeed, this writer, had affinities to the Waldensians, who were most open on the question of baptism, he certainly was not a blind follower of the Novatians, Paulicans and Cathari. Nor could these movements be called 'Baptist', at least in the Fullerite sense of the term. Gill wanted nothing to do, as he declared towards the end of his *Body of Divinity* when dealing with the uprisings in Münster, with 'men of bad principles and bad characters'.[6] He applied this rule to all movements bearing the name of 'Christian'. These split-off parties were, indeed, most divided in their theological appreciations and especially on baptism. The terms 'Anabaptist' and 'Catabaptist' were given them by their critics who had often as little theological appreciation as they had. The term 'Baptist' is especially unfitting when applied to many referred to as 'Anabaptists' because they did not baptise at all! Fuller viewed, it appears, all Anabaptists as being Baptists in his sense of the term but this was far from the case as there were sprinklers, pourers, dippers and 'spiritual Baptists'[7] amongst them. Fuller was not ripe enough as a theologian to understand this. His knowledge of church history remained most

[5] See BOT edition p. xxx.

[6] Book IV, Of the Respective Duties of Magistrates and Subjects, p. 602, 1810 Edition.

[7] Those who believed that as they were baptised in the Spirit already, they needed no water baptism.

rudimentary. I view the Anabaptist movements as being similar to the Covenanters in Scotland who came in all shapes and sizes with quite contradictory theological and political motives. They had their Swordbearers and Staffbearers just like the Anabaptists. One Covenanting party supported James Sharp (1618-1679) as Archbishop, yet another Covenant party murdered him. The major Covenanting parties were, at times, guilty of violent revolutionary practices. One Scottish bookseller told me that my mother née Hume came from a good Covenanting stock, so I asked him which. He thought all Covenant movements had believed alike though some were highway robbers and even Roman Catholics! Bullinger dealt very fairly with the Anabaptists and helped them in their court cases but found that in next to no time twelve different split-offs had emerged of quite contrary views. Here, too, we must remain balanced in our own thinking.

We remember that the famous Dr Guthrie scolded the Baptists for splitting up so often but soon after he helped found a split-off from The Church of Scotland himself which has since divided itself into various other 'churches'. The present Free Church of Scotland (Continuing) is a product of such schism. We must also be aware of how universally split up our Reformed churches are and that many of them have been reduced to nothingness in the process of splitting up.

On February 3, 1781 Fuller mentions having read Edwards on '*Affections*' but when is not stated. Edwards died in 1758 before the New Divinity School pioneered by Bellamy, which influenced Fuller so much, really came into vogue. Joseph Bellamy died in 1790 and his works reached Fuller and his friends possibly soon afterwards. Edwards Junior died in 1801 after a most controversial life and it is well-known that his Liberalism led him from his father's teaching on the human will and the atonement. Samuel Hopkins died in 1803. This post-Edwards group of very mixed theological acumen was apparently Fuller's main source of 'theological' reading but Haykin, who backs the idea, does not feed us with facts as to this 'theological' relationship. As far as Fuller's reading is concerned, his main sources theologically speaking were Non-Baptist Liberals but Fuller founded his theory of baptism on their theology but not their baptismal practice.

Fuller's ministry found no blessings

Fuller's ministry at Soham was not blessed and he was unable to hold the members together. I put this down to his instable theology and gospel doctrines. One by one, the members felt they could not sit under his ministry and within a few years he was preaching to an almost empty church which had a membership of nine though they seldom assembled in bulk and could not pay Fuller's salary. Fuller felt that if he extended the chapel's premises, more would come in but the tiny church asked him where he thought the money would come from and how did he know that the extra space would be filled when the tiny space of their chapel was empty. Then Fuller abandoned them. One would have thought that had Fuller had a gospel worthy of all acceptation, he would have drawn many into his fold. At an Association meeting in May 1781 Fuller asked Gill, Booth, Evans, Guy, Hall, Hopper, the Rylands (father and son) and Sutcliff for help. They all advised him to leave Soham for Kettering, a thriving church who needed a pastor, an offer Fuller gladly accepted. However, Kettering had been founded by an Arian only a few years previously. Then Kettering became the Baptists' Halle.[8]

The aftermath of Fuller's pastorate at Soham

For years after Fuller left Soham, the church went from bad to worse. It was joined by a friend of Fuller's in 1803, John Gisburne an Arminian with Socinian/Arian leanings, who preached regularly there and eventually became the church's pastor on Fuller's recommendation. His appointment caused inner difficulties in the tiny run-down church because Fuller had enabled certain trustees to take over the church property who now quarrelled with Gisburne over the ownership. So Fuller was now guilty of continuing the strife in the Soham church which he had long abandoned. To add to the strife, Gisburne renamed Fuller's old church The Unitarian Church at Soham, Cambridgeshire and brought scandal upon it which ended in the Courts where Fuller was called as a major witness. Fuller pleaded not guilty of association with Gisburne's Socinianism to the amusement of the Press as he had obviously been on Gisburne's side all the time and had supported him as he had supported their mutual Arian friend Robert Aspland. However, Fuller maintained he had not taken sides against Gisburne

[8] Of course, I am being facetious but these parallels are occasionally drawn.

because of theological reasons but on the question of the trusteeship of the church only. Robert Aspland was a General Baptist who ran the Arian Monthly Repository and had been welcomed by Fuller and Ryland into their prayer-fellowship and the Bristol College. Aspland accused Fuller of misleading the court and Fuller protested that Aspland's paper had twisted the facts. Works ensued from Aspland's and Fuller's pens with each giving his own version of the quarrel.[9] This was obviously a kind of shadow-boxing as the two remained the best of friends.

Fuller had to appear before the Court as a witness in the Soham disruptions

The matter only came before the Grand Jury because when Gisburne preached from the pulpit he was challenged from the pews by a Mrs Howe who drowned his preaching by loudly reading Fuller's defence against the charge of following Priestley. This caused a riot which reached the local constable's ears who quickly entered the chapel and sought to gain order. The group around Mrs Howe were subsequently summoned to give an account of themselves before the court. Fuller was then called as a witness for the accused. The British Critic described both the Arianising of Soham and the court and press conflicts caused by it in detail but added that Gisburne's pastorate was at Fuller's instigation and stated that both sides accused each other of lying and the matter was given over to arbitration. Fuller's followers protested against this and strove to stop Gisburne or other like-minded preachers such as Aspland from entering the Soham pulpit by blocking the doors. The reporter relates that arbitration went in favour of Gisburne. Actually, the reporter himself was against Gisburne but argued that the Fullerite section had made a such a mess of their defence so the verdict was inevitable. He also added as a Dissenter that plainly

[9] The two works in question were: A Narrative of Facts relative to a late Occurrence in the County of Cambridge. In answer to a Statement contained in a Unitarian Publication called 'The Monthly Repository', by Andrew Fuller, 1810 and Bigotry and Intolerance Defeated or an Account of the late Prosecution of Mr. John Gisburne, Unitarian Minister of Soham, Cambridgeshire; with an Exposure and Correction of the Defects and Mistakes of Mr. Andrew Fuller's Narrative of that Affair in Letters to John Christie, Esq. Treasurer of the Unitarian fund, by Robert Aspland, Minister of the Gravel Pit Congregation, Hackney-Harlow, 1810.

intolerance and bigotry were not limited to the established churches and ended his article with the words:

> If anybody connected to the cause wishes to read the books, he will find that much coarse, vulgar and improper behaviour was resorted to on both sides, though all claim to be gentlemen of the first reputation, and purest honour.[10]

Again, Fuller emphasised before the court that he was not quarrelling with Gisburne's doctrines but wished to see the problem of ownership solved. Though Fuller's allying with Arians was general knowledge, he surprised many by denying any connection with them. A number of Arian Baptists like Aspland and orthodox Gillites like Button refused to believe him. Fuller had supported Aspland from Aspland's youth on and had placed him under Arian influence at the Bristol college. Even during the period of the court prosecutions, Fuller was witnessed walking arm in arm with Aspland and having him as guest in his home, though Fuller often quarrelled with him concerning his own (Fuller's) ever changing beliefs. Button had long accused Fuller of being a follower of Joseph Priestley.

Fuller associated with Priestley

Fuller could not shake off his alleged association with Priestley's views which was aired in the court case. Indeed, William Button, a Particular Baptist of the John Gill type and a promoter of foreign missions, called Fuller in his book *The Nature of Special Faith*, outright a follower of Joseph Priestly. What Fuller was or was not theologically was never clarified in court but in the press-coverage Fuller received much criticism and ridicule for his wishy-washy conduct and lack of theological understanding.

Coleridge accuses Fuller of being a theological novice

Journalist, poet and prose author Samuel Taylor Coleridge (1772-1834), argued in the press that Fuller's defence against Socinianism was highly questionable as it was built on assertions showing that Fuller did not realise what was at stake theologically and philosophically in the

---

[10] The British Critic, Vol. 36, 1810, p. 538 ff., Internet Archive.

Socinian controversy and lacked understanding in both areas of thought.[11] This was the theological state that Fuller was in when he compiled his *Gospel Worthy*. During this time Fuller as mentioned above, was closely associated with Arian Robert Aspland as also initially with William Adam whom the BMS sent as a rival missionary to ward off Carey's spreading influence outside of the BMS' control. Aspland, like Adam, had studied theology at the Baptist College at Bristol where the college was slow to challenge the widely different theologies of the candidates. Indeed, at the start of Aspland's first term, the Jubilee preacher chosen was a noted Arian. At first, Arianism was hushed up at the college but when this became well-known it caused something of a scandal.

All this led to Coleridge's argument that Fuller did not know where he stood theologically and that the way he handled Socinianism was sheer 'metaphysical meddling' and playing around with the subject instead of an earnest critical study.

Pre-Gillite Baptist errors

The Baptists were strongly infiltrated by Arianism and Socinianism prior to the Salters' Hall Conference of 1719 which demonstrated the influence of Robert Robinson, James Foster and John Gale and their 'Arian baptism'. Arian Baptist Robinson's work *History of the Baptist Church* is sadly still a standard work amongst all Baptists though its historicity is highly questionable. This was before John Gill brought in his cleansing theology and a sound Baptist Confession of Faith after the First and Second London Baptist Declarations had been abandoned by his predecessors who sought an alliance with the General Baptists and wished to close their eyes to theological differences.

Robert Hall Jun., one of Fuller's main supporters and a denier of particular redemption claimed that John Gill's theology was a continent of mud. Raymond Brown in his standard work *The English Baptists of the Eighteenth Century*, rejects what he calls Hall's biting criticism and immediately goes on to show how Gill and Brine steered the Baptists clear of Unitarianism and Arianism and writes:

---

[11] See The Literary Remains of Samuel Taylor Coleridge, Vol. IV, 1839, *Works*, pp, 289-295. This is a review of Fuller's 1793 article 'The Calvinistic and Socinian Systems Examined and Compared'.

> Under the influence of preachers and writers like James Foster, ministers and churches could easily pass from doctrinal freedom to theological indifference, and then to Unitarianism. Gill and Brine helped to keep many a reader in the way of truth when others were hopelessly confused. Given the limited perspective, theirs was a contribution to 18th century theology which did not deserve Hall's censures and ought not to be so summarily dismissed and forgotten. But Gill and Brine lacked natural successors.[12]

Modern Baptists who criticize John Gill so strongly and his stand against the decline in doctrine and lack of practical, pastoral theology are almost invariably of the Fullerite split-off from traditional Baptist and Reformed theology and Fuller's Association was the first to reject the authority of Scripture in matters of faith. If Fuller is not found guilty of the Arianism and Socinianism which affected the Baptists both in Britain and on the mission field then he escapes the verdict by the skin of his teeth. His contemporaries thought Fuller was simply out of his depth in the debate because of his own every-changing theology. I would go further and say that Fuller's aims were more sinister. He now strove to destroy the Trinity by rejecting the Son's Divine Atonement as Christ procured it; reduced the Deity of the Father through rejecting His revelation and placing Him under Natural Law and rejected the Divine Holy Spirit by making Him but an external influence, mostly through 'reasonable and fitting' impressions gained through the witness of other people.

Fuller and Grotianism

Chun in his dissertation on Fullerism entitled *The Legacy of Jonathan Edwards in the Theology of Andrew Fuller* says something very revealing of his own theology: 'It is one thing to accuse Fuller of being Grotian, but I do not see how one could remotely associate Fuller with Socinianism.' This statement speaks volumes. Most scholars who write on Fuller link him with Grotianism; Haykin and Chun being no exceptions. Chun apparently here is also accepting the fact that Fuller was influenced by Grotianism. This would cancel out much of his

[12] Published by the Baptist Historical Society, 1986, p. 93.

defence of Fuller. If Fuller were a Grotian, a verdict which I believe is sadly true, then he was far from orthodox in his Christianity. If Chun accepts this, he must be open to my detailed historical and theological discussion of the close proximity of Fuller to Socinianism which the local press of his day was quick to point out. If Chun had researched this early period in Fuller's theological development, here would have been the place to air his views in his doctoral thesis defending Fullerism without spelling it out.

I find no reference to Fuller's troubles at Soham and the controversies regarding Fuller's involvement with Socinianism and Arianism in standard Fullerite 'histories' of Fuller. I was thus compelled to fill in their omissions by reading up on the Christian and Secular press of the day, though my work which Chun criticises was for the average Christian reader and not a university thesis. Chun has obviously not taken this most necessary trouble in his dissertation. Fuller's carelessness and lack of discernment in his appreciation of Socinianism is not even mentioned by Chun. The Press of the day could not believe that Fuller had not played a part in the scandal for which he was called before a Court of Justice as a witness. There, however, he professed to know nothing about what was going on in the church he had recently pastored and been a member of for many years and still played a part in its organisation. Yet Fuller himself caused the Soham scandal by persuading his much-reduced church membership to take on a Socinian pastor with his full blessing. I suspect that Haykin and Chun are turning a blind eye to this controversy because of their intention to use Fuller as an excuse for their own Grotian and rational view of the Atonement. Where Fuller departs from their programme, they are not interested in him at all. This leaves them with an artificial, lop-sided view of Fuller's overall gospel and all the misunderstandings, errors and unripe ideas concerned in it. Though the feel they are defending Fuller, they are actually giving him a bad name.

Fuller on the necessity of the Atonement

On page 172 of his dissertation Chun criticises me again for challenging the New Divinity School on their Grotianism. He feels I am wrong in accusing the Grotians and Fuller of denying that the Atonement of

Christ is a necessary revelation to man of the righteousness of God.[13] He quotes Fuller as affirming that the Atonement is indeed a necessary display of God's righteousness. He does not tell us that both Grotius and Fuller see no necessity in the atonement as God could have used other means to forgive us our sins. Furthermore, he does not examine Fuller's use of the terms 'necessary' and 'righteousness' as both he and Grotius deny the absolute historical actuality of the Atonement and use the terms in the area of metaphoric imagery which they feel is God's own usage. Revealed religion in Fuller's philosophy is merely arbitrary and thus has no permanence. This is why the New Divinity School echoed John Wesley's criticism of the Biblical doctrine of imputation as put forward in James Hervey's great essay on imputed righteousness *Theron and Aspasio* which I have outlined with strong agreement in my book *James Hervey, Preacher of Righteousness*. Hervey preached real righteousness and not the 'figurative', 'arbitrary' kind which Fullerites teach. The historical, theological necessity of the Atonement is that it was actually wrought out there and then on the cross as an Atonement for sin. There is no Atonement in stages. Atonement is reconciliation, redemption and a covering for and a cleansing from and wiping away of sin both in Old Testament and New Testament usage. Coleridge claims that both Fuller and Priestly strove to follow Spinosa on their doctrine of God's necessary work in salvation but theirs was merely a most undeveloped form of what Spinosa actually taught.[14]

Fuller distances himself from Priestley

Fuller's major task in his essay on Socinianism was not to deal with directly the views of Lelio and Faustus Sozzini and their development after their teaching in Switzerland and Poland, which would have been appropriate and expected, but to distance himself from Joseph Priestley as Fuller had a reputation for being 'worse than Priestley'.[15] The article was personal in its motives rather than theological. A parallel can be drawn with Fuller's handling of Richard Baxter with whom he had been allied even to the point of being called 'worse than Baxter'. These are

[13] See my *Law and Gospel*, pages 167-168.

[14] *Literary Remains*, p. 295.

[15] See Fuller's The Calvinistic and Socinian Systems Examined and Compared, page 50 of the BOT edition.

all signs of Fuller wishing to maintain a good name for himself and that he was still highly unsettled in his own theology. Though Fuller in his essay against Priestly argues that his views on the will are opposite to Priestley's, in reality they are the same as they are based on the 'reasonableness of things'. In his criticisms here, Coleridge gets his facts rather mixed up as he says that Fuller was 'mislead by Jonathan Edwards'. This is a misjudgement as Fuller altered Edwards' teaching so that it was nearer Priestley's. However, after thus criticising Fuller on the will, Coleridge exclaims:

> Why, yours, Dr Priestley, is just as bad! – Yea, and is no wonder: – for in essentials both are the same. But there is no reason for Fuller's meddling with the subject at all, – metaphysically, I mean.[16]

Fuller seems to have understood Priestley as little as he understood Baxter as his critics such as Coleridge and Button pointed out, but he did not wish to be associated with men of dubious report. I have demonstrated how Fuller sided with the Socinians on 10 major doctrines[17] and Coleridge says in his review of Fuller's own book allegedly against Socinianism, published in 1793, how Fuller made exactly the same theological mistakes that Joseph Priestley did and that he objected to thoughts in Fuller on Socinianism, not because they were Calvinistic but because they were ideas that Calvin would have recoiled from. This was William Button's point in his *The Nature of Special Faith*, who likens Fuller's doctrines with those of Priestley. One cannot call either of these writers 'Hyper-Calvinists' and Button was a staunch supporter of foreign missions. Complaining of Fuller's delving into shadowy philosophy to explain his Christianity, Coleridge writes:

> O, why did Andrew Fuller quit the high vantage ground of notorious facts, plain durable common sense, and express Scripture, to delve in the dark in order to countermine mines

---

[16] *Literary Remains* pp. 294-295.

[17] Section headed Fuller and Socinianism, p. 201 ff. and *passim*, *Law and Gospel in the Theology of Andrew Fuller*, 2nd Edition, 2011.

> under a spot, on which he had no business to have wall, tent, temple or even standing ground![18]

This is the best definition of Fullerism I have ever read.

Atonement delayed

Both Grotius and Fuller taught a delay in Atonement until the believer confessed his sins (plural and individually listed) whereas sin itself was put to death with the death of Christ not with the acceptance of the sinner. Christ died to bring death to sin and life to His own. So, though Fuller occasionally uses the word 'propitiation', as Chun points out, the propitiation for Fuller is not immediate propitiation in Christ's baptism of death and glorious resurrection but is worked out when the believer in 'duty-faith' and on hearing the 'well-meant offer' takes them for himself through his own agency. This was once called Liberalism but is now called by Fullerites 'gospel preaching'. The fruits leading to propitiation and thus justification, Fuller tells us, are on a table spread before the sinner. We have only to grasp out and take them.[19]

Furthermore, in the pages Chun refers to, I do not deal with the doctrine of necessity in isolation but bind it synergistically into all the other Christian doctrines denied or re-interpreted by Grotius, Fuller, the New Divinity School and modern Fullerism. I outline this, my strongest commitment, in my book *The Covenant of Grace and the People of God.* There is no such Covenant in Fuller's works published up to date. Indeed, Fuller has a Dispensational view of God's 'covenants'. Fuller's wayward teaching must be studied as a whole not as separate absolute parts bound together by 'the reason and fitness of things', whatever that is. We are saved by Grace and not what we feel is 'reasonable' and 'fitting'. All this is clearly outlined in John Gill whom Fuller knew personally and confessed to having read his major works.

Fuller believed God's revelation was arbitrary

Fuller will have nothing to do with God's revealed will as he feels such revelation in the Scriptures, especially in the Old Testament, is not

---

[18] *Notes on Andrew Fuller's Calvinistic and Socinian Systems Compared* in Coleridge's Literary Remains, p 295.

[19] See Fuller's essay on Justification which is way off the Biblical mark.

permanent but short-termed and arbitrary. It is surprising that neither Chun nor Haykin deal with Fuller's low view of revelation in comparison to his high view of Natural Law and Natural Religion. Chun must know that Fuller argues that God's entire revelation will be wounded up when his eternal Natural Law is understood rightly and even God Himself must return to this Law and place Himself again under it.[20] So it is Fuller's 'Natural Law' (Fuller always gives the term capitals) which persuades natural, fallen man to understand 'the reason and fitness of things'. Actually, 'Natural Law' is Fuller's God as it is the only fixed standard, he believed, for a Christian to follow. This has, of course, nothing whatsoever to do with the Christian's faith and is quite pagan in its understanding of both God's revelation and Law. God's revealed Law is merely that which must be understood 'figuratively' according to Fuller but how he figured this out is any man's guess. However, such as Haykin, Chun and Daniel in defending Fuller are defending a vain philosophy of unfallen nature, against a saving gospel revealed in God's Word.

Standing alongside Warfield in my criticism of New Divinity

Chun, in criticising my objections to the New Divinity School omits to add that in context I am quoting and agreeing with none less than Benjamin Warfield here concerning the real vicarious suffering in Christ's Atonement. This is denied by the New Divinity School and with this denial they include a denial of the real imputation of sin to Christ and His righteousness to the believer. This leaves them totally without a gospel. This is why I entitled one of my published works on Fullerism *A Gospel Worthy of No Acceptation*. Who wants a gospel void of God's Good News? Warfield's strong criticism of New Divinity teaching applies equally to Fuller who followed it. Besides, we know that Edwards Junior, one of the founders of the New Divinity school, had taken over the teaching of Nathaniel Emmons and Nathaniel Taylor which perverted Edwards' teaching on what was 'natural' in man and what was 'moral' and led to the views of Samuel Hopkins which Fuller took over. Chun's association of Fuller with Edwards leaves out the

[20] A full discussion of this central topic in Fuller's philosophy would fill a book. Please consult my index on the subject in my *Law and Gospel* Second Edition where I give well over a hundred documented examples from Fuller's works.

downgrading in Fuller's theology over a decade from Edwards to Hopkins. He will not admit for the sake of his argument that between the time of Edwards Senior and Fuller's continuous development of his theology, a lengthy dumbing down of doctrine had taken place which had influenced Fuller no end.

Chun claims on page 173 that:

> Fuller believed that if there is such a thing as justification by Christ's righteousness, then in his own words, Fuller would be charging himself with perverting the gospel and thereby, denying the very nature of the deity of Christ.

Actually, this is Chun's thought rather than Fuller's but taking this utterance at its face value we find that Chun is building on a false alternative which was admittedly the usual 'either or' method of Fuller's. Chun's falsely put alternative neither applies to Fuller or Ella whom he is criticising. The crucial factor here is the timing of Christ's Atonement. When did Christ actually put an end to sin, imputing that sin to Himself according to repeated Old Testament prophecy? When did Christ cover sin? When did Christ kill off sin? Was it not at His death and at no other time? Christ's penal, sin-killing sacrifice was a once and for all time event. We do not believe in the repetition of this sacrifice as in the Roman Catholic repetition of the mass. Christians are no repeaters but once-and-for-all-timers. There was only one Atonement needed and it was all Christ's vicarious work at one time for eternity. The Just died for the unjust. Christ calls His Baptism the death that He had to die for the dead. With His death many were made alive. As in Adam all die, so in Christ shall all be made alive. This is the gospel placed in baptism which points to the fulfilment of righteousness in Christ. This was Christ's testimony when He showed us the gospel way in His own baptism.[21] This was the teaching of that mighty preacher of righteousness James Hervey whom the New Divinity School condemned for preaching that the Atonement fully accomplished its God-intended and God-given purpose in his prose-poetical work *Theron and Aspasio* which also caused very strong protests from free-willer Wesley. Both Wesley and Hopkins taught that

[21] Matthew 3:15.

the Atonement was conditional on the reception of sinners. The Bible teaches that Christ met every single condition on His very own. By His stripes we are healed. We note that Christ first met all the necessary conditions and then we were healed.

Chun's false Calvinism

Chun, apparently leaning on Nettles, believes that Fuller never forsook Calvinism yet his portrayal of Fuller's rational theology is way outside the gist, tenor and wording of Calvin's gospel. This goes also for Edwards Junior who rejected his father's Reformed theology. I am indeed very critical of Calvin's fatalism and legal approach to many matters of grace and the origin of sin. I find he leaned too heavily on Zwingli's fatalism. Calvin's theology was, however, never as weird as that of Hyper-Fullerites such as Chun, Haykin and Daniel, and even at times Nettles, who describe 'Calvinism' in Fullerite terms.

One of the first articles I read from Nettles' pen was his contribution to the 1984 edition of Reformation Today, a Fullerite organ run by Erroll Hulse which had little to do with Reformed doctrines. Here in his essay 'Andrew Fuller and Free Grace' Nettles cites two authors who question Fuller's Calvinism.[22] Instead of examining these objections to Fullerism, he claims that such statements are 'misleading and make Fuller appear less Calvinistic than he was'. He thus accepts Fuller's claim that he was a 'Strict Calvinist',[23] though Calvin would certainly have not accepted either Fuller or Nettles as representing his beliefs. Nettles then strives to argue why Fuller was a *bona fide* Calvinist by nicely stepping away from the Calvinistic allegations against Fuller and stresses Fuller's Calvinism in terms of moral duties and distinguishing between regeneration and faith. Furthermore, though he cites 'Gillites' as opposing Fullerism, he claims they did not preach repentance and faith. Gill, Brine, Stevens etc. of course did just that, teaching repentance against the background of total depravity where it belongs in contrast and thus going far deeper than Fuller. So, too, the faith which Gill and Brine demanded was not duty-faith but Christ's faith in those whom he made regenerate by His faith. Indeed, those who Nettles looks

---

[22] See pages 3 to 14.
[23] Page 5.

on as 'Hypers' preached repentance and faith to a far greater degree than did Fuller and his followers.

At last, an accurate quote

In his final effort to refute my analysis of Fuller's theology and my defence of a real and actual Atonement, Chun quotes me accurately as writing on page 89 of my first edition of *Law and Gospel in the Theology of Andrew Fuller* regarding Fuller's deviation from the Biblical description of the Atonement:

> Thus, instead of the atonement objectively securing faith and reconciliation for the elect, it is the subjective believing of the sinner, which makes the atonement, working backwards, effective. It is repenting and believing that gives the atonement its power, not the atonement that empowers the sinner to believe.

Obviously, I rejected such a scheme and against my objection Chun quotes Fuller's words in his *Gospel Worthy*:

> If there be an objective fulness in the atonement of Christ sufficient for any number, there is no other impossibility in the way of any man's salvation to whom the gospel comes than what arises from the state of his own mind.

I always think it risky to begin a definitive and creedal statement of doctrine with an 'if' clause. I take this statement however to mean that Fuller is not giving us a display of doubt but a dogmatic statement in these words. Nor do I accept the idea of Christ dying for 'any number', meaning any unspecific number. His death was not a ransom for 'any number' but for the number for whom he died. Even our hairs are numbered according to Christ.[24] His ransom was completed at the ransoming. 'Any number' is not an accurate way of referring to all those known to God specifically and individually in the Lamb's Book of Life who are elected in Christ. Chun, however, sees Fuller's words as indicating a Scriptural proof that there is no 'natural ability' to prevent sinners coming to Christ but only their 'moral ability' fails them and

---

[24] Matthew 10:30.

that 'cannot believe' means 'they will not believe'. This is in stark contrast to Jonathan Edwards' clear teaching on man's natural and moral inabilities and Luther's *Bondage of the Will*. I do not accept this false distinction in man between the natural and the moral but even if we abide by Chun's distinction, we are still faced with a sinner who is dead in trespasses and sins and can only be made alive by Christ's atoning death. When Christ said on the cross, 'It is finished', he meant just what he said in His once and for all time sacrifice. No sinner by accepting a so-called 'well-meant' offer via his 'duty-faith' can equal that. Furthermore, he need not.

Fuller put a burden on sinners which was totally artificial. Christ saves by Grace and not via pseudo-Natural Law efforts to accept Him. This means that the whole debate concerning man's natural or moral destiny is irrelevant to Christ's Atonement for man as man, not man as merely a bunch of naturals or morals. Christ's righteousness has nothing to do with so-called duty-faith. There is no gospel whatsoever in this speculative idea. Dead men have no existence in Christ whatsoever until Christ awakens the dead in the Valley of Bones. Then they receive a true spiritual nature which is Christ given and a true faith which is Christ's faith and a true righteousness which is Christ's righteousness. Fuller repeatedly denies this truth arguing that if man were fully dead in trespasses and sins, he could not respond to God. Perhaps this is what Coleridge meant concerning Fuller's annihilation of real man.[25] Left to himself, at death man is as dead as a door nail. Only Christ can raise him. In other words, Fuller's fictive man does not exist. Neither does Fuller's fictive cut-down God.

Stephen Holmes feels Spurgeon's theology was built on Fullerism

Stephen Holmes' Foreword to Chun's thesis starts off with a great, undocumented exaggeration. He claims that Spurgeon built his theology on Fullerism, translating 'Fuller's evangelical Calvinism into the vernacular of working-class London'. He even believes that Spurgeon's world-wide fame is due to his Fullerism. True, Spurgeon respected the piety of Fuller but also pointed out that Fullerism contained 'thorns' as he told Fuller's son Andrew Gunton on being presented with a copy of *The Gospel Worthy*. Still, theological taste is

[25] See Coleridge's Literary Remains, Book IV, pp. 294-295.

difficult to define; some called Spurgeon an Arminian and Gill, too. That Spurgeon was a Fullerite is rather hard to swallow given the vast evidence against such a fanciful notion. However, Fullerites argue that even Calvin was of their following, too.

Holmes continues, 'It is not an exaggeration to say that all mainstream Baptists in Britain today are descendants, theologically of Andrew Fuller.' He even goes so far as to say that the traditional theological core of Baptist churches is built on what Fuller taught. John Reisinger makes the same claim for his NCT teaching otherwise known as Hyper-Fullerism. I admit that the gangrene (as it was called in the contemporary Christian press), of Fullerism is rotting many a church and that this is not limited to Baptist churches by any means.[26] There are even a number of Presbyterians today who translate the Westminster Confession into Fullerite thinking. It is, however, an unbelievable statement when applied to the bulk of Baptists. During my lecturing visits to Sweden, Norway, Germany, Holland, Britain, Switzerland and the United States through a cross-section of Baptist churches, some numbering thousands of truly Reformed believers, I found they told another, more acceptable, story and even former Baptist associations who toyed with Fuller are now rejecting Fullerism as a false gospel. As a well-informed friend of the historical Baptist faith, I would object strongly with most Baptists against the most far-fetched idea the Fullerism sums up the Baptist faith. Perish the thought!

So, too, Holmes forgets that even Fuller had to admit that Baptist churches outside his shrinking Association and outside his influence grew more in numbers and that Fuller's Association supported the Arian growth amongst their relatively few churches which eventually turned Liberal. Again, Holmes puts Fuller's 'success' down to his allegedly following Edwards' teaching on the natural and moral properties of man. I would suggest that Fuller's failure was through his lack of theological training and his following Grotius through the eyes of the New Divinity School.

[26] See J. A Jones' (pastor of Jireh Chapel, London), A Sketch of the Rise and Progress of Fullerism, or Duty-Faith, That Gangrene now rapidly Spreading in Many Baptist Churches, 1861.

Fullerism was never the backbone of Baptist faith

We can happily conclude today that neither Fuller nor Reisinger, nor Haykin, nor Chun nor such as Curt Daniel who propagate Liberal Hyper-Fullerism represent orthodox Baptist teaching in any way, at least, in the old Particular Baptist sense. The fact that Chun himself views Fullerism erroneously as the backbone of general Baptist teaching is the *a priori* reasoning behind his writing his 2008 thesis published in 2012. He is oblivious to the fact that few Baptist bodies would agree with him, whether Particular, Strict or General, though Fuller sought to combine all three and did not hesitate to accept Arians in his mergers to boot. On the whole, Fuller's theology had as many holes in it as Swiss cheese but all these holes were filled with a rationalism which was fully opposed to the theology of our Reformation and Fuller's contemporary orthodox scholars such as John Gill.

Chapter Seventeen

Fuller the Missiologist and Pastor

The forgotten Fuller

In a recent paper written by Prof. Michael Haykin entitled The Forgotten Missional Theologian, the author keeps alive the opinion that Andrew Fuller sparked of world-wide missionary outreach. He thus does not try to reconstruct the work of the 'Forgotten Missional Theologian' but merely emphasises the traditional run-of-the-mill, modern Fullerite slant on a figure whom they rob of his true historical and theological status and the 'Forgotten Fuller' remains forgotten still. Taking this stance, Haykin claims that:

> Fuller served as the main promoter, thinker, fundraiser, and letter-writer of the Baptist Missionary Society for over twenty-one years. He held that rope more firmly and with greater conscientiousness than anyone else.

Such an argument, though needing much revision, has nothing to do with Missional Theology or preaching the gospel through evangelism world-wide. This over-evaluation of Fuller as an organiser of missionary evangelism based on an alleged theology of missionary strategy is being increasingly used to boost Fuller's popularity today. Nettles tells us that:

> William Carey would not have gone to India apart from Fuller's support; nor could Carey's *Enquiry* have had any effect had it not been for Fuller's *Gospel Worthy*.

He goes on to suggest that the modern foreign missionary movement was founded on Fuller's doctrine of the absolute sovereignty of God.[1]

Not to be outdone by other Fuller fans, C. J. Moore, a Ph.D. candidate at Midwest Seminary and pastor at Liberty Baptist Church, in his paper 'Andrew Fuller and the Genesis of Modern Missions', writes:

> Astonishingly, the modern missionary movement owes its genesis to a man who was never a missionary himself: Andrew Fuller.[2]

Defining 'missional'

The term 'missional' has been redefined by a number of Baptist Fullerite pastors in recent years to mean the very opposite of 'missionary'. They now confined the term to local church work and their digital outreach, reminding us of the old Lutheran Orthodoxy that confronted Francke's and Ziegenbalg's world-wide missional thrust. David Mark Rathel in his small book *Baptists and the Emerging Church Movement*, defines 'missional' as:

> The need for a local church to reach into the community, contextualise its message to its surrounding culture and employ modern technology to reach as large an audience as possible. [3]

This is a too limited view of the Great Commission and, to do justice to Haykin, that writer looks correctly over local borders to realms further afield.

---

[1] Why Andrew Fuller? p. 5 and Andrew Fuller on Free Grace, p. 14 in Reformation Today, 1984 edition, editor Erroll Hulse.

[2] Aug. 13. 2020, online.

[3] *Baptists and the Emerging Church Movement*, Wipf & Stock, Oregon, 2014, p.3.

However, no matter how one boosts Fuller as a missiologist, his endeavours fade away into nothingness in comparison to the work and outreach of such as August Hermann Francke. Indeed, one of the main reasons for the BMS not following the work of the Halle missionaries was to promote Fuller as the pioneer of what Francke had done long before him. In the same way, Carey is given the laurels due to Ziegenbalg. This modern claim by Haykin stands in stark contrast to what the records show as historical, down-to-earth facts. Such as Curt Daniel, Robert Oliver, Chris Chun and formerly Erroll Hulse, now in glory, have re-written Fuller's life but their 'evidence' simply does not fit the case. A Christian lives by God's grace and the Scriptures and not historical novels. I sadly hear now that the publisher who brought out my book on Isaac McCoy, that great supporter of missions, has turned his life, without my being informed, into a 'historical novel'. Cowper criticised this misuse of literature by saying that the taste of the day was 'tickle and entertain me or I die!'

Horst R. Flachsmeier's History of Missiology

In my long search for missiological studies in the sixties, I found for a number of years few historical and theological overviews of missionary work. Then, soon after commencing work for the Evangeliska Fosterlandstiftlsen in Sweden, including itinerant preaching and teaching the Sami nomad children, I came across Horst R. Flachsmeier's work *Geschichte der Evangelischen Weltmission* (1963) and a year later Paulus Scharpff's *Geschichte der Evangelisation.* I read these books time and time again and Flachsmeier's work especially has laid the foundation of my own missiological thinking. This author was a practising physician, theologian and missionary and covers the work of missionary enterprises from Paul to modern times. Scharpff's work is more a history of revival movements and mass evangelism though there is much good, historical information in it. He mentions Carey but once, more or less by the way, not even giving his first name. He does not mention Fuller at all.

I consider Flachsmeier's work to be exact and most precise but it contains a surprise for such as Haykin, Piper, Chun, Nettles and other promoters of Fuller as a missiologist. Flachsmeier spends some fifty pages on the evangelization of India and Pakistan which includes 38 pages on Carey and the BMS. Here he is most supportive of Carey's missiological thinking though he also lists the negative elements of the BMS work. Though the events leading up to the formation of the BMS and Thomas and Carey's involvements are outlined accurately, there is not so much as a single mention of Andrew Fuller in the entire 597 paged accounts. Nor does Werner Raupp in his 475 paged collection of missionary and missiological texts entitled Mission in Quellentexten mention Fuller though he spends four and a half pages on Carey. This was not a careless omission as evidence for Fuller as a leading missiologist simply does not exist.

Fuller was not the originator and prompter of the BMS

Fuller was certainly not the originator and the main initial promoter of the Baptist Missionary Society and Indian Missions. His interference within the Indian mission lamed the Baptist missionary outreach in particular and the entire missionary movement in general. The initial historical impetus for the Baptist work in India came via John Thomas followed by Ward, Marshman and Carey in that order. They carried on an already established missionary work performed by many churches, in particular the Lutheran, Presbyterian, Church of England and Independents. This joint work had already been the means of converting many thousands of Indians to Christ. The part-time missionary Baptist work in Serampore and Calcutta was financed chiefly through large secular earnings; book, pamphlet and newspaper sales of a very mixed, kind; translations of non-Christian works and donations from friends from other denominations and societies in India. Nor can Fuller be counted as having positive influence on the more numerous missions outside of the Baptist fold. These had been doing good, solid work in India for up to two centuries before Fuller strove to have them disqualified as true missionaries in his writings to his own narrow band of followers. Fuller was indeed strictly against the historical international missionary work of at least two hundred years from the Reformed Dutch to the Lutheran, Church of England and Presbyterian periods and ridiculed their pioneering self-offering work as evidence of their being misled by 'Jezebel'. So, too, Ryland had his hand on the BMS rudder far longer than Fuller who died when the East India Mission was steering clear of many of its early troubles caused by Fuller's interference and dropping of the ropes he had promised to hold. Ryland's major part in the home policies and practice has never been clearly studied as the myths say Fuller did it all. Yet, right from the start in October 2, 1792, we find Ryland's signature before all others on documents appertaining to the BMS.

Carey's calling to India was not dependant on Fuller's writings

Haykin emphasises Fuller's importance in aiding the Baptist much-belated thrust into world missions by stating:

> From a merely human perspective, if Fuller's theological works had not been written, Willian Carey would not have gone to India.[4]

We do not view missionary work from a 'merely human perspective', but from a historical, Biblical and theological perspective. It was Carey who persuaded Fuller to follow him in his interest for foreign missions and it is obvious that Carey was basing his motives not only on his personal calling but also on the work of previous Lutheran, Presbyterian, Independent, Moravian and Church of England missionaries to India whom he names. It is also presumed that by reading the American Presbyterian Jonathan Edwards' works that Carey received an interest in overseas missions. Fuller's enthusiasm before Carey eventually moved to India was through his strange fascination with Thomas' charisma. Thus, he first looked to Thomas as a leader of the Mission with Carey as his assistant.

Carey was never as insular as Fuller

Carey was never insular and narrow-minded in his vision to have all evangelical, Reformed Christians take a necessary interest in foreign missions. Here, Fuller, was light-years behind him in appreciating what foreign missions entail. Sadly, Carey failed to keep to such initial ideals himself. The over a hundred Protestant missionaries and their foreign mission societies represented in India from up to 200 years before Thomas and Carey had the aim of evangelising India irrespective of denominational restrictions and Home Board resolutions such as those Fuller strove to enforce on Thomas, Carey, Ward and Marshman. Fuller's denominational, administrational and highly political

---

[4] SBJT, 17.1 (2013) pp. 46-52.

interference in the work of Indian Missions was quite contrary to the Christian's Great Commission and had a most destructive impact on Indian Missions. So, too, Carey was strongly influenced by John Sutcliff's call for 'concerts of prayer', following the Church of England calls earlier in the century such as those of Romaine which must be seen as a major incentive for Carey to take up the gospel call in India. Without Sutcliff's care and guidance, Fuller would have been even more of a failure as contemporaries such as Cox point out. We read that Carey was stricken with shame that the Baptists had waited so long in following non-Baptist missionaries. This reflected the objective truth. Yet we are told by modern Fullerites that their Guru Fuller pioneered Indian Missions. Indeed, if we were to follow the Banner of Truth's trust in David Gay, we would be led to believe that darkness was on the face of the earth until Fuller enlightened it. Gay's book *Battle for the Church* depicts a battle between the Bible and Fullerism.

Fuller as a lobbyist

One of the main arguments put forward by Fullerites to show that Fuller was a missiological pioneer is the fact that he sought contact with the religious and political authorities of his day, mostly indirectly, on Indian policies. This we see in his published work, *An Apology for the late Christian Missions to India in Three Parts with an Appendix* which he composed in letter form to Edward Parry, Chairman to the East India Company and Major Scott Warring. These were not in answer to letters sent to Fuller but remarks on their private letters sent to others of which Fuller had been notified and had jumped on the bandwagon. In these letters, we find how deeply involved Fuller was personally in British Indian politics but also, how he felt that as a Britisher and a Christian he should defend the Baptist missionaries. However, though he sees Carey's work as benefiting both the gospel and Britain's reputation, he is quite wrong when he says that Carey was not financed in his translation work by Government monies but merely by societies (which?) and individual support. Printing orders to the Serampore Press from secular authorities are extant. There are other interesting asides in these 'letters'. We read that in 1807, the gospel had already been preached for twenty years in Bengal but not by whom and that some four thousand converts had been made on the coastal territories a hundred years before his writing. Fuller does mention Schwartz but seemingly as if he were merely acting for the 'English' Government, as he called it. So, too, Fuller mentions Professor White's Bampton Lectures at times positively but also critically on matters which White explained far better than Fuller's unschooled interpretation.

Be this as it may, the lobbying Fuller did in support of missiological principles in India was dwarfed by the actions of such contemporaries as Grant, Buchanan, Brown, Duff, the Clapham Sect and others who kept up a pro-Missions lobby in Parliament and the Press over many years. None of these pro-Mission contenders have been ranked as Missiologists. Nor can Fuller's efforts be compared with those of the Serampore Trio in India.

Fuller motivated by Thomas

Fuller's fascination with an initial blind trust in Thomas besides his extreme emotional ups and down quite overshadowed his interest in Carey. Furthermore, Fuller pulled out of the agreement with Carey when his friend most needed him before he embarked for India and cut the ropes which allegedly had bound him to Carey less than two years after tying them. Carey had likened his services to India as going down a mine and Fuller felt he was the one to pull Carey back to the surface. However, such a situation scarcely occurred and the ropes remained slack until the BMS severed them. Haykin, too, in speaking about Fuller's non-existent 'missional theology', quite ignores Fuller's highly radical and rationalistic theology taken over from the Enlightenment philosophers, Neo-Platonists, Latitudinarians and New Divinity men in a most undigested and amateur way. Furthermore, Haykin must have noted that Fuller's blockade of international, evangelical missionary endeavours led to the unevangelical and un-Reformed promoting of an oecumenical movement void of evangelical gospel theology.

Fund-raising became a major factor in Fuller's 'ministry'

Fuller's much praised solicitations for money for the BMS kept him away from his neglected church for up to four months at a time leaving his sheep without a shepherd. This entailed absence from Sunday preaching from midweek Bible Studies, Prayer meetings, elders' and deacons' meetings and visiting the sick, poor and needy as a good pastor should.

Fuller's unseemly behaviour towards the Church of England ministers and Scottish Baptists who gave him lodgings and generous donations whilst he neglected his own flock, is illustrated by, T. S. Grimshawe in his major work on Church of England minister Legh Richmond who hosted Fuller and his unthankful tongue. Indeed, Fuller abandoned his own flock for long periods over many years, calling for an assistant only shortly before his death. However, the actual funds he raised amongst many British denominations were minimal in comparison to the large sums ploughed into the Mission from Calcutta due to the Lutheran, Presbyterian, Independent, and Anglican churches, the Danish and British East Indian Companies, the Danish King and the British Government. It is here that true Baptist evangelists such as Krishna and Chamberlain reap our praise!

What happened to the funds refused by the Serampore Trio?

Yet we must ask what happened to these large sums of money raised in Britain and the monies paid out to the English BMS from India? It could be that what Fuller and Staughton practised in England encouraged Staughton later to practise in the States. Staughton's misuse of funds came to the public's notice in a more missionary-minded and open U.S.A. society but has not been looked into yet in Britain. Fuller boasted that he had gained a pound a mile in all his canvassing travels. Success in the meetings he took was always mentioned in guineas, pounds, shillings and pence. It is thus rather sickening to read Fuller's reports of his preaching success. We know that some of this money was ploughed into further 'missionary' work in Africa and other countries which was seemingly dealt out with a bucket full of holes as Carey was quick to inform the BMS, but this still needs a good deal of money to be accounted for. Here there is room for much research and explanations from the BMS side. It cannot be said that superfluous monies were sent to India as the Serampore Trio always refunded BMS donations and loans from their own income with interest.

Little research done on Foreign Missions by Fullerites

Haykin's research has yet to justify the idolised position he gives Fuller though he heads a university department for such research. The depth of his work is illustrated by the BOT gigantic tiny print edition of *The Works of Andrew Fuller* which came out in 2007 with Haykin's name on the front cover though Prof. Haykin neither edited the work nor the introductory biography. This was done by Andrew Fuller's son, Andrew Gunton Fuller in 1831.

Prof. Haykin has written a few opening words for the reprint entitled 'Andrew Fuller: Life and Legacy: A Brief Overview' and brief it is. Fuller's early 19th century editors had neither the training nor the facilities to do background and source research on Fuller and had merely put down the obituary thoughts of close friends and family members when a more critical evaluation would have been out of place. Haykin heads a team of researchers who could quickly provide such a critical, complete edition. Fuller's works have, on the whole, not been reset or altered in their layout since the early 19th century. The latest reprints from Sprinkle Publications and the Banner Of Truth represent collections in 19th century garb in a tiny print which is very tiring to read and very bulky to use. Haykin has made no efforts whatsoever to bring Fuller scholarship up to date or provide new material though he has promised such for decades.

A refreshing change of subject

Turning from Haykin's 'forgotten Fuller' it is so refreshing in comparison to read Prof. Sarah Hinlicky Wilson's Christianity Today article concerning Bartholomäus Ziegenbalg as 'The Missionary India Never Forgot'. Wilson shows rightly how Ziegenbalg actually did change the course of modern missions for the better. This was in a way foreign to Fuller's denominational dreams that scorned the evangelical and pan-Christian 'pleasant dreams' of Carey. In England Carey dreamed the same dreams as Ziegenbalg but Ziegenbalg saw his dreams coming true which Carey could not do because of Fuller's interference and his own preoccupation with secular work and business matters. Unlike Carey, Ziegenbalg was a full-time missionary in the traditional and still modern sense. So, too, Fuller's rational theology, in which he replaces the inner working of the Spirit with 'the nature of things' and 'right reason' as did Gotthold Ephraim Lessing, the father of what came to be known as the 'Liberal Movement', was the direct opposite to Carey's more Biblical, pragmatic view of the inner working of the Holy Spirit. Fuller's disdain for revealed religion, God's Law and Christ's Church were also foreign to Ziegenbalg's Biblical teaching. Fuller's gospel which he felt was worthy of all acceptation is one of dry dead bones which have an inner wherewithal to wake up and take on innate Christian duties. There is no such inner spiritual awareness in fallen man. Only God's voice can awaken the dead.

Fuller was not a Calvinist in the Reformed sense

Thus, we cannot possibly speak of Fuller as a 'Calvinist' as does Calvinist Haykin, that is, if we agree with Cowper who told his nephew, a theological student, that the gospel is injuriously called 'Calvinism' as it is the doctrine of Paul and the Scriptures. Nor can we claim that Fuller was Reformed as he denied the very principles of the Reformation based on the character of God, the eternal nature of the Law, gospel revelation, the Fall of man, the means of salvation and the establishment of a true Church. So too, he mistook the fashion of 'morals' for true spirituality as do a number of his followers. Nor was Fuller evangelistic as he severely curbed the work and spirit of evangelism in India and his associate churches. Fuller emptied baptism of its Biblical purpose and filled his view of the Lord's Supper with rational, institutional and quite un-Biblical notions.

Ever since engaging with Haykin decades ago, I have wondered why he forced his own brand of Calvinism onto Fuller and did not allow Fuller to speak for himself. The fact is that Fullerism quickly ousted Reformed thinking from the Baptist churches which followed him in trusting in a faith built on pre-faith duties and post-conversion occupation with 'what is reasonable' and what represents 'the fitness of things'. One would thus think that any Christian scholar on issuing a reprint of Fuller's works would evaluate this modernistic impact of Fuller's and make a thorough-going, critical analysis of Fuller's theological legacy.

Haykin simply misunderstands Fuller

After meeting and fellowshipping with Haykin, I cannot believe that he would accept Fuller's low view of God as being merely arbitrary in salvation; nor Fuller's high view of man and rejection of the doctrine of total depravity. Furthermore, Fuller's ecclesiology which only accepts his kind of Baptists as full Christians; his gospel of Rationalism; his low view of the Work of the Holy Spirit; his unbiblical view of Atonement and Justification, his denial of the permanency of the Law which reveals God's very nature and love for an institutionalised Church based on

'Baptist Principles' must be analysed and judged before it does any more damage. Above all, Fuller's rejection of the permanency of God's revealed will and his hoped-for return to what he calls 'Natural Law' must be scrutinised critically and objectively. This is the Fuller Haykin has totally forgotten and sadly ignored. Haykin has done no such necessary research and is still not doing it and has still not contributed to a better understanding of Fuller *in toto* than his predecessor Andrew Gunton Fuller who merely wished to preserve his father's writings. This was a more honourable reason for printing his father's works than to perpetuate a myth.

Those looking for good, scholarly, studious work, airing new research on the forgotten Fuller will thus not find it in Haykin's Introduction. Indeed, with all the criticism that sound Christians of Fuller's day heaped on Fuller, calling his ideas an evil gangrene in the churches and all the trouble Fuller's radical philosophical thrust is causing in breaking up churches today, one can only say that Haykin has merely attempted to re-paint an idol. Or shall we say whitened a sepulchre?

Further elements of Fuller's life and testimony suppressed by Haykin

As a student of eighteenth and nineteenth century theology I was also hoping that Haykin would tackle the problem of why Fuller who was converted in a Hyper-Calvinistic, Johnsonian church with a tendency to Arianism, stayed so long as a member and pastor of such a society. Why does Haykin skip over Soham's Johnsonism and Arianism? Also, why does he not examine the Arian origins of Kettering? It was John Brine of Currier's Hall, Cripplegate, where his friend John Gill often preached, that combatted Johnsonism, not Fuller. Why does Haykin not examine Fuller's fickle coquetry with nature-based religion, New Divinity, Baxterism, Arminianism, Sandemanism, Socinianism, Scepticism and Enlightenment philosophy? Why, too, if he were the heart and soul of the Indian Mission as Haykin wrongly teaches, did Fuller allow Arians and men otherwise ill-equipped for the task, to work on rival translations of the Scriptures to Carey's? Why, too, do modern Fullerites such as Curt Daniel steeped in Enlightenment Rationalism force on lost sinners a mumbo-jumbo of natural religion, so-called 'common grace' and appeals to man's supposed natural responsibilities and abilities to exercise duty faith and other rigid barriers to belief? Daniel starts his evangelism by stressing what man 'ought'[5] to be doing rather than what God has done. What evangelistic good is to be hoped for from those who believe that man is the co-agent of his own salvation? Why was Fuller and now his followers, so Antinomian in splitting up the Eternal Law of God arbitrarily into 'carnal' and 'moral' parts, yet Neonomian in up-grading a narrow choice of ethical rules to make them their sole guide to faith and obedience? As yet Brother Haykin has provided no answer to these acutely important questions. Yet Haykin must have noticed that it is the Hyper-Fullerites such as David Gay and Tom Wells that have taken Fuller's writings to their logical conclusion and become NCT adherents. If Haykin is really the Fullerite he says he is, then we must suspect him also of having NCT notions.

The down-grading in Fuller's theology must be outlined

I would like to see an analysis of Fuller's ever-changing philosophy of theology and have his works rearranged so as to demonstrate this chronological decline. Why, according to Fullerites, was Fuller at his most 'spiritual' when he emphasised that 'morality' and 'spirituality' were synonyms through which one allegedly attained to 'the nature and fitness of things'? Why do modern Fullerites claim allegiance to Fuller on points which Fuller had long abandoned as he admitted in later works? These Fullerite followers teach that we must accept such paradoxes as being irreconcilable as they demonstrate the two aspects of the truth. They thus patch together ideas that Fuller had rejected but claim they are Fuller's still. How naïve can one get?

Fuller's 'change of sentiments'

So, I would like to know why Prof. Haykin does not recognise the fact that Fuller admitted that he had radically changed his mind numerous times concerning the atonement, imputation, justification and righteousness, yet such as Haykin still insist on reprinting these positions from which Fuller moved as if Fuller would still be teaching his acknowledged former errors today. *The Gospel Worthy of All Acceptation* is a classic example of Fuller's low view of revealed

---

[5] Here Daniel reveals his Kantianism which is the basis of his rational theology.

religion and his love for paradoxes to be solved by the reasonableness of Natural Law. There is no hope for sinners in it. There is no constant evangelical gospel prevailing through it.

It appears from reading Fuller's Change of Sentiments, an almost forgotten work, that on writing the first edition of *The Gospel Worthy of All Acceptation*, he merely stressed that the atonement was 'sufficient for all mankind'. He then discovered that in the Scriptures Christ had 'an absolute and determined design in his death to save some of the human race and not others'. So what did Fuller do? Modify his former statement and update it with one nearer the Biblical truth and more Biblically worded? No, he left his Liberal and Radical religion of Natural Law unaltered in *The Gospel Worthy of All Acceptation* and merely added his Religion of Design to 'complete' his gospel of paradox. A self-contradictory 'gospel' is no gospel at all.

Fuller's supposed 'epoch-making' gospel

Haykin tells us that in later editions of Fuller's *Gospel Worthy* his 'major theme remained unaltered'. However, Fuller's 'major theme', as demonstrated, was not a gospel theme. So, too, he does not say what Fuller altered but argues that 'this epoch-making book sought to be faithful to the central emphasis of historic Calvinism', which he defines as preaching man's 'universal obligations'. Would our Reformers, including Calvin, agree? I think not. 'Universal obligations' neither describe Calvinism nor the Gospel. Preaching 'universal obligations' may be a kind of Humanism but it is not preaching the need for salvation and does not point to the One who saves. The Latitudinarians 'preached' in this way but happily not our Reformers. Fuller's Liberalism is also not 'epoch-making' as it is as old as Adam and did not help Adam much then and has opposed the true gospel since then. Indeed, Haykin's unfounded opinion that Fuller's personal syncretism is 'epoch-making' must be the overstatement of the age and designed only to mislead Christ's lambs. The idea of Haykin's replacing the Reformed faith with Fuller's appeal to man's 'universal obligations' draws the curtains over any claim to 'historic Calvinism'.

In his Change of Sentiments, Fuller also confesses that he altered his mind several times after writing A Reply to Philanthropos. This work is a favourite with most lovers of Fuller as one can pick out teachings from it that will please all sides including utter Sceptics and Hyper-

Calvinists. Nettles in his essays such as his Reformation Today contributions thus leans heavily on Fuller's Reply to Philanthropos without adding a word of caution because Fuller confessed to have changed his mind on what he wrote. Nevertheless, Fuller insisted that though he had altered his opinions several times concerning these letters he would not alter the work itself in future editions. Indeed, very many pro-Fuller quotes by his devotees are taken from works from which Fuller had distanced himself but they are still printed as 'his'. Haykin, too, has changed his mind several times, like Fuller, since first writing on him, coming nearer to Fuller's open Liberalism and Radicalism each time. Originally Haykin was orthodox on the Atonement but his recent works show that he now accepts Fuller's Governmental Theory of the Atonement which robs the Atonement of its once-and-for-all-time accomplishment on the cross leaving the sinner as Fuller expresses it merely to reach out and grasp it throughout all ages.

Fuller knots himself in his own ropes

Haykin mentions Fuller's missionary theology as if everybody understood what it was or took it for granted. A brief study of Haykin's subject here would have been helpful as Fuller differed mostly from Carey who never mixed his missionary strategy with severe right-wing colonial, political thinking as did Fuller. So, too, Haykin ought to examine the 'holding the rope' theory of Fullerites which has reached mythological proportions though Fuller's promise to Carey was broken even before Carey's first letters reached Kettering. As we have seen, Fuller's despotic 'absentee-bishop' manners reached such horrible dimensions that Carey felt he was destroying the lives of the missionaries. He even used the word 'killing' to describe Fuller's political pressure on Fountain. So, too, Ward and Marshman were greatly grieved to find that Fuller was sabotaging their church planting. The severe inner-quarrels between the Baptist missionaries in India because of BMS interference and 'hen-picking' is only being recorded in very recent years. Marshman travelled to Britain to stop the doctrinal downgrading of the BMS but returned a broken man after a mission unaccomplished.

Churches forced into being of the Fullerite Baptist kind

Fuller only recognised BMS-controlled churches in India and would not tolerate indigenous churches with non-denominational names. He saw his work as a means of spreading British Colonialism. For him, as for Marshman, becoming a loyal subject to Britain was half-way to becoming a Christian. Marshman could not even envisage an Indian Christian as a mature, independent being but only as a poor 'imbecile' who needed the British Raj or he would never survive. Has Haykin forgotten or never read that Ryland, whom Haykin sees as one who held the ropes as long as Carey lived, was a chief rope-cutter also? Carey had to tell Ryland Junior that his enormous interference in the practice of the Mission showed he was acting 'evilly'. Furthermore, Haykin does not touch on the very strong differences of opinion as to Church-and-Mission relationships in India and that most of the Baptists were quite against Fuller's 'Baptist Bride' ecclesiology.

The 'expansion myth'

Another point Haykin could have taken up was the expansion myth concerning the alleged vast increase of Fullerite churches through Fuller's ministry which nearly all present day Fullerites strongly believe, especially as surmised in the works of Robert Oliver and Erroll Hulse who even write of 'marvellous expansion'. Haykin tells us that Fuller's church doubled its membership from 1782-1815 so that it reached 175 members, but fails to say that from around 1795 Fuller's church was left more and more in the hands of others and the Association churches in general decreased in membership and theological acumen as they decreased in their hold on Scripture. Fuller's own many descriptions of the state of his Association's churches are far more sober and realistic, showing how they averaged some 70 members[6] but adds that the bulk of these (fifty per church) were not 'real Christians'. Indeed, Fuller distinguished between 'hearers', 'members' and 'Christians' in his congregation. Of, course, other dissenting churches such as William Huntington's had congregations of several thousand and a number of evangelical Anglican churches had over a thousand active members. Indeed, there were at least four large

[6] See Fuller's essays 'State of the Baptist Churches in Northamptonshire' and 'Decline of the Dissenting Interest'.

evangelical churches in Fuller's district which dwarfed the Fullerite churches. When the evangelical Church of England ministers in the district died with no evangelical pastor to take their places many flocked to Baptist churches in the vicinity, so increasing their numbers greatly. These numbers, however, quickly decreased as the Fullerite churches became increasingly liberal. Robert Sheehan, writing in the Banner of Truth magazine in 1985, claimed that rationalistic theology had been accepted by 'the overwhelming majority of non-conformist leaders'.[7] Fuller wrote of 'The Decline of the Dissenting Interest' and his articles on the state of the Northampton Baptist churches were far more sober than estimates made by such as Haykin, Oliver, Hulse and a number of BOT articles. They ought to have first read reports in the many Anglican, Strict and Particular Baptist newspapers of the day such as the Christian Magazine, The Gospel Herald, The Gospel Standard, The Earthen Vessel and the Christian Pathway before blowing bubbles in the air.[8]

Many contemporary Evangelical and Reformed pastors, including many Baptists, were fundamentally opposed to Fuller and complained of the confusion Fuller brought to the Baptist cause. The first major exodus from Fullerite churches and Associations in 1805 came through the more evangelical witness of Gadsby, and the East Anglican Particular Baptists who opposed Fuller increased from 732 members in 1800 to 2,658 in 1829. The reconstructed Norfolk and Suffolk Associations of 1830 who opposed Fullerism grew from seven churches to 35 churches in a few years. In 1833 the London Particular Baptists threw out Fullerite Liberalism from their churches as did twenty-nine churches in the Metropolitan Association of Strict Baptists in 1871. This purging of the Strict and Particular Baptists churches of rationalistic Fullerism continued into the 20th century.

The truth is that the majority of churches in Fuller's county and surrounding districts never fell for his theological dualism and even Hyper-Fullerite Robert Oliver admits that many members of Fuller's Association disagreed with him and split-offs occurred. John Stevens,

---

[7] 'The Decline of Evangelicalism in Nineteenth Century England', Issue 278, p. 16.

[8] See Section 4 of my chapter Andrew Fuller and the Gospel's Evangelical Witness pp. 266-273 in my book *Law and Gospel in the Theology of Andrew Fuller* 2nd edition concerning the downgrading of the Baptist Churches through Fullerism.

who had a church well over twice the size of Fuller's, points out in his *Help for the True Disciples of Immanuel*, (London, 1841) that the Fullerite destruction of churches continued on a regular basis and, truth to tell, it continues its church-splitting work today. Summing up Fullerism some twenty-five years after Fuller's death, Stevens found its scepticism concerning personal salvation denied 'the sure and effectual conversion of all the redeemed'. Stevens goes on to outline the enormous negative influence Fullerism scepticism had on the churches during the first half of the 19th century.

Looking back on the destructive effects of Fullerism amongst certain evangelical churches in 1861, J. A. Jones of Jireh Chapel, London writes:

> I wonder not at its prevailing, as it is exceedingly pleasing to human nature, and very gratifying to a proud man to be told he can believe if he will. But it is too humbling and too degrading to tell the sinner he has neither will nor power. So that those ministers who maintain the hypothesis of the creature's natural ability, will be sure to please the ear of men in general, and so gain what is so much sought after in the present day – vain popularity.[9]

Kenneth Dix on Fuller's influence

Kenneth Dix is widely proclaimed as an orthodox Strict Baptist with a heart for the gospel and one who has a most balanced view of the historical development of the Baptists. He wrote in the Strict Baptist Historical Society Bulletin for 1976:

> It is commonly held that high Calvinism stifled life among the eighteenth century PBs, and no growth was possible until Fuller showed the way. This view ignores much of the available evidence, for there was a continuing growth during the whole period. Certainly, there was a quickening during the last quarter,

[9] Earthen Vessel, Sept. 2, 1861, 'A Sketch of the Rise and Progress of Fullerism, or Duty-Faith, that Gangrene now rapidly spreading in many Baptist Churches.'

> but this had commenced before Fuller's book was written. The influence of Fuller here has been exaggerated.

Dix also affirms that:

> Historically, SBs have consistently maintained that 'saving faith is not a legal duty imposed on unregenerate man'.

Dix tells us in the same work:

> By 1886 Fuller's Association had gone further than perhaps even John Stevens could have imagined and officially reported, 'A few indeed, still cling to the theory of verbal inspiration, in spite of its being manifestly contrary to the facts'.

This is the natural result of rejecting Biblical evidence and deifying 'the nature and fitness of things'. This Rationalistic break with the Scriptures came into Baptist thinking via the Non-Baptist Samuel Chandler. John Gill in his The Moral Nature and Fitness of Things Considered Occasioned by Some Passages in the Rev. Mr. Samuel Chandler's Sermon, lately preached to the Societies for the Reformation of Manners, complains that 'the nature and fitness of things' was on all lips as a sign of 'this enlightened age, this age of politeness, reason and good sense'. He sees the phrase as a retreat from the doctrine of revelation but Fuller did not heed his warning. Of course, Lessing taught that reason was the Holy Spirit in man. Gill argues that one only needs to ask these common-sense-enthusiasts what nature are they talking about and what are 'things' and what is fit about them, and most who use this fashionable phrase 'are at once silenced and confounded'. It is worthy of note that Fuller's Association had formerly taught that it was the teaching of John Gill which had saved the Particular Baptists from decay. It still is![10]

---

[10] See my Strict Baptist Historical Society lecture John Gill (1697-1771): Preserver and Reformer of the Particular Baptists, Bulletin 2019, Number 46.

Expressing evangelical ideas in Biblical terms

Evangelical ideas must be expressed in Biblical terms otherwise confusion arises. Fuller's rationalistic views were admittedly fashionable in his day amongst scoffers of Biblical religion but were not accepted by Bible-believers. The Particular and Strict Baptists as a result of Fuller's novelties split up so that technically more Baptist churches were founded. The quality of theology in the Fullerite churches remained sub-Baptist and sub-Scriptural with no great increase in overall membership. This is exemplified by the work of John Ryland Senior who extended the membership of his Northampton church seven-fold and yet his son and successor, Dr John Ryland, a follower of Fullerism and on the BMS Board let his father's church which he took over shrink at the same swift rate as Ryland gave up his father's doctrines. Ryland Junior then excommunicate members who were of his Father's persuasion and witness and even excommunicated those who talked to the excommunicated. These cast-outs then increased the membership of sounder churches. As Fuller put an end to sound teaching in his own flock besides abandoning them for months at a time, we would have expected Haykin to have dealt critically with this down-grading.

Why did relatively uneducated Fuller despise the 'uneducated'?

A pastoral interest of mine would be to know why Fuller, who had very little education himself,[11] was so critical, mean and arrogant against people whom he felt were 'uneducated'? Was this merely his own way of protecting himself from similar criticism? A case in point is his strictures against Carey's English though in his own uncorrected letters there were glaring grammar and spelling mistakes, even when he was 'correcting' Carey. Fuller, however, felt rightly that when Carey was so careless with his English, he might be equally careless with his Bengali.

John Piper and stay-at-home Fuller

John Piper has the advantage over Haykin as he is internationally known, especially in Europe and has not only gained a doctorate in Germany's Heidelberg but still lectures in this country. As Piper has

---

[11] Cox, who knew Fuller well, said he had received 'rudiments of education' at his Soham school which was visited by Aspland twenty years later.

dealt with far more theological problems and modern ideas than Haykin, he is a man whom everybody in the circles I move in, knows. He is, as I am, a lover of Christian poetry and has said some very nice things about my understanding of William Cowper and the books I have published on him. Yet I found out recently that his theology and theory of missions are radically different from those of Cowper, so I began to dig deeper in Piper's further works though I had already given several my close attention.

Happily, Piper's main work on Fuller entitled *Andrew Fuller: Holy Faith, Worthy Gospel, World Missions* is available as a download on the internet. This is greatly to Dr Piper's credit. The work has a Foreword by Michael Haykin which starts by a quote from Ryland Junior's sermon at the funeral of Fuller in 1815 claiming that Fuller was 'perhaps the most judicious and able theological writer that ever belonged to our [i.e., the Calvinist Baptist] denomination'. The words 'the Calvinist Baptist' prefixed to 'denomination' appear to be Haykin's as at the time and as far as I know even to the present day, the Fullerite Baptists never went under the title 'Calvinist Baptist denomination'. Indeed, with the early merge of Arian and General Baptist theology with Fuller's lax doctrines and those of the free-will Baptists, the title had no relevance in Fuller's ecclesiology and theology. Yet Haykin tells us that his view of Fuller is 'by no means skewed' and that Spurgeon thought Fuller was the best theologian of his century and that David Phillips called Fuller the 'Elephant of Kettering'. On reading this, I thought of elephants in china shops as the old saying goes.

Fuller's 'impact on history' according to Piper

In his first chapter, Piper tells us that Fuller's 'impact on history' is shown in his *Gospel Worthy* thus 'opening the modern missionary movement' of which Carey was the 'morning star', quite ignoring the great gospel work done in India long before Carey arrived there and that most of the 'firsts' attributed to Carey were history long before Carey reached India. Piper, indeed, believes Fuller and Carey founded 'the greatest missionary movement in world history'. This, he puts down to Fuller's theological thinking. Happily, we have most of Fuller's works to keep us sober.

Piper and Hyper-Calvinism

Piper in his defence of Fuller against Hyper-Calvinism shows he has great difficulty in defining terms and deals merely with hearsay and not concrete examples. What he actually says is the usual automatic mantra of Fullerites against their make-believe opponents. Thus, Piper never strives to find out what Fuller is really talking about but keeps to the myths. Fuller certainly never combatted Hyper-Calvinism in the form Piper presents it and, indeed, said little on the subject. He did write against Antinomianism of other kinds than his own but modern Fullerites tar and feather such as Gill, Brine, Romaine and Hervey with the Antinomian brush but these were demonstrably lovers of God's Law to a high degree whereas Fuller taught its abolishment in true NCT style. Hyper-Fullerite and highly Liberal Curt Daniel spends over 900 pages in his anti-Gill thesis quoting Fullerites against the supposed Hyper-Calvinism allegedly in John Gill's theology without airing correctly either Gill's or Fuller's views. He is satisfied to rely on the mere opinions of others who agree with him though lacking evidence. This is why, in my review of Daniel's book, I have termed it correctly a collection of quotes.

Fuller learnt human responsibility from Gill

Indeed, Daniel overlooks much of what Gill taught a thankful Fuller, such as human responsibility before God and argues as if Gill was void of such theology and therefore stood in Fuller's shadow. Daniel never really gets down to any 'scientific' definition of Hyper-Calvinism but nor does Piper, admittedly a better scholar, in his comparison of Calvinism, High Calvinism and Hyper-Calvinism with Fullerism and the present-day Hyper-Fullerism of Piper, Haykin, Hulse and Daniel. Furthermore, Piper never analyses Fuller's definitions of theological terms which he obviously uses in a different way to Piper who appears to follow the standard definitions as if Fuller had never redefined them. Piper ignores the fact that Fuller's theology refers to God's alleged temporary action and revelation of Himself in Law and Grace. The only future for God in Fuller's theology is seen in God's acceptance of Natural Theology as being greater and more lasting than His own revelations. Fuller thus sees an end to the revealed Law, indeed an end to revelation itself and an end to the very nature of God as He has hitherto revealed Himself. Indeed, God's existence after His revelation is wound up is de-personalised by Fuller into pure 'Natural Law' and 'the reasonableness and fitness of things'. This is either a deification of nature or sheer Atheism. Presumably this is why Fuller insists that man's fall and Christ's work in salvation are to be understood 'figuratively', which was the very argument of the old eighteenth and nineteenth century British and German Liberals and the following Down-Grade Controversy stoutly opposed by Baptist Spurgeon.

The idea that God only justifies those of a 'holy disposition'

Piper refers to Fuller on God's justifying the ungodly in the light of Romans 4:5:

> But to him that worketh not, but believeth on him that justifieth the ungodly, his faith is counted for righteousness.

Fuller claims here that the passage is unique and dark and needs to be explained by other passages which appear to contradict it. This is yet another of Fuller's many alleged Scriptural paradoxes. Fuller cites John 3:18, 36; Acts 13:39 and Romans 3:26, 28 to show that man must have what he calls 'a holy disposition' before justification and that God's justification of the ungodly is that he first makes them godly and then justifies them. John Piper underlines this aspect of the supposed godly ungodly by saying:

> What matters, Fuller says, concerning the meaning of the justification of the ungodly is not that we possess no holy affections in the moment of justification by faith, but that, whatever we possess we make nothing of it as a ground of acceptance, 'counting all things but loss and dung that we may win and be found in him'. Faith is a duty. It is an act of the soul. It is a good effect of regeneration.[12]

For all his unclear words, Piper is here obviously following Fuller's view that faith comes from a godly disposition which receives grace, rather than an ungodly disposition which is given grace. This clearly departs from New Testament teaching. Romans 4:5 is no dark, one-off

[12] *Andrew Fuller* p. 51.

passage which cannot stand on its own merit. Romans 5:10 repeats the truth as if to make sure that this doctrine is clearly understood:

> For if, when we were enemies, we were reconciled to God by the death of his Son, much more, being reconciled, we shall be saved by his life.

This wonderful and graceful truth is to be found throughout all Scripture. Grace is not engendered in sinners by the sinner's reception but in God's giving it to lost sinners. Faith by grace is Christ's love demonstrated where no reciprocal love was in existence. The reciprocity comes with the giving as a gift of dependency. It is Christ's faith which is given the hitherto unbeliever for salvation and not the appropriation of the believer's own.

Fuller's arguments here have never been challenged by Fullerite scholars though many orthodox scholars have challenged them and been called 'Hyper-Calvinists' and 'Antinomians' for doing so. Though I have argued for the unchanged status of the Law of God in Christ as God's eternal standard since the commencement of my Christian writings some sixty years ago, BOT Fullerites such as Maurice Roberts still call me an Antinomian on their websites though my respect and love for the Law is demonstrably far greater than theirs as they have no lasting Law whereas God's Law reveals His eternal Nature. I can say faithfully with David that I love the eternal Law of God and will love it eternally. Contrary to knowing that one is safe in the Law because of Christ fulfilling it, Fuller and those who blandly follow him preach in unbelief the temporary nature of God's Law and limit his Church to a holy few who wear his Closed Communion badge. It is no wonder that the NCT is composed of many former Fullerites and they are Fullerites still. This is true Antinomianism without a mask.

Piper, however, goes even beyond Fuller and is worried that people will think:

> If God justifies the ungodly, then faith must be ungodly because God justifies by faith. If the natural man cannot receive the message of the cross, then don't urge him to receive it; it's pointless and cruel. Sound logic is not the enemy of exegesis. But

more errors than we know flow from the claim to logic that contradicts the Bible.

One wonders what has produced this odd and quite bizarre logic in Piper's mind concerning how those who disagree with him think.[13]

So, too, those who pit Fuller against imaginary Hyper-Calvinists represent a 'Calvinism' which was never Calvin's, setting aside especially Calvin's doctrines of both man and God. It is here where their spade-work really ought to start in discovering what Haykin calls 'The Forgotten Fuller. The ground for the major error in Fuller's theology has to do with what Luther rightly called the bondage of the will and Calvin saw as indicating total depravity. Fuller never accepted these fundamental Biblical, Reformed doctrines and would not accept that he was totally disabled from communion with God as a fallen sinner. He argued time and time again that if man were absolutely depraved there could be no hope of salvation for him so he must have a spark of something inside him out of which God could kindle a flame. Man's disbelief, Fuller argues, had nothing to do with lack of ability but with lack of interest and will. The Fall, says Fuller:

> represents man as not only possessing great advantages but as able to comply with everything that God requires at his hand; and that all his misery arises from his voluntary abuse of mercy, and his wilful rebellion against God. It is not want of ability, but of inclination, that proves his ruin.[14]

This is a principle held stubbornly by most modern Fullerites. Erroll Hulse, for instance, wrote:

> There is nothing to hinder him (a fallen sinner) from being spiritual except his indisposition, his rebellion, his sin, his unwillingness. He is absolutely free to do good, to be spiritual, to repent, to believe. That is, he is a free agent.[15]

---

[13] See Piper's *Andrew Fuller*, pp. 55-57.
[14] Three volume edition, Vol. 1, 38.
[15] *The Great Invitation*, p. 60.

If this is 'Calvinism', what is the difference between 'Calvinism' and 'Arminianism' or 'Christianity' and 'Rationalism'? According to many Fullerites, they are all the same on this point.

Fuller's figurative theology and missionary ideals

Strangely enough, it is Fuller's 'figurative' or merely 'moral' understanding of man's state of being aware of his saving duties to God, to use Fuller's expressions, which moves Piper to support Fuller's gospel. This leads him to make the grandiose claim that his mentor transformed world-wide missionary activity and his doctrine of justifying faith led to true gospel preaching and 'the greatest missionary movement in world history'.

The truth is that Fuller brought strife and turmoil to the existing united evangelism of the international and indigenous missionary work in Northern India which had continued harmoniously for two hundred years before Fuller's radical interference. His ratio-political and institutional novelties challenged the Biblical doctrine of the Atonement strongly as I have pointed out in my book *Atonement in Modern Evangelical Thought*. Christ's Atonement was not complete according to Fuller until duty-faith was exercised by the sinner which was confirmed and finalised in Fullerite baptism. Children, according to Fuller, are thus shut out from God's Covenant of Grace, Salvation and true Church Membership.[16]

Fuller's positive influence in India is a myth

Fullerite faked-news is that their idol pioneered the very best of missionary outreaches and was a pioneer missiologist *par excellence.* This is a myth that must be combatted. His interference in the Indian Mission was not only petty, it was disastrous. Fuller cut off the ropes with which he promised to hold Carey only a year or two after Carey embarked for India. Abraham Booth said that Carey was now 'lost' but he said the same of Fuller shortly later. Booth in 1796 was to combat Fuller's gospel of Rationalism in his work *Glad Tidings to Perishing Sinners or, the Genuine Gospel a Complete Warrant for the Ungodly to*

[16] I am not referring to Fuller's idea of an institutionalised adult membership of a Baptist Church here but the Body of Believers, the Bride of Christ and the People of God irrespective of man-made strictures and conditions.

Believe in Jesus. It is quite unbelievable to me to read of Fullerites linking Booth with Fuller when they were two opposites regarding the Biblical gospel which saves.

Fuller the meddler in missionary affairs

Fuller interfered terribly in the theology, organisation, policies, politics and practice of the mission as an absentee bishop aided by John Ryland Junior who opened the doors to Socinian preachers at Bristol. Both 'rope-holders' Fuller and Ryland disagreed radically with the Indian Mission's ecclesiology. Again, we must emphasise that Carey had to complain that Fuller was 'killing' (Carey's actual word) his missionaries and Ryland was acting criminally (again Carey's actual word) and told Fuller that he must realise that the Indian mission could not be run on British political and legal lines when Fuller strove to have the Serampore earnings and property regulated by a British Bank under his control. The BMS claimed full authority over the mission whose funds were their major income and, against Carey's plea for no foreign interference, sent a rival team to oust Carey from his position in Serampore where he was working closely with Lutheran, Independent and Anglican missionaries.

Forbidding Christian communion in India

Fuller refused the Baptist missionaries the right of Christian communion with their missionary colleagues and protested against their coming together to work out missionary strategies. These non-Baptist missionary colleagues had welcomed Carey to Calcutta and paved the way for his acceptance by the Danish and British authorities. The idea that Carey found Calcutta void of Christian witness is a further myth spread by modern Fullerites. There were several Christian mission churches at the time in Calcutta run by missionaries who had won thousands for Christ – more than Carey ever won. This pre-Carey history is almost totally ignored by BMS friendly writers who have just not taken the trouble to research beyond their BMS borders and discarded also much that was good in Baptist missionary work in India in the process. We badly need a Baptist missiologist who will give us a thorough, comprehensive portrayal of international Baptist missionary work in India.

Fuller neglects his church for money-raising activities

Fuller, who saw his missionary task now as a collector of inter-denominational monies, neglecting his own church for as much as four months absence per year[17] to go on canvassing trips, though he did not object to other denominations and international non-Baptist Missionary Societies paying for Carey's translation works. Fuller's begging money for India was hardly better than begging money to build the Roman pontifical palace and which was no help to true religion in India at all. Even Protestants have their Tetzels! Furthermore, the bulk of the sums raised by Fuller for fictive missionary work was a fraction of what the BHS received from Serampore and Calcutta and was not used in India and what little was loaned to the Serampore and Calcutta missionaries was paid back with great interest by the Serampore Trio. Fuller's work as a businessman relying on others to finance his money-machine had nothing to do with pastoral, Christian, employment though most Fullerites trade it as such today.

Evangelical organisations stopped funding Baptist enterprises

When it became most evident that the Baptists were theologically and linguistically not equal to their translation tasks, relying on Hindu and Muslim Pundits, paid by the Danish and British governments and works borrowed from secular sources, the other missionaries and their supporters dropped their funding. They also challenged the Baptists' language competence. Yet the BMS, after cutting the ropes binding them to a joint Christian witness in India, then criticised the other denominations, chiefly through Yates, for being the rope-cutters. They demanded monies from the Bible Societies for their own rather fanciful translations. Yates, one of the better educated Baptist missionaries, now turned against the BMS and supported rival, non-Baptist denominational establishments before striving to finance his own educational facilities. He then gave up missionary work altogether, Roy and Adam faded from the Baptist scene.

---

[17] Aspland Jr. claims that Carey was absent from his church for up to four months per year but authors claim that Carey was absent three months at a time. Aspland is referring to Fuller's total absence from Kettering per annum, pp. 76, 77, *Memoirs*.

Carey, Marshman and Ward failed in their missionary call

Carey was mostly a stay-at-home, tied to his governmental office in Calcutta and his secular teaching in Serampore. Carey's major tasks were to keep living at the high standard he had chosen and to take up dubious linguistic translations. Christopher Smith rightly says, 'Carey was much more of a mission motivator and Bible translator than a pioneer in the heart of India or a missionary strategist.'[18] Francis Augustus Cox, who knew the Serampore Trio personally, wrote:

> Carey, Marshman and Ward had long deplored their inability as missionaries to itinerate as missionaries, on account of their domestic labours in translating, printing, and Superintendence of schools.[19]

As the Trio were fully taken up in business and administrative work, they appointed Krishna (also Krishno) to do their missionary work for them. Wishing to keep control of missionary activities they put him under the supervision of an Englishman who was in no way Krishna's equal as an evangelist. Sadly, the Serampore Trio did not take all this as a sign that they should return to their missionary status but became full-time employees under the British and Danish governments.

The home committee fostered Arianism rather than Christian co-operation

Truly sound Baptist itinerant, church-founding missionaries like Chamberlain are hardly honoured by Fullerite Baptists. Kettering was now upgraded to London for Board meetings but the BMS departed further from the Serampore Trio until they rejected them entirely. Yet why, we may ask, did the BMS employ at least two Arian writers for their Baptist secular newspapers, yet would not have the Serampore Trio hob-nobbling with sound and successful evangelical missionaries whose societies had been working in India for over a hundred years with great success? Church of England missionaries such as George Lewis were evangelising India in the seventeenth century as were the Danes under Worm and then Ziegenbalg from 1706-7 onward. Ziegenbalg

[18] Bu.edu/missionary-biography/c-d/carey-william, 27. 01. 2016.
[19] Cox's *History*, p. 235.

accomplished all the 'firsts' Carey's biographers attribute to Carey simply because they are quite ignorant of India's Christian history. Carey was very much open to working with the international team throughout India but Fuller would not tolerate it.

Carey found strong backing from Danish and British governments
We must remember, too, that Carey came to Calcutta without a permit but was nevertheless very kindly supported not only by the Danish government in Serampore but by the British government in Calcutta. Thus, the idea that the British government suppressed the Baptist mission is yet another myth which Carey's biographers continue to teach. So, too, it is a common belief amongst Baptists that it was Fuller who persuaded the British Government to open India's doors to missionaries in 1813 but this was primarily the work of Grant, Brown, Wilberforce and other Church of England evangelicals. The fact is that there was a strong welcome for Carey in India from the Danes, Dutch, Swedes, Germans and British already working there, besides the many native Christians of the day. The Serampore Trio were all for joining this well-established missionary thrust but Fuller put his foot down urging and commanding the BMS missionaries not to rock his boat.

Admittedly, Fuller rightly criticised Carey for neglecting his missionary duties by reading and translating 'cultural' works which hindered his spare-time missionary work for years. So, too, the BMS were against the founding of the Serampore secular college though modern reports in the Baptist Quarterly maintain that it was a project of the BMS and not founded by the Danes as their third university after Copenhagen and Kiel. However, Fuller had apparently no objection to Carey's work as a full-time civil servant in a BEIC and British government college for budding administrators with a dazzling high salary, most of which Carey ploughed back into the BMS which benefitted mightily from the Serampore secular incomes. There would be nothing wrong in this were it not for Fuller's constant boast that the Serampore Mission was run as a charity depending on individual donations and the missionary society. This was simply not true.

The Carey Center Home Page entry of Feb. 6, 2007 sums up Fuller's life in the words:

> Fuller was a man of great force and energy of character. His turn of mind, according to one of his biographers (J. W. Morris), led him to cultivate the intellectual and practical parts of religion rather than the devotional. His want of fervour and unction in preaching and in prayer was remarked on by several of his friends, who attributed to this cause the want of adequate success in his ministerial work. A friend once stopped him with the remark, 'Brother Fuller, you can never administer a reproof to a mistaken friend but you must take up a sledge-hammer and knock his brains out.' A missionary in India, whom he had sharply admonished, thus replied, 'Thank you, Brother Fuller; your sledge-hammer is a harmless thing at this distance! Samson, too, is sometimes as meek as other men.' Of this tendency he was aware, and he sometimes lamented it; but when he tried to apologise he seemed to make things worse. To his sterling integrity, the nobility of the objects to which he devoted his life, and the spirit of self-denial in which he prosecuted them, all who knew him bore the fullest testimony. He has been compared to John Knox, both in respect to his excellences and his defects.

Comparing the facts with fancy

The above, sober account of Fuller's theology may come as a surprise to some in view of what such Baptist historians as George Winfried Hervey have related. After telling us that Fuller's first meeting with Carey in his cobbler's shop was 'among the great beginnings of modern Christian progress', he says of Fuller:

> He is now only a very obscure Baptist pastor, but destined to become one of the greatest of theologians, the morning star of modern Calvinism, the easy vanquisher of the great Unitarian philosopher Priestly, the exploder of the great Robert Hall's beautiful theory of over-free Communion, the real author of the principle subject-matter of Chalmer's grandiloquent discourse on Astronomy. And yet this man of great thoughts has room in his soul for a world-embracing benevolence.[20]

[20] *The Story of Baptist Missions*, p.1.

Hervey and A. H. Burlingham, the author of his Introduction, can both say this as they quite deny that any substantial missionary work had been done in India before Fuller's days. The result is that Hervey starts his history with Fuller and Carey being obviously unaware of what went on before. Burlingham tells us that previous Bible translations were the work of 'Pedo-Baptists' as if this disqualified them as translators and the results were 'sectarian collocations' and thus could not be compared with the work of 'our missionaries', that is the Baptists and that former missionaries previous to 1792, with the possible exception of the Moravians, were sent sporadically and had no reference 'to the heathens as such' but were chiefly to foreign residents and colonials. The story of Ziegenbalg is left fully out of the historical overview and Burlingham says that such as Schulze and Schwartz were only 'occasional' and 'individual' and 'sporadic' instances of foreign care for the Indians. He complains also that they were not 'institutionalised'. Hervey states that the original Herzog Real Encyclopädie contained most positive reports of Baptist missionaries which the American translators of the Schaff-Herzog translation left out but Schaff began translations work before Herzog finished his German work. Hervey's work was completed before the completed, updated translation of Herzog's third edition which contains an abundant number of testimonies to the Baptists in India placed in their correct historical context. As Burlingham gives neither page nor volume of either Herzog's or Schaff's works and shows no exact textual knowledge of either to back up his statements, one can only assume he is working from hearsay.

The fact is, however, that Carey did little missionary work between 1792 and 1802 and later the Serampore work was mostly amongst Europeans and Colonials. According to the facts aired in the book, as opposed to the fancies, a real Baptist breakthrough first came to the then East Indies in 1878. This, we are told, however, was the work of American Baptists, not the British BMS. Then the era of Carey and Fuller was long over. Meanwhile it was the Indians whom the British Baptists 'employed', as Cox puts it, who mostly evangelized the Indians.

Part 7

The Era of Thomas and Carey

Chapter Eighteen

Thomas Returns to India with William Carey

A fascinating story

Ever since 1966 when my Professor of Missions at Uppsala, Bengt Sundkler, presented his students with facsimiles of Carey's *An Enquiry into the Obligation of Christians to use Means for the Conversion of the Heathen* building on the work of the Tranquebar Mission through Schwartz and told us inspiring tales of Carey's life in Calcutta, I have been fascinated with the story of William Carey and how his various reputations have been handled in subsequent works on Indian evangelism. Prof. Sundkler said he had learnt from Carey to drop all fastidious controversy and put the Church of the Lord Jesus Christ before formal denominationalism. Fired on by Carey's over-confessional and inter confessional views of evangelism, Sundkler became a missionary himself. However, though a Sundkler, a Culross, a Myers, a Pearce Carey, several Smiths, a Jones, a Bullen, a Walker, a George, a Potts and a Webber have written at length on Carey, such as myself feel that the full true life of that very human but godly man has still to be portrayed. What has been portrayed has often passed into the legendary or even mythical. In striving to give Carey a write-up void of historical accuracy, many of his novelist biographers have done both him and the cause of the Indian Missions a deep disservice. Indeed, Carey even in his life time has been picked on in Baptist history to portray the perfect missionary though he protested at this false notion and was never a missionary either in the traditional sense or according to modern dictionaries.

As many biographers, mostly Baptists, have misrepresented and even idolised Carey and merely used him as a name-carrier for their own ideas, Carey's real achievements have been neglected by concentrating on parts, mostly edited or taken from secondary sources, and making them wholes. So, too, Carey's idea of missionary work has never been really studied, acknowledged or examined in Baptist scholarship. Today, we need a large team of inter-national evangelical authors of many categories both male and female to do full justice to Carey's memory. Even then, the danger would be that such authors would compromise on essential features of Carey's life so as to avoid controversy respecting denominational views. Carey himself was quite aware of this falsifying of his beliefs and history and protested that while his work was not yet done and it was far too soon to evaluate the overall impact of his mission, churches, denominations, missionary societies, political parties and philanthropic societies were already inventing 'lives' of him which were pure fiction. Sadly, most modern evaluations have been built on these 'lives'. The search for the historical Carey goes on.

Carey's home background

William Carey was born in Paulerspury, Northamptonshire on 17th August, 1761, and was the first of Edmund and Elizabeth Carey's five children. Edmund was a weaver, a member of the Established Church and he also kept a small school and served as the parish clerk. So, Carey was no mean peasant as so often depicted. Edmund home-schooled William to read, write and study the Scriptures and introduced him to Bunyan's *Pilgrim's Progress* whilst a young child. He was to find Christ through the preaching of Church of England minister Thomas Scott, friend of Cowper and Newton. William's Uncle Peter told him stories of his travels as a soldier and also taught him the joys of gardening. Carey suffered from bad eyesight as a child and could not see in strong sunlight so a gardening career was out of the question. He thus started his adult life at 14 as an apprentice cobbler and remained in the trade for some 28 years. John Warr, a fellow-apprentice and Dissenter lent Carey books which prepared him for Scott's preaching and to respect both the Church of England and Dissent. In the days of his youth, the 'dipped and sprinkled' as William Cowper testified, 'lived in peace'. Neither Thomas Scott nor John Sutcliff the pastor of the Olney Baptist Church at that time put their denomination before Christian unity. The surrounding churches had been strongly influenced by Bunyan so water-baptism was no bar to communion and 'open-communion' was commonly practised. This was sadly to change in the Baptist churches which followed Fuller.

The Particular Baptist Association

In 1764 six churches joined to form the Particular Baptist Association and by 1779 whilst Carey found his fellowship with those of John Bunyan's persuasion in Hackleton and Olney, the immersion issue had become prominent and John Sutcliff (1752-1840), the Olney Baptist pastor became one of the first immersionist-only pastors at Olney. However, he still fellowshipped with the local Church of England ministers such as Moses Brown, John Newton, Thomas Scott, C. Stephenson and Henry Gauntlett and organized meetings with them. It was thus a common sight in Olney to see Sutcliff taking an evening stroll arm in arm with the Olney vicar and his curate. So, too, John Ryland Senior, one of the greatest of Baptist soul-winners communed openly, alongside Booth with such Church of England stalwarts as Hervey and Toplady.

Cowper on Anglican and Baptist sweet fellowship in Olney

The Church of England poet and educationalist William Cowper writes of the great spiritual times he had with the new Baptist denomination as he told his aunt, Mrs Madan on 18th June, 1768:

> We have had a Holiday Week at Olney. The Association of Baptist Ministers met here on Wednesday. We had three Sermons from them that day, and One on Thursday, besides Mr. Newton's (John Newton, 1725-1807) in the Evening. One of the Preachers was Mr. Booth, (Abraham Booth, 1734-1806, was to become the pastor of a Calvinistic Baptist Church at Little Prescot Street, Goodman's Fields some seven months later) who has lately published an excellent Work called the Reign of Grace. He was bred a Weaver, and has been forced to work with his Hands hitherto for the Maintenance of himself and a large Family. But the Lord who has given him excellent Endowments, has now called him from the small Congregation he minister'd to in

> Nottinghamshire, to supply Mr. Burford's Place in London (Samuel Burford was pastor of a Calvinistic Baptist Church at Currier's Hall, Cripplegate). It was a comfortable Sight to see thirteen Gospel Ministers together. Most of them either Preach'd or Pray'd and All that did so approved themselves sound in the Word and Doctrine, whence a good Presumption arises in favour of the rest. I should be glad if the Partition Wall between Christians of different Denominations would every where fall down flat as it has done at Olney. The Dissenters here, most of them at least who are serious, forget that our Meeting House has a Steeple to it, and we that theirs has none. This shall be the Case universally, may the Lord hasten it in his time!
>
> I am my dear Aunt your very affectionate Nephew
>
> Wm Cowper

Needless to say, all these ministers were invited to dine with Newton and later Thomas Scott (1747-1821), supporters of Indian Missions, at the Vicarage.

Carey, after sitting under Olney's Anglican pastor Thomas Scott, wrote later in his Memoir that it was at this time that he was enabled 'to depend on a crucified Saviour for pardon and salvation; and to seek a system of doctrine in the Word of God'. After conversion, Carey was gradually won over to immersionism and was subsequently 'baptised' by John Ryland Jr. (1743-1825) in the River Nene on 5th October, 1783, though he still looked to Christians of all denomination for his fellowship and cooperation in evangelism. His friend Andrew Fuller could never follow Carey's ecclesiological calling. He referred to Carey's interest in world-wide missionary endeavours as but 'pleasant dreams' which he refused to support. Carey's wife Dolly did not join him in his rebaptism being satisfied with her own original baptism. This dividing of the waters and separation from her old life was most likely the cause of Dolly's depressions as later eye-witness accounts describe.

Carey rejected by the Olney Baptists as a preacher

After altering his views on baptism Carey immediately applied to the Olney church to be set apart as a preacher. Carey thus preached a trial sermon in the summer of 1785 but the church turned him down as they felt that he had no ability for preaching. Carey, however, disregarded the views of his pastor and fellow-church members and started to preach in and outside of his new denomination without his own church's blessing. He then accepted a call to Moulton Baptist Church on a salary of £12 per year and applied to the Particular Baptist Fund for further financial support and received a grant of £5 from them.

A search for information on world-wide Christian opportunities
At this time Carey's reading centred around Captain Cook's Voyages and stories of the spread of the British Empire but he soon found access to reports of missionary outreaches in India, North America, Greenland and Abyssinia pioneered by the Danes and Germans, mostly through magazine articles. He then looked back at the appeals of Church of England William Romaine and Independent Philip Doddridge in the seventeen-forties for the evangelization of the world and the calls for the united prayer of all Christians concerning such a world-wide ministry amongst the Presbyterians of America and Scotland. He studied carefully the Anglican missions to the New World and was in agony to find Baptists had taken no initiative in the gospel call for world-wide evangelism. Leaning on German Schwartz and older English writers on India such as White, he began to write down his appeal to the Baptists to follow the Continental missionaries. He now asked Sutcliff to teach him Greek and Hebrew and also tackled Latin, Dutch and French.

Carey finds his pastor's and shoemaker's salaries too low
Carey's vision of receiving a living wage for his pastoral duties seemed an impossibility. He was now reduced to a pittance of £9-10 a year whereas his fellow Baptist pastors were supported by their churches with salaries up to and over £100 a year. They often received higher salaries than Church of England curates and pastors. A benevolent cobbler told Carey to give up cobbling to bring in more money and he would give Carey 10 shillings a week so that he would have more time for language study and another friend gave him £10 so that he could publish his *Enquiry*. Though he left Moulten for a larger church at Harvest Lane with better payment, Carey still could not make ends meet and had to return to boot-making.

Carey accepted back into the Association fold

Harvest Lane Baptist Church was riddled with immorality and many left Carey's new church on his becoming their pastor, fearing he would condemn their practices, which Carey did. At last Carey decided to disband the corrupt Baptist membership altogether and started with a *tabula rasa*. This move was crowned with great success and Carey was now accepted back into fellowship by the local Association. Now Carey was officially recognized as a *bona fide* Baptist pastor and his inauguration was conducted by John Ryland Jun., Samuel Pearce (1766-1799), Andrew Fuller (1754-1815), and John Sutcliff (1752-1814).

Carey and Pearce's plans for a missionary society rejected by the local Baptists

Pearce after reading of the shipwrecked crew of the Antelope now considered a call to the Pelew Islands and Carey, after reading Cook's Voyages felt a strong desire to go to Otaheite as a missionary and shared his plans with Pearce. The two men then put forward proposals for a Baptist Missionary Society to send them off to the lands of their choices. At first their proposals were rejected by their Baptist brethren. Fuller had no part in these pioneering thoughts. However, when Carey published his *Enquiry* in 1792, this moved many to think again about world evangelism. It must be noted here that Sutcliff, Ryland and Fuller were initially against Carey's going to print and told him he must go it alone. When the *Enquiry* was finished, Carey did not tell Sutcliff, Ryland and Fuller for fear of offending them.[1]

When twenty-four association churches gathered at Friar Lane Nottingham in May, 1792, and Carey was invited to preach and expound his ideas concerning foreign missionary work, his ideas were again rejected. His older and more experienced brethren including Sutcliff, Fuller, Ryland and Beddome told him to start evangelizing around his own doorstep before trying to convert Indians to Christ. Now Fuller comes into the scene. Carey then begged Fuller to make a proposal to save his cause so Fuller moved 'that a plan be prepared against the next ministers' meeting at Kettering, for forming a Baptist Society for propagating the gospel among the heathen'. Fuller and his

[1] See Cox's *History of the Baptist Missionary Society*, Vol. I, p. 6 ff.

friends made it clear, according to Cox who knew Fuller, Sutcliff and Ryland well, that he was doing this merely for Carey's sake and a possible future development but Carey's proposals were not for the present day.

A Missionary Society is founded

When the next association meeting was held on 2 October only twelve ministers, a deacon and a student attended. The only minister from another Baptist association was Pearce. Carey called those who attended the meeting 'nobodies from nowhere'. After a rousing plea Carey won over Sutcliff, Ryland, Fuller and Reynold Hogg of Thrapston in Northamptonshire for his and Pearce's proposals and these pledged themselves to becoming the planning executives of a new missionary society. This newly formed society was not initially sanctioned by the Baptist Churches of Britain as a whole, nor even by the local Association but represented a small group of local men who had little idea of the role they should take on.

Sutcliff had planned an interdenominational prayer effort which was said to be the start of the missionary movement in the 1780s and had republished Edwards' *An Humble Attempt to Promote explicit, Agreement and Visible Union of God's People in Extraordinary Prayer*. His thrust was thus not limited to Baptists but for all God's people. Nor was it limited to India. Just when John Thomas came on the scene to modify this Baptist world-wide vision has caused unnecessary debate in missionary literature. His appearance is usually placed today after Carey's decision to go to India. This view must be reconsidered as the records paint quite a different picture. Cox in his BMS *History*, quotes from Leighton:

> Leighton Williams et al. tell us in their collection Serampore Letters: Being the Unpublished Correspondence of William Carey and Others with John Williams 1800-1816 that Pearce and Carey felt the missionary call to Pelew Islands and Otaheite respectively:
>
> But just at this moment a gentleman named Mr. Thomas returned from Bengal, who had repeatedly written

> thence to the leading Baptist ministers in England, giving an account of his conferences with the natives.

They go on to say concerning the foundation of the BMS:

> 'We found,' says Dr Ryland, 'that he (Thomas) was now endeavouring to raise a fund for a mission to that country (India), and to engage a companion to go out with him. It was, therefore, resolved to make some further inquiry respecting him and to invite him to go back under the patronage of our Society.'[2]

This is confirmed in Cox's *History of the Baptist Missionary Society* where the author says:

> At their third meeting, held at Northampton, Nov. 13, 1792, a letter was received from Mr. Carey, stating that a Mr. Thomas, a surgeon from Bengal, was raising a fund in London for a mission to that country, and was also endeavouring to obtain a companion in his work. He expressed an apprehension lest this should interfere with their more enlarged plan, and a wish to amalgamate the funds. Mr. Fuller was commissioned to make inquiries respecting Mr. Thomas, – his character and proceedings.[3]

We read that Fuller was happy with his enquiries and that:

> At the meeting in January, 1793, the report given by the secretary, respecting Mr. Thomas, was highly satisfactory; and 'the committee, being fully of opinion that a door was now open in the East Indies, for preaching the gospel to the heathen, agreed to invite Mr. Thomas to go out under the patronage of the Society; engaging to furnish him with a companion, if a suitable one can be obtained.' Brother Carey was then asked, whether, in case Mr. Thomas should accede to our proposal, he was inclined to accompany him. To this, he readily answered in the affirmative. The same evening, Mr. Thomas himself arrived at

---

[2] *Serampore Letters*, p. 11.
[3] Cox, p. 19.

> Kettering, and fully acceded to all our proposals. 'It was late in the evening', says Mr. Morris, who was an eye-witness, 'while they were in full deliberation, his arrival was announced. Impatient to behold his colleague, he entered the room in haste, and Mr. Carey rising from his seat, they fell on each other's necks, and wept.[4]

It is quite clear from such sources that Thomas, not Carey was asked to represent the BMS in India and Carey was to be his assistant. John Thomas was thus the BMS' first missionary choice.

So, too, according to early chroniclers such as Williams, mentioned above, it appears that the initiative to pioneer a Missionary Society came from Sutcliff and Ryland rather than either Carey, Pearce or Fuller and Carey told the newly formed Society that he would go anywhere they sent him. This means that the BMS missionary candidates had no certain idea of where Carey and Pearce should be sent until they were motivated by Thomas who was looking for funds and an assistant which turned out to be Carey. The BMS funds for India were thus committed to Thomas and not Carey. That Carey eventually took over the leadership from Thomas is a fact that I believe has not been adequately examined by modern missiologists.

Society membership widened theologically to bring in more money The Particular Baptist Missionary Society started on a most humble financial basis. The question arose how they would pay their missionaries' salaries. However, the members at the meeting had not been prepared for what was now decided and a collection revealed that most pockets were empty. Finally promises were gained from the founding members concerning future donations which amounted to the humble sum of £13. 2s 6d. It was decided that a membership fee should be charged all those who wished to join the Missionary Society, irrespective of Christian standing. Spurgeon was later to protest strongly that the Baptist Mission Society allowed anyone to join it, provided they paid a membership fee of 10s 6d. It is quite plain that Fuller's opening the Society to all, though it strengthened Fuller's reputation, did the society no theological good.

---

[4] Cox, p. 20.

This was also the start of Fuller's life-long canvassing for cash, mostly from other denominations, which caused him to neglect his own pastoral duties for months at a time each year. The people of Yorkshire were especially generous and the poor blind curate of Bradford willingly parted with a guinea on hearing that the gospel was to be spread abroad. Not to be outdone, his more affluent Vicar gave the same amount but not a penny more. Many Baptist ministers complained, arguing that the home churches were destitute and ought to be supported with such monies, fully knowing that they often came from non-Baptist sources.

Fuller falls for Thomas' persuasive talk

Fuller was now most zealous to take his part in the running of the new Baptist Mission but had more enthusiasm than understanding of what abilities a missionary ought to have. After meeting John Thomas who was on a fund-raising tour, Fuller discovered that Thomas had intended to visit the founder's meeting at Kettering but had forgotten the date. He suggested by letter that he and the new Society should join hands and funds and they could then provide him with a companion missionary. Thomas had obvious abilities and had studied medicine, but had been something of a rake and was permanently in debt. The idea of being financed by a Missionary Society appealed to him though up to this time Thomas could not be trusted with anyone's money, not even his own. According to Ryland, the BMS was fully aware of this fact. Being totally without money, Thomas had deserted his family, signed on as a ship's surgeon to India and had left his wife and family without a penny to look after themselves. The idea of being a primary missionary in a wage-paying Society appealed to him greatly especially as he was on the run from his creditors for the umpteenth time.

It was Thomas alone who persuaded the Particular Baptist Society as it was first called to turn its gaze on India. Thus, Thomas is the true founder of the Baptist Mission to India, indeed he was the first missionary to be accepted by what came to be called the BMS and Carey was merely seen as one who would accompany Thomas back to India as an assistant. Samuel Pearce was left out of the picture.

Thomas was the Baptist pioneer in India

Thomas, who gained Fuller's interest appears to have been the first British Baptist to preach in Bengali and had already translated parts of both the New and the Old Testaments into the Bengali dialect he had picked up in Calcutta. He had already been the means of converting several high-caste Brahmins and several English noblemen and at least one Portuguese and this must be recognized and esteemed. However, he had always lived far beyond his financial means and felt that living off other people was nothing to be ashamed of. Fuller gazed at Thomas in adoration, so thrilled was he to meet one who had actually evangelized as a foreign missionary. Ignoring Thomas' reputation in financial matters and family responsibility, Fuller recommended Thomas as God's opening door for the Society and urged them to back him and invited the doctor to attend a meeting of the Society on January 9, 1793. Thomas came, saw, and conquered and dazzled and amazed everyone with his news from India. At last, they had a real missionary in their midst and a Baptist at that!

Thomas' weaknesses were not aired at the founding of the PBMS

Although the new Mission knew about Thomas' debts, Ryland now looked into the matter and concluded that Thomas' difficulties would not hinder his plans to return to India. Williams tells us:

> Although a man of real piety, Mr. Thomas had been 'guilty of many faults, many weaknesses, and many failures'; but the result of the inquiry proved on the whole satisfactory, and it was resolved that Carey and Thomas should proceed to India together.

Ryland's verdict seems to have removed any doubts that the committee might have had concerning Thomas' character and financial standing. Obviously, Ryland had not looked deeply enough into the matter. Thomas now told a wide-eyed Carey how easy it was for a missionary to provide for himself on the Indian mission field, without telling Carey how he had been a bhikşuka (beggar) and accrued great debts. So now Carey dropped his idea of Otaheite, opted for India and volunteered to join Thomas on his return to India at the Mission's expenses. Carey had already stated, rather naïvely in his *Enquiry*, that if missionaries were provided with 'clothing, a few knives, powder and shot fishing tackle and the articles of husbandry to cultivate a little spot of ground just for their support', they could maintain themselves. This was certainly true but it was not the path either Carey or Thomas trod when they eventually reached Calcutta and were given the very opportunities outlined in the *Enquiry*.

Carey sent out as Thomas' apprentice

Up to this time it was obvious that Carey was to be sent out as an apprentice to Thomas who was viewed as a star of great magnitude. Sutcliff and Ryland Jun. did not attend the meeting with Thomas but the remaining executives entered formally into partnership with him. Fuller later told Sutcliff and Ryland, 'It is a great undertaking, but surely it is right'. On returning to Leicester, Carey informed Dolly of his decision to depart for India immediately. His wife refused point blank to go, thinking the scheme impossible. She reminded Carey that he was in poor health and she was eight months' pregnant and perhaps she and the child would lose their lives on such a hazardous journey to the other side of the world. Then Carey's church protested strongly and Carey's own father who had nurtured him in the gospel said his son had gone mad. Brave but neglected Dolly lovingly told Carey that if he went, she would follow in three or four years when their unborn child would be old and strong enough for the exhausting journey. Dolly told Carey he could take their eight-year-old Felix with him so as not to be quite divorced from his family. This shows how loving and sensible Dolly was.

Great obstacles delay embarkation for India

Thomas and Carey planned to sail in March 1793 but after their valedictory meetings and tearful departures from their loved ones, they met with great obstacles. Carey did not bother to apply for a permit to India which the East India Company demanded, fearing he would never be given one. He thus decided to smuggle himself on a ship bound for India and stay hidden throughout the long journey of up to a year or even much more. So, he approached 'good old father Newton' and asked if he ought to risk travelling illegally. Newton's advice was 'Conclude that your Lord has nothing there for you to accomplish. If he have, no power on earth can prevent you'. This ambiguous statement moved Carey to risk travelling illegally. The party thus boarded a ship in London and sailed to Portsmouth where a protection convoy was to join them.

Carey finds out that Thomas was on the run

Then Carey realized for the first time that in spite of Ryland's assurances, Thomas was actually on the run from the authorities and would have difficulty leaving England without paying his debts first. Indeed, Thomas' creditors now looked to the Law to stop the party leaving the country. Thomas was apprehended by the law authorities and escorted to London to sort matters out leaving Carey to face extra expenses caused by the delay, now not knowing whether the journey could start or not. Carey was now on the wrong side of the law himself in attempting an illegal passage to India in a British ship.

Carey prepared to neglect his wife and family

Meanwhile, Carey preached in the Baptist and Independent churches along the coastline which helped his funding. On 6 May, Carey heard that Dolly had delivered a healthy child. Instead of rushing to her side where he belonged and was free to do, Carey told Dolly that his sense of duty overpowered all other considerations and insulted his wife by telling her that unlike Dolly, Mrs Thomas was making the journey. So, like Thomas, he was prepared to desert his wife and new born child. Carey's unloving remark was scarcely true of Mrs Thomas as her husband was more or less under arrest and she was a scandalously neglected wife and mother and now she was left forsaken on the harbour-side with her daughter. Thomas returned on 23 May and found Carey, Felix and Mrs Thomas still standing forlorn on the jetty. The ship had sailed without them. The captain had been ordered by the authorities to leave the missionaries behind because of Thomas' debts. This was the start of the BMS mission to India.

Carey promises never to leave Dolly again

Carey now returned home to Dolly and promised he would never leave her again and had given up his missionary plans. However, Thomas with his persuasive tongue had found someone who was ready to pay off his creditors. He even found a Danish ship which would carry them legally to India. So now Thomas dashed to Carey's home and pleaded with his whole family not to give up their enterprise. Thomas was so successful in his persuasive talk that even Dolly relented and agreed to accompany Carey to India with her children and her sister. Now it was Andrew Fuller's turn to draw back. His nerves and stamina broke and he complained about Thomas' 'debts and embranglements'. However, Yorkshire and London friends came to the rescue with extra finances and Thomas quickly found new sponsors and through his enormous energies and powers of persuasion, soon had the party in Dover, ready to board a Danish ship legally as restrictions for Carey were only on British vessels. However, they reached the docks but could not find the ship. Nigh panic gripped the friends again and they had to wait another two weeks, until the belated ship glided into the dock. On 15 June she set sail for India with the missionaries and their families safely on board. The time of anxiety and chaos was to end for a while but Fuller's nerves were broken.

The sea journey

Carey used the sea voyage wisely to learn Bengali from Thomas and he used his knowledge of Hebrew to assist Thomas in his Bengali translation of Genesis. The voyage was surprisingly speedy, taking only five months. The ship's owner-captain known to all as 'Captain Christmas', proved a good and faithful friend and used his Danish connections to make sure that Carey and his family would be warmly received by the Scandinavians in Bengal as Carey had no permit to work under the British regime. The Captain allowed Carey and Thomas to preach freely on board but the interest shown, Carey says, was limited to half a dozen people. Carey began to enjoy sea life and especially his heavy meat suppers with Felix washed down with two glasses of wine. One must ask if this was the start of Felix's alcohol problems as much wine and rum was to be taken at meals in India.[5]Alcohol was not regarded by many early evangelicals as a problem as the Baptists often drank wine or rum together just as the Methodists appeared to prefer brandy according to the brandy bills made public at their association meetings. The Church of England

[5] Carey said the practice of the missionaries even when drinking water was to mix it with rum to avoid contamination. They could have boiled the water which was a known and sensible practice at the time.

campaigned for beer-drinking as tea-drinking was so expensive and founded many breweries.

Smuggled out of the ship on arrival

On arrival in India, the missionary party could not reach the Scandinavian enclave in Serampore quick enough as they were faced with immediate arrest or deportation by the British authorities. Captain Christmas had them smuggled out of the ship on a small fishing boat which took them to Calcutta where they were housed secretly by hospitable Indians. Thomas began to preach the gospel as soon as he had landed. Carey was amazed how willing the Indians were to hear Thomas and he soon believed that missionaries would be welcomed wherever they went in India. Carey and Thomas quickly found a faithful fellow-missionary in Kiernander, the over eighty-year-old Swede, who had dedicated his life to evangelizing the Tamil, Bengali and Eurasian Indians. Kiernander advised the English newcomers to set up their first station at Bandel but they rejected the offer. Thomas was dismayed to find that in his absence his former converts and especially Ramram Basu (formerly referred to by Thomas as Bosu), who later became, on and off, Carey's teacher, had been scorned and ostracised by the British Christians. Some had reverted to their former ways.

The Society had unwisely entrusted their initial funds to Thomas

Despite the clear evidence that Thomas had no head for finances but still recognizing him as their missionary leader, the home society unwisely entrusted Thomas with the £150 which was to cover the first year's expenses. Carey had a better head for money than Thomas but he still played only the second fiddle. Thomas, true to type, immediately squandered the funds on a large villa with numerous servants to 'keep up appearances' so that he might practice as a doctor and thus hopefully pay off his debts. This action forced the Mission itself into debt. Instead of following his *Enquiry* plans Carey turned to the Christians of Calcutta begging them for a loan. They refused to oblige him because of Thomas' bad reputation in Calcutta. Carey then sought secular employment as a gardener but was turned down due to lack of qualifications. Carey had known quite well of Thomas' inability to handle money because of the dockside fiasco before he had condescended to the purchase of a fine, representative villa instead of building a hut in the country and living as a native as he had planned. He had already written in his Journal for January:

> For these two months past I have seen nothing but a continual moving to and fro. For three weeks we were in Calcutta selling our Venture; but the great expense into which Mr T. had inadvertently given of Servants, etc. filled my mind with anxiety and wretchedness, and the continual Hurry of Business took up all my time and preyed upon my Soul, so that the prospect of worldly Poverty & the want of a sense of divine things filled me with constant discontent and restlessness of mind.

As so often in the coming years, Carey gave others the full blame for mistakes which occurred either with his cooperation or at his instigation. This is also seen in the way Carey handled his translators who wrote under his name. This was all too much for Mrs Carey who became more and more depressive. Young Felix became so ill with dysentery that he was at death's door. The Baptists were saved by the Indians led by Ramram Basu who provided the missionaries with a rent-free plot of gardening land in the Sundarbans near Debbatta. So, at the very start of the BMS project in India, it was the Indians themselves who took the initiative in supporting Carey, Thomas and their families. Basu must thus be reckoned with Thomas as a pioneer of Carey's future work. An English official, Charles Short, then offered the Careys accommodation nearby. Carey now strove to keep his family by growing vegetables on the rent-free plot he had been given by the Indians, hunting and fishing as he had formerly planned but Thomas remained a financial problem. The better climate and more abundant supply of food soon rid the family of dysentery and Carey actually confessed that he had never been happier though he was still not doing the work he was called to do.

Chapter Nineteen

Thomas and Carey Drop Their Former Missionary Ideals

Carey, at Thomas bidding, rejects missionary opportunities

Seeing how successful Carey was in producing food, several hundred Bengalis who had fled from the area because of bandits and tigers, returned and became Carey's neighbours and his parish. This would have been a wonderful start for a missionary's life and Carey could have lived as a native as he had planned with native Bengalis around him. Carey was provided with a congregation without aiming for it. Now all Carey's hopes and aspirations were being fulfilled.

Instead of accepting the God-given situation he had dreamed of, been called to, and written about for years, Carey allowed Thomas to influence him again and he left his demi-paradise. Carey was usually quite blind in his trust in friends as we know also from his adherence to Marshman and Fuller with whom he was often in disagreement but gave way for friendship's sake. Thomas was still taking the lead in his and Carey's affairs. Thomas had been offered a post as an indigo producer with a substantial salary and had managed to persuade the Commercial Resident, a Christian man, to find such a post for Carey, too, which Carey, strangely enough, readily accepted. After an initial period of instruction in Malda and Goamalti, Carey and Thomas were placed in charge of the indigo factories in Mahipal and Mudnabati. Thomas, who still thought himself as occupying a leading role, took the larger and gave Carey the smaller production centre.

The 'Missionaries' become financially independent

The men's salaries, however, were now very substantial as the indigo business at first prospered. They also earned extra commission on all sales and believed their initial aim to be financially independent of any home support was now fulfilled. Carey, now apparently taking the initiative for the first time and acting independently of Thomas told Fuller and Ryland on August 5, 1794:

> I now inform the Society that I can subsist without any further monetary assistance from them. I sincerely thank them for the exertions they have made, and hope that what was intended to supply my wants may be appropriated to some other mission. At the same time it will be my glory and joy to stand in the same near relation to the Society, as if I needed supplies from them, and to maintain with them the same correspondence.

Nevertheless, after declaring his financial independence from the Society who had not provided the Careys with anything near the support they needed anyway, Carey asked them to kindly order a long list of tools and provide for an annual shipment of trees, shrubs and vegetable seeds which he would pay for out of his own pocket. Carey also told the Society that he was hoping to offer employment to those Indians who lost their caste through coming under the gospel. So now, Carey was an independent Christian, able like Paul, to earn his own keep and still minister to others. From now on Thomas was to take up the second fiddle. Carey's mention of possible Indian converts, however, was a look into the relatively far future.

The BMS take Carey's news badly

The Society was rapidly developing ideas of its own importance and responsibility as a missionary administration body. The uncertainty as to the success of the mission had seriously affected Fuller's nerves and, after two weeks of partial facial paralysis, after Thomas' and Carey's departure he found himself 'incapable of reading and writing with intense application'. Highly-strung Fuller melo-dramatized this as a sign that he was being martyred for the gospel and his country's sake, writing in 1793:

> Upon the whole, however, I feel satisfied. It was in the service of God. If a man lose his limbs or his health by intemperance, it is to his dishonour; but not so if he lose them in serving his country. Paul was desirous of dying for the Lord; so let me!

Here Fuller was certainly giving himself airs as he had hitherto played but a minor role in the foundation of the Society but had been prompted first by Sutcliff, then Ryland, then Carey and then by Thomas. He was apparently in no danger of losing his limbs, nor was he at death's door. Why certain people have blown up their image of Fuller as if he were the greatest missionary supporter of all time must remain a conundrum. We must also remember that during 1793 William Wilberforce was using Parliament to adopt a Christian attitude to the Indians and allow them the privileges of the Gospel. Fuller was still as good as unknown in Britain and never had the power to Reform India as had such as the Clapham Sect who combined evangelical outreach with legislation permitting and aiding such work. It is praiseworthy that this team of evangelical men and women of great influence, representing all branches of British society, always held a sheltering hand over the Baptist missionaries who had not such influential support.

Fuller becomes too big for his boots

Fuller now cultivated ideas unbecoming of a great missionary strategist himself. He began to exercise a political, patriotic attitude to the evangelising of the Indians he believed were under his control convinced that the more the Indians turned to God, the better support they would be for the East Indian Company and British rule in India. His Mission would be the best way to serve Britain's expansionist interests. Fuller was getting too big for his boots. On the other hand, his contemporary Christians William Cowper and John Newton as expressed in their letters and Cowper's great poems Expostulation, Charity, Hope and The Task believed that liberty of body, heart and soul was a key outcome of true missionary work, so India must be free and divested of colonial shackles. This idea of missionary work was also anchored in Carey's *Enquiry* that the gospel cannot be divorced from religious and political liberty and the one aim in missionary service was 'to use every lawful method to spread the knowledge of His name'. Right at the start, the BMS began to sever itself from its roots.

Thomas' and Carey's business ideas fail

Meanwhile, the indigo business proved to be another of Thomas' highly risky ideas. Of the five years Thomas and Carey had worked at Mudnabati only two had produced good harvests and the rest had been ruined by alternate droughts, storms and twenty-foot-deep floods. Added to this, severe epidemics took their toll of the native workers who worked under severe, badly paid conditions. Thomas gave up the work in despair first, probably as he ran the larger business, and suffered proportionately from the slump but Carey soon felt he must also resign. Mr Robert George Udny, the owner of the plantations and one whom had repeatedly helped Thomas financially, then decided to close both of the plantations.

The missionary-cum-businessman's aim of financial independence from the Baptist Society's support was now in danger. Strangely enough, after all his prompting in England to 'go native', Carey, now acting independently of both the BMS and Thomas, still did not think of becoming the missionary of his dreams. In spite of his business failure, he decided to borrow money to add to his own savings so that he could buy his own indigo plantation himself. He even felt he could find his employees amongst the missionaries such as Fountain and hired him as his assistant on the plantation. There was now obviously something of a Thomas that indwelt Carey.

Carey goes-it-alone

Udny, who had proved a tower of strength to the two Englishmen was now removed from his post in the EIC and a fierce opponent of his Christian stand replaced him, so Udny was of little help now. The two men's aim to found a mission financially independent of the Baptist Society's support now stood on a most shaky foundation. Carey pursued his course and borrowed money in true Thomas-like style and bought an indigo plantation to be run by himself alone by which he could become financially affluent through the profits.

Now Felix's health suffered again and neglected Dolly became severely ill and even more depressive because of the insecure life they lived. She also had the terrible experience of losing a child during the plantation epidemic. Now Thomas began to show signs of mental disorder as everything was going wrong for him and, to be honest,

Carey was pushing him out through copying his more negative ways. He was severing the ropes which attached him to Thomas.

No converts between 1793 and 1800

Though the two missionaries had now been in India almost seven years together, they had not seen a single new convert during this initial period though several of their predecessors had each gained some 150 (Schwartz and Kiernander more) converts for the gospel in the same time. When the break-through came, it was the more or less cast off and now very erratic Thomas, not Carey, who led their first native Indian to Christ who was eventually baptised. Carey insisted on baptizing Krishna as the new leader of the Mission. Krishna had visited Thomas with a dislocated shoulder for treatment and through Thomas' testimony came to a saving knowledge of Christ. Krishna proved to be quite the backbone of the Mission and the greater winner of souls than them all. Perhaps, however, to keep us sober concerning this incident of 1800 we may note Barnes's expression concerning the first two thousand years of evangelism before Carey. He ends his story of Carey in 1800 telling us that:

> Before Carey baptised his first convert in 1800 there had been 40,000 converts in the Tranquebar mission:[1]

Fountain joins Thomas and Carey

By 1795 Carey was still preaching mainly to Europeans but he could now manage to witness in his own brand of Bengali and the people heard him willingly and with great curiosity. It took another six or seven years before Carey felt any fluency in preaching in Bengali. Carey was now learning his Bengali from Pundits who either did not understand English, spoke a different form of Bengali from the local inhabitants or were not Christians. This proved to be a lasting handicap for Carey and perhaps explains why converts were so few in comparison to the work of previous missionaries in India, albeit using mostly different languages. Besides, variants of Bengali were not the most spoken dialects around Calcutta.

[1] P. 106.

Now John Fountain, a printer, arrived from England to join the traders and Carey became quickly fond of him, Pearce Carey commenting, 'Carey was very drawn to him, as a true yokefellow'. However, Andrew Fuller took a strong dislike to Fountain seemingly because Fountain did not share Fuller's extreme right-wing politics, so Fuller accused him of being disloyal to the British Establishment. His 'pastoral' letters to Fountain were thus full of condemnation with no encouragement in them in support of Fountain's strong desire to win souls for Christ. Fountain was just not interested in preaching for the extension of the British Raj like Fuller but solely for the extension of Christ's Kingdom. Fuller's interference became so extreme that Carey had to write to the BMS Secretary, warning him of his great exaggerations and mistrust on political grounds. On 17th July, 1799 he told Fuller diplomatically but firmly concerning his friend Fountain:

> I think your fears arose from the best of principles, but also think they were carried to excess on this occasion and also that your observances thereon were too strong. The miscarriage of the African Mission is a sufficient apology for the greatest jealousy, yet I wish you to be tender. You were near killing him. Be assured, however, that he is a good man, and fear not to place a proper confidence in him.

Here was a gentle hint to Fuller to mind his own business and to remind him that his missionary enterprises were proving disastrous. The BMS thrust in Jamaica also left much to be desired. Fuller was also severely aggravated by the fact that Carey would not register Fountain as a missionary but as an assistant in his factory. Carey did not want his friend Fuller to mess up his own plans for India.

Carey felt he could not be recognized legally as a missionary

Fuller had all along protested that Carey was not working as an out and out missionary and this was obviously a most sensitive topic with Carey who gave as an excuse that he could not legally claim to be a missionary under present colonial restrictions. He explained concerning the yearly survey and control of non-Indians in Calcutta:

> Were a person on this occasion to return his name as a missionary, it would be putting government to the proof, and obliging them to come to a point on the subject whether missionaries should be allowed to settle in the country, as such, or not; and there cannot be much doubt but it would be negative. But when a person returns his name as a manufacturer, no suspicion can arise, if his conduct be good in other respects; and it would be more proper for new persons to appear as assistants to those in covenant with government than otherwise.

Carey thus concludes:

> I should not hesitate to declare myself a missionary to the heathen, though I would not on any account return myself as such to the governor-general in council.

Other full-time missionaries, however, had no inhibitions as to their own true identity and were disappointed when Carey said he could not work with them. When Fountain, a printer by trade, arrived at Calcutta, he was thus not announced to the authorities as a co-missionary with Carey but as Carey's 'general assistant'. Carey employed him at the indigo factory though there was a dysentery epidemic at the time which decimated the workers so that Carey was glad to have Fountain give up his missionary ideals for a while and assist him in the factory. In 1799 Fountain greeted the arrival of a Miss Tidd from Oakham who was apparently betrothed to him in England and the couple were married within a few weeks of Miss Tidd's arrival. Carey, now Fountain's employer, did not officiate at the marriage, probably because he was not registered as a minister. The young couple asked Scotsman Claudius Buchanan now co-pastoring Kiernander's Old Mission Church to perform the service according to the Church of England rites. Again, this shows the intimate fellowship enjoyed by the Baptist missionaries and other denominations at the time which was to be broken on orders from Fuller and his denominational bias. It also shows that Carey was not considered a minister in Calcutta, even by his close Baptist friends as he was only a trader.

Fountain, who had been demoralised and humiliated by Fuller, started his own pioneer work at Dinapoor but died after a short illness.

Fountain had been most successful as a preacher and had often urged his fellow missionaries on to new activity when they felt most discouraged. He was an ideal missionary though Fuller suspected him of Republicanism. There were many Republicans amongst the British Baptists at the time as witnessed by the testimony of John Ryland Sen. and a large number sided with America and sympathised with France during the disastrous late eighteenth and early nineteenth century wars. Almost all the Americans who identified themselves with Carey were Republicans, but no less useful as missionaries for that.

Carey tells Fuller to drop his English ideas for Indian ones

Concerning Fuller's efforts to run the East Indian Mission on British legal lines which had no say in the Indian legal system, Carey tells him, 'You must keep your English ideas, and get Indian ones'. Unlike Fuller, Fountain left his politics out of his missionary strategy. His own understanding of the so-called common man and true missionary motivated him to alleviate the human and spiritual needs of the out-castes, the poor and the needy. He wished to make converts to Christ and not to British Colonialism.

Funds in the Mission were again low but a kind, wealthy Portuguese of independent means from Macao, came to the rescue. Ignatius Fernandez, who had been converted through Thomas' ministry before Carey's time, joined the missionaries in their work and supported them with generous gifts. Fernandez assisted in financing many projects and equipped the missionaries with new books and household necessities before they began earning big money. Macao, now in the Republic of China was a Portuguese Colony until 1999. Fernandez encouraged the Serampore Mission to publish Chinese works. At this time, Carey's main financer and main evangelist were both converts of Thomas. But now Thomas was being kept locked up by Carey, as was Dolly his wife. They were both said to be 'mad' by Carey and his friends.

Fountain dies leaving a widow and child

By the summer of 1800 the Fountains' baby was on the way but Fountain, took ill of the epidemic which had already decimated numerous members of Carey's work force in his indigo plant. Carey called in the East Indian Company's best doctors but they were unable to save Fountain who died on 20th August, 1800 after spending only four years in India. His deathbed testimony caused many to look on the Christian gospel with new eyes. It was a moving scene indeed when the Calcutta missionaries and friends gathered to say farewell to their brave brother until they were reunited in the resurrection. They sang the hymn Fountain had composed for such a time under the title *Rejoicing in Hope*:

> With rapture he'll mount his celestial abode,
> His spirit find pleasure and rest.
> With ecstasy bask in the smiles of his God,
> Partaking the joys of the blest.

Mrs Fountain sadly had to give birth to a fatherless child but two years later married William Ward who, with Marshman, invited Carey to join with them in Serampore.

The death of Fountain had proved a great loss to the Baptists in India as he was the only one besides John Thomas, Felix Carey and William Carey who could preach in Bengali which he had learnt remarkably quickly. The relative numerous Baptists now sent by the BMS to the Calcutta district had yet to learn Bengali and Hindustani. They taught in English in the schools but the poor of Bengal did not understand that language so could not attend the classes.

The arrival of William Ward

In May 1799, Carey received a letter, posted over seven months previously, from William Ward who had once met him after a service at Goat Yard Church, Southwark, which John Gill had pastored but where now John Rippon was pastor. Ward, who was said to be a Gillite, wrote that he wished to live and die with Carey and was setting out forthwith for India 'with the others'! Who the others were, he did not say. As the British government had banned missionaries from entering British India, Ward and the others, i.e. the Marshmans, the Grants and Brunsdon, had travelled to North America where they boarded an American ship bound for Danish Serampore.

Pearce Carey in 1929 whilst commenting on the days before Carey's journey to India mentions Carey's brief contact with Ward in London as being of great consequence writing:

> The week's most influential incident was being met on Sunday, the 31st,[2] after preaching in Rippon's pulpit, Walnut Tree Alley, Carter Lane, by a Christian youth of twenty-three, named William Ward, a printer of Derby, who was visiting friends. They walked almost to the Monument together, and Carey unfolded to him the desire and purpose of his heart respecting biblical translations. Laying his hand on Ward's shoulder as they parted, he said, 'I hope, by God's blessing, to have the Bible translated and ready for press in four or five years (an over-sanguine expectation; it took him seven). You must come and print it for us.' Neither ever forgot this.

The new missionaries seek Danish asylum

When Ward arrived with William Grant, David Brunsdon and Joshua Marshman and their families, they placed themselves under the protection of the Danish flag but the British authorities demanded that they should be sent back to England, fearing the Danes would fit them out with passports so they could preach unhindered throughout Bengal. This is what indeed happened. From now on the Serampore missionaries enjoyed the privileges of Danish citizenship. Thomas was now very ill and Carey was taking the lead though he lived outside of Serampore. He heard that the women missionaries had quarrelled throughout the journey and that now the men were quarrelling in Serampore. The reasons for these quarrels have not been recorded apart from the fact that Marshman had a fiery temper. Carey was unable to enter the Danish enclave but the Danish Governor of Serampore, Ole Bie, gave Ward a Danish passport to take to Carey so that he could enter into the Serampore fold.

Grant immediately caught a fever and died after a very brief illness of only three days leaving a widow and two children. Brunsdon soon followed him to the grave, again leaving a needy family behind. Ward wrote in his diary that Mrs Carey was 'wholly deranged'. However, Bie told the British missionaries that they could count on his support. He, himself, had been converted through the testimony of the Tranquebar Mission's Christian Friedrich Schwartz (1726-1798) and wanted the

[2] 31st March, 1793.

same blessing for all those under his administration. Without the Lutheran Bie and the missionary-minded Danish legislation there would have been no Serampore Trio and no Baptist Mission in India until after the 1813 Charter. Bie thus informed the Baptist missionaries that he wished them to set up a Mission Station in Serampore and help him establish a church, printing press and schools in the colony. It must be noted again here in contrast to the many contrary and unresearched reports on the founding of the Serampore Mission that this initiative was taken by Danish Christians and not the BMS who always stayed aloof to the Serampore scene until later myth-spreading took over.

Living as Danes amongst Danes

The new missionaries were able to make several land purchases including a very large house in the middle of the town with two acres of garden which they bought from the Governor's nephew for £800. This amounted to a mere four years' rent. Ward wrote, 'The price alarmed us, but we had no alternative; and we hope that this will form a comfortable missionary settlement. Being near Calcutta, it is of the utmost importance to our school, our press, and our connection with England'. In no time, Ward had set up his press, sufficient paper was at hand and he began to print the Bengali Bible. Again, we must remark that this was Ward's doing though Carey has been given the honour of setting up a press, some modern writer's even claim that Carey's was the first press in India! Here, too, Fountain's work must not be forgotten as he was a printer by trade.

Due to the generosity of the Danish King, the missionaries were able to add a school, a college, a hostel and private houses to their property so that within a few years, the buildings alone of the mission station covered five acres with several acres of botanical gardens run by a large staff of native workers.

Life in Serampore

The Christian work the Serampore Trio undertook in Danish-held territory in the limited form it took, when the trio were not engaged in their varied secular occupations, nevertheless was a reflection of and built on Ziegenbalg's endeavours and successes. These had been carried on by Ziegenbalg's son in Serampore long after Ziegenbalg's death. Indeed, the Danish influence on Carey started before he sailed to India in the Danish vessel Kron Prinsessa Maria to Calcutta. Helen Holcomb tells us that Bie received a personal and 'stringent command' from the Danish King to take the Serampore Trio under his care and adds:

> But why was Col. Bie so deeply interested in these servants of God? During of the earlier years of his service — perhaps at old Tranquebar — he had come under Schwartz's influence, had received great good through him, and ever after had counted it one of the great privileges of his life to have enjoyed the delightfully evangelical ministrations of this good and great man. Thus, the seed sown in that early Tamil Mission bore fruit for the Serampore work.[3]

Indeed, it was Bie's idea to set up a printing press in Serampore and not Carey's and had been urged on him by Schwartz. In her book on gospel pioneers to India, Holcomb portrays pictures of her four principle Indian missionary stalwarts. These are Ziegenbalg, Francke, Schwartz and Carey. Thus, the three great pioneering forerunners of the Baptists outreach in India, according to Holcomb, were Lutherans from the Tranquebar Mission.

Ziegenbalg's only surviving son Gottlieb Ernst Ziegenbalg became the first Director of the Danish East India Company in Serampore in the 1750s and brought with him missionaries from Tranquebar to preach regularly in the colony. Thus, the Danes welcomed Carey, Marshman and Ward with open arms as being of one mind and calling with them and supported them with a trans-border (Serampore/Calcutta) united effort alongside Kiernander (recently deceased), Brown, Grant and Buchanan.

The town of Serampore now proved an asylum of peace, not only for the Indians but for the many fugitives from the Americo-Franco-British wars and many wealthy investors settled there rather than in more turbulent areas. The Baptist missionaries were able to profit from this mission-friendly background outside of restrictive British laws. Meanwhile, they were combatting grave illnesses. Thomas and Mrs Carey were quite deranged and Thomas who had moved to Serampore died, they say, without coming to his senses. Thomas had been very

[3] *Men of Might*, p. 9-10.

badly treated. The Mission's first converts were through Thomas' preaching and fatherly care for his patients so it would be most wrong to rob Thomas of the privilege of being regarded as a great pioneer of the Baptist East India Mission. Brunsdon died of a liver complaint.

Thomas forced to hand his mantle to Carey

Up to this point, for all his failings, Thomas had proved himself to be the premier soul-winner of the Mission and it grieved him to be shoved more and more to the side. At last Thomas' work was also providing a financial gain for the mission. When wealthy Fernandez died, he left most of his land and property to the work of the missionaries. Carey could now preach Bengali more fluently than Thomas and had begun to preach in Hindustani and was also studying Sanskrit believing the language provided a key to Indian cultures, traditions and thought processes. His aim to make Sanskrit the language which would unite all India failed but the fact that Sanskrit is still used in religious services and poetry in India is a result partly of Carey's work.

Early in 1797, with the help of his pundits, Carey revised Thomas' translation of Matthew, Mark, Luke 1-10 and James and is said to have put the finishing touches to the rest of the New Testament. This was all presented as Carey's own work directly from the Greek text. It was followed by the myth that Carey was so fluent in some thirty-five languages that he could translate the original Bible texts into all of these languages. However, the first printing of a supposed Bible in Bengali at the Serampore press was said to be in 1800 but this was not a Bible production but merely Thomas' translation of Matthew's Gospel worked over by the Indian Mangal Samachar.

The printing posed a major problem in spite of Bie's insistence that a press should be set up. There were a number of presses in use in Calcutta which were open to business with Serampore but the Trio wanted their own. Buying type in England was out of the question but Robert George Udny, another great non-Baptist supporter of the Baptist missionaries, generously provided the £46 for an old, abandoned press with vernacular type which was on sale in Calcutta. Carey was not provided with his first press by the BMS.

Doubts concerning limited research on Indian Evangelism

I have been an enthusiastic reader of William Carey (1761-1834) and his works since the nineteen fifties and stocked my library early with scores of works by or appertaining to him. Several magazine publications on Carey's life and gospel outreach have come from my pen. I have authored several essays published in New Focus Magazine and a larger work included in the Martin Bucer Seminar publication *William Carey: Theologian – Linguist – Social Reformer.*[4] I also placed a number of long essays on Carey on my website and mentioned both Carey and Fuller often in my books. When writing these articles and essays, up to the Martin Bucer publication, I used mainly English-speaking literature, almost ignorant of the vast amount of literature on the evangelization of India in foreign languages which were not foreign to me. The inconsistencies in these English language reports and their obvious one-sided bias began to puzzle me greatly so I decided to study the matter more carefully. I then realised that, on the whole, former authors who wrote in English, including myself, had missed out on over three hundred years of solid missiological work in other languages. Furthermore, it was to this continuing work and support, starting over a hundred years before Carey arrived in India, to which Carey turned on his arrival in Bengal in November, 1793. It also became clear to me when studying Continental and Indian sources that this continuing support, including the backing and financing of the East India Company, the Danish King and the British Government, was greater by far than the sporadic and erratic contributions to evangelising India that the Baptist Missionary Society made.

The need for a multilingual, international approach

Apart from studying modern works by Indian church historians seemingly unknown to English-speaking writers, I turned to Danish, Swedish, Norwegian, Dutch, German and French authors and the Halle multi-lingual missionary archives to widen my appreciation of early Indian missions. Happily, my College Martin Bucer Seminar, Bonn fitted me out with a National License so that I could surf through most of the world's archives and libraries giving me access to works all over the world without paying a penny in fees. Furthermore, I pursued

[4] See BQ, review October, 2016.

personal research at some length in the Angus Library at Oxford and also in several Scandinavian and German archives and Libraries, some fifty in all. The very large number of original and secondary works discovered pointed to a William Carey seemingly unknown especially to English-speaking Baptist writers. Furthermore, I found a Carey who could not be forced into the concepts of those who took over his work in the Baptist Missionary Society such as William Yates, William H. Pearce, William Adam and Rammohun Roy who either brought strife and opposition into the Serampore/Calcutta work or departed greatly from the Christian faith once delivered to the people of India by such as Worm, Lewis and Ziegenbalg.

'Transfer of Training' traps

Though stressing the importance of studying Indian evangelism multi-linguistically in relatively modern languages much amateur historical linguistic work has been detrimental to Indian studies. Though Tamil and Sanskrit 'scholars' each claim to represent the oldest language in India, going back some three thousand years, these were, according to better modern scholarship only two of many languages at the time or had developed from previous languages or dialects now unknown to mankind. This understanding led the earliest Protestant European missionaries to learn the rudiments of Farsi, Sanskrit and Arabic before settling in India in the hope that this knowledge would aid them in learning the Indian languages of their day. With hindsight, we can now say this was impractical, time-wasting and caused the making of faulty translations and grammars. This was one of the traps Carey fell into as he spent many years during his employment in EIC and government colleges studying and reconstructing dead or dying Sanskrit dialects in their ancient literary forms and working out grammars and dictionaries based on these ancient Classical languages whilst using a European metalanguage based on Latin grammars and not that of either ancient or modern Indian writers. One cannot force languages which are probably older than Latin into a Latin framework of grammar including syntax. Nor can one use English styles based predominantly on King James' Authorized Version English for a meaningful rendering of a modern Indian language.

We were told at school that learning Latin, or at least its meta-language, made learning all Indo-Germanic languages, indeed all other languages, easier. Yet we were taught no Latin and we who needed the subject in order to matriculate had to use alternative means than day-schools. This theory of using Latin has never impressed me, nor has it ever really worked. I noticed this first on tackling Finno-Hungarian during my work with the Lapps and my teaching Finnish students English in a London missionary school whilst studying for my B.D. Yet I have learnt to love Latin for its own sake and not as a door-opener to all languages. I have learnt to see that even the still used but very vague term 'Indo-Germanic' languages can be a hindrance to linguistic research, as it fails to see the many relationships between all languages. Especially when dealing with such languages as the pre-Jewish languages of Palestine and Farsi, one sees how artificial divisions restrict learning rather than enhance it. This goes also for the so-called 'Dravidic' language group of India which was the whim of a British missionary who had no overall command of Indian languages and the system has no true historical, linguistic, cultural basis.

Dubious co-workers join the Serampore and Calcutta team

In 1799, Carey witnessed the horrible scene of a Sati or widow-burning but he did not at first protest as a Christian but joined the protest movement of the Hindus under the leadership of Raja Roy who had much influence in India and on the Baptist missionaries. The British left Roy mostly in peace as he often obliged them with large loans. Raja Roy was to write vigorously against the practice of widow burning and, as he frequented with the Baptists, he began to write what he felt were Christian books. Roy's charismatic influence was so great that the Baptists absorbed him into the mission work with disastrous consequences. Through Roy's Arian view of Christ, the accuracy of the Mission's Bengali translation began to suffer. Adam was for Roy's view, Marshman, after a time of encouraging Roy turned against him but Yates, whilst professing orthodoxy, still accepted Roy's Arian views concerning the meaning of the Greek.

Roy writes for the Baptists

Eventually Roy was asked to write for the Baptist newspaper run by Marshman. He was to be supported on the Baptist side by the BMS' Arian missionary William Adam who allowed Roy's pseudo-Christianity to influence his translation work. Yates, an educated man and not a professing Arian, followed Roy's Arian based linguistic ideas closely though he must have known that Roy had only a slight knowledge of New Testament Greek. This was all the result of Fuller's watering down of Biblical theology and allying with the Arians and General Baptists in order to support the mission, his Association, and the Bristol Baptist College. No wonder Spurgeon protested at the way the BMS was organised!

Roy and Yates leave work for the Baptists and join Alexander Duff

After his Baptist days, Roy worked also closely for a time with Church of Scotland missionary Alexander Duff until different theologies and ideologies separated them. Sati was eventually banned in 1829 chiefly through the work of Rammohun Roy, though Carey is said to have played a subsidiary part in wording the British laws which were passed. Baptist Yates allied himself for a time with Duff before giving up his missionary work altogether yet later he voiced his opinion loudly amongst the Baptists in discussions concerning his limited understanding of Greek. Duff's associates, colleagues and converts often proved to be of an inter-faith variety theologically. Krishna Mohan Banerjee (1813-1885) who became a Professor at Bishop's College, Calcutta, claimed, 'Having become Christians, we have not ceased to be Hindoos'. Just a few days ago, I received mail from an Indian scholar telling me he had become a better Buddhist through his encounter with Jesus. Western Christian Missionary Societies cannot claim to be innocent of such 'inter-faiths' development.

Basu arrested for embezzlement, Thomas becomes deranged

Now Thomas, who was responsible under God for the conversion of Ramram Basu who was a great support to the two missionaries, witnessed that his convert, after his wife was divorced from him by the force of her relatives, was living an adulterous and deceptive life with another woman and was soon arrested for 'embezzlement'. This shook Thomas no end, although he himself held to very low views of marriage bliss, and his nerves began to suffer. He realised, too, that he had lost the leadership over Carey and thus over plans for the Baptist Mission which had not yet come into being. Traditionally Krishna is given the honour of being Carey's first convert probably because Carey baptised him whilst Thomas was locked in his room to save him from appearing at the ceremony. It was Thomas, however, who had led Krishna to Christ. It must also be stressed that it was Thomas' converts who proved to be the major soul-winners and financial supporters in the days before Carey came into big money.

Chapter Twenty

David Brown again rescues the Baptists from their difficulties

David Brown appointed Provost of an EIC college

Church of England missionary and chaplain, David Brown, now pastoring Kiernander's Old Mission church came to Carey's assistance after Carey's new independent business ventures failed. The East Indian Company was now absorbed into the British Empire and in 1800, Lord Wellesley, the Governor-General, founded Fort William College at Calcutta for the instruction of colonial civil servants. David Brown, a faithful and energetic Anglican supporter of the Mission, was then chosen by Wellesley as Provost.

A chance given Carey to solve his financial problems

The appointment of a Head for the Bengali and Sanskrit Department was a bit of an embarrassment because there were few Europeans who had qualifications in these languages though obviously many native pundits were available, but the highly paid post had to go to a European. Brown, to help solve Carey's financial difficulties, informed him that if he could show published proficiency in Bengali, he would nominate him for a highly paid post on the College staff. Thomas was given no such promise, most likely because of the poor treatment Brown had received from the missionary doctor. His nerves were also falling apart. Nevertheless, Carey decided to go for the appointment though he had still had no permit to settle in Calcutta, still did not have the necessary linguistic knowledge, still did not know Bengali adequately and practically in either spoken or written forms, and still had no knowledge at all of Sanskrit.

A questionable scheme

In order to gain the post Carey worked out a rather questionable scheme which demanded the cooperation of Basu the Bengali pundit who had aided Thomas and Carey on their arrival in Calcutta. He had provided Carey with a plot of land and had begun to teach him Bengali yet Carey had dismissed Basu from his services in 1796 for his alleged immorality. Carey now needed Basu's help badly, so overlooking his former stark criticism of Basu's private life, he begged multi-lingual Basu to return under Carey's employment in order to help him obtain the post of Head of the Bengali Department. Here over-enthusiastic Carey fans must take note. I must repeat that Carey himself confessed at this time that his own Bengali was still weak and his Sanskrit was virtually non-existent. Yet he aspired to an appointment as Professor in both languages.

With hindsight, it must appear astonishing that Carey aimed for posts such as of Head of Department in Bengali and Sanskrit. His working out a ruse to obtain them is an almost unbelievable act of ambition given Carey's lack of language education, experience and acumen. The ruse worked simply because there was nobody to challenge it. As the old saying goes, 'In the land of the blind the one-eyed man is king'.

The difficulty was that any candidate for the post had to prove that he had authored academic works on Bengali but Carey had done no such scholarly work and had published no dissertations on the Bengali language and was utterly unable to do any such work in Sanskrit. To make matters worse, he was now working on a Bible translation with a pundit who knew no English and communication with him was almost impossible. So, Carey needed Basu's help again and begged him to return, outlining his plan to become the Head of the Bengali and Sanskrit Department in the new College if Basu cooperated. Basu promised he would again help Carey out. Without the native Indian's help, Carey would never have gained his lucrative post which he held until his death.

Carey discovers a copy of an alleged Bengali Grammar

Carey had got hold of an alleged Bengali Grammar which had had a very limited circulation and was knocked together by a former government worker who was an expert at Persian and had developed his own ideas as to the importance of Sanskrit as the root of Bengali. It was the idea of a Sanskrit-based Bengali which was to become a major part of Carey's linguistic work. Somehow, this government official had produced a kind of Bengali-for-dunces out of his own grasp of Sanskrit and Bengali. It was only for temporary inner-British trainees' use as a make-shift arrangement and appears to have been quickly abandoned. By Carey's day, it was forgotten. Carey asked Basu to help him 'Bengalize' this edition and bring it out under Carey's name. Perhaps Carey had picked up the print-offs from this work when taking over an old government or newspaper printing-press given up by its previous owners and users.

The sources of Carey's Bengali Grammar

The Bengali Grammar which Carey published around 1800 after his failure as a businessman in order to be chosen for a position on the Fort William staff is claimed by devoted Carey followers as one of the missionary's many 'firsts'. This is, of course, quite wrong. Such admirers of Carey have simply not taken the trouble to examine the true state of affairs. A number of Bengali linguistic works were already available at the time and this Grammar was neither Carey's own original work nor Basu's but a reprint with 'some distinctions and observations', to use Carey's own words, of a Grammar which he had not authored but which came out under his name. The alterations and additions Carey placed within the 'translation' were indeed Basu's and Carey's work but these had to be quickly erased in the second edition as they were quite faulty. Carey blamed Basu for these faults and dismissed him for the second time to keep his own head above water. This is further evidence, however, that Carey did not yet understand Bengali enough to compose a grammar of the language.

Halhed's 'Grammar'

The Grammar was actually the work of Nathaniel B. Halhed (1751-1830), and was published in 1778, years before Carey arrived in Calcutta and even more years before Carey re-printed it with comments.

Halhed's work was followed in 1799 by Henry Forster's *A Vocabulary in Two Parts, English and Bongalee* which was generally available although Halhed's 'Grammar' was not. Even Carey's second 1805 edition of a Bengali Grammar which many modern commentators still claim was 'Carey's very own' was not his own but Halhed's with various further 'additions', many of which were erased in a following edition because of their unnecessary bulk and speculative nature. Very soon, Carey's alleged Grammar was given up, even in the college department which Carey led, but it had served its intended purpose. Carey thus inherited a most faulty view of the Bengali language from a badly qualified translator and grammarian and was assisted by a multi-lingual native-speaker whom he at times did not understand.

Nathaniel Brassey Halhed (1751-1830)

Halhed was the son of a wealthy bank director and had matriculated from Harrow to Oxford where he majored in Oriental Studies, Persian and Economics with a view to working in India at the invitation of Warren Hastings. He settled in Bengal in 1771 and besides his work for the East Indian Company, he translated Persian and Sanskrit works and in 1776 set up a printing press in the Hooghly district where Kiernander worked and where Carey landed in 1793. This is most likely the old press Carey bought through Udny's connections. Halhed's writings were most varied. He translated the Upanishads into English, probably to balance off the new emphasis on the Vedas, the origin and age of which was highly debated. He wrote material in English for the newly founded Calcutta Theatre besides composing poetry and writing political essays. Halhed's highly limited grasp of Bengali, however, was very much coloured by his Persian (Farsi) which had also developed into several major forms (Southern and Northern) by this time.[1] Indeed, Persian was rapidly becoming a mere Arabic dialect though it was formerly Indo-European. Indeed, Halhed's Bengali Grammar has been shown to be heavily dependent on the *Persian Grammar* of Sir William Jones which he published in 1746 and which ran into many editions. This Grammar was designed for both Persians and Indians. Halhed left India in 1785.

---

[1] In today's Farsi, there are only four letters left of the original Farsi alphabet, all the other letters are Arabic script with slight modifications.

There were many Persian speakers in Bengal at the time but the more educated among them used Jones' *Persian Grammar* and were in no need of a Grammar which was neither truly Bengali nor truly Persian such as Halhed's. Halhed had compiled his Grammar for the use of trainee administrators who knew less than he did and it remained within that circle as a source of pidgin-Bengali. It is strange that Carey, if he had had an inkling of Bengali at the time, would have accepted such a makeshift Grammar as the basis of his own work. This is a clear indication that Carey knew little of the language when he applied for the post of Head of the Bengali Department. This, apparently did not disturb Carey who knew no Sanskrit but applied also for the post of Head of the Sanskrit Department at Fort William.

The Grammar served Carey's purposes until 1821

Halhed's Grammar was not designed for English translations into Bengali nor for Indian Bengali readers and would not have facilitated any mutual understanding between the British and the Bengalis at all. We can thus understand that nowadays a good many academic works, with hindsight, have been written criticizing Carey's use of Halhed's Grammar and Basu's Bengali on which Carey relied for years. This never seems to worry most modern writers on Carey who have knitted a net of myths around the two figures Carey and Fuller. The Grammar was officially dropped in 1821 when better works appeared from other 'compilers'. When criticism of Carey's alleged grammar became strong, Carey claimed the mistakes were the work of his assistants thus indirectly confessing he was not the author. It must be noted here that Carey, also published his *Dialogues, intended to Facilitate the Acquiring of the Bengali Language* for English readers but this was also mainly the work of Ramram Basu. This gifted Indian realised that he was doing the major work but Carey was putting his signature to it, so he published his own Raja Pratapaditya Charitra in 1801 under his own name. Carey's later pundit Mrityunjay Vidyalankar, though he was allegedly working for Carey, brought out his own Batris Simhansan in 1802. Indeed, before Carey produced his own Dictionary, there were many major works published by the Fort William Indian scholars who were at last again placing Indian literature into Indians' hands. We must note that because of the powers of the British authorities Carey had their help free of charge. These were pioneer writers who took on Carey as their pupil but sadly that pupil has gained the honour due to his Indian teachers as if he were their master.

Great Bengali writers translated into English

So, too, there had been a number of great writers in Bengali such as Krittibas Ojha (1381-1461), the mediaeval recorder of the Ramayana stories and from whose works Carey built up his antiquated Bengali and printed translations allegedly his own. After many years of devotion to this enterprise, Carey finally printed a number of Ramayana legends in five volumes on the Serampore Mission printing press. Carey also is said to have translated the Mahabharat of 16th century Kashi Ram Das into English in 1802. These major works with which Carey and his many assistants busied themselves were not translated into contemporary Bengali for the education of Indians but were taken from Old literary Bengali and re-written in English for European usage only. The profits from sales were used to support the 'missionary' work though most of this 'missionary' work was secular business.

'Easy Readers' for Carey's students

So, again, we may question this undertaking of very many years as the Indians did not profit by it but it brought in cash from Europeans for European projects. After the 1820's in Calcutta, a good number of Danish and English classics were, however, translated into Bengali by Indian educators. Denmark's Hans Christian Andersen was popular reading at this time in Bengal as also the Yorkshire Brontë sisters. These were useful in the general education of Indian readers. I feel a personal tie to these ladies as I lived in the same street as the Brontë family in Thornton, Bradford, though many years afterwards and it was in the Haworth Vicarage once manned by their father that I received a call to matriculate at the London Bible College, following in the footsteps of the Haworth vicar whose guest I was.

Carey's unsuccessful compilations

Prof. Fiona Ross, a non-Latin typographer in her British Library paper on Early Indian Printed Books highlights Halhed's Bengali Grammar of 1778. She also deals with Graves Chamney Haughton's 1821 Grammar which quickly took over from Carey's unsuccessful compilation. Ross explains that Halhed's work had not the Bengali speaking Indians in mind but 'native Europeans' and was hardly for Indian usage as 'it accords more with European sensibilities, fitting well with the Latin types that necessarily predominate in the Grammar' and reveals European typographic conventions contrary to most Indian manuscripts'. Prof. Ross also points out that even the punctuation used in the Bengali work was Latin.

Unnatural Bengali

Moving on to G. C. Haughton, Ross explains how that author considered Carey's fonts as being insufficient to express the language as spoken and written by Bengalis so Carey had a new, more 'Bengali' type cast, but even this, according to Ross, was still 'not natural to Bengali chirographic practices'. When one considers how many hundreds of Bengali classical literary works from the past were available to the Europeans, we find them being printed off using the Mission's pseudo-Indian punches which could in no wise contribute to their literary merit. It would be like writing Sámi-giella, gål'li-giella (the golden tongue of the Lapps) in ASCII-Code. Looking back over the printed forms of Sami from the seventeenth and eighteenth centuries on, especially Bible portions, one might truly say that they have helped to corrupt the language and robbed it of its gold. This is my own major complaint about the effectivity and necessity of the Baptist translations into Indian languages. Sadly, this goes for many other languages, too.

A merciless analysis

Perhaps the most thorough-going and absolutely merciless analysis of Carey's work is that of Mohammad Abdul Qayyum who did a Ph.D. on the subject for the London University School of Oriental and African Studies in 1974. His manuscript is kindly made available as a freebie on the net with hand corrections and I recommend anyone who is interested in the subject to download it. Judging by his name, however, Qayyum is a Muslim and Muslim speakers of Bengali have their own version of the language. Be that as it may, even Carey's closest friends Marshman and Martyn were highly critical of Carey's Bengali work though Marshman assisted Carey with his translations into English which had little if any evangelistic purpose.

Carey had no time for academic research for an academic post

There had also been Bengali Grammar printed much earlier than Carey's immediate Halhed sources but I have found no evidence that Carey used them and they appear to have been written in Latin script. Carey was obviously under pressure to publish quickly to obtain the College post and had no time for detailed research. So too, Carey's alphabet or script which he took over from the same sources as Halhed does not cover a number of Bengali sounds due to insufficient consonantal and vowelized forms. It was also not a script commonly used by Bengali speakers. However, most languages, like Old Bengali, have qere and ketiv (what you say and what is written) forms also common in Semitic languages, but also occur in English, French and other Western languages. In our Hebrew Bible this has given us the problem of not knowing really how to pronounce God's Name which was why the qere form was obviously used,[2] giving rise to the artificial form 'Jehovah'. Not realising that Swedish was a tone language like Chinese, I made horrible mistakes by putting the accent on the wrong syllable thus altering the meaning of the word. I was once preaching on the work of the Holy Spirit when the congregation burst into laughter. I had preached about a Holy Duck as the same word in Swedish has two different meanings according to intonation which renders it as a spirit or a duck. I also spoke of my love for beans which through my wrong intonation expressed a love for the fair sex, the same word being used for a bean and a lady though with different intonations. That was most embarrassing. Similarly, Bengali is not pronounced at all, from a foreigner's point of view, as it appears it should be pronounced. This is the same in most languages; think of the two meanings and pronunciations of 'wind' and what do we make of 'Worcestershire'? Carey was simply not aware of such linguistic niceties which were commonly well-known and abound in Bengali so he virtually created a new dialect without them. Nor was Carey apparently aware of the very many indigenous works on the linguistics of various Indian languages, especially those akin to Sanskrit and Farsi. In the sixth century the linguistic scholar Pāṇini had already worked out 4,000 rules for linguistic analysis and wrote extra works on terms which he could not bring under his rules. The semiotics, semantics, morphology and even

[2] Obviously, the Jews used a qere because the ketiv was considered too holy.

the phonetics of Indian languages had been worked out and applied long before Carey's day. These works remained in Indian language versions and were only published in English after Carey's time. Carey, however, is said to have mastered over thirty Indian languages. If this were true, he cannot be excused for not applying these necessary linguistic studies to his own translation work.

Using ambiguous scripts

When one starts on a script from scratch it is easier to eliminate such difficulties as Wycliffe Bible Translators soon learn. Ziegenbalg had opted for a script which excluded ambiguities. Such scripts, however, may soon become antiquated through altered pronunciation. Carey started with an already ancient script which did not adequately cover the modern language and pronunciation. Actually, even old Sanskrit, especially in the Southern dialects, could have helped Carey in providing new letters for new sounds as it did in updating Malayalam, a language close to Tamil, up to six old Sanskrit letters known as Grantha being used. When the Arabs took over Farsi and gave it the Arabic script, they realised that Arabic letters could not cover the language so they added four ancient Farsi letters to their new Farsi Script.

So, too, there are enough vowel and half vowel signs and syllabic signs available in the old Indian languages to keep them up to date in modern speech but Carey ignored most of them. However, alphabets appear to be getting shorter rather than longer world-wide as we are discovering throughout Europe. English, of course has suffered greatly from this devolution. Happily, diacritics are heavily used in Indian languages to add more pronunciation, spelling and grammatical additions and aspects have been changed into verbs through various augmentations to help this development as we observe a little in the Greek language.

Qayyum in his *A Critical Study of the Bengali Grammars of Carey, Halhed and Haughton* says:

> Carey's Grammar follows the grammatical pattern devised for the analysis and description of a dead, classical language i.e. Sanskrit. The early nineteenth century in Bengal was a period of transition. New ideas and words of many diverse origins were

constantly creeping into the Bengali language. Anybody, who wanted to know the idiomatic genius of this living language, would have been disappointed by Carey's Grammar. Nevertheless, during Carey's service at the College, a period of about thirty years, his Grammar was published four times. The main reason for this was that, as long as Carey remained in the College, it continued to be used by him as a textbook. The other reason was that at that time books were printed, in very limited editions. In his Grammar, as we have seen, Carey tried to give as many rules as he could, sometimes without proper explanations or examples. This was because he thought the rules could be supplemented in class. The Grammar was, therefore, not useful as a self-taught book, but as a text-book in class. For this reason, we find that in 1830, when the professorship and posts of other pundits were abolished in the College, the Council of the College decided to commission a fresh Grammar of the Bengali language 'with 156 exercises prepared on an easy and simple plan'.

Carey was not asked to compose the new Fort William Grammar

The work of preparing such a grammar was not given Carey who was still on the staff, but was assigned to a Lieutenant Todd and the Reverend T. Proctor.[3] The appointment was still not given to an Indian Bengali scholar. However, long before this rejection of his make-shift work, and after further dismissing Basu, Carey had hired the services of Mrtyunjay, a Brahmin scholar who was financed through the Fort William College. Qayyum notes:

> It is of significance that all Carey's important linguistic work was accomplished during the fifteen years of Carey's collaboration with Mrtyunjay. After Mrtyunjay's retirement in 1816, Carey published only his two-volume Bengali Dictionary in the years 1818 (volume I) and 1835 (volume II). Nevertheless, the compilation of even this was achieved during Mrtyunjay's time at the College of Fort William.[4]

---

[3] Qayyum pp. 222-223.
[4] Qayyum pp. 231-232.

Here, again, Carey is referred to as a compiler and not translator. He was a 'scholar' only in as much as his servant mentors were scholars. Perhaps we could call him a translator's manager but hardly a translator. However, to call Carey even a 'compiler' is, at times, going too far. Wishing to bring out a Bible in Kassai in 1813, Carey knew of only one person who spoke the language and asked him to translate the whole Bible into Kassai, a group of languages spoken then on the Bengali-Burma border.[5] Of which languages Carey understood nothing. Apparently, Carey chose the Kassai speaker out of the blue[6] as the only person he knew who could speak a Kassai dialect and we can suppose that the 'translation' remained in the 'blue' as Carey had no means whatever of overseeing or checking the work with the aid of his Hebrew and Greek textual knowledge. The Kassai dialects have either Chinese and/or Arabic roots. From Carey's time on Urdu and Hindi was spoken rather than old Kassai. Horne in his Manuel tells us that in 1839 the Bible in Kassai was still being translated by the 'Baptist missionaries' but the New Testament had been translated in its entirety.[7] Actually, the Serampore Trio printed Matthew's Gospel in Kassai in 1816 using the 'Divine' script of Hinduism Devanagari for the Kassai Muslims, which was rather tactless, and the New Testament soon afterwards. The full Bible was eventually produced by Welsh Presbyterian missionaries but they used Roman characters!

There is one interesting element in Carey's earlier Bengali which explains diversities in it. Carey sought the assistance of various pundits one after another in bringing out his four editions of his Bengali Grammar. Few of these pundits knew Bengali well, others knew either no Sanskrit or no English. These men used various spellings according to their educational and religious background so that Carey's works display a variety of spellings obviously influenced by which Pundit he was using at the time. Fuller noticed this practice in Carey's writings and condemned it but he also assumed that Carey would be using

[5] Not to be confused with the Congo Kasai, Africa.

[6] He wrote on 11th December, 1813 to say 'This week we obtained a person to assist in the translating of the Kassai language' as if he had found merely another member to add to a team. However, this 'person' appears to have been when comparing the various accounts, the only 'person' involved.

[7] *A Manuel of Biblical Bibliography*, London,1839, p. 113.

English punctuation in his translations which was sadly true but quite wrong. So, when Carey asked for the term in English, not recognizing the Bengali translation, he was given different spellings of the same terms. One can test this theory easily by comparing the host of Indians scholars' works, male and female, on the subject of Carey available today from people of different backgrounds who invariably use different spellings for the same terms and refer to Carey's work in different meta-languages. Carey invariably, but unavoidably, used different spellings of the same term in his writings.

£1,500 per annum plus extra perks

Brown as the Provost of the college gave Carey the required post which brought a very large salary of £1,500 with it besides many extra perks. Indeed, the salary was soon doubled and Carey was earning well over ten times as much as his contemporary British pastors whether Anglicans or Free-Churchmen. Apparently, there was no Englishman around in academic circles at the time who knew of the history of the Grammar and could challenge its authenticity. Carey, via his 'Grammar' had suddenly risen from a pauper to an affluent man who could now print his own publications through college commissions and had a team of some hundred translators at hand at no cost to himself. No other missionary had, or perhaps ever had afterwards, such a platform from which to work. So actually, Carey climbed into the occupation of his dreams over the back of others who had done the bulk of his alleged work for him. Indeed, it must be further noted that almost every time Carey published a work, it was when he had engaged the many 'expert' pundits to do the work for him. When criticism came, even from his own co-workers, as it gradually did when other missionaries and government workers entered the field, he blamed his pundits and fired them. This also applies to the quality and accuracy of Carey's Bengali Bible which Marshman and Martyn criticized from the start but nobody took any notice of them as Carey's fame was now established.

Carey given the credit for other peoples' work

To give Carey full justice, later in life Carey spoke of his 'compilations' rather than his 'works', but modern biographers invariably refer to Carey's having translated the Scriptures into numerous languages. So, here I must agree with Sindhu Pani in his work *William Carey's Contributions to Bible Translations* and Sunil Kumar Chatterjee in his work *William Carey and Serampore* that Carey has been given the sole credit for the work of a large team of mainly Indian co-workers who ought to be given due recognition but this was not considered necessary under colonial rule.

It now appears that, in time, Indian writers will reset the balance concerning Western and Eastern works on Indian Missions. We remember that Carey was asked to found a department for the translation of Scripture into Indian languages and was also made Head of the Sanskrit Department. Yet there were many learned Brahmins available who were fluent in the ancient language and were far more eligible for the appointment but these experts were made the novice's assistants. Nevertheless, they influenced the work of translation immensely and often Carey and his British friends had no means of checking their assistants' work. To argue that Carey always checked the results by the Greek and Hebrew only makes sense if he were perfect not only in Greek and Hebrew but also in the thirty-odd languages translated.

Carey finds lucrative work for Marshman and Ward

Thus, though foreign missionaries were refused entrance into British Bengal for a number of years and missionaries already there were severely hindered in their work, Carey could now find work for Marshman and Ward in the provision of grammars, text books and translations from the Classics and Scripture. For Chinese experts such as Armenian Johannes Lazar[8] who had spoken Chinese from his childhood on, he provided posts at £450 per annum. Marshman was to work closely with Lazar in translating Bible passages and the works of Confucius. In other words, scholars were being employed though they were not Biblical scholars, with far greater proficiencies than Carey at a fraction of his salary. However, all this work was for the further education of Eton pupils, British soldiers and the Anglo-Indian aristocracy at the Calcutta College. Carey was also quick to create posts for academically inclined converts. Over the years, he was able to build up a library of the greatest works in Sanskrit and other ancient and

[8] There are various spellings of this name including 'Lasser'.

modern Indian and Asian languages, the bulk of these books being still available to scholars behind fire-proof doors in the Regent's Park College Library, Oxford, instead of India where they belong but from where they were removed. For anyone hoping to do missionary work in India or academic work in the ancient Indian languages, a prolonged visit to Regent's Park College is an absolute must. The collection has recently been catalogued.

Developments on the home front

Meanwhile Fuller was also departing from the old pioneering Baptist ways concerning gospel missionary evangelism followed by such as Henry Jessey and John Bunyan. Jessey had shared the same pulpit with Anglicans such as Thomas Fuller for years and Bunyan had joined him in preaching that baptism was no bar to communion. Both had wisely left party politics and denominational squabbling out of their preaching. It was the Bunyan-Jessey idea of Christian Communion that had graced the founding of the Olney and district Baptist churches. We now find Fuller exercising a political, patriotic attitude on behalf of the British Baptist churches and the East Indian Mission, as he called it, obviously claiming sole responsibility for all true missionary work in East India along political lines. He felt that the more the Indians turned to God, the better support they would be for the East Indian Company and British rule in India. Thus, Fuller viewed his serving the mission as the best way to serve the expansionist interests of his country.

The original gospel vision given up at home and abroad

Sadly, Carey's initial vision, shared with Thomas, for a Baptist Missionary Society had not only been given up in India but also in Britain. The Baptists under Fuller were leaving the idea of 'local' or 'home' churches in favour of 'Associations' under a common leadership and a joint and binding theological manifesto. Fuller thus saw the Indian Mission as being his 'association' under the leadership of the BMS committee under him. This, however had not been founded as a joint Baptist Association project but a local one. Indeed, Fuller's own Northamptonshire Association was now busily rationalising away the gospel in God's Word and denying the inspiration of the Spirit in it. Furthermore, the other growing Baptist associations were not as enthusiastic about Indian missions as Sutcliff, Pearce, Ryland and

Fuller were. These associations, with the exception of the growing number of Particular Baptists, were, under Fuller's guidance, allying with the Arminian and Arian Baptists leading eventually to the idea of a united British Baptist Union which caused many churches to break up into multiple rival churches. Fuller saw the dangers of this 'unionism' which he had fostered too late and stated in 1814 that of the eleven association churches in Nottinghamshire and Leicester which had an average of seventy members each, only fifty per church were 'truly Christian people'. As Fuller's own churches were thus so 'mixed' one wonders why Fuller would not share communion with fellow evangelicals in other denominations which he accused of being as equally mixed as his own.

The Society's New Divinity

The fact was that some Baptists, having left their Particular Baptist ecclesiology and, indeed, theology, were going through something of a revolution which had come into Britain from the United States under the title of 'New Divinity' which was really 'Old Rationalism' and now governed Andrew Fuller's theology. Indeed, Fuller's ideas, as we have seen in previous chapters, based on Continental and American Liberal and rationalistic writings outside of the Baptist fold, strove to empty Christianity of all its basic doctrines. Thus, many Particular Baptists who initially supported Carey's mission in any way were now alienated by Fuller's new anti-evangelistic and anti-Christian rational view of natural law and duty faith. These orthodox Baptists looked then and in later years to the teaching of Gill, Brine, Huntington, Hervey, the Gospel Magazine, Toplady and Hawker who carried on the doctrines made clear by our Reformers. These are the doctrines on which this author stands.

Missionary-minded William Button denounces Fuller's Liberalism

William Button, a founder supporter of the Society, now felt compelled to write his *Remarks on the Gospel Worthy of All Acceptation* against Fuller and Ryland. The Anglican Evangelicals and High Calvinists, whom Fuller acknowledged were more successful evangelistically than he, believed that Fuller had abandoned the doctrines of grace, and thus looked on the Society's committee with suspicion. John Ryland Senior's theology was represented by Gill's commentaries which he had placed in his church building in Northampton for all to read. This proved an embarrassment to Ryland Junior, one of the senior members of the Executive Committee of the Baptist Missionary Society who had the commentaries removed when he took over from his father and began to excommunicate the old Particular Baptists and those of 'Gillite' faith and learning.[9] Fuller's own church members were soon complaining that they were greatly neglected by their pastor who was often away on Sundays and even mid-week meetings canvassing for money.

However, Fuller had little time for his pastoral duties in his home church even when he was not travelling about the country. Travis Myers of the Boston University Theological Department comments on the university's current web-page regarding Andrew Fuller:

> Fuller spent up to ten hours per day in correspondence and reporting for the BMS. He contributed articles to Evangelical Magazine, Missionary Magazine, Quarterly Magazine, Protestant Dissenters' Magazine, Biblical Magazine, and Theological Miscellany. He sought financial support via letters and by an average of three months of vigorous itineration each year among various evangelical churches in Scotland, Ireland, Wales and England.

It is thus rather hard to believe that recent writers on Fuller claim he was not only an ideal pastor but he was also a pastor of pastors. What Myers says of Fuller would be an ideal statement to make concerning a Missionary Society Secretary but being both that and an ideal pastor at once would be a task too heavy for anyone. Furthermore, Fuller's Northamptonshire Association theology, viewed on its own, was not Bible-based enough to support any kind of gospel expansion as Fuller's teaching had isolated it from a sound trust in the fundamentals of Christianity and it was the first Baptist Association to go openly Liberal in 1889 denying the doctrine of verbal inspiration.

Indeed, with his emphasis on Governmental Moral Theology as developed By Hugo Grotius with its absolute denial of the Biblical, Reformed doctrine of the absoluteness of the Atonement and his

---

[9] See my introductory chapters and notes to 'Weighed in the Balance', Huntingtonian Press, 1998, for examples.

emphasis on the superiority of Natural Law over God's revelations, Fuller had parted company with orthodox Christianity altogether.

Leading evangelical magazines warn against Fuller's cancerous theology

After 1780, the leading Baptist and Anglican magazines began to point out the danger of Fuller's new philosophy, even calling it a gangrene in the churches.[10] George Wright finishes his 1877 Gospel Magazine article on Fuller's poisoning of theology by saying:

> I am sure you will join with me in the most unfeigned abhorrence of a system that robs God of his glory, and enhances the condemnation of the guilty to an immeasurable degree by increasing their responsibility.

Furthermore, a number of those who stood closer to Fuller, such as Benjamin Beddome, believed that churches who neglected their own local work and funding were not in a position to send out missionaries hoping that they would do better abroad. Joseph Kinghorn, who had collected quite large sums of money for the BMS start-up, was now shocked to find Fuller's megalomania turned on him, saying his work was 'without modesty and sobriety' and that Kinghorn was an 'infidel objector', merely because he had protested at Fuller's suppression of free enquiry within the association. Fuller was quick to threaten that he would go to law against anyone who threatened his Christian understanding. This was certainly much against the spirit of Carey's evangelistic manifesto *Enquiry*. Indeed, Thomas Schirrmacher of the Martin Bucer Seminar in Bonn, in his outline of Carey's missiology, shows how almost all modern Missionary Societies look back on Carey as their founder but contrary-wise hold to a theology of missions which was never his. So, too, all modern talk of the generous support Fuller organised must be seen in the light of Carey's great-grandson Samuel Pearce Carey, to date his major biographer, who stated that if

---

[10] See A Sketch of the Rise and Progress of Fullerism, or Duty-Faith. That Gangrene now rapidly spreading in many Baptist Churches, J. A. Jones, Earthen Vessel, September 2, 1861. Also George Wright's article on Fullerism in the Gospel Magazine, Vol. xii, 1877, p. 343.

missionaries in India had waited for the needed support from the Society, they would have starved long before it came. Furthermore, at this time exporting English goods and monies to India was a risky business indeed and often took up to three years to arrive.

Part 8

The Danish-British Work in Bengal

Chapter Twenty-One

Establishing a work in Danish Serampore

The Serampore Mission was a Danish plan

Serampore was founded as an extension of the Tranquebar Mission and the earliest work there both in the realms of trade and missionary activity were products of the Tranquebar Mission's outreach. It had a governor who was converted through the Tranquebar Mission and an East India Company Director-founder who was Bartholomäus Ziegenbalg's son. The real founder of the Serampore Mission as Baptists later came to know it was thus the Dane, Governor Bie. It must be emphasised that the BMS had no part whatsoever in these plans and were indeed strongly critical of the Serampore work and set up a rival work in Calcutta. Bie gave Ward a passport making him a Danish subject and permitting him to visit British controlled territory and bring Carey back with him to help in the consultations. Bie then gave the Serampore Trio the benefits of Danish citizenship. It was a daring move for missionary-minded Denmark to make at the time as Britain was about to declare war on the Danes and was using every excuse to put pressure on Colonel Bie so that he would surrender the colony. Denmark was now on friendly terms with France which was the main reason given for Britain's declaring war on the Danish colony but it was Denmark's policy of supporting the evangelizing of the Indians which had become the real thorn in the flesh for the British. Today, we might think that such a small nation could scarcely stand up to Britain but Denmark was still a major world power in those days and had access to all the natural resources needed in the Industrial Revolution. Denmark's once great power was on the wane and the British lion, or rather tiger, was now stalking through India.

King Frederick refuses to give up Serampore to the British because of his promises to the Serampore Mission

Brave King Frederick, faithful to the missionary cause, corresponded personally with Carey, Ward and Marshman and later told them that during the troubles with Britain, he had refused to surrender Serampore because, in 1801, he had personally promised the missionaries protection through the Danish Court and refused to break his word. For him, the giving up of Serampore would have meant the end of the gospel in India. It took another ten years for Britain to realise that their opposition to Indians becoming Christians was wrong. During these ten years and long after, what became known as the Serampore Trio (Ward, Carey and Marshman) were under Danish protection in the spirit of the Tranquebar Mission. Serampore was certainly not ruled from England's Kettering and Fen Court[1] as Kettering and especially Fen Court would have nothing to do with them.

Charles Grant's support of missions

Not all the British East Indian officials were anti-missionary at this time. Many had not forgotten that at the birth of the Company in 1600, the spreading of the gospel in India had been one of its major aims. Company Director Charles Grant had been campaigning for missionaries to India since 1787, encouraging Anglicans and Baptists alike to put their hand to the foreign plough. The response to his appeals in India and Britain was slow. However, Grant found himself powerless even to obtain passports for the British missionaries and advised them to remain under Danish citizen protection. He, however, supported the mission financially, bought Kiernander's church building for the use of missionaries after the Swede died and left a substantial legacy especially for the British Serampore Mission workers at his death. It was this church that Thomas had demanded for his own use but the far better qualified David Brown was given the post because of Thomas' fierce attacks on the work of the long-established Mission.

---

[1] Headquarters of the BMS.

Pastor Brown, a close friend of Grant's, in spite of his strong distrust of Thomas, sought to help Carey and his friends as much as possible by mediating between them, the police office and the East Indian officials. He, and several other non-Baptist supporters, would have become communicants at the Serampore Mission services in 1800 according to the wishes of Carey, Marshman and Ward but Fuller opposed the plans strongly, even to denying that those field-workers who were supporting the Serampore Trio and thus also the BMS were 'real Christians'.

Originally open-communion was the norm in Serampore

In these early years, however, Christians of various denominational backgrounds made up the bulk of Carey's fellow-worshippers. They naturally allowed Baptists to conduct their services within their fellowship. Both Thomas and Carey were invited to preach in their services at the Old Church. Thomas made himself unpopular by wishing to turn the church into a Baptist institution but Carey became popular, because of his openness, with the non-Baptists evangelicals who were greatly in the majority.

In Britain, exclusive, closed-shop communion had not been the practice of the earlier generations of Particular Baptists. Andrew Fuller had nothing against begging non-Baptists to finance the BMS in the name of the East India Mission, or give them political support, but he would not have members of the churches who had donated much money to partake of 'the cup of blessing' in the churches they had helped to established and in the church buildings they had provided, financed and even erected. Indeed, Fuller told the Serampore Trio; Ward, Marshman and Carey, as they came to be known, that their idea smacked of the Anti-Christ and fellowshipping with non-Baptists at the Table was like opening the doors to immorality and dangerous heresy. When this news spread around, Fuller defended his interference in the work at Serampore in the Christian press by stating that it was not a question of open or closed communion but of the validity of being a Baptist. This obviously stood higher in Fuller's priorities than the validity of being a Christian. For a Baptist to fellowship with Anglicans and Presbyterians, Fuller argued, would mean he was no longer a Baptist. This is a most extreme, anti-Christian position to take in the opinion of this writer who has preached and lectured perhaps more in Baptist circles than any other and communed with thousands of Baptists in sweet fellowship. Fuller broke such Christian and blessed communion.

Fellowship destroyed by exclusiveness

So, the group of fine, eager Christians at Serampore, could not establish a true church as desired but had to opt for an exclusive denomination which separated them from the very brethren who had made it possible for the Baptists to establish a Mission in India. In spite of the great offerings the Serampore Trio made to keep the Baptist boat from rocking, as Ward described the problem, the BMS now sent a rival team of less able men to elbow them out and reduplicate the work of the Trio for the BMS.

Ward's view of the work his fellow missionaries were doing perhaps explains why his letters to Britain paint a most negative picture of the Indian situation as if there was a void in evangelism. Pearce Carey gives us a lengthy excerpt from Ward's correspondence concerning his view of India:

> On September 20, 1800, Ward writes to one of his friends expressing the confidence of his mind in the vocation he has chosen, and the certainty of its ultimate success.
>
> > You will expect me to say something of what we are doing, and in fact what sort of place we are in; and yet I know not, that I can say any more than I have said to others.
> >
> > Here are priests by the thousands, but they never preach or instruct their flocks, except in a few ceremonies. Here are temples by the thousands, Musselman and Hindoo; but the praises of God are never heard in them. Here are plenty of doctrines, but none of them mend the heart, or in fact touch it.
> >
> > The three great doctrines, which make such havoc of souls in Europe, are universally prevalent here. Both Musselmans and Hindoos believe, that punishment in hell is temporary, not eternal; there is not a man therefore, that cares about future punishment. Antinomianism is universal. With them it is the easiest matter in the world

> for God to pardon or pass over sin. Crimes indeed are necessary, they say, and God is the author of sin. Deism is, I believe, very prevalent, especially among the most refined Musselmans, and almost every European in the public service is a Deist.
>
> The corruption of manners amongst all is dreadful. Instead of Hindoos being that innocent people, which some have pretended, they are as dissolute as any people on earth, though there is nothing ferocious in their manners. If anyone wishes to see the meaning of the apostle's words to the Ephesians, 'without hope, and without God in the world', let him come hither. The baseness and degradation of the people is so great, that many Europeans laugh at us for thinking of their conversion. It is almost the universal opinion among Europeans here, that our design is utterly chimerical.
>
> Here, then, what triumphs will there be for divine grace? It is reserved for the latter days, and for the final triumphs of the Lamb, that Hindoos will be gathered in; as the thief and Jerusalem sinners were among his first triumphs. Doubt not, that our Saviour will certainly famish all these Gods, and lay them prostrate in the dust.

It is clear that Ward believed Indians were as pagan as the British. Indeed, the average British trader or politician was an insult to his own country. Oddly enough, Fuller did not protest at the fact that the British missionaries were gradually coming under the financial and organisational influence of Danish Lutherans who, nevertheless, shared their intense desire to win the Indians for Christ as much as did many Anglicans and a growing number of Presbyterians. Indeed, American Presbyterians such as Captain Wickes were now also supporting the mission. According to the Introduction to Hervey's book *The Story of Baptist Missions* (p. xviii) it was the American Baptists who made the first major breakthrough in the conversion of the Indians. Adoniram Judson was originally sent out to assist Carey as a Presbyterian missionary. Carey expert, Professor Bengt Sundkler, of Uppsala University, a fervent evangelical but hater of blind denominationalism, wrote a fine book showing how William Carey was the father of true,

Biblical ecumenicity. He much regretted the fact that influential believers had failed to rally around him because of their denominational prejudice and the oecumenical movement thus fell into the hands of worldly churches who nevertheless hail Carey as their father.

Suggestions for joint work with the LMS

The London Missionary Society which was of great assistance to the Baptists in India, approached Carey in Calcutta through Nathaniel Forsyth (d. 1816) concerning exercising a joint missionary approach. They were informed through Carey that this was impossible. Through Fuller's mismanagement, inter-communion between the two societies was made inacceptable and the missionaries were no longer pulling on the same rope. Fuller had not only rocked the boat, he had capsized it. Another reason for this break was that though Carey was heavily supported by the British authorities, Forsyth had no such backing, though he did not seem to worry about it.

Nathaniel Forsyth had been actively working in Calcutta since 1798 whilst Carey was still, more or less, dormant. Unlike Carey, he did not hide behind the title of 'trader' or take up secular work but strove to be a full-time missionary from the start. Forsyth proved that the course Carey rejected was clearly possible and Forsyth became what Carey had hoped to be. This brought him into conflict with the British authorities but Danish Serampore gave him asylum and freedom to preach the gospel. He eventually followed in Kiernander's footsteps and worked in nearby Chinsurah, where he served the Lord as he had been called to do. It is interesting to note that Forsyth then moved to Bandel where Kiernander had also recommended Carey to work. From Bandel, a missionary gained easy access to other areas through the waterways which Forsyth used and Chamberlain following him. Carey discovered this effective method shortly before his death. This shows the wisdom based on experience of Kiernander and those who followed him which Carey rejected for so long.

Forsyth and Carey were both for a time in Serampore together

Writing of Forsyth's wish to associate with Carey, the LMS report for 1800 states that Carey:

> owed his gaining a foothold to the providential fact that Denmark held a small patch of Indian territory around Serampore, and threw over him and his colleagues the mantle of her protection. It is one of the ironies of history that while Great Britain, one of the most powerful of European nations from whom Carey sprang, exerted her power to frustrate his benevolent aims, Denmark, one of the least influential of European peoples, was able to hold open the door of blessing through which Carey and his colleagues, and also Nathaniel Forsyth, entered to begin their beneficial labours for the millions of India.[2]

Of Forsyth, one of his successors in the Bengal Mission G. Gogerly wrote:

> Mr. Forsyth is described as being a man of most singular self-denial and large-heartedness, and as generous to an extreme. His whole time, talents, and property he devoted most conscientiously to his missionary work, and to the relief of suffering humanity. From the funds of the London Missionary Society he never received anything, with the exception of a few dollars when he embarked for India. His private resources were exceedingly limited, and, in consequence, his mode of living was most simple and inexpensive. 'For a time' said his friend Mr. Edmond, whom everybody in Calcutta knew and loved, 'he had no stated dwelling place, but lived in a small boat, in which he went up and down to preach at the different towns on the banks of the river.[3]

So here we find another missionary, let down by his missionary Society who joined Congregationalists, Anglicans and Presbyterians to do the work of an evangelist just as Carey had dreamed of doing but never really put into practice. He also lived in the very way Carey had envisaged. We also find Forsyth walking miles to preach and most unlike the Serampore Trio, he refused to have the Indians carry him

---

[2] *The History of the London Missionary Society*, p. 14.
[3] Ibid, p. 15.

around in a carriage or Palankeen. He also cared for and witnessed to the sick and invalid in the Calcutta General Hospital with the help of David Brown who obtained permission for him. We also see how missionary societies were quick to send out missionaries but slow to support them. David Brown often filled the cap or, to use Carey's metaphor, held the ropes. Forsyth died after eighteen years of hard labour in Chandernagore aged forty-seven years.

Carey pays tribute to Ward and Marshman who had invited him to Serampore

Now the Baptists were amongst the largest land-owners in the Serampore District, with the exception of the leading administrators. Soon after settling in Serampore, Carey realised what a godsend Ward and Marshman were. He told the Society, 'Brother Ward is the very man we wanted: he enters into the work with his whole soul. I have much pleasure in him, and expect much from him. Brother Marshman is a prodigy of diligence and prudence, as is also his wife in the latter: learning the language is mere play to him; he has already acquired as much as I did in double the time.' Ward had more difficulties with language learning but Carey found him, 'so holy, so spiritual a man' and he soon became a favourite of the Indian children.

Living like the Moravians

The Serampore missionaries now drew up an order of family rules after the Moravian fashion, regulating who prayed and led the worship at what times, who took care of the common purse, who looked after the medical equipment and who took care of the library. All business and trade that was done was jointly regulated by the missionaries who now called themselves, again following Moravian practice, 'the Family'. The British Baptists had seen this work in their predecessors the Moravians and found that it worked with them equally well. Marshman wrote, 'Thank you, Moravians. If ever I am a missionary worth a straw, I shall owe it, under God, to you.' Sadly, little or no private family leisure was possible and the arrangement was not according to the dictates of the BMS.

Serampore was financially independent of Kettering

Happily, the printing of Bengali Bible portions and many other works both secular and religious now went ahead at full speed. A newspaper was founded and work was taken in from other organisations needing information in print. With the income from the press and the schools alone, the missionary family became 'more than self-supporting' and could pay back BMS funding as if they had been debts. Then there were the high wages received from Fort William. The entire amount that the Mission had received from the Home Front was paid back within five years. Further building projects were financed by the Mission itself, with the added assistance of friends in India. The Mission now owned property valued at many thousands of pounds, but due to BMS pressure and the desire not to turn their missionary work into a business, the missionaries signed over all the Serampore Mission rights and assets which they had hitherto accrued to the Society. This was eventually altered to allow the missionaries a tenth of their profits in order to make provisions for widows and orphans. This meant that the BMS were now dependent on the East Indian Mission which was now one of the Society's major financial supporters though the money came from the Mission itself. It was not the home front which was supporting the Indian Mission but Serampore who was supporting the work of the home front. The funds were used to fund missionary stations elsewhere which, in spite of the funding from India, proved a financial burden through organisation problems. The Serampore Mission, however, wisely retained much of the trusteeship so they had a say in how their monies were being used. Hand in hand with their practice which had brought material progress, Carey prayed, 'If we are enabled to persevere in the same principles, we may hope that multitudes of converted souls will have reason to bless God to all eternity for sending the Gospel into this country.'

Krishna Pal was proving to be a missionary indeed

Though Carey's biographers could now testify to the palatial circumstances under which the missionaries lived, they could also testify that native Indians were turning to Christ through native preachers. Krishna Pal was instrumental in having his wife; his four daughters; his wife's family and several other Hindoos follow him to Christ and formed the first Indian church north of Madras. Krishna Pal became an accomplished speaker, hymn writer, itinerant preacher, soul-winner, pastor, and Carey's major tutor in various dialects. There is a beautiful letter extant in Krishna Pal's hand, dated 12th October, 1800 testifying to the great change Christ had made in his life. On 29th December, Carey wrote: 'Yesterday was a day of great joy. I had the happiness to desecrate the Gunga (River), by baptising the first Hindoo, viz. Krishna, and my son Felix.' In many ways, however, Krishna's baptism was a matter for sorrow. Thomas' joy and praise at being instrumental in converting the first Bengali to be baptised is said to have made him so elated that he lost his mind, and had to be kept behind locked doors during the baptism service. Naturally, the way that Thomas had been forced out of any leadership of the Mission also must have preyed on his mind. One would have thought by rights he should have baptized the two converts as none of them were Carey's but his. Mrs Carey was also thought too unbalanced to witness the baptism of her son so was also locked in her room. History has still to examine this locking up of protesting Mission members.

Thomas' pioneering work is now wrongly attributed to Carey

Sadly, Thomas is still not given recognition by very many Baptists for pioneering the conversions made in the Serampore work. Typical, it appears, of most works eulogising Carey is the claim that he opened up his Indian church by his leading Krishna to Christ. Neither of the first six or so converts were the results of Carey's work but it was Thomas and Ward who led them to Christ. I was happy to read recently Mark Galli's online essay 'William Carey – The Man Who Wouldn't Give Up'. Galli had stated that 'In December 1800, after seven years of labour, Carey baptised his first Indian convert, Krishna Pal'. An observant blogger wrote immediately that Galli had erred and that the honour should be given John Thomas.[4] The blogger felt that Thomas' joy at Krishna's conversion was so great that it made him mad and so different theories of Thomas' sad condition go on being aired. Whatever Thomas' condition, it was not made easier by the horrible fact that he was kept under lock and key, or rather bolted in, so that he could cause no bother and make no public testimony concerning the baptismal candidates.

[4] www.hopefaithprayer.com.

Pearce Carey, quoting Stennett, gives rather a different version of the first baptisms carried out by the Serampore missionaries writing concerning Ward:

> According to Stennett, Ward writes in November, 1800, 'I begin to smatter a little Bengalee. God, I hope, has blessed my labours to the conversion of Mr. Carey's two eldest sons, and towards the close of January, I expect we shall be joined by 2000 (alluding to the New Testaments) more missionaries, of whose success I dare not indulge the least doubt. In a few weeks I hope we shall have to baptize four persons, a native, Mr. Carey's two sons, and Mr. Fernandez. The native has been raised under the ministry of Mr. Thomas, and has been in his service twelve months. He renounces caste, preaches Christ, and appears to be truly converted. Felix Carey has begun to preach, having known the language from his youth. I hope he will make a useful missionary; I bestow much labour upon him for this purpose.

Here Ward emphasises that Krishna Pal was Thomas' convert, and appears to view himself as being responsible for Felix's conversion and also that of his younger brother William. The latter, however is very rarely indeed listed as a convert in further biographies and it appears that William lost fellowship with his father in matters of faith and conduct as a young teenager and took to strong drink as did Felix who was brought up on the bottle but not the milk bottle. This may sound facetious but the fact is that both sons became addicted to alcohol at a very early age. So, too, both Stennett and Pearce Carey mention that Fernandez was also baptized on this occasion but he, too, was led to Christ by Thomas. Pearce Carey also mentions that the next native convert was Fukeer (often spelt 'Pukeer'). He was also led to Christ by Thomas and was one of his factory workers. Fukeer followed Thomas to Serampore and was received into the fellowship there. Apparently, Fukeer had confessed to become a Christian before Krishna as Thomas met Krishna who had come to him with a dislocated arm on the same day that Fukeer was accepted into fellowship in Serampore. Shortly after this event, however, we hear no more of Fukeer.

Native opposition to baptism

There was a great uproar amongst both Europeans and the natives concerning Krishna's baptism and the baptism of other Indians which followed. Many Europeans had the idea of a 'white church' and the Indians feared that Christian baptism was a means of forcing Indians to become Europeans. Abandoning the practice of the previous British churches who kept to the caste system and even used different cups for different castes at the communion service, the Serampore Trio announced that their worship was to be caste-free. This angered many of the Europeans and the Bengalis themselves demanded that the Indian Christians should be severely punished. Crowds of up to 2,000 angry natives hammered at Krishna's door and there were also great protests when his daughter protested that she would not marry the man to whom she had been betrothed against her will. The Governor had to come to their rescue as the crowds were crying 'Feringhi'[5] at the newly converted Indians and protesting that the Europeans were striving to rob them of their status as Indians. Governor Bie's assurance that Krishna and his friends had truly become Christians but not Europeans, failed to calm the enraged mob.

Indians turn to Christ

A fortnight later Jaymani, the first of many Bengali women was baptised, followed soon after by her sister Rasmayi, a leather worker's widow named Annada and a man called Gokool, who had been converted about the same time as Krishna and who was baptised with his wife. Then high caste Petumber Singh, who had sought forgiveness of sin for many years, professed Christ, followed by other high caste Indians such as Syan Dass, Petumber Mitter and his wife Draupadi. These were learned people who soon became teachers and preachers to their people. Then Muslims such as Peroo and Brahmins such as Krishna Prosad became Christians, so that now within four years, forty native Indians were converted and eight from other peoples. A number of these became missionaries and evangelists in their own right and spread the good tidings in other areas right up to the Chinese border. This turn of events was greatly assisted by the publication of the Bengali New Testament the bulk of which Thomas had translated. It

[5] Portuguese for foreigner.

was first placed on the communion table at Serampore on 5 March, 1801.

Cox writes of Krishna:

> For six months the heart of Krishno had been set on an itineracy to the eastern part of Bengal, and having provided a temporary supply for Calcutta, he was sent thither with Gorachund. He accordingly proceeded to Silhet, within about a hundred leagues of the province of Yunnan, in China. Here he found a people without caste, and of good character for probity. He found, also, two European residents, who encouraged his efforts. In a short time he baptized seven persons, and resolved to settle at Pandora, a few miles nearer China than Silhet, where one of the European gentle-men built him a house and a school-room. It was determined to send two native brethren to strengthen his hands. These were Boodheesa and Pran-krishna.[6]

Here, Krishna was truly fulfilling the work of an evangelist and, helped by people outside of the Serampore 'missionaries'. These, according to Cox, had stopped evangelising because they were too busy translating, printing and 'superintending schools so employed others to do their work'.[7] Krishna was now virtually running his own mission and that with great success. However, true to Britain's colonial spirit at the time, Krishna was put under a British supervisor and was said to be a mere employee of the Serampore Trio whose work he was doing for them.

Thomas' translation of Matthew gains the British King's eye

Thomas' work on Matthew was also published as a separate hand out. This action gained the interest of the King of England who recommended this pioneering project to the East India Company. They, in turn, protested that they had not approved of the translation but the King replied that the task of spreading the Scriptures was outside of their jurisdiction and that he was greatly pleased that his subjects were employed in such a manner. However, it was this work of Thomas',

---

[6] Cox's *History*, p. 236.

[7] Cox, p. 235 and *passim*.

edited and extended by Carey which eventually moved the King and the East India Company to reconsider the status of missionaries to India. Here we see that, though locked up, Thomas was still serving the missionary cause in India.

Many now claimed that the printing of the first Bengali New Testament was the first step in turning the Indians from their erroneous superstitions. This was only half of the truth. In the providence of God, this first major translation by the British missionaries built on Thomas' work also helped to turn the British East Indian Company from their erroneous, superstitious attitude towards the citizens of Indian so that restrictions against missionaries were lifted in 1813.

Chapter Twenty-Two

Prudence and Folly at Serampore

'Foreign ornaments' dispensed with

In order to combat the fear that missionaries were forcing the Indians to become Europeans, made stronger by the fact that they actually did force them to adopt 'Christianised' European names, the Baptists realised that they must dispense with what they now called 'foreign' ornaments. The giving of Christian names had severely hindered the work of genealogists and historians in India as often family names quite disappeared. The missionaries insisted on calling their native co-workers solely by their new single names and not in the customary three names. Not infrequently new converts were compelled to take on the first name of the one who led them to Christ. This was rather lacking in respect as the missionaries did not use their own 'Christian' names in everyday speech, rather than their family names, with people outside of their friendship circle. Nor were their family names abolished. They thus only addressed Indian converts by their 'Christian names'. Traditionally, many Indians carried three names similar to the ancient praenomen, nomen and cognomen which helped to trace the ancestry and history of the individual.[1] They were means of identification whereas being called merely 'Aaron' or 'Timothy' were not. This caused the present author great difficulties when tracing the 18th-19th century history of the Baptist mission to the Native American Indians for his book *Isaac McCoy: Apostle of the Western Trail*. He found so

[1] This custom tended to vary according to district and religion.

many Indians called John Gill, John Calvin or Isaac McCoy in the Southern states and Andrew Fuller in the North that it became impossible to determine if they were the same people as those called Hajekathake, Pos-sa-che-haw, Nam-pa-war-rah or Sa-mau-kau before their baptisms. Several Indian chieftains had impressed on me that they valued my work because it took the Native Americans back to their own family roots and identification. The missionaries had severed these roots from their family tree.

Carey believed that the odd idea of previous missionaries to give their converts 'Christian names' as a sign that they had left their own culture behind had no useful function so theoretically his converts carried the same name after baptism as before and were no longer renamed 'Calvin', 'Luther', or whatever, as formerly. This renaming had caused social unrest as members of the same family now carried different names. Carey, himself, however, continued to address his converts and servants by one single name only in the colonial manner.

Ziegenbalg and name changing

Ziegenbalg had had difficulties making up his mind concerning name-changing. He found, however, that Europeans in general could not pronounce the native names of Indians so he arranged that his converts should take on 'Christian names' as middle names for European use and retain their full Indian names for family use and the Indian society. This custom has continued up to modern times but is not free from problems. However, the giving of names connected with religions was not a Western phenomenon seen from a historical point of view. It was an ancient custom in India and had been practised by the Hindus, Buddhists and Muslims for many centuries so the giving of 'Christian names' was really no novelty. For an author and researcher who reads books in several different languages, complications arise. English books recording Indian Church History often give English Christian names to Indians who had Danish or German 'Christian' names, feeling this made for better English reading, not realizing that this makes the Church historian wonder who the named ones really were. Worse still, the British recorded Indian names as they understood them in English letters and many modern Indians have thus pseudo-Indian names which were never given them by their forefathers. This seems to be especially the case with Bengali names which have become pidginised by British and American speakers.

Different attitudes to names in the South and the North

The attitude to the Tamils concerning family names was rather different to the more northern Indians. Family names were eagerly dropped by many and they had nothing against bearing European names as their family names revealed what caste they were in and they desired a caste-less society. However, many Indians were given Christian names like Cecil, Clive or George thinking that these names of high-ranking administrators might help them up the social ladder. The Thomas Christians, however, now spread out through most of India, identified themselves with high caste Brahmins and took on Brahmin names and Brahmin customs. Many so-called European 'Christian names' have now been absorbed into Indian spelling and pronunciation, giving rise to such neologisms as Pranchi (Francis) and Devassya (Sebastian). One often comes across the name of 'Alexander' which comes in many versions such as 'Iskander' or 'Eskander'.

Now the Serampore fellowship decided to stop, at least theoretically, the custom of 'Christianising' by name at baptism.[2] This was a wise move as the families of Indian believers, especially in Bengal, looked upon the giving of foreign names to their dear ones as a form of apartheid, separating one family member from another. The rumour even spread that Indians with English 'Christian' names could now be legally deported to England. Sadly, this caused opposition in the BMS whose 'absentee bishops' insisted on carrying on the old meaningless practice and reintroduced it officially after they boycotted Carey.

The Serampore Baptists were firm in rejecting the caste system

The Baptist missionaries stood firm on their stand against the caste system though this caused an uproar amongst 'Christian' Europeans, Hindus and Muslims alike. When casteless Gokool died, his coffin was carried by Bhyrub, a converted Brahmin and Piru, a former Muslim; besides Marshman and Felix Carey to demonstrate that they were all now one in Christ. So, too, in 1802, Krishna's Christian daughter, a Sudra, was married to a Brahmin convert, said to be the first Indian

[2] I write 'theoretically' because Indian co-workers were still called by one name only.

Christian marriage to occur in North India. A special service was devised for the occasion based on the Church of England rite and not Baptist traditions. The 'Anglican' marriages were most likely so that they could be officially registered by the colonial authorities. Fuller, however, broke with the Church of England on the matter of divorce.

Six silver shillings for each baptismal candidate

However, one well-meant action of the Serampore Baptist missionaries soon proved to be highly impracticable. At the beginning of their ministry, they offered six silver shillings to all who would present themselves for baptism as an encouragement to take this meaningful step. Six shillings to a penniless, 'untouchable' person who had to mostly beg for a living was a small fortune in those days and was certainly the wrong way to go about counting those baptised as 'converts'. Some 'rice' Christians were now in danger of becoming 'silver shilling' Christians. Six shillings was also the amount the Serampore Trio paid their Indian evangelists monthly to do the work that the very high salaried Serampore Trio had promised to do themselves. Happily, the missionaries, though rather too late to ward off just criticism and, too, tempting misuse, dropped the offer.

The problem of non-Baptist or non-Christian spouses

The first Baptist converts whether males or females brought or strove to bring, their wives and children into the fold of the church. Soon, however, newly converted church members sometimes found their spouses most unwilling to become publicly 'immersed'. The missionaries, however, insisted initially that the converts' families be baptized with the believers thus causing extra pressure on the newly converted whose spouses and offspring refused to be baptized.

Help sought on the problem of Indian marriages

At first the Serampore Trio showed great leniency to the Indians requests to preserve their family unity and a number of converted men and women brought their spouses to church so that they could come under the gospel but some of the wives and husbands refused to attend church services. The Serampore Baptists held weekly prayer-meetings all through 1803 for a solution to this major problem but found none. They then became impatient to have all things regimented but having found no solution and although they had told the home committee that they could manage their own affairs, they now passed the puck to Andrew Fuller and the BMS, leaving them to sort out the problem. The solution the home team came up with was most questionable from a Biblical, social and ethical point of view.

Secretary Fuller, serving as the BMS spokesman ruled that marriages 'outside the Lord' were not real marriages and a Christian was thus not bound in wedlock by either an unbelieving husband or wife. According to George Smith,[3] Fuller therefore advised the Serampore Mission that converted Indians should do all in their power to have their spouses worship with them but if this proved impossible after a reasonable period of time, they should divorce their wives or husbands and be free to remarry again. Such Christian divorcees could then take up church offices. Fuller apparently did not think of what misery his decision entailed for those 'put away' by such an un-merciful act. This was the very practice of the so-called 'pagans' which had led Basu to his misery. The poor divorced men, women and children would be thus forced to leave the family nest and be damned to poverty and the scorn of both the 'Christians' and the 'pagans', though it would be difficult to tell who was a pagan and who a Christian in Fuller's system of morals. So, too, not only a number of converted Indians were bigamists but many of Carey's English associates and church-goers were bigamists, too, but it soon became clear that the missionaries were respecters of persons. Carey tells us that the solution found amongst the British in Calcutta who had Indian wives was to dismiss them with a suitable allowance when their hearts were captivated by a British woman. Very many of the children cared for in the Baptist schools, as was the case in Ziegenbalg's schools, were unwanted children through the 'mixed' amours of colonial masters.

Fuller's error of judgment

Fuller's advice ignored the fact that marriage was a natural creation act and love, care, devotion and faithfulness played a large role in maintaining marriage bonds, whatever the religion of the participants was. Adam and Eve were one flesh both before and after the fall. Where most of our Reformers saw marriage as a creative act of God for all

[3] See Smith's *William Carey* p. 105.

peoples, the Baptists moved from this position though the Dissenting churches of Commonwealth times and the Church of England at the Restoration had equally stressed that marriage was both a creation act and a civil contract. The two who became one flesh were therefore not necessarily Christians. Marriage was for an Adam and an Eve, a Cain as well as an Abel; and for an Esau as well as a Jacob. One could not force a Christian to divorce his spouse on the grounds that he or she had married whilst unconverted. Yet true marriage as such was a means decreed by God to illustrate the love of Christ for his Bride the Church. It is an evangelising act which gives even the unsaved a peep into Heaven.

In the early days of the Baptists, marriage 'outside of the congregation' was, according to J. J. Goadby in his most enlightening book *Bye-Paths in Baptist History*, either not recognised as 'legal' or led to excommunication. A Christian could thus be excommunicated for refusing to desert his wife. The Church of England's leading Martin Madan advocated bigamy with concubines so Christians could avoid adultery and woman becoming prostitutes. This was certainly not according to our Lord's teaching on divorce or that of any of the New Testament writers. John Newton was criticised by some of his fellow ministers for not advocating 'Christian' bigamy. Against his cousin Madan and in defence of Newton, Cowper wrote of both respectively:

> Oh rare device! The wife betray'd
> The Modest, chaste, Domestic Woman
> To save a worthless, Wanton Jade,
> From Being, what she would be, Common.
>
> If John marries Mary and Mary alone,
> 'Tis a very good match between Mary and John.
> Should John wed a score, oh! the claws and the scratches!
> It can't be a match: - 'tis a bundle of matches.

Squabbles with the BMS over funding

The wealthy Serampore Trio were now investing nine-tenths of their large income in worldwide missions. The rest was used for the daily needs of the growing missionary family. The Serampore Mission was thus the greatest financial supporter of the British Baptist Missionary Society worldwide. The figures speak for themselves. During Carey's forty years in India, he personally received a mere £600 from the home committee. On the other hand, Carey donated most of the £46,000 he earned as a business man and professor in India to the Society's work. The other missionaries doubled this amount between them and their non-Society friends in India provided another £80,000.

Rather than rejoice at this situation, the sad truth is that the more Carey's Mission became totally self-supporting and expansive, the more the Society wished to have full control over all its financial resources, including the major amount of property provided by non-Baptist Christian friends and the Danish Royal Family and diplomats from Denmark, Germany and England. Furthermore, the Society wished also to have full control over the personal lives and agendas of the missionaries. They demanded a fully transparent East Indian Mission, with themselves as 'Big Brother' watching over and administrating it.

The Serampore Trio wisely saw that the Society was totally lacking in the acumen and experience needed to rule their East India Mission from afar and that Fuller and his associates could not understand the needs of India. Thus, when Fuller and the home committee strove to govern the Serampore Church as absentee vicars, they hampered the Mission's work greatly and dropped the rope they had promised to hold in support of Carey. When Fuller died in 1815, the remaining founders and the new Committee became even more antagonistic towards the Serampore missionary strategy and evangelistic outreach. Indeed, they now complained that the Serampore Trio were making themselves rich at the expense of the Mission and treated them with great suspicion as if they were fiddling the Society's books. They became so grasping that Carey had threatened to give them all the assets of the Indian Mission and go off and found another mission, run by those at the Indian front alone. With hindsight, this would have been the more sensible thing to do. Under the new Secretary John Dyer, whom Carey thought strove to act like a Secretary of State, the BMS did separate themselves from the Serampore Mission but only to hamper their work as less disciplined rivals.

Carey's 'less than perfect' family life

Ruth Tucker in her essay 'William Carey's Less-than-Perfect Family Life' writing in issue 36, 2020 of Christianity Today, has shown that the 'model missionary' did not have a 'model home'. So, too, Shally Hunt portrays what she feels is Felix Carey's 'colourful and tragic life' in her article of that name and in her book *Prisoner of Hope*. Sometimes these two works show exaggerations from a rather feministic point of view but their criticism is timely, given all the modern hype concerning the way Carey has been idolized. It is true that Carey's wife Dorothy was greatly neglected by her husband as were also Carey's children. We must face the facts. It seems to have been highly irresponsible of Carey, too, that whilst Dolly was supposed to be mad, she became pregnant through Carey's visits to her room, locked from the outside, to add to her worries. So, too, Carey spent apparently more time alone with another woman outside of his missionary duties than he did with his wife. Indeed, when Carey joined the Serampore Duo to make up the famous Trio, Marshman was shocked to find Carey's children running around like young savages, void of all care, protection and education. Marshman's first task then in India was to act *in loco parentis* and educate Carey's children, a task Carey failed to do himself. He was assisted both by Thomas and Ward in this task. Nobody could condone such neglect and irresponsibility but Tucker goes too far in her complaint that men in those days looked on their wives and children merely as 'property'. Besides the fact that one has also a responsibility to look after one's property, which Carey failed to do, Tucker's generalizing theory is quite wrong as witnessed by Mr and Mrs Ziegenbalg, Mr and Mrs Chambers, Mr and Mrs Brown, Mr and Mrs Kiernander and, of course this could not possibly apply to Carey's fellow missionaries Joshua and Hannah Marshman. Truth to tell, in some of these marriages, the wives proved the stabilizing and even dominant factor. As further evidence against Tucker's strange notion we might also add the marriages of Bullinger, Gill, Luther and many if not most other men of God who adored their wives and even followed their initiative and enjoyed a marriage of equality. Luther did not call his wife 'Herr (Boss) Käthe' for nothing! Bullinger had a most harmonious marriage with his Anna but was for many years under the thumb of his mother-in-law. So, too, there are even many recorded cases of Carey doing Dorothy's will rather than the other way round.

Besides, more than one Reformer such as Richard Hooker led a hen-pecked family life.

John Gill was criticised by the Keach-Stinton faction for being a family man who even prepared his sermons with his tiny tots on his knees and loved his wife deeply. This criticism was also the lot of Ziegenbalg whom the Roman Catholic priests accused of neglecting his 'office' by living with his family. They even printed and posted up an anti-Ziegenbalg caricature depicting Ziegenbalg called away to preach the gospel with his wife and children clutching at his clothing to draw him back to his family responsibilities. Ziegenbalg's family always stood with him, behind him and in front of him and shared his poverty for Christ's sake but also out of a strong, mutual conviction of love.

It was not only Mrs Carey who was greatly neglected by her husband but also his children Felix and William who as teenagers developed alcohol problems and troubles with the opposite sex. Carey was also only a teenager when he married a woman six years older than he was. They say it was more a mother-child relationship and Carey always continued to act as an irresponsible teenager in Dorothy's motherly presence. Certainly, this does not speak for Carey but we are reminded that the collapse in Dorothy Carey's health under the stress and artificial social conditions beside the hot climate was not solely a feminine factor as the male Dr John Thomas fell a victim of the same pressure at the same time. It appears to be almost forgotten that Thomas pioneered Baptist evangelism in India and not Carey, and that Thomas had started translating the Bible into Bengali long before Carey, and had completed at least Matthew, Mark, James and Genesis before Carey used them as a basis for his own work. Indeed, it was Thomas' translation of Matthew which proved a break-through for the Serampore Mission. Christopher Smith relates in his work on Carey concerning Krishna who was converted under Thomas, 'When Carey led Krishna and his son Felix into the waters of baptism the ravings of Thomas on the one side, and Mrs Carey on the other, mingled with the strains of the Bengali hymn of praise.' So, Carey's background was far from harmonious and ideal and we must ask ourselves if the 'ravings' of Thomas were not because he was butted out from the leadership and ought to have been the one baptizing his own converts instead of being locked up? The worries of Krishna come before our eyes here as Carey put other Indians over him in his evangelistic work who had come to the Lord after him and did not live up to his high ideals of the ministry. Were Dorothy's 'ravings' due to the fact that she had been so greatly neglected and even locked up? The fact that Carey spent so much time with a rich Duchess, giving her private English lessons whom he eventually married when he was supposed to be doing the work of a missionary would have caused any wife to be frantic. Instead, Dolly's protests that Carey was unfaithful were put down to her 'madness'.

Kiernander had quite a wealthy background which provided him with money enough for his long and successful studies and the financial support of the Mission. He also inherited his parents' land and property and was also supported by other family members on his side. Yet Kiernander is generally accused by pro-Carey writers of marrying his first and second wives for their money. This is a preposterous and mean accusation. Yet Carey, formerly a very poor man is not criticised for marrying an affluent Danish Duchess with wide political contacts, though an invalid, very soon after Dorothy's death. The fact is that both Kiernander and Carey as widowers then entered into marriages with stalwart women who loved the Mission as much as their husbands, and were a great blessing to it. If others had been Dolly, they would also have told Carey to mend his ways but Carey had now become a 'cult figure' and, like Fuller, could not stand criticism.

Carey had obviously given up all responsibility over his wife and children. Thus, the many amateur pro-Carey diagnoses of Dolly's and Thomas' complaints as being sheer 'madness' are most disturbing. There is no such undifferentiated, clinical malady as 'madness'. Anyone would wrongly be presumed mad, by those who believed Carey always did right, who protested at such neglect and lack of recognition under which Dolly and Thomas suffered. To be locked up day and night as they were would make anyone rant and rave and become depressed. Indeed, it usually takes others directly or indirectly to make a person 'mad'. It appears there has never been any attempt to examine closely Thomas and Dolly's sufferings in a professional manner but they have both been dumped on the side as 'missionary misfits'. The missionaries who 'misfitted' them must also be held at least partly responsible for their severe treatment of Thomas and Mrs Carey.

The initial tragedy of Felix's connections with his father's Mission was certainly owing to his father's parental failures, bad influence and interference in Felix's four marriages before his death at the age of thirty-seven. Felix's alcohol problem and his love of luxury obviously started in his childhood with his father's fondness of large 'meat suppers' washed down with two full glasses of wine. The Carey's never drank even water without mixing it with rum allegedly to kill off bacteria where boiling would have proved more efficient. Carey lived in palatial circumstances, surrounded by a host of servants, which must have influenced Felix's thirst for the high life which caused him to enter into debt to better his circumstances when sent off by his father to live in what his brother William called 'a wretched wilderness'. It was the horror of living so miserably that had broken Carey's career as a planned backwoodsman missionary.

Shally Hunt says Felix Carey had 'a colourful but tragic life' and feels that his father looked upon him as the black sheep of the family and as an untamed tiger. She quotes Hannah Marshman as saying that Carey saw and lamented the evil but did nothing to remedy it. Under Ward's fatherly care, however, Felix became civilized. Both Tucker and Hunt refer to Ward as Felix's 'surrogate father'.

Hunt, in her effort to describe Carey's obvious neglect of his son is too hard on Felix in her statement, 'his talents were linguistic and medical rather than evangelical' and that, 'Felix was unable to succeed in the mission field'. On the count of being weak in evangelism, Carey was hardly better than his son as Mark Galli truthfully and objectively states when commenting on the relative lack of conversions throughout the history of the Serampore Trio who:

> recognized that as the years went by they spent less time with Indians and more with translation work and administration of the mission and schools. Though other missions to Hindus have rarely done better, Carey's legacy is not primarily in evangelism.[4]

From being a youngster aged only fourteen Felix entered whole heartedly into preaching under the guidance of Ward. He also founded Sunday Schools for children. His father married him off at the age of eighteen to a child of fifteen, Margaret Kinsey, daughter of a Calcutta school-teacher which all seemed rather rushed. It is said that Carey, by

[4] *William Carey – The Man Who Would Not Give Up*, www.hopefaithprayer.com.

this means, wished to prevent his son from entering into sexual adventures. William, also neglected by his father until he could not be corrected, fell into immoral conduct. Chatterjee claims that this was the general lot of the neglected European children in India. Perhaps more fatherly love and care would have saved Felix from what seems to have been a forced marriage between teenagers and saved his younger brother William from ruining his life.

Hunt and Tucker, however, hardly touch on Felix's good side and his youthful excellence, though the records speak of him as a successful preacher and evangelist and excellent at itinerant work. Hunt tells us that in 1807 when Felix had reached the age of twenty-one and had already fathered two children by his young wife now aged 18, Carey Senior 'ordained him and commissioned him to serve as a missionary in Burma' which, at the time, was closely allied with Bengal. The projects Felix now envisaged but could never really carry out, chiefly through lack of backing from Serampore, moved Hunt to believe Felix began to suffer from what she called 'bipolar syndrome' which led her to call her book *Prisoner of Hope*, taken from the honest words written on Felix's grave-stone. One should not drop such a hypothesis into an article or book without clear clinical evidence based on studies by the well-qualified, especially as this syndrome is very difficult indeed to diagnose even by experts.[5] However, Hunt finds one positive thing about Felix and that is his introduction of smallpox vaccine to Burma. She also tells us that 'Felix lost a mother from insanity, a brother from dysentery, his first wife in childbirth, his second wife and two small children in a shipwreck'. His third wife was gored by a bull and left an invalid. Felix then begged his father to allow them back to Calcutta for the sake of his wife. Hard of heart Carey absolutely refused this request at first and told his son that he must put the Mission before his family. He apparently did not consider that the womenfolk in the Mission were also part of the Mission. What happened to Felix's third wife is not clear although Hunt says he abandoned her to live a life as a 'hanger on', scrounging on the Rajahs and that when he died his fourth wife was expecting a child.

[5] I do not write these words as a novice as I have been academically trained in psychology receiving a 'first' for my work and one of my sons with whom I have discussed Carey's, Thomas' and Dolly's cases in depth is a leading expert in such cases.

After reading S. K. Chatterjee's work on Felix entitled *The Tiger Tamed*, one gains a wider view of Felix's abilities and disabilities. When Felix eventually entered government employment, apparently to save himself from starving, he was severely criticized by his father who, nevertheless, lived and died a government employee himself. It was as if Carey wished to force his son into succeeding as a missionary where he had failed.

Actually, Felix had often great success in unevangelized fields without the company of his more stay-at-home father. Chamberlain and Krishna joined readily in working with him in his itinerant ministry which proved most successful. Hunt says she has found her sources on Felix in the Angus Library records to which all writers make a pilgrimage who wish to contribute to a general knowledge of the East Indian Mission with any accuracy. However, reading such sources is one thing, selective understanding and interpretation of their purport and the drawing of conclusions is another. As I have experienced on many occasions Angus Library, Oxford, has provided many such as myself with an enormous treasure open to all for research. Sadly, it is not what one finds but what one makes of it that prove sometimes that conclusions bare little relationship to what they are based on.

There are many negative things said about Felix in Burma in recent accounts which are mere guess-work rather than objective facts but Felix was only there for little more than three years and did much lasting good which is nowadays seldom emphasized. His initial journey to evangelize Burma when little more than a youth was most tragic. When Felix and his wife and children set out for Alva in Burma, their ship capsized and he alone survived. Nevertheless, he carried on in the spirit of his father composing a Grammar in Burmese and Sanskrit and drawing up a Burmese dictionary. He also translated Bunyan's *Pilgrim's Progress* into Burmese besides Goldsmith's *The Vicar of Wakefield* and translated a *History of England* besides a work on Chemistry, all for the Serampore College. He became Burma's ambassador to Calcutta but was apparently incapable of carrying out his duties. He was persuaded by Ward (not by his genetic father who had refused to have Felix back) to return to Serampore/Calcutta where he continued as a member of his father's team but was now recognised outside of Serampore as the most outstanding Burmese scholar amongst the Europeans. He died after been stricken with cholera and his gravestone was inscribed with the words:

Sacred to the memory of Felix Carey,
eldest son of the Rev. W. Carey, D. D.
who departed this life on the
10th of November, 1822,
ætat 36 years and 20 days.
A prisoner of hope released.

BMS did not explain the situation in Serampore to the churches

The Baptist Missionary Society did not reveal the true circumstances of the East Indian Mission to the general public as it would have been detrimental to their fundraising. However, anything coming from Serampore and Calcutta was severely edited. India was certainly the country which captured the interest of British believers the most so the Society kept on advertising the work in India as their prime target for funds. Thus, people thinking they were contributing to the spread of the gospel in India were actually contributing to the mission elsewhere where the methods of the Society were far less successful, indeed where they were often disastrous and ill-planned. A similar state of affairs in North America prevailed where William Staughton, a co-founder of the British Baptist Mission, was guilty of a most deceitful strategy. Monies canvassed for the spread of the gospel to the Native Americans were used for the world-wide mission. A training college set up for the training of Native Americans actually shut its doors to Native Indians as they were considered sub-human but allowed all others in. However, through mismanagement the college was soon bankrupt. This scandal brought the American Baptist Society to its knees and Isaac McCoy, pioneer missionary to the Native Americans, who strove to follow in Carey's footsteps, eventually formed a new mission and helped found the Southern Baptist Convention. In those days, the Southern Baptists were mostly Gillites and the Northern Baptists Fullerites and Free-Willers. Staughton was made responsible for American funds in support of Carey's Serampore work but instead of passing them on, he kept them back claiming that Carey's educational policy was false as he had botany and physics taught in the Serampore College. This, Staughton argued, was unbecoming for a Christian missionary. The difference between the western 'Indians' and those of the East was that McCoy's 'Indians' suffered greatly because they did not receive funds earmarked for them, whereas Carey's Indians were chiefly aided by the missionaries' own earnings and interdenominational support. Such facts quite disprove the teaching of modern Fullerites who would have us believe that Carey and the Home Committee where always of 'one heart and one soul' and that Carey's success was because he put into practice all that was dictated to him by Staughton, Fuller, Ryland, Hall and company.

Carey sat on the fence regarding the BMS

Though Carey did not agree with the Society over the financing of the mission and was often tempted to break with them, he believed initially that his influence would be greater within the Baptist Missionary Society than outside of it. When one reviews the accounts of the Society's own fundraising work soberly, it is clear that the larger donations came from outside of the Committee's denominational circle and that the amounts raised by the BMS were far too modest to finance a large world-wide mission, not to mention a single mission in India. The two great exceptions were the Society's success in raising over a thousand pounds for Bible Society work and in meeting the costs caused by a fire in the Mission's printing department in India. However, the bulk of these monies came from outside of the denomination and such rare donations were paid back with interest by the Carey Mission.

Even when members of Carey's wider 'Missionary Family' were fitted out materially for their pioneer work by the Society, Carey regarded this act as one of mere supply on demand and paid the Society in full. Thus the Serampore Trio were not in any debt regarding the BMS who ignored them for long periods of time.

The British Charter of 1813

The British Charter Act[6] of 1813, brought great relief to both foreign and British missionaries in Bengal. Later Baptist writers have, however,

[6] The Charter Act of 1813, also known as the East India Company Act, was an Act of Parliament in the United Kingdom which renewed the charter issued to the British East India Company, and continued the Company's rule in India.

greatly exaggerated the role Baptists made in producing this charter and also, oddly enough, see only the Church of England as benefiting from it. For instance, Crockett and Noonkester in their Carey.edu article The Vicar of Wakefield state under the heading 'Consensus Evangelium':

> Prior to charter renewal in 1813, some Anglicans and many dissenters appealed for the necessity and prudence of Christian missionary outreach to Hindus and Muslims. Proof texts for this view were the sayings of Jesus 'Go and teach all nations' and 'Go into all the world, and preach the gospel to every creature'. A universal context is clear in the statement of Oxford's Joseph White that 'Christianity, whether we consider the promises of its founder, or the spirits of its laws, is calculated for universal use, and claims universal belief.'

We note that this remark came from a pioneer missiologist from the ranks of the Church of England, not the Baptists. At the time leading to the charter, EIC Directors such as Grant, Lutherans, Presbyterians and Anglican ministers and missionaries were arguing for such a charter long before any large number of 'dissenters', especially the newly arrived Baptists, were on the scene. The main engineer behind the new Charter was certainly Grant who had often rescued the Baptists from grave financial difficulties. The Great Commission to evangelize the world had been emphasized in conjunction by Anglican Joseph White's 1785 appeal for missionaries to follow their Christian obligation to propagate the gospel in foreign parts, especially in India. Nor was this a new thing as the Church of England had already been supporting Indian missions for decades, using Tranquebar, Madras and other places as their bases. British Church of England evangelicals had been campaigning for an India open to the gospel without denominational fetters decades before Thomas and Carey came along. The quote from Mark 15:1 indicating the universal scope of the Commission was used by Anglican minister White in his tenth sermon on evangelizing India in his 1785 series of Bampton lectures on the duty of attempting the propagation of the gospel in India. Carey felt he should follow with his *Enquiry* eight years later. Many of White's points in his work of 526 pages with another 87 pages of notes are to be found in Carey's brief *Enquiry* and his efforts to 'attempt great things', which was not original to Carey. Nevertheless, though Crockett and Noonkester admit that the Anglicans, who were in company with many missionaries from other nations and denominations, were invariably first in their ventures, not to be thus outdone, they promote the idea that Baptists bettered them. For example, the two authors argue:

> Anglicans like White and David Brown, later to become an Anglican chaplain in Calcutta, brought their arguments to the public before the Baptists did. Brown circulated a proposal for establishing a protestant mission in Bengal in 1787 and sent it to the Archbishop of Canterbury and the Bishop of Llandaff. Nevertheless, unconstrained by ecclesiastical bureaucracy and safe under Danish protection, the Baptists surpassed the Anglicans during the first decade of the nineteenth century by producing numerous Bible translations and mission stations.

This statement can hardly be beaten for its bias and falseness. The Baptist 'translations' were mostly the work of non-Baptists and, indeed, non-Christians who obviously lacked the linguistic acumen of the large number of missionaries who had gone before them and they were far more short-lived. Indeed, it was Church of England evangelicals who encouraged the Baptists to engage in necessary Bible translations and who funded their first efforts generously, giving Carey the benefit of their expertise. Previous Bible translations prior to the translating methods of the Baptists were subject to decades of scrutiny and improvement and are still widely used such as that of Fabricius who died shortly before Carey's arrival in India. Nor did the Baptists found more mission stations than other inter-denominational missions had done but demonstrably far fewer. The Danes protected the Serampore Trio out of Christian love for the Lord's people and because they hoped they would continue the work already established there by the Danes, Swedes, Germans and English of other denominations.

Crockett and Noonkester's argument that the 1813 Charter provided more freedom for the Anglicans than the Baptists is, again, a false conclusion. The two authors continually confuse the difference between the EIC officials and Anglican missionaries and ministers and contradict themselves as the great works of the Baptists they boast of could only have been possible within the strictures of the 1813 Charter which the two highly biased writers strongly criticise. In other words, the 1813 Charter helped greatly in promoting the Baptists' work and did not hinder it. For instance, according to the Christian Observer, Vol. XII, pp. 741-743, Carey was able to set up schools in and after 1813 outside of Serampore which catered for 1,000 pupils. This would have been impossible before 1813. These schools, however, could not be called Mission schools as they were most secular in nature and were run by what Carey calls 'Heathens' who were unbelievers. Such schools, however, are seemingly always counted as Baptist missionary centres or 'stations'. However, as part of their paid duties, the 'pagan' teachers read the Scriptures to the children 'without making any objections'. It would be interesting to find out what Scriptures these were and in what language.

So, too, Crocket and Noonkester write as if the Baptists were free of any form of colonial thinking but both Marshman and Fuller, and to a lesser extent Ward insisted on the privileges of being colonial British and saw the gospel only working under British control. Former missionaries, on the whole, had not mixed their nationalism and patriotism with the gospel as my overview of the history of missions above shows.

Jeyaraj on the 1813 Charter

Indian scholar, pastor and theologian Daniel Jeyaraj, speaking of Schwartz' influence on subsequent missions claims:

> The life and work of Schwartz had a considerable impact on the East Indian Company, so that by 1813, it allowed British missionaries, and from 1833 all Protestant missionaries, to work in India.[7]

In other word's Germany's Schwartz was behind the 1813 Charter as he was behind Grant's and Carey's plea for missionaries and it was most certainly not an anti-Baptist political campaign. Grant disagreed

[7] 'Mission Reports from South India and Their Impact on the Western Mind', p. 32, from *In Converting Colonialism: Visions and Realities in Mission History*, ed., Dana L. Robert, 2008.

with Carey's translation strategy but nevertheless left Carey a most generous legacy.

There were thus many missionaries, chaplains and pastors working in Calcutta with the approval of the British traders and political authorities. So, there was a strong, evangelical, continuous witness in the city awaiting the arrival of people like Carey to strengthen it. However, instead of linking with the over 50 years' Christian witness of the Swede Kiernander in Calcutta, and the great work of Schwartz between Tranquebar and Serampore and beyond, and instead of supporting Brown and Buchanan in their relatively large and growing Calcutta churches, Carey entered into risky and speculative secular business enterprises such as running Indigo plants on borrowed money. As these did not bring him the desired income, he taught in an English college for civil servants under the British Government at Calcutta and later boosted his large salary of now £1,500 a year by teaching in a secular Serampore College backed by the Danish Government. Most of the time Carey commuted between his two secular posts, spending a few days a week in Calcutta and then a few days a week in Serampore with luxurious apartments and many servants in each place.

Chapter Twenty-Three

The Founding of Denmark's Third University at Serampore

The Danish Bengali trading centre

In 1755 the Danes founded Frederiksnagore near to their trading station Dannemarksnagore which they had used from 1698 to 1714 but had been forced to give up because of conflicts with the local landowners. The new trading centre named after King Frederick V (born 1723) soon became known as Srirampur which was pronounced by the Danes 'Serampore'. This time it seemed that Srirampur would have a longer life as it was built through the interests of the Governor of Bengal Alivardi Khan on behalf of the Mogul Emperor who resided in Delhi. Governor or Nabob Khan secured agreements with the local landowners allowing them mutual benefits with the Danes. The conditions laid down were that Serampore should not be turned into an armed fort and that Nabob Khan should receive two and a half per cent of the customs duties on all goods. The trading centre which became a crown colony and one of Denmark's and Norway's largest cities was given rights to trade in all of the state of Bengal and draw work forces from the local landowners' and their employees' families. This proved to be a thorn in the flesh to Great Britain especially as Serampore became more internationally important after the Napoleonic Wars. Serampore and Tranquebar were thus taken over by the British in 1845. Nowadays Serampore and Calcutta have grown into one large city

Britain at war with Denmark

During all the transactions going on between Serampore and Copenhagen regarding setting up a College in Bengal, Britain was at war with Denmark and Lord Nelson was besieging Denmark's capital in the Battle of Copenhagen during 1801. As Denmark was a neutral state at the time and no challenge whatsoever to Britain, the trumped-up war with Denmark brought great criticism on bullying Britain both at home and abroad. Robert Brook Aspland recorded in 1850:

> The history of war scarcely furnishes us an instance of a more indefensible and unrighteous attack on a brave and neutral power than the seizing of the Danish fleet, consisting of eighteen ships of the line and fifteen frigates, by the English Fleet. The defence offered by the Government was, that the Danish Fleet would have fallen into the hands of France, and it was expected that the Danes would quickly surrender. This anticipation, if really entertained, was disappointed. The Danes resisted, though vainly, at the cost of two thousand lives of their citizens and the conflagration of a portion of their capital. By a national outrage like this, where might the spirit of a Christian minister be stirred within him, and the outpouring of his heart be listened to without 'offence'.[1]

During these scandalous attacks on Denmark and her overseas territories by Britain, the Danish King kept his protecting hand over the British Baptist missionaries.

The Serampore Trio serve both sides in the disputes

In 1801, Wellesley made it clear to the Serampore Trio that their Mission was now treated as a British enclave in Danish Serampore and would be tolerated and even supported by the Company and British Government. The British Colonial powers called the Trio 'our men behind the enemy lines' or, in other words, 'British spies'. The Serampore Trio welcomed this move as they truly thought they could function as mediators between Denmark and Britain. Thus, the Danish Serampore leadership who had supported the Serampore Trio as Christians now had to view their guests as political representatives of

---

[1] *Memoir of the Life, Works and Correspondence of Robert Aspland*, p. 220.

Britain. From now on the Trio served as middlemen between Britain and Denmark, including in the realms of education. Because they were now politically secure on both sides of the Danish-British border, they could operate for the gospel's sake on both sides, too. Both Carey and Marshman supported Lord Wellesley's colonial ambitions fully as Carey made clear in his speech as moderator recorded in Buchanan's book on the Fort William College but they continued to profit from the political immunity and financial support Denmark afforded them. They had now the best of two worlds.

The number of missionaries in Serampore was shrinking

By 1801, the number of Baptist missionaries in Serampore was shrinking. In that year Brunson died after being ill most of his time in India at the very early age of twenty-four. John Thomas also died on 13th October, 1801, so now four of the Mission's first seven missionaries were dead. Dorothy Carey died in 1807 at the age of 51. She had never been recognized as anything but a bed-comforter for her husband. No one seems to have researched whether her claims that Carey was unfaithful to her were justified. They were put down, or covered up, by claims she was 'mad'. On the positive side, a number of Indian converts and enquirers had broken their castes by eating with the missionaries.

Myths surrounding Serampore College

Now we must deal with the myths spread so widely in modern missionary literature concerning the Serampore College which had been planned for years by the Danish authorities to be their third university after Copenhagen and Kiel. Originally the College was set up in 1818, ten years after the Serampore Trio came to the Danish colony, as a secondary school providing a general educational centre for the children of Asiatic Christians, and Non-Christians nation-wide, providing the latter fulfilled certain criteria. University status was to come some ten years later but this, too, was to be of a primarily secular nature. The brochure announcing the opening of the College gave its official title as 'A College for the Instruction of Asiatic Christians and Other Youth in Eastern Literature and European Science, at Serampore, Bengal'. This brochure was not printed from the Serampore Press as was usual for the Trio but printed in London in 1819.[2] What was extraordinary about the school was that most of the tuition was based on Sanskrit and its dialects which was the equivalent in Europe of basing education on Latin as was still the custom in Carey's day though neither Carey, nor Ward, nor Marshman had enjoyed such an education. Marshman began to learn Latin at the Bristol Training College for ministers.

The authors of the brochure outlined the ten aims of the College as:

> The pupils should be given a knowledge of:
> The 'Pouronic and Boudistic systems'.
> Arabic.
> Chinese.
> Christianity in conjunction with learning Sanskrit.
> European science and Information.
> English for a 'select number'.
> Latin for those of Portuguese and French extraction. This was added to their studies of Sanskrit followed possibly by Greek and Hebrew.
> The principles of education for future teachers.
> Further Scripture for those encouraged to enter the ministry.

When outlining the basis of the education supplied by the College the main pedagogical aim of the school was to provide a knowledge of Sanskrit to children from Christian homes and Arabic and Persian for a certain number of others, probably those whose families followed other religions. Also, a foremost place was given in the curriculum to the learning of 'Hindu, Pouronic and Boudhist systems', which apparently meant instruction in individual religions or in Comparative Religion. This is a far cry from the current common belief amongst Western Baptists that the Serampore Trio founded a Theological Seminary such as that founded by Danish and German missionaries a hundred years before.

The 'Pouronic' Pouranic or Puranic systems mentioned, refer to some eighteen works termed 'the Purana' which contain legends,

[2] The brochure is available in the Public Domain.

histories, and literary tales possibly dating from the first to the eleventh centuries. These are held by many as the original documents forming the basis of Hinduism. The term 'Boudhist' (Buddhist) refers to such writings as the Sutras which were early translated into Sanskrit but poetical works were preserved in Pali and many very early works were in Chinese.

Concerning the missionaries' wish to further the gospel by all this concentration on ancient languages and Indian religions, the authors claim:

> From those who understand the real state of things, the answer to these will be, that it must be done by publishing the gospel in its native excellence, and comparing it with all that now holds possession of the public mind. To do with this, however, they must make it known, must be acquainted with those doctrines which hold the great mass of the people in such captivity that they fear even to hear of the gospel. That this knowledge can scarcely be obtained without an acquaintance with the language in which alone these doctrines are contained, the Sŭngskritŭ language; and this points out the necessity of a Collage for native Christian Youths, in which, while instructed in the Scriptures, they shall be taught Sŭngskritŭ in the most efficient manner, and be made acquainted with the philosophical doctrines which form the soul of the Boudhist and Pouranic Systems.

In other words, the pupils were to be guided through Carey's recently 'translated' Bible into his own reduced form of Sanskrit which he was busy learning at the time. This was all propaganda for the Mission as there were a number of Bibles available in a number of Indian languages or imported ones such as Syriac which were both ancient and had been modernised. Why thus confine Scripture learning to an artificial, dead language? There were already Bibles in Indian languages which the pupils already knew. It was thus insisted in the brochure repeatedly that learning Sanskrit was the gateway both to Non-Christian and Christian learning so that the authors could write:

> And while the instruction of Christian Youth in all the learning of the Brahmŭns, will be so much more effectual, that it

> may possibly accelerate the work of full age, it will remove the reproach of ignorance from the Native Christians, and enable their children to enjoy the highest literary advantages of their own country, as fully as the highest castes amongst the Hindus.[3]

The authors stress repeatedly that just as our Reformers were enabled to use Latin and Greek in their studies the same benefits would be gained by Indians who learnt Sanskrit. This is a very lame comparison as Latin and Greek opened the doors for our Reformers to study the Scriptures and the history of the church, whereas Sanskrit, as the Serampore authors stress time and time again, opens the door to Hinduism and Buddhism. The amount of time teaching such subjects as Hinduism and Buddhism was apparently greater than that spent on any other subjects including Christianity. The doors to these religions were, however, open to most Indians in their native languages without having to learn Sanskrit. The Buddhists were still using Pali as their classical language. However, no amount of 'transfer of training' can make the Vedas and the Tripitaka suitable as an introduction to the Christian faith especially in a dumbed-down version.

Of the ten aims of the school, the first four are taken up with Sanskrit learning followed by Arabic and Chinese. As there was already a school for Arabic in Calcutta with a hundred students, the authors argued in their brochure that they were cheaper in their fees and could cater for a hundred-and-fifty students. Indeed, there was a strong spirit of rivalry between the Serampore college and the growing number of other colleges in Calcutta and surrounding districts which were being set up by various denominational and secular authorities.

The fifth aim of the College was to teach general history which should go beyond 'elementary reading', the solar system laws of attraction, gravitation, motion and 'mechanical powers'. The sixth aim was to give 'a select number' lessons in English and the seventh aim was to give those of Portuguese and French extraction the chance to learn Latin and Greek. The eighth and ninth aims were to foster an interest in becoming either teachers or entering the Christian ministry.

The tenth aim was to take in youths from all over India irrespective of caste, religion or Christian denominations including Roman

---

[3] P. 6.

Catholics. The matter of tuition fees and who should pay for them is not clearly stated. The first mention of fees indicate that the College would cover all fees but then we read that the system was that those who were recommended by friends of the college should be financed by such friends. Other pupils, apparently those who did not live in, should provide for their own learning media.

Jacob Krefting to be President

The President of the College was to be the new Danish Governor Jacob Krefting who backed the formation of the college and was on its governing board. The brochure says that Krefting was to be President 'for the time being' possibly because news was ripe concerning a second British government takeover. Britain had 'confiscated' Serampore towards the end of the Napoleonic era but through the agencies of Governor Krefting, the Danish King and Commissary Gordon Forbes, the colony was restored to Denmark in 1815. There was then a push-me-pull-you state of affairs for the next thirty years when, in 1845, Serampore was finally placed into British hands. The resulting 'deal' did not affect the Danish Christian work in Serampore and all institutions such as missionary work, the hospital and Serampore College had business as usual. The entire history of this period can be followed in the Collection of Treaties, Engagements and Sanads[4] Relating to India and Neighbouring Countries, Calcutta, 1892 available on the Public Domain.

So the Serampore College was obviously not a theological training college as so often stated in Baptist literature but rather a school for secondary education open to all races, confessions and castes. It was not founded by the BMS for graduate theology or missionary strategy but was an arrangement solely between the Danish Government and the Serampore Trio with the approval of the British authorities. Indeed, it was the disagreements between Marshman who took the lead in the Serampore College proposals, and the BMS that prompted N. P. Hancock to claim that this caused the breach between Serampore and

[4] A deed granted in British India to native rulers in exchange for their allegiance. An extensive list of such sanads is also available in the Public Domain.

Fenn Court.[5] The Serampore College was simply not on the BMS agenda. So, too, most of the teaching was to be done by Indian pundits and Carey himself taught such subjects as botany and gardening supported by a subscription to Curtis' Botanical Magazine and Sowerby's English Botany Magazine and did not teach say, Sanskrit, Latin, Greek or Hebrew. According to Staughton, this was one of the reasons why the BMS did not help to finance the college.

Those who still hold to a theological college being founded in Serampore refer to two colleges run parallel in Serampore by the Trio, a secular college and a Bible College but we only know of one college being founded in 1818, mostly staffed by Indians under European supervision, and the college of 1827 which was given a Danish University status which did not materialize until the Serampore Trio were all dead.[6] As Carey and Marshman had become key figures in pacifying both the Danish and British sides during Britain's attempts to take over Serampore, the Danish Governor of Serampore sent Marshman as a representative of both the Danish and British authorities to Copenhagen in 1827 to obtain a university charter for Serampore College. We remember that Marshman was acting as a Danish citizen with a Danish passport at this time. This Danish arrangement was not altered by the British for a number of years and by then the College had been merged with Calcutta University. After 1883, the Serampore-Calcutta University gave degrees but those in Theology were first awarded after 1915. Neither the Serampore Trio nor the BMS had anything whatsoever to do with this development.

Brian Stanley on the Serampore College

Brian Stanley of Edinburgh University insists in his Baptist Quarterly article, Vol. 51 (1) 2020,[7] that the Serampore College contained a theological department from the start for the training of 'Indian Christian missionaries to their own people', he gives no evidence to back this up other than his repeated emphasis that the Serampore

---

[5] The Headquarters of the BMS. See Healing the Breach: Benjamin Goodwin and the Serampore 'Schism', Baptist Quarterly, pp. 121-133.

[6] Ward died of the cholera in 1823, Carey died in 1834 and Marshman in 1837.

[7] The Vision of a Christian Higher Education for India: 200 years of Serampore College History.

institution was indeed a theological college. He equally claims, however, that the College was open to 'non-Christian students'. This hardly points to a theological training for the ministry. Stanley produces what he believes is evidence by referring to the Newbigin Commission of 1969-70 chaired by Presbyterian Lesslie Newbigin, Bishop of Madras, who describes the Serampore College of his day as 'a theological college (which) remains physically part of an institution teaching secular subjects'. However, the College's ownership and status in 1970 has no bearing on the original work for which the Danes employed the Serampore Trio. The 1818 brochure clearly defines what scope Bible teaching had in the College and it was only one of many subjects.

Furthermore, when Serampore was given a charter, Frederick VI, according to Stanley, ruled that degrees were only to be conferred on students 'that testify their proficiency in science'. Again, this does not give the impression of a Theological Training Centre. Stanley also quotes Marshman who brought the Danish Royal Charter to Serampore after a visit to Copenhagen as saying that he wished 'to give a superior education to the children of Christian natives', feeling that instruction in history, geography and science would help free them from 'the Hindoo System'. Also, far from affirming that Carey taught theology at the school, Stanley tells us that:

> Chemistry – along with botany and agriculture (both taught by Carey) and geography – was duly an integral feature of the first curriculum of Serampore College. Chemistry was taught by John Mack, the son of an Edinburgh solicitor, and graduate of the University of Edinburgh; he was the first foreign missionary to be supported by Charlotte Chapel in Edinburgh.

John Mack (1797-1845) was recruited by Ward whom he met at the Bristol Baptist College and encouraged to join the Serampore teaching staff. The Trio paid for his journey and he was not sent out as a BMS missionary. He was helped financially by Charlotte Chapel, Edinburgh though he was not a member of that church. When both the Serampore teachers and BMS board parted company, Mack campaigned for a reconciliation between the two parties.

Laying a foundation for further language study

Stanley emphasises that Carey taught Botany and Agriculture, for which he had no academic qualifications, but does not list him as a teacher of Scripture. The evidence shows indeed that the Serampore College was more akin to the Fort William College than a University, though it reached the latter standard over the years via amalgamation with Calcutta University. Stanley also says Carey intended 'to found an institution that would lay the educational foundations for advanced linguistic study'. Here again, this does not necessarily sound like plans for a theological college. Perhaps Stanley is confusing Carey's work at Serampore College with that of his work at Fort William College where intense linguistic work of the translation kind was carried out. Indeed, the evidence suggests that a number of teachers employed in Calcutta were also employed in Serampore so their work was united. Such a language education was also given in the Government sponsored Arabic College in British Calcutta which Marshman sought to outrival. Stanley is also obviously using the word 'linguistic' to mean the translation of languages and not in the modern sense of Phonetics, Phonology, Morphology, Syntax, Semantics, Socio-Linguistics, Historical Linguistics and Pragmatics. A linguist is not merely one who learns many languages. Such a person is a Polyglot.

Clarity found in the sources

However, we must again look at the sources: the college deeds contradict Stanley's opinion by stating that it was founded as 'A College for the instruction of Asiatic, Christian and other youth in Eastern literature and European Science'. The term 'Asiatic' included Hindu and Muslim youth. This does not sound like a Bible College or Theological Seminary either. Furthermore, the BMS could never make up their mind as to what relationship they wished to have to the Danish College and as Stanley rightly states, limited their meagre support, when it was forthcoming before the break with Serampore, by offering to help only students who were 'pious natives' and members of Baptist Churches, thus shutting out those for whom the College was chiefly founded which was for all countries, classes and creeds.

The Baptist Missionary Society breaks with the Serampore Trio

From 1815 to 1820, Carey gradually realised that the BMS was systematically striving to hinder his work in India and destroy his missionary ideals. They had begun to send out very young inexperienced, albeit gifted, men in their early twenties who were told not to join the Serampore Trio's 'Family' but take their orders directly from the Home Committee. This is exactly what happened to Bartholomäus Ziegenbalg under Wendt and almost put an end to the Tranquebar Mission. These new Baptist missionaries would be salaried directly from England and there was to be no pooling of income. Ignoring the great pioneer work of Carey, Ward and Marshman, these greenhorns started up a work of their own calling themselves the 'Calcutta Missionary Union', professing to be the 'real' British Baptist Mission in India. This work included duplicating schools and churches to compete with those of the old Mission which was typical of the Society's own chaotic waste of their supporters' good money. They even set up a rival printing press. Thus, those who seek for statistics concerning Baptist work in India should take note of all these duplications which broke the joint witness of the Baptists though it extended the numbers of Baptist missions.

Deliberately basing their work in areas where the gospel was already thriving, the newcomers refused to do pioneer work. They were obviously merely 'cashing in' on the Serampore Trio's success. It was not long before some of these untrained youngsters promoted the Liberalism of Fuller, Ryland Jun. and the Halls and erred into Unitarianism which influenced the Baptist impact on Hinduism and caused the entire missionary movement to be questioned. Marshman made a journey to England to sort out the mess but found the Society had lost the missionary zeal present at the time of its foundation. All the old Fullerites, including Robert Hall, were now against them. When Marshman returned home to India, Carey was shocked to find him looking fifteen years older and told the rebel home committee so. Furthermore, Carey complained that John Dyer, then the full-time Secretary of the BMS, treated the Serampore Trio as if he were The Secretary of State.[8] Again, we are reminded of Wendt and the Danish Mission.

[8] See Hancock's 'Healing the Breach' op.sit.

The BMS's counter Baptist Mission

The 'old mission' was now greatly restricted in their work of expansion as the new missionaries just would not cooperate with them. No wonder Carey wrote, 'I am greatly afflicted' and called the Society's hostile strategy 'a Counter-Baptist Mission' which, of course, it was. When Baptist authors such as Robert Oliver tell us that through Fuller's ministry Baptist churches increased, they merely increased by Fuller founding a new form of Baptist churchmanship, which can rightly be called a 'Counter Baptist Mission, and then all Baptist split-up churches were counted as having increased. Again, Carey protested that he had understood the work of the Society as supporting their brethren on the mission field by 'holding the rope for them' but they had now removed their brethren from the India end of the rope and placed mere Society servants in their place. The Serampore Trio refused to become servile to the incompetent and un-Biblical whims of the Society, yet throughout this period they continued to use their income magnanimously for the support of the Society's work. The grasping Society, however, claimed that more ought to be forthcoming. Carey replied that he kept so little for his own daily needs that if he were to die on the spot, his widow would not have funds to pay for his funeral. However, Carey told Ryland privately that he refused to take action against the new policies of the Society and would carry on as usual not wishing 'to mortify anyone by proving they were wrong'. Now, even Ryland turned against the missionaries, especially Marshman of whom Carey said 'I wish I had half his piety, energy of mind, and zeal'. Ryland's letters became plainly insulting and the Society poured 'hailstorms of accusations' on Marshman and Carey (William Ward had died in 1823) via the Christian press.

Carey declared 'unrighteous' by the BMS

Carey's correspondence was now even severely edited, cut and reshaped by the Society to 'prove' that he had been 'unrighteous' since first going out as a missionary. Carey told Ryland firmly that he was acting evilly and regretted that his former brethren now looked on him as a renegade servant of the Society. Now, even members of Carey's family were encouraged by the Society to 'squeal on' Carey and Marshman. By March, 1827, Carey and Marshman were officially no longer considered the Society's servants and were cut off from the

Society's pseudo-fellowship and support. We now read in the BMS Fen Court minutes that there were two missionary societies operating in Serampore, the BMS and the Serampore Trio.

The East India Mission leaves the BMS to its folly

Carey and Marshman were too stalwart in character to be put off by such unjust and unworthy action and sought to bridge the great gap which had come between them and the Society. In 1830, they now did what they had long threatened to do. They signed over the entire Serampore property and income to the English Society's trustees, though the Society had no legal right to it, and merely asked to be able to live rent free with their families for the rest of their lives. The Society responded with glee but divine justice intervened; the Calcutta banks crashed so that the Society was not able to cash in on the revenues from the buildings as hoped.

By this time, Carey had become well known and respected in India and both the East India Company and the British Government now viewed Carey most favourably and joined with the Danes in supporting him. So, Carey was free to get on with his own way of doing missionary work without, as he said, the Society wasting his precious time. He continued with making the Scriptures available in various dialects and the last sheet of his new Bengali edition of the Bible went through the press in June 1832. With the British Governor as his patron and financial supporter, Carey founded a seaman's mission in Calcutta and purchased a boat for use as a mobile missionary station. Apparently, he was now free from his duties in both the Serampore and Fort William Colleges. Carey was even able, though now over seventy years of age, to establish new stations in a number of unevangelized areas. Carey confessed to his colleagues that, in his old age, he had 'scarcely a wish ungratified'. He was becoming the missionary of his youthful dreams. On 9 June, 1834 William Carey passed peacefully through death to eternal life. Before his home-call, he asked for a few words from a hymn by Isaac Watts to be placed on his grave and nothing more:

> A wretched, poor and helpless worm,
> On thy kind arms I fall.

Carey died happily and contented in Jesus' arms and that is more than many mortals can hope for. He was not able to live up to the ideals he had laid out in his *Enquiry* but this was also very much the fault of the para-church organisation which had pledged itself to support him but had done its level best to hamper his work. Fuller's and the BMS's enormous lack of understanding concerning Carey's theology, missionary strategy and evangelistic fervour remain as a warning for future generations of those called to obey the Great Commission and win the world for Christ. Happily, there are enough examples of such brave defenders of the faith in the history of Missions to help them start on this the very best of callings.

A new thought for most Baptist historians

The depiction of Carey's biography as a would-be missionary who somehow failed to live out his calling throughout the bulk of his time in India will perhaps be a new thought to Baptist historians as also the hitherto ignored disastrous interference of Fuller in the evangelization of India. Such depictions are, however, necessary to show friends of India and friends of Missions that there is a better way. Much more sound work on the history of the evangelization of India needs to be undertaken. It is quite astonishing that such work has not yet been done and the Baptist world seems to accept uncritically so many myths and legends. Friends of India are waiting for the Baptists to explain why Carey spent so many years in India marking time and turning all his former plans and ambitions on their head. Is Roy Lazar correct in stating that Carey's initial lack of missionary success is quite simply because 'for the first seven years Carey did not do any missionary activity'?[9] However, even in the ensuing years, Carey's missionary outreach was far less than that of Ziegenbalg and his many followers throughout the hundred years separating the two. Carey, for instance, cannot be compared to Schwartz in any way positive for Carey

Too tied up with business activities

Actually, for most of the rest of their lives, the Serampore Trio was so tied up with business activities and secular educational employment

[9] Theory and Praxis in India: Practical Theology in a Multi-Religious Context, International Journal of Practical Theology, Part II, 20.02.2018, p. 5.

that they could not give the uneducated Indians the Christian attention which Ziegenbalg offered his hearers. In the same way Fuller was so tied up with raising cash that he neglected his pastoral duties. Though other Baptists opened doors for the Gospel northwards to Delhi following the work of earlier missionaries of many denominations in the North, Carey remained more or less sedentary until his life was almost over. When Ziegenbalg's initial three years' trial period had ended in 1709, he was already preaching to two hundred newly converted souls, mainly from the lowlier classes and castes and had no intention of leaving his post. Carey is said to have not reached that goal before 1833. The numbers of Carey's converts seem to have been left to guess-work as even contemporaries of Carey speak of a mere twelve or so in his congregations whereas others speak of hundreds. Claudius Buchanan, the Anglican Vice-Provost of Fort William College under Brown in Carey's days and one of Carey's supporters in his translation work, speaks of six Baptist missionaries in Calcutta though some 18 Baptists were working outside of the Serampore Trio's area.[10] The Baptists were thus always a minority of witnessing brethren in Serampore-Calcutta.

[10] See Buchanan's *Christian Researches in India.*

Chapter Twenty-Four

Early Printing Presses in India

The advent of moveable type
Much has been written, especially in very recent years, on the pioneering activities of Carey motivated by Fuller, with reference to the use of printing presses in India. However, such printing presses were turning out Christian literature in India a good hundred years before Carey entered the country.

Block type which allowed for the printing of whole pages from one piece of wood, with carved letters protruding from the base block, had been in vogue in India from at least the beginning of the first millennium A.D. Though it is still widely taught that moveable type was invented by the German Johannes Gutenberg in 1450, we now know that movable type was used in the East, particularly in China and Korea some four hundred years previously. We also know that moveable type was being experimented with in Goa, India by the Jesuits from 1550 on, ten years before the great Inquisition in Goa started against the Thomas and Nestorian churches. These first moveable type printing presses, however, could still only print page after page by inking a block of type and then pressing it on separate paper using one single block per page. No mechanism was involved in the process. Mechanical duplicating presses using rolls of paper, cutting and folding them as far as we know, and we do not know very much about these times, came in towards the end of the 17th century in India.

Printing presses in India were thus far from a new feature in Carey's day although Carey is widely said to have been a printing pioneer.

Madras, which became an essential area of the Tranquebar mission, already boasted of ten such presses and claimed they were abreast of most large cities in the world as a printing centre. The Armenian Christians set up a press there in 1772. This Madras 'press boom' ended in the middle of the nineteenth century as by that time printing presses were being set up all over India and competition was very great. The Armenians were printing in Calcutta from 1796 on, though a Rev. J. Stephens was printing for them in Calcutta even before. The Roman Catholics, especially the Jesuits, had printing presses long before Ziegenbalg and Carey and Goa established a mechanical sheet printing press in 1556 which began turning out books a year later. M. Siddiq Kahn in his 'The Early History of Bengali Printing' [1] refers to three books printed in the Bengali language in the 16th century by the Portuguese. These, as the 1692 Paris printing of a Bengali book demonstrate, were probably printed from copper plates though turned duplicating moveable type and moveable plates became common after Ziegenbalg's initiative. Ziegenbalg's first works were written on palm leaves but by 1712 he was using a mechanical press financed in conjunction with the Danish Court and the SPCK which was imported from England through the mediation of George Lewis in Madras with paper rolls for immediate use. Ziegenbalg engaged a German Heinrich Schöricke, a soldier employed by the Danish East India Company, as a printer. Schöricke brought two book-binders with him. He appears to have only known Portuguese besides German and printed a work in Portuguese on the order of salvation and Christian doctrine. The DEIC soon re-enlisted Schöricke because of his useful military skills but he continued to help the mission whenever free until 1731. A man by the name of Johann Gottlieb Adler was sent to the Tranquebar Mission to learn how to run a press but he proved incapable and so was assigned in 1718 to font-making. His younger brother Dietrich Gottlieb, took over the work but also showed no competence and as he also led a wicked life, he was dismissed from the Mission. Governor Hassius who had been so hateful against the Mission was then also dismissed from his services by the Danish King so the two returned to Europe together. Nevertheless, the printing press struggled on and a number of works were already printed before 1718. The Bible translations in Tamil which

[1] The Library Quarterly, Vol. 3, Number 1, Jan. 1962, p. 51.

were now forthcoming, however, demanded a great deal of paper so Ziegenbalg built a paper mill in 1713. Ziegenbalg wrote to George Lewis a Church of England missionary and chaplain working amongst the slaves in Madras on 7th April, 1713 saying:

> We may remember on this Occasion, how much the Art of Printing contributed to the Manifestation of divine Truths, and the spreading of Books for that End, at the Time of the happy Reformation, which we read of in History, with Thanksgiving to Almighty God.[2]

Colloquial Tamil appears to have been first printed in moveable type in Tranquebar but Ziegenbalg's paper mill was not the first of its kind in India and more printing presses and paper mills were founded during Schwartz' and Kiernander's time. Schwartz persuaded his ward the King of Tanjore to set up a press for the printing of Sanskrit and Marathi literature and by Carey's day printing presses had become widespread and Governor General Warren Hastings set up multiple presses in British controlled India and allowed the Indians to build their own. Carey's printing press in Calcutta, often praised as a 'first', as we have already noted, was far from an innovation. Indeed, according to Graham Shaw's work *Printing in Calcutta to 1800*, between the years 1700-1800 there had been no less than 40 printers working in Calcutta, mostly doing newspaper work but Kiernander and Stephens were printing Christian literature besides calendars, almanacs and news reports. The Reverend J. Stephens had a press up and running in 1774 and Kiernander's Mission Press had been running in Calcutta since 1778, long before Carey's day. According to Shaw this was only one of *seventeen* presses [3] working in Calcutta before Carey arrived in the city, though never more than ten were being used at one particular time. These presses were turning out material in Armenian, Bengali, Hindustani and Persian, mostly government publications, regulations and treaties. These included the Bengali Grammar Carey used and two Bengali dictionaries. As India was becoming more aware of her

---

[2] The original letter is found in the Franckeschen Stiftung Hauptbibliothek, Nr. 63 B6.

[3] My italics to show the folly of claiming that the Baptists pioneered printing in Calcutta or even India.

Classical past, a good number of Sanskrit works of poetry, drama and history were translated into English. Shaw lists some 368 works printed in Calcutta before 1800. Rather than pioneering printing in Calcutta, Carey was something of a late-comer.

There are many works coming from Indian presses today concerning India's printing history and obviously research is still at a primary stage. The first moveable type for the Bengali language is said to have been made by an Englishman named Joseph Jackson according to Kahn in his Ph.D. thesis 'History of Printing in Bengali Characters'. The first Bengali book printed in India is said to be Halhed's *Grammar of the Bengal Language*. Henry Forster came out with his *A Vocabulary in Two Parts, English and Bongalee* in 1799. William Carey produced his *Dialogues, Intended to Facilitate the Acquiring of the Bengali Language* in 1801 and Ramram Basu's *Raja Pratapaditya Charitra* (a kind of novel) in 1801. From 1801 on many Bengali works were printed in Bengali by native Indians. Here, there is obviously room for further research.

The background behind the Serampore Trio's Bengali press

In our quest for the true, full story of Carey's printing workshop and fonts we must go back a number of years before Carey arrived in Calcutta. Then a Roman Catholic missionary named Brother Andrews[4] set up a press in Tribeni on the Hooghly near Calcutta in order to further his outreach. Nathaniel Brassey Halhed, in conjunction with a typographer by the name of Charles Wilkins, who appears to have been knighted for his work, approached Andrews with a view to his printing a Bengali Grammar. At that time there was apparently no appropriate Bengali printing type available which could be used for modern works. There was, however, a local inventor and calligrapher of a long line of calligraphers named Panchanan Karmakar (usually referred to as simply Panchanan) who was asked to create a moveable type. He did so and soon came up with punches which revolutionized printing in India but also created a variant script from normal hand-writing and that used by previous presses. Panchanan then designed other variant types for printing some thirteen languages including Persian, Telugu, Tamil, Burmese and Chinese which were, however, also markedly different

[4] Some sources call him 'Father Andrews'.

from the original handwritten forms. The Indian languages have gone through massive changes in their scripts from this time on with some of them, including Bengali having several scripts at one time. This has caused the reading of ancient texts in northern India to be a pastime only for linguistically trained academics and has cut away much of the culture of especially northern India, particularly in its relation to religious roots. Many modern developments in Hinduism, for instance, are a feature of the age of printing and not gathered from handwritten literature which had been used for three thousand years. Carey's own efforts at printing an understandable Bengali were altered considerably by Carey's successor at the Fort William College Ishwar Chandra Vidyasagar who simplified the fonts and altered the alphabet for more modern usages. This could hardly be called an improvement. Though the Serampore press is supposed to have printed Bibles or rather Bible portions in 44 languages, 36 of them going through Carey's hands, according to George Smith and R. Kilgour the press printed in only eight languages, these being Persian, Hindustani, Malayalam, Burmese, Sinhalese, Javanese, Malay and Lazar's Bible version in Chinese. According to Kilgour, many of these printed translations were of little practical use and many Bibles or New Testaments said to have been printed contained only small samples of translations or single gospels.[5] Furthermore, several 'translations' were in Roman characters which would be of little use to those who read only the vernacular script, that is the bulk of the natives. Furthermore, many of these saw no active circulation but remained in their experimental forms. Far from all these translations arising from the skills of the Serampore missionaries, a good number were produced by Hindu and Muslim scholars attached to the Fort William College where William Hunter had the say. The Urdu and Hindi translations were not the work of Carey. Furthermore, apart from the Bengali Bible printing which has an unclear background, much of the early Serampore printing came out under the Serampore missionaries' name but these Bibles and Bible portions had been translated many years before by other missionaries and their teachers. A typical example is Tamil which the Serampore Trio told the BMS on 19th February, 1813 had taken them 10 months to translate but there were at least four translations of the Bible into the Tamil language

[5] See especially Kilgour's *The Bible Throughout the World*, p. 115.

dating up to a hundred years before the Baptists arrived in India. This goes for the Teluga, Arabic and Hindi translations also.[6] Bibles in these languages were relatively easy to come by in Carey's Calcutta and Serampore. What seems to have happened is that these translations were put into the Serampore new scripts or Roman characters which would seem a waste of time and money. Indeed, the Serampore press mismanaged their financing and went bankrupt in 1837. It was taken over for a number of years by the Baptist Mission Press, set up as a rival to Serampore, but that press also went bankrupt in 1855.

Panchanan is only recently given credit for his work

Panchanan's basic script was actually a Devanagari script based on Classical Sanskrit of the northern kind which was seen as having divine origins by many Brahmins. Panchanan's work was not initially recognized for what it was and usually British diplomats or missionaries, who employed Panchanan reaped the laurels for his work. Thus, modern India calls Panchanan 'The forgotten pioneer of type-making'. It was Panchanan who made printing Bengali in Calcutta and Serampore possible, not Carey. However, Panchanan's designs brought in textual novelties and unusual, unknown types in writing such languages as Marathi and Bengali which caused a break for many with their old literature and culture. The press also used Devanagari for their Bible portions for Muslims which was hardly a wise thing to do.

'Dumbing down' languages and scripts

A similar development has occurred in present-day Israel. Those now used to modern Ivrit scripts which appear to be copies of Japanese Manga-Katakana would probably be in difficulty if the Hebrew press, political and advertising agencies revived the Classical Aramaic block script used for the traditional Torah. The exclusion of a number of radicals, vowels and pointings (punctuations) has impoverished the language. Type printing has also destroyed much of the Sami culture in northern Europe, made more disastrous by the forced merging (mixing up) of some six Lapp languages by order of non-Sami governments. Even printed Scripture portions by the late 17th century and early 18th century Danish missionaries are now unreadable for most Sami. I

[6] See the BMS publication *Brief Narrative of the Baptist Mission in India*, p.80.

distributed Scripture Gift Mission tracts amongst Sami peoples throughout the nineteen sixties. These Sami spoke various Finno-Ugric dialects but none could understand the literature so I gave up and stopped learning the old Sámi-giella (the Sami language) as it was not so much dying out as being killed-off. I preached solely in Swedish with a few Norwegian inserts when preaching over the border.

It is interesting to note that the first Protestant missionaries to Lapland and the first Bible translators were trained and appointed by the same highly successful group of people who sent missionaries out to India. The three peoples I have studied more closely than any others; the Sami, the Native Indians and the Indians have all nowadays a cultural, social and religious deficit due to European and 'American' suppression. My old friend from my Bradford and Pudsey days, Frank Baggot who founded the Sahara Desert Mission lamented the same trends in North Africa. Indeed, the original Tuareg script as a method of communication had been given up and Frank strove to revive it.

The situation in India was also like that of Turkey when Ataturk changed the Turkish script in 1929. This closed the literature of the past to all but the privileged who were able to study Old Turkish. The radical move also altered the Turkish language, particularly in the region of vowel sounds as they could not be represented by the 'modern' script. Then came further changes in the 1930s, separating the language from its form only a few years previously. Turkish, however, was only one language among many to which new scripts brought difficulties.

The Indian languages have gone through massive changes in their scripts. Some languages, including Bengali had several scripts at one time but the would-be Bible translators around the educational establishments pioneered by such as Carey, dumbed down the array of languages and Hinduized their translations which actually left post-Carey Hindus claiming that their obviously altered language was the original Hindu and their religion was the original Indian religion. However, it is obvious that through standardizing old Bengali script, signs for half vowels and sibilants have now fallen by the wayside. The result is that the people speak 'as written' but 'as written' does not represent what 'was written' and spoken and many sounds have thus disappeared from the language, thus actually causing new dialects to occur. Concerning the religious claims of modern Hindu converts to Christianity there is a great similarity with Welsh Druidic Christianity.

I have often met Welshmen and those boasting of a 'Celtic' ancestry who claim that Christianity is an extension of Druidism which was originally Davidic in origin. Similarly, one often meets Indian Christians who claim their New Testament belief is actually an extension or continuation of the Vedas.

Ziegenbalg's printing compared with Carey's

Ziegenbalg used a modern metal press with metal punches and types but over 100 years later, Carey commenced printing on an old-fashioned wooden press with wooden punches. Besides, though Carey set up a press for religious and secular printing as Kiernander and others had done long before him, several Hindu presses were working parallel to Carey's and partly in competition. Indeed, non-English newspapers were being printed in Bengali, Urdu, Hindi and Persian by the time Carey began his own printing work. These were also printing the works Carey compiled for the Fort William College. Marshman who brought out his Samachar Darpan first in 1818 strove to jump on the native bandwagon but his newspaper, as the Serampore printing press in general, only lasted until 1852. Rammohun Roy started his Sambad Kaumudi in 1821 but this had a very short life, too. By 1870 of all the 38 Indian language newspapers published in India, over half were printed in Calcutta. When the Colonial powers realised that news-making was being taken out of their hands and placed in the hands of the Indians, they clamped down on their 'subjects' initiative through severe legislation as they believed that if newspapers were run by the native Indians it would cause them to think for themselves and perhaps one day throw out the British.[7] Carey's total printed output was greater than Ziegenbalg's but the bulk of this output was in secular works for use in secular schools, colleges and administration and not for missionary and evangelistic purposes as was Ziegenbalg's.

So, Carey was merely one amongst very many when he set up the Baptists' first printing press in 1800. This step was very far from being the pioneering novelty one often reads about in English-speaking accounts of Carey's life and times. Carey's press with its wooden punches was, according to many commentators, destroyed by fire in

[7] See 'History of Media in Bengal: A Chronological Overview' by Avani Basu, Transcience Journal, 2013, Vol. 4, Issue 1.

1812 just as the Mission's translation work was growing and much translation work was burnt besides most of Carey's funds and stores of paper. Carey then used metal punches[8] but these were the invention of Indians who have until very recently not received due recognition for their ingenious work. Due to lack of paper, the Serampore Trio started building a paper mill in 1812, again, a hundred years after Ziegenbalg. This was run by William Ward who was a printer by occupation and Marshman directed most of the printing. Again, here, Carey is falsely given the laurels.

The BMS set up a rival printing press to Carey's

Ziegenbalg brought out a missionary magazine called The Halle Reports in 1708 to gain European missionary interest and after 1812, Marshman published several newspapers, both secular and missions-oriented, mostly in English. Both, Ziegenbalg and the Serampore Trio, however, published numerous newsletters and reports in the native languages, Ziegenbalg adding English and Portuguese to his Tamil and German publications.[9] Other languages such as Teluga, Hindi and Arabic were added long before Carey's time. Carey's team under his supervision published many works both large and small in a number of Indian languages. However, when the BMS elbowed Carey out of the BMS leadership and ostracized him in India gradually through 1815-17, they set up a rival printing press to Carey's under William Pearce. The Indian native presses, however, soon left the missionaries' printing technology far behind. Indeed, Carey's own college printed through Hindu printers during Carey's years at Fort William.

Jewish presses

Though there was a long-stablished Jewish community in Calcutta, it does not appear that they were consulted by the European missionaries as to the particularities of Hebrew exegesis. Nor do we hear of Carey consulting their expertise. There were Hebrew printing presses in Bombay, Pune, Cochin and Madras, from the 18th century on, the first

---

[8] According to Carey's report on the fire, he spoke of molten metal which might indicate that he was already experimenting with metal punches or metal framed presses.

[9] See *The Printing Press in India: Its beginning and Early Development*, Anant Kakba Priolkar, Bombay, 1958.

Hebrew printing press in Calcutta, however, was not founded until 1840 by Eleazar ben Aron Saadiah 'Iraqi ha-Cohen who cast his own type. 'Iraqi is said to have been a scholar, author and poet whose productions rivalled those of Western Europe. His press printed various publications until it closed down in 1856.

Ziegenbalg designed his own punches

Ziegenbalg had no Tamil script in either punch or type form so he drew the Script by hand for the local dialect with his own additions where suitable characters were missing and sent them off to Germany to be copied and moulded. When the punches arrived, they were far too big for ordinary printing work and Ziegenbalg and his co-workers had to make new punches themselves out of 'cheese tins'. Carey took over Bengali wooden punches already made whereas Ziegenbalg had very quickly moved from wood to the more durable metal. The tradition goes that Carey like Ziegenbalg had to design new punches himself. This is merely a myth spread by those who will not have Carey bettered by Ziegenbalg. Such a 'pioneer' work was not necessary as the type-maker family who designed and cut the type for Halhed was still in Calcutta working on the press set up by Hastings in 1779 some 20 years before Carey set up his press and they continually worked on Carey's press and designed and cut out new type for him. True to tradition, they used wood much of which did not survive the fire of 1812 which destroyed much of Carey's early writings not just the press. Thereafter, Carey stuck to metal fonts.

Five weekly newspapers printed on Indian private presses in Calcutta alone in Carey's days

A. K. Priolkar in his *The Printing Press in India* writes of five weekly newspapers being printed in Calcutta, each on different days. Carey might have read these during his leisure time to keep himself up to date on news. Indeed, between 1800 and 1819 various dailies such as The Bengal Hurkaru and Chronicle were being printed in Calcutta.[10] James August Hicky (Hickey) had a press up and running in 1777 printing government papers and then his own newspaper in 1800. His press, however, was already old-fashioned by the time he started printing.

[10] The Bengal Hurkaru was founded in 1795 and printed in Calcutta until 1866.

Kiernander approached Hicky with a view to printing missionary news through him but Hicky demanded exorbitant prices for his services so Kiernander decided it would be cheaper to print himself. So Kiernander set up his own press in Calcutta in 1779, bought from English sources. He had familiarized himself with the work of printing in the Halle University printing shop so running a press was no new enterprise for him. Hicky, who was about to go bankrupt, fought Kiernander in the courts for taking on 'his' custom but lost his case. He complained that Kiernander's press was ruining his livelihood. Kiernander quickly brought out his own newspaper named The Christian Companion. In this measure Kiernander was supported by the SPCK as were the bulk of missionary-printing missionaries before him. The Frenchman G. Duverdier wrote a most interesting book in 1985 entitled *Deux Imprimeurs en Process a Calcutta: Hicky contra Kiernander*, outlining Hicky's failure to prevent Kiernander from printing material for which he strove to hold rights.[11] The East India Company, fearing that Hicky was too open in criticism of British policies forced him to close down his rather antiquated newspaper work and confiscated his press in 1802. So, there were quite a number of presses at work in Calcutta before Carey started on his own printing, though a number of these had a very short life. This was all known to the BMS and it was no secret that Carey used not only the type from these printing presses but also employed their staff-members. So, Carey's printing press was virtually an extension of the press work which had been founded long before his coming and whose owners assisted Carey in all possible ways. It is thus difficult to see why Carey's first press which was very old-fashioned and which was ruined a relatively few years later by fire could be described in many books as a 'first' in India. It might have been a 'first' for the BMS, but it came hundreds of years after India's true 'firsts'. Besides, the BMS set up a rival press in Calcutta to Carey's and thus took custom from him.

'Missionary' Hindi and Bengali

Native Indian humour quickly called the Serampore efforts at translations 'Missionary Hindi', or 'Missionary Bengali', 'Missionary

[11] I have failed to obtain a copy, even a digitalized one, in Germany, but the book must make for very interesting reading.

Marathi, etc., irrespective of the fonts used. Carey realised too late that though other print forms such as Modi,[12] ought to have been used, his own Devanagari script was now in general use among the Anglo-Indians and the literate so he could not change matters without reaping much criticism and causing financial loss. Modi, is commonly called Broken Devanagari due to the head-strokes being broken whereas in the Balbodh script which Carey used they are continuous except for numerals. Modi, however was the script of prose and had been so since the early 13th century if not before. The Balbodh script, for which Carey opted, was used for poetry and its more formal calligraphy gave it a more classical look. It was, however, not the script of the humble literate or every-day prose. Charles Wilkins designed a Modi script commissioned by Governor Hastings, forged in metal for use by Halhed. Why Carey used wooden Devanagari types rather than metal Modi or other every-day scripts is probably because, being antiquated, they were cheaper and also easier to repair though they easily warped and were not fire-proof. Perhaps Halhed or Hicky merely wanted to get rid of a discarded script and sold them to Carey for a song. The odd thing is that it is generally supposed that Charles Wilkins' Modi script at this time disappeared mysteriously. However, we find Carey bowing before public criticism because he used the old poetical script for prose work and so he printed his second edition of his Marathi Grammar in the prose script Modi in 1808 using metal fonts. I have failed to discover who made Carey's Modi fonts so could it be that Carey eventually got hold of Wilkins' creations? It appears that Carey also did not know Modi and other scripts when first setting up his press and became acquainted with them later when his Devanagari had been printed profusely. Carey's action, however, caused the old script to become acceptable as Carey's publications became popular reading in his missions and schools through Serampore usage. Still Carey complained that though he could now preach for an hour in Bengali, the poor could not understand him. His own Bengali was quite different to theirs.

The day before writing these words I had a visit from a highly educated Bombay family who use the Devanagari script to write their own Marathi. In the Bombay district Modi has only given fully away to Devanagari in modern times. So eventually Carey established the more

[12] Thought to have originated in Sri Lanka.

permanent script but perhaps not the one to be most easily understood. However, new signs in Devanagari covering chiefly half-vowels and vowels have been added for fluency of reading and pronunciation which Carey obviously did not use. These cause reading difficulties when taking a back-glance at Carey's old script.

Ziegenbalg's Tamil script remained fairly constant but the Bengali script was subject to many variations and even versions in Arabic script were used as also in Punjabi which has developed an Arabic-Farsi alphabet.[13] There was never truly a standard Bengali language or script as social, religious and philosophical connotations modified and altered older meanings. Tamil has fared rather better, if being more conservative can be called better. However, Tamil Bibles were produced by well-meaning 19th century European missionaries in Roman characters, probably more for use by undiscerning Europeans than Indians and sensible Europeans. The greater stability of Southern Indian languages compared to the ever-varying northern languages because of religious and cultural variations, the interference of the British and the northern trade routes bringing with them ever new loan-words helped them survive. However, even Tamil Bibles have been tampered with to make them conform to Latin syntax and Western punctuation.

English has become merely a mixture of 'loan languages' and perhaps there will be a pan-Indian native language one day when each absorbs the other's language. I noticed this when a good Punjabi friend of mine spoke to further friends who spoke Urdu, Bengali and Hindi. There seemed to be no difficulty in understanding one another though there was much polite laughter concerning different pronunciations.

[13] I am merely judging from the way the script looks. I have no deep knowledge of the development of Punjabi scripts.

Part 9

Linguistic and Political Difficulties Facing Indian Missions

Chapter Twenty-Five

The Dangers of using Non-Christian Cultural and Religious Terms in Bible Translations

Translations should not involve cultural exchange

It soon became clear in Carey's day that translation work was becoming more an involvement and interactivity with the religion and culture of the target people besides the denominational preferences of the English editors and translators. This brought with it such grave theological and ecclesiological problems that an evangelist could no longer preach 'Thus saith the Lord' as various names for 'the Lord' in their translations were either based on a polytheistic background or a Unitarian denial of the Person of Christ as testified in the Scriptures. So, too, words to describe the Lord's Supper and baptism were taken from ancient Indian and Persian myths and legends, noble in themselves but lacking in Biblical meaning. The idea of a strict scholarly and academic attention to the original languages of the Bible played an inferior role. This was not only true of Baptist translators but also of those Church of England missionaries who compiled quick translations such as Henry Martyn who relied on the ancient Esfandiyār Homer-like stories for his language. These epics were apparently written to commemorate the Zoroastrian Wars and the ideals of the Avesta. This is probably because Martyn put his translation into the hands of Baghdad scholars such as Nathaniel Sabat. Sabat used to persecute Christians to their deaths but was converted to Christ and placed himself in Martyn's services. In India, Martyn had Muslim pundits to assist in his translations. Yet most of these 19th century translators were sure to affix a statement on their title pages that they had translated directly from the Hebrew and Greek into the target language.

Indian languages even before the gospel was heard then as even more today were most touchy on religious and social issues depending on the former religion and caste of the translators and readers. I realised this only recently when employing a group of young unemployed Punjabis to clean up my garden on standard wages and insurance. I greeted them with 'Saat siri akaal'. The men did not reply and looked annoyed. On apologizing for my badly pronounced greeting, they told me rather haughtily that they would not respond to the language of unbelievers as they were Muslims. They expected and then obtained from me the greeting 'As-Salam-u-Alaikum'. Punjabi, like many other Indian languages has now a Hindu form and a Muslim form.

One of the greater weaknesses of the translations Carey's large team of European and Indian translators made is that they had no 'common language' into which they could translate, nor had they a common language from which to translate. Nor did the majority have a common faith but one strongly leaning on Indian religions and their many variants. So, too, Carey had no special 'target group' in mind when employing multi-cultural translators who were not familiar with the Scriptures in any language. He certainly did not translate for what is falsely called 'the common man'.

The problem illustrated in modern Bangladesh

The difficulties of adapting old Bengali translations such as Carey's into the Bengali of today is illustrated by the modern dialects spoken in Bangladesh. On looking into a modern Bangladesh Mission's web site entitled Bible Translation in the Chittagong Hill Tracts, I found the following statement:

> The William Carey Bengali Bible, translated in the early 1800's, was the first Bengali Bible to be used in Bangladesh (formerly East Pakistan). Unfortunately the language of this Bible is archaic and highly stylized, which makes it incomprehensible to the ordinary Bengali reader. Early Bible teachers discovered the problem; and an adaption of the Carey Bible into what is called the Bengali Common Language (BCL)

version was started in 1966 by Lynn Silvernale.[1] The New Testament of this version was finished in 1976 and the Old Testament in 1995. During this same period, a Muslim Bengali Common Language version (MBCL) was written for the Muslim population in Bangladesh by a group of translators led by Dr Viggo Olsen. These two Bibles (which use theological terms familiar to Hindus and Muslims respectively) have had a dramatic effect on the dissemination of God's word among Bengali speakers. They are hugely popular even among non-Christians. It is sadly true to say that these 'mixed and muddled' translations were the work of modern missionaries and not native citizens.

The BCL Bible translations have impacted the tribes living in the Chittagong Hill Tracts; but Bengali has never been a unifying language for Christians because of their different cultural and religious differences. For years, the tribal Bible teachers have used the dubious Bengali Common Language Bible in their teaching but the scriptures were always translated by the teachers into the language, dialect and cultural background of their audiences. The BTBM association has members from 8 different tribes. These tribes are the Tripuri, Chakma, Marma, Rakhine, Mro, Khumi, Chak and Khyang. Translators in Bangladesh have worked towards providing the New Testament for the principal tribal groups within the BTBM association.[2]

Even a 'Common-language Bible' does not work

The idea of a 'Common-language Bible' has obviously misfired here as it appears to be a Bible from which all that might offend either Buddhists, Hindus or Muslims has been erased, leaving Christians who have separated themselves from other religions the task of Hinduizing or Islamizing the contents of such as Carey's Bible, or any Bible as the case may be. Viggo Olsen, Baptist medical missionary to Bangladesh

---

[1] An American nurse who undertook the translation with a retired school teacher Mrs Basanti Dass

[2] Chittagong Hill Tracts of Bangladesh online. Silvernale was an ABWE missionary in the then East Pakistan.

mentioned above, rightly pointed out the folly of using Carey's translation because of the use of the Hindu god 'Ishwar' (Iswar, Iswa) for God.

If we look into Hinduism, we find that Ishwar is a god amongst thousands of gods and is also used to describe such a god as Rama who was an allegedly human elevated for his services to a senior god. Christ is often compared with Rama in Indian religious debates. Here we see how easily Arianism can infiltrate Christianity through faulty and misguided translations. We must also mention the name of Avatar used for Christ in Bengali. Like Ishwar, this term is used in Hinduism as an epithet for various gods. Thus, in the Western world we are presented with the blue-coloured fairy-like humanoids in James Cameron's film of that name but also the far more dangerous flood of Avatar-Christ occult 'theologies' and the idea that Christ, Krishna, Buddha and Chaitanya are all incarnations of 'god' which merely means they are humans entrusted with a divine task. Thus, the term Avatar does not mean 'One who is truly God and truly Man' whom we call Christ the Lord.

Olsen rightly objected to this misuse of Bengali terms arguing that they might suit Buddhist, Hindu and Pantheistic interpretations but not Muslims. So, he composed what he called 'Muslim-friendly' Bengali and English translations for Bangladesh readers which we might call a further Babel Edition leading to confusion. The samples I have seen in this 'translation' are quite horrific as Olsen has merely erased Carey's Buddhist and Hindu terms and replaced them by Arabic terms such as 'Allah' for God which have no common appeal. Of course, 'Allah' is just as heavily loaded with non-Christian ideas as 'Ishwar' and robs God of His Triune Being, thus ranking Christ and the Holy Spirit as Hindu deities or Muslim 'prophets'. In spite of its obvious failings, Olsen's 'Muslim-friendly' Bible, published in 1980 became Bangladesh' best-selling book.[3] The question here is what Bible texts did Olsen use on which to base his 'translation'? On a web site discussing Olsen's methods, I found an article written online by Jay Pratt dated 2008 that states:

---

[3] See Mark Ellis' 'Legendary missionary doctor works on Muslim-friendly English translation of the New Testament', www.godreports.com, May 29, 2012, online.

> I thought that we had planned for a successful CPM by translating the eminent Train and Multiply leadership training course and activity guide written by George Patterson. However the Buddhist background leaders turn up their noses at the existing Bible translation that these excellent materials were based on. Many of the exercises in those materials that we translated read, for example, 'Find in Acts 10, whom Peter brought with him to start the first Roman church.' Well, they could not find anything, because they did not have Bibles, and my apprentices would not distribute the Bible in the majority language.
>
> Currently these new church leaders from a minority people group have formed their own translation committee and are translating from the United Bible Society's, Contemporary English Version into the majority language. They have completed the Synoptic Gospels and Acts as of first importance for them. New believers and seekers prefer Matthew's gospel, after asking for evaluations from their Buddhist family and highly educated monk friends. In contrast, most international Bible consultant organizations have agreements with the National Bible Society that they will not work on newer translations of the existing Bible.

What is obviously happening is that Bibles are being translated from old, far from accurate translations and not from the original languages. This is seen also in the many 'Children's Bibles' used in the Western world. They are translations of translations and often depart widely from the original Bible. We have also 'Reformed' Bibles, 'School Bibles', Roman Catholic Bibles, Baptist Bibles, Jehovah's Witnesses' Bibles, Feministic Bibles and Politically Correct Bibles. Tragically, Greek, Hebrew, Aramaic and Latin as also early Early-English Bibles and those translated in Reformation times are disappearing from our churches, homes, schools, libraries and universities. Happily, my own University Marburg where I did my doctorate in Theology demand a knowledge of Latin, Greek and Hebrew of their post-grad theological students, a number of whom become deeply involved in Bible work. I notice that even modern translations of the King James Bible introduce elements not in that Bible and not in the ancient texts. Translations of translations do not result in a correct, original Bible translation.

If Olsen used such an English rendering as the United Bible Society's translation and the many different tribal translated versions which use terms from their former religious languages, we are in for a return to pre-Babel times. Few Hindu, Muslim or Buddhist religious terms are of use Biblically, theologically and linguistically in Bible translations. This confusion is enhanced by dialects of Bengali being written in different scripts, some written from left to right and others written from right to left. Southern Hindi, a Sanskrit derived sister language is written from left to right but its northern Urdu form is written from right to left.

Indeed, Indians such as journalist-author Khushwant Singh now actually declares his own country to be a 'Babel' because of its language confusion.[4] Even if we remain within the context of one language allegedly rooted in Sanskrit such as Hindi and compare Bombay (Mumbai) Hindi with Lucknow Hindi we must ask whether it is the same language or not. We must also consider the fact that because of a presence of over 200 years in India, modern English has more 'pure' Hindi words in it (about 2,000) than many northern Hindi-speakers use as they have mixed their language with Persian and Arabic.[5]

Obviously using Ishwar or Krishna is inappropriate for a Bengali translation as Olsen rightly realised. Terms like 'Ishwar' and 'Allah', were used of either a plurality of gods or one god amongst many. This is why we give the Christian God a capital letter to distinguish Him from many gods. However, the God of the Bible is not to be confused with 'Ishwar' and 'Allah'. Especially the latter term is highly misleading as a name for our triune God. The generally accepted meaning and usage of 'Allah' shuts out the divine character of Jesus and the Holy Spirit who are essentialities of the Godhead. The Muslim

---

[4] I am grateful to journalist Reiner Krack for putting me in touch with Khushwant Singh's humorous criticisms of Indian foibles in his helpful book *Hindi Wort für Wort*, Kauderwelsch Band 17, Bielefeld, 1998.

[5] A few of the more colloquial ones which immediately come to mind are chitty, blighty, cushy, thug, loot, hooligan, bungalow, bandana, dinghy, pyjamas, cashmere, chutney, bangle, shampoo, jungle, juggernaut, punch and cot but there are many, many more.

'Allah' has no such Trinitarian properties. This means that Jesus and the Holy Spirit are separated from the Godhead, leaving a pseudo-Christian god who is much less than God the Heavenly Father of Christians. Olsen is merely treading in the footsteps of the translators he seeks to correct who fell into Unitarianism. So, in avoiding a Hindu god, Olsen has given us a Muslim Unitarian god but Christians know only the Christian triune God. Even, however, in his English rendering of the Bible, Olsen refers to Jesus as Isa al-Massih and John the Baptist is rendered 'the Prophet Yaha'. This may suit an Arabic Bible but hardly a Bengali Bible and certainly not an English Bible. Anyway, the office of 'Al Massih' (or Masih) in Arabic and Muslim thinking is quite different from what the Bible means by 'Messiah'.

So, too, Hindi was a far more widespread Indian language than Bengali and had a long literary background so why start with a new form of a language such as Bengali which had even in Carey's days no real past and a divided future? Chamberlain saw this and worked on a Hindi Bible but such Bibles had been around for very many years and only needed to be revised though they were still usable.

Carey's methods of translating or rather having Scriptural passages translated by a team mostly composed of non-Christians with no skills in the Biblical languages was most questionable. A number were not even Bengali speakers or familiar with associate languages. The translation work was thus done most unprofessionally. He appears to have used the Authorised Version and his own Sanskrit Bible, which took him years to translate though not really needed, as a basis for his dictations to his mostly Hindu translators. The Bengali of Carey's day, if it were really based on Sanskrit, which was only Carey's theory, was nevertheless strongly anchored in different, often opposing, Sanskrit forms which may or may not have provided the different Bengali dialects and caste vocabularies which were available in Carey's day and still are. One wonders indeed, why Carey went to such time-consuming labour in translating the Bible into the dead language of Sanskrit which he nevertheless 'modernised' on his own bat but which few would find useful as anything other than a linguistic exercise or merely a time-consuming hobby. It is as if a modern Englishman would attempt to translate the Bible into ancient Anglo-Saxon without a deep and profound knowledge of that language and also the ancient Hebrew and

Greek texts. Perhaps this was to stabilize his position as Head of the Sanskrit Department at Fort William.

Carey's professional background would account for his Bengali Bible's overload of Anglicisms, ancient vocabulary and the use of Hindu vocabulary and strange syntax. Bengali was not yet a unified, stable standard language and had no standard written form but Carey sought to create such a language using new methods. However, some of his limited linguistic ideas were hardly helpful. For instance, Carey used the metalanguage of Latin Grammars into which he squeezed Bengali which is hardly helpful. Indeed, Bengali literature seems to have received an artificial boost and newness of life through the use of Carey's linguistic creations. One wonders why Carey did not use a Hindi Bible from scratch as this was readily available and Hindi was spoken all over the North but also in southern regions. So, too, both the Bengali and Hindi of the missionaries were brought very close together so that they hardly represented two different languages. Nevertheless, Carey and his team seemed unaware that the same word used in the two languages had different meanings. This is paralleled in the Swedish and Norwegian forms of 'Bokmål', the different meanings given to the same words being often a cause for amusement.

As a security in using words which were not religiously loaded by non-Christian translators, Carey is said to have compared the Old Testament material with Biblical Hebrew. Carey also worked industriously on the Bengali New Testament and we can infer from what he said of his Old Testament work that he compared the New Testament with the Greek. He most certainly did not translate directly from the original languages as so often presumed. Yet Carey did not understand a number of the languages into which the Bible was allegedly translated so how could he check their accuracy with the Greek and Hebrew? Reports on how Carey translated are most varied and often quite contradictory, varying according to the educational status of his commentators and their background languages. This would have meant, too, that Carey was as fluent in Hebrew, Greek, Aramaic, Bengali, Chinese, etc. as he was in English, though the languages he allegedly used were weighted down with religious and philosophical elements quite foreign to Christianity. So too, there were many critics, including Fuller, of Carey's brand of English.

Translating ancient forms of a language, whether Indian or Chinese and culling linguistic constructions and figures of speech from them to be put into Christian usage does not seem to be a fitting way of preparing a modern translation of the Bible. If one wishes to translate the Bible into Modern Greek, it would hardly help to re-translate Homer as a leading-up exercise. Whilst swatting for my Classical Greek matriculation exam at night school, I had to translate hundreds of verses of Homer before going on to do Koiné at Uppsala and never knew how this would help me. As my class mates were budding theologians and I was elected Speaker for my class, I asked the Minister for Education, Moberg, if we could halve Homer and do the same number of verses in Mark's gospel. After being invited by Moberg to a discussion with Prime Minister Palmer, this was allowed and prepared us much better for our Bible work at the university.

Luther and Ziegenbalg perfected their target languages by talking to people in the market place. It appears that Carey relied too much on pundits who either spoke different Bengali dialects or, like Carey, had just learnt or were learning Bengali. He wished for quick translation to be used to convert the Indians but made too many compromises with Indian religious terminology. What Carey was aiming at was a new Bengali lingua franca. However, Carey's Bengali Bible was variously rejected as either totally useless, good in parts or as a revelation of Christianity which was acceptable to the reader for want of anything better. The fact that Carey's Bengali was taught in the Mission's schools and colleges for almost thirty years, provided Bengal with a new dialect of Carey-Bengali. Otherwise known as 'Missionary Bengali'.

What was Carey's real contribution to the Bengali Bible?

Baptist accounts of Carey's translation work are most puzzling and there are no clear Baptist records of how Carey and his large team translated the entire Bible into Bengali from the original languages which was claimed on the title page of the first printed edition which is said to have been published in 1793, 1801, 1806, 1809 and 1811 according to the various accounts. The disastrous fire of 1812 destroyed much of Carey's work. The state of the press at this time and what exactly the damage was is also recorded differently in various works.

Some say that it was devastating, others, however, claim that the loss was not great.

Carey had gained some rudiments of New Testament Greek and Hebrew before embarking on his journey to India with John Thomas, a doctor by profession. It is also known that during this journey, he learnt some Bengali from Thomas who went through Genesis with him. Was this Bengali confined to Thomas' rendering of the Genesis text? How much Bengali Thomas himself had gained, we do not know. He knew enough to lead people to Christ. This, preparation on Carey's part could not possibly suffice as a basis for translating the Bible immediately on reaching India, setting up a business and preaching mainly in English in a church for Europeans. Besides, the Bengali grammars Carey used were written by British diplomats who had picked up more Farsi than any other language. They were used to enable British employees to obtain a quick grasp of basic Bengali and would have been a hindrance in translating from the original tongues into Bengali.

Many other earlier and contemporary foreign missionaries to India were academically trained in Hebrew and Greek both as translators and expositors. This had been the Scandinavian and German practice for centuries. Even today in oral Hebrew finals in Continental universities, Hebrew or Greek texts which are seemingly picked at random must be read aloud, translated without dictionary help and then expounded. Neither Thomas nor Carey had such a most necessary background. We are repeatedly told, however, that Carey had mastered Latin, Greek, Hebrew, Dutch and Italian before sailing for Calcutta and after a few lessons from Thomas on board was able to translate the Bible into Bengali immediately on reaching India in 1793. This story must surely belong to merry myth-making. Another story concerning the origin of Carey's Bengali Bible is more credible. Carey was conducting a meeting one Sunday morning in Calcutta but was interrupted by someone demanding that the Bible be translated into Bengali. Carey is supposed to have been so struck by the idea that he immediately asked a friend to continue the service, went home and started on a Bengali translation. When this translation ended, the story does not say. What language Carey and his friend were using for the church service, we do not know. We do know that Carey initially campaigned for preaching to the Indians in English and it took many years before he could preach in Bengali.

A reassessment of Carey's work as in recent Ziegenbalg studies is urgently needed

The Swedes, Dutch, Germans and Danes continued to send out missionaries to India throughout the 18th century, supported also by Church of England institutions such as the SPCK who encouraged Ziegenbalg and his successors to publish in England through them. The Swede, Kiernander, had been appointed to his task by Clive of India and Governor Hastings who were missionary-minded men. Kiernander founded a church and free schools in Calcutta and built a printing press there so neither tasks were pioneered by Carey as so often claimed. Indeed, when Carey reached India his future friend David Brown, an evangelical clergyman, was pastoring Kiernander's Old Mission Church and at least two printing presses were at work in the city before Carey set up his press from cast-off parts from the other presses.

Kiernander also evangelized the Bengalis long before Carey and the oft repeated statement that Carey found no Christian in Calcutta contradicts the historical evidence which shows that there were many Christians of many Western and Eastern denominations working in Calcutta at the time gaining numerous converts and Carey was warmly received by most. Testimonies to the sturdy Christian faith of such people often occurred in local newspapers. During Carey's early sojourn in Calcutta, it was still common for Kiernander's converts to give their children the middle name of Kiernander after the Swede. The thriving church, schools, hospitals, alms-houses and the local Christian cemetery Kiernander founded were all still living institutions and there for Carey to visit. Indeed, Baptist missionaries such as Fountain were married in Kiernander's Mission Church then pastored by Brown and Buchanan. They wished for an 'Anglican' service. The Kiernander family blog on the internet tells us that 'Not a year went by without a reference being made in print' in the English press to Kiernander so his work was internationally revered.

Carey's alleged flight from Calcutta for Serampore as commented on by most modern British Baptist writers is also something of a myth. Carey used Serampore merely as a weekend or part-time residence for all the years he worked at the Fort William College founded in Calcutta by Lord Wellesley in 1800 for the training of civil and military officials connected with the East India Company. Initially, Carey worked at least five days a week in Calcutta in the Civil Service College and then was rowed up the river to Serampore on Friday evenings and brought back to Calcutta Monday mornings for year after year. This altered as Carey who was Head of the Sanskrit Department was given the freedom to let others take over his lectures. He then spent a mere three days a week in Calcutta which left him plenty of time to do his own secular translating work for publication and sales. According to the Christian Herald and Seaman's Magazine, for the year 1821, Carey kept up two spacious houses, one in Serampore and one in Calcutta with 'every comfort one could wish for'. He kept 'a large number of Hindu servants' and earned 6,000 dollars a year besides support from within India and overseas. Here this former cobbler lived in stark contrast to his academic forerunners who dwelt amongst the casteless with no display of 'upperclassness' at all. Yet Carey only paid his co-working Indian evangelists, pastors and pundits a mere 6 dollars a month though he was paid hundreds a month himself. Indeed, Carey paid his co-workers the same salary he had received as a near bankrupt cobbler and on which he said he could not live. There was no social and financial equality between the British Baptist missionaries and their Indian co-workers.

Nevertheless, though Carey never seemed to have much authority in India outside of Calcutta during his missionary life time, his importance together with his team of workers, on the whole, is seen with hindsight as massively influential and important to the history of India. Here we think of laws Carey and his Serampore and Calcutta friends and fellow-workers helped establish in their translation works prohibiting widow burning, infanticide, and human trafficking and the fact that the Serampore Trio reintroduced many ancient cultural works for the study of Europeans in translated form. These were not go-it-alone actions but Carey and his friends worked hand in hand with Hindu reformers whose beliefs they nevertheless condemned.

In the face of such evidence given above it appears strange to this author that the massive number of new works on Indian missions world-wide has still not moved Baptist writers in England to revise radically their 'histories' of Carey the individual and the part the Baptist Missionary Society played in his life. Many stories about Carey the missionary are pure myths or what one calls today 'fake news'. The picture they present does no justice to Carey as a man deeply involved in national politics and one who eventually got on well with the Danish

Governors, the East India Companies of several nations, the British Government and the Calcutta Bible Society, nor does it do justice to early Indian foreign missions, nor especially to the Indians themselves. Indeed, the present 'Baptist Picture' certainly does not honour the thousands of Christian Indians who served Christ throughout the century before Carey and parallel to Carey and after him.

Chapter Twenty-Six

Grappling with Secular, Institutional, Political and Denominational Borders

The new Baptist brand of 'modern missionary' work

Carey was employed chiefly as an educationalist by the British Government and also later by the Danish Government. The Baptists' first schools pioneered by the Marshmans were for Anglo-Indians and none of the Serampore Trio taught in schools organized by Indians. Furthermore, they provided initial tuition for fee-paying pupils which thus denied education to most of the native population. This was no incentive to church planting outside of the academic area. The missionaries then lived on the profits they made from teaching, printing and the other businesses they founded besides their high wages as Government and EIC employees. They were then in a position to provide scholarships for Students at the Serampore College under certain strict conditions. This was a great break with earlier missionary strategy which was solely for the spiritual benefit of the common people at great cost to the missionaries who did not think in terms of financial profit. Gradually means tests were made to enable the poor to attend the Serampore and Calcutta Baptists' schools but this meant that the fee-payers were also paying for the poor though the profit went to the missionaries. Carey spoke of rich Armenians whom he had likened to 'worse than Muslims' but he had Armenian children besides other nationalities from the international upper classes in his schools. Apparently, this tuition was in English. In the evenings, he spoke with native Indians when he had time. Ziegenbalg did not cater for the upper classes and his schools, like those of Francke, were almost exclusively set up for the poor.

Ziegenbalg brought the old paths up to date

Ziegenbalg did not charge his pupils for their tuition and no fee, class, nationality or caste system was allowed to break the unity of the schools. There was little encouragement given in Carey's ministry for the local natives to plant indigenous churches, but the Indians themselves under such stalwarts as Krishna compensated this loss. After only a year or two, Ziegenbalg built his Jerusalem Church with his converts but a few more years on and the Tamil Christians themselves built their New Jerusalem church entirely by themselves which was considered indigenous. When he was permitted by the authorities, Ziegenbalg also preached, baptized and catechised in the garrison churches and those of the East India Company's chaplaincies. Soon native Indians began founding churches through the work of native pastors. Ziegenbalg's New Jerusalem Church has now gone through well over 300 years of uninterrupted ministry on the same site and its latest pastor, S. Abraham Navaraj is its 117th Indian pastor in succession.

The free boarding school with some 45 boys so praised by Carey's biographers was limited to the male children of Christians only but provided difficulties even for poor Christians as school books, writing paper and other accessories had to be provided by the parents. Commentators such as Buchanan says in his 'Christian Researches in India' that there were no conversions amongst the Baptists' school children. We read, however, of numerous children in Ziegenbalg's schools who came to profess a lively evangelical Christian faith and witnessed to other children about it at home and abroad.

The Caste System and Sati

Ziegenbalg did all in his power to suppress the Indian caste system but Carey was cautious in castigating the caste system and centred his criticism on the barbaric practice of Sati or widow-burning though, here, too, Carey backed Indian protests rather than voice his own as a missionary. The Hinduism of Carey's co-workers was built on the caste system so he had to tread carefully. Ziegenbalg had the great advantage of being able to use several classical Tamil anti-caste writings which he could turn into the vernacular so there was already openness on the subject in Tranquebar. Ziegenbalg also pioneered the opposition to slavery in India as probably the first European to do so. Up to Ziegenbalg's time the Portuguese, Dutch and Danes bought slaves, some of which were even imported from Africa. Ajith George says in his work on the Serampore Mission:

> Although Carey knew very well about the caste system Carey neither encouraged nor attacked that evil system but he was very careful to see that his converts had a casteless Christianity.

My co-authors of our book *William Carey: Theologian – Linguist – Reformer* claim:

> Carey was just as outspoken in his opinions on slavery and the caste system, which he in no case wanted to allow within the church, even at the cost of advantages for his missionary efforts. In this point he differed from the Halle-Danish Mission and the Society for the Promoting of Christian Knowledge (SPCK).

This is too much of a generalization as Ziegenbalg combatted the caste system strongly but had a different understanding of the caste system and Hinduism in the early 18th century to Carey's view a hundred years later. Both the caste system and Hinduism had developed quite radically by Carey's time. I took up this matter in detail under the sub-heading Ziegenbalg and the caste system and ended the section by saying:

> Anyone, however, dealing with the Hindu caste system from the earliest times to the present age will see that caste theories have altered considerably over the centuries. Though Ziegenbalg taught that all were equal in Christ, some of his successors built churches with three or four wings to isolate caste from caste.

There was no general policy of toleration for the caste system in the Halle Mission, although some gave in to pressure from those who wished to be Christians but keep their caste as their livelihood hung on the system. Furthermore, though racism appears not to have been accepted by Carey, several of his fellow Baptist missionaries were out and out racists. This could not be said of the Tranquebar Mission with perhaps the exception of Bövingh but he was not from Halle and was not sent out as a missionary.

Ignoring denominational borders

Neither Ziegenbalg nor Carey worked on a strictly denominational basis, but Ziegenbalg far less than Carey who was compelled through his love-hate adherence to the BMS to toe a party line. Ziegenbalg remained independent of Missionary Societies' efforts and won most critics over to his side. The Serampore Christians practised open-communion until Fuller challenged the practice. Carey bowed to this ruling following Ward who did not want to 'rock the Baptist boat'. Indeed, it was Andrew Fuller's alternative view to the supra-confessional Church both Ziegenbalg and Carey wished to further which hindered Carey from success whereas Ziegenbalg had continued his way irrespective of his denomination's urging. In 1806 Fuller began to put enormous pressure on the Serampore Trio to be first Baptists, then Christians. However, Carey found the fellowship with the evangelicals from various churches just as he desired and he was warm in his praise of non-Baptists Henry Martyn and George Simeon as they also were thrilled with fellowship with him. Carey's reports of the sweet fellowship he was enjoying with Christian men and women, who were in the majority on the mission field, left Fuller cold. When Carey urged Fuller and Ryland in 1810 to join hands with his English, German, Danish and American brethren and take part in conferences at regular intervals to discuss missionary strategy, Fuller argued that it would be to no avail and could lead to no agreement. He could not grasp the fact that there was already complete agreement between those ready to support the move in India and Fuller had no idea of the fellowship Carey was experiencing as he boycotted such fellowship himself.

Actually, Fuller stopped Carey from becoming a true, evangelical world leader. Fuller could not envisage what true evangelism and church planting meant, nor does it seem that he understood Christian fellowship beyond his own denomination. Even when Ward pleaded with Fuller not to rock the Indian boat, he had to stop rowing himself and give the BMS the directive who then capsized the boat of mutual Christian cooperation in evangelizing the needy. In spite of this BMS' interference a number of evangelicals happily attended Carey's church though fellowship through the Lord's Table was denied them.

Carey's plans for a General, Ecumenical Council of missionaries world-wide

On 15th May, 1806, as recorded by most biographers, Carey wrote to Fuller outlining his plans for an inter-denominational General Council to be held at regular intervals to discuss joint missionary strategies. Delegates should be both individual missionaries and representatives of the Missionary Societies. Andrew Fuller gave Carey's proposals an absolute veto. Grandson of Carey, Samuel Pearce Carey who probably remains the most popular writer on William Carey, comments:

> Carey's keenness for all possible inter-church and inter-mission cooperation prompted him to conceive the plan of bi-decennial World-Missionary Conferences at strategic centres, and to urge Andrew Fuller to get the first summoned for 1810 at the Cape. And his spirit glowed with the possibility of meeting Fuller himself and Ryland there, and the zealots of the London Missionary Society, and the Haldanes of Edinburgh, and his own fervid correspondents in Philadelphia and Boston, and the successors of Eliot and Brainerd amongst the American Indians, and Moravians from the West Indies, and the Germans from Sierra Leon, and Robert Morrison from Canton, and Henry Martyn from Cawnpore, and Daniel Corrie from Agra, and Dr Taylor from Bombay, and Danes from Tranquebar, and Dutch from Ceylon, and his own son Felix from Burma! He had kept so abreast of things that he seemed to have personal friends in every field.[1]

If Carey had succeeded in persuading Fuller of the wisdom of such a venture at that time, he would certainly have deserved the title 'Father of world-wide missions' but Andrew Fuller gave him a complete, incomprehensible veto to his needy proposals. Pearce Carey thus continues his warm and obvious acceptance of his grandfather's plans by stating:

---

[1] *William Carey*, p. 72.

> The Conference would have been the intensest reaction of his (Carey's), life for the pooling of experience and the planning of advance.[2]

In this matter and in the matter of refusing 'his' missionaries the right and duty to share the Lord's Table with his brethren in Christ, Fuller forced Carey out of the ranks of the great missionary pioneers and church planters.

A hundred wasted years

It took another hundred years before Carey's 'pleasant dream', as Fuller termed it, was realised but then the partakers had lost much of the evangelical zeal of Carey and his multi-denominational, evangelical colleagues. Ruth C. Rouse in her article 'William Carey's Pleasing Dream' remarks that the international missionary conference organized in 1910 was not according to Carey's suggestions and was 'chiefly great missionary demonstrations, fitted to inform, educate and impress'. The great chance under Carey's leadership was not taken up by the Baptist Missionary Society.

It is difficult to trace Pearce Carey's sources in this matter and this led to his contemporary Ruth Rouse writing concerning the question of Fuller's refusal to cooperate with Carey in 'William Carey's Pleasing Dream':

> The facts in this study have been gathered from contemporary letters, journals and reports, e.g. the journals of Henry Martyn and Claudius Buchanan: The Periodical Accounts (herein referred to as P.A.) Relative to the Baptist Missionary Society: and the Minutes and Reports of the S.P.C.K. It is unfortunate that the original correspondence between Carey and Fuller has disappeared. Information as to its whereabouts will be welcome.

As subsequent biographers such as Payne either refer to Pearce Carey or Ruth Rouse for documentation on this subject in lieu of original sources, the question must be raised as to why and how this correspondence disappeared though so much has been preserved

---

[2] S. Pearce Carey, *William Carey*, 1942, pp. 71-73.

concerning Carey's dealings with the Society. We know that Fuller, aided by Sutcliff suppressed much sound advice which came from India and presumably also their written reactions to it. Carey's sound idea was entirely in the spirit of his *Enquiry* which had allegedly won Fuller over to the missionary cause. Was this part of the later campaign to present Fuller as the initiator, leader and brain behind Carey's mission to India and not Carey himself? It is true that Fuller strove to clip Carey into his own paper-doll.

Ziegenbalg and Carey worked side by side with Indians

Apart from siding with their colleagues from other denominations both Ziegenbalg and Carey worked side-by-side with Indians, recognizing them as being equal status to themselves. There was, however, a difference, Ziegenbalg sought out the poorer classes and had no colonial attitude to them whatsoever. Carey allied more with the better educated as a British Government employee. Marshman, however, could not accept Indians as his equals. Ziegenbalg shared his life fully with the poorest poor of India. This the Serampore Trio never did.

Chamberlain's exemplary missionary successes in India

Not all of the Baptist missionaries in Carey's team were 'residents' in the sense that they declined to 'go out into the highways and byways' to plant churches. John Chamberlain who had heard of the Indian mission through reading London Missionary Society reports, being a Baptist decided to follow his calling to India through the auspices of the BMS. As he was of very humble stock, being but a farmhand, he hesitated in following a call to India but Sutcliff took him in hand to train him for a year, after which Sutcliff pronounced him unfit for the task just as he had formerly advised Carey not to take up the ministry, so Carey went ahead on his own bat. Chamberlain was spared this course as Dr Ryland gave him an opening at the Bristol college. Here, his fellow student, Cox, the author of the *History of the Baptist Missionary Society* highly praises Chamberlain's efforts and dedication as he mastered a number of languages with holy zeal in preparation for work in India and began to evangelize the Bristol slums in preparation of his future work with the poorest of the poor. Cox, however, mentions that neither the students nor the teachers at Bristol approved of his work amongst the poor but he was able to convince them of the need for the gospel and good works amongst the needy.[3] At Bible College we were warned against inviting the poor and homeless into the College premises because of the danger that they would 'steal the College's silver cutlery'. None of the students were aware that the college had any such silver and enquiries proved that it had no such articles. The poor-loving Chamberlain's joy was great as he was not only approved of as a missionary but was able to marry the girl of his dreams, a Miss Smith of Walgrave.

The Chamberlains sail for India

John Chamberlain and his wife were set apart for the Indian mission field on 21st April, 1802, two years after Carey began work as a Government and EIC civil servant, and a few days later embarked for India via the USA to avoid permit difficulties for those travelling on British ships. The couple departed from the states on 17th August for India with Mr and Mrs Nott, Mr and Mrs May, Dr and Mrs Johns, Miss Green, Miss Chaffin and Mr Hall, all Baptist missionaries sadly long forgotten. During the voyage Mrs Chamberlain gave birth to a daughter who sadly died about a week later. During their time at sea Chamberlain read widely, including books by Jonathan Edwards, Bishop Hall, James Hervey, Plato on Socrates and Isaac Watts. The couple also sang a number of Watts' hymns. Chamberlain also read diligently in his Greek New Testament and in books concerning much esteemed missionaries such as David Brainerd.

The Chamberlains reach Calcutta in 1803

On 26th January, 1803, the Baptist missionaries arrived at Calcutta where they were welcomed by Carey and Ward and proceeded to Serampore on the following day. There were now some 25 Baptist missionaries in and around Serampore who were given absolute freedom by the Danes and in no way handicapped by the British who were particularly lenient to Carey who now worked both in Calcutta and nearby Serampore under the auspices of both governments. We remember that Carey himself had no British permit. I have often been critical of Baptist missionary William Yates' handling of the original texts in his Bible translations and his insistence that Christian baptism

[3] Cox's *History*, p. 107.

was immersion, confusing meaning with his symbol for it. However, his compiled *Memoirs of Mr John Chamberlain Late Missionary to India* published in 1826 is a real gem and a great tribute to Yates' subject. Most of the contents came from Carey's and Chamberlain's journals and letters. My information on Chamberlain is mostly taken from this work. However, I also used Francis Augustus Cox's account in Chapter IV of his *History of the Baptist Missionary Society*. Cox knew Chamberlain more or less from his conversion to his death and admired him greatly. His chapter on Chamberlain, however, leans strongly on Yates.

From the start Chamberlain confessed that he did not wish to settle in Serampore but tour the country as an itinerant missionary. This plan had been largely given up by the Serampore Trio, though they encouraged their Indian converts to engage in such work. Thus, Chamberlain sought out Krishna at once to organize itinerant tours with him. As Chamberlain moved from Bengal to the Punjab, he wrote:

> Preaching and riding about are what suits me; and here I conclude, that it is my work to itinerate, and to publish abroad the holy Scriptures, which through the divine favour, you will have been enabled to prepare thus far for the nations, some to sow and some to water; some for this department, and some for another. It is not to be expected that all should be qualified alike.[4]

Chamberlain was never happy at Serampore because of its emphasis on business and setting up trading stations rather than Mission stations, throughout the north. Indeed, he complained that as soon as he approached Serampore, he felt sin surge up within him. He was called to evangelize not to serve tables. He wanted nothing to do with the kind of life the Serampore Trio were engaged in. On writing the above, Chamberlain had set up a base at Cutwa, before setting off to the Punjab. His aim being to enter the unevangelized fields of Hindi and Punjabi speakers whose languages he was learning to speak diligently. It took Chamberlain a year to master Hindi before leaving Bengal for even more Northern parts. At first Felix Carey often joined him on his long journeys but Chamberlain's most faithful companion over months

[4] Yates, *Memoirs of John Chamberlain*, p. 261.

at a time was Krishna, whom he called Krishno. Chamberlain's new Indian friend, companion and teacher had become a first-class itinerant preacher going on tours of up to five months at a time quite alone and unafraid. Many European missionaries have had centuries of praise but most of them lagged behind Krishna in their endeavours and Krishna should be remembered all the more diligently. Chamberlain was often accompanied by his wife who stood with her man despite the dangers of entering unknown territory where the people looked on Christians as evil, drunken rogues. Sadly, their son John Sutcliff Chamberlain, named after their friend, the Baptist pastor in Olney, who was born on 17th of November, 1803 died on 2 February, 1804.

The boating pastor

Soon Chamberlain gave up the idea of riding through the country on horseback because of the difficulties involved due to the rough country and many rivers and lakes. He realized that the natives usually travelled by boat and followed their advice and practice which made his work easier and speeded it up. Needless to say, Chamberlain became one of the greatest Baptist soul winners. However, his hard life took its toll and by the time he turned 40 he was a very ill man. Still, however, if he did not preach three times a day in the highways and byways, he felt he was not doing his Christian duty. His sickness gradually broke him down and at the age of forty-four it was decided to send him back to England for a while hoping that the climate and the doctors there would be able to restore his health. After only three weeks during the long voyage to Britain, Chamberlain went to meet his Saviour, rejoicing in his trust in the Lord but sad that he had not lived a more fruitful life. Compared to most others his life was as fruitful as could be. A co-passenger wrote that Chamberlain 'died on 6 December 1821, 20 days after we set sail, and his remains were committed to the deep in Latitude 9. 30. North, Long. 85 East.'[5] I look upon Chamberlain as a real Baptist pioneer missionary and we ought to hear more of him.

Richter wrong in his references to Chamberlain

The fact that Baptist Chamberlain was wrongly mentioned by the German author Richter as a victim of British governmental suppression,

[5] Yates, p. 418.

is worthy of note. Chamberlain's missionary ideals were far closer in practice to the theoretical missionary aims formerly held by Carey and from which Carey very soon departed. Thoroughly trained in missionary strategies and well prepared by his Christian calling, Chamberlain was as near as one perhaps could possibly get to the ideal missionary and did not let ideas of secular employment, business and high wages tempt him away from his calling. Rather than not being able to evangelize the North as Richter wrongly supposes, Chamberlain spent 19 years witnessing to the Hindus and only once in 1810, as far as his own letters show, was he advised not to go to the border territories at that particular time because of great unrest there. No one was allowed then to visit the border regions apart from soldiers and British officials. Contrary to the picture painted by Richter, it can be said, on the whole, that Chamberlain was treated very well by the British authorities even when we would have expected him to have been hindered by them. He, like Carey, went to British India without a permit.

Chamberlain given British permission to evangelize without a permit

Chamberlain relates how he was once questioned on entering a northern territory by a British official concerning his lack of credentials to prove that he was of British nationality and free to travel through the British colony. Such credentials were demanded of all at this time of unrest which was growing in the North and would eventually spread throughout all India. The Black Hole of Calcutta was now history but the Great Indian Mutiny was in preparation. Though Chamberlain had no documents to prove he was a British citizen, he found a friendly officer who, after questioning Chamberlain vouched for the fact that he was British and allowed Chamberlain to evangelize the area though he had had no official permit to do so.

Beyond denominations

Ziegenbalg aided indigenous and self-financing churches which did not use the appellation 'Lutheran'. Carey often called his church the Union Church whose membership was multinational. Both men believed earnestly that their churches were composed of God's people, not denominational members and therefore Carey liked the title Union Church as a place of worship. However, as soon as Carey died, the

Baptist Missionary Society insisted on calling the churches under Carey's control whatever their history 'Baptist Churches', oddly enough, not 'Immersionist' Churches, so camouflaging the immersion issue which had caused the Indian Church to split up into a denominational tangle. As so many Baptists protest that 'baptism' is a Greek loan-word and does not represent 'immersion', which is a Latin loan-ward, I cannot understand why they do not keep to the old traditional and Biblical term and why they argue that their Latin is allegedly more scriptural than the original Greek. Besides, to call one's church after a rite and not the instigator of that rite is putting effects before causes. So, too Carey's work had been chiefly financed through secular income; Lutherans, Independents, and Church of England people. Many of these had joined Carey's Union Church for the sake of Scriptural preaching and fellowship even though they could not accept the Baptist position on baptism and were thus denied membership. Such supporters of Carey's work were not allowed to take communion with the so-called 'Baptist Bride' and had to remain in Fullerite eyes second class Christians. There was a caste-system in Fullerism, too. Fuller's doctrine of baptism was radically opposed to normal Baptist procedure. It was the rite, not faith in Jesus Christ, that opened the door to the Lord's Supper, as he allowed those in his churches whom he considered non-Christians (an average of some fifty per church) to gather around the closed communion table on the grounds they had been baptised according to his strictures. Fuller's understanding of church discipline was quite different to that of such as Gill, Brine, Ryland Senior, Sutcliff and Booth. He founded an institutionalised order as against a community of saints. Even the Halls, father and son, disagreed with him!

The New Jerusalem Church in Tranquebar still upholds its witness
Ziegenbalg's New Jerusalem Church, is still an indigenous church today as his churches, manse, schools, colleges, printing press, printing mill and library were taken over by the Christian congregation at Tranquebar. Ziegenbalg founded a National Southern Indian Church but Carey cannot be said to have founded the Church of North India which was already growing rapidly in Carey's day despite the blockading interventions of Andrew Fuller and his even more hard-liner successors both at home and in India. Indeed, Carey's outreach in India

can be said to be the first and last of its kind. It is thus not possible to call Carey the 'Father of Indian Missions' or even the 'Father of Modern Missions' nor did he continue what the Fathers of modern missions in India had accomplished. Though Carey's reputation seems to be growing in our modern age, most of the work he did is neither followed up nor accepted today and Carey has almost become a mythological figure like many a saint before and after him. Besides, both Carey's former colleges and the BMS went ways which were certainly not in the spirit of the *Enquiry*. If the BMS and Carey had based their work on the principles of the *Enquiry*, they would not have been far off the right path.

Educational pioneers and school founders

In 1707, Ziegenbalg established schools for the education of both Tamil boys and girls, mostly from the penniless classes. Ziegenbalg dealt cautiously with local prejudice against female education so the girls were at first allowed to follow the teaching behind a curtain partitioned off from the boys but in 1710 Ziegenbalg overcame local prejudice and had a girls' school built. Soon we find him teaching co-ed classes. Carey found a number of schools already in existence but founded a mission school for boys in 1800 and Hannah Marshman one for girls sometime later. These, however, were fee-charging schools. Here, Carey has been widely praised for founding schools for girls but it is Hannah Marshman who pioneered them for the Baptist late-comers in that field. Again, Carey has been given the laurels for other people's work. Again, too, the work of Hannah Marshman has not been given adequate credit and her biographers hitherto have been criticised unfairly.

Much is made of Carey's 'modern' methods of using audio visual means via map-work and globes but these reforms had been introduced in 17th century Britain and Europe by educational reformers such as John Durie. Ziegenbalg also used such visual methods with much interactivity between teachers and pupils. Such methods were also promoted in the 18th century by educationalists and home-schoolers such as William Cowper, well-known to Carey from his Olney days when, according to Cowper 'the dipped and sprinkled lived in peace'. Both Ziegenbalg and Carey, in their various times, introduced the study of horticulture and agriculture, relying on the works of horticulturists before them, Ziegenbalg on Indian/Dutch sources, Carey on English. However, horticulture was a favourite study of many Protestant missionaries who cultivated their own vegetables, fruit and flowers from the seventeenth century on. The Jesuits had done this long before them. Again, Carey was only following in their train. Ziegenbalg built a large vegetable garden to cater for the hungry mouths of the poorer Tamils and Carey became quite a botanist in Calcutta. However, he was relying on English gardening magazines and ordered his plants, rather unsuitable for the Indian climate, from England. Ziegenbalg used indigenous literature and grew 'home products'.

Jeyaraj gives Carey the credit for pioneering the education of native Indian pastors but Ziegenbalg founded a theological seminary in Tranquebar in 1716 for the training of indigenous pastors which Carey is said to have built on over a hundred years later. However, Carey instigated no such college. Carey's work, like Ziegenbalg's, was financed strongly by the Danish King and supported by the Danish Governor Colonel Ole Bie who ruled Serampore from 1776 to 1805 before being forced from his position by the British. Without strong Danish support based on the Tranquebar Mission's ideals, there would have been no Serampore for the Serampore Trio. Bie himself was a convert of Schwartz of the Tranquebar Mission whose writings had fired Carey's initial missionary thoughts. In 1827 King Frederick VI of Denmark (1808-1839) granted the Serampore College the right to confer university degrees, following plans first put forward by Frederick IV in 1714. Carey was seen as a suitable teacher for the secular British Fort William School and also, through Marshman's influence in Denmark, for the royal university at Serampore. These, however, were secular appointments.

Personal trials and family affairs

Ziegenbalg lost several family members to the Indian climate and Carey and his first wife are said to have lost eight children which must have been an almost unbearable burden on the Careys, chiefly on Dolly.

Carey's first wife was of peasant stock but Charlotte, Carey's second wife, was a wealthy Countess of Danish-German extraction and already part of the pre-Carey Serampore Christian outreach and, unlike Dorothy, was content to live a life within the Serampore/Calcutta atmosphere programmed by her husband. Charlotte was instrumental in securing Carey's attachment to and support from the Danish government. In spite of her being an invalid, she could stand up for herself against Carey much better than Dolly and was quite at home in India. She was a woman used to managing her own business. Carey's son Felix supported his father though he was often either harshly treated or neglected by him, but also introduced to drinking more alcohol than was healthy for him. This was also brother William's lot who failed in his father's appreciation before Felix. The problem of strong drink in the Carey household still needs to be vigorously investigated.

The vantage point of ignorance

Carey's nephew Eustace must have been a further disappointment to Carey as he helped organize a rival mission to elbow the Serampore Trio out of their mission work. He was to write two works justifying his, Yates, and Adam's action as if William Carey had supported him all along. His lengthy evidence merely boils down to the fact that Carey had told his nephew to go his way and allow his uncle to go his own way, too. Eustace Carey condemns the defence of the Serampore Trio against the rival BMS missionaries as being either unjustified or irrelevant and is severe in his condemnation of the work hitherto done by the Trio. Eustace's main argument was that the 'older missionaries' had not kept to the ruling of the BMS which was quite true. It is also true, however, that the BMS Board had little notion of what confronted the Serampore Trio in India and virtually had no idea of what was going on in India. Yet from this 'vantage point' of ignorance the BMS demanded that they not only ruled the Indian mission field but the Indians themselves. The BMS had certainly not kept to their side of the original founding agreements.

Several members of Carey's wider family in India turned their backs radically on him and can be truly said to have worked against him. This was often Carey's own fault as he interpreted the BMS status in India as he wished. For instance, he refused to be dictated by the BMS concerning himself but refused to accept Adoniram Judson as a fellow missionary in India because he was not authorized by the BMS, a fact Eustace was quick to point out. Judson's decision to move to Burma must be understood in this context.

Ziegenbalg's son Gottlieb became Denmark's EIC Director

It is quite evident that the Serampore Trio's acceptance in Serampore rested on Serampore's long connection with Danish and German missionary work rather than the BMS. Ziegenbalg's first son Gottlieb who became the first Director of the Danish East India Company with its headquarters in Serampore and his work, backed by the Danish King and the Danish Governor, helped open the doors for Carey and his missionary friends to Serampore. Schwartz who had motivated Carey in his interests for India had been Gottlieb Ziegenbalg's tutor, mentor and supporter, as he had been Bie's. When Ziegenbalg came to India, he met hostile governors and hostile traders but managed to win them over in the end and convince them of the need for evangelism amongst the Indians carried out by trained people of whatever nation, thus preparing the way for further missionaries such as Schwartz, Kiernander, Brown and Carey.

Languages translated into Bibles or Bible portions before Carey's time

The reoccurring theory in critical assessments of Ziegenbalg that he and his fellow-missionaries knew no Danish is quite incorrect. Both Ziegenbalg and Plütschau were fluent enough in Danish to learn Portuguese and Tamil through that medium. Many of the earlier missionaries came from areas which were then Danish dukedoms and which have become German only in modern times. Kiel, for instance, in present Germany was part of Denmark and a Danish University in Ziegenbalg's and Carey's times. When I visit my son and his family in Schleswig-Holstein, now part of Germany but then part of Denmark, we worship at a Danish Church and the language spoken throughout the service and afterwards at coffee is Danish although now all these Danish-speaking people are Germans. Ziegenbalg founded a school for Danish speakers in Tranquebar and a number of the first missionaries there were Danes, though they would now be considered Germans because of the extension of Germany into former Danish areas.

There were also other language translations to follow in the early years of the spreading of the Tranquebar Mission's outreach which extended to Serampore and Calcutta. Co-workers and successors such as Schwartz and Kiernander also published in a good number of other living and classical languages such as Sanskrit, Urdu, Farsi, Marathi,

Telugu, Arabic and Bengali throughout the 18th century. With such works they extended their gospel influence from Tranquebar, throughout northern India to Afghanistan and Persia. Schwartz was the man who had motivated the Serampore authorities to allow foreign missionaries to enter the colony. Without Schwartz, who walked in Ziegenbalg's footprints, there would have been no Baptist Mission. Thus, Helen Holcomb writes in her *Men of Might in India Missions*:

> To Ziegenbalg and Schwartz, Carey, Marshman and Ward owed their home at Serampore.[6]

J. Sandegreen, a Swedish Serampore College Professor, says in his Carey Lecture:

> Without Ziegenbalg there could be no Carey; without Tranquebar no Serampore.[7]

Indeed, as Frykenberg points out, it was the influence of Lutheran Schwartz' on Carey that prompted the Baptist to write his *Enquiry*.[8] Jeyaraj in his many works on Indian evangelism mentions Ziegenbalg's works written in Tamil, German, Portuguese and Latin. These were soon translated into a number of other languages indigenous and foreign.

Unitarian, Socinian, Arian opposition within the East India Mission

On the Indian side, the Arian controversy in Calcutta was started by the BMS co-worker Rammohun Roy and on the European side by William Adam sent to India by the BMS. On the 'home front' side were the Arian Baptists at the Bristol College and those Arian churches who were invited to merge with the Particular Baptists by Fuller. This Arian influence amongst the early union of Baptist churches was principally the work of Andrew Fuller and Dr John Ryland as Fuller sent Ryland who presided over the Bristol Baptist College Arian candidates such as Robert Aspland. Ryland then engaged Arian lecturers such as ex-

[6] *Men of Might*, p. 66.
[7] Calcutta, 1955.
[8] Robert Eric Frykenberg *Christianity in India*, p. 270.

student Job David for the 'edification' of his students. The controversy was heightened when Fuller backed a Socinian to become pastor of Soham which Fuller had given up for Kettering.

William Yates, William Adam and Rammohun Roy had begun work on a separate translation into Bengali of the Bible as a rival to Carey's but the three quarrelled over Arian issues and their various unorthodox leanings destroyed the value of their work. It was Roy's limited understanding of Greek which moved Adam, who had joined Carey's translator team in 1818 after graduating from Bristol Baptist College and Glasgow University, to now join the Indian Arians. Yates seems to have remained orthodox but took over Roy's Arian interpretations of New Testament Greek for his 'Baptist' Bible translations. The Bristol College had opened their doors to Arians but then, on changing their theology, had difficulties keeping them out and different opinions had been aired as to how far doctrinal tolerance could be accepted in the Baptist institutions.

The *Dictionary of Unitarian and Universalist Biography* states concerning Adam:

> After mastering the classical Sanskrit and Bengali languages, Adam joined a group of men who were revising the Bengali translation of the New Testament. The group included the cordial and scholarly Hindu cum Christian, Rammohun Roy who convinced Adam that the meaning of the Greek preposition dia required that John 1:3, in their Bengali translation should be rendered in the sense of, 'All things were made through the Word', and not 'by the Word' as Christ was a mere instrument of God. In 1821 the view of the nature of Christ, propagated by Roy's and Adam's translation and espoused by the Baptist missionaries, was rejected by orthodox Christians as the Arian heresy (named after the 4th century CE dissident, Arius). For this reason Carey is said to have nicknamed his rival Adam as 'the second fallen Adam'.

Raja Rammohun Roy (1772-1833)

Roy, who has been called 'The Father of Modern India' was born into a high caste Brahmin family and studied Bengali, Persian, Arabic and

Sanskrit from his youth on. As he commented so dogmatically on Biblical texts, he was reported to have a profound knowledge of Hebrew and Greek but his Biblical knowledge appears to have been fostered by the Authorised Version of the Bible as he had never studied the original languages. As an adult, he took up the professions of banker and money-lender, making a large fortune, the latter occupation bringing him in favour with the British in Calcutta. The Baptist missionaries were drawn to him initially because of his knowledge of Bengali and his opposition to Sati which was practised in Calcutta perhaps more than anywhere else. As Roy professed to be a better Christian than other Christians, and wrote quasi-Christian articles and books, he was welcomed into the Serampore Baptist fold and encouraged to write for their newspaper Samachar Darpan. Roy gradually took part in the Baptist gatherings and attended their church services and helped them with their understanding of the Greek text in their translation work. This shows that the missionaries could hardly have been proficient in that language themselves. Roy was the chief instrument in having Sati banned in 1829 contrary to claims in modern Baptist reports that it was at Carey's initiative.

The Samachar Darpan was a Baptist secular newspaper

The Samachar Darpan came into the hands of John Clark Marshman, after his father had given up as editor and producer. John immediately classified the former Baptist weekly as a secular newspaper and put it into the hands of Hindu pundits yet the Baptists still claimed ownership but no longer financed the paper which was now heavily subsidised by Government grants. Again, the BMS were supported by secular monies.

Joshua Marshman makes no headway with the BMS

John's father, Joshua, decided to take up the Arian matter with the BMS as he feared Arianism was becoming acceptable under the Baptists. So he travelled to England to clear up the matter. Once in England, he found the BMS and Baptist Association void of sympathy for his orthodox venture so he returned to India a broken man. Carey said he had aged 15 years during his brief visit to England. At that time, in its search for paying members the BMS and the once Particular Baptists who followed Fuller were now saying that they refused to look closely at their members' doctrines. At that time the Fullerite Baptists would share communion, prayer meetings, preaching activities and other forms of Christian fellowship with Arians but not with Reformed evangelicals of other denominations.

Theological and political peculiarities of the Baptist fold

Roy's influence amongst the Baptists because of his rendering of the Greek and Bengali was relatively strong until his long strife with Marshman concerning which of them was the true Christian. Roy had written a series of books on Christianity with an Arian bent such as his *The Precepts of Jesus: The Guide to Peace and Happiness*, arguing that his brand of Hinduized Christianity was the true religion. Roy's work was published in 1820 and appeared both in Bengali and English. The Indian nobleman saw Christ's work as that of a Guru according to the Hindu pattern arguing that the Christ of Marshman was not the Christ that Jesus claimed he was. We must remember that Joshua Marshman confused being a Christian with his high view of British rule. Roy believed he taught Christ as Christ witnessed to Himself and therefore his Christianity was better than Marshman's political theories. This led to a further series of works and counterworks from both Marshman and Roy.

Marshman's great blunder

Though much of Roy's theology was based on highly selected passages from the Authorised Version seen through Hindu-Arian eyes, and was open to correction from a man more versed in the Bible, Marshman spoilt his corrective to Roy's works by stooping to sheer racism, calling the writer of alleged Christian literature and Bible translator Roy a 'Heathen' as if that was condemnation enough to stop the controversy. He clearly did not follow Carey's policy of the equality in God's eyes of all peoples. This was not just a one-off outbreak of temper as Marshman was well known as one who quickly became hot under the collar, especially over politics.

In his political manifesto arguing for the subjection of the Hindus under British Colonialism written in 1813 and entitled 'The Advantage of Christianity in Promoting the Establishment and Prosperity of the British Empire in India', Marshman clearly claimed that the preaching of the gospel in India, was a way of putting a permanently immature India under the far superior British yoke. Confessing, obviously with his tongue in his cheek, that he did not wish to enter into politics, he immersed himself deeply into that genre by writing:

> It is neither my business nor my wish even to glance at anything of a political nature: my calling as a missionary, however, can never abate my affection to my native country, nor can I cease to feel deeply interested in its welfare. I am conscious too that no one in Leadenhall Street,[9] nor even in Britain, more ardently wishes for the permanence and prosperity of the British empire in India than myself; and I cannot at all times avoid weighing those ideas respecting the probable means of securing these objects, which my situation among the natives and my acquaintance with their notions and feelings naturally suggest; and I am fully convinced that one of the most effectual means of perpetuating the British dominion in India will be the calm and silent, but steady and constant, diffusion of christian light among the natives. Little is at any time to be feared from the Hindoos, they are too much divided and too indolent to be formidable. It is my firm opinion, that to the very end of time, through their imbecility of character, which christianity itself will never remove, they will be dependent on some other nation: and happy will it be for them, should Providence continue them under the mild and fostering care of Great Britain; provided she act in her proper character, as a nation professing Christianity.[10]

One would have thought such racist sentiments would prevent any Christian from becoming a missionary to Indians especially as Marshman felt he was a missionary to permanent imbeciles whose imbecility could never be removed by Christianity. I must admit that when I read these shocking words, I became hot under the collar and wept over the wrongs done to India by such evil foreign thinking! Similar statements came from the Serampore press concerning the Muslims. When this was questioned, the blame was put on the writers but not the Serampore missionaries who had appointed them. It was no wonder that Roy disagreed with Marshman and his 'Christianity' as any

---

[9] The Headquarters of the BEIC.

[10] *The Advantage of Christianity*, pp. 6, 7.

decent-minded person would, whatever their faith. At this time, Marshman was not doing missionary work but assisting Carey in translating Indian philosophical works and the writings of Confucius into English besides teaching at the Anglo-Indian school he and his wife had founded to finance their life in India. This literary work both secular and religious and his political book production and vendetta against Roy scarcely gave him time to be more than a spare-time missionary at best. He was but a guest in the India of Roy who lorded it over his hosts. The odd thing is that Marshman claimed in his racist politics that he was walking in the footsteps of Bartholomäus Ziegenbalg and the Moravians.

Ziegenbalg never covered his Christianity in political propaganda
Ziegenbalg had never combined politics and Colonialism with his Christian outreach and he made himself an Indian amongst Indians, recognizing many 'Christian' features amongst the Tamils which were lacking in the Scandinavians and Germans. Nor were the Moravians hyper-patriotic to foreign governments as Marshman. It was sadly not clear to Marshman that by calling professing Indian Christians of whatever quality 'imbecile' and 'heathen' he was behaving in a most un-Christian manner and a shame to his missionary calling. If he felt that Christianity was no match for the Indians without external force, he had no business to be a missionary who is called to transform sinners.

Roy declared the winner over his battle with Marshman
It was thus clear that Roy was declared the winner of his verbal and written battle with Marshman and he kept his temper to boot. This did not do the Baptist testimony any good and several riots were put down to Christian tyranny. This boosted Roy's image in India and the Hindu community were also quick to sympathise with Roy who has ever since been respected as a benevolent Indian who thought in Indian terms. Indeed, Roy's philosophy of religion and social activity was indeed thereafter called the 'Bengali Renaissance'. The BMS and the Serampore editors, were very late in realizing that they were doing nothing to promote evangelical, Reformed Christianity via their quite un-Christian propaganda newspaper so they wisely stopped production in 1841.

Unitarianism in India

In the years following the alliance with Christian humanist Roy and Baptist Arian Adam, there was an upsurge of Unitarianism in conjunction with great evangelical fervour in the East Indian Company's circles which emphasised moral civilised improvement rather than the Christian faith. Moral Government was all the rage. During this upsurge of Rationalism, humanist Roy and Baptist Adam founded the Calcutta Unitarian Society. Soon the two friends quarrelled because Roy supported a more Hindu form of Arianism and Adam a more 'Christianised' form of the same error. Roy who moved naïve Baptists to follow him in his one-to-one narrow interpretation of Greek words had seemingly forgotten that his own language was well-known for its multitude of synonyms concerning very many words and that the Greek 'dia' carries at least eight meanings in English and 'baptizo' over forty. The Indian languages are themselves a lexicological treasure chest here. Roy, and those who followed him, obviously translated restrictively for their own purpose as the case of Yates shows. However the non-Arian Baptists disagreed with Roy, they kept to his narrow interpretations of the Biblical Greek, probably knowing even less Greek than Roy. Even in the translations which are claimed to be Carey's own, great weakness was shown in translating key words such as Christ's 'blood' and 'love' with faulty Bengali or Hindi terms and the quite unprofessional opting for one Indian word for one Greek or Hebrew term quite out of context. This is especially dangerous given the many connotations of 'love' in many Indian languages several of which represent anything but Biblical Christianity.

I remember a guest-speaker at a German Reformed Conference who was the Principle of a British Theological College and a convinced Fullerite. Though knowingly speaking to Greek and Hebrew experts, he attempted to base his Liberal views on the Greek text. I was astonished to hear that this 'Greek expert' did not know the difference between Aspects and Tenses, confused the Perfect with the Imperfect and made a number of lexicological errors. Immediately after his rather pitiful lecture, with no gospel in it whatsoever, a number of young, active academics came over to me, shaking their heads at what they had heard. The lecturer, noticing this, cried out in the lecture hall, pointing at me, 'Don't talk to that man. He is a heretic!' He was not invited again to lecture. There are obviously 'experts' and 'experts'. The shoddy scholarship of so-called Fullerite experts saves us from being overflooded by their followers.

Fuller, Arianism and Socinianism in Fuller's circles

Meanwhile, in England, the Particular Baptists were winning ground against Fuller's followers and several Baptist churches had to be excluded from the churches supporting the Bristol Bible College for their attachment to Arianism or Socinianism. That Socinianism was eventually banned from Broadmead is illustrated by the Unitarian Aspland family. Robert Aspland had gained a scholarship to Gresham College but Andrew Fuller persuaded him to matriculate at the Broadmead College in 1798 with a view to becoming a Baptist minister, though Dr John Ryland was for Aspland settling down under his Professor Ward scholarship at Battersea. Aspland reached Bristol just as the anniversary celebrations were in progress. The preacher chosen for the remembrance sermon was an old boy of the College, Job David, who was a noted Socinian. Writing in 1850, after the first generation of Socinian-friendly leaders had passed away, Aspland's son, Robert Brook Aspland wrote in his footnotes to his father's *Memoirs*:

> What holy horror would be roused by a 'Socinian' preacher now entering the pulpit of Broadmead!

Fuller complained that his churches were small but those of his opponents were increasing in membership. It is well known that the former Johnsonite church Fuller pastored at Soham from 1775 to 1803 shrank rapidly under his ministry. As he spent a quarter of his time whilst pastoring Kettering in other pulpits, especially on the Lord's Day, we cannot speak of a sustained ministry at Kettering under Fuller's pastorate there. Fuller never really settled down at either Soham or Kettering.

By 1797 his Soham feet were itching to move on to larger churches. The final break came with Soham when the church refused to invest money in expanding the church building as Fuller demanded because their numbers were too small and they were too poor to pay Fuller a higher salary. Fuller was greatly disappointed because he thought a larger church premises would tempt more visitors, nor realising that sound gospel preaching attracts sinners in need of a Holy God and not marbled halls. So Fuller opted for the much larger Kettering. It is to be noted that the Soham Socinian Baptist Church which Fuller had taken over with a membership of 47 was reduced to nine members under Fuller's ministry. It was, however, during his eight-year pastorate of this far from orthodox church that Fuller wrote his far from orthodox *Gospel Worthy of All Acceptation.*

The author's criticism of modern Fullerite Liberals

My own criticism of Fullerite Liberals such as Michael Haykin, Curt Daniel, Chris Chun, Robert Oliver and the late Erroll Hulse, is that what they falsely declare to be a gospel worthy of all acceptation is as The Earthen Vessel describes it, in reality, a gangrene in the churches and a completely false gospel. Fuller's major works were written at a time when he was openly courting error and welcoming Socinians such as twenty-year younger Aspland to his house prayer meetings, and placing him under Socinian teaching. Aspland was far from orthodox in his understanding of Christ but Fuller himself was clearly Grotian in his views of Christ's work. So, in spite of Fuller's altered theology, both men removed Christ from his gospel Throne. Aspland was certainly more 'Christian' in his views concerning the work of the Holy Spirit than was Fuller. Many of Aspland's views concerning the Old Testament and the Jews as being ousted by New Testament principles were in harmony with Fuller's views and those of the modern NCT people which clearly evolved from Fuller's negative attitude to the Old Testament, the Jews and, above all, the revealed Law of God. One of my main criticisms of David Gay, now a notorious NCT man though still going his own way, was that in his book *Battle for the Churches*, he argued that darkness was on the face of the earth before Fullerism flourished.

The missionary unity which Carey in India enjoyed with his evangelical, Bible-believing fellow missionaries from several church backgrounds and countries was spoilt when Fuller pitched his dark and dismal radical cancerous theology and no-communion tent in their midst. It had been Aspland's criticism all along that Fuller's ideas of religious freedom stopped where his opponents differed from him.

It is strange to note that Gisburne is claimed to have run down Soham, and not Fuller, whereas when Aspland preached for Gisburne at Soham on 14th August, 1808 whilst court enquiries were continuing, he records that he spoke to 'a large and respectable' congregation though many whom he called 'Calvinists' under the leadership of a Thomas Emons strove to prevent him from entering the church.[11]

The Socinian Soham Church eventually joined the General Baptist Churches as also did Robert Aspland's Arian New Port Church on the Isle of Wight and thus gained access to the BMS and a continuing presence in the Bristol Baptist Training College. This was obviously one of the reasons why the BMS had to drop its honourable title of the Particular Baptist Missionary Society. This down-grading and opening of the theological basis for the Mission was criticized by Spurgeon because the so-called Baptist Missionary Society now accepted anyone willing to pay a membership fee of ten shillings and sixpence. Quite a sum in those days. It was not the end of the Particular Baptists, however, as their churches grew and remained orthodox whereas those who followed Fuller lost many members and became Liberal. We note, too, that Arians Robert Aspland and William Adam, the latter being sent out by the BMS to India, had both studied theology at the Baptist College at Bristol which was obviously under Socinian influence when presided over by John Ryland Jun.

All this backs up Coleridge's argument that Fuller did not know where he stood theologically and that Fuller's defence of his handling of the Soham church in his 'A Narrative of Facts Relative to a Late Occurrence in the County of Cambridgeshire; in Answer to a Statement Contained in a Unitarian Publication called The Monthly Repository' dealing with Soham's Socinianism was guilty of 'metaphysical meddling' and playing around with the subject instead of writing an earnest critical defence. Actually, as Fuller was charged with being 'worse than Priestly', this work as clearly seen from the contents was written to wash Fuller clean of this accusation. When he learnt that the court findings were not to his liking, Fuller was man enough to apologize to his former brethren saying that some of his criticisms of his brethren 'were not deserved'. Dr Ryland does not mention the Soham matter at all in his biography of Fuller but Fuller's biographer Morris, who challenges a number of myths perpetuated by Fullerites, says of Fuller's 'A Narrative of Facts' that when Fuller wrote it he must have had 'a most unhappy lapse of memory'. This must also be said of

---

[11] *Memoirs*, p. 221 ff.

the present Soham Baptist Church who in their brief online histories of the Soham church give a glowing presentation of Andrew Fuller as he never was at Soham and merely add a few words concerning the church's decline into Unitarianism which cannot be beaten for their understatement. The present-day church, now an FEIC church tells us on their web-site:

> It is true to say that there were some difficult periods in the church's history. Indeed, by around 1810 things had got so low that it was left to the remaining nine determined members to call a Pastor and re-establish the church work.

The British Critic, after describing the Arianisation of Soham and the court and press conflicts, ended in the words:

> If anybody connected to the cause wishes to read the books, he will find that much coarse, vulgar and improper behaviour was resorted to on both sides, though all claim to be gentlemen of the first reputation, and purest honour.

The writer claimed that both sides (Gisburne's and Fuller's) had brought disgrace on the Dissenting cause and criticized Fuller's move in backing Gisburne by adding that Soham, 'must have been tolerant; to a degree of idiotism, to have winked at such an intrusion.'[12] I take this also to be a dig at Fuller.

Baptist Arianism before and after 1719

The Baptist Liberals, who did not represent the bulk of Baptist churches by any means, were strongly infiltrated by Arianism and Socinianism prior to the Salters' Hall conference of 1719 which demonstrated the influence of John Gale (1680-1721) and James Foster (1691-1753). Later Arian influence was strengthened by ex-Methodist Robert Robinson (1735-1791) and Robert Aspland (1782-1845) and their 'Arian baptism'. Arian Robinson's work *History of the Baptist Church* is still a standard work amongst Baptists. Robinson was very active in the Soham-Kettering region and well-known to both Aspland and

[12]The British Critic, Vol. 36, 1810

Fuller. It is also well-known that Fuller's Kettering Church was founded by an Arian, William Wallis. To counteract this downgrading of the gospel John Gill brought in his more orthodox theology. His sound Baptist Confession of Faith (Goat Yard Confession) came out after the First and Second London Baptist Declarations had been abandoned by his predecessors who had sought an alliance with the General Baptists and had decided that one should not be so particular about doctrine. Modern Baptists who criticize John Gill so strongly are almost invariably of the Fullerite and New Divinity split-offs from traditional Baptist and Reformed theology and have substituted the rationalism of the so-called Enlightenment for Christian doctrine. Gill saved Baptist theology from inner corruption. His enemies called Gill's stabilising reforms a 'dunghill' but it was such as Fuller who piled up the dung. Fuller's defence in the public hearing was that he did not know what was going on in Soham which many found hard to believe and accused him of lying. Perhaps Fuller was simply out of his depth in the debate because of his own every-changing and ever weak theology but, nevertheless, he thus supported movements which endangered the churches and did much damage in the progress because, as Cox says, he liked to command and had organized both sides of the trouble makers. So, too, Fuller obviously misrepresented his opponents but was man enough to confess that he had been untruthful in his criticisms when that truth came out. We know from the records, especially via Cox, that when Fuller opened his mouth too wide in the condemnation of others, Sutcliff would tap him on the shoulder and say, 'Could I talk with you alone for a moment', after which Fuller changed his tune but Sutcliff was not always there to help restrict Fuller's busy-bodying. Expressing his views on Sutcliff and Fuller, Cox tells us that once when Fuller lost command of his tongue regarding Cox, Sutcliff came up to him and said:

> 'My dear young brother Cox, I see that my brother Fuller has somewhat hurt your mind.' It was admitted. 'Well', said he, 'don't be disconcerted or discouraged. It is his manner; he does not mean anything unkind; he really loves you. My brother Fuller sometimes serves me just the same: he speaks, on a sudden, perhaps very harshly; but I know him, and let it pass; and he will soon be as confiding and affectionate as ever.' Here were the

> men; – Fuller severe, prone to command, little disposed to make even proper allowances, yet capable of strong attachment; Sutcliff, kind, peaceful, humble, generous-hearted, and wise.[13]

There are interesting examples of Fuller's lack of command over his tongue recorded by Robert Aspland who went to school in Soham and became Fuller's protégé. In his 'Bigotry and Intolerance defeated, or An Account of the late prosecution of Mr. John Gisburne, Unitarian minister of Soham, Cambridgeshire with an exposure and corrections of Mr. Andrew Fuller's narrative of that affair in letters to John Christie in 1810', he wrapped Fuller's knuckles verbally for not speaking the truth and cited quite severe quarrels between Fuller and himself. He adds also that, when quarrels were at their height, he and Fuller could be seen walking arm in arm together and even dining together. Further examples are given by Aspland's son in his *Memoir of the life, works and correspondence, of the Rev. Robert Aspland* in 1850. Aspland Senior complained that his friend often addressed him in a priestly, intolerant, high and mighty, manner with occasional outbreaks of bad temper. He also criticised Fuller's fanatical way of demanding legal punishments for those who disagreed with him theologically. When Fuller died, Aspland wrote in his journal:

> Poor Andrew Fuller is, it seems, gone. It will, I doubt not, fare better with him than he was disposed to allow or to wish with regard to some others. An infirm temper, and a narrow education kept him the dictator of a mere party, though his talents were adapted for more extensive usefulness. However, it is pleasant to think he will rise, or soon become a different man, at the resurrection of the just.[14]

Aspland's remarks concerning Fuller's meagre education were entirely unfair as Fuller was the driving force in finding scholarships for Aspland and arranging for his further education and placing him in an Arian educational nest. Aspland was often guilty of biting the hands that fed him. Yet even Cox who kept faithful to Fuller was prone to

---

[13] Cox, *History of the Baptist Mission*, p. 265.
[14] *Memoir*, p. 363.

criticise Fuller for his mere 'rudiments of education' and high and mighty bossy manner.[15]

Today Soham is a member of the Fellowship of Independent Evangelical Churches (FIEC). This fellowship is described as an 'open communion' group of churches as, unlike Fuller, they allow for freedom of Christian conscience on modes and methods of baptism.

The BMS's disdain for Carey's work

The BMS had been very critical of Carey's translation work and Arian Adam in his 'Correspondence Relative to the Prospects of Christianity and the Means of Promoting its Reception in India' sided with the 'junior brethren' who had been sent out to India to elbow out the Serampore Trio and castigated Carey's compilations of Biblical translations sternly. He supported Ellerton's Bengali New Testament against Carey's and accused the Serampore Trio of promoting 'phantom languages' which had no relation to the ones spoken by the Indians but were purely artificial written languages. This, of course, was correct. Though Adam believed that the Baptists were now making more professed converts than the Church of England missionaries, he argued that the testimonies of such converts were hardly convincing. Allowing for the fact that Adam was an Arian, and may have been biased in his criticism, it must be confessed that also sound Christians like Brown and Martyn, besides missionary educators such as Duff, agreed with much that he said as also the Bible Societies who ceased to support both Carey's supposed Grammar and his 'compiled' translations. Even the Fort William College soon departed from Carey's grammar and dictionary because of their insufficiencies.

Baptists were not alone in adjusting Christianity to Hindu thinking

The Baptists were not the only missionaries to patronise a Christianity which dealt disproportionately with Hindu culture in Calcutta and un-Christian matter and compromised in their Christology. The Scotsman John Nicol Farquhar (1861-1929) arrived in Calcutta as a London Missionary Society representative in 1891 but showed little of the Christianity of his LMS evangelical forerunners who had paved the way for Baptist Chamberlain's call to India. He is chiefly remembered for

---

[15] *History of the Baptist Missionary Society*, p. 263.

his works *The Crown of Hinduism* (1913), *Modern Religious Movements in India* (1915) and *The Apostle Thomas of Southern India* (1927). He left India in 1922 to become Professor of Comparative Religions at Manchester University.

Farquhar adapted the then current 'Fulfilment Theology' to win Hindus for Christ by telling them that Christ was the goal of all Hindus and thus the Crown of Hinduism. He built his theory on Matthew 5:17, 'I came not to destroy but to fulfil', interpreting the text quite out of context. So he argued that missionaries should not seek to destroy Hinduism but point out to Hindus how their religion finds its fulfilment in Christ. He emphasized that Christ is beyond denominationalism and sectarianism and that every religion has some truths in it which help a person find Christ. Many of Farquhar's convictions were obviously influenced by the writings of Arian Roy who allied with the Baptists for a number of years, so we are not surprised to find that Farquhar uses a portrait of Roy in full noble Indian regalia for a frontispiece to his work on religious movements.

Chapter Twenty-Seven

The Dano-Norwegian-German Mission and the Baptist Missionary Society: A Comparison

Britain hears of Ziegenbalg's work

Although reports of the work of the Dano-Norwegian-Halle Mission and Ziegenbalg's books on the state of religion in southern India reached England in the very early 18th century and quickly went into many editions with the backing of the Archbishop of Canterbury, the Royal Family and The Church of England Missions to India, they kindled little interest in the Dissenting Churches although very few of the missionaries whose works were published were of the Church of England. Indeed, from the British point of view, they were all Dissenters! It is now well-known, at least amongst Methodists, that Susanna Wesley's family was attached to the East India Company and that Samuel Wesley, a Church of England minister, had not only considered going out as a missionary to India at the beginning of the 18th century but had begun to study major Indian languages and save up for the journey, determined to preach the gospel there.[1] This was thwarted by a sudden change in his finances and he became an inmate in Lincoln Castle Debtors' Prison. However, these records of God's work in India from the early 18th century on remained in the Wesley family library and were used by Susanna in the education of her

[1] See 'The Influence of Danish Missionaries to India on Susanna Wesley's Methods of Education', Methodist History, 2014.

children John and Charles. Thereafter, reports from the Dano-Norwegian Mission as also those of Church of England missionary-chaplain George Lewis continued to reach Britain. The British Royal Family and their German chaplains were keenly interested in Ziegenbalg's work and hosted him in London on his first and only furlough. Ziegenbalg was very grateful for British support which included the gift of a printing press and many rolls of paper, with the help of the SPCK and George Lewis as also great help in establishing the charity schools and church founding.

A need for a biography of Lewis and his work in India

There is a great need for a reliable, well-researched biography of this 17th and 18th century missionary today as Lewis is quite forgotten by even his own denomination who have nevertheless written many times about the area in which Lewis evangelized and cared for the souls of Indians and Eurasians but especially slaves. A. Wescott, for instance, one-time Principal of the Society for the Propagation of the Gospel in Madras wrote in 1897 of the Vepery Mission in Madras as the 'oldest Mission connected with the Church of England in India' without so much as mentioning Church of England Lewis's pioneering name within that community.

The Tranquebar missions 'Firsts'

Indeed, by the time of John and Charles Wesley's parents, the Danish-Halle Protestant Mission at Tranquebar had already provided India with all the 'firsts' that English writers, mostly Baptists, on the whole, claim were the achievements of William Carey, though Carey came on the Indian scene so very many years later and obviously built on centuries' old church planting. His denomination, too, the Baptist Church, was a young church development in contrast to the long-established Indian churches whether of Western, Eastern or Indian founding. The 'newness' of the Baptist faith in India was not grounded in the old evangelical Reformed doctrines which had been preached in India for almost two centuries. The Fullerite Baptists merely brought a new and different approach to Baptism with an ecclesiology and soteriology attached to it which were historical novelties culled from Enlightenment philosophical thinking which denied the Atonement as a once and for all time fiat of Christ's.

Today's Tranquebar remembers Ziegenbalg

One has only to walk down the High Street of Tranquebar, now called Tharangambadi to see a monument and plaques in honour of Bartholomäus Ziegenbalg (1647-1719). There are lots of similar statues all over India, often painted gold to make them appear more impressive, and they are usually set up in remembrance of great statesmen, military heroes, or local Rajahs. This statue, also painted in gold, is, however, quite different. It is set up to commemorate the first Dano-German missionary to India, Bartholomäus Ziegenbalg, sent by courtesy of the Danish King over 300 years ago to found the Tranquebar Mission. Behind the statue there are two large though unusual plaques for this mostly conservative Hindu town[2] which surprisingly commemorate a foreign Christian missionary. However, the inhabitants of Tharangambadi are too grateful to forget the great impact young Ziegenbalg's work had in placing the town firmly on the map and in the Indian history books and Tamil lexica. Indeed, the Indian historian and theologian Daniel Jeyaraj has called Ziegenbalg 'The Father of Modern Protestant Missions' and 'The Morning Star of India'.[3] There is none other, at least to date, in the history of Western missionaries to India who could challenge such well-deserved titles though they are given to Carey and Fuller in ignorance of India's history of evangelization. Thus, as soon as one reaches Tranquebar from the sea, one finds on the promenade a large stone edifice commemorating the landing of the good ship Princessa Sofia Hedwiga which brought Ziegenbalg to the town. Should you have sent postcards off to Europe from Tharangambadi in recent years, they will have been sent from the Post Office with stamps bearing a portrait of Ziegenbalg produced during a week of official celebrations in Ziegenbalg's honour.

Tranquebar says 'Be like Ziegenbalg'

The plaques on the High Street bear the admonition in capital letters 'BE ALWAYS THE FIRST', followed by the words, 'ZIEGENBALG WAS'. Then twenty-four prime attributes of Ziegenbalg's ministry are

---

[2] Tharangambadi has now a population of 77 per cent Hindus, 12 per cent Christians and 10 per cent Muslims.

[3] See Jeyaraj's book *Bartholomaus Ziegenbalg, the Father of the Modern Protestant Mission*, The Indian Society for Promoting Christian Knowledge, New Delhi, 2006.

listed engraved on the two plaques like the two tablets of Moses. His work for the gospel is listed as a 'First' but also his 'practical divinity' in founding schools for both girls and boys, establishing a Seminary to train Christian leaders; promoting home crafts; building an orphanage; setting up factories; engaging in strenuous social work including establishing a free meals' kitchen for the poor, widows and ex-slaves;[4] founding the town's tailoring trade; building and running a paper mill; creating an alphabet for the local language, translating the Bible; teaching the printing trade; authoring books in Tamil and even translating Tamil works into German dealing with the religious history of the area. Indeed, Ziegenbalg seemed to have had his finger in every pie, pulling out all the plums in order to nourish the hundreds whom he suddenly found under his care both spiritually and bodily. He was indeed a modern missionary pioneer who believed that the whole gospel was for the whole man and embraced body, soul and spirit. This calling to the whole man angered many of his Christian contemporaries such as Wendt who felt that evangelizing was merely peripatetic preaching.[5]

Ziegenbalg is credited with founding the first Christian congregation in all Asia since the days of the early Church and helping his congregation to build a church through their own energy and work. This church building is still standing and in regular use as also the Manse built for Ziegenbalg though the latter has recently been opened as a cultural museum. Ziegenbalg's grave is also still standing in the church cemetery, looking as if it had been newly erected. So, too, are the graves of other missionaries to India in the century before Carey's arrival.

Ziegenbalg influenced Hinduism positively

The local Hindus confess that Ziegenbalg even influenced their own ever-changing religion which adopted the idea of grace from Ziegenbalg which was not present in Hinduism before. Carey had great difficulty in keeping Hindu influence out of his own Bible work.

---

[4] Tharangambadi cooking is famous and almost the first 'tourist attraction' of the town was to set up a school of cookery where visitors are taught how to cook delicious meals by the local housewives.

[5] See Ziegenbalg's letter to Wendt dated 15th August, 1718 in which Ziegenbalg tells Wendt that his call is to the whole man physical and spiritual and one cannot separate the one from the other. Were he to view man as either merely spiritual or merely physical, he would deny his calling.

Ziegenbalg's Christian witness strongly affected Hinduism in the district and opened it for the gospel. All over old Tranquebar one is reminded of Ziegenbalg by the New Jerusalem church, public buildings, schools and machinery, including his old printing press, which he set up, all still kept in good condition by a thankful community. Modern travel brochures boast in a positive sense that because of this, time has stood still in Tharangambadi. Time might have stood still but Ziegenbalg's gospel is still continuing there. When the British 'bought' Tharangambadi from the Danes in 1845 they wisely did not interfere with the Danish-German missionary witness. However, resistance came with the events leading to the First World War. More than one commentator I have read remarks that it is not so much that time has stood still in Tharangambadi but that Ziegenbalg's ideas are still ultra-modern.

Ziegenbalg's missionary success almost unknown in Carey's Britain and up to modern times

Yet, in spite of this, when Carey was called to walk in the footsteps of Ziegenbalg and Schwartz, he found very few amongst his colleagues back home who knew of the long history of Indian missions so they presumed that Carey was pioneering the work. This is most surprising as many books, magazines, missionary reports and private correspondence had reached Britain and the United States outlining the good and hard times the Halle missionaries were going through. The lack of attention given to the pioneering missionary work in India with the misunderstandings accompanying it continues very much today, though writings on the Dano-Halle Mission continued in publications pointing to the importance of Ziegenbalg, Schwartz, Kiernander and their associates and were and are still numerous. They began in 1716 with Ziegenbalg's *Grammatica Damulica*, his *Propagation of the Gospel in the east: being a collection of letters from the Protestant missionaries, and other worthy persons in the East-Indies, &c. relating to the mission; the means of promoting it; ... chiefly on the coast of Coromandel* in 1718, and his *An Account of the Success of Two Danish Missionaries Sent to the East Indies, for the Conversion of the Heathens in Malabar* of 1718, besides his *Genealogie der Malabarischen Götter: aus Eigenen Schriften und Briefen der Heiden Zusammengetragen und Verfasst* in 1865. These works were followed by Joseph White's, *On the Duty of Attempting the Propagation of the Gospel in India*, in 1785, a work which obviously influenced Carey's *Enquiry*.

In 1813, Eleazer Lord of the Andover Theological Seminary published a number of letters from Ziegenbalg's pen in Boston. Reinhold Wurmbaum followed him in 1830 with his work *Bartholomäus Ziegenbalg und Johann Ernst Gründer die deutschen Heidenboten in Südindien*. Hugh Pearson published his *Memoirs of the Life and Correspondence of the Reverend Christian Frederick Swartz to which is Prefixed a Sketch of the History of Christianity in India*, in 1835., Christian G. Schmidt's *Kurtzgefasste Lebensbeschreibungen merkwürdige evangelischer Missionare* came in 1836. Johan Hartwig Brauer published his *Die Heidenboten Fredrichs IV von Danemark* in 1837 and Joachim Heinrich Jäck (ed), published his *Taschen-Bibliothek der Wichtigsten und Interresantesten Reisen Durch Ost-, West- und Süd-Indien* in 1839. Scotsman Claudius Buchanan, who knew both the Tranquebar and Calcutta work at first hand brought out his, *The College of Fort William in Bengal*, in 1805 and his *Christian Researches in India*, in 1840 which are packed with the author's own eye-witness accounts. James Hough followed with his *The History of Christianity in India*, Vol. 2. 1706-1816, in 1845 but by then numerous Danish works on the Tranquebar Mission were being translated into English such as those of J. Ferd. Fenger, Director of the Dano-Halle Missionary Society who will be mentioned in more detail below. Julius Richter's work *A History of Missions in India* with all its failings came out in 1862. Wilhelm Germann's *Ziegenbalg und Plütschau: Die Gründungsjahre d. Trankebarschen Mission* was published in 1868. Then we have Lemuel Call Barnes, *Two Thousand Years of Missions before Carey*, of 1902.

Other older works which I have consulted are mentioned throughout this book. Since then, there has been a bevy of works published in many languages, including English to which my Bibliography testifies.

The Baptist were very late in following a call to India

The quite substantial and constant supply of news from India to the Western world led to the Lutheran churches, Church of England, the Reformed Churches, the Independents, the Congregationalists and the American Presbyterians gradually taking a keen interest in the work of the Danes, Norwegians, Swedes and Germans and they strove to work closely with them concerning their plans to provide India with missionaries. However, with the arrival of Carey in India, the resulting massive BMS concentration on the work of their own missionaries led to the ignoring of the great work already done in India and which was still going on. They produced a massive flood of Baptist publications which referred almost solely to Baptist endeavours.

The reaction on the European Continent to British silence regarding their missionary work

There was, however, an early Danish reaction to the British silence regarding Continental missionary endeavours up to the 1830s. Johannes Ferdinand Fenger of the Danish Missions Board researched the initial official history of the Danish-Norwegian Christian work in India which resulted in his *Den Trankebarske Missions Historia*, of 1842. Fenger explained in his Preface that his work was an attempt to 'clear up a remarkable portion of modern church history'. The fact was that with the arrival of British Baptist missionaries in India, 180 years after first the Dutch and then the Dano-Norwegians, the early history of the Protestant evangelization had become lost to most missionary-minded Westerners not conversant with Continental missions and languages. These now, for want of better knowledge, tended to date the major evangelization of the Indians from the formation of the Particular Baptist Missionary Society and William Carey's work in India from 1793 on. Yet substantial Baptist missionary work in India had to mark time for almost a decade after 1793 before it had any impetus in India. Most surprising, therefore, are the number of Baptist works which give time-lines concerning Indian evangelization jumping directly from the Jesuit outreach in the early 16th century to Carey's work in the early 19th century. The entire Protestant outreach before Carey is left out. The historical fact is that Carey was most unsuccessful for many years in areas which had been open to the gospel for many decades and in which others had been most successful. Carey only blossomed as a missionary after he joined an evangelical work of long standing in Serampore where he spent most of his weekends and leisure time from his college responsibilities at Fort William and later in the early years of the Danish University in Serampore. Because the Baptist missionaries had no British permits to settle in Calcutta, they were given Danish passports by the Danish authorities in Serampore and travelled as Danes under the Danish government. Indeed, the move to Serampore had nothing to do with the orders from the BMS who had as little influence in Serampore as in Calcutta which was none. It was entirely the initiative of Danish Christians working under Danish authority. So too, the Mission's first converts even then were led to Christ by John Thomas, the true initiator of the BMS and not William Carey. So here, another of Carey's 'firsts' must be challenged.

Misleading accounts concerning Carey

Obviously, Carey was not the first to start up missionary work in Serampore by very many years yet even Christopher Smith in his more open and sometimes critical account of the Serampore Trio tells us 'The founding father of the Baptist mission at Serampore was William Carey', which is in several ways misleading as it gives the impression that there was no missionary outreach there before Carey arrived on the scene and the BMS stood solidly behind him. Besides, Ward and Marshman were in Serampore before Carey and the two had been welcomed to Serampore by missionaries already there under the jurisdiction of the Danes and had received the backing of the Danish Government and the Danish-German churches. Once established in Danish Serampore, they called Carey to come over and help them. So Carey increased the Danish-supported Duo to a Trio. The BMS had no hand whatsoever in this arrangement. However, rather than move his home and College work from Calcutta to Serampore, Carey remained fully settled in Calcutta which remained his home base until his death.

Furthermore, Thomas had been doing missionary work in the area a decade before any of the so-called Serampore Trio. So, too, there were a number of missionaries from old established Christian missions in Calcutta and Serampore before, during, and after 1793. Concerning the various works of Carey on the one side and those of Marshman and Ward (politically two entire opposites) on the other, Christopher Smith bursts the romantic missionary bubble of unity in their ranks by stating that from then on:

> Carey ran his professional literary business in the heart of British Calcutta, while the Marshmans and Ward ran schools and industries on their mission estates in Serampore and Calcutta.

This, of course, was post-1800. The simple truth is that Carey was never really stationed in Serampore and commuted between Calcutta and the Danish colony for the rest of his life. This hardly sounds like traditional missionary work or very much inter-missionary cooperation between Carey and his Baptist colleagues.

Smith goes too far in criticizing the enormous costs of the so-called Serampore Trio's general educational work, especially in the Serampore College when he says, 'the work of the Serampore Mission revolved around two colleges. Their bold collegial venture, however, consumed huge amounts of money, to the detriment of the Baptists' overall mission work in Asia'.[6] It is true that the Serampore Baptist missionaries lived in the relative luxury of Indian Nabobs but they were on very high Calcutta government salaries and believed in living up to their status. Sadly, the wages the Serampore Trio paid their servants and native evangelists were very meagre to say the least. Furthermore, the Serampore Trio's work in fee-paying schools with a broad curriculum and two salary-bringing colleges that had little to do with Christian outreach are two of the factors which occupied so much of the Serampore Trio's time and efforts. This can hardly be called 'missionary work'. If the trio had become simply pastors of churches at home or abroad, they would have had far more opportunities to evangelize.

So too, the fact that Carey never left Calcutta for more than a very few days but was employed there by the British as a teacher in an Anglican supported college for British civil servants will come as a surprise to many who have based their knowledge of Carey on popular and rather romantic 'biographies' attaching him almost solely to Serampore, where he allegedly worked as an itinerant preaching in the highways and byways instead of teaching Botany and Physics at the Serampore College when time allowed from his Calcutta college duties. The 'Mission stations' the Serampore Trio were supposed to have set up outside of Serampore were chiefly the work of others and were more cash-bringing trading stations than anything else and the schools run by non-Christian staff.

---

[6] 'The Legacy of William Ward and Joshua and Hannah Marshman', A. Christopher Smith, International Bulletin of Missionary Research, July 1999, pp. 120-129.

It must not be forgotten that Kiernander pioneered Missionary work in Calcutta decades before Carey

It ought to be made common knowledge amongst devout Christian readers keen on Indian missions that the Swedish Kiernander who had already spent over forty years evangelizing both the south of India and Bengal, after much itinerant preaching, had founded a congregation in Calcutta for whom he built a mission church in 1770 and the work was greatly increased by David Brown, a Yorkshireman and a passionate evangelical and soul-winner who had arrived in Calcutta some ten years before Carey and was supported by the Scottish scholar-pastor and missionary Claudius Buchanan. Brown was very kind in offering Thomas financial support and cooperation. Thomas took Brown's money but treated Brown most harshly for not being a Baptist. There was nothing 'original' or 'pioneering' about the work of the Serampore Trio and the ties to Continental Christians were mostly stronger than their ties to the BMS from whom they officially separated in 1827.

Carey's first translations were financed without the BMS

Furthermore, Carey would never have been able to start on any Bible translation whatsoever if his missionary friends of several denominations, who were on the mission field before him had not given Carey a free grant of £1,600, collected mainly from non-Baptists to begin the work. Carey's translation was, however quickly contested and abandoned but translations into Indian languages based on far sounder scholarly and theological principles had been progressing in India for well over a hundred years and were published outside of the Baptist fold and continued to be so. Eventually, the BMS itself gave up Carey's Bengali translation work.

A rare critic of Baptist Serampore Trio research

Christopher Smith is one of the few Baptist writers who deals with the Serampore Trio critically and objects to the myths surrounding them in his repeatedly emphasized 'quest' to separate the 'Carey of tradition' from the 'historical Carey'.[7] In his essay 'A Tale of Many Models: The

---

[7] See Smith's Introduction to his essay 'Mythology and Missionology: A Methodical Approach to the Pre-Victorian Mission of the Serampore Trio', International Review of Mission, Vol. 83, Issue 330, 1994.

Missiological Significance of the Serampore Trio' he writes under the sub-section 'Historical Quest':

> First, it is amazing how little in-depth missiological research has been carried out on the Serampore Trio. A fine array of primary sources is waiting for use by a new generation of mission scholars. Likewise the value remains to be discovered of many fine inter-disciplinary studies (produced since the sixties) that shed copious light on the contents in which the troika operated. Failure to realise this has resulted in the perpetuation of tunnel vision, misunderstanding, and unfounded mythology by mission promoters and most popular biographers of Carey phenomenon. All it will take to begin to rectify this is careful examination of the correspondence of Carey's team, of their secular associates, and of other missionaries. Along with this body of first class evidence, we need to take seriously the voluminous statements and accounts of the altercations between the Trio, the Baptist Missionary Society (BMS), and the second generation of Baptist missioners to India, especially in the 1820s. Taken together, these disclose that myths about Serampore were already in the making several decades before Carey passed away, and that their exposure in the middle 1820s caused something of a furore, leading to the split between the Trio and the BMS in 1827.[8]

Smith's thoughts on the Dano-Halle think-tank

Smith also finds it difficult to comprehend why Carey did not persuade the Baptists to take advantage of the enormous think-tank the Danish-German Mission and many supporting colleges and universities had built up at the Halle University organized initially by Francke. This could also be said for the BMS. Indeed, Smith writes that Marshman aimed at making the Serampore College into an 'Indian Halle'[9] which becomes obvious when reading Marshman's Serampore College reports. This aim was far too ambitious and was perhaps thus mostly hidden from British and American readers by Baptist writers. Smith

[8] 'Missiology: An International Review', Vol. XX, No. 4, October 1992, pp. 481-482.
[9] See the 1818 Serampore College brochure.

demonstrates that Marshman's vision was not built on what the Danish-Halle Mission had accomplished and, we may add, was to accomplish. When speaking of the difficulties the Serampore Mission had in reconciling the modern world to their Biblical endeavours, Smith says:

> Yet there is something puzzling about this historical scenario, namely this: Why did the courageous troika not appeal to a well-known pious Protestant precedent, albeit in continental Europe, for their enterprise in Asia? Why did they not make much of the magnificent model provided by August Hermann Francke's Stiftungen, or philanthropic 'Foundations' that were erected in the Halle area of Saxony, in Prussia, a century earlier?[10]

My verdict would be that the Serampore aims in education and missionary work were to break with the old, well-trodden paths and lay out their own in an effort to be innovative and outdo Halle. They viewed themselves as a more modern and more effective Tranquebar. This is the feeling one gains when reading one of the Serampore Trio's rare mentions of Halle in their 1818 College brochure. So, too, the on-going history of Continental missionary work outside of the Baptist contribution did not interest those writers, and there have been many who simply were happy to weave stories around Carey's symbolic figure for want of further knowledge.

Three simple reasons

There are three simple reasons why the BMS did not build on the comparatively successful hundred years of Halle missions and Dutch missions before them.

Kettering and Fen Court were ignorant of the affairs in India

The first reason is that though the Mission led by David Brown looked to Francke's missionary strategy as a model for their own work and Carey was so dependent on Brown for his Calcutta and Serampore work and financing, the Baptist Board in England had no idea of what was going on in India and Fuller felt that all the missionaries in India apart from the few Baptists were seduced by what he called 'Jezebel' and one

[10] Ibid, p. 486.

should not cooperate with them. The historical missionary work in India was thus of no interest to them. So the Baptist Board insisted that the Serampore Trio should regard India as unevangelized and ignore the long history of the Church in India. Such an ostrich position can hardly be successful.

The BMS and allied writers ignored Indian mission sources

The second reason is frankly given by Michael Mann in his 2007 review of *The Beginnings of Protestant Mission in India*. He sees the neglect of acquiring a true knowledge of Indian Missions on the British side simply because they:

> hardly knew (and for some reason still do not know) anything about the immense value of the Franckesche Stiftungen's impressive archive because they were (and are) not able to read German and did not care about this capacity.

This goes also for the British reluctance to consult Danish, Swedish, Norwegian, French, Dutch and German archives which has been my privilege and delight, as they lack the language expertise needed. It is worth learning at least a smattering of these languages if only to read the vast information which they provide concerning world evangelism unknown to 'English-only' readers. A missiologist or writer on missionary studies must work hard to gain reliable material.

Sadly, this enormous amount of material on Indian evangelization dating back to well over a hundred years before the founding of the British Particular Baptist Missionary Society is still largely ignored from the British side though today, foreign language learning is made easier than ever before.

However even the American Baptist Christopher Smith in spite of all his criticism of the faulty mission strategy of the BMS does not bother to research this foreign material as illustrated by his copious notes and bibliographies in his series of articles on the Serampore Trio. Indeed, I have found in his works only one reference to an Indian scholar, Sunil Kumar Chatterjee author of a work on Hannah Marshman, which Smith calls 'simple' besides a few Dutch writers listed in his bibliographies in English translations and a translated work of Francke's. Chatterjee in his work *Hannah Marshman: The First*

Woman Missionary in India (p. 43) gives some interesting information on how Marshman was providing half of the mission's funds at one time through the fees he charged in his school. Again, such information is not always desirable by certain pro-BMS authors as it does not fit their idealized image of a missionary's work and their own ideas of how the Serampore work ought to have been run.

Andrew Fuller ignored the historical evangelization of India thinking it sub-Baptist

One might ask here why the great work of Western Protestant missionaries over two hundred years starting with the Dutch, long before Ziegenbalg who worked long before the BMS entered India, was merely ignored. These successes were denied because the BMS believed they were established by unbelievers and those seduced by Jezebel. Baptist Institutionalism of the Fullerite kind simply refused to be recognized as a movement which stepped very late into the work of Christ in India but claimed they were the very first real Christians in India.

Having studied a great variety of Continental records in the original languages for the last ten years and the life and works of Carey since my early student days, over sixty years ago, I felt it high time that something should be written to correct what Mann calls 'national ignorance'. I would add to this 'denominational ignorance and blindness'.

Carey was not a missionary in the sense that Ziegenbalg was

The third major reason for the break between the work of the older missionaries and Carey was that the Englishman was not a missionary in the sense that Ziegenbalg and his followers were. The Tranquebar Mission was run by full time missionary pioneers. Ziegenbalg lived and preached regularly in the slums of Tranquebar and went constantly into the highways and byways to promote the Gospel and evangelized a number of Southern Indian cities besides the working amongst the country-dwellers. Carey was mostly a stay-at-home, tied to his governmental office in Calcutta and his secular teaching in Serampore and his many secular translations of non-Christian folk-lore, religions and Asian philosophers. Carey was not a slum-dweller for Christ's sake. So, too, Carey is attributed with feats of translation work which were never his. A case in point is Carey's alleged translations from the Chinese. Carey is reported to have spent much time translating Confucius from that language but if so, which of the many versions did he work on and from where did he obtain his sources? Actually, it was Marshman who had taken Chinese lessons in India but the main work was done by a Macao-born Armenian, Lazar whom the Trio used as a translator and amanuensis. The pioneers in India of Confucius translations were the Jesuits well over a hundred years before Carey and we must ask if the Serampore and Calcutta College teams used the Jesuit Latin translations as their source language or were they imported from Macao? Even if Carey's and Marshman's Latin was up to it, there is much doubt as to the genuine nature of these Jesuit editions, some scholars even suggesting that they invented them. The Macao sources also provide many different versions of Confucius' alleged work. The first published versions of Confucius in English, however, were those of James Legge in 1867, long after the Serampore Trio's Home-call. What had thus happened to the alleged Serampore translations? We may, however, ask why Christian missionaries occupied themselves with the philosophy of Confucius and other Asian philosophers when they had so little time available for evangelistic and pastoral work. Indeed, Serampore brought out a number of 'translations' of secular works years before they printed out the mass of their supposed nigh fifty Bibles in as many languages. For instance, the *Works of Confucius* came out in 1809 but the Chinese Bible was printed in 1822. Furthermore, Carey spent much time giving a rich countess private lessons in English instead of going into the highways and byways with the gospel, so it was no wonder that Dorothy challenged his faithfulness to her. Shortly after Mrs Carey's death, Carey married the wealthy widow.

Carey and 'crowd sourcing'

Such as John Chamberlain were the real Baptist missionaries in the still accepted Western sense of the term but these great Baptist pioneers are mostly unknown today. Biographers have been kind to a few true Baptist missionary pioneers but apparently missed most. Carey's major tasks were to keep living at the high standard he had chosen in two secular colleges financed and organized by others and to take up dubious linguistic translations which Yalin Xin of the William Carey

International Development Journal claims were the first 'crowd-sourcing' translations. Christopher Smith thus says, 'Carey was much more of a mission motivator and Bible translator than a pioneer in the heart of India or a missionary strategist.'[11] Ziegenbalg was a most successful mission motivator, translator, pioneer and missionary strategist.

Danes and Germans also suppressed much of Ziegenbalg's work

Ignorance is a human failing and sadly very widespread amongst all peoples and denominations. The effort to give the Christian public a strongly edited picture of a missionary's work was not just a Baptist feature. The wide scope of Ziegenbalg's work often shocked his Lutheran supporters. Halle was the centre of the Pietistic outreach in Denmark and Germany yet such as Ziegenbalg had a far wider view of the Christian gospel than the home base. To him, the gospel dealt with all aspects of mankind; spiritually, socially, educationally and intellectually, and he laid great store on scientific linguistic work, medicinal studies and agriculture. Francke went so far as to tell Ziegenbalg to concentrate on converting the heathen and not dabble in 'other matters'. Wendt even felt that 'other matters' which included feeding and clothing the poor and teaching them to read and write were a waste of time and money.

Making Ziegenbalg a 'pukka pietist'

August Hermann Francke and his Halle associates and successors edited Ziegenbalg strongly before publishing his missionary reports to make him appear to conform to their 'pietistic principles'. This was no better than Sutcliff's and Fuller's severe editing of material from Carey before publishing what was left of his material. The two sought to display Carey as a 'pukka Baptist' of the Fullerite kind which he never was. Some of Ziegenbalg's major academic works and missionary studies only saw the light of day in the middle 1850s. It would appear, according to modern Indian scholarship, that 'the half has not yet been told'. This fact led Hugald Grafe, in his contribution to *Halle and the Beginnings of Protestant Missions in India*, compiled by Andrew Gross, to entitle his contributing chapter, 'Errors, Legends and

[11] Bu.edu/missionary-biography/c-d/carey-william, 27. 01. 2016.

Uncertainties in Ziegenbalg's Biography', showing how severely Ziegenbalg's reports were edited before publication. Thus, it is better to read such collections of Ziegenbalg's works as those published by Arno Lehmann in the nineteen fifties under the titles 'It Began in Tranquebar: The Story of the Tranquebar Mission and the Beginnings of Protestant Christianity in India',[12] and 'Alter Briefe aus Indien: Unveröffentlichte Briefe von Bartholomäus Ziegenbalg 1706-1719',[13] to obtain a fuller picture of this missionary pioneer.

Making Carey a 'pukka' Fullerite

One of the major reasons why Carey has survived in history as a much different person than he was is to be blamed on the BMS manipulation of his records. According to F. A. Cox, whenever the BMS received reports from India, Fuller would take the material to Sutcliff. Both then sat down together cutting and pasting the documents, so that much was suppressed though the Indian missionaries had thought the BMS would publish it.[14]

A slowness in India to take up the theme of missions

Indian Christians up to around the year 2000 were also slow to take up the theme of the history of evangelization in their own country but this has changed most positively since the Ziegenbalg celebrations of 2006 in India and now there is a flood of books, articles and even films on Ziegenbalg's missionary endeavours, many of a very high theological and academic standard. My explanation of this late awakening was that it took India some time to recover from suppressive Colonialism which mixed Christianity with political and British nationalistic policies. Now India can breathe and think alone and view her own history through independent eyes.

The need to revalue and perhaps rewrite the Baptist Indian story

We are now therefore in a good position to reassess the story of the Particular Baptist Mission to the Indians and take a new look at those who proclaim in numerous publications that Carey sowed seed on

---

[12] Christian Literature Society, Madras, 1956.

[13] Evangelische Verlagsanstalt, Berlin, 1957.

[14] Cox's *History*, p. 262.

entirely new ground in India. The works of Stephan Charles Neill (1900-1984) whom I heard as a conference speaker on Christianity in modern India as a student must also be mentioned here for its pioneering historical survey. Sadly, Neill's vision of a Christian based, prosperous India has not yet been accomplished on a general scale.

In spite of the overwhelming evidence pointing to the pioneer work of the Tranquebar Mission which stretched out to Bengal, we find an authoress writing as recently as 2019 under the name 'McKenne' telling us that Carey was 'the father of modern missions', and 'the first missionary to India'. Cook, in his *The Story of the Baptists* tells us that:

> To William Carey, however, more than to anyone, is due the origin of modern missions: He was the first to catch the inspiration, and his zeal and enthusiasm surpassed all others.[15]

On consulting the Bethany Global website (bethanygu.edu), I find, that they feature a lengthy essay entitled 'William Carey: Pioneer to India and Father of Modern Missions'. In this work they claim that 'Carey was the first missionary to India' and compare Carey's conversion positively with that of Eliot and Luther instead of every Christian who is blessed with repentance and faith. Even John Piper who is a well-trained scholar calls Carey 'the Morning Star of modern missions' and claims that 'Andrew Fuller stayed at home that he might save the world' whereas stay-at-home Fuller did his level best to wreck Carey's work.[16] Ajith George, leaning heavily on A. Jayakumar, tells us that Carey was 'patriarch, apostle, prophet and pioneer of the modern missionary movement' and claims Carey founded 'India's first Christian missionary organisation'.[17] George Smith writes:

> William Carey had no predecessor in India as the first ordained Englishman who was sent to it as a missionary; he had

[15] R. B. Cook, *The Story of the Baptists in all Ages and Countries* p. 303.
[16] See Piper's 'He stayed at Home to Save the World', May 7, 2019, *Desiring God*, online.
[17] Serampore Mission - History of Christianity in India.

> no predecessor in Bengal and Hindostan proper as the first missionary from any land to the people.[18]

On the same page Smith tells his readers that 'Carey practically stood alone'. Carey's own testimony refutes this error as he joined an international team already working in Calcutta. He wrote to Andrew Fuller on 10th December, 1805 saying:

> The British and Foreign Bible Society Centre letter to Mr Udney, wishing him, Rev. Messrs. Brown and Buchanan, brethren Marshman, Ward, and I, form a committee to cooperate with them in this country. In consequence of this brother Marshman drew up a memorial, which was much improved, showing the practicability of translating and publishing the Bible, for a comparatively small sum. From this Mr. Buchanan drew up an address, which was immediately forwarded to the governor general, and is intended to be circulated all over India, get subscriptions for this work, and I doubt not of its success. This will, if obtained, take off the heavy expense of translating and printing and enable us to employ them in spreading the word when printed.

We see here that the initiative to translate the Bible into Bengali which is here referred to did not come from Carey alone or the BMS but from missionaries in cooperation with Carey of other denominations who also funded the work until they had to withdraw their support because of Fuller's interference. It was a great privilege for the Serampore Trio to be working with such fine men of God. Buchanan, of course, besides being a former curate under John Newton was recognized internationally as a fine Hebrew, Chaldaic and Syriac scholar besides being well-qualified in Greek and Latin and several Indian languages. None of the Baptist missionaries could compete with him. The biography prefixed to Buchanan's own work on *Christian Researches in India* shows how well Buchanan was prepared for his translating tasks and his book shows how well he fitted in to his Indian background as a missionary, pastor and administrator. However, Fuller

---

[18] *Life of William Carey*, p. 78.

thought him 'deceived by Jezebel' because he would not accept Fuller's institutionalism based on Liberal Enlightenment philosophy. Yet Fuller, like Thomas was not averse to accepting Buchanan's, Brown's and Director Grant's financial support whilst refusing to cooperate with them as brethren in Christ.

The letters mentioned below stretching over a period of years show how closely Carey still worked with missionaries from all over India, the vast majority being ordained men including Englishmen and Scotsmen. Indeed, were it not for the cooperation of Anglican ministers in and around Serampore, the Baptists would have never been able to work there. In a very long letter written on September 2, 1806, Carey wrote of the strong support the Baptist missionaries had from their British Brethren who were Lutherans, Anglicans, Presbyterians and Congregationalists and who opened the doors for his own work:

> The Rev. Mr. Brown called on Saturday last on the magistrate at Calcutta, and has sent us the following memoranda of what he learned from him. After a long discussion with the magistrate, I find as follows, viz.:
>
> 1. The missionaries remain at Serampore in full powers.
> 2. There is no objection made to their circulating the Scriptures.
> 3. There is no objection to their preaching in their own house at Cossitollah, or in the house of any other person, provided they do not preach openly in the Lal Bazar.
> 4. Natives may teach and preach wherever they please, provided they be not sent forth emissaries from Serampore.
> 5. There will be no objection to their exercising in the Lal Bazar, or anywhere else, whether they can procure permission from the port of directors, or the British government.
>
> The magistrate informed Mr. Brown that he had never received any complaint against us, or any of our brethren, and that he knew nothing of any report to our prejudice having ever been sent to government.

Here we see how the Church Missionary Society men did their level best to have Carey's work legalized in the British Colony.

In a letter to Sutcliff dated from Calcutta on 11th February, 1807, Carey tells his friend and former pastor:

> Three evangelical clergymen have been stationed in different places under this presidency, and one has just left this for Madras. The very places which we desire to occupy, but could not obtain permission, are thus supplied by men who are as desirous of the conversion of the heathen as we are, and who heartily coincide with our measures.[19]

From poverty to affluence

Whilst Carey, however, writes of the full-time work of other missionaries in evangelizing India, he tells Sutcliff:

> Until lately I was teacher of three languages in the College, on a monthly salary of Rs.500 per month; but, on 1 January past, I was, by the governor general in Council, appointed Prof of the Sanskrit and Bengali languages, to which Mahratta is added, though not specified in the official letter, with a salary of Rs.1000 per month. This will much help the mission.

Obviously, Carey began to alter his views of a missionary's life on leaving Britain. Even on 6th May, 1793 at the start of his journey to India after eating on board ship he boasted:

> My health was never so well. I believe the sea makes Felix and me both as hungry as hunters. I can eat a monstrous meat supper, and drink a couple of glasses of wine after it without hurt.

This new idea of a life as a missionary nabob continued. Perhaps the 'hurt' did come after all in the form of sea-sickness on a monstrously full stomach and too much alcohol. Apart from the wine, there was always a bottle of rum on Carey's Calcutta or Serampore table, allegedly to purify the water though, as has been noted, boiling would have done the trick. This became the general practice of the Serampore

---

[19] These were the very men whom Andrew Fuller says were seduced by Jezebel.

Trio and a number of the Serampore-Calcutta missionaries, including Felix and William, Carey's sons, had alcohol problems. On 26th June, 1807, we read in Ward's Journal that charges were brought against BMS missionary Richard Mardon of Calcutta and Burma (1803-1812) by his wife for 'drinking too freely'. Often the missionaries' behaviour shocked the Indians, many of whom did not touch alcohol.

Once in India, Carey surrounded himself with numerous servants who cared for Carey's every need but neither they, nor Carey, made any effort to bring up Carey's children in the nurture and admonition of the Lord. No provisions for the education of his children seem to have been made until Marshman and Ward took over Carey's parental responsibilities. It is only in recent years that Carey's neglect of his wife and children has reached public hearing.

When Thomas and Carey landed in India on 11th November, 1793, it was the very year of the new British Charter which rejected the need for Christian missions to India and which demanded applications for permission through the East India Company's office and British Government channels. Carey had not applied for permission. Nor did Carey apply to go out with other missionary societies which would have secured permits for him.

The year 1793 freed from myths and legends

The legends surrounding Carey's 1793 arrival in India were popularized well over a hundred years ago. Julius Richter has been used as a source for many later biographies of Indian missions, including the works of Bishop Stephen Neill, yet Richter's work is often very unreliable as a historical survey. Amongst other historical errors, he wrote in 1906, in his *History of Missions to India*, that 'Modern Missionary work in India dates from November 11th, 1793 the day upon which William Carey landed in Calcutta.'

Two alleged decades of gloom

Richter, however, often contradicts himself as he does in the example given above. This is because he is obviously dependent on conflicting sources for his 'history' and had no first-hand knowledge of what he was writing. This goes for many would-be biographers of Carey who have not researched their subject carefully enough but merely collected and repeated former legends. So, Richter seemingly takes back the one exaggerated utterance mentioned above by presenting a further great exaggeration though perhaps truer than his former praise. He states that from the time of his arrival in India Carey entered into a 'gloomy' period of two decades in which there was no preaching of the gospel and that the Mission was as good as dead because of this. However, missionary work by non-Baptists did not stagnate in this way. Richter's dismal picture of the Baptist missionaries would bring us up to 1813. However, some form of missionary activity had been going on after 1800 both in Serampore and Calcutta and Carey had done a good deal of preaching albeit as a part-time missionary and mostly in English.

Richter also perpetuates the myth that Carey was not accepted at all by the British authorities which Carey's letters, especially of 1807 clearly contradict. Richter makes another historical howler in his example of the suppression of Baptist missionaries by British authorities exemplified by the case of John Chamberlain who, he claims was rejected by the British in his attempt to convert the Hindus. Richter's remarks on Chamberlain would make one think that Chamberlain's great work amongst the northern Hindus never happened.

Hunting for a house and secular work

Many writers, ignorant of India's past, refer to the 1793 arrival as if it were a great reforming pivot in the history of missions. Yet all that date indicates for those who admire William Carey is that it was the year in which Carey hunted for a house which took him well into 1794 with further time spent looking for secular work in keeping with many other Europeans within the various East India Companies. Carey's first efforts to finance himself and his family which had been implemented by Thomas, failed and Carey was soon made redundant. He then entered into several most speculative business schemes for another six years or so which left him again redundant. This indeed was a 'gloomy' period compared to Carey's thoughts outlined in his *Enquiry*.

Where the Baptists were failing, other denominations were active

During this 'gloomy' period for the Baptists, Church of England missionaries, Presbyterians, Independents, Greek Orthodox, Armenians, Nestorians and Roman Catholics were evangelizing Calcutta according to their own ways. The Moravians from Tranquebar who had been working in Serampore since 1777 left just prior to Carey's arrival and Carey and his friends bought up the Moravian property for 6,000 rupees. This including a large communal building with a two-acre garden and Carey declared that he would now carry on where the Moravians left off.[20] Not to be outdone Marshman is said to have proclaimed, 'Thank you, Moravians. If ever I am a missionary worth a straw, I shall owe it, under God, to you.[21] The Moravians had left behind them a number of Bengali works, including a Bengali dictionary and a number of the books of the Bible translated into Bengali. These works are hardly referred to in Carey biographies but they must have made the British missionaries initial learning of Bengali easier as there were also a number of linguistic and Biblical works in print before his day.[22] However, we know that it took Carey years to master the Bengali tongue though he clearly used former works about and in Bengali for the compilations which came out in his name. We may surely ask, given the circumstances, how much Carey relied on Moravian publications in producing his own works.

It must also be taken into account that before Carey had any idea of what his future plans in India were, many of the evangelical Christians both in secular and missionary employment in Calcutta were assembling under Kiernander's, Brown's and Buchanan's preaching at the Old Church. Baptists, too, were also reckoned amongst their hearers and joined in worship with their Lutheran, Church of England and Presbyterian brethren. Indeed, it can be said with no disrespect to any nation as all are equal in God's sight, that red and yellow, black and white Christians met under that roof of the Calcutta Old Church showing that there was no racism in Christianity. The pastors of the Old Church emphasised their international and interdenominational state. Marshman and Fuller were both sadly to show marked racist and imperialistic tendencies.

---

[20] See letter from Carey to Stedman, May 17th, 1801, BMS Archives.

[21] *William Carey Theologian –Linguist – Social Reformer*, p, 63.

[22] See 'William Carey, Modern Missions and the Moravian Influence', David A. Schattschneider, International Bulletin of Missionary Research, 1998, 01, 008, pp. 8-13.

The fluctuating number of Baptist missionaries in Serampore and Calcutta

By this time there were over twenty British and American Baptist missionaries working in and around Serampore and Calcutta but the number of missionaries from other countries was even larger. Several of the Baptists did not get on well with the other missionaries whether non-Baptist or Baptist. Several, such as Luther Rice, who had arrived in Serampore in 1812 with another eleven missionaries from the United States of America, soon returned home. Judson went to Burma as he was not found acceptable by the British Baptists. This suspicion might have been caused because of the American Union's unilateral declaration of war against Britain in 1812. Soon the number of 'Baptist' missionaries, however, was severely reduced. Congregationalist Rice actually became a Baptist in India with his friend Judson and then Rice returned home to collect money for the Indian Mission but did not return. His life is catalogued *passim* in my book *Isaac McCoy, Apostle of the Western Trail*. He went from serving the East Indians to also serving the Native Americans. Rice spent the rest of his life raising money for Baptist missions but was scandalously treated by the American Baptist Board of Foreign Missions as was his friend Isaac McCoy, the great missionary to the American Indians.[23] The Mission Board under Staughton, a former BMS Board member, confiscated Mission money for its own use and thus misused the many thousands of dollars Baptists Rice and McCoy raised for the training of Native Americans. In the scandal that ensued through misapplication of funds at the Columbian college and the banning of Native American students for whom the college was originally planned and funded, Staughton managed to get off scot-free by placing the blame on Rice and the College. He sold all the land financed by friends of the American Indians to pay off the college debts for which he had chiefly himself to blame. Then the college was bought by non-Baptists and the George Washington University was founded on the premises. The new owners recognized the great work of Rice in his endeavours to educate the Native Indians and honoured him as the true founder of the George Washington University. This great Baptist's life's work has still to be

[23] See Appendix 1, 'Luther Rice and the Columbian College Fiasco: A Vindication', pp. 591-610 in my *Isaac McCoy: Apostle of the Western Trail.*

detailed by sympathetic biographers but I wrote a detailed appendix concerning his work in my above-mentioned book and *passim* within the main body of the book.

To make matters worse, a number of the leading Baptists in the American Union turned out to be outright racists and refused to admit the Native Americans to the very college which the generous American public had financed through Rice and McCoy. It was the ex-member of the British Baptist Missionary Board William Staughton who led the attack against true missionary endeavours as Wendt had done in Denmark and Fuller had done in England.

It is nevertheless strange that most of the Baptist missionaries surrounding and aiding the Serampore Trio, including Chamberlain, have received either weak write-ups from modern Baptists or no write-ups at all, though they were a strong part of the ongoing most positive Baptist witness in India. Indeed, the Serampore Trio are often written about as if they were the sole missionaries in Serampore and Calcutta though there were many missionaries there from some six countries and numerous denominations besides the Baptists. Many of these were missionaries in the truest sense of the word but they are sadly no longer honoured.

Carey did not father modern missions

Sadly, the historical facts briefly presented above still remain little known to British Baptist Christians though happily the Baptist Quarterly is now examining the historical, international, denominational and over-denominational issues involved. It would, however, come as an educative surprise to modern Baptist authors at all levels who constantly praise Carey as the 'Father of Modern Missionary Outreach' and see him as the 'Morning Star' of India, to read Professor Daniel Jeyaraj's mammoth work on the origins of modern missionary outreach to his home country under the title *Bartholomäus Ziegenbalg, the Father of Modern Protestant Missions: An Indian Assessment* (2006). In this work, Jeyaraj says:

> William Carey's achievements in Serampore, reported to the English reading public in Europe, received much recognition. His work in Serampore included translations of the Bible into Bengali. He also translated the two most famous Indian epics

Mahabharata and Ramayana from Sanskrit into English. These and other achievements earned him worldwide recognition. At the same time, similar pioneering works, accomplished by Ziegenbalg almost a century earlier in south India remained unnoticed and unrecognised. This negligence led several scholars to wrongly consider William Carey as the father of modern Protestant mission. Ziegenbalg preceded Carey by a century, and accomplished many things now attributed to Carey. In terms of quality achievements and also in terms of time, Ziegenbalg is and remains the father of modern Protestant mission. William Carey can be viewed as the father of modern theological education in India.

Liverpool Hope University testifies to Jeyaraj's enormous research into the full scope of Ziegenbalg's work to modern friends of India by writing:

> The research, on early 18th century South India through the writings of German missionary scholars, has expanded knowledge of the Tamil people, languages and cultures; identified more than 160 Tamil and Telugu texts engraved on palm leaves; and recovered numerous paper manuscripts that were considered lost. The work on manuscript recovery has contributed to the professional practice and discourse of professional archivists and librarians and, through examining these manuscripts in Tamil, German, Latin, Portuguese, and English, a new picture about the Tamil emerges. This has important implications for Tamil cultural identity, heritage and pride, currently a matter of social and political emphasis in the Indian public sphere. It also contributes to government initiatives for the revival and celebration of the Tamil language.[24]

Even the high praise of Ziegenbalg missionary endeavours in the above-mentioned book by Jeyaraj falls short of emphasizing all that Ziegenbalg and his Danish-German-Indian team achieved and the way

---

[24] 'Reclaiming Cultural Memories of the Tamils in European Missionary Writings', REF 2014 Impact Case Studies, Liverpool Hope University.

his successors picked up his mantle. Indeed, Jeyaraj's remark on Carey's pioneering theological training in India is also refuted by the historical evidence which shows that Carey, who is widely reported as having set up a theological academy in 1818, never taught theology in a theological training college which did not come into being in Carey's days. Ziegenbalg founded a pastor's training college for native teachers over a hundred years earlier in 1716. Indeed, Carey criticized the Danes and Germans for sending missionaries out only after years of training. Carey was seemingly aware of Ziegenbalg's pioneering missionary outreach prompted by Ziegenbalg's successor Schwartz but shows no first-hand knowledge of his works. However, he wrote in his *Enquiry*:

> In 1706, the King of Denmark sent a Mr Ziegenbalg, and some others to Tranquebar on the Coromandel Coast in the East Indies, who were useful to the natives, so that many of the heathens were turned to the Lord.[25]

Clifford G. Howell, an American, wrote in 1912 that:

> Providentially, a Danish colony had been planted at Serampur, about sixteen miles above Calcutta. Its governor, Colonel Bie,[26] had enjoyed the friendship of Schwartz and extended to the lonely missionaries a friendly welcome to his 'city of refuge'. He resisted all attempts to deprive them of protection, declaring that 'if the British government still refused to sanction their continuance in India, they should have the shield of Denmark thrown over them if they would remain at Serampur.' And there they remained; and there Carey joined them.

He concludes:

[25] *Enquiry* p. 36. This appears to be a corrected edition as Carey invariably spells the names of Danish-German missionaries incorrectly, calling Ziegenbalg 'Ziegenbald'. His renderings of other missionaries to the Tamils makes it nigh impossible to recognize them. This would indicate that Carey was not familiar with their written works but knew of them from hearsay.

[26] He is often called 'Bea' by modern Indians. Bie was a convert through the Danish Mission's missionaries such as Schwartz.

> to Ziegenbalg and Schwartz, Carey, Marshman, and Ward owed their home in Serampur.[27]

This is undeniably true and ought to be recognized by all writers on Carey. In estimating his progress as a missionary, they must go back to the roots of any positive work which Carey, the branch, sought to continue a hundred years later. Though Carey spent over forty years in India, Ziegenbalg's missionary thrust lasted only thirteen years beginning 1706 and ended with his early death aged 36 years in 1719, yet he accomplished so very much more than Carey in such a short time as a full-time missionary.

---

[27] *The Advanced Guard of Missions* by Clifford G. Howell. Mountain View, Calif: Pacific Press Publishing, 1912, (www.wholesomewords.org/missions).

Part 10

Quo Vadis India?

Chapter Twenty-Eight

Giving Credit to the True Pioneers of Indian Missions: A Summing Up

The enormous importance of Ziegenbalg's lasting work

Daniel Jeyaraj in his many comparisons of Ziegenbalg with Carey and the languages they used clearly shows how Ziegenbalg's writings and life had been well recorded from the early 1700s on. These reports are in over ten languages including Latin. It was whilst reading such documents after the publication of our Martin Bucer Seminar work *William Carey: Theologian – Linguist – Social Reformer* that I first began to realise the enormous importance of Bartholomäus Ziegenbalg and August Hermann Francke in the evangelization of India; a work which Schulze, Fabricius, Schwartz, Kiernander and Carey took up, consolidated and extended. These documents present a very different picture of Carey's work to that provided by British Baptist authors who have been far too insular in their research and paid far too little attention to the many sources available in English and to the religions of India. They have, too, on the whole, backed a theology which is anti-evangelical. There has also been a stubborn refusal to deal with original sources because they were not in English and, sadly, these abundant sources were often thought to be of no interest if they were not written in English. I have been publicly attacked by reviewers who have scolded me for quoting 'foreign literature' and not keeping to English works as if the historical truth could be culled from English sources only and it were folly to search for the truth elsewhere. In keeping with this unwillingness to tackle foreign languages, modern writers have also been far too uncritical of translations said to be from Carey and his associates and the dubious theology expressed in and by them. Happily, the Carey Center now lists in their home page Bibliography a few Dutch and Indian authors, one work in Danish, one in French and one in Latin. The writings of Chatterjee have recently been noticed, chiefly by lady writers as he deals very much with the Careys' family life and Hannah Marshman. At last, the Baptists are waking up to the solid work done in India by lady Baptists.[1]

The British East India Company supported the early Lutheran and pietistic missionaries

Concerning Lutheran Schwartz alone, who pioneered much of India with the gospel before Baptist Carey started his work in that country, the Scottish Presbyterian George Smith, writes:

> The East India Company, who gave him and his companions a free passage in their ship in 1750, turned out William Carey forty-three years after, and forced him and his colleagues to seek an asylum from Little Denmark in its Bengal settlement. But Schwartz owed the peace and protection which enabled him to lay the foundation of the Native Church of Southern India – now numbering half a million souls – to the Company.[2]

The question now arises why Schwartz, who died in 1798, was given so much freedom by the Danish and British East India Companies and was fully backed by the Church of England and other denominations but this freedom and support was allegedly denied Carey who arrived in India whilst Schwartz was still alive? Indeed, whilst Carey was in India, monuments and epigrams were being set up to Schwartz' honour by no less than John Flaxman (1755-1826), the Wedgwood designer and John Bacon (1777-1859)[3] for the East India Company and the

---

[1] I use the term 'lady' honourably as I was brought up to use. The words 'woman' and 'female' have sadly suffered in the modern dumbing down of the English language.

[2] See Smith's *Short History of Christian Missions*, p. 141. I take it that Smith is referring to the numbers of the South India Church at the time of his writing in 1884.

[3] Bacon also did sculptures of Wellesley and Hastings of India and the most prominent British leaders.

British in thankful memory of this great missionary. The Indians themselves had already set up a number of monuments in memory of Ziegenbalg. This work of remembrance was carried out with strong inter-denominational and international backing.

Carey was more the protégé of the Danish and British governments than the BMS

The truth is that Carey, unlike the contrary picture in many Anglo-American biographies and articles, actually experienced little neglect from the East India Company and the British Government should he stick to their rules, which he usually did. He then found himself also backed strongly by both Danish and British officials and chaplains and his literary endeavours, before the BMS set up barriers, were heavily supported financially by the interdenominational Bible Societies and the non-Baptist Missionary enterprises in the India of his day and sporadically until the time of his death. The East India Company never set up statues in honour of Carey's missionary services as he was a mere EIC employee. They did honour Schwartz' missionary stance and diplomacy because they profited enormously by it as Schwartz enlightened both natives and Europeans in India.

This tolerance and encouragement contradict many Baptist claims

Such acts and such toleration of former missionaries and Carey stand in stark contrast to Baptist claims that the early British Christian work in India supported by the Church of England and the East Indian authorities would not tolerate 'Dissenters'. Organisations such as the SPCK worked interdenominationally and they were founded interdenominationally and neither Ziegenbalg, nor Fabricius, nor Schwartz, nor Kiernander were Church of England men though they gladly worked in fellowship with that Church as long as the SPCK did not interfere too much in their work as in Kiernander's case. The SPCK itself was a product of Danish and German evangelical action and was not strictly of Anglican or British origin. Carey found acceptance amongst the Continental and Church of England missionaries and employment under the British and Danish Government after abandoning his initial wild business schemes. Fuller's interference, however, made this difficult. This means, however, that the Baptist Missionary Society's version of Anglican opposition to the Baptist missionaries needs to be radically re-evaluated. Indeed, when the British began to force out the Danes from Serampore, they were proud to have the Serampore Trio as their agents and middlemen.

Fuller refused to accept the progress made before the Baptists in evangelising India

Carey was certainly criticised more by his own people than foreign churches, the EIC and government officials. The more radical opposition to Carey was certainly on the BMS side, and Carey protested strongly against their interference in missionary affairs in India. However, Fuller and his followers would not accept the vast Christian work done in India by other denominations as being true evangelism, bringing with it true conversions. To Fuller as he early emphasized, any apparent missionary success of non-Baptists was the work of 'Jezebel'. Ward had written to Fuller with a plea for Fuller's understanding that at Serampore they should fellowship around the Lord's Table with all 'real Christians'. In a long reply written to Ward in 1800, Fuller maintained that non-Baptists were not real Christians. With a most legal and institutional understanding of a form of baptism he thought was Scriptural, he told Ward that Baptist baptism was a positive command of God which is given believers as a 'trial of our obedience' and must be obeyed. For Fuller, baptism as determined by him was an eleventh commandment to be followed by only condemnation and dismissal from God's grace for those who broke Fuller's restrictions.

Here surely Fuller is misinterpreting Scripture. He claims, applying this to non-Fullerite churches:

> One thing alleged against the church at Thyatira was that she suffered that woman, Jezebel, to teach and seduce God's servants, Rev. ii. 20.

What the Scriptures say here about Jezebel is a historical truth but to apply this prophetically to baptism of the non-Fullerite kind both in Thyatira and the history of the Christian Church in general is merely a dogmatic institutionalized supposition with neither Scripture nor history, nor the practice of the Church in general to back it up. To use Revelation 2:20 to castigate all Christians who do not adhere to Fuller's legalistic views is sectarianism and false legalism at their worst. If such

Baptists as Fuller wish to be outsiders that is their business alone but they do not thus need to insult the Scriptures and their brethren in Christ as an argument for separation. Fuller's Liberal rationalizing away of the Christian gospel until all that is left is to follow Natural Law, as God Himself must, would, if accepted, be the end of the Gospel of reconciliation between fallen men and God. However, Fuller did not believe in a full fall as it would then disable man from thinking rationally.

Furthermore, Fuller confused the Biblical teaching on baptism with his interpretation of whom should be baptised and the mode in which the rite should be carried out. He convinced himself that no Christianity can be accomplished outside of his personal and quite radical conviction and commanded those he felt were under his authority to act like himself. Fuller outlined his views of Baptist baptism as being a 'positive command' of God in his Thoughts on Open Communion, writing:[4]

> To dispense with baptism as a term of visible communion, is to connive either at a total neglect of an ordinance which by the authority of Christ is binding to the end of the world, or at a gross corruption of that ordinance; and in many cases at both:

This is just what Ward was not saying in his plea for tolerance on Fuller's part but that it was faith in Christ that determined their visible communion and not a rite. To misuse baptism as a legalistic trial of faith robs baptism of the grace which it signifies. Fuller continues:

> for there are great numbers who do not believe themselves to be baptized according to the Scriptures, who yet content themselves with the baptism they have. To connive at a known omission of the will of Christ must be wrong, and must render us partakers of other men's sins; yet I see not how this can be avoided on the principle you espouse, provided you account such persons to be real Christians.

---

[4] Letter to the Rev. William Ward dated 21st September, 1800.

Again, this is avoiding the issue dogmatically and judgmentally believing that 'great numbers' of Christians know that they are wrongly baptised but are not prepared to do anything about it. I have met very many Baptists – whole churches full of them – who have had themselves re-immersed because they felt they had not come up to Baptist specifications in their own first baptism into their local Baptist Church. To them, (until they joined this particular Baptist church with better teaching) baptism had become a work of supererogation to be repeated if the baptised person found himself back-sliding. One Baptist author of note and a dear friend died without being baptised as he felt he was unworthy to stand up to the 'trial of faith'. Yet baptism is especially taught by Jesus as a promise of the gospel of grace,

Ward was simply pleading for a joint communion of evangelical, Bible-believing Protestants who were one in the faith. He certainly was not dealing with believers who 'connive' at disobeying God though Fuller did connive at unchurching Thomas and Carey's predecessors and contemporary fellow Christians. Ward's fellow missionaries and friends in other Reformed denominations certainly did not hold to a baptism which they believed was un-Scriptural and a form of works-righteousness. Yet Fuller goes on to write about his 'conniving' ideas again:

> But supposing them to be sincere in their attachment to paedobaptism, or that they really believe it to be the mind of Christ as revealed in the Scriptures; yet still if you admit them to the Lord's supper, you must connive at what you consider as a gross corruption of the ordinance of Christ a corruption that amounts to a subversion of every good end to be answered by it, and that has introduced a flood of other corruptions into the church. To me it appears evident that paedobaptism opened the door for the Romish apostacy; and that the church will never be restored to its purity while it is allowed to have any existence in it. The grand cause of the church's having been corrupted so as to become apostate was its being MINGLED WITH THE WORLD. Paedobaptism first occasioned this fatal mixture, and national establishments of religion completed it. The one introduced the unconverted posterity of believers; the other all the inhabitants of a country, considering none but pagans, Jews,

> and deists as unbelievers. The one threw open the door; the other broke down the wall. It is manifestly thus that the church and the world have been confounded, and will always be confounded, more or less, till paedobaptism is no more.

It is strange that Fuller here refers to the Calcutta Christians other than Baptists as 'Paedobaptists' though they obviously did not baptise children simply because they were children just as 'adult baptism' does not mean baptising adults merely because they are adults. The insistence, which is thankfully rarely kept to, that only those of an 'Age of Discretion' may be baptised totally begs the question as to how 'discretion' or reaching the age of 'accountability' fits one out as a Christian. Neither discretion nor accountability ever made a Christian. So, too, baptism must never be separated from the fact that when we talk of baptism, we are talking of Christ's righteous act in defeating death and not 'steps' in our own obedience. To deny baptism to educationally subnormal or greatly handicapped people is not part of the Christian Gospel.

Most converts in India were adults

Actually, the thousands of converts to Christ in India before Fuller's day were first and foremost adults who said, 'As for me and my house, we shall serve the Lord and taught their children the Scriptural purpose of baptism. They also saw household baptisms as the Scriptural norm and the way of following Christ's commands as did the early Baptists such as those in Switzerland.[5] The claim sometimes heard that the New Testament term 'household' does not apply to the children in it is a lame excuse indeed as the term itself *ipso facto* includes parents, children and even servants. When a Christian says, 'As for me and my house, we shall serve the Lord, he is obviously including his children. Baptism is a pointer to serving the Lord and experiencing His baptism. It is part and parcel of Gospel preaching.

Concerning Roman Catholic apostasy, it was Rome who first introduced baptism by immersion as a total washing away of sin, thus misusing the rite as a grace-gaining means. In the first centuries after

---

[5] I go into this matter in depth in my book, *The Covenant of Grace and Christian Baptism* when referring to the early Swiss Baptists.

Christ, talk was about baptism using the Greek loanword and not the Latin neologism 'immersion'. Fuller's insult to evangelical Christians as being akin to Roman Catholics, pagans, Jews and Deists is attempting to tear the robe of Christ into shreds. Fuller, however, continues by writing:

> If you admit Paedobaptists to communion, you will not be able for any continuance to secure your own principle that none but 'real Christians' should be admitted. It is like inviting a friend to your table whose company you value, but who cannot come without bringing his whole family with him. In the earlier ages baptized children were actually and consistently admitted to the Lord's supper. In national churches they are still generally admitted I believe as they grow up, if no gross immorality appears in their conduct, and in some if it does. And even in congregational churches they are taught to consider themselves, either on account of their birth or baptism, or both, as somehow members of the visible church. Such an idea might in some measure be suppressed, where the great majority were Baptists; but, by admitting members on your principle, it would soon be otherwise.

Here again, Fuller is barking up the wrong tree, besides arguing rather absurdly that baptism was not administered correctly until the Baptists took the field. All that he says of any possible misuse of family baptism goes for any possible misuse of adult baptism also. Besides, when I invite couples to visit me, I expect them to come as a family, I do not turn their wives and children away. Fuller's argument that non-Baptist churches invite unbelievers to take part in the Lord's supper show his total ignorance of most non-Baptist denominations. Also, he forgets his own confession that many baptised Baptist partakers of the Lord's Supper are acting in unbelief as they are not yet converted.

I myself have seen enough in Baptist churches of five-year-old little girls with painted faces and frilly dresses baptised on their mother's testimony that their daughters had reached the correct age of discernment and had professed Christ and could thus be baptised. The ensuing party and presentation of gifts rounded off the ceremony. I say this because my Baptist friends often, to criticise non-Baptist baptisms, paint pictures of the folly of baptising infants, quoting Spurgeon's well-known illustration. Physician heal thyself! The misuse of baptism in all Christian denominations whether Baptist or not is quite appalling.

The point, however, which Fuller makes time and time again is that only Baptists are 'real Christians' because their rite unites them in Christ. Here, again, Fuller puts belief in a rite before faith in the Lord Jesus Christ. To be frank and honest, I have not, on the whole, seen less worldliness, less alcoholism, less adultery, less family disharmony and less hypocrisy in Baptist circles than in other Bible-believing, evangelical churches. Even the Baptist churches in Fuller's Association had their disciplinary problems regarding theft and drunkenness and cases of child abuse. The Olney church being no exception. There are even stories currently being spread throughout the U.S.A. of one Baptist pastor shooting a rival pastor dead because he was simply a rival pastor. I know one of these stories to be true. John Gill's church even had a member who was imprisoned for armed highway robbery! Christians are still in Adam until the resurrection which Christ's baptism depicts, whatever their denomination.

When teaching in Sweden, my school invited a church choir to sing at some event or other. I knew several choir-members personally so also knew that they were a mottled lot. We were all surprised when the choir-leader told us that all his singers had been documented as being baptised in the Spirit without exception. To me, this is just as questionable as saying that all our baptised church members are born of God. I wrote a history of a Baptist church which was never published because some of the baptised I had mentioned had later 'stopped' following the Lord. Sadly, there are back-sliders in all Christian institutions.

A Landmarker's testimony

One ardent internet Baptist Blogger who claimed to be a Landmarker with whom I corresponded boasted that in each church that he took over, and he appeared to wander from church to church, to be on the safe side, he re-baptised every member. Many Christians I have met whilst striving to care for their souls have told me that they have had a multiple of Baptist baptisms as their pastors who never seem to have stayed more than a few years in their churches seemed to be convinced that their flock was never 'done properly'. When I told my multi-baptism pastor friend that I could not agree with him, he called me on a

Landmarker blog site 'a son of a whore and married to a whore' and claimed that John Gill, whom I had quoted, was an 'apostate'. His friends told me that I had all the arguments but they had 'The Faith'. I found their 'Faith' highly immoral. But Fuller has more to say:

> The religion of Jesus was never suited to the spirit of this world. Its subjects require to be born again, and to make an open avowal of it. Therefore, when worldly men took it in hand, they knew not what to make of it, nor what to do with it, till they had framed it to their mind by explaining away these uncouth principles. Paedobaptism was of essential service to them in this business. Its language was, and still is, One birth will do, at least for the kingdom of heaven upon earth, provided it be from a believing parent. And now, the great difficulty being removed, the smaller is easily surmounted. 'There is no necessity for an open and public avowal; a little water in a private house will do.' Thus the two grand barriers that should separate the church from the world are broken down.

Fuller is scraping the bottom of the barrel of scandalmongering here. The denominations he condemned all emphasised a public testimony of their faith and insisted on the New Birth otherwise called being born again, as an entrance into true church fellowship, visible or invisible. The Articles of the Church of England express the need to be born again clearly and emphatically. Scriptural arguments for the need to be born again, I would say, are more expressive and direct in the Thirty-Nine articles than in Baptist creeds. The omission of teaching the New Birth is a pan-Christian failure, present sadly amongst the Baptists as elsewhere. Baptism was never meant as a guarantee of faith but faith in Christ's baptism is Christ's guarantee for sinners. I have met many a Presbyterian who denied the need for a public testimony of faith. Baptism as an avowal of one's own faith is not the same thing. Calvin complained that his church refused to have a public confession of faith as was the Church of England practice in Confirmation or any such public testimony. He believed he was correct in wishing for such a Confirmation practice but his members who were all at sixes and sevens at the time voted against him as he complained to his English friends. Calvin's time at Geneva was never a bed of roses and the threat of exile was so great that he decided to give up his flock from time to time but his friend and advisor Heinrich Bullinger persuaded him on several occasions to stick to his post. It was Bullinger that had Calvin reinstated after Geneva actually exiled him and banned him from the city church.

The Baptists' stance on excommunication

The usual Baptist stance on excommunication is a case for deep consideration. This disciplinary measure is used in Baptist churches in direct contrast to what the Bible teaches and appears to me to be more common within the Baptist movement than even within the Roman Catholic Church. Indeed, I have preached in Baptist churches who claimed to have almost a hundred percent membership of those excommunicated from other Baptist churches. The fellowship was most sweet but the scars caused by pastoral arrogance and legalism were deep. I have experienced this on my own body. Having preached several times at a local Baptist church I was informed by the pastor that he had felt divinely led to place me on his membership list. When people were converted through my ministry, he visited me in anger asking me if I were trying to steal his church from him. He also told me that I was disobeying his church principles by preaching to the local soldiers and, in anger, said he had struck me from his membership list and thus excommunicated me from the fellowship of the saints. As I never asked to be on his membership list, it did not upset me to be taken off it. The pastor's name translated into English was 'Pride'. When the elders told him his teaching was frightening members away, he resigned and was 'called' to another church miles away. I have received letters recently from a man who invited a person to preach in his church, allegedly 'Strict Baptist' but would not allow him to partake in the Lord's Supper in the church to which he had just ministered. My 'friend' told me that his church was a closed shop as trade unionists express it. Trade Unionism has its place but not in the Church of God.

However, Fuller has still more to say to Ward's request for Fuller's blessing on their joint communion church. Commenting on the name of Jezebel and her seduction of the church at Thyatira mentioned in Revelation 2:20, he says:

> The allusion is doubtless to the wife of Ahab, who corrupted the pure worship and ordinances of God in her time, and mingled

> them with idolatry. Whoever they were that were thus denominated, it was doubtless some person or body of persons that strove to draw off the church from her purity, and to introduce for doctrines the commandments of men. It seems, too, that some of God's servants were seduced by her; good men, whom your plan of admission would have tolerated. And it is worthy of notice that, the censure is not directed against her for doing so, but against the church for suffering it.
>
> You allow immorality or dangerous heresy, even in good men, to be a just cause of a refusal of communion. But is not God as jealous of his sovereign authority as he is of his truth and holiness? The ruin of mankind was by means of the breach of a positive institution. The corruption of instituted worship forms a large part of antichristianism, and is to the full as severely censured as its heresies and immoralities. Positive commands, like the bathing of Naaman in Jordan, are designed for the trial of our obedience. And with respect to the gross deviation from the command in question, after it has once opened the door for the grand apostasy, (an apostasy from which we are not cleansed to this day,) shall it be pleaded for as innocent, and ranked with meats, and drinks, and days? Rather ought we not to set our faces against the seductions of Jezebel; and, instead of conniving at God's servants who are seduced by her, to assure them that much as we love them, and long for communion with them, we must, while we have ears to hear, 'hear what the Spirit saith unto the churches?' Rev. ii.7.

So here we have it black on white that Fuller looked on his evangelical friends who were strongly supporting the BMS work as those whom Jezebel has seduced. Readers must note here, however that Fuller, in his works on Law, distinguished between what is 'right' in itself as an eternal truth, which he calls 'Natural Law' but 'positive institutions' or 'positive laws' are merely right because God commands them and thus are not intrinsically 'right' in themselves as they are part of God's arbitrary revelation which is of a mere temporary nature and will give way in the long run to Natural Law.

Fuller back-pedals fourteen years later

It is interesting to note that Fuller appeared to back-pedal from this strict view in a letter to the Instructor dated 28th January, 1814. Here he relates that the Serampore Trio are free to commune with other Christians without having to compromise on their own beliefs. But this was fourteen years after the damage was done which greatly hindered the work of the Indian mission as a whole. So, too, Fuller does not mention his own strictures on baptism and the Lord's Supper or whether he had dropped them or not. Besides, the worthiness of a Christian to attend communion is a matter between the communicant and God as the Scriptures make plain. Ward told Fuller that he was not talking about people who made themselves publicly unworthy by their non-Christian behaviour but about 'real Christians'. However, Fuller radically changed his theology at least three times as I have pointed out in my published studies of his ever-changing theological fancies so no Baptist can use his ever-changing strictures at one given time as a permanent Christian norm or as a measure of the man himself. Indeed, there was no such thing as a 'permanently revealed Law' for Fuller as all that was revealed was of a temporary and arbitrary nature so that God's pronouncement of what was right was merely because God said it was right but Natural Law shows us what is always right.

Arguing for the triumph of reason over Law

In his work On Moral and Positive Obedience,[6] Fuller argues for the triumph of nature and the fitness of things over the Law given to Moses as a confirmation of the Covenant of Grace with Abraham. Gospel ends are, for Fuller, to be reached by man's innate powers of reason as a categorical imperative as taught by the Enlightenment philosophy of Paine, Kant and Lessing. Here he follows Grotius's rationalism in claiming that there are eternals such as the order of nature and temporals such as God's Law and Revelation to man which are entirely arbitrary. He forgot that God's revealed Law speaks of a new Creation which transcends Natural Law and reveals God's eternal character which is *per se* unchangeable. This is why I claim that Fuller was one of the

[6] *Works*, Vol. iii, p. 352 ff.

several fathers who parented the so-called New Covenant Theology.[7] Perhaps readers may think I am hard on Fuller as a Baptist but I do not consider Fuller as a normal Baptist of the Particular Baptist persuasion but as one who bases his baptism on a legalism engendered by his low view of God and high view of man. We do not baptise because it is thought reasonable by those who place Natural Law and 'the fitness of things' over God's revelation. We baptise because it is part of the practical Gospel of the Great Commission. So our gospel is a purely revealed gospel and not worked out by either our 'reason' or our view of 'the fitness of things'. I believe that baptism is part of God's gospel revelation to me and has an eternal significance. It is not a part of fallen Natural Law.

Inter-Christian tolerance in India stopped by Andrew Fuller
In India there was a healthy inter-denominational fellowship until Fuller opened the closed communion debate and a new Fullerite Baptist ecclesiology was established. Thus, the former 'open communion' practised in Serampore became in reality 'no communion'. Fuller argued that originally the Baptist missionaries practised closed communion then turned to open communion which he strove to stop. What he really meant was that the early Baptist missionaries had communion with one another but then, when they were received into fellowship by their evangelical brethren from other denominations their fellowship around the table was opened up and expanded. Fuller speaks of a resulting 'mixed communion' but there was no mix-up in Serampore until Fuller started to rock the boat, denying Christians from various denominations the right of communion.

However, the Company's and the British Government's initial openness to Baptists is seen by Carey's very warm reception by Lord Wellesley, Governor General of British India, at the Fort William College at a time when it was clear that the college's aim was to establish Church of England establishment within the British Indian Empire.[8] Apart from Fuller in Kettering, William Yates, William Adam

[7] See my analysis of Fuller's view of Universal Law in relation to Positive Law in my book *Law and Gospel in the Theology of Andrew Fuller* (2nd ed.) and especially Part II entitled The Letter Law and the Spirit Law.
[8] See Frykenberg, *Christianity in India*, p. 244.

and Rammohun Roy, on the receiving end of the BMS's policies, were obviously a furthering cause, wittingly or unwittingly, of the breach between the Baptist missionaries and those of the major denominations in India who were almost all sound Evangelicals. Linked with the Baptist method of translation work with its denominational emphasis on restricting the meaning of the Greek, and forcing non-Biblical meanings into the New Testament text, there was also the Unitarian controversy which broke out amongst the Baptists at this time. Each party allowed their 'translation work' to isolate them from the traditional methods of translation which Ziegenbalg and his successors had used. Extra-Biblical usage whether linguistic or religious determined the translations.

Need for Baptist reassessment of pioneer missionary work in India

The mass of information provided by mainly non-British authors thus demands a completely new assessment of the way the Baptist Missionary Society in England sought to re-run the Serampore Mission and organize it according to their own plan to which none of the Serampore Trio agreed. Such a new examination needs to look into the way the Baptist Mission blocked out in their write-ups much of the work of scores of other missionaries on whom Carey based his own service to the gospel. So, too, the reasons not only for Andrew Fuller's early break with the traditional evangelism of India but also the break-up of relations between Carey and the 'home front' at the beginning of his ministry in India and especially during the years 1815-20 and 1830-4 after Fuller's death need to be re-examined rather than ignored. The go-it-alone nature of Fuller's would-be dominance of the Mission with his closed-shop institutionalism was the first major blow against the unity of the Indian Church,[9] but the Baptist Missionary Society went

[9] See Andrew Fuller's Thoughts on Open Communion: In a Letter to the Rev. William Ward Missionary at Serampore, dated 21st September, 1800, *The Works of Andrew Fuller*, one volume Banner of Truth Reprint, 2007, pp. 854-855. See also On Terms of Communion, p. 852 and Strictures, p. 853, Strict Communion in the Mission Church of Serampore, p. 855. The Admission of Unbaptised Persons to the Lord's Supper inconsistent with the New Testament: A Letter to a Friend in 1814, pp. 855-859. Also Clary, Ian Hugh. 'Throwing Away the Guns: Andrew Fuller, William Ward, and the Communion Controversy in the Baptist Missionary Society.' Foundations 68 (May 2015): 84-101, Clary, Ian Hugh, 'Andrew Fuller and Closed Communion, SBJT Forum

further during Carey's ministry and set in motion plans to elbow the Serampore Trio out of the institutionalized Baptist missions altogether. This led to the Fen Court edict of 1827 claiming that the BMS and the Serampore missionaries were two different missionary bodies. All threadbare ropes binding the two were cut but the BMS continued to demand the Serampore earnings and property.

The BMS elbows Carey out

Beginning in 1815, the Baptist Missionary Society, highly dissatisfied with Carey, decided to make a fresh start in India according to their plans and not Carey's. They started by putting pressure on the Serampore Trio to sign over all their assets, funds and property to the English 'Mission'. Carey was forced to say 'no' to this demand as he believed that the Indian Mission should not be governed from abroad and most of the Serampore and Calcutta assets consisted of funds and salaries from non-Baptist institutions. Furthermore, Carey had always sent the bulk of his private earnings to help finance the English Mission and continued to do so. The response in England was to send a new team led by William H. Pearce in 1817 to operate as if the Serampore Trio had never existed. Worse still, instead of opening up a new area for evangelization where they could go their own way, they set up their rival headquarters in Calcutta and even a rival printing press.[10] Carey was especially distressed to find his own nephew Eustace at the head of the rebel faction. Carey wrote, 'Nothing I ever met with in my life – and I have met with many distressing things – ever preyed so much on my spirits as this difference has.'

The BMS was against the Serampore College from the start

In 1818, Arian William Adam was sent to Serampore and the Missionary Society's home committee caused further disturbance by protesting at Carey's leading participation of the interdenominational Serampore College with its Danish license to train both English

---

(ed Michael Haykin), Southern Baptist Journal of Theology, 17. 1. 2013, pp. 46-52 and Potts, E. Daniel, 'I throw away the guns to preserve the ship', Baptist Quarterly, pp. 115-117, 20.12. 2000. See also Bibliography.

[10] William Hopkins Pearce, son of Samuel Pearce was a printer by trade having worked for years at the Clarendon Press and was originally supposed to assist Ward.

students and Indian citizens (mostly Hindus) in, at first, equal numbers. Staughton protested that Carey only taught secular subjects such as gardening there. So, the Home Committee protested that they would not send a penny to support it. Much of their protest was valid from a missionary point of view. The refused 'help' was not needed as the Danes' and Carey's English friends from a number of different confessions provided huge sums for new buildings and the Serampore Trio were able to provide four thousand pounds from their own joint savings. Through a Royal Danish decree, the Serampore College became the first degree-awarding University in Asia and Denmark's third university after Copenhagen and Kiel which by 1829 was providing hundreds of Indian citizens with a good, all-round education. However, the College had to wait another century before they had the professional staff to undertake university work.

Ajith George in his most helpful work the *History of Christianity in India: The Serampore Mission* sums up the many rifts between the Serampore Trio, who mostly worked from Calcutta, and the grasping and domineering BMS:

> During 1815 to 1837, there was a close rift between the parent society, BMS, and the Serampore mission. The roots of the controversy were embedded in the status of the Serampore Mission as a largely self-supporting entity – a status which was founded on fundamental principle, and not merely on economic necessity. Over the years of Fuller's secretaryship, the Trio built up a complex of buildings at Serampore, purchased with their own money, supplemented by loans from the Society. The premises were held on behalf of the Society, but the legal status of the trust deeds was unsatisfactory. To the home committee it seemed imperative after Fuller's death that the mission property at Serampore should speedily be placed on a basis which would secure its proprietorship to the Society … The Serampore mission was self-supported and the missionaries had begun a convent community, where missionaries were taken at request. Until March 23, 1827 negotiations were attempted but the Committee publicly announced that the BMS and the Serampore mission parted ways.

> From 1827-1837 Serampore mission was supported by an independent committee. In 1837 a reunion negotiation took place where the BMS excluded the Serampore College from its control. Late in 1855, after the death of Marshman, the last of the Trio in 1837, the BMS committee included Serampore College into its governance.

So here the bubble of a faithful missionary body giving full support to a dependent Serampore Trio for whom they held the ropes bursts. There was never a full union of the BMS either with the work of the Serampore Trio or the founding and organizing of the Serampore College. Indeed, the Trio had a precarious position all along as they neither wished to ally too closely with the international evangelicals but also did not wish to be bossed about by the Baptist Missionary Society.

Yates sent to oppose Carey

The lack of interest by the BHS in the Serampore College is illustrated by their backing of William Yates whom they sent to Calcutta in 1815. Baptist Yates not only rejected Carey's translation work but also questioned the position of the Serampore College, eventually supporting Alexander Duff in the founding of his Scottish Church College in Calcutta in 1831 which very soon out-rivalled Serampore College as an academic establishment. Duff's establishment started off by providing a basic education but soon entered into academic work long before Serampore College stopped being a mere preparatory school. It was Yates who chaired a committee of those interested in higher education, urging Duff to set up a Calcutta University. However, Yates was soon to set up rival establishments himself and prepare 'Easy Readers' for his school as Felix Carey had done for the Serampore work. Yates gradually isolated himself from the BMS, the Serampore Trio, the Serampore College and Duff's educational projects and in 1829 he asked the BMS to be relieved of his missionary duties. Sadly again, this instability in the BMS appears to be ignored by those who prefer a more highly edited and romantic version.

Yates' energies in language learning and education were enormous but as so many missionaries before and after him he is best described as a jack of all trades and a master of none though the John Brown Baptist University granted him an M.A. in 1831 and a D.D. in 1839 as they had already honoured other Baptists before, such as Carey who was given a D.D. in 1806 and Marshman received the title in 1810. Yates academic status, however, was certainly far higher than Carey's and Marshman's. Nevertheless, Yates cannot go down in history as having served the Indian church more than he hindered it. Nor has his image been blown up by modern Fullerite Baptists as that of the Serampore Trio, as though to clear their conscience concerning the lack of positive cooperation with the three men by the BMS and their other failures in India.

Baptists in Europe worked well with State Churches and still do

I do not claim at all that all Baptists go to the extremes of Fullerite Baptists as my many works on many Baptist heroes prove. I have fellowshipped for many years with a gigantic Baptist Church in Enid, Oklahoma who practise a baptism of which Fuller had apparently not even heard in the old sense of Henry Jessey, John Bunyan and John Ryland Sen. Yet whilst the British Fullerite Baptists were quarrelling with their evangelical brethren from other denominations, the European Baptists were busy being accepted by the Reformed and Lutheran churches who thus voted for Baptist participation in the German Kirchentag. Since then, German Baptists are treated with the same respect as the various state churches in Germany and the state churches through their church taxes help to finance Baptist churches who pay no church tax. The German Christians and public authorities had been so impressed by the bravery of the Baptists in catastrophic areas caused by fire and plague from which other ministers fled. By their Christian works they became known and not by denominationalist legislation or squabbles over rites.

In the North-Rhine Westphalian schools where I taught for over 25 years, all Scripture teaching is under the auspices of the state churches but Baptists and Free Church people may also obtain their Vokation with their State Church brethren after suitable training and be ordained to teach Scripture up to matriculation level without compromising in any way. I was not a member of the Rhineland Established Church on taking my Vokation but was asked to join the Religious Textbooks Committee editing books on religious education and audio-visual help which employed me, parallel with my teaching and lecturing, for over ten years. Our editorial committee was quite inter-denominational.

All this was primarily due to the work of Johann Gerhard Oncken (1800-1884) who started his ministry through a joint project with the Lutherans to establish Sunday Schools. His wife was a former member of Charles Haddon Spurgeon's church and Spurgeon preached at the opening service of his Hamburg chapel. In the congregation, he found state politicians and representatives of other churches and speaks very highly of Oncken's work. Prof. Helmut Thielicke who was known as 'Germany's Spurgeon' because of his fine evangelical preaching and under whom I sat as a post-graduate student at Hamburg University, is commonly acclaimed as Germany's expert on Spurgeon though he was a Lutheran minister.

Oncken started training missionaries for overseas' work in the early 1840s but was challenged by the Berlin Baptists led by Gottfried Wilhelm Lehmann (1799-1882) over the meaning of Baptism and the Lord's Supper, Lehmann took a more institutional and denominational approach. Lehmann thought baptism was not only a sign of but means of acquiring faith. As the national church authorities felt that Oncken's more evangelical and Reformed position was becoming lost, they demanded a new joint Baptist Confession which Lehmann drew up though also relying on Oncken's Hamburg Confession. It was a formal compromise which foretold division especially after Oncken's death in 1884. Oncken's principle was that every Baptist should be a missionary and he envisaged the Church as a growing and spreading community rather than a local organisation. Since then, it has become a moot question of who founded the German Baptists; Oncken or Lehmann. This question was put to my tutor in Baptist History Dr Hans Luckey at the Oncken Seminar, then in Hamburg, now in Berlin, to which he answered that Oncken was the pioneer but Lehmann brought the organisation into existence. I thought Lehmann had rather messed things up for the German Baptists. Oncken's chief theological background was amongst the Scottish Calvinists.

One of my favourite stories of Oncken records his 1862 visit to Edinburgh to meet the famous Dr Thomas Guthrie (1803-1873) who helped found the Free Church of Scotland. This staunch Scottish Calvinist was most missionary minded and he quickly asked Oncken how many missionaries the German Baptists had. Oncken answered promptly 'Seven thousand'. The good Doctor gasped and then thought that Oncken had misunderstood him and posed the question again receiving the same answer, 'Seven thousand'. Then Oncken said in English, 'We consider every member a missionary'. Guthrie then paced about the room lost in wonder exclaiming 'That is it! That is the way to evangelize the world. Every Christian a missionary!'[11] Would that every denomination felt as Oncken did!

[11] Read Günter Balders' thrilling account of the life and work of Oncken. See Bibliography. There was always some rivalry between Berlin and Hamburg. Shortly after my post-grad year at the college it moved to Berlin with its library and archives.

Chapter Twenty-Nine

The Future for Indian Missions

What we learn from the Indian story

Personally, I feel that the history of Indian evangelism shows us clearly what are the right things to be done and what are the wrong things that have been done. The wrong way of going about gospel evangelism has been aired intensely in this study as also the right way. We can obviously now gain right insight into the wrong done and learn to draw positive help for the future from all that was according to the Scriptural Commission.

Foreign Missionary Societies bring in foreign thoughts

The first question we should perhaps ask here is to what extent did the policies of Foreign Missionary Societies favour Indian evangelism. Our concentration on the BMS under Fuller and Dyer, a look at the Danish Missionary Society under Wendt and the SPCK under the Anglicans, I believe, teaches us that foreign Missionary Societies bring in foreign thoughts and tend to become a law unto themselves when these thoughts are planted abroad. Thus, we can say positively that Foreign Missionary Societies are not the ideal way of fulfilling the Great Commission.

Denominationalism divides the gospel and thus the Church

The second question worth asking is what has denominationalism done to convert India for Christ? Again, we can learn from mistakes here as denominations, especially on the foreign mission field have usually separated one Christian from the other over inessentials, rites and ceremonies which have become a pseudo-gospel in lieu of the real Gospel of the Good News of Christ our Saviour. They have also developed abroad as a kind of home-from home where ex-patriots can delight in one another's denominational company and practise their own traditions. That may provide 'Happy Hours' for ex-patriots but it hardly gives them a reason or excuse for enforcing such practices on the Indians. One must beware of modern churches in India which bear the name of their foreign origins of British, German, French or American, as the case may be, and sadly continues. This is spiritual colonialism.

So, too, whether one is sprinkled, or dipped or immersed, or ducked backwards or forwards one, two or three times, or confirmed, or has had hands laid on or been prepared for the 'agony bench' or for sitting in the confessor's box, these are happily non-essentials and most secondary to declaring 'Repent and believe' and explaining from the Scriptures how it is done. Entering into the arms of Christ is far lovelier than labouring under the fetters of mere traditions. I gather from this that the way ahead for India and indeed for the rest of the world, is not through the denominational door but through the only Door worth going through as recorded in John 10:9:

> I am the door: by me if any man enter in, he shall be saved, and shall go in and out and find pasture.

This is the way to gain abundant life. Preaching Christ as the only way, the truth and the life[1] is the work of an evangelist whether in India or anywhere else. We have gloriously true stories to tell!

Political culture also divides the gospel

The third question which comes to my mind on reviewing the previous chapters of my book is how much of our own political culture should we take with us when evangelising India or anywhere else. Christ tells us to render unto Caesar what is his and render unto God what is his. He said this even in the colonial times of His day when *Pax Romana* governed Palestine. However, there is now no imported Caesar thrust on that Free State of India. When an overseas missionary is in that vast

[1] John 14:6.

country, he is responsible to the government of his second home and not his past home. His 'powers that be' are now Indian governmental powers. So many missionaries in the past have loaded themselves with a little England or a little America or a little France on their backs and have been too overburdened by their load to preach the boundless and borderless gospel Biblically. So, whether you are from the great Chinese, Australian, African, European or American Continents or from little Brexit Britain you must leave these lands behind you and become all things to all men in India. When you leave your home-country to take up a new home you are then a citizen of that new country. The idea of going to India on a six months 'Tentmaker' contract, for instance, will only do you good but hardly India. Happily, most Indians are highly proficient in understanding and speaking English and, with their natural politeness overlook the Western folly of remaining mono-lingual in the land of a thousand languages.

Settle down in a local church and do your part in it

Anyway, once you have tasted Indian food, you probably will repent of your prolonged holiday ideas and want to stay for such 'human' reasons, though animals like to eat well, too. My advice here is to settle down in a good local Indian church and if you are not prepared to do that, go back to your old home quickly. Here in Germany, we have British Churches, Russian churches, American churches and gigantic Korean churches full of enthusiastic Christians who want to do something for Germany. As long as they remain in their nationalistic pseudo-holy-huddles they will do very little to awake the sleeping churches and the self-righteous atheists here. British or American 'Christian Clubs' in India will be just as useless.

Foreign missionary culture exemplified

At a school run by the Swedish Inner Mission for whom I worked for several years, we prayed for and supported a Swedish missionary family in the land then called Ethiopia. One day, we received a letter from the family begging money for a wooden floor. They told us that the natives had no wooden floors and they wanted to show them something of Swedish Christian civilisation. We sent them the money, they put in the floor boards and the 'natives' had a good laugh. Exactly a year later, our 'civilised' missionaries sent us a begging letter once again. Their house needed new floor boards. 'How strange', we thought, 'their old boards were but a year old.' However, the termites had eaten up the wooden boards, this was why the 'natives' never used them. These missionaries, however, insisted that a civilized house had floorboards. They were doing the wrong job in the wrong country and were a financial burden on those who felt they were doing the Lord a service with their widow's mites. 'Missionary floor boards' are just not part of our gospel.

East is East and West is West

Many missionaries, whether long term or short term, fail to see that East is East and West is West. This goes for North and South too. In the case of Westerners going to India we must note the wisdom of Sri Ramakrishna Paramahamsa who said: 'If you want to go east, don't go west'.

I started my walk down the Memory Lane of my youth regarding India at the beginning of this book with a quote or two from Rudyard Kipling who opened my eyes to the Northern frontiers of India as she then was. Here I think of his fine tribute to human bravery and honour in his Ballad of the East which ought to be still taught in schools and also learnt off-by-heart. Kipling said:

> Oh, East is East and West is West, and never the twain shall meet,
> Till Earth and sky stand presently at God's great Judgment Seat.

Of course, Kipling wrote this in order to contradict it immediately by arguing that when brave people are prepared to put away the accidentals of origin, birth, family, race and nationality in mutual respect, borders fall down. Idealist Kipling thought this was possible in India under the British Raj by means of a gentleman's agreement between a triumphant Britain and a conquered India, but events and common sense proved him sadly wrong. Fallen man is no gentleman. The only valid method of making East and West meet is in the Kingdom of our Lord Jesus Christ. A Western Christian who is called to serve the Lord in India is then an Eastern Christian. Of course, this works the other way, too. Europe and the U.S.A. are happily now receiving missionaries from India.

The importance of language proficiency

Again, we must return to the problem of languages. A few decades ago, I visited the Angus Library, Oxford, to do research on Carey. I was confronted with several thousand Sanskrit books once owned by the Serampore education authorities and wondered why they were in Oxford. I thus informed the most cooperative Librarian Sue Mills, explaining that I had academic training in Librarianship and was interested in Indian languages and would like to see the catalogue. Sue promptly told me that in spite of the antiquity of the Library after being place into Western hands, nobody had ever showed any interest in cataloguing the books. We discussed ways of doing this and I suggested an Indian scholar could best do the work. One was quickly found and the catalogue was prepared. The point is here that such priceless treasures were neglected through lack of language proficiency and lack of interest. The collection had not been put to public use and would have been of far more use in India as after the work of Ishwar Chandra, called Vidyasagar (1820-1891),[2] Sanskrit in the Carey and post-Carey period was re-shaped into a modern language and literature was eagerly sought in that language. Records of its foundation, however, lie dormant in Oxford. I feel most strongly that the Baptist college should give the books back to India. Colonial claims are no longer valid.

The 'moral' here is that if and when you are called to India, be prepared to prepare yourselves in at least three Indian languages before otherwise going out as a burden to the people. Most Indian languages are of what one might call 'modern invention' as witnessed by the simplified 'Missionary Indian' forms of today. Becoming all things to all men begins with the capacity to speak with the people to whom one is witnessing. In the old days, missionaries refused to prepare themselves in Indian languages for work in India on the grounds that they would pick up a faulty pronunciation when taught by Europeans. This is no problem today as there are hundreds of competent Indian scholars now working in Western universities and colleges who can teach you to pronounce, read and write Bengali, Punjabi, Hindi, Urdu or Tamil etc., to perfection. They perhaps cannot teach you Scripture

---

[2] 'Vidya' means knowledge and 'sagar' means ocean. Chandra was called 'Oceans of Knowledge' because of his illuminating works.

because their own Bibles have become too 'cross-cultural', to put it lightly.

One must find a taste for Indian food

The question of food is also a matter of missionary complaints. One often hears the quite unfounded moan that Indians only eat goats. This is like saying that the Germans only eat curried sausage, the British fish and chips and the French live on bread, cheese and onions. Carey was not impressed with the variety of Bengali food as he preferred 'heavy meat suppers' washed down with alcohol and had obviously an untrained palate. The Indians are especially famed for their fine cooking but many Western mouths and stomachs are used to coarser fare. Those returning from India complain of the high cost of Indian food. On further questioning, one finds they are Western bound in their culinary tastes and order 'English Food' from around the world so that they could live like a 'civilised' European under a South Asian roof. This is a very expensive folly. Before moving for India Western immigrants should befriend a local Indian cook and take cooking lessons to prepare themselves for a new life of culinary surprises and joys!

Do not go to India as a 'foreign missionary'

There is yet a better way. Do not go to India at all as a 'foreign missionary' with all its negative attachments to the point of making yourself anti-Christian. Go to India by all means but as a normal Christian Indian amongst Indian brethren within the scope of the Great Commission. Do not give yourself 'airs' as if you were a privileged Angel come directly down from Heaven to convert a heathen land, but, like our Lord, take upon yourselves the calling of a servant, and definitely lower than the angels. Your 'emptying' yourself in this way will lead to a greater fulness in usefulness to the gospel.

Tourist missionaries are an abomination

The modern Tent-Maker idea and misuse of the term has led to a new kind of rucksack-tourism amongst 'missionaries' who are here today and gone tomorrow. Such a hit and run evangelization does neither the harassed short-term missionary any good nor the Indian peoples. I notice too that most of these would-be missionaries either work temporally for foreign firms in India for their 'tent-making' occupation or let their extended holiday be paid for by their home churches. Others are supported by 'tent-making' organisations in the home country which are run on business lines almost like private employment agencies. Yes, they even charge for their services! This is obviously the wrong way to do things. Furthermore, of the numerous adverts on the Internet calling for world-wide partnerships, the pictures of many hands clasped as also the pictures of conferences do not reflect world-wide partnerships but usually show people of one racial background only. The picture of a young European-type man climbing the blank wall of a cliff-face as an introduction to one online tent-maker organisation soliciting help from businesses seemed most inappropriate to me. This scarcely depicts a promising start for either the tent-maker business or its training programme for a short-term 'missionary' service.

There are plenty of opportunities in India for people prepared to join a local church, take on Indian citizenship and work in education or the natural sciences or medicine or an almost endless range of other trades. If they wish to take the gospel to unevangelized fields, if they can find them, then let them be called to this work by their local Indian church.

Choosing a local Indian church

I know choosing a local church will be difficult, as it is in the Western world. Through mainly foreign interference we have in India a great 'pneumatic' movement of blown-up religious fervour which acknowledges the one Spirit only with the Father and the Son as its prophets. Then we have those 'Christo-centric' organisations who tell us that they have found Christ through their various Hindu, Islamic, Buddhist, Jainistic or Zoroastrian religions. This is no wonder as foreign missionaries have mixed their gospel of Christ for centuries with elements of these religions in a misunderstood 'cross-cultural' religious fervour. We remember that even Henry Martyn used Zoroastrian images culled from the epic feats of ancient heroes in the Avesta in his translation work. These images influenced his ideas of Christian baptism and influenced his translation work.[3] Thus Zoroastrians today tell us that they have one God, a Heaven and Hell and Christian baptism so what more can be expected from them by 'Christians'?

[3] The old Zoroastrian epics tell of their heroes being baptised in blood.

To look for pseudo-Christian organisations and institutions for an emphasis on the Fatherhood of God is an easy pastime in India as even those religions which Westerners condemn as polytheistic, extol the one Father and Creator of all. When Indians tell you that they also believe in one Father and Creator of all, it is a good basis for further discussion but no guarantee that one is talking to a Christian. Let us be honest, not everyone who says the same thing in our Western churches can be stamped as a 'pukka Christian'. Even Fuller argued that fifty or so per cent of his own church members were not 'true Christians'. This would mean that Fuller accepted the bulk of Baptist membership at the Lord's table on account of their Baptism and not their faith. Where then is the difference between Fuller's closed communion and his colleagues' open communion? For Fuller, a specific rite decides the issue not clear gospel teaching.

The best advice to be given

So, I believe the best advice one can give to those who have received a call to India is to follow the wisdom of friends in India concerning the relative many churches who still remain in the old paths and join a small local church of not too many members who believe in the one Atonement of Christ for His entire elect Bride without any 'and', 'but', or 'or' and the Divine Authority of the Word of God in as good a translation as they can find. The latter will be the more difficult task but the Lord will certainly provide as He has done for me in this multi-cultic, racist, sexist, myriad of apostate churches in Britain, Europe, North America and the rest of the world. The gospel is there for those who seek it but it is not there for unsaved souls to grasp out and take it, as far too many erroneously teach. Spiritual things must be spiritually given, spiritually received and spiritually understood. This has been possible since the dawn of creation and we have God's own word that this manna from Heaven will be provided for ever until we enter the blessed mansions of the New Jerusalem awaiting us as our promised and secured inheritance. This is certainly why Ziegenbalg built his New Jerusalem Church in Tranquebar and whether we stay at home to clean out the stables here or find new stables to clean out in other lands, we are all doing the work of an evangelist and thus Christ's Kingdom will come on earth as it is in Heaven.

Appendices

Appendix I

Tom Nettles on Fuller, Edwards and Ella

Some time ago, much belated, I came across an online essay by Tom Nettles, originally published in Issue 53 of the Founders Journal for 2003 and entitled 'Jonathan Edwards: An Appreciation'. It had not come to my notice before although I am referred to often in the article. This work deals very much with my own study of Fuller's theology in my book *Law and Gospel in the Theology of Andrew Fuller* but quite ignores the documentary evidence I give in an attempt to paint a picture of Andrew Fuller after Nettles' own heart. As usual, the Fullerite argument is that Fuller based his theology on Edwards. However, Nettles tends to portray Edwards in a Fullerite way rather than in the evangelical Reformed traditions in which Edwards stood.

In pursuit of his aim to 'Fullerize' Edwards Nettles states:

> In an article entitled 'Inward Witness of the Spirit', Fuller summarizes the substance of a couple of Edwards's arguments in Religious Affections. *He argues that the inward witness of the Spirit is not a special revelation to any individual that he in particular is a child of God. Instead, such assurance comes by inference from the presence of spiritual perceptions and actions in one's life.* The truth of the Gospel, no matter how its impressions come to our minds, must be 'cordially' embraced. That is, an 'approving view of God's way of salvation, such a view as leads us to walk in it' is the foundation of peace and is the way that 'God speaks peace to the soul'. No sooner is 'the gospel in possession of the heart than joy and peace will ordinarily accompany it'. Since the New Testament promises

> eternal life to believers, 'we cannot but conclude ourselves interested in it'. *He does not deny the personal work of the Spirit in this, but emphasizes that the internal work of the Spirit accompanies the knowledge of and heartfelt reception of what Scripture itself actually teaches.*

George Ella represents this as 'Grotian rationalism and Socinian skepticism'. He says Fuller 'preaches as a wolf amongst the sheep' and that he 'boils Christian assurance down to reason rather than revelation'.

I have placed two passages in this quote in italics as of special note. The first is an accurate picture of Fuller, but not of Edwards. Fuller has copied parts of a passage from Edwards who warns against a false way of discerning religious affections. He has interpreted this freely and concluded that Edwards believed as he did. Edwards, however, true to Scripture, goes on to describe the right way of judging religious affections through the Holy Spirit's action on the heart. Fuller has badly copied the ailment but has not even considered Edwards' cure but sought that cure in 'impressions' on the mind, which Edwards had rejected for God's working on the heart. Nettles here, follows Fuller but not Edwards.[1]

The second passage in my italics is true of Edwards but not Fuller. In other words, we must distinguish between Fuller and Edwards on this issue. Founders Journal people are always affirming that he who reads Fuller reads Edwards as if Fuller were the greater theologian and we find Edwards incorporated in Fuller. The latter thus leads us further on into Reformed theology than Edwards. Indeed, Nettles does not call Fuller, the 'Baptist Edwards' but argues that after starting with Edwards Fuller became 'the Baptist Luther'. However, what Nettles writes concerning Fuller's essay 'The Inward Witness of the Spirit', and defends against alleged arguments coming from me without citing them, does not reflect what I wrote about the essay at all, nor do I 'represent' Fuller in the manner envisaged by Nettles. Furthermore, my findings concerning Fuller's Grotianism and Socinianism were not based on a few sentences regarding Fuller's un-Biblical view of the Spirit but on a most detailed and broader analysis which Nettles ignores

[1] Edwards on 'Religious Affections', BOT two-volume reprint of 1979. Vol. 1.

in his misapplication and mismanagement of my words. Indeed, instead of meeting my arguments in my book *Law and Gospel in the Theology of Andrew Fuller*, Nettles overlooks them but then invents new accusations which he does not even attempt to justify. I can understand Nettles wishing to defend Fuller as in defending Fuller, he is defending his own departure from Orthodoxy, but he ought at least to tackle the arguments of those with whom he disagrees, especially when those brethren are open to debate with him and have considered his views carefully. So, too, in claiming that I rightly associate Fuller's views with those of the Grotians and the Socinians, he implies that I include Edwards in this association, which I do not.

Striving to understand Nettles, I would be the first to accept that the gospel is there to be 'cordially embraced' and that once the Spirit has enlightened us and equipped us to take the path of salvation, we are enabled to walk in it and receive an interest in it and a joy and peace when pursuing that path. This is what being in Christ and Christ being in us is all about. I do not denounce this as Grotian etc. at all as this is my faith and the faith once committed to the saints.

Here, Nettles has gravely misrepresented me, jumbling too many different things together at once under a faulty common heading. Furthermore, Nettles, himself, has associated Fuller with Grotius in several of his writings so why blame me for doing the same? So, too, in this statement, especially in the first passage placed in italics, Nettles is echoing Grotius himself and not Paul who does not write of human inference concerning the Holy Spirit but on the actual indwelling of the Spirit in the Christian, indeed, also the indwelling of Christ. This aspect is entirely absent from Fuller's essay which is not an essay on the inward work of the Spirit at all but about 'inferences' through outside influences, relying, as Nettles admits on certain 'dispositions'. If this is anything worth noting, it is secular, amateur psychology and not Biblical theology and practical divinity.

The very little Fuller has to say about the Spirit is, furthermore, clothed in words redefined as to their meaning which is part and parcel of Fuller's constantly redefining terms to suit his own gospel.[2] For

---

[2] See Fuller's 'The Proper and Improper Use of Terms'. As I have shown in my various works on Fuller, there is not a major, essential Christian doctrine which Fuller does not re-define whilst keeping to traditional Reformed terminology.

instance, when Fuller speaks of 'inward witness of the Spirit', he is not speaking of the actual indwelling of the Spirit but of man's own inner assumption regarding the Spirit's external work on him which leads him to make 'inferences'. What I actually wrote was:

> With such passages in mind (concerning God's inner work in man), I turned to the promising title of the Inward Witness of the Spirit in Fuller's works, hoping against hope that here, at least, would be some uplifting and comforting teaching on the Spirit to assist the believer in his holy walk. The essay is an exposition of Psalms 85:8 and 35:3 'I will hear what God the Lord will speak: for he will speak peace with his people, and to the saints: but let them not turn again to folly.' 'Draw out also the spear, and stop the way against them that persecute me: say unto my soul, I am thy salvation.' This might be thought an unusual passage to be used in describing the inward work of the Spirit.

Fuller starts his exegesis by arguing that the texts prove that God bestows prosperity on His people. This is the true meaning, Fuller argues, of 'God will speak peace unto his people'. Fuller goes on to say that, 'There is no doubt but that true Christians do possess, though not without interruption, peace of mind, joy in the Holy Ghost, and a solid, well-grounded persuasion of their interests in eternal life'. This is welcome information. One would suppose that Fuller was now about to outline what he means by the indwelling of the Spirit and how this helps the believer in his union with Him and in his holy service to Him. Such people, longing for the Spirit's indwelling holiness must remain disappointed.

This is the only time Fuller mentions the Holy Spirit in the sermon. He then goes on to reinterpret this one passage and tells us that Christians who hold this view misunderstand what is meant by it. They have relied on the truth being a matter of revelation and Christian experience which is the greatest of errors, according to Fuller. Those who trust in Scripture and their own experience of its truths in this way, Fuller emphasises, have been 'deluded into great errors, to the dishonour of God and the ruin of their future peace'. Fuller adds that he has seen more than a few evils attached to such a view.

Fuller warns against letting hearts rule heads

Here, as so often in Fuller's exegesis, he strives to teach truths by shocking his hearers and forcing them to leave their old views of piety, going to great stretches of exaggeration regarding their position to do so. He tells them that they are letting their hearts rule their heads. They are putting revelation before reason. He preaches as a wolf amongst the sheep, rather than a good shepherd who feeds his sheep with heavenly food. If God does not speak to Christians by the revealed Word and the indwelling of the Spirit, how does He communicate with His people? Fuller answers with the full weight of Grotian rationalism and Socinian scepticism behind him.

Knowing God by 'inference' put to the test

Fuller claims, we can only know God's working in us by 'inference'. Here we have the Grotian a posteriori view again. Faith, for Fuller, is not an exercise in using the gift of love to God, it is that which comes through inferring what is fitting or not. It is obvious that Fuller looks down his nose at those believers who can say with Paul, 'I live by the faith of the Son of God, who loved me, and gave himself for me' (Galatians 2:20). The apostle's words to Timothy might also appear suspicious to Fuller when he says, 'Henceforth there is laid up for me a crown of righteousness, which the Lord, the righteous judge, shall give me at that day' (2 Timothy 4:8). Fuller is so far from a belief in the inward witness of the Spirit in man, bearing witness with his spirit that he is a son of God that he deems such testimonies presumptuous. The Scriptures only speak to characters, Fuller maintains, (we would perhaps say 'types' nowadays if we were wayward enough) and only if we can ally ourselves by inference with such 'characters' can we speak in such a personal way of what God has done for us. There is never a direct personal appeal to a person from the Scriptures. One wonders, as so often, what has happened to Fuller's doctrine of the work of the Holy Spirit here. Fuller does not reveal if he considers Paul to be one of these 'characters' from whom we can infer like experiences with ourselves or whether Paul himself was merely taking on the role of another character as Fuller expects the Christian to do. Be this as it may, Fuller is adamant in insisting that God, through His Word, does not speak directly to individuals but such individuals can only infer their own salvation by comparing themselves with Bible patterns. Again, he boils Christian assurance down to reason rather than revelation. The sinner is left on his own in judging what is 'moral' and what is 'positive', what is 'carnal' and what is 'spiritual'. Fuller's arguments are, to use his own categories 'carnal' as they are not spiritually discerned but come via impressions of the 'reason and the fitness of things'.

Fuller places rational 'impressions' before revealed facts

All this talk about Bible revelation and religious impressions is all unimportant secondary material to Fuller. He seeks to force his hearers' attention away from the means God has used to the mere rational fact, as Grotius taught, that belief is present by an a posteriori inference through hindsight. However, this begs the question of how the sinner is led to believe the gospel if not by the inner working of the Spirit. Faith does not come after the believing but sinners believe by a divine gift of grace, whilst they were yet sinners. Belief is a direct gift not a rational 'impression' of a gift given to 'characters' for our imitation.

Misapplying and altering Scripture

After all this philosophical, though certainly not convincing, logic, Fuller again strives to take on the 'character' of the orthodox pastor, even appealing to the use of the heart. He closes his sermon, seemingly altering Romans 5:1, with the words:

> Believing on the Son of God, we are justified; and being thus justified, we have peace with God, through our Lord Jesus Christ.

This, however, is not what Romans 5:1 says. Fuller omits to say how belief comes to the sinner. Paul in Romans 5 is not speaking of belief by rational impressions. This would make the sinner the agent of faith. The verse actually reads:

> Therefore being justified by faith, we have peace with God through our Lord Jesus Christ.

Paul is speaking of faith given by Christ's agency (v. 1) through the outworking of the Spirit (v. 5), entrusted to sinners by the Father (v. 8) as a ground of justification, not the act of believing which procures justification. He is speaking of faith given to the ungodly (v. 6). The apostle is certainly not speaking of prosperity when he refers to 'peace' but he is clearly talking about hope in the glory of God even in tribulation (v. 3). He is speaking about justification being given to people whilst still in their sins (v. 8). This is all procured, Paul argues, by Christ's atonement. Rather than experiencing God by inference, we read that 'the love of God is shed abroad in our hearts by the Holy Ghost which is given to us as we have been reconciled with God' (v. 5). The Gospel, when it comes to a person, comes personally and straight from God. The Spirit does not reach us by a gospel of inference but by illuminating our hearts and granting us grace to experience God's direct and undeserved love in Christ.

Fuller's 'witness' versus the Spirit's inward witness

In carefully choosing a Biblically promising title, the Inward Witness of the Spirit, which nowhere finds echo in his sermon, and in ending on a pseudo-Biblical text which Fuller has altered to suit his theology, Fuller believes he has done the work of an evangelist. His effort is, however, a caricature of the pastoral calling of a preacher and he misuses the Spirit's name to promote a gospel without means, based on pure rational inference to fulfil its end. Hardly the stuff to promote true holiness! Furthermore, what has all this to do with Edwards? Absolutely nothing! Indeed, what has Fuller's supposed précis on Edwards brought us? Again, absolutely nothing as the two works cannot be compared in any way. Furthermore, my copy of Edwards' 'Affections' (1821) has over 450 pages but Fuller's wee sermon on an entirely different subject runs into a few paragraphs only.

Nettles' weakness in defending Fuller

Nettles errs as an apologist for his Fullerism in that:

1. He does not describe accurately the setting in which his arguments take place.
2. He does not correctly describe the position taken by the person he is defending.
3. Furthermore, he is most careless in presenting the views of the one he has chosen to attack which are so contrary to his own witness.

4. Though my book clearly shows many reasons for holding that Fuller is guilty of Grotianism, Latitudinarianism and New Divinity teaching, Nettles makes no effort whatsoever to define these views and argue the one way or the other concerning them.
5. My critic fails to see the weakness of Fuller's philosophy, especially in his doctrine of 'inference' and in his method of claiming that 'inward' really means 'outside'.
6. Nettles has not examined critically Fuller's doctrine of Scripture and how it should be used in context and quoted correctly.

Doing the work of an evangelist
Nettles continues to back Fuller against Ella by further asserting:

> Though Fuller believes he has 'done the work of an evangelist', according to Ella his effort is a mere 'caricature of the pastoral calling of a preacher and he misuses the Spirit's name to promote a gospel without means, based on pure rational inference to fulfil its end'. Fuller's use of inference cannot be evidence that he promotes reason over revelation. He avoids the error of enthusiasm by adhering to the clarity of biblical revelation over any supposed private revelation in discerning the evidences of salvation. It is not clear why Ella prefers the word 'revelation' in speaking of individual assurance.

Against this I must point out the polemic lack of care in expression shown by Nettles and a dire misunderstanding of the doctrines involved. The work of an evangelist according to 2 Timothy is to preach sound doctrine and not follow one's own lusts; keep to the truth and not follow fables, inferences and dispositions. In my evaluation of Fuller which has grieved Nettles so much, I demonstrated how Fuller is found wanting in all these respects. Most of his ideas indeed were admittedly 'modern' at the time, coming from apostate Presbyterianism, Congregationalism, Socinianism and Latitudinarianism based on Enlightenment theories but, as the bulk of the Christian Press of the leading denominations said at the time, Fullerism was a gangrene that threatened not only the Church but also society. This is witnessed by the just suspicion that Fuller was a Socinian. His own church whose pastorate he filled with a Socinian and which declared itself to be Socinian and the court case it involved indicate this. Fuller's second church had been founded by an Arian and Fuller supported and encouraged an Arian presence in the BMS and the Bristol Bible College as did its Head, John Ryland Junior. At the time, the BMS did not know theologically what was fish, fowl, flesh, cheese or chalk.

If Fuller's theory of 'inference', as described by him and not re-sugared by Nettles, is as he explains it in 'The Inward Witness of the Spirit', this is radicalism pure and thwarts the doctrine of the inner revelation of the Spirit. This, of course, is not revealed in its fulness through Nettles' tactics of throwing snippets of quotes out of context from my work at me but not examining my book as a whole and dealing with its arguments as a whole. This is truly 'criticism with a penknife', a criticism also raised against the Marcionites whom Fuller and New Covenant Theology people often imitate.

Fuller's faulty view of man and God

We remember that Fuller distinguishes between natural ability and moral ability and teaches that the natural faculties of man are sufficient to understand the 'nature and fitness of things' leading to salvation. We know that true salvation for him is not looking to the Word of God which he regards as arbitrary and temporary but to Natural Law which is eternal and under which even God must bind Himself and will do so after the gospel dispensation. Hence, he believes that all men have the duty to respond savingly to the gospel which he defines as following Natural Law, because their sin has not destroyed their natural capacities to respond. Indeed, he even denies that man is dead in trespasses and sins and that the Spirit gives no further revelation to the sinner above what he has already in his natural state. This my book and numerous essays, I trust, clearly show. I outline this further in my expanded edition and in my writings concerning Michael Haykin, Chris Chun, Curt Daniel and other Fullerites on Fuller.

Confusing revelation with reason

Furthermore, the idea suggested by Nettles that I prefer the word 'revelation' to the phrase 'individual assurance' is a red-herring indeed. I prefer no such thing as they are not synonyms and interchangeable.

Nettles has merely attacked me out of the blue thus misleading his readers and being unjust to his chosen opponent. I do, however, believe that Fuller confuses 'revelation' with 'reason' and 'the light of nature' as the followers of the Enlightenment did at the time (see Lessing's *Die Erziehung des Menschengeschlechtes* and Rutherford's *Lex Rex* and the Westminster Confession on the Sabbath). It is also clear that he confuses 'individual assurance' with a rational inference drawn from observing the actions of external things. At Uppsala, we theologs had to go through a university course in psychology. Our professor had just written a book on religion and the role-playing of Christians. He argued that when we read the story of a Biblical character such as David praying, we infer the benefits he gains and identify ourselves with him in prayer, hoping for the same blessings. I told my professor that blessings of the spiritual kind do not usually come through human inference but when I pray, I go to the Lord as a repentant sinner just like David did and often then receive the inner testimony and strength of the Spirit that David experienced. We both have the same needs and both the same God. This was not a matter of my playing at being David but being, like him, a sinner saved by grace.[3] This was not a 'character' role we take on but actual experience in which we were both engaged.

Using the right means

Nettles goes on to say:

> What Ella has in mind when he portrays Fuller as promoting a 'gospel without means' is also unclear, for Fuller's advocacy of means is virtually impossible to challenge. If Ella is asserting that Fuller had no place for the Spirit's work in empowering the Gospel, his case could hardly be made. Fuller's challenge to the thought of Robert Sandeman puts to flight any suspicion that Fuller denied the necessity of the efficacious working of the Spirit. Though agreeing with Sandeman that the sinner's immediate closure with Christ should be the goal of gospel preaching, he argues against Sandeman's unspiritual view of faith.

---

[3] See Hjälmar Sundén's *Religion och Rollerna.*

This is another quite false deduction concerning what both I and Fuller say. In 'The Inward Witness of the Spirit', Fuller starts his paper by stating that he is speaking about 'shalom' in the lives of the believer which, as said above, he interprets as 'prosperity' and not peace. He then asks his leading question:

> In what form or manner does God communicate peace to our minds, and the knowledge of our interest in his salvation?

Here, Nettles will, I trust, agree with me that Fuller is apparently seeking the means of gaining peace (or prosperity as he argues) with God. Then Fuller, as so very, very often in his method of determining the 'proper' and 'improper' meaning of his words, explains that it is wrong to believe that God reveals this peace directly to us or through His Word. The kind of revelation whereby the Word convicts man of his sin and points him to His Saviour according to Fuller is not perfect revelation as God has various kinds of arbitrary revelation and is continually revealing different forms of revelation. Fuller is apparently speaking of revelations which are more perfect than what Scripture tells the mind. Of course, Fuller is evading the true issue when arguing that God's Word merely speaks to the mind. By this means, Fuller is denying God's major means of salvation, the reading or preaching of the Word as applied to the soul. Fuller is refuting the teaching that God speaks directly to the sinful soul through His Word and thus changes the very being of the sinner through the entrance of Christ and the Holy Spirit into the sinner's life. Here, we must note again, Fuller was very far from Edwards' point. Then Fuller quotes several examples of the fatal progress of the sinner because of following impressions on his mind without inferences, caused by reading God's Word or thinking that God speaks privately to him, two views which seem to be indistinguishable to Fuller. Here Fuller outlines his theory of salvation via 'inference'. He has denied that 'impressions' received from the Word of God can do any good but believes that 'inference' describes the believers trust in the Spirit. However, contrary to what Fuller says 'impressions' can refer to a godly influence on the heart by God but 'inferences' refer to what the human mind deduces from certain experiences through its own powers. 'Inference' is merely rational, 'impressions' can be spiritual.

Rejecting the work of the Holy Spirit as a means of enlightening the heart and referring to other revelations, Fuller concludes that, 'It is very *indifferent* [4] by what means we are brought to embrace the gospel way of salvation, if we do but cordially embrace it.' This is all very well but Fuller is telling us 'for as to the interest that any individual has in spiritual blessings, be it ever so much a truth, it is nowhere directly revealed in the Scriptures; nor is there any possible way of proving it thence, except by inference'.[5] Thus Fuller rejects the God given means of bringing a soul to Christ and replaces it by a personal exercising of the mind whose natural abilities are not fallen.

Now though this two-and-half-page article is on the work of the Spirit, as I have outlined above in more detail, Fuller mentions the 'Holy Ghost' but once referring to the true Christian's joy in Him. However, his doctrine that this joy is merely through inference is actually a denial of the inner-working of the Spirit in the believer which produces this joy. So too, how can one profess to write an article on the Spirit when He is mentioned but once by the way and the true means whereby a soul is brought to repentance and faith ignored? Indeed, one can read through all Fuller's works on the spirituality of man in his moral conduct such as 'The Holy Nature and Divine Harmony of the Christian Religion', 'The Nature of True Virtue', 'Morality not Founded in Utility', 'The Great Aim of Life' or 'The Goodness of the Moral Law', or any of his other moral essays dealing with walking along the paths of righteousness and holiness and you will never come across the inner or inward work of the Spirit. You will, however, encounter Fuller's teaching on the moral law, (which Fuller often confuses with the gospel); his positive law; his Natural Law (nearly always used with capitals as it is Fuller's LAW *par excellence*); and his revealed law which is a mere temporary law. These laws he uses in different circumstances according to what is now called 'Situation Ethics' to be applied through what Fuller calls 'parity of reason', always emphasising that it is the spirit of his different laws one should obey not its letter. At times this is altered, as in Christ's case, as a law demanding but a token obedience rather than a full obedience. Yes, Fuller indeed argues that Christ did not put Himself under the whole Law as our

[4] My italics.

[5] 'The Inward Witness of the Spirit', *Works*, Vol. 1, p. 624.

Vicarious Substitute but only obeyed a 'token' of God's Law. If there were no actual fulfilling of the whole Law, there can be no ransom. Furthermore, in relation to law there are no 'cannots' for Fuller but 'will nots'. The way to salvation is by loving Christ as if man had not apostatised which is in the natural power of all. Indeed, Fuller says:

> I maintain that men have the same power, strictly speaking, before they are wrought upon by the Holy Spirit, as after, and before conversion as after; that the work of the Spirit endows us with no new rational powers, nor any powers that are necessary to moral agency.[6]

Missing the mark

Salvation has nothing to do with man's moral agency but solely with the Grace and Love of God. Fullerites, such as Michael Haykin are confusing spirituality, which comes as God's gift, with the believer's moral agency. But what has the sinner's morals to do with salvation?

Nettles then goes on most strangely to speak of my 'severe missing of the mark' which, he claims does neither me, Fuller nor Edwards justice. This is, of course, mere prejudiced polemics as I have not commented on the part-quotes he gives out of context either in relation to myself, Fuller or Edwards. Nettles' own marksmanship appears to be dangerous here as he shoots at imaginary targets. Furthermore, it is obvious that Nettles has different views of how the Holy Spirit works to Fuller, Edwards and myself. Concerning the relationship between Fuller and Edwards, I believe that Fuller was more influenced by New Divinity and the Moral Government teaching than Edwards' theology out of which he picked bits and pieces to enrich his own vocabulary, though he gave Edwards' terms different meanings. Though blessed by many of Edwards' writings, I do agree with John Newton that they get rather philosophical and speculative at times and one is tempted to philosophise and speculate with him. However, I do not agree that we ought to interpret Edwards' view of moral and natural abilities in the light of his son's, New Divinity's, and Andrew Fuller's rational interpretation. To make an Andrew Fuller of Jonathan Edwards is folly

[6] *Works*, Vol. 1, p. 38, fn.

indeed. Yet, Nettles sees Fuller as greater than Edwards and a second Luther.

Duties based on natural, unfallen abilities

Nettles now refers to Fuller's words 'I believe it is the duty of every minister of Christ plainly and faithfully to preach the gospel to all who will hear it'. I say 'amen' to this as I believe Nettles would. But Nettles continues with Fuller's quote saying 'and as I believe the inability of men to spiritual things to be wholly of the moral, and therefore of the criminal kind, and that it is their duty to love the Lord Jesus Christ and trust in him for salvation though they do not'. To this, I cannot say 'amen' because it is an unscriptural position to take. Though we are called to preach Christ to all as He has commanded us, we do not preach to a man of two beings, one moral and fallen and in need of salvation and one natural who is unfallen and aware of his duty to be saved. Man as man is blind, nay, dead in trespasses and sins and he has no knowledge of duties or abilities leading to saving faith no matter what his disposition is or what he might infer. The idea of man's moral status being different to his natural status in salvation is totally unscriptural. Yet Fuller, who sees the gospel as a natural law tells us in Nettles' correct quote of him, 'Were they but of a right disposition of mind there is nothing now in the law of God but what they could perform'. Fuller can say this because of his probation ideas of the Fall. Each man is on probation like Adam and only falls when he finally rejects Christ. This, of course, is New Divinity teaching and has nothing to do with Edwards' teaching. The Bible tells us that man is dead to the gospel but Fuller tells us that man cannot be totally dead otherwise he could not respond to the gospel. That gospel, however, tells man that he cannot respond and that Christ must respond for him. The gospel in its true Biblical sense must be preached to all in their full capacity as fallen sinners. This is the duty of all Christians, that is, to be always ready as fishers of men to cast the net on the other side in obedience to God. It is God, however, in the Spirit's inner work on the soul, who provides the increase and not man's natural, unfallen ability to make himself moral again by inferences and dispositions.

Appendix II:

Arthur Kirkby's contribution to studies of Andrew Fuller

Arthur Kirkby in his doctoral thesis *The Theology of Andrew Fuller and his Relationship to Calvinism*, written in 1956, opened the doors for a more balanced study of Andrew Fuller, free from the exaggerations of many Fullerite enthusiasts. Apart from my own confessed indebtedness to Kirkby, modern Fullerite scholars have ignored his major arguments and evidence for them. Kirkby breaks the myth of Fuller's alleged reproduction of Edwards' theology.

Chris Chun, for instance, does not refer to Kirkby's doctoral work anywhere in his thesis, though he lists Kirkby in his Bibliography as if he had read him. As Chun must have read my remarks on Kirkby's important piece of scholarship in my *Law and Gospel in the Theology of Andrew Fuller*, which Chun criticises in his own thesis, it is odd that he leaves Kirkby's most relevant research concerning Edwards' allegedly direct influence on Fuller out. He would be thus pleased to know that with all his criticism of Fuller, Kirkby still described him as a 'Calvinist'. However, the term 'Calvinist' is a lid for many different kinds of pots.

Why ignore Kirkby's work on Fuller?

As Kirkby's work was the most thorough academic analysis of Fuller's theology up to his day, why is he ignored by modern Fullerites such as Chun and Haykin in their academic works? They have so little to go on from a scholarly point of view so they ought to have considered this scholarly work on Fuller. Dr Kirkby kindly supported my work on Fuller and gave me some good advice concerning my book which I followed in my *Law and Gospel* which Chun chooses to criticise strongly. Chun ignores the evidence I give and my references to Kirkby which he ought to have taken into consideration in a professed scholarly work. It is the usual practice in a doctoral thesis that all previous relevant academic works are reviewed before the scholar brings in his own, entirely new research. There is no such research done in Chun's work and no new research added.

Ignoring the many biographical and theological works on Fuller

Haykin in his alleged search for the historical Fuller makes one of his usual historical howlers. He tells us that there were only two biographies written in the twentieth century on Fuller. These were penned by Gilbert Laws and Arthur H. Kirkby and that 'Neither was a major study, and Kirkby's was but a booklet. Thinking that Haykin must be referring to Kirkby's lengthy dissertation which gained for him an Edinburgh University Ph.D., I was astonished to read that Haykin called this pioneering work 'but a booklet', especially as such words were uttered in a foreword for Piper's very brief fifty-odd paged booklet. Furthermore, Haykin, with his great staff and libraries to which Kirkby did not have access, has never produced a like work. On looking at Haykin's footnotes, I was further surprised to see that Haykin had indeed ignored Kirkby's major work on Fuller, which gives more insight into Fuller's life and works than anything yet produced by Haykin, Chun or Piper or anyone else up to that date. Instead, he listed a brief essay from Kirkby's pen entitled Andrew Fuller (1754-1815) written in 1961 which, nevertheless, certainly provides us with more facts on Fuller than Piper does. However, this was not Kirkby's major 20th century work mentioned above which Haykin also ignores. Though Haykin lists other theological studies of Fuller's life and works in the bibliography at the end of his Foreword, (including twentieth century works), he still omits to mention Kirkby's major work and two other important minor works also authored by Kirkby.[1] Either he did not know of them or he did not agree with them and thus dropped them as unsuitable for his own personal stand in the same way that he ignores

[1] See my Bibliography.

Fuller's reading of Mosheim. Similarly, though Chris Chun lists Kirkby's important thesis in his Bibliography of *The Legacy of Jonathan Edwards in the Theology of Andrew Fuller* (2012), he does not deal with this work in his supposed analysis of Fullerism in the body of the book. This would have prevented Chun from stepping out into the dark as Kirkby shows how the very traditional Fullerite dogma on which Chun based his thesis must be revised.

Prof. Nathan A. Finn prepared a very large bibliography of works on Fuller for the South Eastern Baptist Theological Seminary. He, too, fails to cite Kirkby's major work on Fuller in his overview of works before 1980 but does include him in his Bibliography as also Kirkby's 1954 work for the Baptist Quarterly which Haykin and Piper also omit to mention. In my book on Fuller, I quoted from this essay and Kirkby's further BLQ essay of 1961 to show how Kirkby argues that Jonathan Edwards' influence on Fuller was far less than commonly supposed. Fuller's own references to Edwards would bear this up.

My recommendations of Kirkby's work on Fuller

It is interesting to note that a few early Fullerite reviewers of my *Law and Gospel in the Theology of Andrew Fuller* advised me to consult Kirkby's dissertation, not realising that I had quoted from this work in the very book they were reviewing which showed that they had neither read my work diligently, nor Kirkby's. Indeed, I wrote in both editions of this work that I recommended Kirkby's thesis as the best book up to date on the subject of Fuller and stated that I agreed fully with Kirkby's conclusions concerning Fuller's doctrine of the human will and human abilities. I also placed in my Bibliography a large number of popular, academic and unpublished works on Fuller (*pro* and *contra*), many from the twentieth century, which both Haykin and Piper have overlooked.

Judging by the difference in our ages, I must have known Arthur Kirkby much longer than Haykin as our correspondence and telephone-calls go back some three decades before his death in 2001. Kirkby kindly sent me a MS copy of his dissertation and he helped me considerably with my writings on Fuller from the late eighties on. With his permission I referred to Kirkby's pioneering work on Fuller a number of times in my book *Law and Gospel* and other shorter essays on the subject. Though this has come under harsh criticism from Chun in his dissertation, ignoring my main arguments, Kirkby is also ignored.

Calvinism and Fullerism

Kirkby's main concern, however, was to deal with Fuller's Calvinism, whereas my great interest was to examine Fuller's Christology and his doctrines of God and Man, Ecclesiology, Rationalism and alleged influence on spreading the gospel abroad. Calvin catalogued the doctrines of the English, German and Swiss Reformation for French readers rather than create a theological synthesis of his own. Besides, much of Calvin's alleged doctrine in the eyes of modern Reformed writers is really based on student's notes and secondary material. Most Calvin 'scholars' are content to quote one another to back up their own interpretation of 'Calvinism' and thus often quite contradict the real Calvin's ideas such as on the Fall and on Redemption. Calvin was bettered by Bullinger on Gospel essentials within the Covenant of Grace. Happily, too, early Reformers such as Lambert, Tyndale, and Jewel were more consistent and comprehensive. Somewhat later Hooker showed he was better at systematising the gospel and Davenant, Ussher and Durie were more practical and pastoral. The world had to wait for John Gill for a combination of all these features as the Anglo-Saxon world had grown to forget Bullinger, a greater than Calvin who always stood in Bullinger's shadow. Personally, as one who has read most of Calvin in Latin, French, German and English over many decades and found much that was beneficial, I could still not take his works as my guide for Biblical and Practical Theology because of his leanings towards Zwingli's harsh, rational doctrines as expressed in his 1530 work on the Covenant and election. Here, Zwingli expressly excludes a Scriptural or theological analysis from his philosophical reasoning. The fact that the rebels, led by John Knox, at the Frankfort Refugee Church during Mary's persecutions mistranslated Calvin's Latin was one of the reasons why I wrote my book *Trouble Makers at Frankfurt* in defence of the British Reformation.

The Westminster Confession does not depict historical Calvinism

Recently, however, much has been written claiming that the Westminster Confession is Calvinistic through and through.[2] I would

[2] I am thinking chiefly here of Andrew Woolsey's doctoral thesis of 1988 published very recently by Reformed Heritage Books without taking into consideration the last thirty years of intense research on the subject.

strongly contest that statement as the confession was compiled by people of radically different theologies, as Warfield demonstrates, all of whom wished to leave their distinctive denominational and philosophical marks on Biblical and Practical Theology. It was an attempt by various Separatists to draw up a rough agreement where all could have their say apart from the reforming Church of England men. Furthermore, the confession was rushed through when the Presbyterians, led into error by Rutherford's enlightenment philosophy, lost power and efforts to iron out the internal differences were dropped because of the change in powers due to Cromwell's bad health, lack of funds and death. The Westminster Confession has sadly become the Bible of many so-called Reformed people. Its mangled Covenant theology has opened the doors for the modern NCT with their old-fashioned heresies adequately refuted in Church History in the third and fourth centuries.

Kirkby on Fuller

Coming back to Kirkby, what did he say in the works Haykin has forgotten or ignored in his own research? First of all, he pointed out that the supposed influence of Jonathan Edwards on Fuller was an incorrect hypothesis as the dates usually given do not tally with Fuller's development and own testimony. We do know, however, that Fuller turned to the Neo-Platonists, to which Edwards had turned in younger years but shaken off. However, Fuller obviously did not know Jonathan Edwards, when recommended to him by Robert Hall Sen. in 1775. Fuller then confused the North American Edwards with the Church of England's John Edwards of Cambridge whom he found good. He first learnt in 1777 that he had confused the two authors. So, there is no proof that he turned to Jonathan Edwards and took over his teaching whilst writing his first edition of *The Gospel Worthy of All Acceptation* at all.

I am most indebted to Kirkby for pointing out to me Fuller's Enlightenment 'free-willism' in summing up man's abilities to believe as a product of his being naturally able to do so. Kirkby thus tells us that Fuller taught that man, 'could if he would' exercise duty-faith. Kirkby also admitted that Fuller quoted much from Calvin but his manner of interpreting Calvin was not Calvinistic.[3] This was

[3] *The Theology of Andrew Fuller*, p. 160.

Coleridge's complaint against Fuller when comparing him with Priestley. This can also be said of most modern Fullerites who have read Calvin as little as they have read Fuller. Indeed, one of my fiercest American Baptist critics who called my analysis of Fuller 'immoral', admitted, after I had asked him for his source in my works and also Fuller's, that he had neither read me nor read Fuller but he 'was entitled to his own opinions'. The Banner Of Truth writer on whose behalf his 'agent' was writing had written a review of my book on Fuller for Michael Haykin though he had only read my Introduction. In an after-dinner speech in which he cracked jokes at my expense he was asked if he had read me on Fuller. Back came the answer that he did not need to read me to condemn me. The person who posed this question sent me a recording of the scoffer's speech. This group of opinionated critics, once ardent supporters of the Banner of Truth, are now deep within the New Covenant Theology fold, nesting in its dead branches after destroying the roots of their faith. Here we may mention David Gay, Tom Wells and Fred Zaspel.

Bibliography

Alban, D. J., Woods, R. H. & Daigle-Williamson, M. (2005). The Writings of William Carey: Journalism as Mission in Modern Age. Mission Studies 22. 1.

Allen, S., William Carey: A Missionary Who Transformed a Nation. Mission Frontiers (2011). www.missionfrontiers.org, accessed 08/01/2017.

Ansorge, Catherine, The Revd George Lewis: his life and collection, University of Cambridge, 2018.

Armitage, Thomas, A History of the Baptists: Traced by their Vital Principles and Practices, Baptist Standard Bearer, Vol. 3. 2001, reprint of 1890 edition.

Baptist Missionary Society, Brief Narrative of the Baptist Mission in India, 1819.

Baptist Union, The Baptists and the Bible Society: Memorial Relating to the Bengali and other versions of the New Testament, BU Committee, London, 1840.

Balders, Günter, Theurer Bruder Oncken: Das Leben Johann Gerhard Onckens in Bildern uns Dokumenten, Oncken Verlag, Wuppertal, 1984.

Barnes, Lemuel Call, Two Thousand Years of Missions before Carey, The Christian Culture Press, 1902.

Beck, J. R., Dorothy Carey: The Tragic and Untold Story of Mrs William Carey, Baker, Grand Rapids,1992.

Behera, M. N., William Carey and the British East India Company. American Baptist Historical Society. Vol. 29. 4, (2010).

Belcher, Joseph, William Carey: A Biography, A.B.P.S., Philadelphia, 1853.

Bergunder, Michael (ed.), Missionsberichte aus Indien im 18 Jahrhundert, Neue Hallische Berichte 1, 1999 and 2004.

Beyreuther, Erich, August Hermann Francke 1663-1727: Zeuge des Lebendigen Gottes, Verlag der Francke-Buchhandlung, Marburg, 1956.

Beyreuter, Erich, Bartholomäus Ziegenbalg. A Biography of the First Protestant Missionary in India 1682-1719, Madras, 1955.

Boehme, Anton Wilhelm, The Propagation of the Gospel in the East: being an account of the success of two Danish missionaries, lately sent to the East-Indies, for the conversion of the heathen in Malabar. In several letters to their correspondents in Europe. Rendered into English from the High-Dutch, London 1709 and 1711.

Brauer, Johan Hartwig, Die Heidenboten Fredrichs IV von Danemark, Altona, 1837.

Brekke, Torkel, Mission Impossible? Baptism and the politics of Bible translations in the early Protestant mission in Bengal, Peace Research Institute, Oslo, Feb. 2006.

Bregy, Sabine, Quellen zur indischen Geschichte bis 1858: Zum Beispiel Bartholomäus Ziegenbalg, Alois Payer, 2008.

Brewster, Paul, Andrew Fuller: Model Pastor Theologian, Nashville, 2010

Buchanan, Claudius, Christian Researches in India, Society for the Promotion of Popular Instruction, 1840.

Buchanan, Claudius, The College of Fort William in Bengal, 1805, Internet Archive.

Bullinger, Heinrich, Der Widertöufferen ursprung, fürgang etc., Zürich, 1561, 1975 Leipzig Facsimile Reprint.

Bunke, Ernst, August Hermann Francke der Mann des Glaubens und der Liebe, Brunnen Verlag, Giessen, 1939.

Carey, E., Memoir of William Carey. Stamford Street, London: William Clowes and Sons, 1837.

Carey, Mrs Eustace, Eustace Carey, A Missionary to India, Pewtress & Co, 1857.

Carey, W., An Enquiry into the Obligations of Christians to Use Means for the Conversion of the Heathens. Leicester, UK, Ann Ireland, 1792.

Carey W., Eine Untersuchung über die Verflichtung der Christen, Mittel einzusetzen für die Bekehrung der Heiden, translated by Klaus Fiedler and Thomas Schirrmacher, Verlag für Kultur und Wissenshaft, Bonn, 1998.

Carlile, John, The Story of the English Baptists, London, 1905.

Carson, Penelope, The East India Company and Religions 1698-1858, The Boydell Press, 2012.

Carman, John B., Protestant Bible Translators in India: An Unrecognised Dialogue, Harvard Divinity School, Hindu-Christian Studies Bulletin 4, 1991, pp. 11-20.

Carne, John, Lives of Eminent Missionaries, 2 Vols, London, 1832

Chatterjee, Sunil Kumar, Mission in India: A Catalogue of the Carey Library, Council of Serampore College, 1984.

Chatterjee, Sunil Kumar, Hannah Marshman: The First Woman Missionary in India, Hooghly, 1987.

Chatterton, Eyre, Bishop of Nagpur, A History of the Church of England in India Since the Early Days of the East India Company, SPCK, 1924.
Chute, Anthony L. et al, The Baptist Story from Sect to Global Movement, Bang, 2015.
Chute, Arthur C., John Thomas, First Baptist Missionary to Bengal, 1757-1801, Introduction by A. J. Gordon, Baptist Book and Tract Society, Nova Scotia, 1893.
Chun, Chris, The Legacy of Jonathan Edwards in the Theology of Andrew Fuller, Brill, Leiden, 2012.
Clark, Davis W., Death Bed Scenes of Dying With and Without Religion, Designed to Illustrate the Truth and Power of Christianity, Lane and Scott, N.Y., 1852, pp. 228-230.
Clary, Ian, Throwing Away the Guns: Andrew Fuller, William Ward, and the Communion Controversy in the Baptist Missionary Society, Foundations 68 (May 2015): 84-101.
Clary, Ian, Andrew Fuller and Closed Communion, SBJT Forum (ed Michael Haykin), Southern Baptist Journal of Theology, 17. 1. 2013, pp. 46-52.
Clipsham, E., Andrew Fuller: A Study in Evangelical Calvinism, Parts One to Four, Baptist Quarterly, XX, 1963, London, pages 99-114; 146-154; 214-225; 268-276.
Clipsham, E., Andrew Fuller and the Baptist Mission, Foundations, 10 (1), 1967, pp. 4-18.
Coker, J. L., Developing A Theory of Mission in Serampore: The Increased Emphasis upon Education as a 'Means for the Conversion of the Heathens' Mission Studies, Vol 17, No 1-35, (2001).
Cook, Richard A., The Story of the Baptists in all Ages and Countries, Baltimore, 1884.
Crosby, Thomas, The History of the English Baptists, (4 Vols.), London, 1738.
Cross, Antony R., Reversing 'The Amazing Ignorance and Stupidity of Some Persons': Baptists, the Biblical Languages, and Bible Translation, Baptist Quarterly, Vol. 50 (2), 2019, pp. 44-57.
Culshaw, W., 'William Carey – Then and Now', The Bible Translator, 18 (2) April, pp. 53-60.
Dansk Biografisk Leksikon, 1933-44, Bartholomaeus Ziegenbalg.
Davis, W., William Carey: Father of Modern Mission. Chicago, IL: Moody, (1963).
Dorairaj, S., Of the German who took Tamil to Europeans, Frontline, Vol. 27, Issue 15, Jul. 2010, pp. 17-30.
Douwes, P. A. C., William Carey Schoenmacher-Zenderling-Professor-Taalgeleerde, 1761-1834, The Hague, 1934.

Dix, Kenneth, Particular Baptists and Strict Baptists: An Historical Survey, The Strict Baptist Historical Society, Annual Report and Bulleting, Number Thirteen, 1976.
Drewery, M., William Carey: Shoemaker and Missionary. Hodder and Stoughton Limited. London: T. J. Press, (1978).
East India Company, The Asiatic Journal and Monthly Register for British India and Its Dependencies, Vol. 24, London, 1827.
Ecke, Karl, Fortsetzung der Reformation, Mission Verlag Memmingen, 1965.
Ehrlich, Joshua, The East India Company and the Politics of Knowledge, Havard doctoral thesis, August 2018.
Ella, George M., John Gill and the Cause of God and Truth, Go Publications, 1995.
Ella, George M., John Gill and Justification from Eternity: A Tercentenary Appreciation 1697-1997, Go Publications, 1998.
Ella, George M., Weighed in the Balance: Excommunicating the Sheep in Order to Feed the Goats, Texts by William Huntington, John Ryland and Samuel Adams. Introductory Chapters and Notes by George Ella, The Huntington Press, 1998.
Ella, George M., The Free Offer and the Call of the Gospel, Go Publications, 2001.
Ella, George M., Law and Gospel in the Theology of Andrew Fuller, 2nd edit., Go Publications, 2011.
Ella, George M., John Gill (1697-1771): Preserver and Reformer of the Particular Baptists, Strict Baptist Historical Society, Bulletin 2019, Number 46.
Ella, George M., The Covenant of Grace and Christian Baptism, Verlag für Kultur und Wissenschaft, Bonn, 2007.
Ella, George M., The Covenant of Grace and the People of God, Go Publications, 2020.
Ella, George M., The Atonement in Modern Evangelical Thought, Go Publications, 2021.
Elliot, Kelly R. C., Baptist Missions in the British Empire: Jamaica and Serampore in the First Half of the nineteenth Century, MA thesis, Florida State University, 2007.
Fenger, J. Ferd., Den Trankebarske Missions Historie, Verlagt av Universitäts-Boghandler C. A. Reitzel, Copenhagen, 1843.
Fenger, J. Ferd., Geschichte der Trankebarschen Mission nach den Quellen Bearbeitet, Glimma, 1845. This was translated into English from Emil Francke's collection of Fenger's papers by K. Pamperrien K. in 1863 which he entitled History of the Tranquebar Mission – worked out from the original

papers by J. Ferd. Fenger, Translated into English from the German of Emil Francke, Tranquebar 1863.

Flachsmeier, Horst R., Geschichte der evangelischen Weltmission, Brunnen-Verlag, Giessen und Basel, 1963.

Fox, Richard, Was the Sanskrit Bible the English Bible in Disguise?, International Journal of Asian Studies, 2018.

Francke August Hermann, Brief von August Hermann Francke an Bartholomäus Ziegenbalg und Heinrich Plütschau, Franckesche Stiftungen, Halle (Saale), 1708.

Frykenberg, Robert Eric, Review articles of Stephen Neill's 'A History of Christianity in India to AD 1707', Journal of Asian Studies: Vol. 46, No 1, 1987, pp. 195-197.

Frykenberg, Robert Eric (ed), Christians and Missionaries in India: Cross-Cultural Communications since 1500, Eerdmans, 2003.

Frykenberg, Robert Eric, 'The Legacy of Christian Friedrich Schwartz', International Bulletin of Missionary Research, Wisconsin University, July, 1999.

Fuller, Andrew, Thoughts on Open Communion: In a Letter to the Rev. William Ward Missionary at Serampore, dated September 21, 1800, The Works of Andrew Fuller, one volume Banner of Truth Reprint, 2007, pp. 854-855. (See also On Terms of Communion, p. 852 and Strictures, p. 853) Strict Communion in the Mission Church of Serampore, p. 855. The Admissiion of Unbaptised Persons to the Lord's Supper inconsistent with the New Testament: A Letter to a Friend in 1814, pp. 855-859.

Frick, Gita Dharampal, Indien im Spiegel deutscher Quellen der Frühen Neuzeit, Tübingen, 1994.

George, Ajith, Serampore Mission – History of Christianity in India, Leonard Theological College, Jabalpur, Jan. 30, 2016, academia.Edu.

George, Timothy, Faithful Witness: The Life and Mission of William Carey. Birmingham, AL: New Hope, 1991.

Germann, Wilhelm, John Philipp Fabricius: Seine fünfzigjährige Wirksamkeit in Tamulenlande, Erlanged, Verlag Andreas Deichert, 1865.

Giorgi, Lotte, Maria Dorothea Ziegenbalg, Tatsacheberichte aus dem Leben der ersten deutschen evangelischen Missionarsfrau in Süd-Indian, Evangelische Verlagsanstalt, Berlin, 1958.

Germann, Wilhelm, Ziegenbalg und Plütschau; ein Beitrag zur Geschichte des Pietismus/ nach handschriftlichen Quellen und ältesten Drucken, Erlangen, 1868.

Germann, Wilhelm, Ziegenbalg und Plütschau: Die Gründungsjahre d. Trankebarschen Mission, Erlangen, 1868.

Gilbert, Christopher, St Bartholomäus Ziegenbalg, the Morning Star of India, undated, Academia.edu. download. Gilbert has filmed Ziegenbalg's life.

Gilbert, Christopher, The Archived Wisdom of a Twenty-something Missionary – Christopher Gilbert, undated Academia.edu.download.

Gilbert, Christopher, Tamil Studies Beyond Empires: Why India Celebrates Bartholomäus Ziegenbalg, sixty-nine minute film, 2013.

Glover, R. (1960). The Progress of World Wide Missions. New York: Harper.

Gross, Andreas, Halle and the Beginning of Protestant Christianity in India, 3 Vol. Halle, 2006.

Guite, Mercy Vungthianmuang, Die Darstellung der indischen Gesellschaft bei Bartholomäus Ziegenbalg in 18.Jahrhundert in Tranquebar, India: Eine Analyse, Grin, 2015.

Haldane, Alexander, Memoirs of the Lives of Robert Haldane of Airthrey and of his Brother James Alexander Haldane, New York, 1854.

Haus, Håkon, Christian Friedrich Schwartz – Et 150 Års Minne, internet download.

Haykin, Michael (ed), The Army of the Lamb: The Spirituality of Andrew Fuller, Sola Scriptura, 2019.

Haykin, Michael, 'The Honour of the Spirit's Work' Andrew Fuller, Dan Taylor, and an Eighteenth-Century Baptist Debate over Regeneration, Baptist Quarterly, Vol. 47, (4), 2016, pp. 134-161.

Haykin, Michael, 'Dipping is God's Appointment': The Mode of Baptism among the Early Particular Baptists, Baptist Quarterly, Vol. 49, (1), 2018, pp. 3-12.

Herzog, Johan Jakob, Real-Encyklopädie für protestantische Theologie und Kirche (18 vols.), 1854-1913. See also Schaff-Herzog 'translation' Encyclopedia of Religious Knowledge.

Hervey, George Winfred, The Story of Baptist Missions in Foreign Lands: From the time of Carey to the Present Date, Chancey R. Barnes, 1884.

Horne, Thomas Hartwell, A Manuel of Biblical Bibliography, London, 1839.

Houghton, S. M. (ed.) Five Pioneer Missionaries: Brainerd, Burns, Eliot, Martyn and Paton, B.O.T., 1965, 1987 reprint.

Indo-Asian News Service, Bartholomäus Ziegenbalg – the German who printed the first Tamil text 1682-1719, 4th July – 2006.

Isaiah, Sudir, Thirumalai, M.S., Three Hundred Years of Evangelization in India – The First Missionary to India: Bartholomaeus Ziegenbalg, Globe Serve, June 1, 2007.

Israel, Hephizibath, Protestant Translations of the Bible in Indian Languages, 7th Feb. 2010.

Israel, Hephizibath, Some Challenges for Scholarship on Protestant Translations of the Bible: The Tamil Context, Religion Compass, 4/2, 2010, pp. 99-113.

Israel, Hephzibath, Religious Transactions in Colonial South India: Language Translation, and the Making of Protestant Identity, Palgrave Macmillan, 2011.

Ivimey, Joseph, A History of the Baptists, London, 1814.

Jäck, Joachim Heinrich (ed), Taschen-Bibliothek der Wichtigsten und Interresantesten Reisen Durch Ost-, West- und Süd-Indien, Nürnberg, 1839.

Jahn, Christof, Die Unruhe Gottes: Eine Chronik um Bartholomäus Ziegenbalg in fünf Bildern und einem indischen Vorspiel, Erlanger Verlag für Mission und Ökumene, 2005.

Jeyaraj, Daniel, Bartholomäus Ziegenbalg the Father of Modern Protestant Missions: An Indian Assessment, I.S.P.C.K., 2006.

Jeyaraj, Daniel, Deutsche Pietisten im Spiegel indischer Quellen: Über die Anfänge der Dänisch-Halle'schen Mission im südindischen Tranquebar Anfang 18. Jh., Lecture given at the Ludwig Maximilian-Universität, München, 2008.

Jeyaraj, Daniel, Early Anglican Involvement in India: Theological Reflections, Mission Theology in the Anglican Communion, 31.05.2017, online.

Jeyaraj, Daniel, Maria Dorothea Ziegenbalg, the First German Lutheran Female Missionary to the Tamil People in South India, International Journal of Asian Christianity, Brill, 29 March, 2019.

Jeyaraj, Daniel. Der Beitrag der Dänisch-Halleschen Mission zum Werden einer indisch-ein-heimischen Kirche, 1706-1730. Erlangen: Verlag der Ev.-Luth. Mission, 1996.

Jeyaraj, Daniel, The First Lutheran Missionary Bartholomäus Ziegenbalg: His Concepts of Culture and Mission from a Post-Colonial Perspective, SMT, Svensk Missions Tidskrift, Vol. 93, No. 3, 2005.

Jeyaraj, Daniel, Making Missionary Heritage Alive through Archival Research: Experiences of a Researcher-Archivist. Online essay, not to be quoted without the author's permission. Missions, International Bulletin of Missionary Research, New Jersey, USA: Overseas Ministries Study Centre, 1986.

Jeyaraj, Daniel, Mission Theology in the Anglican Community, Annual Mission Theology Lecture, Durham University, 3 May, 2017 and Lambeth Palace, 30 May 2017.

Jones, T. K., History's Lessons for Tomorrow's Missions, International Bulletin of Missionary Research, New Jersey, USA: Overseas Ministries Study Centre, 1986.

Kanjamala, Augustine, The Future of Christian Missions in India: Towards a New Paradigm for the Third Millennium, Pickwick Publications, Oregon, 2008.

Kidd, Ronald A. N., Finding Pieces of the Puzzle: A Fresh Look at the Christian Story, Wipf and Stock, 2011. See Chapter 9, 'Protestants in India 1706 A. D.'

Kilgour, R., The Bible Throughout the World: A Survey of Scripture Translations, World Dominion Press, 1939.

Kirkby, Arthur H., Andrew Fuller: Evangelical Calvinist, Baptist Quarterly, XV, 1954, London, pp. 195-202.

Klauber, Martin, The Great Commission: Evangelicals and the History of World Missions, B&H Publishing Group, Tennessee, 2008.

Koschorke, Klaus (ed), Tamil Language for Europeans, Ziegenbalg's Grammatica Damulica, with Annotations by Daniel Jeyaraj, Wiesbaden, 2010.

Koschorke, Klaus, Asia in the 19th and Early 20th Centuries, Chapter 9 of Global Christianity edited by Schørring and Hjelm, Brill, Leiden and Boston, 2017, pp. 267-300.

Krajewski, Ekkhard, Leben und Sterben des Züricher Täuferführers Felix Mantz, 1957.

Lehmann, Arno, It Began in Tranquebar: The Story of the Tranquebar Mission and the Beginnings of Protestant Christianity in India, Christian Literature Society, Madras, 1956.

Lehmann, Arno (ed.), Alter Briefe aus Indien: Unveröffentliche Briefe von Bartholomäus Ziegenbalg 1706-1719, Evangelische Verlagsanstalt, Berlin, 1957.

Lewis, C. B., The Life of John Thomas: Surgeon of the Earl of Oxford East Indiaman, and First Baptist Missionary to Bengal, Macmillan, London, 1873.

Lord, Eleazer, A Compendious History of the Principle Protestant Missions to the Heathen (2 Vol.), Boston, 1813.

Lovett, Ashley, Baptists on the Lord's Supper and Christian Character, Baptist Quarterly, Vol. 5, October, 2019, pp. 155-169.

Lovett, Richard, The History of the London Missionary Society, H. Frowde, 1899.

Mallick, Sovan K., 'Nineteenth Century Missionary Encounter with other Religions', Academia.edu., 2019.

Mann, Michael, Review of Halle and the Beginning of Protestant Christianity in India, Andreas Gross, s.o., International Asian Forum, Vol. 38, No. 3-4, pp. 410-413, 2007.

Mantena, Sundari, The Origins of Modern Historiography in India, Antiquarianism and Philology 1780-1880, Palgrave Macmillan, 2012.

Marshman, John Clark, The Story of Carey, Marshman and Ward, London, 1864.

Moon, Penderel, Warren Hastings and British India, Hodder & Stoughton, London, 1947.

Moore, C. J., Andrew Fuller and the Genesis of Modern Missions, Aug. 13, 2020, online.

Morden, Peter J., Andrew Fuller and the BMS, Baptist Quarterly, Vol. 41, July 2005.

Mulholland, K. B., From Luther to Carey: Pietism and the Modern Missionary Movement. Bibliotheca Sacra 156, 1999.

Nagy, Silvia, Colonization or Globalisation? Postcolonial Exploration of Imperial Expansion, 2010.

Nehrbass, Kenneth, Gospel and Culture Blog, Biola University, see his various blogs on Indian (and other) missions, mostly 2017-18.

Neill, Bishop Stephen, A History of Christianity in India 1707-1858, Cambridge, 1985.

Neill, Bishop Stephen, A History of Christianity in India: The Beginnings to AD 1707, Cambridge, 2004.

Neill, Bishop Stephen, A History of Christian Mission. New York: Penguin, 1986.

Nettles, Tom, 'Why Andrew Fuller?' and 'Andrew Fuller and Free Grace', Reformation Today, 1984, pp. 3-14.

Nuttall, G. F., Northamptonshire and the Modern Question, JTS, NS, XVI, 1965, pp. 101-23.

Oliver, R. W., Historical Survey of English Hyper-Calvinism, Foundations (Engl), 7, 1981, pp. 8-18

Oliver, R. W., Significance of Strict Baptists Attitudes to Duty-Faith, SBHSB, 20, 1993, pp. 3-26

Pearce, Carey, S., William Carey: The Father of Modern Missions, The Wakeman Trust, 2008 reprint.

Pearson, Hugh, Memoirs of the Life and Correspondence of the Reverend Christian Frederick Swartz to which is Prefixed a Sketch of the History of Christianity in India, New York, 1835.

Piper, John, He Stayed at Home to Save the World: Andrew Fuller (1754-1815), May 7, 2019, Desiring God online articles

Potter, Claire, 'The Influence of Danish Missionaries to India on Susanna Wesley's Methods of Education and its subsequent Influence on John Wesley', Methodist History, 52:3, April 20

Potts, E. Daniel, 'I throw away the guns to preserve the ship', Baptist Quarterly, BQ, XX, 1963-64, London pp. 115-117, 20.12. 2000.

Pratt, Jay, 'Can Bible Translation Movements get the Job done faster'? Paul/Timothy net., 2008.

Qayyum, Mohamed Abdul, A Critical Study of the Bengal Grammars of Carey, Halhed and Houghton, School of Oriental and African Studies, University of London, Ph. D. thesis, 1974.

Randall, Ian M., Henry Martyn 1781-1812) and the Baptists in India: An ecumenical vision? Baptist Quarterly, Vol. 45, April, 2013, pp. 87-113.

Reddy, Kelly, Review Article on Paul Brewster's Andrew Fuller: Model Pastor Theologian, Toronto Baptist Seminary, June 2017, (student paper).

Reitzel, C. A., Den Trankebarske Missions Historie, Copenhagen, 1843.

Richter, Julius, , Fleming H. Revell Company, 1862. Online edition from 1908.

Roberts, Liardon, God's Generals the Missionaries, Whitaker House, 2014.

Rubiés, Joan-Pau, Tamil Voices in the Lutheran Mission of South India (1705-1714), Journal of Modern History, 19, Pompeu Fabra University, Barcelona, 2015, pp. 71-81.

Roebuck, Thomas, The Annals of the College of Fort William With Appendix, Calcutta, 1819.

Roy, Raja Rammohun, The Life and Letters of Raja Rammohun Roy, eds, Sophia Dobson Collet and Hem Chadra Sarkar, Calcutta, 1914.

Rubiés, Joan-Pau, The Concept of Cultural Dialogue and the Jesuit Method of Accommodation: Between Idolatry and Civilization, Activum Historicum Societas Jesu, 2005.

Rubiés, Joan-Pau, Reassessing 'the Discovery of Hinduism': Jesuit Discourse on Gentile Idolatry and the European Republic of Letters, International Encounter and the Jesuit Mission in South Asia (16th-18th Centuries), Bangalore, 2014, pp. 113-155.

Sackety, Evelyn, The Historical Circumstances that Led William Carey (1716-1834) to the Serampore Trio, Academia.edu.download.

Scharpff, Paulus, Geschichte der Evangelisation, Brunnen-Verlag, Giessen und Basel, 1964.

Schirrmacher, Thomas (ed.) William Carey: Theologian – Linguist – Social Reformer, Verlag für Kultur und Wissenshaft, Bonn, 2013 containing a biography of Carey by George M. Ella.

Schirrmacher, Thomas, Aufbruch zur Modernen Weltmission: William Carey's Missionstheologie, RVB, Hamburg, 2001.

Schmidt, Christian Gottlieb, Kurtzgefasste Lebensbeschreibungen merkwürdige evangelischer Missionare, Leipzig, 1836.

Schouten, Jan Peter, Jesus as Guru: The Image of Christ among Hindus and Christians in India, Amsterdam-New York, 2008.

Schwabe, Fabian, Mission und Obrigkeit in Tranquebar im frühen 18. Jahrhundert unter Berücksichtigung einzelner Briefe Ziegenbalgs, Grin Verlag, Hauptseminar Hausarbeit, 2005.
Settgast, Ann-Charlott, Der Mann in Tranquebar, Evangelische Verlag, Berlin, 1981.
Shaw, Graham, Printing in Calcutta to 1800, A Description and Checklist of Printing in Late Eighteenth Century Calcutta, The Bibliographical Society, London, 1981.
Sherring, M. A., The History of Protestant Missions in India From their Commencement in 1706 to 1881, Religious Tract Society, 1884.
Singh, Brijraj, The First Protestant Missionary to India – Bartholomäus Ziegenbalg, O.U.P., New Delhi, 1999.
Smalley, W., Translation as Mission: Bible Translation in the Modern Missionary Movement, Macon, GA: Mercer, 1991.
Smith, Christopher, The Legacy of William Carey. International Bulletin of Missionary Research. New Jersey, USA: Overseas Ministries Study Centre, pp. 120-129, 1992 and 1999.
Smith, Christopher, Mythology and Missionology: A Methodical Approach to the Pre-Victorian Mission of the Serampore Trio, PDF smith-wc-irm, 1994 pp. 1-25.
Smith, Christopher, The Protégé of Erasmus and Luther in Heroic Serampore 1812-1855, Indian Journal of Theology,
Smith Christopher, A Tale of Many Models: The Missiological Significance of the Serampore Trio,
Smith, George, The Life of William Carey: Shoemaker and Missionary. New York: E. P. Dutton, 1909.
Smith, George, Short History of Christian Missions from Abraham and Paul to Carey, Livingstone and Duff, Edinburgh, 8th undated edition.
Smith, George, The Life of Alexander Duff, Hodder and Stoughton, 1899.
Smith G. E., Patterns of Missionary Education: The Baptist India Mission 1794-1824, Baptist Quarterly, XX, 1963-64, London, pp. 293-312.
Stanley, Brian, The Vision of a Christian Higher Education for India: 200 years of Serampore College History, Baptist Quarterly, Vol. 51, Number 1, Jan. 2020.
Stennett, Samuel, Memoirs of the Life of the Rev. William Ward, London, 1825.
Stock, E., History of the Church Missionary Society. Vol. 1. London, 1899.
Sundkler, Bengt, Missionens Värld: Missionskunskap och missionshistoria, Svenska Bokförlaget, 1963.
Sundkler, Bengt, Missions-Forskningens Arbetsuppgifter, Svenska Institutet för Missionsforskning, Lindblads Verlag, Uppsala, 1952.

Sweetman, Will; Ilakkuvan R., Bibliotheca Malabarica: Bartholomäus Ziegenbalg's Tamil Library, Vol. 119, Collection Indologie, Institut Français d'Indologie, 2012.
Sweetman, Will, Heathenism, Idolatry and Rational Monotheism among the Hindus: Bartholomäus Ziegenbalg's AKKIYANAM (1713) and Other Works Addressed to Tamil Hindus, taken from Halle and the Beginning of Protestant Christianity in India, 3 Vol., Verlag der Franckeschen Stiftungen zu Halle, 2006, eds Andreas Gross et al.
Sweetman, Will, The Dravidian Idea in Missionary Accounts of South Indian Religion, (From Religion and Modernity in India), New Delhi, O.U.P., 2016.
Sweetman, Will, The Prehistory of Orientalism: Colonialism and the Textual Basis Bartholomäus' Account of Hinduism, Journal of Asian Studies, 6, 2. New Zealand, 2004. Pp. 12-38.
Thomas, Fr. B. M., Impact of Christianity on Indian Society and Vice Versa, Academia. Edu, 2019.
Thomas, John, 'Letter to John Rippon', The Baptist Annual Register, 1790, 1791, 1792, and part of 1793, pages 353-370.
Vaiphei, Suantek, The Contribution of the Protestant Missionaries in India, academia.edu. download.
Vethanayagamony, Peter, It began in Madras: the 18th century Lutheran-Anglican ecumenical ventures in mission and Benjamin Schultze, ISPCK, Delhi, 2010.
Walton, Alexander, A Christian Republic in the Hoogley: A Contextualisation of William Carey's Missionary Vision, Master's Thesis, Birmingham University, 2014.
White, Charles L., A Century of Faith, The American Baptist Home Mission Society, 1932.
White, Joseph, On the Duty of Attempting the Propagation of the Gospel in India, Oxford University Bampton Lecture, 1785.
Wilkinson, Michael, Memorials of an Indian Missionary, London 1859.
Wilkinson, Michael, Sketches of Christianity in North India, Seeley, Burnside and Seely, London, 1844.
Winter, John (ed), The Claims of the American and Foreign Bible Society Maintained and Vindicated, Ohio, 1845.
Wood, Nicholas J., 'Pity, Humanity and Christianity? The Work of William Carey in Postcolonial Perspective', Baptist Quarterly, Vol. 44, Oct. 2012, pp. 487-503.
Yeh, Allen and Chun, Chris, Expect Great Things, Attempt Great Things: William Carey and Adoniram Judson, Missionary Pioneers, Wipf & Stock, Oregon, 2013.

Yoder, John H., Täufertum und Reformation im Gespräch, EVZ Verlag, Zürich, 1968.

Young, Doyle L., Andrew Fuller and the Modern Missionary Movement, Baptist History and Heritage, 1982, 17 (4), pp. 17-27.

Ysrael, Muzeon, The Jews of India: The Story of Three Communities, The Israel Museum, Jerusalem, 1995.

Ziegenbalg, Bartholomäus, Alte Briefe aus Indien. Unveröffentlichte Briefe von Bartholomäus Ziegenbalg. 1706-1719, Berlin, 1957.

Ziegenbalg, B. and Grundler, J. E., A letter to the Reverend Mr. Geo Lewis, Chaplain to the Honourable East India Company at Fort George: Giving an Account of the Method of Instruction used in the Charity Schools of the Church call'd Jerusalem, in Tranquebar by the Protestant Missionaries there. London, 1715.

Ziegenbalg, Bartholomäus, Grammatica Damulica, Hale, 1716. This work has recently been translated from the Latin and Tamil with annotations and comments by Prof. Daniel Jeyaraj, Harrassowitz Verlag, Wiesbaden, 2010.

Ziegenbalg, Bartholomäus, An Account of the Success of Two Danish Missionaries Sent to the East Indies, for the Conversion of the Heathens in Malabar, London, 1718.

Ziegenbalg, Bartholomäus, Genealogie der Malabarischen Götter: aus Eigenen Schriften und Briefen der Heiden Zusammengetragen und Verfasst, SPCK, 1865.

Ziegenbalg, Bartholomäus and Plütschau, Heinrich, Propagation of the Gospel in the east: being a collection of letters from the Protestant missionaries, and other worthy persons in the East-Indies, &c. relating to the mission; the means of promoting it; ... chiefly on the coast of Coromandel, London, 1718.

Ziegenbalg, Bartholomäus, Gründler, Johan Ernest, Die Malabarische Korrespondenz: Tamilische Briefe an deutsche Missionare, Eingeleitet und erläutert von Kurt Liebau, Jan Thorbecke Verlag Sigmaringen, 1998.

Ziegenbalg, Bartholomäus, Thirty-Four Conferences Between the Danish Missionaries and the Malabarian Bramans, translated by J. Thomas Philipps, London, 1719.

Index of Works Cited

Index of Scripture Citations

Old Testament

New Testament

New Testament

Index of Geographical Places and Languages

Index of Colleges, Universities, Religions, Churches and Institutions

Index of Names

www.ingramcontent.com/pod-product-compliance
Lightning Source LLC
Chambersburg PA
CBHW060316100426
42812CB00003B/793

* 9 7 8 1 9 0 8 4 7 5 2 4 4 *